Biological Anthropology

A Synthetic Approach to Human Evolution

Noel T. Boaz

International Institute for Human Evolutionary Research

Alan J. Almquist

California State University–Hayward

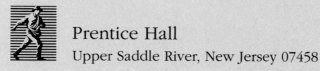
Prentice Hall

Upper Saddle River, New Jersey 07458

Library of Congress Cataloging-in-Publication Data

BOAZ, NOEL THOMAS.
    Biological anthropology : a synthetic approach to human evolution
/ Noel T. Boaz, Alan J. Almquist.
       p.   cm.
    Includes bibliographical references and index.
    1. Physical anthropology.   2. Human evolution.   I. Almquist, Alan
J. II. Title.
GN60.B67 1997
573—dc20   95-37820
ISBN 0-13-369208-6   CIP

Editor-in-chief: *Nancy Roberts*
Acquisitions editor: *Fred Whittingham*
Development editor-in-chief: *Susanna Lesan*
Production editor: *Barbara Reilly*
Buyer: *Lynn Pearlman*
Interior and cover design: *Levavi & Levavi*
Creative design director: *Leslie Osher*
Line art coordinator: *Michele Giusti*
Design supervisor: *Anne Bonanno Nieglos*
Cover art: *Landscape with Bat at Twilight by J.W. Webb.*
      Courtesy of SuperStock, Inc.
Photo researcher: *Diane Austin*
Copy editor: *Mary Deebe*
Editorial assistant: *Pat Naturale*
Line art studio: *Vantage Art, Inc.*
Illustrators: *Dorothy Sigler Norton; Raymond E. Smith*
Chapter opening photography: *Douglas Mazanovich*

 © 1997 by Prentice-Hall, Inc.
Simon & Schuster/A Viacom Company
Upper Saddle River, New Jersey 07458

Printed in the United States of America

10 9 8 7 6 5 4 3 2

ISBN 0-13-369208-6

*This book was set in 10/12 ITC Garamond Light by Compset Inc
and was printed and bound in Canada by Transcontinental Printing Inc.
Color separations by Lehigh Colortronics.
The cover was printed by The Lehigh Press, Inc.*

Prentice-Hall International (UK) Limited, *London*
Prentice-Hall of Australia Pty. Limited, *Sydney*
Prentice-Hall Canada Inc., *Toronto*
Prentice-Hall Hispanoamericana, S.A., *Mexico*
Prentice-Hall of India Private Limited, *New Delhi*
Prentice-Hall of Japan, Inc., *Tokyo*
Simon & Schuster Asia Pte. Ltd., *Singapore*
Editora Prentice-Hall do Brasil, Ltda., *Rio de Janeiro*

To our children

Lydia, Peter, and Alexander

Christopher and Emily

Brief Contents

1. Evolutionary Perspectives on Human Biology and Behavior   *1*

2. Earliest Beginnings: DNA, the Cell, and the First Animals   *33*

3. Evolution and Natural Selection   *66*

4. Populations, Species, and Evolution   *100*

5. Stages of Vertebrate Evolution   *131*

6. Introduction to Primates: Origins and Evolution   *172*

7. Primates: Patterns in Social Behavior   *210*

8. The Florescence and Decline of the Hominoids   *246*

9. Evolution of Hominoid Behavior   *278*

10. Australopithecines   *320*

11. The Genus Homo   *359*

12. The Evolution of Human Social Behavior   *397*

13. Human Biology and Variation   *438*

14. The Human Life Cycle: Human Biology, Growth, and Adaptability   *478*

15. The Modern Human Condition in Evolutionary Perspective: Applied Biological Anthropology   *514*

Contents

Preface   *xi*

---

1. *Evolutionary Perspectives on Human Biology and Behavior*   *1*

Anthropology   3
*The Scientific Method   5 • Paradigms of
Biological Anthropology   7*

**Subjects That Biological Anthropologists
Study   10**
*Human Differences   10 • How Human
Populations Adapt   11 • Origins   11 • The
Role of Molecular Biology   13 • Behavior   13*

The Language of Biological Anthropology   15
Species   17 • Subspecies   18

**Phylogeny: Reconstructing the Evolutionary
History of Species   20**
*Phylogenetic Systematics   20 • Gene Lineages
and Organismal Lineages   23 • Ecology and
Evolution   25 • Evolution Versus Creationism   25*

The Perspective of Human Evolution   27

**Summary / Critical-Thinking Questions /
Suggested Readings   31**

---

2. *Earliest Beginnings: DNA, the Cell, and the First Animals*   *33*

Ultimate Origins   34
The Big Bang Theory   34

Continental Land Masses Drift Apart   36
*The Process of Continental Drift   37 • Effects
on the Earth's Geography   38 • Effects on the
Fossil Record and Living Species   39*

The First Evidence of Life   39
*Early Explanations   39 • The Search for
Secular Explanations   40*

Cells Evolve   42
*The Role of ATP   42 • The Role of
Photosynthesis   43*

**DNA: The Reproductive Machinery of the
Cell   44**
*How DNA Replicates Itself   44 • DNA and
Protein Synthesis   46*

The DNA Molecule Evolves   47
The Increase in Amount of DNA   47

The Cell Nucleus Evolves   51
The Earliest Organisms   51

**Evolution of DNA Repair and Sexual
Reproduction   55**

Mitosis and Meiosis Evolve   60
Mitosis   60 • Meiosis   61

The Earliest Animals Appear   62

**Summary / Critical-Thinking Questions /
Suggested Readings   64**

3. *Evolution and Natural Selection* 66

Influences on Darwin 67
Malthus's Theory of Populations 68 • Lyell's Theory of Uniformitarianism 69

Darwin Develops His Theory of Natural Selection 71
Collecting Evidence for Evolution 71 • Investigating Differential Reproduction 74 • Wallace's Co-Discovery of Natural Selection 75 • The Problem of Inherited Variation 76 • Darwin's Theory of Inheritance 80

Development of a Theory of Inheritance 80
The Laws of Heredity 81 • The Principle of Segregation 82 • The Principle of Independent

Assortment 84 • Chromosomal Theory of Heredity 86 • Gene Linkage and Crossing Over 87

Mendelian Genetics and Molecular Genetics 89
How Protein Synthesis Works 89 • Gene Structure 93

Mutation: The Source of Genetic Variation 93
Selection Acts on Mutations 97

The Puzzle of Sexual Reproduction 97

Summary / Critical-Thinking Questions / Suggested Readings 98

4. *Populations, Species, and Evolution* 100

Populations 101

Individuals Within Populations 102

Hardy-Weinberg Equilibrium and Population Genetics 104
Mutation 110 • Inbreeding 112 • Migration 114 • Chance Sampling 115

Evolution Changes Population Allele Frequencies 118
Selection 118 • Microevolution" Leads to "Macroevolution" 121

Speciation 122

Evolution of Behavior 123
Sexual Selection 124 • Ethology 126 • Fixed Action Patterns 127

Summary / Critical-Thinking Questions / Suggested Readings 130

5. *Stages of Vertebrate Evolution* 131

Homologous Structures 132

Clues from Morphology, Embryology, and Paleontology 134

Phylum Chordata 135

The First Vertebrates: Our Fish Heritage 139
The Evolution of a Bony Skeleton 142 • Early Life in Fresh Water 143 • Evolution of Biting Jaws 143 • Evolution of Limbs and Lungs 144

First Forays onto Dry Land: The Amphibians 145

Reptiles Conquer the Land 148
Adaptive Radiation 149 • The Evolution of Skull, Teeth, and Limbs 150

Mammals Evolve and Radiate 155
New Reproductive Strategies 155 • Homeothermy 157 • Enlarged Brain and Related Structures 158

The Human Brain in Evolutionary Perspective 159
The R-Complex 160 • The Limbic System 161 • The Neocortex 163

Mammals and Adaptive Radiation 166

Understanding Human Morphology 169

Summary / Critical-Thinking Questions / Suggested Readings 170

6. Introduction to Primates: Origins and Evolution 172

What Is a Primate? 173
Suborders of Primates 181 • Insectivore Ancestry of Primates 183

The First Primate Radiation: Plesiadapiforms 183

The Second Primate Radiation: Prosimians 187

Behavior and Social Organization of Prosimians 190

The Third Primate Radiation: Anthropoids 194

Origins and Evolution of the Monkeys 200
New World Monkeys 202 • Old World Monkeys 204

Summary / Critical-Thinking Questions / Suggested Readings 208

7. Primates: Patterns in Social Behavior 210

History of Field Studies 211

Advantages of Group Living 213

Development of Behavioral Modeling 215
Causes of Behavior 218

Male and Female Reproductive Strategies 219
Female Behavior 219 • Seasonality and Behavior 222 • Male Strategies and Behavior 224 • Female Strategies 227

Primate Foraging and Feeding 228

Primate Defenses Against Predation 230

Communication in Nonhuman Primates 232

Aggression and Dominance Interactions 236

Birth and the Mother–Infant Bond 238

Learning as Adaptation to Sociality 240

Summary / Critical-Thinking Questions / Suggested Readings 243

8. The Florescence and Decline of the Hominoids 246

Introduction to the Hominoids 247

The Apes 250
What Is an Ape? 250

Anatomy of a Climbing Heritage 257

Proconsulids: The Earliest Hominoids 259

Hominoids with Thick Molar Enamel Appear 267

Ape Evolution in Eurasia 268

Evolutionary Relationships of Hominoids 270

Summary / Critical-Thinking Questions / Suggested Readings 275

9. Evolution of Hominoid Behavior 278

The Lesser Apes: The Gibbons and Siamangs 279

The Great Apes 283
The Orangutan 283 • The Gorilla 287 • The Chimpanzee 290 • The Bonobo or Pygmy Chimpanzee 299

Human Social Behavior 302
Human Fixed Action Patterns 303 • Other

"Innate" Behaviors 305 • Human Sociobiology 307 • Human Behavioral Ecology 312 • Culture and Biology 313 • Future Prospects 316

Summary / Critical-Thinking Questions / Suggested Readings 317

10. Australopithecines 320

Definition of Hominidae 321
The Earliest Hominids 322
What the Earliest Hominid Looked Like 325
Taphonomy and Hominid Paleoecology 326
The Australopithecines 327
Australopithecus africanus 327 • Further Discoveries of the Australopithecines 329 • The Subfamily Becomes Defined 333 •

Interpretation of the Evolutionary History 335 • Australopithecine Phylogeny 344
Hominid Morphology and Behavior 346
Australopithecine Paleoecology and Behavior 348
Robust Australopithecines 353
Summary / Critical-Thinking Questions / Suggested Readings 356

11. The Genus Homo 359

The Brain, a Hallmark of Humanity 360
Teeth 362
Skull and Jaws 363
Body Size and Limbs 364
Homo habilis 364 • Age of Homo habilis 367 • Homo habilis and Other Species of Early Homo 368
The First Stone Tools 369
Paleoecology and Behavior 371
Homo erectus Comes onto the Scene 373
Paleoecology and Behavior of Homo erectus 375 • Homo and Robust Australopithecines 376

The Appearance of Homo sapiens 377
Evolutionary Origins of Homo sapiens 382 • Archaic Homo sapiens 384 • Homo sapiens sapiens 385 • Homo sapiens neanderthalensis 385 • Behavior of Early Homo sapiens 388 • Evolutionary Relationships in Homo sapiens 389
Summary / Critical-Thinking Questions / Suggested Readings 395

12. The Evolution of Human Social Behavior 397

Human Behavioral Evolution 398
Primate Behavior 401 • Baboon Models 403 • Ape Models 403 • Studies of Modern Carnivores 406
Archaeology's Insights into Cultural Development 407
Paleobehavior 407
Model Building and Ethnographic Research 412
Reconstructing Early Human Behavior 413
Historical Overview 413 • New Behavioral

Models Emerge: Bipedalism 414 • Brain Size 421 • Cerebral Laterality: Two Brains in One 425 • Speech Areas of the Cortex 427 • Language 428 • Art, Symbolism, and Speech 432 • Anatomical Evidence for Speech 433
Summary / Critical-Thinking Questions / Suggested Readings 435

13. Human Biology and Variation 438

The Nature of Human Genetic Variation 439
How Variation Is Measured 441
The Process of Geographical Isolation 444

Early Studies of Human Variation 446
What is "Race"? 447 • Inadequacy of Traditional Racial Classifications 452

Genetic Markers Can Trace Population Relatedness 453

Natural Selection Causes Human Variation 456
Blood Group Polymorphisms 461 • The HLA System 464 • Lactose Intolerance 465 • Skin Pigmentation 466

Genetic Influence on Behavioral Variation 469
Twin Studies 470 • Race, IQ, and Social Class 470 • Alcoholism 472 • Schizophrenia 474

Summary / Critical-Thinking Questions / Suggested Readings 475

---

14. *The Human Life Cycle: Human Biology, Growth, and Adaptability* 478

Human Growth Studies 480
How Growth Is Defined 483 • How Growth Is Measured 485 • The Seven Stages of Human Growth 485 • Genetic and Hormonal Control of Growth 491 • Growth and Development: A Guide to Evolutionary History 492 • Secular Trends in Growth and Maturation 494 • Growth and Development in Different Human Groups 495 • Responses to Modernization and the Urban Environment 498

Human Adaptability to Environment 500
Heat and Cold 501 • Light and Solar Radiation 503 • High Altitude 504

Nutritional and Dietary Aspects of Adaptation 505

Modern Life and Human Evolution 507

Summary / Critical-Thinking Questions / Suggested Readings 512

---

15. *The Modern Human Condition in Evolutionary Perspective: Applied Biological Anthropology* 514

Premises and Goals of Applied Biological Anthropology 515
Definition 515 • Human Adaptation and the Modern Environment 516

Biomedical Anthropology and Evolutionary Medicine 519
Sudden Infant Death Syndrome 520 • Neonatal Jaundice 521 • Coping with the "Diseases of Civilization" 522 • Human Populations, Infectious Diseases, and Parasites 524 • Structural Problems 526 • Proper Birth Environment for the Human Primate 528

Forensic Anthropology 528
Facial Reconstruction 528 • Criminal

Investigations 529 • Human Rights Investigations 531

Applied Aspects of Anthropometry 533
Eugenics 533 • Design Uses 534 • Biometric Security Uses 535

Evolutionary Perspectives on Brain and Behavior 535
Treating Brain-Injured Children 535

Anthropological Lessons for Education 538

Biological Anthropology, Human Ecology, and Quality of Life 539

Summary / Critical-Thinking Questions / Suggested Readings 540

Appendix 1: The Language of Biological Anthropology: Human Anatomy 542

Appendix 2: The Language of Biological Anthropology: Geology 547

Appendix 3: The Language of Biological Anthropology: Biology and Taxonomy 548

Glossary   550
References   565
Illustration Credits   575
Index   578

Frontiers Boxes

Evolution and Creation: Current
Controversies   *Eugenie C. Scott*   28
Molecular Clocks and Human Evolution
Vincent Sarich   58
The Interaction of Climate, Environment,
and Evolution   *Lloyd H. Burckle*   78
Frontiers in Morphological Analysis   *Glenn
C. Conroy*   164
Predation, Feeding Strategies, and Primate
Origins   *Matt Cartmill*   192
Insights from Field Primatology   *Linda D.
Wolfe*   234
Miocene Apes and Modern Hominoids
David R. Begun   260

Chimpanzee Hunting Behavior and
Human Evolution   *Craig B. Stanford*   308
The Earliest Australopithecines and Human
Origins   *Alan Walker*   345
Multiregional Evolution in the Genus
Homo   Milford Wolpoff   378
Were Our Ancestors Hunters or
Scavengers?   *John D. Speth*   418
Dissecting the Human Genome   *Kenneth K.
Kidd and Judith R. Kidd*   450
The Growth of Pastoral Turkana
Children   *Michael Little*   510
Evolutionary Medicine   *S. Boyd Eaton*   530

Preface

This book has been a long time in the making. It represents not only what we hope will be a useful approach to the teaching of human evolution at the introductory college and university level, but also a new restatement of the coherency and fundamental compatibility of all the many and varied subdisciplines in which biological anthropologists have become specialized. In all, there is the uniting thread of evolution by natural selection, which forms the basic paradigm of our discipline. The subtitle of the volume underlines this concept by using the term "synthetic" to define our approach. Our hope is that our exposition does justice to the elegant theoretical framework of modern biological anthropology and that we have succeeded in communicating the exciting diversity so apparent in this rapidly developing field.

This book is a narrative treatment of human evolution, organized along lines of increasing organismal complexity, leading from prebiotic replicating molecules through to modern *Homo sapiens*. Following this organization, the text proceeds generally from very early time to the present, and from broad taxonomic categories that include human beings to progressively more specific categories, ending with *Homo sapiens sapiens*. We have used available paleoecological data to set the stage and provide the context of the morphological and behavioral adaptations characterizing our ancestors at each major time period. We believe that this organization serves to build students' understanding of the biological, genetic, and anatomical basics of biological anthropology so that the complex questions of hominid phylogeny, human sociocultural behavior, human variability, and modern-day adaptation to our increasingly demanding environment can be approached in more meaningful ways. The table provides an overview of the text's organization.

Many individuals have shaped this book. Sherwood Washburn and Jane Lancaster were instrumental in developing our ideas of a text that brought together fossils and behavior. Joe Birdsell was an important influence in our incorporation of ecology and population perspectives. Jack Cronin deserves credit for contributing the concept of a textbook that fully integrated molecular and fossil approaches. We are indebted to the authors of the text's Frontiers boxes who agreed to share their perspectives and insights, Eugenie C. Scott, Vincent Sarich, Lloyd H.

Time (Years)	Taxonomic Level	Taxa	Structural Complexity	Behavior/ Adaptation	Chapters
10^4–Present	Populations and "Races"	*Homo sapiens sapiens*		Adaptability and Disequilibrium	11,12, 13,14,15
10^5	Subspecies	*Homo sapiens sapiens*		Culture	11, 12, 13,14,15
	Species	*Homo sapiens*	Cerebral Expansion	Language	10
10^6		*Homo erectus*	Body Size Increase	Fire Use	10
	Genus	*Homo*	Cerebral Expansion	Stone Tool Use	10
	Family	Hominidae	Thick-Enamelled Molars	Bipedalism/ Omnivorous	9
10^7	Superfamily	Hominoidea	Body Size Increase	Climbing/ Hanging	8
	Order	Primates	Vision	Social/Arboreal	6, 7
10^8	Class	Mammalia	Limbic System; High Metabolism	Nocturnal/ Insectivorous	5
		Reptilia	R-Complex/ Kidney	Terrestrial	5
		Amphibia	Hand/Foot	Semi-Terrestrial	5
		Pisces	Limb Elements	Aquatic	4
	Phylum	Chordata	Multi-cellular	Instinct	3
10^9	Kingdom	Animalia	Cellular/Multi-cellular	Active Movement	2,3
2–3×10^9			RNA/DNA		1,2

Burckle, Glenn C. Conroy, Matt Cartmill, Linda D. Wolfe, David R. Begun, Craig B. Stanford, Alan Walker, Milford Wolpoff, John D. Speth, Kenneth K. Kidd, Judith R. Kidd, Michael Little, and S. Boyd Eaton.

In the book's long history our editors and publishers, Peter Dougherty, Jerry Lyons, Nancy Roberts, Fred Whittingham, and Barbara Reilly have all believed in the book and have uniquely contributed to the outline, structure, and content in their own ways. Readers and reviewers have helped us immensely in refining passages and editing muddled text. We particularly thank Marc Feldesman, John Fleagle, Paris Pavlakis, Sue Parker, and many anonymous reviewers. Our students have contributed tremendously to the development of the book by their many questions and careful reading, particularly Margaret Streloff, Leslie Khayatpoor, Jean Henderson, Heather Harlan, and Levon DerMikaelian. A special thanks goes to Sabina Johnson for the long hours of copyediting she put in. Finally, the forbearance, support, and encouragement of Meleisa McDonell and Barbara Almquist ensured that this book did not take a second decade to complete. For that we are all grateful.

Evolutionary Perspectives on Human Biology and Behavior

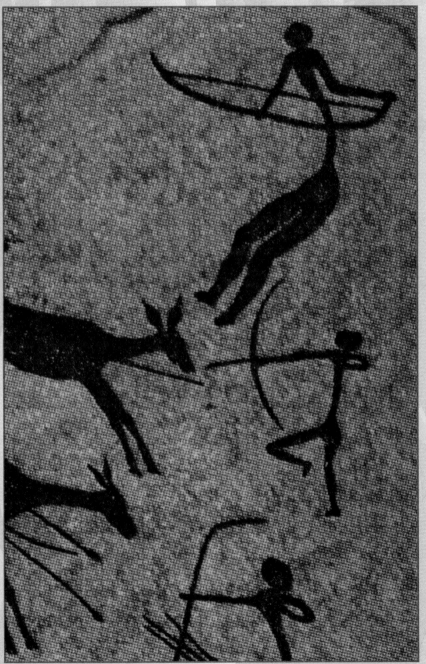

Anthropology Studies Humankind
The Scientific Method
Paradigms of Biological Anthropology

Subjects That Biological Anthropologists Study
Human Differences
How Human Populations Adapt
Origins
The Role of Molecular Biology
Behavior

The Language of Biological Anthropology
Species
Subspecies

Phylogeny: Reconstructing the Evolutionary History of Species
Phylogenetic Systematics
Gene Lineages and Organismal Lineages
Ecology and Evolution
Evolution Versus Creationism

The Perspective of Human Evolution

Summary

Critical-Thinking Questions

Suggested Readings

Biological Anthropology is about humankind's place in nature, how we came to be, how and why our bodies and brains are built the way they are, and why we behave as we do. Portions of these subjects are studied by scientists in many diverse disciplines, but the general, or holistic, study of them is the domain of **biological anthropology.** This broad-based understanding of the human organism is the strength of biological anthropology, and in today's increasingly specialized world of science, it is an important perspective.

The basic scientific framework of modern biological anthropology is *evolution by natural selection,* Charles Darwin's theory to explain the origin and diversity of species on earth. This theory provides scientists with a way to make predictions about human evolution, biology, and behavior, and to test their predictions against observations made in nature. For example, these observations result from laboratory experiments, field studies of our living primate relatives in remote rain forests, or excavations of fossils millions of years old. To give our readers an overall appreciation of human adaptation, anatomy, behavior, and evolution, this book integrates the advances that biological anthropologists have made in understanding human evolution and biology. We draw upon many different lines of evidence to demonstrate both the uniqueness of the human condition and those continuities that make humans part of nature.

Human beings evolved out of and are still today intimately connected with the natural world. The "natural world" does not connote only the "forest primeval" or the African savanna homeland of our early ancestors. Our ancestors lived as gatherers and hunters for the last several million years. We have been "civilized"—living in permanent structures packed into villages, towns and cities, growing food plants, tending domesticated animals, and using metal tools—only for the last few thousand years. This period is less than one-half of one percent of our evolutionary history, which began approximately 2.5 million years ago when we became stone tool–using early humans. But regardless of the diversity of our modern habitats, our biology is still that of hunter-gatherers, quick-witted opportunists who can eat almost anything and who can survive under conditions of great hardship as well as prosperity.

biological anthropology–the study of human evolution, biology, variation, and adaptation (also known as physical anthropology).

ANTHROPOLOGY STUDIES HUMANKIND

Anthropology is the science that studies humans, their biology, adaptations, behavior, and variation within the context of a specialized adaptation of learned social behavior called **culture.** Anthropologists study such broad ranging phenomena as physical and cultural differences among human groups, the structure of the many human languages, the adaptability of human groups to different environmental conditions, the patterns of growth, and the changing patterns of culture over time. This broad scientific agenda makes anthropology a discipline with many specialists and many subdisciplines. For this reason, anthropological research is frequently described as "multidisciplinary." One characteristic of all anthropologists is a commitment to understanding humanity in its entirety, as a functioning whole. For this reason anthropology is also termed holistic.

Anthropology grew out of the Enlightenment, the period of European intellectual discovery in the eighteenth century when interest arose in the diversity of the natural world and scientists became committed to the empirical method. As foreign lands became better known, the perspective of Europeans became more global. People with different customs, living in environments that seemed strange to Europeans, speaking unknown and unwritten languages, and lacking historical records, required explanations. Where did they come from? Why did they live where they lived? How did their customs and languages develop? Anthropology arose as a means to answer these questions.

Although many of the earliest contributors to anthropology were European, today scientists throughout the world contribute to the anthropological data base. For example, Japanese researchers have offered new, ground-breaking insights into the behavior of the non-human primates, the monkeys and apes; and African biological anthropologists have made some of the most important fossil discoveries, leading us closer to an understanding of our origins.

Anthropology in the United States is generally made up of four fields: biological or physical anthropology, cultural anthropology or ethnology, archaeology, and linguistics. Biological anthropologists, also referred to as **physical anthropologists,** study the physical makeup, evolution, and variations of human populations, the relationships of humanity with the natural world, and the biological bases of human behavior. **Cultural anthropologists** study living societies of people, their customs, their myths, their kinship systems, their rituals, and all aspects of their social behavior within the uniquely human adaptation of culture. **Archaeologists** look at how human culture has adapted and evolved over time through the study of artifacts and sites. **Linguists** study language: its many varieties, the forces governing how languages change, the relationships between language and the

anthropology–the study of humankind.

culture–learned aspects of behavior passed on from one generation to the next in human societies.

physical anthropology–the study of human evolution, biology, variation, and adaptation (also known as biological anthropology).

cultural anthropology–the anthropological study of human societies, their belief systems, their cultural adaptations, and their social behavior.

archaeology–the anthropological study of past cultures, their social adaptations, and their lifeways by use of preserved artifacts and features.

linguistics–the anthropological study of languages, their diversity and connections, and the interaction of language and culture in society.

Figure 1–1 • Paleoanthropologist at work.

brain, and the interactions between language and cultural concepts. The four disciplines are joined, sometimes loosely, by their shared focus on human adaptation within culture, that set of learned behaviors which, shared by each member of a society, mediates all social interactions.

Culture has not been such a uniting theme in continental Europe. There "anthropology" is generally regarded as synonymous with American "biological anthropology." In Europe ethnology, archaeology, and linguistics are treated as related but separate sciences.

Biological anthropology, the subject of this book, is closely related to the branch of biology known as **human biology.** Biological anthropologists strive to accurately describe human physical structure both in the present and in the past. They seek to understand how human structure functions in real life and how human individuals with that structure "behave." In addition, biological anthropologists investigate how function and behavior are integrated into the environment in which human beings live. Because they want to understand the origins of structures, biological anthropologists also explore human genetics, growth and development, and evolutionary history.

There are some strong connections between biological anthropology and other anthropological subdisciplines. Biological anthropologists may come into close contact with archaeologists in the cross-disciplinary area of **paleoanthropology,** the study of human evolution through fossils and artifacts (Figure 1–1). Archaeologists may find a fossilized human skull, but the job of describing and studying the specimen falls to the biological anthropologist. Or biological anthropologists may find it essential to put together their knowledge of skeletal biology with that of the cultural and living contexts that the archaeologist has discovered in order to better understand the adaptations of a past human population. Biological anthropologists who study the behavior of the nonhuman primates may have close intellectual ties to psychologists. Specialists on human growth and adaptation may feel particularly at home among a group of biologists who specialize in human biology. And biological anthropologists who investigate molecular biology and the genetics of human populations may work closely with geneticists and molecular biologists. Because biological anthropology is an interdisciplinary field, there are many areas of cross-communication and cross-fertilization, limited only by the scientific ingenuity of individual researchers.

Many of the subject areas relevant to understanding human evolution and biology discussed in this book are taught not only in Anthropology departments but within departments of biology, genetics, biochemistry, anatomy, geology, geography, environmental sciences, and psychology. Researchers in human evolution may call themselves biological anthropologists, biologists, geneticists, biochemists, geologists,

human biology–the branch of biology that studies human physiology and adaptation; closely related to biological anthropological study of the same topics.

paleoanthropology–the study of the physical characteristics, evolution, and behavior of fossil humans and their relatives, incorporating parts of biological anthropology and archaeology.

anatomists, paleontologists, or psychologists, depending on their research specialty. We will use "biological anthropology" and "biological anthropologists" as the most inclusive terms to refer to this broad, interdisciplinary field and to those scientists studying human evolution.

Most biological anthropologists work in university departments of anthropology, where they teach courses in human evolution, human biology, and related subjects. The second largest number of biological anthropologists work in medical schools as instructors and researchers in departments of anatomy or in other research departments. The third largest number work in natural history museums or research institutes where their responsibilities include care of collections of specimens and basic research. A smaller number of biological anthropologists are found in departments of biology, psychology, genetics, biochemistry, forensic studies, and in industry.

The Scientific Method

Anthropology, biology, and other branches of science use a "hypothetico-deductive" scientific method that requires the framing of ideas in the form of **hypotheses.** A hypothesis is a preliminary explanation of observations phrased as a proposition: if "x" is true, then "y" is true. The most significant characteristic of a hypothesis is that it must be *falsifiable*; that is, we must be able to disprove it. Testing and experimentation determine if a given hypothesis explains or conforms with what is observed. If it does not it is rejected or modified. A **theory** is a hypothesis or a series of hypotheses that has stood the test of time and has withstood numerous attempts at falsification. This methodology of hypothesis testing distinguishes science from the humanities.

The most widely understood application of the scientific method is the experiment. Scientists formulate a question that they want to answer, devise a test in which the variables are all held constant except those being tested, run the experiment while varying the conditions of interest, and compare the results to a "control" in which all the variables are held constant. This is the standard mode of operation in experimental sciences such as physics and chemistry.

Biological anthropology also is an experimental science. In the 1950s Sherwood Washburn advanced the approach of "experimental anthropology," later termed the "new physical (biological) anthropology."[1] Thereafter the testing of specific hypotheses in biological anthropology

---

[1]Some anthropologists make a distinction between the older term, "physical anthropology," and the newer term, "biological anthropology." In this book and in most common usage the two terms are synonymous and interchangeable. When a distinction is made it refers to "physical anthropology" being a more specialized field within biological anthropology dedicated to studying human anatomical structures and variation.

hypothesis—an explanation of a set of observations that can be disproved or falsified by additional observations or facts.

theory—usually a set of hypotheses that withstands attempts at disproof and continues to successfully explain observations as they are made, thus gaining scientific support over time.

has been standard procedure. Earlier generations of biological anthropologists tended to go out into the field and gather masses of facts and observations on human populations, but without clearly defined hypotheses to test. Modern biological anthropologists must articulate the hypotheses they want to test before they set off on expeditions. It is not sufficient simply to write in to a funding organization expressing interest in observing monkeys in the wild, for example. A scientist must present a research plan. A researcher might propose testing the hypothesis that a male in a particular monkey species, when he displaces the dominant male in the social group, tends to kill infants that have been fathered by the previous male. This is a testable hypothesis. Either the males kill the infants most of time or they do not.

Biological anthropology is also an historical science, concerned with reconstructing past events. Hypotheses relating to events that happened millions of years ago in the human evolutionary past may seem to be beyond the scope of "experiment" for the most part. But even in these cases experiments have been designed that recreate the conditions of the past in order to test hypotheses about early behavior patterns. Paleoanthropological studies, for example, may be designed to discover how and under what circumstances fossils or artifacts were buried in sediments. In attempting to answer these questions, scientists conduct experiments to see what sort of changes occur in bones in modern environments. They may observe hyenas at a kill, collect the bones after the hyenas are finished, and look at the bones under a microscope. They may examine the scratches on bone after trampling by a herd of cattle. Or they may cut meat off bones using stone tools and examine the cut marks made this way. These sorts of experiments may tell researchers whether a particular scratch pattern found in a fossil site was made by the teeth of predators, trampling under hooves, or the hands of ancient humans while obtaining meat for food.

In the natural sciences the concept of "experiment" has carried over to encompass comparative study of animals and plants in different habitats, environments, or time periods. In a real sense these scientists are doing "experiments," but instead of varying experimental conditions themselves, they allow nature to vary the conditions. For example, Charles Darwin undertook these sorts of studies in the Galápagos Islands off South America (see Chapter 3) when he compared the animal species to see how they had responded biologically to conditions on the various islands. In addition, for both ethical and practical reasons, biological anthropologists cannot perform controlled laboratory experiments on human beings for many of the questions that they want to answer. Here comparative study of human groups can be an "experiment" designed to test alternative hypotheses for human biological differences. For example, anthropologists interested in the causes of the unique physical attributes of people living high in the Andes Mountains (see Chapter 14) can compare the anatomy of members of the group who moved to the lowlands as children with those relatives who stayed at home. In this way, they can test whether environmental conditions or inheritance was the main cause of the mountain group's physical characteristics.

The Paradigms of Biological Anthropology

Like other fields of science, biological anthropology has a method of inquiry and an associated set of questions that serve as an organizing framework of inquiry or **paradigm.** Observations that are made and tests or experiments that are undertaken are grounded in theory. For example, if we observe that different peoples around the world have different colors of skin, we must explain how these differences are caused, how they originated in the past, and how they are affected by today's world.

Typology The paradigms of biological anthropology have changed significantly over the years. In the early phases of biological anthropology, when scientific interest lay in putting the vast array of new information about human diversity that was pouring into Europe into some sort of order, the paradigm of biological anthropology was **typology.** Typology is the designation of one individual drawn from a larger group as "typical" of that group. It is defined as the "type." Typology was an attempt to define a clear set of criteria that could be used to characterize any given species and to classify individuals within those groups. For example, if a typologist was interested in studying dogs, he or she might choose a "type," say an individual German shepherd, to exemplify the concept of "dog" (species *Canis familiaris*). Although there might be an awareness that there is quite a bit of variation in dogs, from Chihuahuas to Great Danes, typologists de-emphasize individual variation from the "type" because the goal is to classify the diversity of life. There is nothing wrong with typology, which is still the first step in biological investigations, because we must know and define what species with which we are working. But other paradigms have come into play that are important as well.

Typology was the first organized approach to studying the human species. The founder of biological anthropology, German scientist Johann Friedrich Blumenbach (1752–1840), whose interest lay in chronicling the worldwide diversity of modern human beings, used typology to define different human "races" or biological groups. He established "types" that were ideals of whole groups of people. His grouping of five major divisions of the human species (Figure 1–2), based on physical characteristics and geography, became known as "races," and was accepted for many years. Today's biological anthro-

paradigm–a framework for understanding and interpreting observations.

typology–"idealist" definition of an entire group by reference to a "type" which tends to ignore variation from that ideal.

pologists have much more data on modern human biological variation than were available to Blumenbach, and few would now agree with his five-fold division of the human species. Yet Blumenbach's pioneering work was important in establishing the groundwork for later development of biological anthropology.

Culture   Culture, the human adaptation of learned social behavior, became a second important paradigm in biological anthropology. In the early phases of the history of anthropology, all attributes of a human group were considered innate characteristics—that is, inherited and not affected by environment, much like the plumage and song patterns of bird species. Early anthropologists might describe a group of South Sea Islanders, previously unknown to Westerners, by the color of their skin, the color and curl of their hair, the clothes they wore, their marriage customs, the language spoken by the group, and even individuals' psychological attributes, all in the same context of innate characteristics. But as the European countries established colonies, and indigenous peoples began to migrate to Europe for a Western education, it became apparent that culture was not innate to a particular human group. A young Australian aborigine or a Masai from Kenya could be transplanted to England, attend Eton and Oxford, and end up speaking, acting, dressing, and thinking about things just as someone else of similar educational background who was English. However, nothing changed the essential physical characteristics of the Australian or the Masai even if they did speak with an "Oxbridge" accent. Clearly physical and cultural traits were under the control of different laws.

For the last century and a half anthropology has struggled to understand the laws that govern cultural and physical diversity. It has often been a confusing struggle, and the fact that modern anthropology departments contain such diverse specialists as excavators of fossils, geneticists, experts on American Indian languages, archaeologists, and researchers on the symbols in myths and legends is testimony to this confusion. Anthropology can accurately be called a "multidisciplinary" subject. But rarely, if ever, does it become an "interdisciplinary" one, in which there is active cross-communication and significant cross-utilization of ideas and methods. Despite their joint embrace of "culture" as an organizing paradigm, especially in American universities, cultural anthropologists and biological anthropologists have pursued their own research methodologies largely independent of one another. Ethnologists, archaeologists, and linguists share the same cultural paradigm: They study how and why cultures vary one from another and how a particular culture meshes with its environment. A question that an anthropologist studying culture might ask, for example, is why a Polynesian tribe would have elaborate prayers, ceremonies, and gear for the dangerous fishing on the open sea, and simple and few cultural attributes for relatively safe fishing in lagoons. One possible answer is

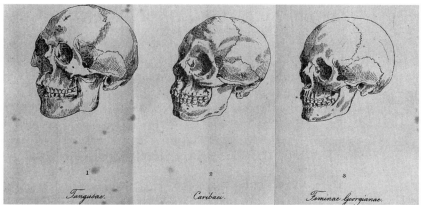

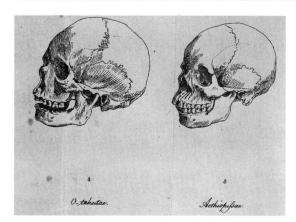

Figure 1–2 • Johann Friedrich Blumenbach (top, right), the founder of biological anthropology, and (left) his classification of human "races": (1) Mongolian, or "yellow" (*Tungusae*); (2) American, or "red" (*Caribaei*); (3) Caucasian, or "white" (*Georgianae*); (4) Malayan, or "brown" (*Taheitae*); and (5) Ethiopian, or "black" (*Aethiopilsae*).

that magic and religion, along with material culture, help humans cope with the environment. Culture then is one of the primary ways that humans adapt to their environment; and as such biological anthropologists should be aware of its importance today and in the past.

Evolution by Natural Selection   The third paradigm of importance to biological anthropology is **evolution by natural selection.** Evolution by natural selection is the theory advanced by Charles Darwin which holds that nature will favor those individuals, the "fittest," who possess traits that allow them to survive and to have more offspring. This process leads to biological differentiation over time and eventually may result in the formation of new species (see Chapter 3). And it is this paradigm that biological anthropologists use for the most part as the basis for most modern research. Because biological anthropologists study human biological variability, which is inherited and not profoundly affected by one's social environment, culture alone has not proved a very useful paradigm for this research. Some of this variability

evolution by natural selection—Darwin's theory that inherited variability results in the differential survival of individuals and in their ability to contribute to offspring in succeeding generations.

is associated with geographic location of human groups. Other variation is due to biological and physical adaptation to particular environments. The evolutionary paradigm that biological anthropologists use helps to explain the biological variability seen in human groups, and it provides a means to make predictions and to test hypotheses. Chapters 3 and 4 deal at length with evolution by natural selection, and it provides the organizing framework for the succeeding chapters. Yet it is not quite accurate to say that the evolutionary paradigm has supplanted and totally replaced the earlier typological and cultural paradigms in modern biological anthropology. For example, the discovery and naming of a new species of lemur living in a remote forest in Madagascar (see Chapter 6), new genetic evidence supporting the separation of a third species of chimpanzee (see Chapter 8), or the naming of a new species of a presumed early human ancestor (see Chapter 10)—all basic typology—can still generate a lot of scientific interest. As for culture, studies of primate behavior that shed light on some of the basic social behaviors of humans (see Chapters 7 and 9); research revealing early human behavior, such as evidence of early human cannibalism as well as the florescence of art in late Stone Age peoples (see Chapters 11 and 12); and studies of the complex but important interactions of health and lifestyle in modern urban environments (see Chapter 15); are some of the most compelling in biological antropology. All of these studies are now undertaken *within the context* of evolution, and herein lies its importance as a paradigm in the modern field of biological anthropology.

SUBJECTS THAT BIOLOGICAL ANTHROPOLOGISTS STUDY

Biological anthropologists deal with the problems of understanding how and why groups of people differ physically and genetically from one another, how they adapt biologically to their environment, how they grow and develop, and how the human species ultimately originated in the animal world. These questions can be framed broadly as questions relating to human evolution, that is, the laws that underlie human variation, adaptation, and patterns of physical change through space and time.

Human Differences

variation—the range of differences in physical or genetic makeup across, within, and between populations of modern humans.

Biological anthropologists study human **variation** and ask questions that can be termed "human differences" questions. Two such issues are: "How and why do people around the world look different?" and "Are differences in human groups primarily the results of inheritance or of different environments?"

Human beings around the world look different partly because they are adapted to different environmental conditions and partly because each population has a different history of migrations and infusions of peoples from elsewhere. Untangling the causes of variation can be complex. Human beings have a remarkable ability as individuals to change their behavior and as social groups to change their culture, depending on the environment in which they find themselves. These changes can and do have biological effects. Humans have been able to adapt successfully to many different habitats in the world today. How and under what conditions adaptability is expressed in growth patterns, physiology, or anatomical traits is an area of ongoing research in biological anthropology.

How Human Populations Adapt

The biological change to accommodate environmental conditions is called **adaptation.** Adaptation within the existing physical or physiological capabilities of humans, which occurs within the lifetimes of the individuals involved, is known as **adaptability** (see Chapter 14). Such *short-term* reversible responses to immediate environmental challenges are part of the universal human biological heritage. Human adaptability includes biochemical, physiological, and behavioral responses to variable environments.

The *long-term* adaptation of humans and other populations of living organisms to the varied habitats into which they may have spread over time is a focus of evolutionary studies. This adaptation occurs by anatomical change and is little modified by environment during individuals' lifetimes. Much of this book deals in one way or another with evolutionary adaptations of humans.

Origins

One of the most interesting and controversial issues that biological anthropologists have pursued, both today and in the past, is human origins. "Origins" questions have always exerted a strong influence on the field. Such questions as "What living animals are most closely related to humans?" and "What was the ancestral form of the living relatives like?" are still issues today, as they have been for over a century in one form or another. The time of appearance of the unique human lineage has been the topic of lively debate, and estimates range a span of more than 30 million years. Paleontologist Bjorn Kurtén (1972), for example, suggested that the hominid lineage appeared very early, approximately 30 million years ago, while molecular anthropologist Vincent Sarich (1967) suggested that the human lineage separated from that leading to the African apes much later, not much more than 5 million years ago (Figure 1–3). Other individual scholars have taken intermediate stances, although the consensus is now for a "late" or "recent" diver-

adaptation–biological change effected by evolution to accommodate populations to different environmental conditions.

adaptability–the range of physiological and behavioral responses that an individual can make to adjust to environmental changes.

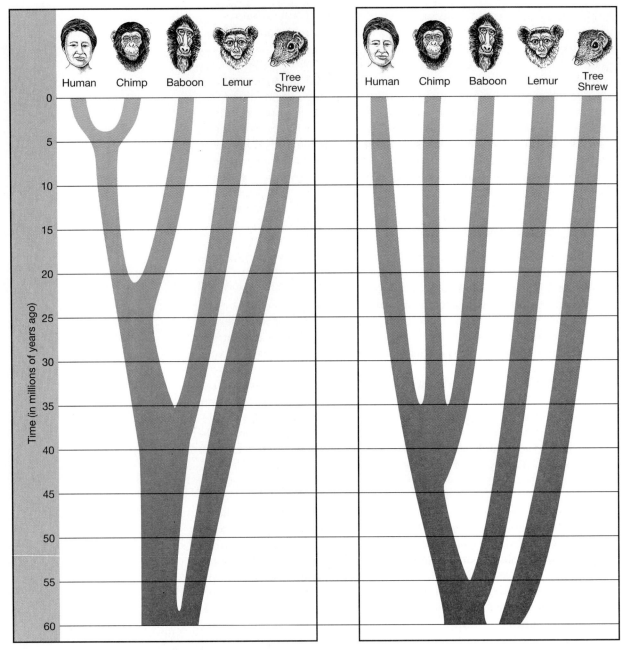

Figure 1–3 • Comparison of two widely varying hypotheses on the timing of the evolutionary divergences of the apes and hominids.

gence, that is, 5 to 10 million years ago. Many "tests" of the various hypotheses of human origins have been carried out over the last century. We will discuss them in Chapters 8 through 11.

Phylogeny, from the Greek word for "originating from branches," refers to the lineal relationships of fossil humans and other **primates**— "animals of the first rank,"—including monkeys, apes, and prosimians. Determining these relationships has been a primary consideration of biological anthropologists since fossil specimens were first found and recognized. The German naturalist Ernst Haeckel (1834–1919) produced the first phylogenetic tree for the human species by making use of comparative anatomy (Figure 1–4), because almost no fossil humans were known at the time. Traditionally, phylogenetic studies have been "vertical" in their orientation because they extend back into history. In contrast, understanding the ecology and behavior of fossil species, now gaining as much attention by researchers, is more "horizontal" in research design. Biological anthropologists are no longer satisfied with hypothesizing only evolutionary relationships between fossils. They want to know how early people and their primate ancestors adapted to their environments, to their diets, and to their social living arrangements and behavior.

The Role of Molecular Biology

A number of problems in human evolution are now addressed through the methods of molecular biology. Molecular evidence concerning the actual biological relationships of humans to the other primates is now rapidly accumulating. The data show that humans are most closely related to the African great apes, the chimpanzee and gorilla (see Chapter 8). In fact, human and chimpanzee are so close that they differ by only 1% to 2% of their DNA sequences. How humans and chimps can be so closely related genetically but quite different in their overall anatomy and behavior is a question that biological anthropologists are attempting to answer. Molecular data can serve also as a test of hypotheses based on the fossil record. For example, molecular data were used to disprove the hypothesis that a unique hominid lineage existed prior to 8 to 10 million years ago (see Chapter 8), and molecular data have played important roles in interpretations of the evolutionary history of modern *Homo sapiens* (see Chapter 11).

Behavior

Behavior—the patterning of animal activity over time—and how it relates to evolution and adaptation has become an important research focus in biological anthropology. Today's scientists want to know what animals did (not just what they were), what period of time they lived in, and what other animals they were related to. Contemporary human behavior is the evolutionary result of the behaviors in our ancestors

phylogeny–the study of evolutionary relationships of organisms.

Primates–the zoological order of animals to which human beings, their ancestors, and their closest living animal relatives belong.

behavior–patterns of animal activity over time.

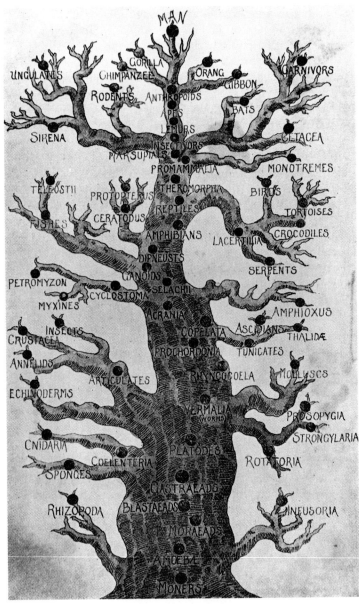

Figure 1–4 • Ernst Haeckel (top) and the first phylogenetic tree (right) depicting the evolution of the human species.

that led to reproductive success; that is, successfully reproducing off-spring in worlds long vanished and in ways of life quite different from today's. With a fuller knowledge of the behavior of our own closest living relatives, we can better understand how modern human behavior came to be. This comparative approach works because the early social and environmental situations to which the hominid lineage adapted in times past are similar to those of many nonhuman primates today. One of the keys, then, to understanding human evolution is a full appreciation of nonhuman primate social systems, and how and under what conditions they developed.

Biological anthropologists, known as **primatologists,** study primates, usually nonhuman primates, also sometimes termed "alloprimates." Primatologists are interested in questions relating to the behavior of the nonhuman primates, such as "How and why do primate species behave differently from one another?" and "What can an understanding of this behavior tell us about the behavior of early humans?" These questions may be approached in a number of ways. For example, anatomical study can be used to deduce the movement capabilities of joints, or researchers may explore what sort of environment and animal–plant relationships may have existed. Archaeology can indicate what sort of cultural behavior took place; and the comparative study of behavior can assist in making deductions about humans in relation to other primates.

Figure 1–5 • Naturalistic field research in primate behavior.

Most of our knowledge of the behavior of the nonhuman primates is derived from recent fieldwork and new controlled laboratory experiments (Figure 1–5). These studies, especially long-term fieldwork by primatologists, have clarified many misconceptions of how different primate species behave in the wild and what their true behavioral capabilities are. For example, Jane Goodall's thirty-year field study among the chimpanzees at Gombe, Tanzania, has resulted in fundamental changes of how we view the human condition. We no longer think of ourselves as the only tool-using animals, as chimps have been observed regularly making and using simple tools. We no longer consider meat eating as uniquely human, because chimps have been observed catching and eating animal prey. Recent laboratory studies of chimps have also shown that humans are not the only animals that can communicate symbolically; chimps can use pieces of colored plastic and sign language to refer to objects and abstract thoughts. Primatological studies now seek to understand nonhuman primates based on fact rather than folklore. As previously stated, living primates help anthropologists interpret the fossil remains of our ancestors, as well as providing case studies of evolution. These studies in turn help in our understanding of fossil bones and evolution when we consider the fact that these bones were once parts of living animals.

THE LANGUAGE OF BIOLOGICAL ANTHROPOLOGY

The language of biological anthropology is composed of the specialized jargons of a number of scientific disciplines, as well as some jargon unique to biological anthropology itself. Much of this terminological detail is unnecessary at an introductory level. Some general categories of terms are, however, necessary for an understanding of the field.

primatology—science that studies primates, usually primate behavior and ecology.

Many of the basic descriptive terms in biological anthropology are anatomical. In fact biological anthropology is frequently called "physical anthropology" because of its roots in investigating the physical structure of the human body. In our discussions of human evolutionary anatomy and fossil remains we will use a number of terms referring to the bones of the skeleton, the parts of the brain, and the teeth. Appendix A provides a synopsis of anatomical terms used.

There are a number of geological terms that come into biological anthropology via the work of paleoanthropologists, who extract fossils from the ground and thus have much in common with earth scientists. The interaction of evolution with climate change, the drifting of continents over time, and the reconstruction of the ancient environments in which our ancestors lived keep this a lively area of research. Appendix 2 discusses basic geological terminology and illustrates the geological time scale.

A large component of the terms making up the biological anthropological lexicon comes from biology. The proliferating terms of the rapidly developing fields of genetics and molecular biology make their way into biological anthropology, as do the terms of ecology, evolutionary biology, zoology, and behavioral biology. Perhaps the largest source of new terms for the beginning student is the **taxonomy** or naming of all the different animals that are relevant to understanding human beings' place in nature. These organisms are largely unfamiliar to most people and they generally have long Greek or Latin names that are difficult to pronounce. Sometimes this array of unfamiliar terms can be daunting. We provide the English translations of the names when they are first mentioned, and they can also be looked up in the glossary. There is an order to the organization of these names, appropriately termed **systematics,** which is based on the closeness of relationship among the animals. Appendix 3 provides the taxonomy and systematics of the primates, that group of animals most closely related to human beings. The taxonomic classification of the human species is presented in Table 1–1.

taxonomy–the science of naming different organisms.

systematics–the science of classifying and organizing organisms.

Table 1–1 • Taxonomy of the Human Species
Kingdom Animalia
Phylum Chordata
Class Mammalia
Order Primates
Infraorder Anthropoidea
Superfamily Hominoidea
Family Hominidae
Genus *Homo*
Species *Homo sapiens*

In this book we discuss many different kinds of animals, and taxonomy gives us a clear-cut and unambiguous way to refer to them. Taxonomy begins with the **species,** originally a term that simply meant "kind," but now indicates a formal taxonomic unit basic to biological classification. A species is defined as a group or population of organisms, the individuals of which naturally interbreed and produce fertile offspring (see also Chapters 3 and 4). Species are designated scientifically by a system of *binomial* ("two-named") *nomenclature.* Our species designation is *Homo sapiens* (Latin for "human the wise"). When only the first part of the binomial name is used, it refers to the level above the species in the taxonomic hierarchy, the **genus.** A genus groups species that are similar in adaptation. We are classified in the genus *Homo.*

Genera (the plural of genus) are placed within **families.** Our zoological family, the **Hominidae,** is defined on the basis of our mode of movement or *locomotion.* Hominids walk on two legs. How two-legged walking or bipedalism evolved and what type of locomotion preceded it are among the oldest and as yet unsolved questions in biological anthropology (see Chapter 10). But bipedalism serves as a useful definition for all the known members of the hominid family.

Species

The concept of the biological species is important because we rely on it for purposes of constructing taxonomies and phylogenies. Ernst Mayr (1963) defined a species as "actually or potentially interbreeding populations which are reproductively isolated from other such populations." We will discuss the concept of "populations" in greater depth in Chapter 4, but now it is sufficient to realize that a **population** is a group of related individuals in one species that live together in one place. Only within a species are male and female animals able to mate and produce offspring who themselves are capable of reproducing. Sometimes animals in different species can mate and produce offspring, as in the case of a horse and donkey producing a mule, but the offspring will be infertile and incapable of having offspring themselves. We would say biologically that the horse and donkey species are "reproductively isolated" from one another.

Mayr's definition works well for living species, but it poses special problems for interpreting the fossil record. For example, we cannot determine whether animals that we know only from their bones and teeth could or did interbreed. Instead, we must use a concept of anatomical distance: how distant in physical form species are in the modern world. That is, we compare extinct and living species and extrapolate this into the past. Also we can ascertain whether the anatomical differences between two fossils are about the same as, less than, or greater than, those between two known living species that can mate and produce fertile offspring. Because species possess their own unique adaptations, understanding the functional anatomy of fossils also helps to de-

species—an actually or potentially interbreeding group of organisms in nature.

genus—a taxonomic grouping of similar species.

family—a taxonomic grouping of similar genera.

Hominidae—the zoological family to which living humans and their bipedal relatives, all now extinct, belong.

population—a portion of a species occupying one area and sharing more genes in common among members of the group than with other members of the species.

holotype–the single specimen on which a taxonomic name is based.

paratypes–a group of specimens on which a taxonomic name is based.

morphology–the study of the form and anatomy of physical structures in the bodies of living or once living organisms.

subspecies–a formal designation of a population within a species that is characterized by biological differences from other such groups within the species; also termed **races.**

cline–a geographic gradient of biological variants in populations from one population center to another.

cide whether they were truly separate species in the past. Species determined from the fossil record are known as *paleospecies.*

Species, whether living or extinct, are defined in taxonomic usage by reference to a type. This may be a single specimen (a **holotype;** Figure 1–6) or a series of specimens (**paratypes**). **Morphology** is the study of form and structure in organisms. Morphological characteristics of the type are described and used to define an entire population of organisms, a species. However, because individuals vary one from another in all biological populations, adequate allowance must be made for slight differences. We may expect a type specimen and an unknown specimen that may possibly be tagged with a new species designation to differ in detail, but before a species designation is made this difference must be seen as greater than would be expected between any two individuals within a normal population. In the past, variation within populations was seldom recognized and, consequently, every new fossil discovery was given the name of a new species. Today, biological anthropologists study anatomical difference to discover at what point observed differences between two specimens are within the species limits or are large enough to place them in two different species.

Subspecies

Subspecies, also known as **races,** are populations within a species that are usually geographically distinct from one another, and may be distinguishable from other subspecies by external morphology and by genetic and behavioral differences. Members of subspecies may interbreed with one another and frequently do so at the fringes of their distribution. This pattern of interbreeding creates gradients of physical or biological variations called **clines,** which sometimes make clearcut distinctions between population centers in a species difficult to discern. Modern human beings may be one such species (see Chapter 13) but numerous species of African and Asian monkeys form well-defined

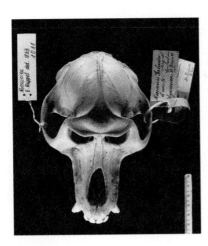

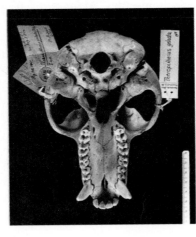

Figure 1–6 • Holotype of the gelada baboon, *Theropithecus gelada,* in the Senckenberg Museum, Frankfurt, Germany.

subspecies over their geographic ranges (Figure 1–7). The gorilla is well known for its three subspecies: two lowland subspecies in central and West Africa, and the well-studied mountain gorilla in the east. In taxonomy a species name is a binomial, but a subspecies name is a trinomial. Thus, the mountain gorilla is termed formally "*Gorilla gorilla beringei.*" As we shall see later, geographically differentiated groups of a species form the bases of future species.

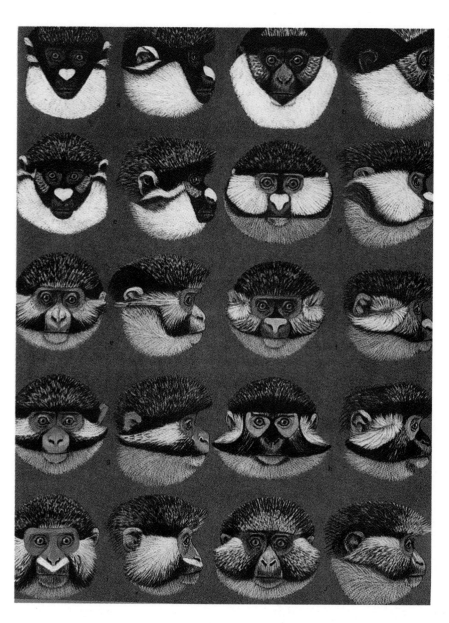

Figure 1–7 • Subspecies of the forest guenon of the genus *Cercopithecus,* by pelage. (From Napier and Napier, 1985)

PHYLOGENY: RECONSTRUCTING THE EVOLUTIONARY HISTORY OF SPECIES

Classification of any set of organisms needs to be based on an easily understood and reproducible set of criteria, so that scientists may communicate effectively about the organisms. In biological theory the ideal for classification is that species classified together should be more closely related to each other than to more distantly related species. Phylogenetic relationships are those that link species through their evolutionary history: a "family tree" through which species B is related to species C through an earlier **common ancestor** A (Figure 1–8). Classification schemes, then, should reflect our current knowledge of evolutionary history. This means that as further discoveries improve our knowledge of this history, they may change our classification schemes. Higher levels of classification above the species (the levels of genus and family) should reflect true evolutionary groupings; in other words, there should be successive levels of more distantly related species as one goes up the hierarchy. However, this ideal is not always realized. A recent example of a taxonomic problem is the family of the great apes, the chimp, the gorilla, and the orangutan (Pongidae). In older classifications, the orangutan, chimpanzee, and gorilla were all classified in this family. Through both biomolecular and fossil discoveries (see Chapter 8) it became apparent that chimps and gorillas as a group were more closely related to humans, classified in the Family Hominidae, than to orangutans. Pongidae therefore was recognized as a mixed classificatory term. In this book we use the family names of Panidae for the chimpanzee, Gorillidae for the gorilla, Pongidae for orangutans and their fossil antecedents, and Hominidae for humans and their fossil antecedents. Some authors, such as Delson (1989) and Andrews (1988), resolve this problem by including all the great apes and humans in the same family, which by the rule that the name first proposed has *priority,* is termed Hominidae. We feel that this approach has the disadvantage of understating the significant morphological, physiological, and behavioral differences among these groups. Here we use Hominidae to refer only to bipedal, large-molared primates closely related to modern humans (see Chapter 10), a position also adopted by Fleagle (1989) and by most specialists working on this group (e.g. Howell, 1978; Simons and Pilbeam, 1978; Johanson and White, 1979; Boaz, 1983; Hill and Ward, 1988).

Phylogenetic Systematics

Before the discovery of molecular measures of genetic relatedness between organisms (and even afterwards), scientists have been concerned with determining which morphological characteristics to use in classifying fossil species. For the purposes of classification, which were the important defining characteristics and which should be discarded?

common ancestor–an ancestral population that gives rise to two or more independent evolutionary lineages of organisms and the succeeding species that represent each lineage.

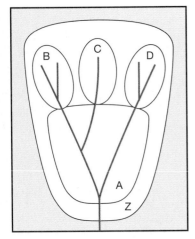

Figure 1–8 • A hypothetical phylogenetic tree with correlation between levels of taxonomic classification and taxonomy, based on single evolutionary origins (monophyly). A, B, C, and D represent species belonging to taxon Z. (From Schoch, 1986)

For example, if we wish to classify horses and cows, it hardly does any good to note that they both have four feet. Why? Because many other animals are also quadrupedal. Thus, the morphological characteristic of having four feet does not serve to distinguish horses and cows either from each other or from other animals.

The German biologist Willi Hennig instituted the field termed "phylogenetic systematics" during the 1950s, now more frequently termed **cladistics** (Greek for "splitting apart"). Cladistics is a way of analyzing relationships among animals in the fossil record by using only newly arisen or "derived" traits, or characteristics. It offers a clear method for determining which characters to use in classification. Characters that have been inherited from ancient, primitive ancestors are thrown out, and only the derived characters that are unique to the taxon are kept for classification. These characters are termed **apomorphies** (Latin *apo*—"away from"; *morphy*—"body or form") or "derived characters." In the example of horses and cows above, an apomorphy of cows might be taken to be the presence of horns, whereas four-footedness is discarded for purposes of this classification because it is a primitive character. Once derived characters are determined for a group of organisms, it is possible to draw a diagram of relatedness, or **cladogram.** The cladogram can then be used to construct a series of phylogenies, which hypothesize ancestor–descendent relationships (Figure 1–9), which must then be tested.

Scientists reconstruct the phylogenetic history of a species by using a basic principle of evolutionary biology: descendants will resemble their ancestors because they are related genetically; that is, they share a large number of genes. A corollary to this principle is that descendants far removed in time from an ancestral population will be more dissimilar than populations not so distant in time from each other. The key assumption here is that anatomical similarity reflects closeness of relationship. The fact that virtually every anatomical structure of a human body can be matched in the chimpanzee body led Thomas Henry Huxley (1825–1895), for example, to hypothesize a close relationship between the African apes and humans (Figure 1–10). Sometimes, however, overall anatomical similarity may be misleading. Species that are unrelated or distantly related may adapt to similar environments and end up looking very similar (see Chapter 4). This phenomenon is known as **parallelism** or **convergence.** Parallelism is sometimes difficult to discern, especially if we have incomplete information about the overall form of the animals, as in the case in which only a small portion of a fossil skeleton is discovered. But if enough of the structure is present, it is usually possible to tell the difference between anatomical similarities evolved in parallel and those that are due to common inheritance. For example, the wings of a bird and a bat are formed by different bones, which indicates that they are evolved in parallel and not inherited from a common ancestral source.

Some species evolve very slowly, and a modern descendant species, a "living fossil," can closely resemble an ancestor. For this reason

cladistics—the common term for the study of the phylogenetic relationships among a group of related animals by reference to only derived traits shared in common.

apomorphy—in cladistic terminology, a newly arisen or derived trait used in systematics.

cladogram—branching diagram showing relative relationships among taxonomic groups of animals; not to be confused with a phylogenetic tree, which postulated ancestor–descendent relationships.

parallelism—the evolution of similar traits in two closely related species, such as elongated hind legs for jumping in two small rodent species.

convergence—the evolution of similar traits in two distantly related animals, such as similar streamlined body form for swimming in dolphins and sharks.

Figure 1–9 • A cladogram and how it differs from a phylogeny. Any single cladogram can generate a number of different phylogenies. (From Schoch, 1986)

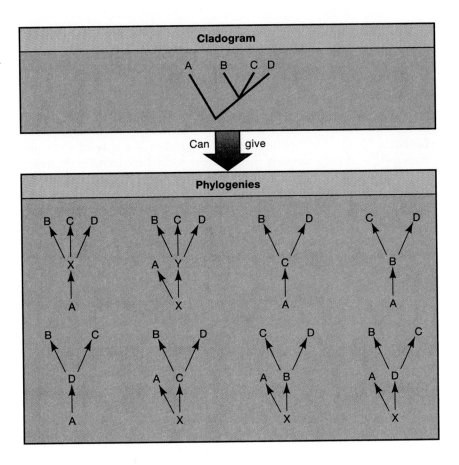

evolutionists use the geological record to determine the age of fossils. Armed with data on anatomical similarity and geological age, they can then assemble a phylogenetic tree for the fossil forms under study.

Figure 1–10 • T. H. Huxley's dissection of a human and a chimpanzee brain, showing the close anatomical similarity between the two: *(a)* posterior lobe, *(b)* lateral ventricle, *(c)* posterior cornu, *(d)* the hippocampus minor.

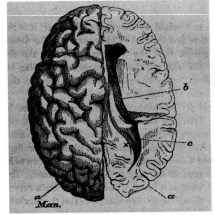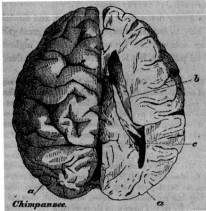

Gene Lineages and Organismal Lineages

Molecular biologists have devised an alternative way to investigate the phylogenetic history of living forms. They reason that if the goal of evolutionary research is to discover the genetic relatedness of organisms in order to reconstruct their phylogenetic histories, why not measure genetics itself? By using techniques to determine the actual structure of the DNA molecule that makes up genes (Figure 1–11), they are able to assess the genetic relatedness of species directly.

Molecular approaches to phylogeny are much more recent than those which use fossils only, and the relationship between the two approaches has sometimes been rocky. Two major areas of difference have separated the two disciplines. First, molecular studies are limited in their data base to using only living species for reconstructing phylogenies. Although it is theoretically possible, extracting DNA and other organic material from fossils has proven difficult. However, some recent progress has been made in isolating DNA from insects preserved in fossil amber. Second, there is not necessarily a close relationship between genetic distances, as measured by molecular techniques, and morphological distance. Quite similar species of frogs, for example, may be very divergent genetically, whereas species very different morphologically, such as humans and chimpanzees, are quite similar genetically (see Chapter 4 for more discussion of this paradox).

Despite numerous recent debates between paleontologists, who use fossils to measure evolution, and molecular biologists, who use genes to measure evolution, their approaches attempt to measure the same

Figure 1–11 • Chromosomes of human and chimpanzee compared. Within each pair, the human chromosome appears on the left, the chimpanzee chromosome on the right.

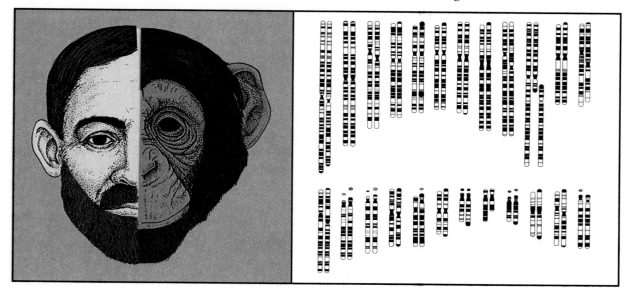

phylogenetic history. They must, therefore, ultimately be compatible. As indicated, their data are not overlapping. Paleontologists have access to some species that have become extinct and have left no living descendants. Those species can contain clues about the twists and turns of phylogeny that cannot be discerned by molecular biologists who have no living descendent from which to work. Molecular biologists, on the other hand, have a superior method of determining true relatedness between species based on genetic similarity—a level of resolution that paleontologists can only approximate.

When molecular biologists reconstruct phylogeny, they are actually reconstructing gene lineages—ancestor–descendent lineages of specific sequences of DNA. When paleontologists reconstruct phylogeny, they are attempting to reconstruct population lineages of whole organisms (Figure 1–12). These two measures of phylogenetic change may not always coincide. Genes may evolve faster, more slowly, or stay the same,

Figure 1–12 • Gene phylogeny versus organismal phylogeny. Species evolve through time both in body form and in molecular structure. The rates of both types of change can be remarkably constant, or they can vary significantly from one another. Biological anthropologists and other evolutionary biologists look at both types of evolutionary change.

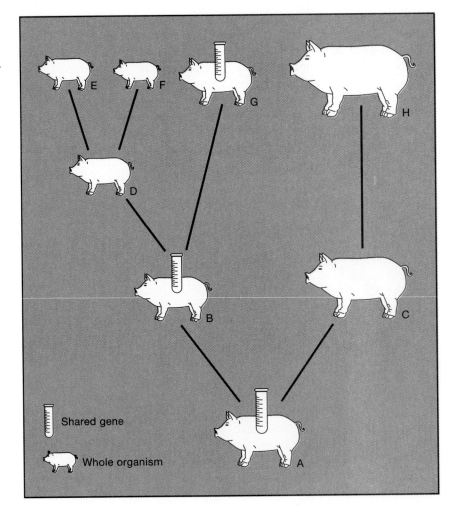

depending on selection, as organisms evolve within populations. But often the two measures will coincide. When they do not, the challenge will be to determine which of the many evolutionary forces have been at work to put the molecular and paleontological assessments at variance to one another. A better and more complete view of evolutionary history will ultimately emerge from a successful interaction of both disciplines.

Ecology and Evolution

Ecology (from the Greek, meaning "study of habitation") is a field of study that dates back to Ernst Haeckel, who coined the term in 1868. In the modern usage of the term, ecology integrates study of the habitat in which a population lives with its genetic, morphological, and behavioral adaptations. Each species is part of a complex ecosystem made up of a community of plants and animals. Within this ecosystem a species occupies its own **ecological niche,** a unique way of life to which it alone is adapted. A species' niche is defined by where it lives, what it eats, and how it goes about its daily life.

Change in the environment in which a species lives is the driving force behind evolutionary change in populations. If the environment stays the same over eons, there is very little morphological change. But earth scientists have accumulated more and more evidence that shows that our planet has undergone many episodic and sometimes rapid climatic and environmental changes. A dynamic interplay has existed between ecology and evolution. Evolutionists are now looking at the geological record of climatic change, molecular phylogeny, and the paleontological record of species to piece together how the forces of evolution have formed the species that have existed on earth.

Evolution Versus Creationism

A natural outgrowth of anthropological curiosity in human variability is how it came to be. Early in the development of biological anthropology the subject of the evolution of the human organism began to be considered. The earliest ideas on human origins were derived from studies of the anatomy of many different kinds of animals, compared to human anatomy. Human beings share many traits with apes, fewer traits with monkeys, fewer with cats, and fewer still with birds, reptiles, fish, and insects, respectively. The existence of fossil forms that bridged the gaps between the living animals was debated. Particular attention was focused on the human–ape common ancestor, which was given the popular nickname of the "missing link."

Two of the primary methods of modern biological anthropology in its investigations of human evolution involve, (a) the use of **fossils,** usually represented by bones that have maintained a resemblance to their original form and shape but have been mineralized over time, and

ecology–the science that studies the biological relationships between species and their environment.

ecological niche–the "ecological space" to which a species is adapted, including its habitat, diet, and behavior.

fossils–remains of animals and plants preserved in the ground.

(b) the analysis of molecules in the body. But early evidence for the great antiquity of human beings (and therefore premodern origins) came first in the form of stone tools discovered in France in the late 1700s. Later, fossilized bones of people were found associated with those of extinct animals. Actual evidence of a form of human so different that it would fit into no known living human group was not recognized until 1856, when the Neandertal "caveman" was discovered (see Chapter 10).

Even before scientists were beginning to delve into questions of human origins, religious scholars had questioned the status quo. As one of the founders of the scientific method, Sir Francis Bacon (1561–1626) had pronounced in the early eighteenth century that scholars should look to nature, not to books for enlightenment. Theology was affected by Bacon's teachings. Monks began to calculate the amount of food necessary to sustain the number of animals on Noah's Ark, the amount of space needed to house them, how much dung they would have produced, and how animals from different environments could have been maintained in such a small space. They strove to make their observations correspond to the Bible. But it was the rise in Europe and America of a theological movement known as Biblical Criticism that led to the acceptance of evolution within a theological framework. Internal evidence in the Bible, when read in the original Hebrew, began to reveal that the Old Testament was written down over a number of years by many authors. A major theological debate raged over whether the Bible *was* the word of God or *contained* the word of God. Those who still maintain the former position, that every word in the Bible is literally true in a modern scientific sense, face difficult problems in interpreting the internal evidence of the Bible. For example, the book of *Genesis* has one account (*Genesis* 1) in which human beings are created last of all the creatures, and another one (*Genesis* 2) in which the first human being, a man (Adam), is created before the animals and names them as they are created. Woman (Eve) is created from one of Adam's ribs in this version. (Men and women actually have the same number of ribs—twelve pairs or twenty-four). Both accounts cannot be literally true because they are contradictory.

A solution, for those who desire to seek one, is to accept that religious scripture, such as the Torah, Bible, or Koran, represent documents of spiritual and symbolic importance to many people throughout the world, whereas science deals with empirically testable hypotheses about the world. Because the two areas of endeavor do not purport to achieve the same ends, a dichotomy between them is unnecessary. Stokes (1988:16) makes this point in his restatement of the creation passages in *Genesis,* a version with which many scientists could agree:

> All known matter appeared in the simplest, elemental form through a single, unique event called the "big bang." With time, as things quieted down, heavier elements and compounds including watery mixtures of gas and dust

appeared. The gathering, and compression of matter into galaxies produced light, nuclear reactions, and massive explosions (supernovas). Eventually all elements were produced and dispersed. From enriched mixtures of gas and dust came suns with attendant systems of planets. In one case, at least, a body (our earth) unusually rich in water was produced. A copious supply of water came from within and remained attached to its surface as liquid oceans and seas. Life as we know it emerged from water; and the oceans, as shown by fossils, were well populated by varied species before land life was in existence. On land, a great variety of bony vertebrate animals appeared and eventually occupied all continents and islands. Man was one of the last creatures to appear; his unique physical and mental attributes allow him to dominate all forms of life.

Evolutionary science, like all sciences, is neutral regarding theological beliefs. Supernatural events are not invoked in scientific explanations of phenomena because science seeks the simplest possible *natural* explanations to understand observations. Religion, on the other hand, deals with the spiritual, symbolic, and moral spheres of human life. Science deals with falsifiable hypotheses, ideas that can be disproved; religion depends on faith, which is not subject to proof in a scientific sense.

In upholding the teaching of evolution in the public schools the American courts have reasserted the division between Church and State. Yet science and religion can coexist, and both responsible scientists and theologians resist efforts to bring the two into unnecessary conflict. Most major Western religions accept evolution as part of the process of creation. In the Anglican Church evolution has been formally accepted since the 1890s; the Catholic Church officially accepted evolution as "an open question" when Pope Pius XII issued an encyclical on the subject in the 1953; other major denominations have followed suit.

THE PERSPECTIVE OF HUMAN EVOLUTION

The study of human evolution has much to contribute to a general understanding of human beings, their origins, adaptations, and way of life. The popular interest that surrounds biological anthropology is derived to a large extent from the high-visibility discoveries of fossils directly or indirectly relevant to human ancestry. Initially, the fossils themselves were considered of paramount interest, but increasingly the *contexts* in which the fossils are found have become of equal, if not of more, importance. The context can tell how old the fossil is, what the climate was like when the species was alive, what other animals and plants were in the environment, what the species may have eaten, what other species may have eaten it, and many other aspects of its evolutionary history not discernible from its bones or teeth alone (Figure 1–13). In short, the total contexts of fossil discoveries have become

FRONTIERS

Evolution and Creation: Current Controversies

By Eugenie C. Scott

"**C**reationism" in its broadest sense refers to the belief that God created, an idea foundational to Christianity, Judaism, and Islam. "Evolution," in the broadest sense, refers to the scientific idea that the universe has had a history: that the galaxies, solar system, planet Earth, and plants and animals exist today in a different form than they did in the past. *Organic* evolution describes the concept that living things share common ancestry and have, in Darwin's terms, "descended with modification" from ancestors who differed from them.

Creationism is therefore concerned with cause, specifically, Ultimate Cause. Evolution is concerned with what happened during the history of the universe, and, as a science, is incapable of saying anything about Ultimate Cause. *Whether* God created is thus truly not part of the creation/evolution controversy. Individuals who believe that God created the world using the process of evolution are known as "theistic evolutionists," and include Catholics and mainline Protestants (such as Episcopalians, United Church of Christ, Presbyterians, etc.), as well as Reformed, Conservative, Reconstructionist, and most Orthodox Jews.

The term "creationist" has recently taken on a narrower meaning to refer to certain conservative Christians who attempt, through political and legal means, to insert into public school curricula a literal version of creation

as found in the Book of Genesis. I will use this more narrow definition of "creationist" in this essay.

Creationist Opposition to Evolution

Antievolutionism has had a long history in the United States. Although the theory of evolution (change through time) was embraced by the scientific community by the beginning of the twentieth century, acceptance was slow to trickle down to the general public.

During the first decades of this century, a series of twelve pamphlets called "The Fundamentals" outlined a conservative Christian theology stressing biblical inerrancy and, for the most part, literal truth of the Scriptures. Fundamentalists read Genesis literally; they believe not only that the earth was created by God, but that it was created in specific stages over a span of six twenty-four-hour days, and only a few thousand years ago. Other Christians interpret the Genesis reference to "days" in a more metaphorical sense.

Between 1915 and 1922, a number of states attempted to legally ban the teaching of evolution. John T. Scopes, the subject of the fictional *Inherit the Wind,* was brought to trial in 1915 for violating a Tennessee antievolution law. He was convicted, and the laws remained on the books (although rarely enforced) until 1968, when they were declared unconstitutional by the U.S. Supreme Court. In *Epperson* v. *Arkansas,* the Court cited the First Amendment of the Constitution, which states that "Congress shall make no law respecting the establishment of religion, or prohibiting the free exercise thereof." It ruled that the "establishment clause" makes it

unlawful for a government entity such as a school to "advocate" religion, which it construed to include the teaching of creationism.

Although textbook publishers had quietly reduced their coverage of evolution—virtually eliminating it by the mid 1930's—by the late 1960's, evolution had begun reappearing. The ready availability of evolution material in textbooks generated a new response from the antievolution forces.

Because the teaching of evolution could no longer be banned, creationists devised a new strategy to counter it. Creationists hypothesized that they could avoid problems with the first amendment if their version of the origin of matter could be presented as an alternate scientific theory, rather than as a Bible-based religious doctrine. Thus, "scientific" creationism was born.

In the late 1970's, model legislation was drawn up by creationists that would require "equal time" for the teaching of creation "science" and evolution. During 1980 and 1981, such legislation was proposed in twenty-two states. Because the "science" inherent in creation science was so sketchy, many physical anthropologists testified against such bills, and through their efforts and those of other scientists, the majority of these bills were defeated. Only Arkansas and Louisiana passed "equal time" bills, and legal challenges were immediately filed. It is interesting to note that these equal-time bills were not, for the most part, supported by mainstream religious groups. In Arkansas, the effort to strike down the bill was led by Methodist minister William McLean, who was joined by clergy from the Episcopal, Roman Catholic, Presbyterian, Southern Baptist, and African

Methodist Episcopal churches, and the American Jewish Committee, the American Jewish Congress, as well as several educational associations.

The trial resulting from the Arkansas challenge, billed as "Scopes II," resurrected some of the circus atmosphere of its predecessor. Creationists presented witnesses in support of the scientific validity of creation "science." They failed. Even the creationists' most highly-credentialed scientist, Chandra Wickramasinghe, stated under cross-examination that most of the law was "claptrap" and totally unscientific. (See Futuyma, below, for an examination of creationist "science.") Judge William Overton ruled in Arkansas Superior Court in January, 1982, that creation science did not meet the tenets of science, and that the Arkansas "equal time" law was unconstitutional.

The similar Louisiana case took several years to make its way to the U.S. Supreme Court. In *Edwards* v. *Aguillard,* the Court declared in 1987 that the teaching of creationism constituted religious advocacy. The strategy of "equal time" for creationism and evolution had met its final doom.

Current Events

Losing so thoroughly in the courts, creationists moved back to local school districts where they historically have been successful. Within a year of the 1987 Supreme Court decision, creationist leaders were promoting the avoidance of terms such as creation science and creationism, which involve the idea of a Creator. Instead, they began speaking in terms of "Abrupt Appearance Theory," "Intelligent Design Theory," and "arguments against evolution." The content of these new "sciences" is identical to the no-longer legal "scientific" creationism, but by using euphemisms, creationists hope to avoid entanglement with the First Amendment.

During the early 1990's, it has still been possible to find the full range of antievolutionist activities, from attempts to ban the teaching of evolution (declared unconstitutional by *Epperson*), promotion of the "two model" approach (declared unconstitutional by *Edwards*), to use of the newer euphemisms, not yet tested in court. The next legal battlefield is likely to be at the school district level, over requirements that schools teach "arguments against evolution" or "weaknesses in evolutionary theory" wherever evolution is taught.

To this day, teachers pressed by parents (or administrators) to avoid the teaching of evolution frequently do so, not wanting to jeopardize either their jobs or community harmony. As a result, many students entering college have never been exposed to evolution, or they have only a fuzzy notion of what the term means ("Man evolved from monkeys?!") This is a great shame, because as the famous geneticist Theodosius Dobzhansky said,

> Seen in the light of evolution, biology is, perhaps, intellectually the most satisfying and inspiring science. Without that light it becomes a pile of sundry facts—some of them interesting or curious but making no meaningful picture as a whole. . . . Nothing in biology makes sense except in the light of evolution.

The same holds true for physical anthropology. Students who are not taught evolution do not have the preparation that they need for further scientific study, or even to be educated citizens.

Additional Readings

Futuyma, Douglas J. *Science on Trial: The Case for Evolution.* Sunderland, MA: Sinauer Publishing Co., 1995.

Larson, Edward J. *Trial and Error: The American Controversy Over Creation and Evolution.* NY: Oxford University Press, 1985.

McCollister, Betty. *Voices for Evolution.* Berkeley: National Center for Science Education, Inc., 1989.

Morris, Henry. *The Twilight of Evolution.* Grand Rapids, MI: Baker, 1963.

Numbers, Ronald L. *The Creationists. The Evolution of Scientific Creationism.* NY: Knopf, 1992.

Eugenie C. Scott is Executive Director of the National Center for Science Education in Berkeley, California and is a member of the Executive Committee of the American Association of Physical Anthropologists.

Figure 1–13 • Paleoecological reconstruction of Swartkranns, South Africa, showing the context of plants and animals from this site in their original surroundings. (From California Academy of Sciences, San Francisco).

important because we now want to understand how early humans lived and behaved, as well as how they are related to other life forms, including today's humans. In this way, we seek to understand the natural history of our ancestors and of ourselves.

What an individual does during his or her lifetime affects the passing on of his or her hereditary characteristics. Behaviors that contribute to a longer childbearing or reproductive life and increase the number of offspring contributed to the next generation are those behaviors that will tend to become more prevalent as evolution proceeds. Our behavior today is the result of millions of years and hundreds of thousands of generations of evolution. If we understand how our ancestors behaved and the conditions under which their behavior evolved, we will have a much better insight into our behavior today. It is also true that our evolution is continuing, and that by understanding how our past has shaped us we may better plan for the future.

The increasingly well-documented human fossil record now demonstrates that for the longest part of our history we have evolved to social and technological conditions that now no longer exist. Only in the last century or so have the dramatic technological changes that we take for granted become a regular part of our existence. Most of human evolution took place before even the advent of agriculture, some 10,000 years ago, when humans lived in small social groups and dealt with one another daily on a face-to-face basis. During this immense span of time, humans "evolved to feel strongly about a few people, short distances, and relatively brief intervals of time . . ." (Washburn and Harding 1975:11). The final chapter in this book will discuss how a species with such an evolutionary heritage can cope with such issues as crowding and overpopulation, international conflict, pollution, health, and education.

SUMMARY

The goal of this book is to provide a coherent integration of our knowledge of human evolution and biology. This synthetic approach focuses on the interrelatedness of biology, behavior, and evolution as well as the connections between humans and the natural world.

Anthropologists are scientists who study humans. They have used three basic paradigms (organizing frameworks of inquiry) in their study of the human species. Typology is a classificatory paradigm now largely superseded as a research enterprise, but still relevant as the basis for taxonomic classification. A second paradigm involves the relationship between culture and evolution to explain human biology and behavior. It is the paradigm that supports anthropology as a discipline. The third and most important paradigm for biological anthropology is evolution through the mechanism of natural selection, which provides us with the basic theoretical framework with which to test hypotheses of human biology and behavior.

Evolutionary science does not address the issues of religious belief, with most scientists feeling it unnecessary to confront or attempt to disprove theological beliefs with scientific arguments. On the other hand, scientists do respond to attempts by creationists to insert untestable religious dogma into the scientific arena, where it clearly does not belong. Many theologians and scientists do, however, find a compatibility between religion and science.

Biological anthropologists pursue many questions about humans and use a wide range of techniques and methodologies, which may include comparative anatomy, behavior studies of living animals, both in the wild and in the laboratory, molecular biology, genetics, and population biology.

For biological anthropologists to communicate in the same scientific language, a system of naming and description must be uniformly followed. Taxonomy, a system of nomenclature or naming, is used to designate a species. Systematics places the species within the hierarchy of more closely related and, then, increasingly distantly related, categories.

One goal of biological anthropology is the reconstruction of primate, especially human, evolutionary history. Phylogenetic questions ask how humans are related to other primates, other mammals, and other vertebrates. To answer these questions scientists rely on cladistics—the discovery of an overall framework of relatedness; a time framework that marks the point when humans shared a common ancestor with the other primates; and a knowledge of the proper sequence of anatomical and behavioral events that occurred through time.

The perspective offered by this book on human evolution takes into account both cultural and ecological variables. The environments under which humans evolved for about 99% of the time that the species has existed on this planet were very different from those under which a majority of humans live today. These environments, which biological anthropologists are studying, have left a legacy for us to deal with as we confront the problems of living within the highly technological and multicultural complex societies of today's world.

 CRITICAL-THINKING QUESTIONS

1. Discuss the paradigm that biological anthropologists use to explain variability in human populations. How has this paradigm changed over time?
2. What role has molecular biology played in addressing human origins?
3. What is the biological definition of species?
4. What is the difference between a species' phylogeny and its cladogram?
5. Why is it important to study extinct hominids?
6. What role has ecology played in understanding evolution?

 SUGGESTED READINGS

Eaton, S. Boyd, M. Shostak, and M. Konner. 1989. *The Paleolithic Prescription: A Program of Diet and Exercise and a Design for Living*. New York: Harper and Row. A book on how human evolution holds many and varied lessons for modern medicine and health.

Eiseley, Loren. 1957. *The Immense Journey*. New York: Random House. Still one of the most readable accounts of a naturalist's approach to human evolution.

Fleagle, John. 1988. *Primate Adaptation and Evolution*. New York: Academic. A general and thorough text on the evolution and diversity of the primate order.

Kingdon, Jonathan. 1993. *Self-Made Man: Human Evolution from Eden to Extinction?* New York: John Wiley. An original and engaging introduction to human evolution from the perspective of one of Africa's great zoologists.

Napier, J.R., and P.H. Napier. 1985. *The Natural History of Primates*. Cambridge, Mass.: MIT Press. A brief but excellent introduction to the living primates, their adapations, and their behavior.

Steele, D. Gentry, and Claud A. Bramblett. 1988. *The Anatomy and Biology of the Human Skeleton*. College Station, Texas: Texas A & M University Press. A good general book on the study of human bones and their biological significance.

Washburn, Sherwood L., and Ruth Moore. 1982. *Ape into Human*. Boston: Beacon. A mature restatement of Washburn's "new physical anthropology" and the views on human evolution of one of its most influential students.

Earliest Beginnings: DNA, the Cell, and the First Animals

Ultimate Origins
The Big Bang Theory

Continental Land Masses Drift Apart
The Process of Continental Drift
Effects on the Earth's Geography
Effects on the Fossil Record and Living Species

The First Evidence of Life
Early Explanations
The Search for Secular Explanations

Cells Evolve
The Role of ATP
The Role of Photosynthesis

DNA: The Reproductive Machinery of the Cell
How DNA Replicates Itself
DNA and Protein Synthesis

The DNA Molecule Evolves
The Increase in Amount of DNA

The Cell Nucleus Evolves
The Earliest Organisms

Evolution of DNA Repair and Sexual Reproduction

Mitosis and Meiosis Evolve
Mitosis
Meiosis

The Earliest Animals Appear

Summary

Critical-Thinking Questions

Suggested Readings

We human beings are literally part of the universe in which we live. The chemical elements, such as hydrogen, carbon, and iron, that make up our bodies are the same elements that make up the planets and stars: They differ only in proportions. These basic building blocks of physical matter on earth are constantly being recycled. Thus, our bodies may contain elements that were once parts of ancient sea algae, trees, dinosaurs, or mammoths. Each form of life has this basic bond to the earth and uses the elements found in nature to carry on its daily life functions and to reproduce more of its own kind.

The evolution of human beings, just as of any other species that has existed on earth, ultimately begins at the earliest appearance of life. The shared characteristic of all living things—the same basic chemicals used in the same ways for reproducing and carrying on life—is a monumental testimony to the shared ancestry of all life. We all go back to one primordial ancestor. Although it may stretch the imagination to realize that you and the salad that you ate for lunch have distant shared relatives, this is in fact the case.

Much of modern biology has become focused on the molecular level of organization. But although exciting new advances in genetics and molecular biology are important, they are only the part of the story. To put the molecular biology of human beings into perspective, we must understand how the molecules of life came to be and how they evolved into and within the more complex systems called animals.

ULTIMATE ORIGINS

The Universe originated some 10 to 20 billion (1 billion = 10^9 or 1,000,000,000) years ago. Despite continuing research by physicists and earth scientists, this beginning is still less than fully understood.

The Big Bang Theory

The most widely accepted hypothesis is the **big bang theory,** a theory that the Universe formed during a "big bang," an explosion of an infinitesimally small speck in space of almost infinite weight (mass) and extremely high temperature. The matter dispersed throughout the early universe and cooled down as it expanded. Astrophysicists measuring

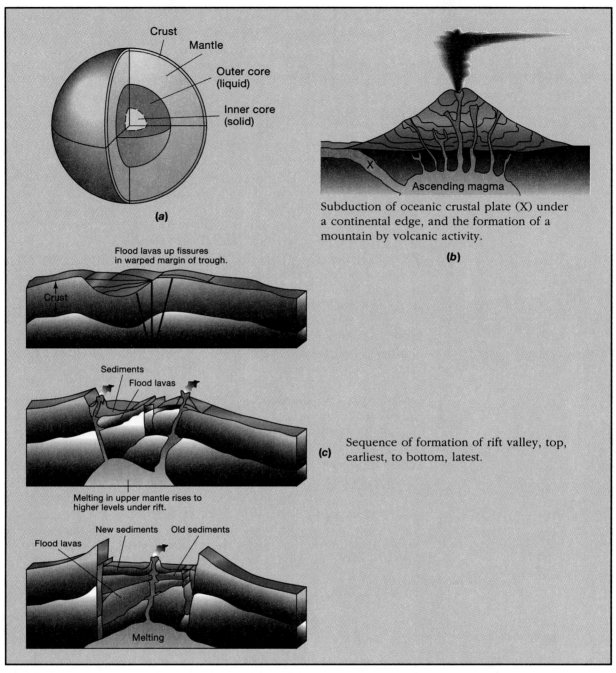

Figure 2–1 • (*a*) Structure of the Earth's crust, mantle, and core; (*b*) Subduction of oceanic crustal plate. The crust and upper mantle of the earth are composed of between 10 and 25 semi-rigid plates that float on the liquid underlayer of the mantle. Each plate moves more or less independently, interacting with others at its boundaries, causing seismic and volcanic activity along the periphery. (*c*) Formation of rift valley between two plates. (From *Earth and Life Through Time* by Stanley. Copyright ©1986 by Freeman and Company. Used with permission.)

Pangaea–the ancient super-continent encompassing all of the earth's then-emergent land masses.

the movements of stars have determined that they are moving away from one another, and they have taken this apparent expansion of the universe as additional proof of the big bang theory: stars are still being pushed apart as a result of the energy released during the initial explosion.

But what are the stars expanding into? If there is a boundary to the universe, its expansion will come to a halt several billions of years in the future. In such a "closed" system, gravity will act to pull all matter together again, and there will be a fiery reconsolidation of matter analogous to the big bang in reverse. If the universe is "open" and the expansion of the stars continues indefinitely, matter and energy will eventually become evenly distributed throughout space, and the end of the universe will be a "cold death" (Pagels, 1982).

From potassium-argon dating of the oldest rocks, geologists have surmised that the earth coalesced out of swirling gases some 4.5 billion years ago. As these and similar gas clouds around the universe cooled down and released their energy, the heaviest chemical elements, the ones containing the most subatomic particles (neutrons, electrons, and protons), were formed. These elements, such as carbon, nitrogen, and oxygen, were to become the basic components of all of earth's organisms.

Ultimately, the earth's surface hardened into a *crust,* below which lay the thick, semiconsolidated *mantle.* At the center of the earth lay the still liquid core (Figure 2–1), maintained to the present day at high temperature and pressure. The oldest dated rocks on the earth and moon allow us to deduce that by 4 billion years ago, large-scale volcanic eruptions had built up highland areas on the earth's surface, areas that eventually became the continents. Water accumulated in the low-lying areas, probably as a result of condensation from the water vapor released by volcanoes. These areas became the ocean basins, which at this early time were filled by fresh water. Over many eons, salts were leached out of continental rocks by rain water and carried to the sea, where they slowly accumulated while the water evaporated back into the atmosphere.

CONTINENTAL LAND MASSES DRIFT APART

Volcanic eruptions accounted for the formation of a large continental land mass surrounded by seas, called **Pangaea** (Greek, meaning the "whole earth") by earth scientists who study early land formations. Over time this supercontinent (see Figure 2–2) broke into a northern part, subsequently labeled Laurasia (from the Laurentian Shield of Canada), and a southern part called Gondwanaland (from a geological locality in India). The nascent continents were bare rock, subject to erosion by wind and rain but otherwise unaltered by any forms of life.

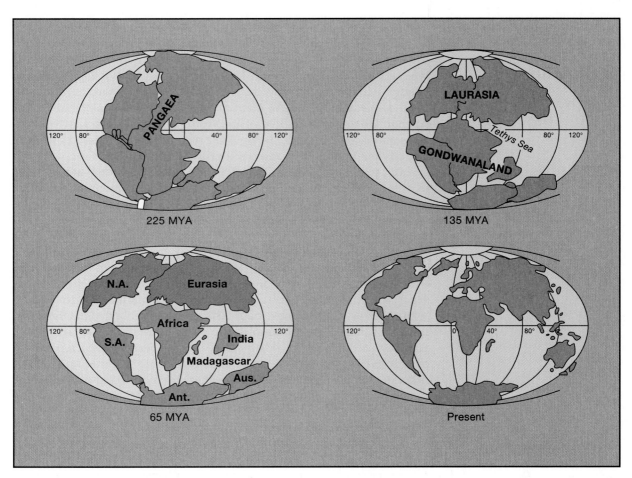

Figure 2–2 • Reconstruction of the early pre-rift southern continent, Gondwanaland, and the northern continent, Laurasia, with outlines of modern continental margins.

The Process of Continental Drift

These land masses have been breaking up, moving and colliding ever since by a process known as **continental drift,** according to a theory developed by the German physicist Alfred Wegener (1880–1930). The process is driven by "hot spots" in the earth's mantle, probably the result of upwelling of the swirling molten core. These hotspots melt the underside and thinning of the earth's crust, which in turn causes splits or **rifts** to occur (Figure 2–1). Molten mantle then flows out to the surface of the earth in the form of lava from volcanoes. This is how new continental crust is formed.

continental drift–theory that continental plates move in relation to one another through and over the earth's crust, also known as "plate tectonics."

rifts–splits in the earth's crust where portions of crust begin to move apart.

plates–the portions of crust that move as a unit during continental drift.

subduction zone–an area where one plate is moving under another plate, creating earthquakes and volcanic activity.

Figure 2–3 • Fossils similar in form to modern blue-green bacteria, from the Figtree Formation of Swaziland, southern Africa. Their age is estimated at 3.2 to 3.5 billion years old. (From J. William Schopf. 1993. "Microfossils of the Early Archean Apex Chert: New Evidence of the Antiquity of Life." *Science* 260: 640–646)

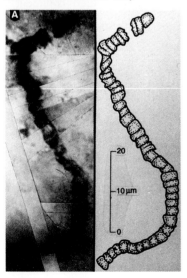

New crust pushes older crust before it. Continents and their underwater margins or shelves move as units known as **plates.** We need only look at the fit between the east coast of South America and the west coast of Africa to trace the line of rifting that split this ancient southern continent into two parts (Figure 2–2). Plates are moved apart by the mechanism of *sea floor spreading.* Research along the Mid-Atlantic Ridge in the middle of the North Atlantic Ocean between Europe and North America shows that crust immediately adjacent to the ridge is the youngest in age. Farther away to both sides the crust becomes progressively older. Therefore, we must conclude that new crust is being formed through underwater volcanic eruptions at the ridge and that crust is being pushed away from the ridge by this process. Geologists now accept the idea that entire continental plates move in relation to one another.

If new crust is constantly being formed, then there must be places where older crust is being destroyed or compacted. Indeed, the process of sea floor spreading causes plates to collide with one another. India, for example, is a separate plate from the Asian mainland which slowly crashed into south Asia some 60 million years ago. The impact of this collision crumpled the older Asian crust and created the Himalaya Mountains. In other cases, where there is a discrepancy in the relative densities of the plates, a lighter plate will ride up over the other denser plate as they come together. The denser plate will then be pushed down closer to the hot mantle and begin to melt. The result is a geological "hot spot," with faulting and volcanic activity in the leading edge of the overriding plate. A region where this is happening is known as a **subduction zone.** A good example is the western coast of North America. The San Andreas Fault of California and Mount St. Helens of Washington are each on a subduction zone, as the North America plate moves westward over the Pacific plate.

Effects on the Earth's Geography

Continental drift explains much of the changing geography of the earth, which, in turn, has profoundly affected the history of life on the planet. The building up of mountain chains such as the Himalayas in Asia or the Andes in South America greatly affects the movement of air masses and thus influences weather patterns over large areas of the globe. The colliding of continental plates, such as North America and South America at the Isthmus of Panama, cuts off ocean circulation patterns. In this case the collision creates the northeasterly flowing Gulf Stream, thus effecting major changes in climatic patterns in eastern North America and western Europe. The splitting apart of continents, such as Antarctica separating from South America and Australia, opens up new circulation patterns. For example, the circumpolar current that now encircles Antarctica prevents warm northerly waters from reaching the South Polar regions, thereby helping to keep Antarctica constantly covered with ice. The abundant animal and plant life that once flourished in Antarctica has been frozen into extinction.

Effects on the Fossil Record and Living Species

Distributions of animal and plant life as seen in both the fossil record and living species have been affected by the changing positions of the earth's land masses and the connections between them. When Europe and North America split apart species became separated by the ever-widening Atlantic Ocean. When North America and South America drifted together, previously isolated species came into contact. Later, in Chapter 4, we will learn that geographical isolation is the most powerful force in forming new species, and the changing composition of species communities is a major determinant of the evolution of the earth's ecology. Thus, continental drift has played a significant role in the earth's natural history.

THE FIRST EVIDENCE OF LIFE

For at least a billion years after the earth's formation, the oceans and continents were barren and lifeless. But paleontologists in Swaziland, southern Africa, have found microscopic fossils of **blue-green bacteria** in rocks 3.2 to 3.5 billion years old (Figure 2–3). Blue-green bacteria are single-celled organisms which simply duplicate themselves and split apart to reproduce. They use energy from the sun—like modern plants. They are also called cyanobacteria or, incorrectly, "blue-green algae." Other microscopic fossil evidence suggests life as early as 3.8 billion years ago. Virtually identical single-celled organisms are alive today.

Blue-green bacteria possess two basic capabilities that define life: **metabolism,** the ability to take substances from the environment and use them to promote survival and growth; and **reproduction,** the production by organisms of other organisms which have the necessary chemicals in them for survival. How did these organisms come into being? What did they originate from?

Early Explanations

In the beginning life came ultimately from nonlife. This is a modern scientific concept that is different from the early notions that living organisms originated from inanimate substances. In sixteenth century England, for example, people believed that bread and cheese wrapped in rags and placed in a dark corner "spawned" rats. By the mid-nineteenth century French chemist Louis Pasteur (1822–1895) and others had shown that life could *not* be spontaneously generated from nonliving substances or

blue-green bacteria–simple, single-celled organisms, also called cyanobacteria, which are similar to the earliest life forms on earth.

metabolism–converting energy sources in the environment to the uses of cell growth and activity.

reproduction–the creation of a new individual from a parental organism with the ability to survive and reproduce.

objects. Souring milk does not create bacteria (they are introduced from the environment and reproduce in milk); flies do not originate from putrifying meat (their mothers lay eggs in the meat that develop there into maggots); and rats are not spontaneously generated in piles of rags (their mothers make nests there). But the question of where the ancestors of the bacteria, flies, and rats originated remained unanswered.

The Search for Secular Explanations

Although some early scientists believed that life had been created miraculously, others continued to search for secular explanations. They hypothesized a planet of barren rock surrounded by oceans containing an abundant supply of organic but not yet living molecules, a sort of "primordial soup." Organic molecules or compounds are those containing the element carbon. (Original usage implied origin from vegetal or animal sources but after the mid-nineteenth century it was understood that "organic" molecules could also derive from mineral and nonliving sources.) The element carbon was also the basis for the construction of these large organic molecules. Carbon atoms are unique in being able to attach themselves chemically to one another to an extent not possible for atoms of any other element (Morrison and Boyd, 1974). In recent decades researchers have attempted to design experiments approximating conditions of the early earth and simulating the evolution of life from nonlife. One important experiment by Stanley Miller in 1953 used sterilized glassware into which was pumped a mixture of gases thought to have been present in the early atmosphere and oceans: ammonia, methane, hydrogen and carbon dioxide (Figure 2–4). Miller passed an electric spark through the mixture to simulate lightning in the early atmosphere. After several days he analyzed the contents of the flask and found that **amino acids** had formed. Amino acids are chemical compounds necessary for life; the "vital amines" or "vitamins" are major components of the proteins that make up all the tissues of our bodies and are also necessary for normal cellular function. Amino acids are the units of which proteins, are found in all living systems, are built. Neither amino acids nor proteins are "alive" but their presence is a necessary prerequisite for life. Other researchers have subsequently repeated the experiment using different concentrations of gases and different energy sources, such as ultraviolet light simulating sunlight, and found that amino acids are also produced under these conditions.

    Scientists think that several steps were necessary to transform the world of preliving molecules into a world in which there were living, one-celled organisms. The evolution of these first cells can be divided into five steps: (1) formation of the earth with a mixture of gases necessary for life: ammonia, hydrogen, methane, carbon dioxide, and water vapor; (2) synthesis of simple biomolecules, such as amino acids and

amino acids–chemical building blocks of proteins.

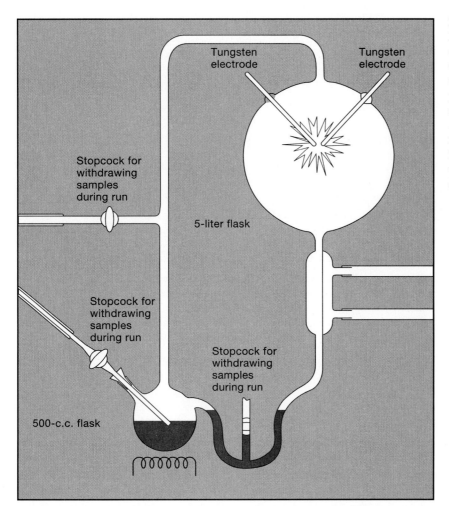

Tungsten electrode

Tungsten electrode

Stopcock for withdrawing samples during run

5-liter flask

Stopcock for withdrawing samples during run

Stopcock for withdrawing samples during run

500-c.c. flask

Figure 2–4 • The design of the Miller experiment, which replicated some of the conditions of the early earth and resulted in the production of organic compounds from inorganic substrates. (From *Chemical Evolution and The Origin of Life* by Richard E. Dickerson, illustration by Allen Beechel, copyright © 1978 by Scientific American, Inc. All rights reserved.)

sugars from these gases; (3) the linking of these simple biomolecules into long chains or "multibodied" molecules known as **polymers,** including proteins; (4) isolation of these polymers into droplets (coacervates, or pre-cells) which carry out chemical reactions necesary for life (metabolism); and (5) the development of a method of reproduction to pass on the chemical capabilities of the parent to the daughter cells (Figure 2–5). The "primordial soup," as the early oceans have been called, contained little or no oxygen and no living organisms. This was the environment in which the earliest cellular life originated. In today's environment life cannot spontaneously arise because the high concentration of oxygen makes the spontaneous formation of organic compounds from gases chemically unlikely. If any complex molecules or "protocells" were to form they would immediately be eaten by any number of life forms or broken down by oxygen-mediated reactions in the oceans.

polymer–a long chained molecule.

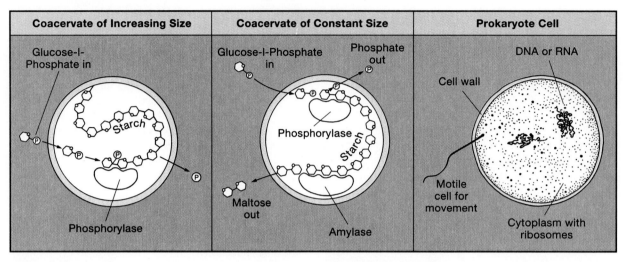

Figure 2–5 • The first coacervate (nonliving pre-cell), mimicking growth, takes in sugar and uses an enzyme to break it down and build a starch molecule, thus increasing in size. The second coacervate mimics metabolism by utilizing a second enzyme to break down starch for energy. The true living cell, a prokaryote, is capable of both growth and metabolism and, in addition, has ribonucleic acid, enabling it to reproduce. (From Dickerson, 1978)

CELLS EVOLVE

The dual functions of metabolism and reproduction may have evolved hand-in-hand (co-evolved) in the first cells. The metabolic molecules that promoted the cell's chemical reactions while using substances from the environment for energy must have acted also to further the survival and enhance the reproduction of early cells. The reproductive molecules, for their part, must have acted to ensure that, as the parent cell broke up or divided, the metabolic molecules were transferred to both of the daughter cells along with the rest of the cell's makeup.

The Role of ATP

Critical to all life today is the breakdown inside the cell of the "multi-bodied" molecule known as *ATP* (adenosine triphosphate) to produce energy. This process is the most primitive form of metabolism. The chemicals that comprise ATP are easily synthesized in experiments reproducing conditions of the primitive earth. The first molecules may have formed polymer chains, or "polymerized," on the surfaces of minerals, in evaporated ponds, or in conditions where water molecules would not have interfered with the chemical construction of these long molecules. Subsequently washed into water, the ATP molecules would have become available for use in supplying energy to the earliest cells.

ATP supplies energy by the breaking of its chemical bonds. All molecules are held together by these bonds, which take energy to form and which lock up energy once they are made. Once a bond of ATP is broken by chemical interaction with water molecules, a process known as *hydrolysis,* a large amount of energy is released (Figure 2–6). Because all cells need energy to survive, as the supply of ATP in the ancient ocean environment was used up, competition for ATP among cells increased.

As a consequence of this competition for ATP, a major evolutionary advance occurred. Some cells became capable of attacking and "eating" more complex molecules, such as glucose sugar molecules, and making ATP from them. Because no oxygen is involved, this process is known as *anaerobic* (*an* meaning "without"; *aerobic* meaning "air or oxygen") *fermentation,* or **glycolysis.** It is the oldest energy-extracting chemical pathway found among life forms on earth today and is present in the most primitive living organisms, the anaerobic bacteria. When our own cells are deprived of oxygen, for example, such as in the late stages of running a marathon or when rapidly running up a long flight of stairs, they also use this energy pathway. We have inherited this ability from our earliest bacterial ancestors.

glycolysis—the metabolic breakdown of sugar molecules to ATP in an oxygenless chemical environment.

The Role of Photosynthesis

The next major step in evolution emerged probably as a result of competition for glucose. Cells arose that could synthesize their own glucose

Figure 2–6 • The chemical reaction (hydrolysis) of the molecule ATP, which releases energy through the breaking of chemical bonds. This reaction is the basic mechanism by which cells use energy.

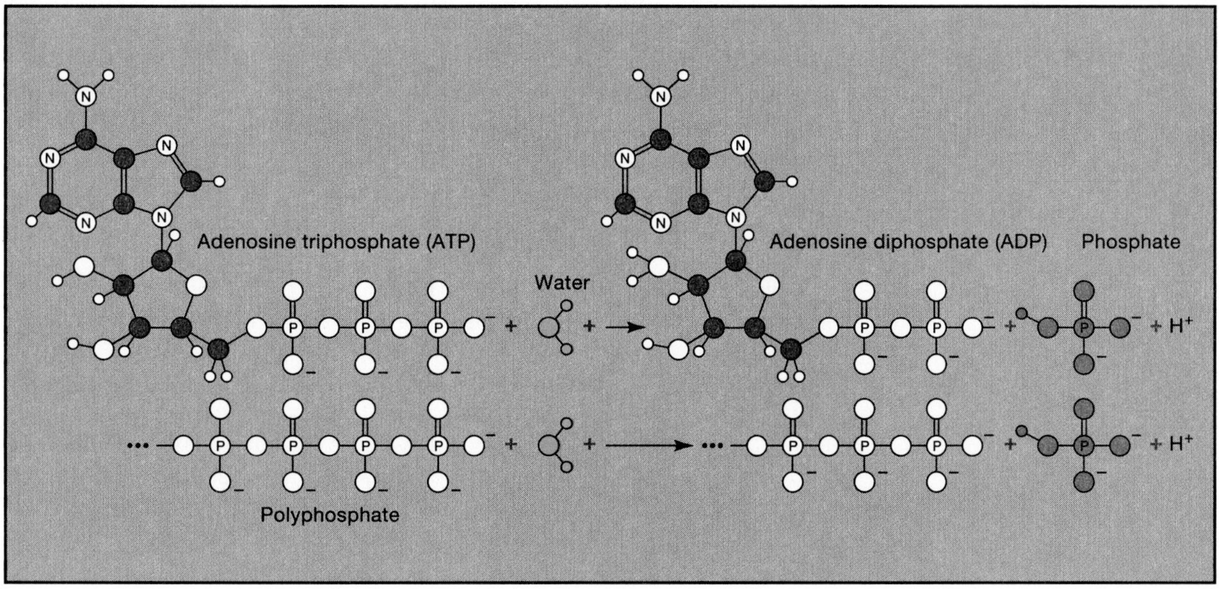

photosynthesis–synthesis of energy containing glucose from carbon dioxide using sunlight; the major metabolic method of plants.

DNA–deoxyribonucleic acid, the chemical that carries the genetic code for all organisms.

from a common environmental molecule, carbon dioxide. This process, called **photosynthesis,** allowed organisms 3.2 billion years ago and similar to today's blue-green bacteria, to obtain glucose by combining water with carbon dioxide, using the energy from sunlight. The byproducts of this reaction, water and oxygen—at that time a gas poisonous to the cell—were then expelled. Over the next 2 billion years oxygen accumulated in the atmosphere. The formation and maintenance of an oxygen-rich environment was a key development in the evolutionary history of later higher organisms. Today's plants, descendents of these early photosynthesizing organisms, still use photosynthesis as their method of metabolism.

DNA: THE REPRODUCTIVE MACHINERY OF THE CELL

Origin of the reproductive machinery of the cell is difficult to reconstruct because there are no forms surviving that show the intermediate stages of reproductive development between the earliest and present life forms. We do know that all life today uses a variant of the same molecule, **DNA** (deoxyribonucleic acid) for reproduction, an indication that this adaptation is a very ancient one. DNA is a long, double-chain molecule composed of alternating units of a five-carbon sugar called deoxyribose and a phosphate (Figure 2–7). The most important aspect of its structure is that to each of the sugar units is attached one of four chemical base units of two types: purines called adenine (*A*) and guanine (*G*); and pyrimidines called thymine (*T*) and cytosine (*C*).

The rungs of the ladder are hydrogen bonds attaching the appropriate bases on both sides. *A* pairs only with *T*, and *G* pairs only with *C* at their bonding points or ladder rungs. This characteristic insures that, during DNA replication and cell division, the new cells receive exactly the same DNA components. Once a sequence of bases is constructed along one side of the DNA, the other side of the ladder may be precisely determined. The DNA bases on either strand are exactly *complementary* in sequence.

How DNA Replicates Itself

When DNA starts to replicate, or make copies of itself, as the cell begins to divide the two strands of the DNA unwind from each other. The cell machinery carries new bases, sugars and phosphates into the nucleus. They attach themselves in sequence so that a *T* attracts a new *A* to bond with it. On the opposite strand its former partner *A* attracts a new *T,* along with its sugar and phosphate. The new bases as they are added are linked by enzymes and a new chain is fashioned alongside the old chain. After replication there are two double strands, each composed of one entirely new strand and one entirely old strand. Because each half of the DNA directs a new complementary sequence to be

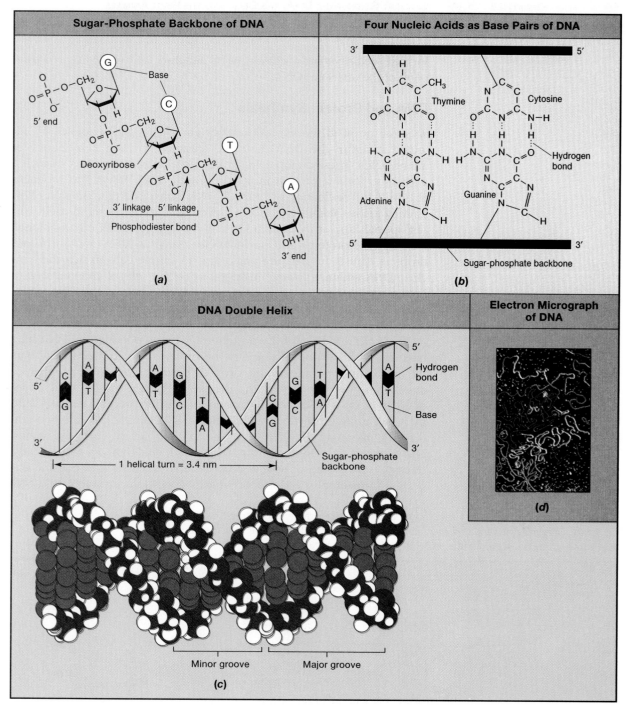

Figure 2–7 • The chemical structure of DNA. (*a*) The repetition of sugar and phosphate to form the backbone of the double helix. (*b*) The chemical construction of the four nucleic acids of the DNA code. (*c*) Diagrammatic representation of spiralled DNA molecule showing A-T, C-G bonds (top); molecular configuration of the molecules (bottom). (*d*) The actual DNA molecule, magnified by an electron microscope. (From Barrett et al., 1986)

formed, cell division results in each daughter cell receiving a faithful copy of the ancestral DNA.

DNA and Protein Synthesis

At some point in the evolutionary origin of life, the sequence of adjoined bases in the DNA molecule attracted to itself a sequence of amino acids. These amino acids linked up alongside the DNA in such a way as to form a protein molecule (Figure 2–8). Why? The probable reason that free-floating or "naked" DNA developed this function of attracting amino acids was to form a protective barrier around itself. Under special laboratory conditions simulating early earth environments, a mixture of proteins and nucleic acids (such as DNA) will form into droplets. These droplets are analogous to simple cells in that they enclose DNA within a protein envelope as do the cells of all living organisms today. A protective envelope would have helped the DNA molecule to withstand turbulent water currents and helped concentrate chemicals useful for cell functions near itself.

The exact structure of the protein molecules coded by the DNA may have been unimportant so long as the proteins served their function as the bounding membrane of the droplet. However, once this problem of maintaining the integrity of the droplet had been solved, distinct sequences of DNA bases began to code for specific proteins which would carry out unique functions within the "cell," extending its lifetime and thereby extending the lifetime of the DNA molecule enclosed within. One type of protein formed the cell wall while others (the earliest enzymes) promoted or speeded up cellular reactions and became important in metabolism. Under laboratory conditions, droplets (and pre-

Figure 2–8 • Diagrammatic view of amino acids being attracted to a free-floating DNA template. Specific polymerizing enzymes make the peptide bonds that link the amino acids and, in turn, assemble the protein. (From Watson, 1976)

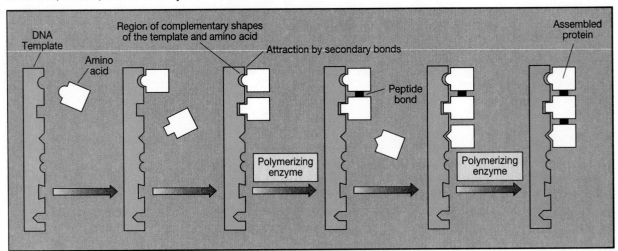

sumably early cells) with metabolic activity have been shown to survive intact longer than metabolically inactive droplets. Metabolism then was an important contributor to longevity in early cells.

One hypothesis to explain the origin of cellular reproduction is that a chemical relative of DNA, the more simply constructed single-chain molecule called **RNA** (ribonucleic acid), was the first molecule to be able to replicate itself. As the parent cell divided into two, the original RNA and its copy, with whatever information they carried, were transferred to the next generation in each daughter cell. What exactly RNA did in the early cells is unknown. RNA survives today in the cell but it has less complex chemical tasks to perform than DNA, and its reproduction has to be aided by cellular enzymes. In some way, early RNA may have evolved into DNA, which is a more stable molecule and capable of producing copies of itself spontaneously without the help of enzymes.

THE DNA MOLECULE EVOLVES

Besides reproducing itself, DNA has the function of producing proteins in the cell. The production of protein molecules on a consistent basis requires some kind of code. The DNA code consists of the bases *A* and *G* (adenine and guanine) or the *C* and *T* (cytosine and thymine) (Table 2–1). The bases are organized into groups of three known as **codons,** that are chemically recognized by a particular amino acid. Codons exist for all of the 20 amino acids that make up every protein manufactured by the cells.

All life forms on earth share the same DNA code. This deceptively simple system is able to code for the stunning amount of variety that we see in organisms. Species' body form, internal chemical makeup, and behavioral capabilities are all derived ultimately from sequences of DNA. In one way of looking at it, the only difference between a human being and a virus is simply a different sequence of the bases that make up their respective DNA's.

Because of the simplicity of the code, only two types of changes are important in the evolution of life. The first is an increase or decrease in the amount of DNA in the cell. The second is a change in the base sequence of the DNA.

The Increase in Amount of DNA

The earliest cells had a relatively small amount of DNA, if we assume they had about the same amount of DNA possessed by living primitive organisms like bacteria (Figure 2–9). As early cells increased in size, perhaps from competition with other cells (a bigger cell is more difficult to attack and ingest), their DNA content increased. In living organisms cell and nuclear size increase with increased amount of DNA.

RNA—ribonucleic acid, a molecule similar to DNA except that uracil (*U*) replaces thymine (*T*) as one of its four bases; the hereditary material in some viruses, but in most organisms a molecule that helps translate the structure of DNA into the structure of protein molecules.

codons—three-unit bases of DNA that code for one of 20 amino acids.

Table 2–1 • The Genetic Code

1st ↓ 2nd →	T	C	A	G	↓ 3rd
T	PHE	SER	TYR	CYS	T
	PHE	SER	TYR	CYS	C
	LEU	SER	STOP	STOP	A
	LEU	SER	STOP	TRP	G
C	LEU	PRO	HIS	ARG	T
	LEU	PRO	HIS	ARG	C
	LEU	PRO	GLN	ARG	A
	LEU	PRO	GLN	ARG	G
A	ILEU	THR	ASN	SER	T
	ILEU	THR	ASN	SER	C
	ILEU	THR	LYS	ARG	A
	MET	THR	LYS	ARG	G
G	VAL	ALA	ASP	GLY	T
	VAL	ALA	ASP	GLY	C
	VAL	ALA	GLU	GLY	A
	VAL	ALA	GLU	GLY	G

The names of the twenty amino acids and their abbreviations are:

ALA	Alanine	LEU	Leucine
ARG	Arginine	LYS	Lysine
ASN	Asparagine	MET	Methionine
ASP	Aspartic acid	PHE	Phenylalanine
CYS	Cysteine	PRO	Proline
GLN	Glutamine	SER	Serine
GLU	Glutamic acid	THR	Threonine
GLY	Glycine	TRY	Tryptophan
HIS	Histidine	TYR	Tyrosine
ILEU	Isoleucine	VAL	Valine

DNA content per cell over the history of life on earth has on average increased. However, the amount of DNA does not correspond closely to organismic complexity. Ferns and salamanders, for example, have much more DNA per cell than do human beings. Hinegardner (1978) has classified organisms into 4 classes based on their DNA content (Figure 2–9). Classes 1 (bacteria) and 2 (fungi) have relatively small

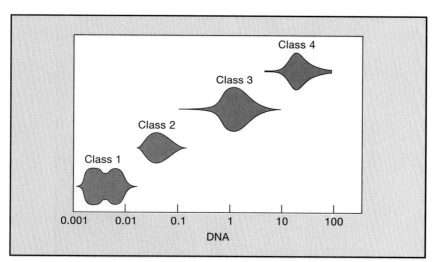

amounts of DNA because of their simplicity. Class 3 includes most animals and some plants. This group is subdivided into 3a—those organisms in which DNA content does not differ greatly among species, and 3b—those organisms whose DNA content may differ within a group by as much as 100%. Finally, Class 4 is characterized by species with very high amounts of DNA. Human beings are in group 3a. How did this rather odd (to us) scatter of DNA patterns evolve in various organisms?

Change and Loss of DNA in Evolution   Hinegardner explains the pattern by noting that for a set amount of DNA in an organism's cells, evolution over time will produce two changes. One, the base sequences will change, as the organism adapts to changing environmental conditions, and two, DNA may be lost. It may be lost, for example, through an adaptation that provides an animal with a longer, stickier tongue to eat ants which renders the unnecessary development of teeth and strong jaw musculature. Consequently, the DNA that coded for these body parts is removed by evolution. The species becomes more specialized, uniquely adapted to its environment and different from other related species. Research on the DNA of fish has shown that specialized species have less DNA per cell than more generalized species (Figure 2–10). Over a long period of time, a lineage of organisms can become very specialized and lose so much DNA that extinction results with even the slightest change in environmental conditions.

On the other hand, for unknown reasons, the DNA content of some species has increased at certain irregularly spaced intervals. We may presume that these increases conferred some advantage at each occurrence. New DNA can produce entirely new proteins which may have evolutionary significance to the species. Thus, DNA increase is quite important in the evolution of life because it provides a template of flexibility for future change.

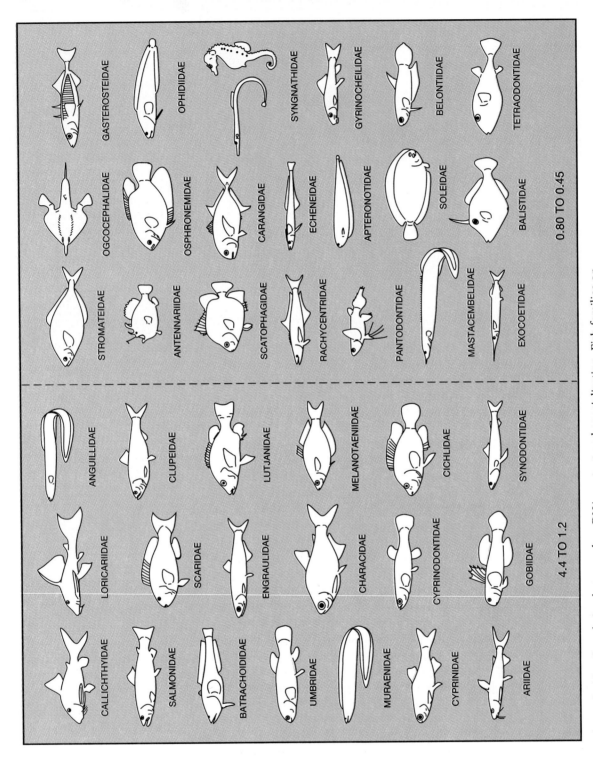

Figure 2–10 • Correlation between low DNA content and specialization. Fish families on the left are generalized and have high cellular DNA contents. Those on the right are specialized and have low cellular DNA contents. (From Hinegardner, 1976)

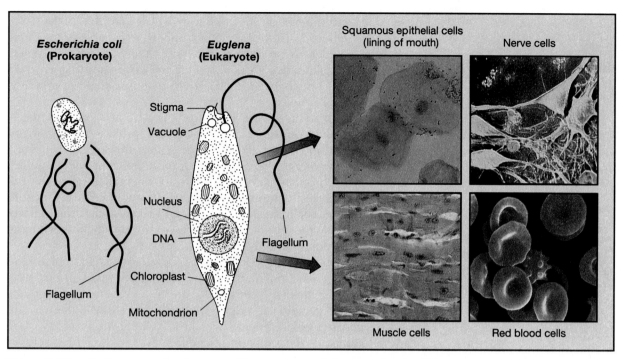

Figure 2–11 • Prokaryote and eukaryote cells, with some of the specialized cell forms that have evolved in higher organisms. (From Schopf, 1978)

THE CELL NUCLEUS EVOLVES

The Earliest Organisms

The earliest organisms were only slightly more complex than the droplet precells scientists have synthesized in the laboratory. These organisms possessed a cell wall composed of proteins, with a double strand of DNA inside, and they reproduced by splitting in two. The earliest of these organisms metabolized anaerobically, but some later ones began to use oxygen as an energy source. These early organisms were either stationary, attached to the shallow sea bottom, or they moved around with a simple tail made up of protein. Called **prokaryotes,** they were the sole life on earth for some two billion years (Figure 2–11). Prokaryotes have a cell membrane, but the DNA inside the cell is floating about along with all the other chemicals in the cell. The DNA is in a chemical environment within the cell that necessitates that it direct all cell activities; it cannot be isolated from any of the subsidiary activities that the cell undertakes. This limits cell size and the diversity of tasks that prokaryote cells can perform.

The fossil record contains large fossilized cells dating between 1.5 and one billion years ago (Figure 2–12). These cells are called **eukaryotes** (Greek, for "true nucleus") because their DNA was separated by a

prokaryotes—organisms like bacteria that lack a differentiated cell nucleus.

eukaryotes—organisms that have a nucleus containing DNA in their cells.

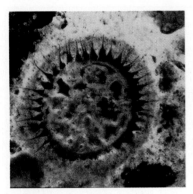

Figure 2–12 • One of the earliest eukaryotic cells, larger than its prokaryotic ancestors. The fossil cell comes from 590-million-year-old sediments in the Doushantuo formation, China.

mitochondria—organelles within the cell with their own DNA that carry on energy metabolism for the cell.

Figure 2–13 • Molecular evolution as indicated by changes in the DNA code (nucleotide substitutions) for 4 protein molecules (cytochrome C, fibrinopeptides, hemoglobin, and histone IV), plotted against time. (From Fitch, 1976)

membrane from the rest of the cell into what is called the nucleus. Scientists have deduced that these cells not only were capable of tolerating oxygen but used it to produce more energy than prokaryotes could. Consequently, eukaryotes were able to grow larger and move faster. The cells in our bodies have nuclei, a characteristic that we inherited from the early eukaryotes.

The early eukaryotes were predatory. They could eat and digest large particles and even other cells. In contrast, prokaryotes can ingest only particles of molecular size that can diffuse through their cellular membranes. Eukaryotes also had a much more efficient energy utilization system. Each cell contained structures or organelles called the **mitochondria.** These structures provided the energy for cellular functions by extracting energy from the nutrients and oxygen that the cell absorbs. In addition, the chromosomes of the eukaryotes held much more genetic information than did those of the prokaryotes.

The approximate date of divergence of prokaryotes and eukaryotes is about one to 1.5 billion years ago, based on both fossil and molecular evidence. The timing of this split can be determined by studying *Cytochrome C,* a protein present in early cells that allowed them to live in an oxygenated environment. Cytochrome C is present today in all plants and animals. By comparing the differences in the amino acid sequences between any two species whose estimated dates of divergence have been determined from the fossil record, an average rate of change in Cytochrome C can be calculated. The molecule changes about two amino acids every 100 million years. For example, a comparison between the Cytochromes C of a human and a moth yields 27 differences, indicating a date of evolutionary divergence of about 675 million years ago (Figure 2–13). Comparison with a primitive eukaryote, baker's yeast, indicates an evolutionary split from the lineage leading to humans at about 1.2 billion years ago.

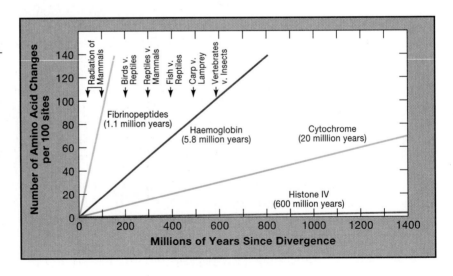

Symbiosis and the Origin of the Mitochondrion Today no life forms intermediate between simple prokaryotic bacteria and complex eukaryotic organisms exist. This fact and the relative rapidity of the appearance of eukaryotic multicellular organisms in the fossil record have suggested to some microbiologists a new theory. This theory is called **symbiosis** (Greek, meaning "living together") defined as "the merging of organisms into new collectives" (Margulis and Sagan, 1985:18). According to this view, the eukaryotic cell is a chimera—two primitive bacterial cells with disparate parts—that began to live as one unit. Each of the two subunits derived benefits from its association with the larger unit and eventually both subunits co-evolved so that they could not survive without the other.

The evolution of mitochondria (Figure 2–14), is an example of symbiotic evolution. **Mitochondrial DNA** is separate from the DNA of the cell nucleus, and mitochondria reproduce by simple division like a bacterium. Early in the history of life a bacterium, ancestral to the mitochondrion of today, that could use oxygen combined with other microorganisms in a symbiotic relationship. The ancestral mitochondrion derived food and shelter from the new arrangement, while providing energy (ATP) from breathing oxygen, and removing waste (fermented food molecules) from this new combination of organisms that was to become the cell.

The ancestral mitochondrion may have been similar to modern predatory bacteria, such as *Daptobacter* (or *Bdellovibris*) (Figure 2–15). These bacteria attack, invade, and reproduce within their bacterial prey, resulting in the death of the prey. The symbiotic explanation suggests that the ancestors of the mitochondrion were restrained predators. That is, they developed an adaptation whereby they could obtain continuing sustenance from the prey cell, while not killing it off. Co-evolution and genetic interchange between prey and predator culminated in a single, mutually interdependent system.

Symbiotic Origin of Microtubules Some of the functions and capabilities most important to eukaryotic cells involve structures called *microtubules*. Within the cell, microtubules drive the circulation of fluids, chemicals, and proteins in a much more organized way than in prokaryotes. Compared to the sluggish activity within bacterial cells, eukaryotic cells are a pulsing beehive of activity. Additionally, microtubules orchestrate the process of cell division.

At present the evolutionary origin of microtubular systems remains unclear. One intriguing hypothesis holds that cellular microtubules derived from a symbiotic combination of whiplike bacterial spirochetes (Figure 2–16), similar to those spiral-shaped bacteria that cause syphilis today. Spirochetes have a cross-sectional structure of 9 pairs of microtubules arranged in a circular pattern around two individual microtubules, a so-called 9 + 2 pattern. The *undulipodia* (Latin, for "waving feet"), or the cell whips on many eukaryotic cells, such as sperm cell

symbiosis–the theory that formerly free-living primitive organisms came together to form a single organism, capable of metabolism and reproduction as a unit.

mitochondrial DNA–the DNA within the mitochondria, abbreviated as mtDNA; mtDNA evolves approximately 10 times faster that the DNA in the cell nucleus.

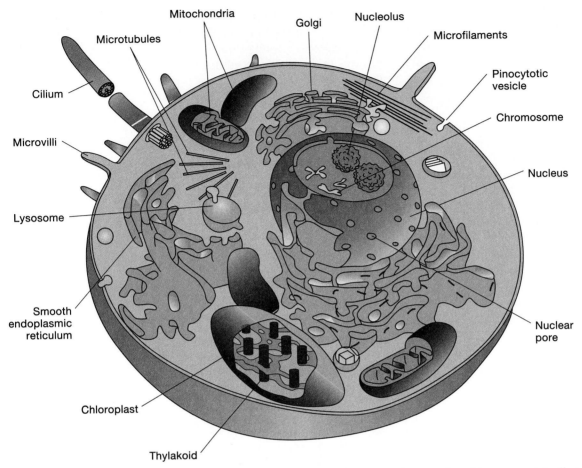

Figure 2–14 • View of cell subunits and organelles. Like the chloroplast, the mitochondrion was originally incorporated into the cell as a "parasite"; these subunits have their own DNA and have now evolved indispensable cell functions related to energy extraction in the cell. (From Barrett et al., 1986)

tails, cilia in our lungs, and the microtubules within eukaryotic cells, all share this 9 + 2 structure. Undulipodia may well be the incorporated descendents of once free-living bacteria, but unlike mitochondria they now lack any residual DNA of their own. Their earliest symbiotic function may have been to provide movement to the pro-eukaryotic cell to which they became attached and, by their proximity, to feed on cell byproducts.

If the hypothesis of spirochetal origin of microtubules is correct, significant light is shed on an additional aspect of eukaryotic evolution, the differentiation of germ (or sex) cells from somatic cells. Living single-celled eukaryotes, such as fungi, have cell division but lack external undulipodia for movement, implying that the microtubular system

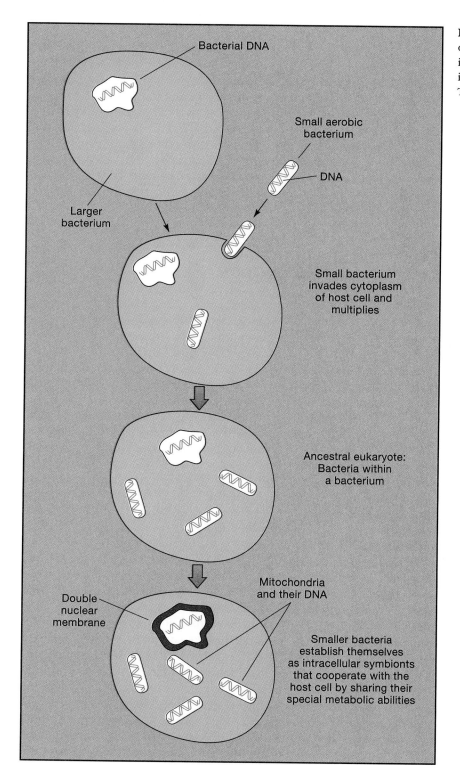

Figure 2–15 • The speculated origin of mitochondria from the invasion of predatory bacteria into a host cell. (From Talaro and Talaro)

enzymes–proteins that have evolved to promote or carry out certain reactions in the cell.

sexual reproduction–reproduction resulting from the exchange of genetic material between two parent organisms.

could be used evolutionarily only for cell division or for movement, not for both. Multicellular eukaryotes hypothetically solved the problem of dividing while retaining movement by evolving *cell specialization:* some cells kept undulipodia and did not divide whereas others became germ or sex cells. The sex cells came to contain the blueprint for developing both their own progeny and those of the undulipodial cells. Once developed, this basic distinction between sex and somatic cells became the framework on which all later multicellular organisms may have evolved. One set of somatic cells that seems to have a particularly close resemblance to spirochetes are brain and nerve cells. These cells have many microtubules, termed *neurotubules,* and possess proteins also found in abundance in living spirochetes.

EVOLUTION OF DNA REPAIR AND SEXUAL REPRODUCTION

We are descended from ancient anaerobic photosynthesizing bacteria that moved out of the airless mud to the sunlit near-surface of the water. As atmospheric hydrogen was used up, these organisms took sunlight and hydrogen sulfide wastes from fermenting bacteria to derive hydrogen molecules. But in the early earth atmosphere a shielding layer of ozone did not exist to block out harmful ultraviolet radiation from the sun. This radiation harms DNA by breaking the molecules apart and by creating *T–T* pairs (called thymine dimers) rather than normal *A–T* pairs, thereby rendering the bacterial DNA inactive and unable to function. DNA repair systems no doubt originally evolved to straighten out this ultraviolet light damage by creating specialized **enzymes**—specialized proteins that promote chemical reactions in cells—to cut out a damaged part of the DNA (Figure 2–17). A new undamaged section of DNA was either borrowed from another bacterium or a virus and then re-inserted into the DNA by enzymes that can "cut and paste" sections of DNA.

Sexual reproduction is the production of new cells through the contribution of genetic material from two parents. Why this form of reproduction first evolved is not simple to understand. First and foremost, as organisms adapt to their environment, selection favors a complement of genes that tends to maximize the organisms' successful adaptation. That is, over time selection would favor genes that, in combination, would anatomically, physiologically, and behaviorally promote an individual's survival and favor its ability to reproduce. Under these circumstances it is logical to think that evolution would favor the situation wherein individuals that are well suited to their environment would pass on to their offspring their genetic package with as little modification as possible. This would assure that whatever successful adaptation was originally made would be maintained throughout later generations. Such a form of reproduction is asexual and is called

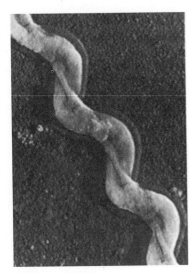

Figure 2–16 • Bacterial spirochete.

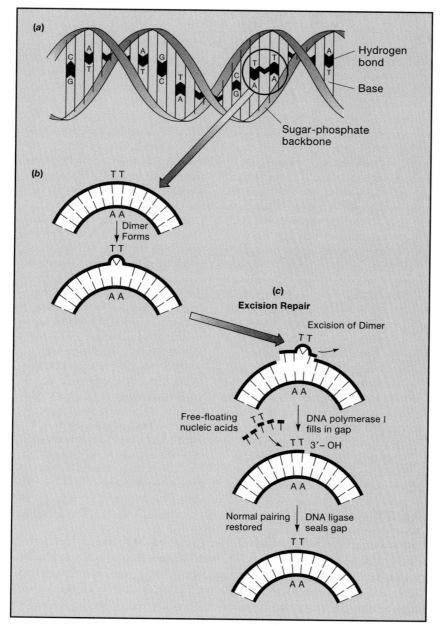

Figure 2–17 • The actions of enzymes in DNA repair. DNA repair is one possible reason for the origin of DNA exchange and later sexual reproduction. (*a*) Normally spiralled DNA molecule. (*b*) Section of DNA molecule where dimer (distortion) appears. (*c*) Excision repair of damaged section of DNA through the actions of enzymes. Free-floating nucleic acids are used to repair damage to DNA. (From Barrett et al., 1986; Klug and Cummings, 1994)

cloning. It involves individuals that simply split in two, or bud, to generate identical genetic copies of themselves. Cloning exists today as a successful form of reproduction in many single-celled organisms, some plants, several insect species, and among the higher vertebrates some fish, amphibians, and reptiles.

The idea for the origin of sexual reproduction through DNA repair is credited to Richard Michod of the University of Arizona, Tucson. In his view gene exchange between individuals originated as a mechanism to

FRONTIERS

Molecular Clocks and Human Evolution

by Vincent Sarich

Any two species, living or extinct, that derive from a unique common ancestor, will show similarities that are retentions from that ancestor. They will also show differences that have accumulated along the separate paths they have traveled from that ancestor to whenever we encounter them.

This pattern is also true at the molecular level, where humans and chimpanzees show 98.3% identity in their DNA sequences, and 100% identity in the amino acid sequences of their major hemoglobins, while for the more distantly related humans and rhesus monkeys the figures are 93% and 96%. This striking similarity between ourselves and chimpanzees at the molecular level was first noted almost a century ago, in 1902, when British parasitologist G.H.F. Nuttall found

himself unable to distinguish between the serum proteins of the two species using antisera made against ours, even though he saw substantial differences when he substituted any other primate serum for that of the chimp.

No one really knew what to make of Nuttall's results, however, and it was not until Morris Goodman began his studies in the late 1950s that we saw progress in the field. Goodman made three major contributions. First, he made use of a technique that gave far better quantitation than was available to Nuttall. Second, he showed that the serum proteins of gorillas were just as similar to those of both humans and chimpanzees as the latter two were to one another. This was a particularly surprising result, as it was almost universally accepted at the time that chimpanzees and gorillas shared much more recent common ancestry with one another than with us. Goodman's results implied that this was not the case—that the most recent common ancestor of the two African apes was in fact our ancestor as well. Finally, and this was his most important contribution, he saw that a critical question had re-

mained unasked since Nuttall's time: Were the striking similarities among human, chimpanzee, and gorilla serum proteins due to the fact that they had evolved more slowly than those of other species, or because the three had shared such recent common ancestry that there simply had not been enough time for their proteins to differentiate very much from one another?

Goodman looked to paleontologists for the answer, and they told him "slowdown," arguing that the divergence times indicated by their reading of the fossil record showed that chimpanzees and gorillas had been separated from one another for longer periods than had certain hoofed mammals, who nonetheless showed larger protein differences than the apes.

This was the state of affairs in 1964 when I, and, independently, the late Allan Wilson, came to see that Goodman's question could be answered without any reference to the fossil record, or indeed any reference to anything besides the protein data themselves. We reasoned as follows: If the slowdown explanation were correct, then our serum proteins, and

---

repair damaged strands of DNA. The bacterium *Bacillus subtilis* uses a mechanism of DNA capture called **transformation**—independent bits of free-floating DNA from dead bacteria of the same species are captured and then used to repair damaged DNA in live bacteria. Experiments show that damaged bacteria incorporate more free-floating DNA than do undamaged bacteria. Undamaged bacteria also replicate more successfully than those damaged in laboratory situations by excessive ultraviolet light or excessive oxygen.

Transformation might be considered a form of proto-sex, a behavior which has obvious short-term individual benefits. But, according to Rosemary Redfield of the University of British Columbia, it is not the only possible explanation for the origin of sex. Redfield contends that hunger is the driving motivation behind DNA capture. She notes that

transformation–incorporation of another cell's DNA into a cell's own DNA structure.

those of the apes, had changed less than had those of Old World monkeys (such as baboons) from the time the two groups had shared common ancestry. This would mean that they would be more similar to each other than the serum proteins of the Old World monkeys would be to the corresponding proteins of the next further out primate unit (New World monkeys). The same logic would allow us to compare amounts of serum protein change in the three higher primate groups (apes, Old and New World monkeys) using prosimians as the reference species, and in all primates using non-primate species.

We decided to do all our early work with albumin, the major protein constituent of serum. Working in Allan Wilson's Berkeley Biochemistry Department laboratory, I purified numerous albumins (including my own) and produced antisera against them by injecting them into rabbits. The strengths of the reactions between those antisera and the various albumins in our sample were then measured. It rapidly became obvious that the slowdown hypothesis was wrong. Human albumin did not react better with antisera

to spider monkey albumin than did baboon albumin. Human or baboon albumins did not react better than that of the spider monkey with antisera to prosimian albumins. But neither could "better" be replaced by "worse." Human and ape albumins reacted about equally well with antisera to Old World monkey albumins. Human, ape, and Old World monkey albumins reacted about equally well with antisera to New World monkey albumins. And so on.

Allan and I then had to conclude that we had found a protein that seemed to keep very good time—thus "molecular clock"—and we decided to use it to calculate the time of separation among the chimp, gorilla, and human lineages. We had found the albumin differences among the three to be about 7-8% of the maximum found among primate albumins. Allowing the latter to refer to, at most, about 65 million years of separation gave us an age for the last common human/chimp/gorilla ancestor of no more than about 5 million years, Since we published that date in 1967, a great deal more in the way of relevant molecular data has appeared, virtually all

of it entirely consistent with "about 5 million years." What has been added is the strong likelihood that in fact we share a brief period of common ancestry with chimpanzees (perhaps 0.5 million years) after the gorilla line split off, leaving my best current estimate of the time of origin of our lineage at 4.5 million years ago.

My ultimate goal is a narrative which, among other things, answers the questions: what, when, where, why, how. I think we are very close to being able to provide the beginnings of such a narrative for our lineage over the past 15 million years or so, and a good deal more for the last 7 million years, that is, the period of the origin and evolution of the African apes. The molecular clock dates provide anchor points for such a narrative. Over the last three decades our understanding of ourselves has taken a great leap forward—and the molecular clock has been a critical part of the equation.

Vincent Sarich is Emeritus Professor of Anthropology at the University of California, Berkeley.

the molecular spine of DNA is made up of alternating sugar and phosphate molecules and when DNA is broken down ("digested"), an organism can use the sugars and the attached base for energy. For example, when a bacterium runs out of internal sugars, it might find and capture external DNA as a new food source. Quite by accident undigested DNA, if it matches a bit of the organism's own DNA, might be incorporated into its host's genetic code. Thus, what started out as a unique feeding strategy may have turned out to be the ultimate origin of sexual reproduction and consequent genetic exchange. Redfield's analysis is provocative in that it explains why sugar molecules are part of the DNA molecular structure. That is, they act, like nectar in a flower, to encourage and bring about the exchange from one individual to another of at least parts of the whole DNA molecule itself.

MITOSIS AND MEIOSIS EVOLVE

Mitosis

When the first cells grew too large they spontaneously split apart. DNA, enzymes, and metabolic activity would then have been carried into two new daughter cells. But this process could be haphazard: if important parts of the DNA molecule and important cellular chemicals did not make it into a daughter cell, cell death would occur. The process of cellular reproduction became more organized so that the same amount of DNA made it into the new cells as had been in the parent. This solution for efficient parcelling out of the parent cell's DNA to offspring cells is accomplished by the process of **mitosis** (Greek, meaning "threading"). Mitosis takes place when DNA in a cell is replicated and then migrates to opposite poles of the cell as the cell divides into two new cells (Figure 2–18).

mitosis–the replication of the DNA during splitting of a cell and migration of each duplicated portion to a new cell.

Figure 2–18 • The cellular processes of meiosis and mitosis (from Barrett et al., 1986).

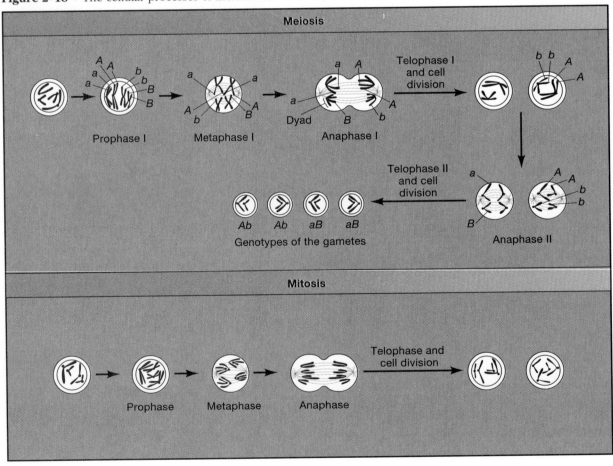

The new cells can then carry on the same metabolic functions as the parent.

Meiosis

The cell and its functioning became more complex in the eukaryotes. The DNA in the nucleus was folded up into thicker thread-like structures known as **chromosomes** (Greek for "colored body" because of their appearance under the light microscope) (Figure 2–19). The eukaryotes possess sex cells, or cells with half the number of chromosomes as the body cells of each parent possess. Human egg and sperm cells are sex cells. As a sex cell divides, the chromosomes split into complementary halves without replicating. A sex cell with half its chromosomes then combines with another such sex cell to form a new cell with the normal number of chromosomes. This process is known as **meiosis** (Greek for "lessening," referring to the splitting in half of the pairs of chromosomes in the nucleus). The eukaryotes thus mix up the DNA from two parents in their offspring. One set of chromosomes is provided by the father and another set by the mother. Eukaryotic sexual reproduction originated at least 850 million years ago. This is the time from which fossilized eukaryotes with complex morphology become abundant and diverse in the fossil record (Figure 2–20).

chromosomes—structures composed of folded DNA found in the nuclei of the cells of eukaryotic organisms.

meiosis—the process whereby eukaryote sex cells halve their DNA for combination with the sex cells of another individual.

Figure 2–19 • Diagrammatic view of folded strings of DNA known as chromosomes. These structures are characteristic of eukaryotes.

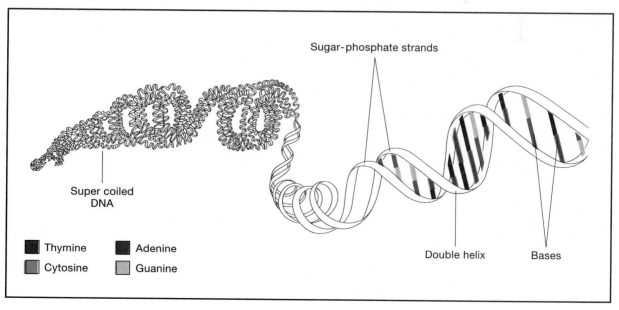

Sugar-phosphate strands

Super coiled DNA

■ Thymine　■ Adenine
▨ Cytosine　▨ Guanine

Double helix　Bases

THE EARLIEST ANIMALS APPEAR

The highest taxonomic category is that of the Kingdom. Prokaryotes are all classified within the Kingdom Protista, which includes not only living species such as blue-green bacteria and viruses but extinct ancestors of the Kingdoms Metaphyta (plants), Fungi (mushrooms and their relatives), and Metazoa (animals).

The earliest indications of animals from the fossil record are burrows made in the shallow sea floor about 700 million years ago, in the latter part of the Precambrian Period (Appendix 2). Although some casts and burrows of soft-bodied animals and isolated skeletal parts are known from the latest Precambrian Period, the Cambrian Period (550–500 million years ago) ushers in the first significant animal faunas. By the middle of the Cambrian Period (about 530 million years ago) a large diversity of animals had evolved. At one site in western Canada, the Burgess Shale, over 50 species are present. Most are *arthropods* (Figure 2–21), distant relatives of the living crabs, insects, and spiders; several types are worms. There is a single representative in this fauna of the Phylum Chordata, the group of animals from which all higher metazoans, including ourselves, evolved (see Chapter 5 for more discussion of chordates).

Metazoans are organisms capable of active movement, at least at one stage of their development. What advantage does active movement confer on an organism? In ecological terms the ability to move is an adaptation that increases the probability of an organism's ability to find food. In contrast, "sessile" or non-actively moving organisms must rely on water or air currents to move them to where their food is. Active movement also makes possible escape from life-threatening situations: animals can move away from environments that are too hot or too cold, too congested, or too dangerous.

Along with the ability to move, animal evolution is characterized by an increase in the size of individual organisms and by cellular specialization. Increase in size is of understandable selective advantage primarily because it prevents predation by all organisms except those of similar or larger size. But a disadvantage with increasing body size is the need for the ingestion of a larger quantity of food.

Specialization of cells within an animal's body necessarily accompanies increase in body size. Why should this be so? Why, for example, could there not exist a fish-sized amoeba-like animal with undifferentiated cells? The primary problem is maintaining an appropriate cellular environment, and when many cells, that is, more than two cells thick, come together to form tissues, they lose contact with the watery medium of their environment. Therefore, they cannot pick up nutrients and exchange waste products. For large animals, circulating fluids made of specialized cells, such as blood, mimic the environment of the ancient seas by bathing all cells. Other cells become specialized to form vessels for transporting this fluid around the body. And still other

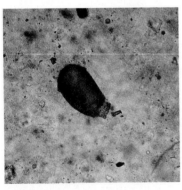

Figure 2–20 • A vase-shaped early eukaryote fossil, likely capable of sexual reproduction, from 700- to 800-million-year-old sediments, Spitzbergen, Germany.

Figure 2–21 • Reconstruction of arthropods and other organisms from extinct groups from the Burgess Shale of British Columbia, Canada, dating from 530 to 550 million years ago. These were the dominant animals in a fauna that included only one species of our own Phylum Chordata (genus *Pikaia* in foreground).

cells develop into appendages such as tails, limbs or fins, and contractile tissues, such as muscle, to enable movement. Finally, sensory and neural cells develop to direct an animal's movements.

Reproductive functions in animals were taken over by only certain cells. Why did this occur? Perhaps an analogy can suggest an explanation. Imagine what would happen if suddenly all the cells in our body began replicating to form a new individual, as cells do in simple eukaryotes. A new individual would not result. We would just grow larger and larger until the tissue could no longer bear the weight of our body. If some cells proliferated too rapidly, other tissues would become crowded out and cease to function. Indeed, this is what occurs in cancer. To organize reproduction, the sex cells—the male sperm and female egg—specialized for their unique function in generating a new individual. Organs in the body specialized for bringing these two types of cells together and nurturing them. Reproductive organs were part of the specialization of body parts that accompanied the evolutionary appearance of the first animals.

In this chapter we have discussed the evolution of life, so far as we know it, from inorganic sources present in the environments of ancient Earth. From simple single-celled organisms more complex multicellular life forms developed, along with new internal organelles, which carried out specific cellular functions. What was the process or mechanism that effected changes in life forms from the simplest to the most complex? The answer to this question plagued natural scientists and philosophers alike, yet it was not until the mid-nineteenth century that the pieces of this old puzzle were finally combined into a biological theory, evolution, which made sense of it all. In Chapter 3, we investigate the evolutionary principles by which organisms and the DNA inside them modify and change through time.

 SUMMARY

The universe is some 10 to 20 billion years old. The earth is considerably younger, having formed about 4.5 billion years ago. Continental drift accounts for movements of plates on the earth's crust which result in climatic and biotic change. The first evidence of life on earth is in the form of microscopic fossils of blue-green bacteria over three billion years old. This early life emerged in oxygenless environments and was capable of metabolic function and reproduction. The DNA molecule, which has the chemical ability to attract free-floating amino acids, became the important ingredient in the production of proteins needed for cellular life and cellular reproduction. Diversity was promoted as many organisms became multicellular, or composed of many cells. All animals and plants visible to the naked eye are composed of millions and sometimes billions of cells, which act cooperatively to sustain the organism. Multicellular organisms have certain advantages over single-celled organisms. Because of their larger body size, they maintain a more constant internal physiological environment (to prevent death of cells) and minimize predation by other organisms. Their adaptations have been modified by evolution in ways to enhance reproduction, metabolism, locomotion, and ways of finding food. Symbiotic evolution of single-celled organisms accounts for the presence of cellular organelles in eukaryotic cells. Sexual reproduction originated as part of the process to repair DNA, a process which transferred DNA from one organism to another. The earliest animals of some 700 million years ago were metazoans capable of movement and characterized by an increase in size and further cellular specialization. Mitosis and meiosis are mechanisms that evolved in early eukaryotes for sexual reproduction.

 ## CRITICAL-THINKING QUESTIONS

1. How has continental drift affected the evolution of life forms on earth?
2. Briefly explain the big bang theory.
3. Name the oldest microscopic fossils found. What capabilities did they possess that allow scientists to classify them as a life form?
4. Describe the difference between prokaryotic and eukaryotic cells.
5. Briefly explain the evolution and function of mitochondria.
6. What is the selective advantage of sexual reproduction over cloning?

 ## SUGGESTED READINGS

Gould, Stephen Jay. 1989. *Wonderful Life: The Burgess Shale and the Nature of History*. New York: Norton. The story of the Cambrian-aged Burgess Shale of Canada and the near-surrealistic animals that first populated the earth's seas.

Margulis, L., and D. Sagan. 1986. *Microcosmos: Four billion years of evolution from our microbial ancestors*. New York: Summit. A good general book on the intimate biological interconnections between our everyday macroscopic world and the teeming microorganisms that share it with us.

Stanley, Stephen. 1991. *Earth and Life Through Time*. New York: W.H. Freeman. A synthetic treatment of geology and paleontology during earth history.

Evolution and Natural Selection

Influences on Darwin
Malthus's Theory of Populations
Lyell's Theory of
    Uniformitarianism

**Darwin Develops His Theory
    of Natural Selection**
Collecting Evidence for
    Evolution
Investigating Differential
    Reproduction
Co-Discovery of Natural
    Selection
The Problem of Inherited
    Variation
Darwin's Theory of Inheritance

**Development of a Theory
    of Inheritance**
The Laws of Heredity
The Principle of Segregation
The Principle of Independent
    Assortment
Chromosomal Theory of
    Heredity
Gene Linkage and Crossing
    Over

**Mendelian Genetics and
    Molecular Genetics**
How Protein Synthesis Works
Gene Structure

**Mutation: The Source of
    Genetic Variation**
Selection Acts on Mutations

**The Puzzle of Sexual
    Reproduction**

Summary

Critical-Thinking Questions

Suggested Readings

In Chapter 3, we discuss how the processes of DNA replication, protein synthesis, and cell biology—the subjects of Chapter 2—relate to the biology and evolution of whole organisms. In the early history of life, replicating molecules and single cells were whole organisms. Today, the ecologically dominant species on earth are much more complex, composed of many thousands of cells. However, these complex organisms evolved from those simpler life forms and, in the process, incorporated the earlier modes of reproduction and metabolism into their own biology.

We begin this chapter with a discussion of the development of the theory that explains the many known facts about the origins and diversity of species of organisms on earth: the theory of evolution by natural selection, first conceived of and developed by Charles Darwin (1809–1882). Darwin's theory successfully explained the observable diversity and adaptations of animals and plants, but not inheritance of characteristics, because the knowledge of genetic mechanisms and the genetic basis of variability escaped him. Next, we discuss the synthesis of the laws of genetic inheritance, developed by Gregor Mendel (1822–1884), and Darwin's theory of natural selection, which together form the basis for the modern synthesis of evolutionary theory. Finally, we discuss the integration of modern cell biology and molecular genetics with the synthetic theory of evolution and how this integration has contributed to a more complete understanding of the intricate workings of the DNA molecule and the process of mutation.

INFLUENCES ON DARWIN

In 1830 the English astronomer Sir John Herschel (1792–1871) wrote that "[T]o ascend to the origin of things, and to speculate on the creation, is not the business of the natural philosopher" (Herschel, 1830:38). Yet one undergraduate at Cambridge University who read those words in 1831 was not dissuaded from a career that eventually led him to investigate the origin of biological species, "that mystery of mysteries" (Darwin, 1887:141). The student's name was Charles Darwin (Figure 3–1).

Darwin prided himself on his **inductive scientific method,** defined as the collection of data without preconceived notions or hypotheses (Hull, 1973:9–10). Nevertheless, the work of several influential scientists

inductive scientific method—inferring a generalized conclusion from particular instances.

Figure 3–1 • Charles Darwin.

deductive–inferring conclusions about particular instances from general or universal premises.

profoundly affected his later thoughts and views of his data, and they contributed to the **deductive** framework for his theory of evolution by natural selection.

Malthus's Theory of Populations

In his *Essay on the Principles of Population* (1798), English economist Thomas Malthus (1766–1834) observed that human population numbers increase geometrically (multiplication by a constant factor) and food resources increase only arithmetically (addition by a constant factor) (Figure 3–2). He put forward the idea that the world always tends to have more people in it than it has food to feed them. Population checks, such as famine, disease, and war, were to Malthus unavoidable facts of society. Malthus made his observations when the population in Britain had begun to swell as the Industrial Revolution gained momentum. In the first edition of his book he advanced the unpopular thesis that human progress was impossible because of the specters of starvation, disease, and war. In the second edition, however, he suggested that delayed marriage and sexual restraint could allay some of the dire societal consequences of overpopulation.

In 1838 the young Charles Darwin read Malthus's book "for amusement" (Darwin, 1887:120), anticipating a parallel between his observations on plants and animals and Malthus's "struggle for existence" theory about human beings. Instead, Darwin hit upon a crucial ingredient that he would later incorporate into his theory of natural selection:

Figure 3–2 • Plot of Malthus's theory of population increase versus food resources, showing the rapid outdistancing by the former of the latter. Numbers on the x and y axes are arbitrary units.

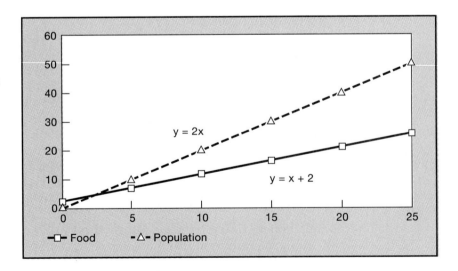

. . . it at once struck me that under these circumstances favorable variations would tend to be preserved, and unfavorable ones to be destroyed. The result of this would be the formation of a new species. Here, then, I had at last got a theory by which to work . . . (Darwin 1887:120).

Lyell's Theory of Uniformitarianism

During the latter nineteenth century, some earth scientists disagreed that small changes observable at work today could account for observed geological phenomena. They suspected that large-scale catastrophes, such as floods, earthquakes, or volcanic eruptions, were the primary forces that molded earth history.

The theory of **catastrophism,** which holds that earth history is explicable in terms of violent and sudden cataclysms which destroyed most living species, after which a new set of creations established new species, was popularized by the French naturalist Georges Cuvier. It accounted for change within a relatively short, and, at that time, generally accepted time frame. This presented a large obstacle for Darwin in that he could not reconcile the idea of a short geologic time scale with his idea of gradual morphological change in evolution. If the world had indeed been formed at 4,004 B.C., as Anglican Bishop James Ussher had calculated in 1654, then there would be very little time for animals to change, let alone for new species to evolve. In Darwin's theory many hundreds or thousands of generations of breeding were needed to account for the differentiation over time between species. In fact, one of Darwin's severest critics at the time was paleontologist Richard Owen, who believed that this form of evolution would simply take too much time for species to appear.

Connected with catastrophism was **special creation,** an idea proposed by Cuvier and others to account for the repopulation of the flora and fauna after a catastrophe had wiped out previous species. Although both these explanations were of the miraculous type and, therefore, nonscientific, "special creation" was distinguished from the original "creation" because it had presumably occurred numerous times in earth history. Although this mechanism could explain a number of observations relating to the geological and paleontological changes seen in earth history, there was no way to test the mechanism. It was an assumption, and as such it was impossible to test directly.

Sir Charles Lyell (1797–1875; Figure 3–3), a Scot trained at Oxford as a lawyer, became one of the most influential geologists of the day. His landmark work, *The Principles of Geology* (1830–33), propounded the view that the earth's geological history could be explained entirely by heat and erosion, processes that we can observe at work today. This idea had been advanced a generation before by Lyell's countryman James Hutton (1726–1797), the founder of geology, yet it was Lyell who extended and popularized the theory. Lyell appealed to a "principle of uniformity," and William Whewell, a reviewer of *The Principles,*

Figure 3–3 • Sir Charles Lyell.

catastrophism–theory that earth history is explicable in terms of violent and sudden cataclysms that destroyed most living species, after which a new set of creations established new species.

special creation–the nonevolutionary theory associated with catastrophism that held that totally new species, unrelated to prior species, were created after extinctions.

coined the term **uniformitarianism** for Lyell's theory. Uniformitarianism is the principle that processes observable today can account for past events in geological history.

Charles Darwin first read a copy of Lyell's book on the round-the-world voyage of the British ship *H.M.S. Beagle* when he was employed as the ship's naturalist. In 1836 on his return to England, Darwin states in his *Autobiography* (1887:83,84) that he "saw a great deal of Lyell" and that "his advice and example had much influence on me." One historian of science has suggested that Lyell's influence was such that Darwin's *Origin of Species* "could almost literally have been written out of Lyell's book, once the guiding motif of natural selection had been conceived" (Eiseley, 1958:100).

Uniformitarianism became one of the founding principles of modern geology, and, through Darwin, a major influence in biology. Lyell's uniformitarian theory was important to Darwin's theory of natural selection because it provided the long time periods necessary for the slow and gradual change that Darwin envisioned. Four of Lyell's propositions are presented here (Rudwick, 1972; Gould, 1984). Propositions 1 and 2 are assumptions. Propositions 3 and 4 are empirical claims that require testing.

1) *Uniformity of Law*   In order to explain phenomena in any place and at any time a law must be invariant. This is an assumption of uniformitarianism. For example, the law of gravity is invariant; that is, it operates in all places and, so far as we know, it has operated at all times during the history of Earth. This assumption is universally accepted by scientists.

2) *Uniformity of Process (Actualism)*   When causes are observable, there is no need to hypothesize more complicated explanations. This assumption is a specific application of the more general practice in science termed "Occam's Razor," which holds that the simplest hypothesis to explain the observed facts is the preferable one. This assumption is also universally accepted by scientists.

3) *Uniformity of Rate (Gradualism)*   Agents of change in the past have always acted with the same degree of energy with which they act now. The Grand Canyon, for example, was not cut by a single great flood, but by a slow, gradual process of continual erosion over millennia. This assumption is widely accepted as a general rule but a number of scientists today also see specific examples of catastrophic change.

4) *Uniformity of Conditions*   The history of life is cyclic and non-directional. For example, should environmental conditions approaching those of 150 million years ago return, dinosaurs would return with them. This aspect of Lyell's theory is no longer generally accepted because there is no evidence to support these hypothetical cycles.

uniformitarianism–principle that processes observable today can account for past events in geological history.

DARWIN DEVELOPS HIS THEORY OF NATURAL SELECTION

Collecting Evidence for Evolution

Much of the data that Darwin used to construct his theory came from his experiences as ship's naturalist aboard the *H.M.S. Beagle,* which circumnavigated the globe in 1833–36 on a mission mapping the South American coast for British shipping interests. On the recommendation of his former botany professor at Cambridge University, Darwin was chosen for the job of ship's naturalist.

When Darwin sailed from England on the *H.M.S. Beagle,* he carried with him the idea of evolution advanced by French naturalist Jean Baptiste de Lamarck (1744–1829; Figure 3–4). Lamarck believed that species could evolve and did change over time. How these changes in anatomy and behavior occurred or whether the changes could produce a new species were still major questions. Lamarck's theory proposed that changes or differences in the environment cause a "need" for organisms to change. This need causes biological change within the organism and makes it better suited to its new environment. Biological change, in turn, may be passed down to offspring. Lamarck believed that the traits an animal acquired in changing could be inherited by its offspring who would be better adapted because of the changes. Thus, he proposed the idea of the inheritance of acquired characteristics (Figure 3–5) to explain the origin of variation among and between different species.

In South America Darwin found evidence of evolution, but his observations forced him to question Lamarck's idea of the inheritance of acquired characters. If Lamarck's explanation of the mechanism for evolution were correct, similar environments would produce similar species.

When Darwin arrived at the Galápagos Islands, off the northwest coast of South America in September of 1835, he discovered some important facts. The Galápagos are volcanic and much more recent in origin than the neighboring mainland. Darwin immediately set to work collecting animal and plant specimens from the many closely spaced islands, suspecting that they differed from those on the mainland. In accordance with Lamarck's ideas, he expected the fauna and flora of the various islands to be quite similar to one another, because the islands were so close together and they lay in the same climate. He found, in fact, quite a unique spectrum of species of birds, lizards and tortoises on the islands. They were related, but also quite distinct from mainland South American forms.

As the work progressed Darwin became aware of a strange and unexpected fact—the tortoises from each island differed from the tortoises of other islands. In fact people could tell what island a tortoise

Figure 3–4 • Jean Baptiste de Lamarck.

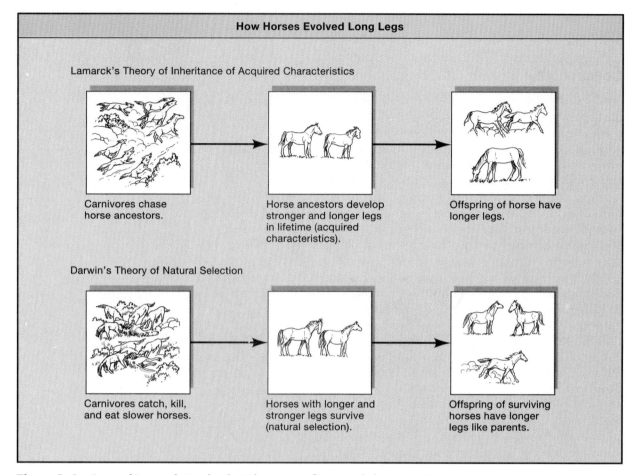

Figure 3–5 • Lamarckian evolution by the inheritance of acquired characteristics, in contrast to Darwinian evolution by natural selection.

came from by looking at the shell alone (Figure 3–6). How could this be so if species were adapted to the same environment?

Darwin began to think that because all the types of island tortoises were in most ways similar, they must have all descended from a common ancestral tortoise and had diverged over time in their adapting to the various island environments. He concluded that geographic isolation was crucial to an understanding of evolution. Geographical variations were not separate "special creations" of species, but rather, they were local modifications of a single species.

Darwin found fossil evidence in South America that showed that evolution had occurred. He discovered in an ancient geological formation a fossil glyptodont, an extinct giant relative of the modern armadillo (Figure 3–7). An extinct llama skeleton discovered in Patagonia showed a clear connection to living South American llamas. In his *Jour-*

Figure 3–6 • Natural selection in tortoises of the Galápagos Islands. A tortoise of the island of Santa Cruz (left) is compared with one found on Isla Isabella (right).

Figure 3–7 • Comparison of a modern armadillo (top) to a fossil representative of a group now extinct (a glyptodont) in South America (bottom).

nal of Researches (1839), Darwin noted that "the most important result of this discovery is the confirmation of the law that existing animals have a close relation in form with extinct species." Darwin termed this "the law of the succession of types," an idea that formed the theoretical basis for connecting the fossil record with the diversity of living animals.

Investigating Differential Reproduction

Darwin returned home in 1836 and devoted the remaining years of his life to the study of natural history. He began to study domesticated animals and to breed pigeons. He also wrote a number of classic studies on organisms like the barnacle and on the evolution of behavior (see Chapter 11). He observed that, through the process of artificial breeding or *selection,* one could obtain populations or strains of animals that were quite different from each other and from the original parental form.

Almost all the pieces of the puzzle of evolution were in place: individuals vary and forms could be artificially selected to breed so that change could come about; and these differences were heritable from generation to generation. What Darwin lacked was knowledge of how this inherited variability could be connected to his deduction that animals could change over time to adapt to their natural environments. Part of the answer, of course, came from Malthus's essay.

Malthus wrote in his essay that not all individuals born reached maturity. Many die from one cause or another before adulthood. A species does not continue to reproduce until it completely covers the earth with its offspring. Rather, there is some upper limit to population growth and populations maintain a stable number of individuals.

Darwin's argument started with the observation that individuals within a species vary one from another (Figure 3–8). A second observation was that this variability could be inherited. Because of variability, some individuals were better suited to survive in their environments than others. Because variability could be inherited parents passed on to their offspring their characteristics. Invoking Malthus's ideas that species produce more offspring than can survive, Darwin reasoned that those individuals best adapted to their environment would survive longer on the average and produce more offspring than those less well-adapted. He called the new theory **natural selection,** to distinguish it from the artificial selection practiced on domestic animals by breeders. Natural selection is the process whereby populations of living organisms change or evolve through time because of differential rates of production of offspring by the parental generation.

In 1859, Darwin published the *Origin of Species by Means of Natural Selection,* a book that he intended to be an abbreviated version of his thesis. While acknowledging the intellectual debt that he owed to Malthus, Lyell, and the codiscoverer of natural selection, the naturalist Alfred Russel Wallace, it was Darwin who fully developed the argument in *Origin of Species.* Darwin reasoned that differential survival occurred because individuals had different abilities (*fitnesses*) to cope with their environment. Differential reproduction would be the result of the survival of those individuals who were better adapted. Over the

natural selection—the process of differential reproduction whereby individuals well-adapted to their environment will be "favored," that is, they will pass on more of their heritable attributes to the next generation than other, less well-adapted individuals.

Figure 3–8 • Individuals vary one from another and variability is inherited.

generations there would be selection by environmental conditions among the various individuals, with the better adapted individuals producing more offspring. Those individuals disfavored by selection might not reproduce at all or would have relatively fewer offspring than the better or more fit animals.

Darwin's work proved quite persuasive to some and quite controversial to others. It generated so much debate, which Darwin addressed in numerous revised editions of his book, that his longer contemplated work never saw the light of day. Later philosopher Herbert Spencer coined the sobriquet "survival of the fittest" to characterize Darwin's theory. Although Darwin was to use the phrase himself later, it fails to underscore the essential element of natural selection—relative success in *reproduction,* not merely in the survival of the individual.

Wallace's Co-Discovery of Natural Selection

By the end of the 1830s Darwin was convinced that evolution or change occurred by the process of natural selection. Still, he continued to accumulate data and make observations for another 20 years without formally publishing his ideas on evolution, although several of his colleagues in England knew of his work. In the late 1850s, Alfred Russel Wallace (1823–1913) observed a division line between the types of animals in Australia/New Guinea and those of Asia. This faunal boundary is today called the Wallace Line (Figure 3–9). Wallace realized that the primitive pouched mammals, such as the kangaroos, were limited to

Figure 3–9 • Sundaland and Sahulland were land masses formed as the ocean levels lowered, a phenomenon that resulted from serial glaciation during Ice Age Pleistocene times. Wallace's Line represents the faunal division between Southeast Asia and Australia. (From Howells, 1993)

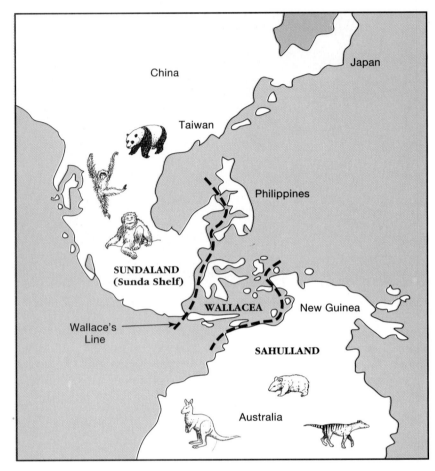

the Australian/New Guinean side and that modern mammals were on the other side. The presence of similar looking species in both groups despite the fact that they had evolved in isolation led Wallace to formulate the general principles of natural selection. Whereas Darwin had seen the principles of natural selection at work between the mainland of South America and the Galápagos Islands, Wallace saw results of the same process expressed between the two continental land masses of Australia and Asia. Wallace independently discovered from his work much of what Darwin had come to believe more than 20 years before. Darwin's first paper on his theory of evolution, along with Wallace's ideas on the subject, were together presented to the Linnaean Society in London in 1858, a year before Darwin's *Origin of Species*.

The Problem of Inherited Variation

Darwin had linked the concepts of excess reproductive capacity, differences in heritable adaptations, enhanced survival, and reproduction of the fittest. What the theory of evolution by natural selection did not ex-

Figure 3–10 • The problem of maintenance of variation: blending inheritance.

plain was how variation had come into existence. The problem for Darwin was how to explain the origin of that variation that led to the differential success in reproduction and ultimately to the formation of new species. Darwin at various points in his life believed that Lamarck was correct in his explanation of the inheritance of acquired characteristics, and he died before the explanation for the inheritance of new traits became known.

How variation was maintained in populations was the second profound problem that Darwin considered. He believed that most traits, when combined in an offspring, were blends of the parental types. For example, the mating of a tall and a short individual would produce an offspring that was intermediate in height (Figure 3–10). Two intermediate height individuals would produce an intermediate height offspring. The consequence of this **blending inheritance,** however, is a loss of variation in the population. In reality it would lead to a homogenization of the next and future generations until almost all of the variability, the raw material of natural selection, was reduced to nothing. If inheritance by blending did occur, then after only nine generations one would have less than 0.1% of original variation left. This fact was noted by a Scottish engineer, Fleeming Jenkin, who published in 1867 an article that criticized Darwin's hypothesis of blending inheritance. How, he asked, could a single favorable change, a heritable **mutation** arising in one member of a population, ever come to predominate if at each successive reproduction its benefit was halved by blending with an individual lacking the trait? The problem presented to Darwin was that some other mechanism must

blending inheritance–the mixing in equal halves of the contributions of parents in their offspring.

mutation–a heritable "change" leading to physical or physiological changes in offspring.

FRONTIERS

The Interaction of Climate, Environment, and Evolution

by Lloyd H. Burckle

Earth scientists have speculated for many years about the relationship between major changes in the earth's climate and periods of rapid evolutionary change. Many new areas of research have now shown that there is a general correspondence between times of major climate change and episodes of evolutionary change. Why should this be so? One idea is that during periods of worldwide cooler temperatures ("global cooling") the animal and plant species in the far north and far south, most affected by colder temperatures, suffer some extinction and tend to be pushed toward the equator. Great ecological pressure is placed on the species already resident in the lower latitudes near the equator as the immigrant species compete for food and space. A great deal of extinction of the resident low latitude species results. When conditions become warmer, species are free to repopulate the higher latitudes again, and evolution acts to increase the diversity of species. In this scenario most of the newly evolved species in the world derive ultimately from higher latitude populations.

Even if this scenario is accurate, and it is not by any means the only explanation for evolutionary change, there are many other factors that may complicate the story. For example, there have been periods, unlike the present, during which climatic cooling was not the same at both the North Pole and the South Pole. If, because of continental drift, a continent was centered at one pole, and the open ocean was centered at the other, the pole without the insulating effect of water would suffer greater temperature change, and hypothetically would witness the greater effect on its animal and plant communities. Further changes can occur on land as ice builds up during periods of cold. These episodes are known as glaciations. The massive build-up of ice on land takes up so much of the earth's water that sea level is lowered worldwide. Islands can become connected with mainland areas and previously open land connections can become blocked by ice formation. These changes in land routes can have important effects on dispersal of species and their subsequent evolution.

What causes the changes in the earth's climate that we see? Major changes are dictated by astronomical cycles related to the earth's relationship to the sun. These so-called Milankovich cycles, named after their discoverer, lead to periodic and predictable changes in global climate. However, the severity and mosaic pattern of that climate change is dictated by other factors as well. Surface and near-surface earth movements, known as tectonism, are one of the most important factors. Tectonic effects include mountain building, continental drift, and long-term vertical uplift or subsidence. Only recently have geologists and climate modellers come to appreciate the role that tectonism plays in climate and climate change (and, by extension, its effect on evolution). Another impor-

tant factor affecting climate is weathering, or the physical and chemical wearing away of the rock of the earth's surface. Increased rates of weathering, caused by higher continental elevations (in turn related, of course, to tectonic activity), will cause greater amounts of calcium carbonate from chemical weathering of rocks to be deposited into the world's oceans. This, in turn, reduces the amount of carbon dioxide in the atmosphere, and in a reverse greenhouse effect, reduces global temperature. The relationship among mountain and plateau uplift, increased chemical weathering, and global climate cooling seems to hold both for the recent periods of earth history during the Tertiary and for much of geological history.

The Tertiary Period is particularly important for primate and hominid evolution and provides a good illustration of the interaction of tectonic change, regional climate, and evolution. Within the past 50 million years, Antarctica separated from South America and Australia, while the north polar regions became landlocked. India collided with Asia some 40 to 50 million years ago and initiated the rise of the Himalayas. In addition to the formation of this large mountain barrier, uplift of the Tibetan plateau was initiated. The American West also witnessed uplift during this time, the most significant result being the Colorado plateau. Finally, regions such as eastern and southern Africa underwent broad vertical uplift, which served to cause fracturing and rifting at the earth's surface.

The climatic effects of these tectonic changes included the thermal isolation of the south polar region and the initiation of major glaciation in

Antarctica after 54 million years ago. This ice sheet increased 34 million years ago, leading to a global drop in sea level. The rise of the Himalayas not only caused increased weathering and reduction ("drawdown") of atmospheric carbon dioxide, thus reducing global temperature, but their height redirected wind patterns in the entire Indian Ocean area, creating a seasonal, or "monsoonal" rain pattern in Africa and southern Asia. Uplift of the Colorado and Tibetan plateaus, besides influencing local climate, diverted high-level jet stream and low-level winds to the north, causing further cooling globally and particularly in the northern hemisphere. Two more recent global cooling events are recorded at 14 million years ago when the Antarctic ice sheet greatly enlarged, and at 7 million years ago when the Greenland ice sheet was initiated. There were many interrelated changes in environment that accompanied these broad changes in climate. The subtropical and temperate belts, for example, had been of broad extent some 50 million years ago, but they have moved progressively closer to the equator through the Tertiary, and have created a series of new climatic zones in their wake. The interplay among climate, tectonics, and evolution is an active field of research, and we can expect to see much progress as research proceeds.

Lloyd H. Burckle is senior research scientist at Lamont Doherty Earth Observatory, Columbia University, New York.

Figure 3–11 • King Philip II's protruding lower jaw, known popularly as the "Hapsburg lip," was characteristic of members of the Hapsburg Dynasty beginning with Holy Roman Emperor Frederick III of Austria (1415–1493). Darwin was puzzled at how this trait could be retained when "blending" with non-Hapsburgs should have reduced the appearance of the trait. Later research showed that the trait is caused by a dominant gene.

be at work to generate the enormous quantities of new variation that replace the loss of so much every generation. To find such a mechanism, Darwin began amassing data from plant and animal breeders in England.

Darwin's Theory of Inheritance

Like many of his contemporaries, Darwin originally conceived of heredity in terms of *force*—the force of inheritance that transmitted likenesses from parents to offspring, counteracted by the forces of variation, which created individual differences in offspring. "Reversion" accounted for the appearance of characters from distant ancestors in some offspring (Olby, 1985:63). Sometimes the "force of inheritance" could be very strong, as in the case of the "Hapsburg lip" (Figure 3–11), which Darwin marveled could have been preserved for so many generations in the male line despite mixing with unrelated female ancestors. (The "Hapsburg lip," also known as "mandibular prognathism," is now known to be caused by a dominant gene [McKusick, 1989].) In other cases, the force of reversion could be strong, as in domestic pigeons that, even after many generations of breeding, show the wild-type plumage of their distant ancestors. Darwin held that the environment caused most variability, albeit in an unspecified way. In this conception he differed from others who considered that most variation in offspring came from assortment of characteristics at reproduction.

Darwin finally developed his hypothesis of heredity which he called **pangenesis.** History has proved pangenesis incorrect but it is important to understand how this influential theory of Darwin's was transformed into our modern understanding of inheritance. Darwin came to believe that there were little particles called "gemmules" in every part of the body that could be modified by some environmental demand. Once altered these gemmules would migrate from the *soma* (body) to the *germ line* (sperm or egg) and modify this material so that the offspring would be similarly modified. Gemmules circulated in the blood or protoplasm and were responsible for causing growth of the same body parts from which they originated in the parent. Traits, he asserted, were still produced by blending, but both parents would have had to have been subjected to the same environmental forces for changing the trait. This modification by Darwin of natural selection to incorporate the inheritance of acquired characters, as had been earlier put forward by Lamarck, substantially weakened the theory and gave cause for arguments against it.

DEVELOPMENT OF A THEORY OF INHERITANCE

Experimentation did not support Darwin's hypothesis of the free circulation of gemmules in the body. Sir Francis Galton transfused the blood of rabbits with different coat colors and then inbred the resulting strains, crossing offspring from the same parents. He found no mixing of coat colors. Rudolf Virchow in Berlin in 1865 showed that all animal and plant cells are formed by division and that "free cells," such as Darwin's hypothesized gemmules with reproductive capabilities, do not exist outside of the reproductive system. The German biologist August Weismann (1834–1914) hypothesized that all hereditary information resides in the reproductive cells, the "germ plasm," and that no changes in the body cells resulting from the environment could affect these germ cells. The nature of the units of heredity was still unknown, but Weismann's hypothesis won out over Darwin's pangenesis and formed one of the bases for modern **genetics,** the science that studies the mechanisms of heredity. The term "genetics" was coined by the English biologist William Bateson in 1900. In its rejecting the inheritance of acquired characteristics and embracing the modern concepts of genetics, Weismann's theory is also referred to as **Neo-Darwinism** (Grant, 1985:17).

In 1889 Sir Hugo De Vries developed a modified hypothesis called "Intracellular Pangenesis," which took recent discoveries about the cell into account. De Vries disagreed with Darwin that the hereditary units ("gemmules") were freely transported in the body, but he did agree that they determined specific traits. Spurred on by Weismann's work, De Vries worked from 1889 to 1900 on proving that hereditary qualities were independent units, and he grew large populations of plants from controlled crossing experiments. De Vries' experiments, along with those of two other workers, Correns and Tschermak, led to the rediscovery in 1900 of elementary principles of inheritance. Unknown at the time to these scientists, this research and conclusions similar to their own had been completed and published thirty-four years earlier.

The Laws of Heredity

Many scientists and historians have pondered that, had Darwin but known of the work of the then-scientifically obscure monk Gregor Mendel (1822–1884; Figure 3–12), he would not have needed to make many of the compromises, such as the theory of pangenesis, that he was forced into by criticism of the *Origin of Species*. Unfortunately, Mendel's work was either ignored by or unknown to the scientific world until 1900, partly because his approach to studying heredity did not take into account and explain organisms' development, a critical research question in the mid-nineteenth century (Bowler, 1989).

Mendel, born Johann, was rechristened Gregor on his acceptance in 1843 at the Augustinian monastery at Brno, in what was then Austria and is now Czechoslovakia. He was trained at the University of Vienna, spent his life as a high school teacher of physics and natural history, and was later appointed abbot of the monastery (Olby, 1985).

In 1856 Mendel began a series of breeding experiments involving crosses of individuals of the edible pea, *Pisum sativum*. His goal was to investigate the problem of why certain plant hybrids all looked alike in

pangenesis–Darwin's mistaken theory of inheritance based on hypothetical particles called "gemmules" that accounted for the inheritance of acquired characteristics.

genetics–the study of heredity and variation.

Neo-Darwinism–the combined theory of evolution by natural selection and modern genetics.

Figure 3–12 • Gregor Mendel.

the first descendent generation (called first filial or F1 generation) but had a tendency to revert to their original states in the second generation (second filial or F2 generation).

Mendel's results are important because they established a **quantum theory of heredity,** distinguished from Darwin's blending theory of inheritance by having clearly defined units which remained discrete, generation after generation (Figure 3–13). A trait in *Pisum* was caused by two irreducible "factors," now known to be **genes.** Genes are discrete DNA sequences that code for amino acids, the constituents of proteins. The Danish biologist Wilhelm Johannsen proposed the term "gene" in 1909 to refer to Mendel's "factors."

Mendel found that in the garden pea one "factor" or gene was *dominant* to the other, which was called *recessive.* Alternative versions of genes occupying the same place on a chromosome, which may be termed "*A*" for a dominant gene and "*a*" for a recessive gene, are called **alleles.** Individuals who have the same alleles, as in the dominant alleles, *AA,* or in two recessive alleles, *aa,* are termed **homozygous** (Latin, for "similar yoking together"). Individuals who are *Aa* are termed **heterozygous** (Latin for "different yoking together"). The combination of genes, *AA, Aa,* or *aa,* is referred to as the **genotype.** Genes do not blend together in the heterozygote, but remain in an individual as two different alleles.

quantum theory of heredity– passing of traits as clearcut quantifiable units not subject to subdivision; characteristic of Mendelian genetics.

genes–units of the material of inheritance, now known to be sequences of DNA.

allele–alternate form of a gene.

homozygous–bearing two identical alleles at a genetic locus.

heterozygous–bearing two different alleles at a genetic locus.

genotype–the genetic composition of an organism, as compared to phenotype, the manifestation of its genes.

segregation–the separation of recessive and dominant alleles during reproduction, allowing maintenance of their separate identities and later full expression of their traits; sometimes referred to as Mendel's First Law of Segregation.

The Principle of Segregation

Mendel's experiments were important because they disproved blending inheritance once and for all. Mendel observed when crossing two pure-bred strains of his pea plants that the hybrids in the F1 generation exhibited only one form of the parents' traits. For example, if plants that produced only green seed pods were crossed with plants that produced only yellow seed pods, invariably the F1 offspring produced green seed pods. If later crossed together, F1 plants would give rise to offspring whose seed pods typically appeared in a ratio of 3 green-seed-pod-producing plants to 1 yellow-seed-pod-producing plant, regardless of the number of plants involved. These results were exciting because clearly they did not support the idea of mixing or blending of equal parts of the parents' inheritance in their offspring.

Mendel discovered that the "factors," now known as *alleles, A* and *a,* which in different combinations were responsible for seed pod color, split apart independently during the production of sex cells. This important principle is termed **segregation,** sometimes also called Mendel's First Law. Mendel determined that a "true-breeding" plant produces only one type of "allele," either *A* or *a. A* in this case is dominant to *a,* so when the two come together in a fertilized plant, *A* is expressed and *a* is not. Only in *aa* plants is the trait "*a*" expressed. Thus, Mendel's hypothesis could explain why all the first generation plants look the same

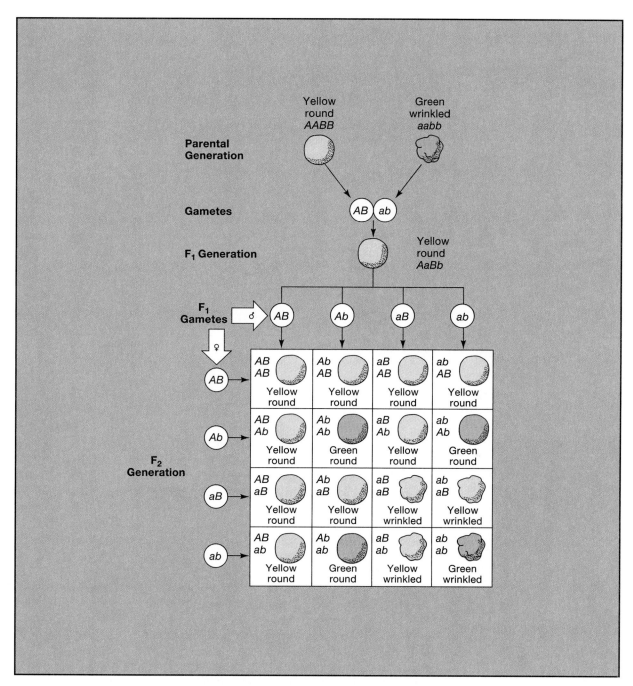

Figure 3–13 • The results of Mendel's breeding experiments with *Pisum sativum*. Two genes were responsible for each trait, they sorted out (segregated and assorted) independently, and the numbers of each type of plant resulting from the crosses were predictable. (From Barrett et al., 1986)

(all are *Aa*) and why the second generation plants show traits that had apparently disappeared (¼ are *aa*). The old mystery of "reversions" was solved.

The Principle of Independent Assortment

Mendel studied seven traits of *Pisum sativum,* and he found that all seven traits were randomly combined with one another in their offspring. Wrinkled seeds, for example, separated independently from yellow pods, as did the other five traits. It is now known that Mendel's seven traits are all coded for by genes which exist on separate chromosomes of *Pisum.* Thus, while alleles, which are situated at comparable places on a paired set of chromosomes, are said to segregate, chromosomes and the genes which they carry are said to **assort** independently. This conclusion means that during sex cell formation the genes on the different chromosomes are split up and combine randomly. Thus, whether a pea plant inherited a pair of alleles for a wrinkled or smooth seed was irrelevant to the combination of the other six traits that Mendel examined. They were all scrambled up each generation in an independent way. The principle of independent assortment is also termed Mendel's Second Law.

Mendel's dramatic results were to some extent fortuitous because the seven traits which he studied were situated on one of each of seven chromosomes of *Pisum.* Had they not been, they would not have assorted independently, as Mendel found, because if two traits were on the same chromosome pair they would have been transmitted to the next generation together. The traits that Mendel chose to study also showed clear dominance and recessiveness. Mendel could have studied many other traits that have a much less straightforward heritability as, for example, those traits found linked together on the same chromosome pair, or those traits occuring as a result of the interaction of many genes. Some historians of science have suggested that Mendel's choice of seven characters to study, ones that just happen to be on the seven chromosomes of the pea plant, and the nearly ideal statistical ratios of his crosses, are a little too good to be true. Whether Mendel selectively presented his data or whether he was just quite lucky in his research design, his discoveries have stood the test of time and they formed the basis for the new science of genetics.

Later the Swedish botanist Herman Nilsson-Ehle proved that traits could be carried on the same chromosome pair when he crossed red-kernel and white-kernel wheat strains and did not find segregation in a clear cut dominant–recessive allelic system. Instead of white and red kernels segregating in a 3 to 1 ratio as expected in the F2 generation, he found five color classes grading from red to yellow-white. It was clear from these results that one externally observable phenotype—the external appearance caused by the genetic complement, the genotype—could be under the control of more than one set of genes. These

assort—the independent separation of pairs of genes on one chromosome from pairs of genes on other chromosomes; also known as Mendel's Second Law of Independent Assortment.

genes could be located at more than one place or **locus,** on the chromosome, or on different chromosomes (Figure 3–14). Furthermore, these genes, when combined in offspring, did not necessarily follow a dominant–recessive relationship. The cases described above are examples of **polygenic** inheritance that may result in a gradational or quan-

locus–a "place" on a chromosome or segment of DNA where a gene is located.

polygenic–referring to genes at two or more loci affecting a single trait.

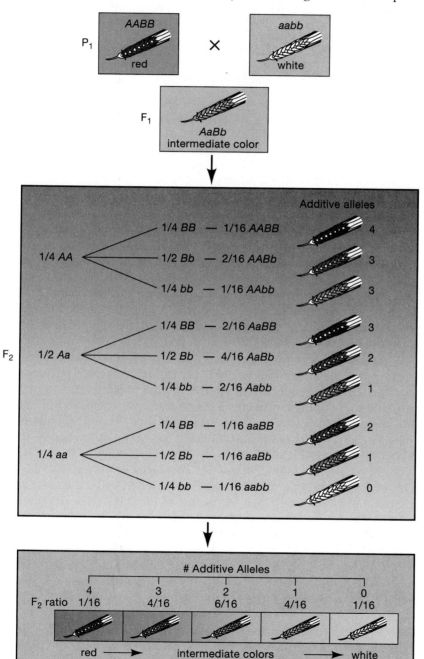

Figure 3–14 • Phenotypic traits can be determined by several genes, sometimes on different chromosomes as shown initially by the work of Nilsson-Ehle on wheat. This polygenic inheritance could explain the observations of Darwin and others that had been used in support of "blending inheritance" and helped to reconcile "Darwinism" and "Mendelism."

titative set of phenotypes. **Epistasis** is a term used to describe the dominance of one gene on one chromosome over that of another on a different chromosome. In cases where genes are clearly dominant or recessive, such as in human eye color, ratios of phenotypes can be calculated. On the other hand, in most cases where genes are co-dominant, that is where they are both expressed to some degree, or in which there are many genes determining a trait, such as height or skin color, Mendelian ratios do not appear.

Chromosomal Theory of Heredity

In 1903 two researchers, Sutton and Boveri, independently hypothesized that Mendelian factors behaved very much like chromosomes. It is now known that humans have 23 pairs of chromosomes. Our closest relatives, the African apes, chimpanzees, and gorillas, have 24 pairs of chromosomes. Human females have 23 identical pairs of chromosomes that include the sex chromosomes (two X chromosomes). Males have 22 pairs of identical chromosomes (called **autosomes**), and one pair which is different: the sex chromosomes, one X chromosome inherited from the mother, and one Y chromosome inherited from the father. The 23 pairs of chromosomes are called the full **diploid** (*diplo* meaning two) set. During meiosis, the diploid set of these chromosome pairs split, with only one chromosome of each pair going to a sex cell or gamete. The 23 chromosomes contained in each gamete constitute the **haploid** (*haplo* meaning single) set. When gametes unite during the process of fertilization to form a new individual, the diploid number of chromosomes is reestablished.

Chromosomes are now known to consist of very long strands of DNA, complexly folded and twisted (see Figure 2–19, p. 61). Genes, as we have seen, are sequences of the DNA found at particular loci on the chromosomes. In human beings a chromosome is composed of about one meter of DNA coiled upon itself many times. Because each human cell contains 23 pairs of chromosomes, it has about 46 meters of DNA (Margulis and Sagan, 1986:279).

Traditionally, the human set of chromosomes is labeled 1 to 22, by size, with number 1 being the largest, and the sex cells, X and Y, constituting the twenty-third pair. A picture of chromosomes arranged in order is known as a **karyotype.** Advances in staining chromosomes known as "banding techniques" allow us to see more structure in chromosomes (Figure 3–15). These techniques involve the use of enzymes or fluorescent stains to reveal consistent patterns of chromosomal morphology. Geneticists are able to identify each human chromosome by its different band morphology.

Chromosome number by itself tells us little about genetic organization, as some mammals may have as few as 6 or 8 chromosomes, whereas flies have 4 or 6 and some plants have hundreds of chromosomes. Even within the higher primates, chromosome counts vary from

epistasis—gene masking the effect of another gene.

autosomes—referring to chromosomes other than the sex (X and Y) chromosomes.

diploid—having two sets of chromosomes, as normally found in the somatic cells of higher organisms.

haploid—having a single set of chromosomes, as found in the sex cells or gametes of higher organisms.

karyotype—identified and numbered arrangement of chromosomes.

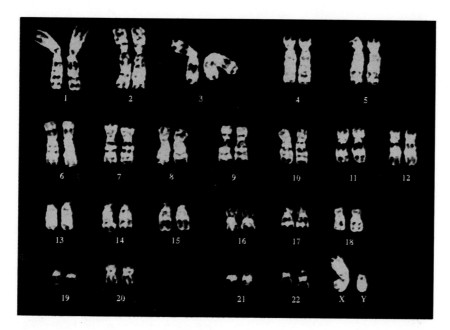

Figure 3–15 • The human karyotype. Banding techniques show the intricate structure of the human chromosomes.

8 to numbers in the seventies. What is important is that each individual has a full set. Without a complete or full set, the individual may not develop properly and may have anatomical abnormalities.

Prior to cell division the chromosomes of dividing cells are usually visible as coils wound up in the nucleus of the cell. During *interphase,* the phase between cell division, chromosomes duplicate and carry out their specific activities. At some point, varying with the tissue, cells divide into two new daughter cells with a complete complement of all of the organelles, chromosomes, membranes, and enzymes necessary for cell function (Chapter 2).

Gene Linkage and Crossing Over

As they studied the inheritance of more traits caused by single genes, researchers found that some genes do not follow Mendel's law of independent assortment. Remember that Mendel's Second Law, which holds that genes assort independently, is only true if the genes are located on separate chromosomes. Groups of specific genes found on closely associated loci on the same chromosome are usually passed on together and, thus, they are termed **linked.** In humans one example of linkage is that between two blood group genes called Rh and Duffy, both located on chromosome 1.

Linkage of genes was found to vary from nearly complete to about 50%. Or, in up to 50% of the cases, linked genes on chromosomes were

linkage–the tendency of genes to be inherited together because of their location and proximity to one another on one chromosome.

Figure 3–16 • The mechanism of crossing over in chromosomes that is the basis for constructing gene maps.

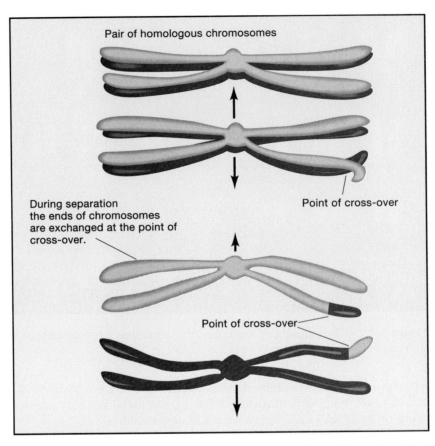

crossing over–the exchange of genes between paired chromosomes during cell duplication.

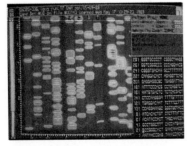

Figure 3–17 • The human gene map. Most of the traits found on genes relate to biochemical activity and specific diseases. (From McKusick, 1989)

not passed on together. This observation was explained by a hypothesis of the Belgian biologist Janssens. He suggested that paired duplicate homologous chromosomes would become tangled up during meiosis, and, as they were pulled apart by the spindles, they would break. Because they were lined up, the homologous sections of the paired chromosomes would get traded by hooking on to the broken ends of the other chromosomes. The process is called **crossing over** (Figure 3–16). Genes that were close together on the chromosome very rarely had a break occur between them. They were thus closely linked, that is, near 100%. Genes more distant on the chromosome had a higher probability of intervening breaks or crossing over, hooking up with another chromosome, and thus being distantly linked.

T. H. Morgan of Columbia University used Janssen's hypothesis to "map" genes. The more often that two traits caused by single genes were inherited together, the closer they were on the chromosome. By quantifying all known genes in fruit flies (*Drosophila*) Morgan was able to discover on which chromosomes and in what sequence genes occurred. Using largely the same techniques, human geneticists have constructed maps of all 23 pairs of human chromosomes (Figure 3–17). Discovering the entire DNA sequence of the human genome is the goal of the Human Genome Project, currently a major genetic research effort in the United States.

MENDELIAN GENETICS AND MOLECULAR GENETICS

With the discovery of DNA as the genetic material by Watson and Crick in 1953, the era of molecular genetics began. Although the relationship between segments of DNA and genes, together with their relationship to observable traits (phenotypes) still is a major question in biology, most geneticists and historians of science agree that the principles and findings of Mendelian genetics are now translatable into molecular terms (Sober, 1984).

Today it is estimated that there are some one hundred thousand billion (10^{14} or 100,000,000,000,000) cells in the human body. Almost all of these, except for the red blood cells and the mature sex cells, carry exactly the same kind and amount of DNA. All of these cells result from the one-cell embryo at fertilization. During development these cells become progressively different depending on which genes are turned on or off and at what time. Cells proliferate into the different tissues of gut, brain, kidney, and eye. Although nerve cells, for example, carry the same DNA as skin cells or as kidney cells, they all differ in function.

The DNA, or more strictly the segments that we speak of as the genes, are responsible for (1) carrying the instructions necessary for the organism's development from its origin at fertilization to maturity; (2) the cell's ability to metabolize (utilize energy) or catabolize (break down products of metabolism); and (3) carrying the essential genetic information for the next generation. How DNA fulfills these functions via proteins and enzymes is the subject of the next section.

polypeptide chain—a molecule consisting of a long chain of amino acids joined together by peptide bonds.

How Protein Synthesis Works

The genetic code specifies chains of amino acids that are combined to make up parts or all of a protein. Each amino acid consists of a basic chemical structure which is similar for all amino acids, and a unique side chain, that accounts for the different chemical and physical properties of the amino acids. One DNA sequence specifies the number, sequence, and types of amino acids in a linear fashion in what is correctly called a **polypeptide chain.** "Peptide" refers to the type of bonding between amino acids and *poly* indicates "many." A protein is a *functioning* unit composed of one or more polypeptide chains that can have several genes controlling them. Some proteins such as *albumin,* a blood protein, are composed of and function with only one polypeptide chain. Other proteins, such as *hemoglobin,* a protein in the red blood cells that carries and releases oxygen, are composed of several polypeptide chains (Figure 3–18). Hemoglobin has four polypeptide chains and the molecule functions only when all are combined. Geneti-

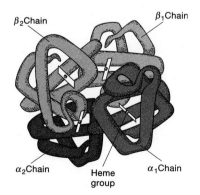

Figure 3–18 • The molecular structure of hemoglobin.

cists have now modified the "one-gene-one-protein" hypothesis to the more accurate "one-gene-one-polypeptide" hypothesis.

Most of an individual's DNA carries genetic information through a specific sequence of nucleotides or bases. A **codon** consists of three base positions in a row; at any one of those positions one of four bases can be inserted. Consequently, we have a potential of 4^3 or 64 different codons that, in turn, specify the 20 different amino acids used to construct a polypeptide (see Table 2–1 on page 48). Because there are more codon combinations than amino acids we find that more than one codon combination may specify the same amino acid. Proteins are molecules that can carry on many of the body's functions: for example, proteins can be involved in making up the structure of the body, such as the protein *collagen,* which helps to form the hard substance in bones; other proteins can have transport properties, such as a *transferrin* which carries iron in the blood. **Enzymes** are proteins that work to promote chemical reactions so that they will go faster at body temperature. An important enzyme is carbonic anhydrase, the protein that catalyzes the reaction in the lungs of $H_2O + CO_2$ to H_2CO_3 (bicarbonate), an important acid/base buffer in the body. One molecule of carbonic anhydrase, one of the fastest enzymes, can perform this reaction 100,000 times in one second! This is 10,000,000 times faster than the reaction would occur without the enzyme there. There are thousands of these different proteins in our bodies. Each protein has its origin in a certain sequence of DNA in the nucleus of the cells.

Other proteins in the body act as chemical messengers called **hormones** (Greek, meaning "to excite or set in motion"). Hormones can be released from the brain or other organs, travel through the bloodstream, and act on distinct target organs such as the breast, inducing it to produce milk, the testis to make sperm, or the kidney tubules to reabsorb water. Hormones have important functions in moderating behavior (see Chapters 9 and 12).

The "central dogma" of molecular biology involves three substances—DNA, RNA and proteins—and three processes—**replication, transcription,** and **translation,** to derive all three (Figure 3–19; Watson, 1970:331). The central dogma explains both how the genetic material passes on its inherited message and how it operates the cell, directing cell and tissue growth. Replication of the DNA was discussed in Chapter 2.

The DNA code is converted into a protein molecule by an involved sequence of interactions among DNA, enzymes, and RNA. In *transcription* the DNA double helix molecule unwinds, the hydrogen bonds holding the molecular backbones together are broken, and the two sides fall apart. New bases are brought to the DNA and are combined until the end of the DNA message is read, much as in DNA replication. However, here only one side of the DNA is copied to make a coded message, called *messenger RNA* (or m-RNA). Codons are read from the DNA without overlapping. For example, bases *AAATTTGGG* are

codon–the triplet of adjacent nucleotides that codes for a specific amino acid or that codes for a stop on termination of translation of that particular segment of DNA.

enzyme–a polypeptide that catalyzes or accelerates chemical reactions.

hormone–a chemical substance produced by an organ or structure of the body which acts on or affects another distinct organ or structure.

replication–a duplication process requiring copying from a template, in this case the DNA molecule.

transcription–transfer of genetic information encoded in a DNA sequence to an RNA message.

translation–synthesis of a polypeptide chain from an RNA genetic message.

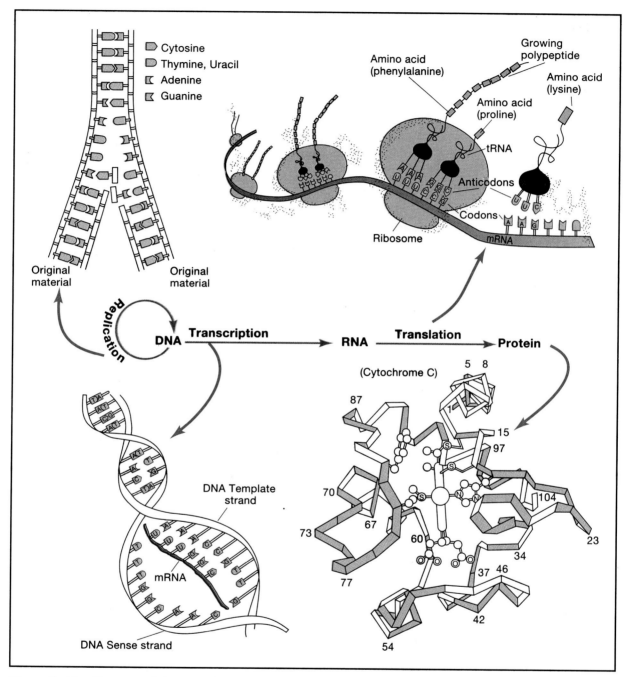

Figure 3–19 • The "central dogma" of molecular biology relates the processes of replication, transcription, and translation of the genetic message.

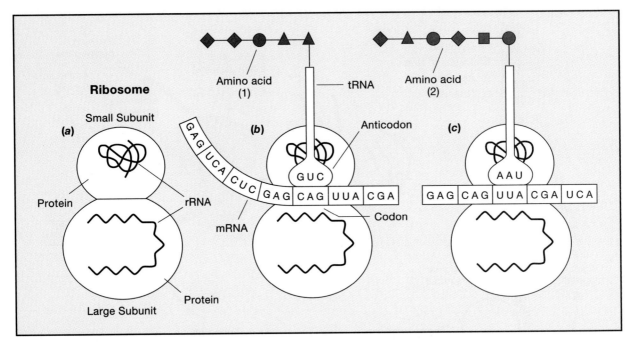

Figure 3–20 • Protein synthesis, the molecular mechanism by which the DNA message is translated into polypeptide chains. The two subunits of the ribosome become attached to the mRNA during translation. The tRNA carry their amino acids to the proper position in the polypeptide sequence, configuring their anticodon to the mRNA codon. Polypeptide synthesis is accomplished when the amino acids join as the ribosome moves along the mRNA strand. (From *The Processing of RNA* by James E. Darnell, Jr., illustration by Jerome Kuhl, copyright © 1983 by Scientific American, Inc. All rights reserved.)

read in sequence: 123, 456, 789—not 123, 345, 567—which would result in codons *AAA, ATT, TTG*. Overlapping would obviously change the intended message. Within the protein-coding message in m-RNA, and unlike DNA itself, thymine (*T*) is replaced by a chemically similar base called uracil (*U*) that pairs with an adenine (*A*). The DNA message has been transcribed into RNA and this molecule now carries the genetic information necessary to make the protein.

When the messenger RNA molecule has been completely transcribed, it slips off the DNA and exits from the nucleus. The m-RNA proceeds to the *ribosome* (described in Chapter 2) where the proteins are actually assembled. On the surface of the ribosomes another type of RNA called ribosomal or r-RNA is found to which the m-RNA binds. The m-RNA message is "read" as it travels along a ribosome, and the message is *translated* into a chain of amino acids. This translation of the message is the second step in protein synthesis (Figure 3–20).

Amino acids, found floating free in the cell cytoplasm, are attached to a molecule of a third type of RNA called transfer RNA (t-RNA). On t-RNA is a three-letter sequence of bases that recognizes a specific three-letter sequence on the m-RNA and binds to the m-RNA, carrying with it its specific amino acid. When the base sequence of the m-RNA is matched to the complementary base sequence of the t-RNA, the t-RNAs are aligned in order on the m-RNA and the genetic message is translated again down the chain. Because the amino acids are positioned on the m-RNA, they are linked together by enzymes that form the peptide bonds and create the polypeptides. If more polypeptides are needed, the m-RNA may be read again to make another copy, or it may be destroyed and its parts reused.

Gene Structure

Genes are composed of segments that are called **introns** and **exons.** Exons are parts of the gene that actually code for the amino acid sequence of the functioning protein. Introns are segments of DNA that are found between the exons, but their DNA sequences do not affect the amino acid chain in the protein. Introns are spliced or edited out of the genetic message during protein synthesis with only the exons remaining in the message.

Within the structure of the gene certain regions have been discovered, so far mainly in prokaryotes, that act as switches, turning on or off other functional parts of the gene. These are called *regulators*. In embryological and fetal development the process of regulating the genetic material programs the cells to different destinies. When it is necessary for cells to produce a protein, the regulator region turns on the protein specified by the gene or genes. Normally many genes are turned off. It is obviously an advantage to the cell to make these proteins when necessary and not have the whole protein-making machinery turned on all the time. Gene regulation is important in conceptualizing how two species that are genetically very similar, say, humans and chimpanzees, which share 98 to 99% of their genes, may differ so dramatically in their external or "phenotypic" appearance. Because gene regulation determines when and for how long certain genes are active, it thus has a major effect on resulting morphology and behavior. Regulatory mutations have been considered important in the hypothesis of "punctuated equilibrium" and have been used to explain how major shifts seen by some investigators in the fossil record could be explained genetically (see Chapter 5).

intron–noncoding sequence of DNA that is not transcribed by the m-RNA.

exon–the expressed segment of a gene, separated from other exons by introns.

MUTATION: THE SOURCE OF GENETIC VARIATION

We have seen how Darwin's theory of natural selection required "inherited variability" in organisms as the raw material with which evolution worked, and how Mendel's findings provided a mechanism for

transmittal of genetic material from one generation to another. Darwin had called attention to what animal breeders termed "sports," novel forms of animals, such as short-legged sheep or tailless cats. Sometimes breeders could trace the lineage of such a breed to a single animal. To Darwin such heritable changes could be of great importance if natural selection were to produce new species. But what was the real nature of these heritable changes?

Hugo De Vries, in his attempt to answer this question believed that if Mendel's system worked perfectly, no new genes would ever be produced. Parents' genes would simply be passed on to offspring shuffled up a bit, but still basically the same. De Vries then focused attention on the evidence for heritable genetic changes, changes that he termed **mutations,** as the source of genetic novelty.

De Vries' hypotheses were affected by results he obtained from the plant that he chose to work on, the evening primrose (*Denothera lamarckiana*). Individuals of this species produce offspring that at times look quite different from their parents. De Vries ascribed these large-scale changes to mutation, and he suggested that evolution generally proceeded by such large jumps. As more was learned of the genetics of *Denothera,* however, it became apparent that its genetic system was rather unique. The occasional discontinuities between parents and offspring were due to crossing over in the usually variable chromosomes of the parents, not to newly introduced genetic variability.

Mutation is the sudden change in the characteristics of an organism which can be inherited by an offspring and, thus, increases the genetic variation in a group of organisms. All the differences at the genetic level we see today in human beings are because of mutations in a sperm or egg somewhere in our evolutionary history. Occasionally in DNA replication a mismatch between bases occurs. On average somewhere between 1 in 100,000 to about 1 in a million cases a mistake is made. An *A* may be paired opposite a *C* rather than opposite a *T.* The altered sequence of DNA is called a mutant. Probably the most important cause of gene mutation may be mistakes in DNA replication in which the wrong base is substituted. Changes can also occur on a larger scale and may affect the number or structure of chromosomes. (Figure 3–21).

Mutations, while they may be important to the individual they occur in, are important to evolution only if they can be inherited. **Mutations** that occur in the sex-cells can be passed on. **Somatic mutations** occur in non-sex-cell tissue, such as skin or neurons. These cannot be inherited. Because we have many thousands of genes, each of us has a high likelihood of carrying a new mutation in our genes.

New genetic input into a population via a mutation can be beneficial or detrimental to the organism that possesses it. The mutation may help

mutation–any novel genetic change that may affect both genes and chromosomes. Such changes are spontaneous and random in occurrence. Mutations are the source of all variability in populations, and, if they occur in the sex-cells usually during the formation of gametes, they hold the possibility of altering the Phenotypes in succeeding generations.

somatic mutations–a nonheritable change in the genetic material of the cells of the body.

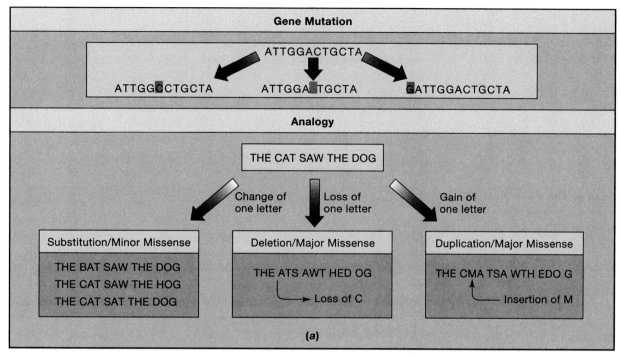

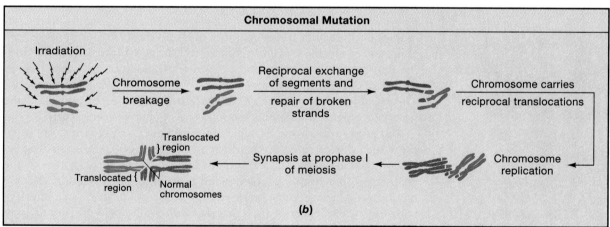

Figure 3–21 • Examples of mutation: (*a*) gene mutation, in which a single base is changed (from Barrett et al., 1986), and (*b*) large-scale chromosomal mutation (from Klug and Cummings, 1994).

the individual adapt better to its surroundings. For example, a new gene can make an enzyme work faster, or at a different temperature, or on a different molecule. This may result in an organism that can respond to the varying demands of the environment in a better manner than in the past.

On the other hand, and much more frequently, a new mutation may result in a defective enzyme or even no enzyme at all. This latter case would occur if a codon specifying an amino acid mutated to a "stop" codon and the amino acid chain was only partially complete. Such a change might make it difficult on the individual, or if it were a critical enzyme or critical gene for gene regulation, the organism might die *in utero*. A mutation might lead to infertility, even if life itself were not compromised. Such an outcome is called a *genetic death*. The outcome so far as evolution is concerned is almost the same whether a person lives, but does not reproduce to pass on genes to the next generation, or if the individual dies before reproductive age.

Mutations can be caused by many agents ranging from X-rays to ultraviolet light to specific chemicals used in industry. Some specific food additives have been shown to cause mutations in bacteria. Some chemicals in our environment from cigarettes, air pollution, and chemical waste may cause mutations in genes. When altered, specific genes, called *oncogenes,* may be responsible for the unregulated cell growth that characterizes cancer.

Mutations can run the gamut from lethal to beneficial. A vast majority of them may be neither, but may be "neutral" in evolutionary terms. **Neutral mutations** at the biochemical level have no effect on the function of a protein. It may not matter if a codon substitution in the DNA results in a different amino acid substitution at a certain position in a polypeptide chain. For example, we have discovered that there are over two hundred different genetic variants found in the human hemoglobin genes, all coding for different amino acid substitutions in the hemoglobin molecule. In the majority of cases these substitutions do not affect the molecules' primary function, that is, to transport oxygen to the tissues. An example of a type of neutral mutation is a new base in the second or third position in a codon (see Table 2–1 on page 48). This mutation may not change the amino acid in the protein. Thus, the function remains unaffected, even though a change has occurred.

Mutations are constantly recurring phenomena in biological populations, and they create genetic diversity that can be used by natural selection. For example, some bacteria are evolving in response to the challenges that antibiotic medicines present to them. Antibiotics are naturally occurring substances excreted by molds that may interfere with the construction of the bacteria's cell walls, or with protein synthesis. Certain mutational changes in a bacterium called *Gonococcus,* responsible for a type of venereal disease, now make it difficult for the antibiotic, penicillin, to work. A newly evolved bacterial enzyme called penicillinase can now break up penicillin, allowing the bacterium to continue to survive and replicate.

Chance, not necessity, dictates the occurrence of new mutations. The exposure of a new drug to inhibit bacterial growth does not cause a new mutation. Instead, the changed conditions allow those individual bacteria with a pre-existing mutation to survive, whereas "old type" bacteria would be killed. Mutations, even though they are random, occur at a rate

neutral mutations–genetic changes that have no phenotypic effect and thus are not acted upon by selection.

consistently high enough to allow evolution to work with the new genetic variability introduced into the population, as we shall see in Chapter 4.

Selection Acts on Mutations

We speak of natural selection operating for or against certain specific genes or genotypes, yet it is the individual (and all the genes that he or she has) that lives or dies. Natural selection acts on individuals on the basis of their phenotypes, and these in turn reflect the genotype. Evolution, then, occurs when the frequency of one genotype changes over time in relation to other genotypes. The change in genotypes, and thus in gene frequencies, in subsequent generations is due to the sum of many individuals' differential survival and fertility under a set of specified environmental conditions.

Selection is the difference in reproductive success between two genetic alternatives. As an example at the simplest level of selection, two alternative alleles, *A* and *a,* may be said to exist within a population of organisms. Environmental conditions change so that individuals with the "*a*" allele begin to reproduce more often and thus propagate more organisms with the characteristic physical form caused by that allele. The "*a*" allele will become more common and can thus be said to have been favored by natural selection. However, recessive alleles in low frequencies are removed very slowly by natural selection. We will discuss how changes in gene frequencies occur in response to selection within populations in Chapter 4.

THE PUZZLE OF SEXUAL REPRODUCTION

We reviewed, in Chapter 2, two ideas about the origin of sex and genetic exchange. The puzzle of sex and its overwhelming success as a form of reproduction in the vast majority of living organisms remains to be explained. Darwin viewed sexual reproduction to be critical to the maintenance of genetic variability in populations. This variability was the grist upon which natural selection operated to produce individuals better adapted to a slowly changing environment. However, to John Maynard Smith (1978) along with Lynn Margulis and Dorian Sagan (1986) sex was a mechanism that did nothing more than scramble up a perfectly good existing combination of genes, and that undid every good recombination it had created in the previous generation. To these authors the logical evolutionary outcome for reproduction should be a mechanism that reverts from sex to cloning once a successfully adapted gene combination has been produced so that the combination remains intact generation after generation. The question these authors ask is why sex endured and became the predominant form of reproduction. The argument in favor of cloning is compelling: clones are, usually, much more efficient in terms of quantity in their reproductive effort, producing more individuals than does sexual reproduction.

Part of the answer comes from research which suggests that, once sexual reproduction develops, it sets up its own blocks to reverting to some other form. Experiments on mouse embryos, in which both copies of a chromosome were engineered to come from the same parent rather than one from each parent, consistently showed that such embryos died early *in utero*. For as yet unknown reasons, the mechanism of sex coupled with the necessity for two parents, has produced a situation which maintains itself and inhibits change.

Sexually reproducing organisms may have an advantage over clones if both were to live side by side in stable environments where competition between many different forms of life is intense. For example, results of a two-year study of sweet vernal grass by Steven Kelley of Washington State University suggests that sexually reproducing variants of these plants out-reproduced the clone variant by about 1.5 times. Although his experiments documented a situation in which sexually reproducing forms showed a large edge over cloning forms, it did not provide a clear reason why this was the case. Kelley believes, however, that the sexually reproducing grass variants flourished because they were less prone to attack by pathogens which could cause disease, and, perhaps, early death. The idea that all living organisms must evolve mechanisms to protect themselves from pathogens that generally reproduce and mutate more rapidly than themselves may well explain the success of sexual reproduction. Through sexual reproduction organisms stand a chance of survival in the face of disease by creating genetic barriers to pathogen attack through a continual reshuffling of their genotypes. We will pursue this idea further in Chapter 14.

 SUMMARY

This chapter reviews the evidence for Darwin's theory of evolution by natural selection and the influences that affected the development of the theory. The influences of Charles Lyell's work in geology and Thomas Malthus's work in population growth were important. Darwin's voyage on the ship *H.M.S. Beagle* provided him with the raw data on which to build his theory. Darwin realized that animals were variable, that much of this variability was inherited, and that limited food supplies would not allow all offspring to survive and reproduce. He reasoned that those best suited to environmental conditions would have more offspring and pass on their characteristics to future generations. Yet Darwin failed to discover the mechanism whereby variability could be passed on to offspring. Much of the solution to this problem lay in the undiscovered work of Gregor Mendel, which furnished the foundation for modern genetics. The chromosomal theory further explained how genes could operate under Mendel's laws. Changes in genes, called mutations, provide the raw material on which natural selection acts. Gene linkage and crossovers explain the anomalous behavior of traits which seemingly do not conform to Mendelian predictions. Molecular genetics and the discovery of DNA by Watson and Crick in 1953 finally provided the bases for understanding how genetic information was transferred from cell to cell and how proteins necessary for cellular life were produced. Molecular biology explains the structure of the gene, how mutations arise, and the kinds of different structural changes which occur because of them. Natural selection acts to remove deleterious mutations from the population, and acts to increase the numbers of advantageous ones. Natural selection moves a species over time closer to maximum fitness (survivability leading to reproductive success) within its environment.

 ## CRITICAL-THINKING QUESTIONS

1. Who were the two men who independently came up with the theory of natural selection? Briefly explain the theory of natural selection.
2. What contributions did Malthus and Lyell make to Darwin's theories?
3. Whose work was eventually a primary factor in the acceptance of Darwin's theory of evolution? Explain.
4. What are genetic mutations? Explain the role natural selection plays in maintaining mutations in the gene pool.
5. Describe the role of sexual reproduction in maintaining genetic variability.
6. What role do amino acids play in the structure of DNA?

 ## SUGGESTED READINGS

Mayr, E. 1991. *One Long Argument: Charles Darwin and the Genesis of Modern Evolutionary Thought*. Harvard University Press. An historical account of Darwin's formulation of the theory of natural selection by a major evolutionary biologist.

Williams, G. C. 1992. *Natural Selection: Domains, Levels, and Challenges*. Oxford University Press. An up-to-date review of how natural selection works in evolution.

Populations, Species, and Evolution

Populations

Individuals Within Populations Vary

Hardy-Weinberg Equilibrium and Population Genetics
Mutation
Inbreeding
Migration
Chance Sampling

Evolution Changes Population Allele Frequencies
Selection
"Microevolution" Leads to "Macroevolution"

Speciation

Evolution of Behavior
Sexual Selection
Ethology
Fixed Action Patterns

Summary

Critical-Thinking Questions

Suggested Readings

major steps in the history of life were taken when simple replicating molecules first organized into cells and eventually into free-moving animals (see Chapter 2) and when natural selection began acting on these organisms to change their genetics, anatomy, and behavior (see Chapter 3). This chapter deals with how animals, by exchanging genetic information, have become organized into groups of interacting individuals called **populations**. Through sexual reproduction of males and females, genes are reshuffled in the resulting offspring. From the gene's standpoint it finds itself first enclosed within a cell, then within an individual organism, and finally within a **gene pool**, the total genetic makeup that is shared by all members of the species. How evolutionary forces affect genes at this third level of organization, and how genes affect the physical and behavioral traits that we see today are the subjects of this chapter.

POPULATIONS

In Chapter 1, a species was defined as a "genetically distinct population." These genetically distinct, or isolated, species are incapable of producing offspring with members of another species. Such barriers to reproduction are called **reproductive isolating mechanisms** and may be of different kinds, from those genetic (two species may have different numbers of chromosomes) to those behavioral (two species may have different mating rituals).

There are varying degrees of differences between species. Some species may be similar to one another in behavior and anatomy because of a recent split from their common ancestor. For example, species of the genus *Macaca* (an Old World monkey) are close genetic relatives. In the wild, separation has occurred because of their wide range and geographic isolation. However, in captivity or on the natural boundaries of each species' home range, individual macaques of any two species have been known to interbreed and produce hybrid offspring (those that share the genetics of each parental species). Such examples show that some populations may be considered separate species because they are geographically isolated from similar forms, but are not truly reproductively isolated because they are too closely

population—a group of individual organisms within the same species living in one area and sharing genetic material.

gene pool—the shared genetic makeup of a population.

reproductive isolating mechanisms—genetic separation of populations by geography, ecology, behavior, physiology, or anatomy.

related in time through their common ancestor for these mechanisms to develop. If given the opportunity, because of this genetic similarity, they remain capable of interbreeding.

The fact that some species can interbreed and produce hybrids complicates a simple definition of a genetic population or gene pool. In addition, when defining the genetic limits of a population, some species, like humans, have such extensive geographic ranges that they should be viewed as having many geographical subdivisions that define *local* populations, called demes. A **deme** is a local population within which gene flow is common among its members and outside of which gene flow is limited. The precise definition of a population, therefore, depends upon the genetic cohesiveness of its members and may or may not be synonymous with the term species. Because a population is a group of interbreeding individuals that is located in a definable space, each population has a specific genetic profile described by noting percentages or frequencies of alleles. Forces that change allele frequencies over time may be the result of differential patterns of births, deaths, immigration, emigration, and selective mating, as well as natural selection. This constellation of forces and their effects constitutes evolution.

INDIVIDUALS WITHIN POPULATIONS VARY

In Chapter 1, it was pointed out that some traditional taxonomists have tended to think typologically—conceiving of only one morphological ideal as typifying the entire species. Although taxonomy requires a "type specimen" for every named species, in reality, there is no "typical" individual. Individuals within a population vary for any trait or characteristic (Figure 4–1). This variation may be described by using the concept of the **mean;** a statistical measure of the average for any trait in the population. But no single individual in the population will exhibit the mean for all traits. Individual "A" may be average for height, but his hair and eye color are lighter than the mean. Individual "B" may be average for eye color but taller and with darker hair than the mean. Perhaps even more important than the average is the amount and range of variation within each characteristic. Range is the limit to which a characteristic can be expressed. For example, average human height is about 5.75 feet, but the range in height for normal adults is from about 4.5 feet to more than 7 feet. To quantify the amount of variation for a single characteristic or trait, the **standard deviation** is used, which is defined as the extent of the observations found on either side of the mean. In a normal, bell-shaped curve (Figure 4–2), 68% of the individuals measured for a trait will lie within one standard deviation from the mean, and almost 95% of all individuals will lie within two standard deviations.

New genetic methodologies and techniques have demonstrated just how much variability there is at the genetic level in natural popula-

deme–a population within which there is a high degree of gene exchange.

mean–the statistical average of a measurement of a population.

standard deviation–in statistics, a measure of variance about the mean within any population; defined as the square root of the average of the squares of the deviations from the mean.

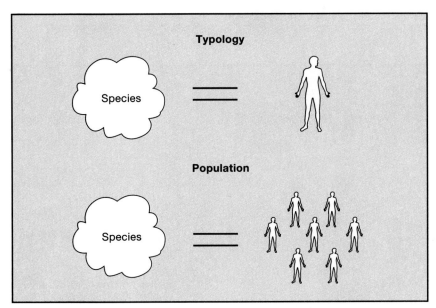

Figure 4–1 • Two ways of looking at species: the "typological" approach (top), which results in the choice of an ideal type to represent the species, and tends to underestimate or ignore normal population variation; and the "population" approach (bottom), which recognizes a statistical range of variability around a mean for any trait within a population. Modern biologists and anthropologists use the latter approach because it conforms with our current understanding of population genetics and morphological variation within species.

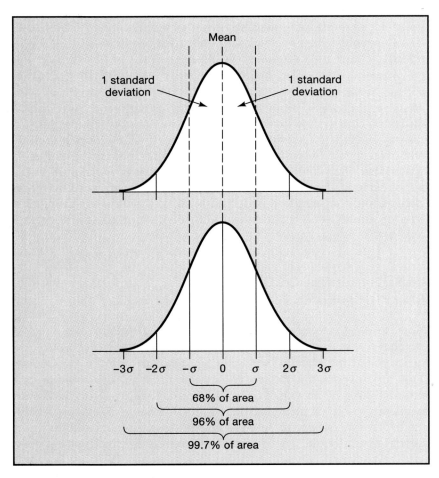

Figure 4–2 • Bell-shaped curve showing standard deviations ("σ") from the mean.

Figure 4–3 • Gel electrophoresis, a method used to measure genetic variation in populations.

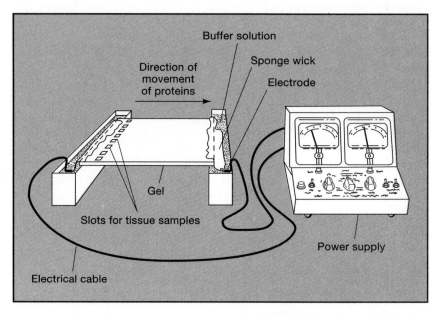

electrophoresis—a technique of measuring the mobility of proteins in an electrified field, thereby testing the structural composition and genetic blueprint of the protein.

Hardy-Weinberg equilibrium— a hypothetical condition in which there is no selection or other forces of evolution acting on a panmictic population and in which gene and genotype frequencies stay the same from one generation to the next.

tions. For example, one measure of genetic variation comes from studies of enzymes and proteins using **electrophoresis** (Greek, meaning "electrical carrying") (Figure 4–3). Proteins differ in their amino acid composition, and amino acids carry either a positive or a negative charge. Studies have shown that, on the average, up to one in three amino acid changes result in a net charge change, and these can be measured electrophoretically. Because the amino acid sequence results directly from the underlying DNA sequence, any differences at the protein level reflect differences in the DNA. Electrophoresis has demonstrated that on average 25% to 30% of proteins or enzymes vary within a population. However, as the technique shows detectable charge changes only, it underestimates the level of variation for the 70% to 75% of amino acid changes that do not involve detectable charge changes.

HARDY-WEINBERG EQUILIBRIUM AND POPULATION GENETICS

How do the forces of evolution work in natural populations to effect changes in the frequencies of alleles? A model basic to population genetics called the **Hardy-Weinberg equilibrium** explains how alleles should be expected to behave in populations. This idea was first proposed in 1908 by an English mathematician, Godfrey Hardy, and independently by a German biologist named Wilhelm Weinberg. These models show us how to test predictions about natural selection and how to assess the relative importance of the various forces which affect allele frequencies. The model states that, if there are no evolutionary forces at work on a particular gene under study, the frequency of the alleles of that gene will remain the same generation after generation. By definition a population in Hardy-Weinberg equilibrium is not evolving. With this expectation, any observed changes in allele frequencies are clues that one or more evolutionary force is responsible. Determination of evolutionary change is based on the comparison of expected allele frequencies in Hardy-Weinberg equilibrium to what is actually observed and measured in nature.

The Hardy-Weinberg model is based on several assumptions about the evolutionary forces that might affect equilibrium (Figure 4–4). The first assumption is that individuals in the population must mate randomly for any particular characteristic. This is true, for example, in the case of blood types because most people are unaware of what blood type (A, B, or O) their prospective mate might have. This is not true, however, for all characteristics. If mating is based on some visible trait or characteristic, then mating is not random. For example, height is one trait that individuals might use as a criterion in choosing a mate; that is, taller individuals might favor taller mates.

The second assumption concerns the size of the population. It is unrealistic to assume that the sample of individuals under study comes from a population that is infinitely large. This assumption can be stated as follows: the smaller the population, the greater the probability that chance factors or **sampling error** will occur. Because sampling error in small populations can cause results that deviate from what is expected under the Hardy-Weinberg equilibrium, this factor must be taken into consideration.

The third assumption concerns mutations. If the rate of a mutation from "*A*" to "*a*" is recurrent and continuous, eventually all the "*A*" alleles will mutate to "*a*". Because all mutations are chance events, it is just as likely that the same allele "*a*" could show a reverse mutation to "*A*." Under these circumstances an equilibrium will be reached if the losses of "*A*" by mutation to "*a*" are balanced by the gains from "*a*" to "*A*". When such an equilibrium is reached for any single gene, the frequency of mutation does not affect the Hardy-Weinberg model. In actuality, the frequency of mutation is usually so low that, even without equilibrium, Hardy-Weinberg frequencies are not affected. Only in extreme cases where mutation rates might be expected to soar, such as in the Chernobyl nuclear disaster in the former Soviet Union, could these rates produce deviations from Hardy-Weinberg equilibrium.

The fourth assumption relates to a shift in population numbers caused by immigration or emigration. By these movements of individuals a shift in allele frequencies may result. If a population is large, the effect of shifts in its membership may not affect Hardy-Weinberg frequencies. However, small populations can certainly be affected. If one can disregard the effects of the possible disruptive forces discussed

sampling error–the degree that a sample of a population misrepresents or is not reflective of the composition in some trait of a larger population because of chance.

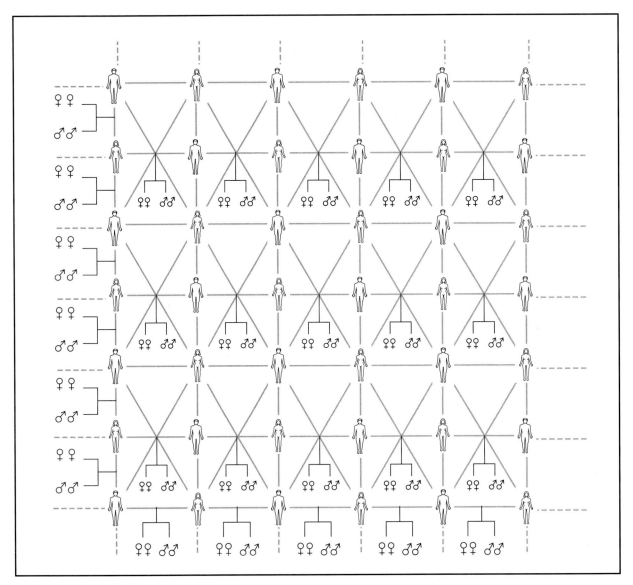

Figure 4—4 • Assumptions of the Hardy-Weinberg model: random mating, infinite population size, no mutation, no migration, and no selection.

here, then any changes in allele frequencies from Hardy-Weinberg equilibrium must be accounted for by natural selection.

The following example will demonstrate how the Hardy-Weinberg model can be used to show that evolutionary change is occurring. By examining a small population of individuals who live in a village in Kenya we might discover that a number of individuals show symptoms for a disease called sickle-cell anemia. Sickle-cell anemia is a malformation of the red blood cells that on the one hand protects individuals against endemic malaria as heterozygotes (*AS*), but on the other hand as homozygous recessives (*SS*) the condition can result in death (Figure 4–5). Sickle cell anemia is a condition resulting from a single base substitution in one codon on the DNA molecule affecting the beta chain of hemoglobin. This base substitution changes the amino acid at position number 6 (from glutamic acid to valine), which in turn, produces a defective hemoglobin "*S*." A different amino acid substitution at position number 6 produces hemoglobin "C" (Table 4–1). The significance of these hemoglobin variants will be discussed more fully in Chapter 12.

Hemoglobin is a four-polypeptide chain molecule consisting of a pair of Alpha chains and a pair of Beta chains. Each chain has the ability to carry one oxygen molecule from the lungs to the various tissues. The "*S*" allele affects the structure of the hemoglobin molecule and the ability of hemoglobin to bind oxygen. The change in structure of the hemoglobin molecule causes the abnormal or "sickle-shape" of the red blood cell (Figure 4–6). When these cells are exposed to low oxygen tensions such as exists in veins or at high altitudes the red blood cell tends to collapse and clump, clogging the smaller capillaries of the body. In the heterozygous condition, this effect is less severe than in the, usually lethal, homozygous recessive condition. Among heterozygote (*AS*) individuals, protection against malaria is related in part to the less than optimal oxygen carrying capacity of hemoglobin and, perhaps, to the premature death of the red blood cells themselves. Either of these conditions lowers the standards of the blood environment in which the parasite thrives.

In examining the hemoglobin type of 100 individuals of this African sample by electrophoresis, exactly four individuals have sickle-cell disease; 64 individuals have normal hemoglobin, and 32 individuals are found to have both hemoglobin alleles, *A* and *S*. In this example, observed genotype frequencies are calculated to be 64% *AA,* 32% *AS,* and 4% *SS*. The sum of these is 100% or 1.0.

The frequencies of the genotypes in the population have been determined by directly counting the individuals. To calculate the allele frequencies in the population, first count the number of alleles in the various genotypes and total the *A* alleles and the *S* alleles. Totaling all the

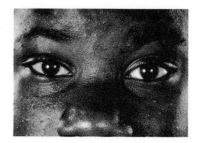

Figure 4–5 • An individual with sickle-cell anemia.

Table 4–1 • Structural Relationships Between Three Variants of Hemoglobin			
Amino Acid Position in the Beta Chain	**Hemoglobin A**	**Hemoglobin S**	**Hemoglobin C**
4	Threonine	Threonine	Threonine
5	Proline	Proline	Proline
6	Glutamic Acid	Valine	Lysine
7	Glutamic Acid	Glutamic Acid	Glutamic Acid
8	Lysine	Lysine	Lysine

Figure 4–6 • Normal (left) and sickle-cell (right) red blood cells.

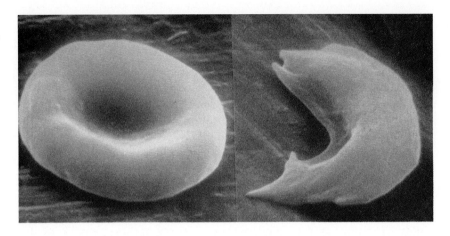

hemoglobin alleles for 100 people there will be 200 alleles (as each person has two alleles). By calculation four *SS* individuals have 8 *S* (4 × 2) alleles; 32 *AS* individuals have 32 *A* and 32 *S* alleles; and 64 *AA* homozygotes have 128 *A* (64 × 2) alleles. In total there are 40 *S* alleles (8 + 32) and 160 *A* alleles (128 + 32). The frequencies of the 200 total alleles are *A* = (160/200) 0.8 or 80% and *S* = (40/200) 0.2 or 20%.

Given these actual allele frequencies the expected genotype frequencies can be calculated based on Hardy-Weinberg expectations, to see if this Kenyan population is undergoing evolution. The following equation for Hardy-Weinberg equilibrium is used: $p^2 + 2pq + q^2 = 1$, in which "*p*" equals the frequency of allele *A* and "*q*" equals the frequency of allele *S*,

$$p^2 = (.8)^2 = .64 \text{ (frequency of } AA \text{ genotype)}$$
$$2pq = 2(.2)(.8) = .32 \text{ (frequency of } AS \text{ genotype)}$$
$$\text{and } q^2 = (.2)^2 = .04 \text{ (frequency of } SS \text{ sickle-cell genotype)},$$

which again totals 1.0. In this example, the expected genotype frequencies are exactly the frequencies originally observed and counted in the population. The assumptions of Hardy-Weinberg have been met, the population is in equilibrium, and thus, no evolutionary change is occurring.

If the expected genotype frequencies do not come out the same as those originally observed, one of the assumptions of the Hardy-Weinberg model has been violated (Figure 4–7). Under such circumstances an investigation is needed to determine, for example, whether or not matings in the population were really random (Figure 4–8). The fact that a small population was sampled might also affect the calculations. Or, perhaps, natural selection may have been acting to remove unfit genotypes from this population. It is just such a deviation from expectation

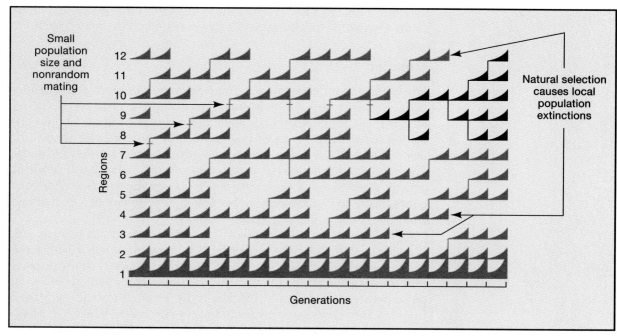

Figure 4–7 • Circumstances in a population that lead to a deviation from the expected gene frequencies predicted for the Hardy-Weinberg model (nonrandom mating, small population size, or natural selection). (From Sewall Wright).

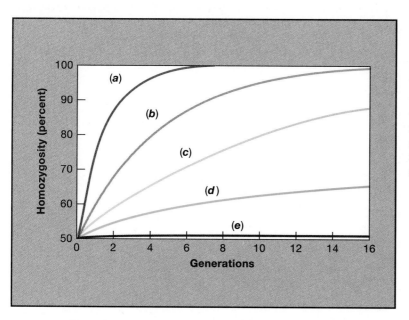

Figure 4–8 • Nonrandom mating changes allele frequencies by increasing the percentage of homozygosity over time, thus effecting Hardy-Weinberg equilibrium. The number of generations required to change allele frequencies from 50 percent is shown for mating systems that involve (*a*) self-fertilization, (*b*) full sibs, (*c*) double first cousins, (*d*) single first cousins, and (*e*) second cousins.

that allows us to pinpoint evolution in action. These forces that affect Hardy-Weinberg equilibrium will now be examined in greater detail.

Mutation

When considered gene by gene mutations are rare in human populations. It is estimated that new mutations occur in 1 in 10,000 (1×10^{-4}) to 1 in 1,000,000 (1×10^{-6}) per allele per generation. In the entire population between 1% to 2% of new births may show genetic abnormalities. Table 4–2 lists some common human diseases caused by mutations and their estimated mutation rates. Today some 2,000 different genetic diseases have been catalogued. Given the number of human genes, many of us probably are born with new mutations, all of which contribute to population genetic variability.

Gene mutations, as opposed to chromosomal mutations, are changes in the DNA base sequence. If a mutation is lethal before the age of reproduction, then it never increases in frequency in the population, causing the death of its carrier before it has a chance of being passed on. However, not all mutations are lethal. They run the gamut from lethal to detrimental to neutral to, in rare cases, beneficial. Mutations as a force in evolution are the ultimate source of new genetic ma-

Table 4–2 • Mutant Traits Caused by Single Gene Mutations

Mutant Trait	Appears Once in Each	Mutation Frequency per Million
Dominant		
Pelger Anomaly (abnormal white blood cells; reduces resistance to disease)	12,500 gametes	80
Chondrodystrophic Dwarfism (shortened and deformed legs and arms)	23,000 gametes	42
Retinoblastoma (tumors on retina of eye)	43,500 gametes	23
Anirida (absence of iris)	200,000 gametes	5
Epiloia (red lesions on face; later tumors in brain, kidney, heart, etc.)	83,000 gametes	12
Recessive Autosomal		
Albinism (melanin does not form in skin, hair, and iris)	37,700 gametes	28
Amaurotic Idiocy (Infantile) (deterioration of mental ability during first months of life)	90,900 gametes	11
Total Color Blindness	35,700 gametes	28
Recessive X-linked		
Hemophilia	31,250 gametes	32

From Winchester (1972).

terial, and they alter the Hardy-Weinberg equilibrium by automatically changing gene frequencies with the input of new alleles.

A dominant mutation, which is rare but observed in all human populations, is a type of dwarfism known as achondroplasia (Figure 4–9). Individuals with this allele possess limbs and vertebral columns that are often deformed making walking difficult. Because the allele is dominant, all individuals who carry it will pass it on to 50% of their offspring. The incidence of this condition is approximately 1 in 100,000 live births. Of these about 80%, or 8 per 1,000,000, must be the result of new mutations, because neither parent had the disease. If two affected individuals mate the homozygous achondroplastic offspring die *in utero*. This allele has an extremely low fitness value of only 0.2×10^{-7} compared to normal. If there were no recurring mutations to keep this allele in the population, it would eventually be eliminated by natural selection. By calculating the frequency of the allele and determining its fitness we see that 80% of the existing alleles are lost each generation. Because in reality the condition seems to be present in all populations, recurrent mutation maintains the allele at a low frequency in the face of natural selection operating against it. Unlike dominant mutations, recessive mutations cause conditions that can only become apparent when they are in the homozygous state (that is when an individual carries both recessive alleles).

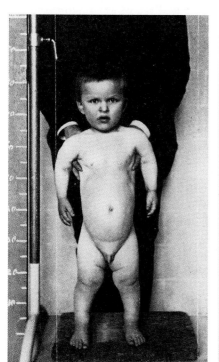
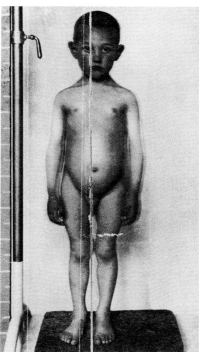

Figure 4–9 • Achondroplastic dwarfism (left) in humans, resulting from a dominant mutant gene, compared with normal growth (right).

Mutations that are "invisible" to selection are known as **neutral mutations.** New "neutral" mutations can, over time, replace original alleles simply by chance, although this occurs at a much slower rate than if selection had affected replacement. The rate at which a mutant substitution occurs and the rate of fixation of that mutant allele determine whether and how rapidly a mutation will become fixed in a population.

The rate of substitution of neutral mutations within a population, as, for example, in many protein molecules, appears to be fairly uniform. This rate, termed "K," is defined as the long-term average of mutants that are substituted in a population per locus per unit time. For the hemoglobin molecule the observed rate of amino acid substitution is close to 10^9 amino acid sites per year. "K" is independent of the size of the population involved. It is simply a function of the rate of occurrence of the mutation.

This rate is different from the rate at which a single mutation increases its frequency in a population or the amount of time that it actually takes for one mutation to fix itself by chance. Having more than one mutation present in a population will raise the odds that it will ultimately become fixed, but the time it will take for fixation by chance is dependent upon population size. The equation $K = 4N_e$ describes this situation. In a population of 10,000 (N_e), it will take 40,000 generations to fix a neutral mutation. On the other hand, if the rate of mutant substitution is the result of natural selection, then fixing a mutation with a selective advantage may be expressed by $K = 4(\mu)(S)(N_e)$, where "μ" is the mutation rate and "S" is the selective advantage. For the same population of 10,000 individuals, a mutation rate of 10^{-7} exists and a selective advantage of 0.2, $K = 0.8 \times 10^{-3}$ substitutions per generation. In this case the mutation would be fixed in only about 1,000 generations (Figure 4–10).

Inbreeding

The mating between individuals who are genetically related is called **inbreeding.** In humans, culture and social customs, such as incest rules or taboos, place restrictions on inbreeding. In rare situations matings may occur among members of the nuclear family and among relatives as close as first cousins. Some human groups have sanctioned inbreeding as a method of maintaining the "purity" of a particular lineage. For example, in dynastic Egypt, inbreeding in the royal family, even between brother and sister, was encouraged in an attempt to preserve "pure" blood lines. The important result of inbreeding is an increase in the level of homozygosity, and the subsequent loss of heterozygosity in the population. Because inbreeding is a form of non-random mating, it alters genotype frequency, which affects the Hardy-Weinberg equilibrium.

neutral mutations–mutations that are not acted upon by selection; neutral mutations accumulate at a more or less constant rate over time.

inbreeding–the increased incidence of mating within a deme or population that results in an increase in homozygosity within the population.

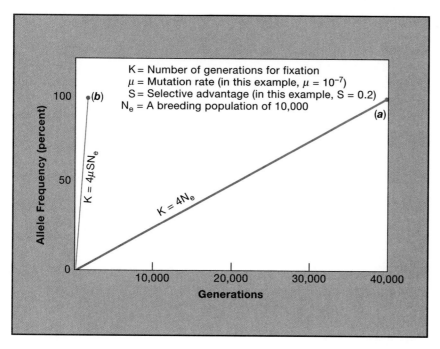

Figure 4–10 • (*a*) Fixation of a neutral mutation by genetic drift depends only on effective population number, in this case 10,000 breeding individuals. (*b*) Fixation by natural selection depends upon the selective advantage of the mutant allele and the rate of mutation, as well as the effective population number.

Inbreeding affects a population in other ways besides increasing homozygosity. For example, if a recessive deleterious allele is present in both mates their offspring have a one in four chance of having a disease caused by the homozygous condition. In a randomly mating population, however, the chance of incurring a recessive homozygous condition of this sort is probably no more than one in 10,000.

The consequences of inbreeding in a population can be shown by the following example. Initially, let two alleles be present in equal frequency (*A* and *a* =.50). At Hardy-Weinberg equilibrium one expects 0.25 *AA*, 0.5 *Aa*, and 0.25 *aa*. After one generation of inbreeding (*AA X AA, Aa X Aa*, and *aa X aa*), the frequency of genotypes becomes 0.375 *AA*, 0.25 *Aa*, and 0.375 *aa*, a decrease of 50% in the heterozygotes. In the second generation the frequency of heterozygotes decreases to 0.125, one-half of the previous generation. For each suceeding generation inbreeding lowers the frequency of the heterozygotes by one-half. Allele frequencies have not changed, however, remaining at 0.5 for both A and a alleles.

The degree to which an individual is inbred or the rate at which inbreeding occurs is measured by the *coefficient of inbreeding,* or "F." "F" is the probability that two alleles found at any given locus come from a common ancestor. As inbreeding reduces variability in a population, "F" is also a measure of the average overall reduction in population heterozygosity. In a large randomly mating population the value of "F" may range from 0 to 1.0 when all show complete homozygosity. For example, any offspring of a first-cousin marriage will have $1/16$ of their genes in common (one-half of their common grandparents' genes passed to their respective parents, which are then respectively passed on to one-half to their offspring (1 in $2^4 = 1/16$). Offspring of a brother–sister mating have a one-quarter probability of having recessive homozygous states for alleles.

The rate of human inbreeding varies from one population to another, but is generally very low. The effects of inbreeding are noticeable in populations that are usually remote geographically or are isolates within a surrounding large population due to religious or cultural practices. For example, the Dunkers of Pennsylvania, a religious isolate descended from German immigrants in the nineteenth century, marry almost exclusively within their own community. Consequently, average inbreeding coefficients are high. In contrast, Arctic Eskimo populations, though remote and with small population sizes, have maintained a low level of population inbreeding because of cultural practices that prohibit marriages between closely related individuals. Population numbers of our early ancestors were probably quite small; inbreeding may well have played an important role in human evolution.

Migration

Migration is the movement of people, hence their genes, from one area to another. There are two extremes in migration. The first is an outward expansion of a population where individuals reach an area that may be sparsely inhabited or perhaps even unoccupied. Although migrations may continue over time, at some point gene flow diminishes between the migrant and its parent population. As gene flow diminishes, the migrant population becomes increasingly distinct genetically from the parent population. New mutations occur in each population and natural selection operates to adapt each population to its separate environment. Consequently, over generations the populations may become different not only in terms of gene frequencies but also in terms of morphological characteristics such as height, weight, and hair color. In all probability such situations have taken place many times in human evolution. For example, the Neandertals in Europe were likely the result of populations that were partially isolated by the geography of Ice Age Europe.

The second extreme is when two populations come into contact, the result is eventual homogenization. Let us suppose that two populations originally differ in terms of allele frequencies. As one migrates into the geographical range of the other and mating takes place between them, the gene pools of each population become less different as genes are shared by both groups. When mating becomes completely random the populations eventually fuse into one group.

An example of homogenization in progress can be seen in the United States between Americans of European ancestry and Americans

migration–the movement of a reproductively active individual into a population from a distant population, thus bringing new genes into that population.

of African ancestry. Mainly between the years 1619 through 1808 Africans, primarily from West Africa, were brought to America as indentured servants and slaves. The genetic composition of the present African-American population is different from the ancestral population, the result of admixture with European-Americans over some 350 years. The presence of European alleles in African-Americans indicates gene flow. The average gene flow, which has been primarily in the European-American-to-African-American direction in previous generations, has been estimated to be as high as 30%. Spread over the last five or six generations this averages out to be about 5% per generation. For example, today the frequency of sickle-cell anemia among African-Americans is about 10%, compared to about 22%, estimated to be the frequency among individuals of the founder African population brought to this country. This reduction in the frequency of this trait can be partly accounted for by gene exchange with other groups of Americans. In addition natural selection has worked to eliminate this gene in America, a nonmalarial environment, through selection against the *SS* homozygote.

Chance Sampling

Sometimes change in the frequency of alleles occurs by chance. How rapidly such changes occur depends upon the size of the population. The chance that an allele becomes fixed in a population rather than lost through the process of genetic drift is related to how frequent that allele is in the population. The rarer the allele, the more likely that it will become lost. Given an original population with two alleles in equal frequency, one will replace the other with a chance of 50%. If the original frequencies of the alleles are not equal, their chances of becoming fixed in the population are the same as their frequencies. For example, if "*A*" is at 90% and "*a*" is at 10%, then "*A*" has a 90% chance of becoming fixed in the population and "*a*" has a 10% chance. Change by chance is called **genetic drift.** Genetic drift is not consistent from generation to generation as is the case with natural selection, as the rate can fluctuate, producing higher frequencies in one generation and lower frequencies in a succeeding one. Change, in other words, is erratic.

One special case of genetic drift is called the **founder effect.** In this situation colonization of an isolated area by a small number of individuals determines the genetic characteristics of a new population. Small founding populations usually possess allele frequencies that are quite different from the parent population. The causes of this difference are twofold. First, imagine a small group setting out to inhabit an isolated South Pacific atoll or an isolated African valley (Figure 4–11). The small group of founders of perhaps 25 individuals would not by chance exactly represent the genetic complement of the larger population to which they belonged. They would not have the same frequencies of alleles and even whole alleles might be absent. The 25 individuals, thus, represent only a sampling of the larger group.

genetic drift—gene frequency changes due to chance effects, not affected by selection; most common in small population sizes.

founder effect—a type of genetic drift caused by sampling a small amount of genetic variation from the original population in a group of individuals colonizing a new area.

Figure 4–11 • An example of the founder effect: syndactyly, the genetically inherited "lobster claw" deformity frequently found in this isolated African population near the Mozambique-Zimbabwe border, traceable to one group of immigrant ancestors.

For example, consider the ABO blood group system; it may have been that of the 25 mutineers, 20 had Type O blood and 5 individuals had Type B blood. Because none of the mutineers had Type A or AB blood, the A allele would be absent in this population. Alternatively, an example is also possible in which all 25 individuals by chance alone were Type A, with alleles O and B not being represented. In this case the A allele is fixed in the population, and all descendants would henceforth have only blood type A (genotype *AA*). The alleles for B and O would be lost unless reintroduced through migration or perhaps mutation. Second, if no further immigration takes place eventually inbreeding levels will rise after a few generations as all of the descendants of the original founders become related through intermarriage.

Deleterious mutations can become common in small populations by inbreeding, or by selection favoring their position in heterozygote combinations as in the sickle-cell anemia example. The following three cases are found in different human populations, apparently introduced by a small group or a single founder and increased to unexpectedly high frequencies. The first example concerns a rare dominant trait associated with the degeneration of the central nervous system called *Huntington's Chorea,* popularly called "St. Vitus's Dance." Recently this allele has been located on a specific chromosome, allowing for early detection in individuals who may carry it. Previously the only way to detect the gene was to observe the onset of symptoms, which usually occurred in individuals at about 30 years of age. The first appearance of chorea, or dance-like jerking motions of the limbs, usually meant death for those individuals who displayed it, yet unfortunately at the age where the disease could be detected many individuals had already passed it on to their offspring. In many populations around the world the frequency of the heterozygote where this dominant allele expresses itself is about 1/10,000. However, in Tasmania, a state of 350,000 people there are 120 cases of this disease or about 1/3000. The spread and higher frequency of this condition is no doubt part of an effect of in-breeding within a small population. Researchers have determined that the dominant allele for Huntington's Chorea was brought to Tasmania by one woman who immigrated there in 1848.

In the second example homozygous recessive alleles produces *Tay-Sachs disease*. This disease results from a reduced production of an important enzyme, hexosaminidase A, which produces a build up of complex fatty compounds (lipids) in the central nervous system leading to mental retardation and usually death by the age of 2 or 3. In most populations in the world the frequency of Tay-Sachs is low, about 1 in 500,000. As affected individuals die at a very young age, the low frequency of the condition is probably maintained by new mutations of the normal allele. However, among Ashkenazi (European) Jews this disorder is found in high frequencies. Again, a founder effect, originating perhaps six to seven centuries ago in eastern Europe, no doubt contributed to the incidence of the allele in Jewish populations; as Jewish people fled the persecutions of the Crusaders, they carried the allele to Europe. The high frequency of the disorder in this population, estimated today at about 1 in 6000, requires further explanation. Unlike the first example, inbreeding or drift are unlikely factors to produce frequencies as high as are reported. One possibility is that the allele in the heterozygous form provides some selective advantage that is not yet clearly understood. For example, there is some evidence that carriers of the allele show greater resistance to pulmonary tuberculosis, an important contributor to death in Europe for many centuries. This example shows that the processes of genetic drift and natural selection may not be mutually exclusive as factors contributing to change in allele frequencies.

The final example concerns a disorder called *Phenylketonuria* (PKU). As in the previous example, recessive alleles in the homozygous state result in a deficiency of an enzyme, phenylalanine hydroxylase. As a consequence, the amino acid phenylalanine accumulates in the blood stream and ultimately causes mental retardation. A diet low in phenylalanine, however, can alleviate the symptoms.

The incidence of PKU varies among different populations. The Japanese reportedly have the lowest rate (1 in every 60,000 newborns) whereas Caucasians are affected on the order of 1 in 15,000. The highest incidence of PKU, about 1 in 5000, occurs in Ireland and western Scotland and among Jews of Yemenite origin living in Israel. Although researchers have identified about 20 different mutations that can cause PKU, suspicion was that only one mutation was responsible for the cases involving the Yemenite Jews because their population of only 250,000 was so small. By retracing Jewish history genealogist Yosef Shiloh of Tel Aviv University was able to determine that all of the present carriers of the allele descended from individuals who had lived in a single village, San'a in Yemen, until at least the late seventeenth century. This mutation must have arisen in a single individual sometime before that time and was later spread in other parts of Yemen and finally to Israel (Figure

Figure 4–12 • The spread by migration of PKU from Yemen to Israel. (Adapted from an illustration by Ian Warpole, © 1990 *Discover* Magazine.)

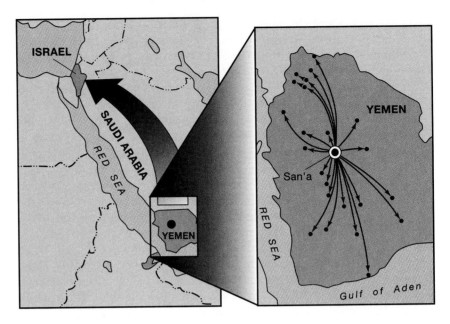

4–12). The high frequency of this allele is, as it is with Tay-Sachs condition, a curious genetic anomaly, and suggests a selectively advantageous situation for the heterozygote carriers. There is some evidence to suggest that a different mutation for PKU in Irish and Scottish women may result in lower rates of spontaneous abortion (Wright, 1990).

EVOLUTION CHANGES POPULATION ALLELE FREQUENCIES

Selection

Natural selection is the mechanism by which a population becomes better adapted to its environment over time. For natural selection to work, the adaptations must be at the genetic level so that they can be passed on to offspring. Those individuals who are more "fit" leave more offspring on average than do less "fit" individuals. **Fitness** is defined as the percentage of offspring a genotype has, relative to the number of offspring of the maximally fit genotype in the population. Fitness values for a population relate to a specific point in time for a specified environment. Fitness of specific genotypes may change over time as a result of changes in the environment.

fitness–the extent to which the genes of an individual survive in its descendants.

directional selection–selection that acts to move the mean of a population in one particular direction.

Directional Selection   **Directional selection** provides a typical example of natural selection in which a given genotype is favored among individuals, eventually becoming homozygous for the favored allele. One of the best examples of directional selection was witnessed in a population of the English peppered moth, *Biston betularia* (Figure

4–13). All of the individuals in the population were colored in a light gray variegated pattern. However, suddenly in 1848 a very dark colored form of the moth appeared and over the years gradually increased in frequency to greater than 90% and spread throughout England. The biologist H. Kettlewell studied this phenomenally rapid change in the moth population. He noted that the first dark colored moths occured at about the same time that major environmental effects of the British industrial revolution were being felt. The lighter color of the original moths blended in with the lichen-covered tree trunks they rested on and provided an effective camouflage from bird predators. However, with the sooty pollution from coal-burning factories covering tree trunks, the lighter moth stood out against the darker background. The darker moth under these new conditions experienced much less predation by birds. Experimenting with this hypothesis, Kettlewell decided to release different colored moths in polluted and unpolluted areas, and then recaptured as many of them as possible at a later time. He demonstrated that the lighter gray moths in sooty polluted conditions were more vulnerable to predation by birds than were dark moths and vice versa. Further work demonstrated that the new dark moth phenotype was caused by a mutation that was dominant to the "gray color" allele, and under the conditions of a polluted, sooty environment it quickly became favored. In one generation of random mating, given a fitness of the black dominant allele of 1.0 and a fitness of the gray allele of 0.5, a rapid change in gene and genotype frequencies will occur. In only a few generations the gray allele would be practically eliminated. Because of decreased levels of pollution today the proportion of gray colored moths is once again increasing.

Figure 4–13 • The English peppered moth (*Biston betularia*) shown in light and dark gray variants.

Balanced Selection Leads to Genetic Polymorphism When selection acts to favor alleles in certain combinations and to act against those alleles when they occur in different combinations, genetic diversity is maintained in the population. This balancing of selection both for and against certain alleles is termed **genetic polymorphism.** In the example of sickle-cell anemia, *AS* individuals may be less prone to disease in an environment where malaria is prevalent. If individuals move away from this environment or if the environment is changed through the eradication of mosquitoes that carry the malarial parasite, *AS* individuals lose their selective advantage. They suffer from the effects of the sickle-cell allele itself, whereas normal *AA* individuals do not.

In Figure 4–14 we show how the sickle-cell allele is maintained over time in a malarial environment. In this case the fitness of the *AA* individual is 0.9 and the selection coefficient is 0.1. The *AS* genotypes are given the fitness value of 1.0 where selection (S) equals 0. Let us assume that the *SS* homozygotes never reproduce; their genotype is lethal and therefore fitness equals 0.0 (S = 1.0). If we start out with an initial structured population of 100 people with 80% having genotypes *AA* and 20% having genotypes *AS*, the allele frequencies are *A* = 0.9 and

genetic polymorphism—the existence of two or more genetic variants within a population; can be a balanced polymorphism when selection favors the heterozygotes, as in sickle-cell anemia.

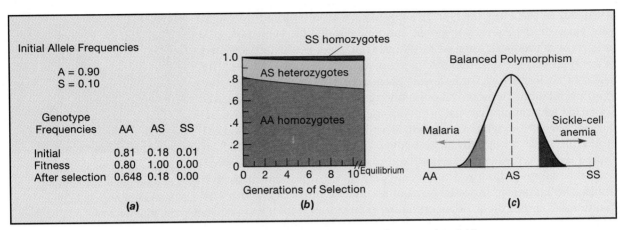

Figure 4–14 • Diagrammatic representation of how selection acts in relation to the sickle-cell trait on a population living in a malarial environment: (*a*) calculation of allele frequencies A and S after one generation of selection, (*b*) graph of allele frequencies A and S carried to 10 generations (equilibrium), and (*c*) graph showing proportions of the population (shaded areas) who do not survive because of malaria or sickle-cell anemia.

$S = 0.1$. Given random mating by the parental population, after only one generation of selection 10% of the *AA* population die of malaria, leaving only 73 new *AA* individuals. Eighteen people who have the AS genotype are protected. However, we lose one individual (a lethal *SS*) who was produced from the mating between *AS* people. We now have 91 survivors but, the allele frequencies have not changed from the original population and remain 0.9 and 0.1 for *A* and *S,* respectively. What *has* happened is that, whereas some people die of malaria, more of the sickle-cell disease people live than would be expected, because of the effects of the *S* gene in the population. Everything else being equal, allele frequencies would not change generation after generation. What has changed is the total number of people in the population. With malaria, only 91 survive when the *S* gene is in the population. If the population existed in a malarial environment and *S* alleles were not present, only 90 people would survive because the fitness of the AA individual is still equal to 0.9. So the population is better off with the sickle-cell gene than without it, even though a new type of genetic death has been added with the *SS* lethal.

This is a balanced polymorphism because the heterozygote is more fit than either of the homozygotes, and because there are at least two alleles at the locus. The net result of this system is to keep both alleles present in the population so long as conditions do not change.

Average Population Fitness   Because natural selection operates for or against a specific genotype in a population, the net outcome is the removal of unfavorable alleles. If this process continues long enough and the environment does not change, homozygosity in the population increases, to the point that all individuals become homozygous for the loci favored by selection. The fitness of all individuals, then, would be 1.0. However, this situation is never realized in the real world; the average fitness in the population is always less than 1.0, simply because unfavored alleles are never completely eliminated from the population. The average fitness of the population increases as the number of unfavored alleles decreases (Figure 4–15).

In some cases, such as with balanced polymorphisms, selection acts to maintain heterozygosity. Although the effect of this heterozygosity may be to lower the overall fitness of the population, it also serves to increase the genetic variability of the population. This variation may be very important to the future of any population when environmental conditions change and new selection comes into play on the population. A population with little genetic variation to call upon faces the possibility of extinction.

microevolution—small-scale change in gene frequencies or other biological traits in a population or species over a relatively brief period of time.

"Microevolution" Leads to "Macroevolution"

Evolution is defined as genetic change in a population over time. **Microevolution** describes small-scale genetic changes, ones that occur over a few generations. Microevolutionary change occurs within the confines of a single species, resulting in a shift in percentages of alleles

Figure 4–15 • The relationship between fitness of a population and homozygosity. Heterozygosity decreases average population fitness but increases the population's variability and consequent future ability to respond to new selection pressures. In small marginal populations (*a*), selection favors the homozygote and leads to the fixation of specific adaptive features. In large populations (*b*), the scale usually tips in favor of the heterozygote but suffers from decreased average population fitness because homozygotes, which are less fit than the heterozygotes, are continually produced.

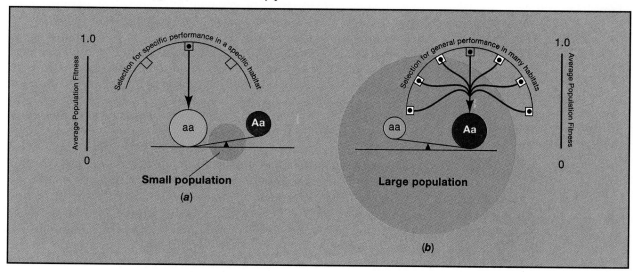

and of morphological characters. The change in coloration of the English peppered moth is an example of microevolutionary change. Microevolutionary change begins the process by which populations diverge from one another, that can ultimately lead to the formation of new species. **Macroevolution** is long-term, producing changes that result in new species over time. The discussion of the evolution of the eukaryotes in Chapter 2 is an example of macroevolutionary change.

SPECIATION

Macroevolutionary change results in speciation, the process by which new biological species form. There are essentially two competing theories in macroevolutionary studies (Figure 4–16). First, Darwin clearly believed that macroevolution is essentially microevolution extended over long periods of geologic time. Small changes over time gradually accumulate to constitute the large changes, which ultimately serve to distinguish new species from older ones. This process known as **phyletic gradualism** was, subsequently, criticized by some scientists who saw what they considered too many "gaps" in the fossil record.

The concept of sudden "jumps" or "leaps" in evolution spawned the second theory that was outlined by the geneticist Richard Goldschmidt in an attempt to reconcile the sporadic fossil record with modern genetic theory. He suggested that large-scale mutation could cause such jumps in evolution. Paleontologist George Gaylord Simpson (1944) disagreed and argued that gaps at the level of the species could probably be accounted for as byproducts of incomplete or poor fossil preservation. Yet he was concerned about the gaps that existed between the higher taxa. As a consequence, he developed the concept of **quantum evolution** that could explain how some populations rapidly shifted in their adaptations. In terms of geologic time such leaps could be so rapid that the chance of finding an intermediate fossil form that reflected these shifts would be quite slim.

Though the predominant viewpoint concerning the rate of evolutionary change leaned towards the gradualistic model, the idea continued. Stephen J. Gould and Niles Eldredge (1977) promoted the idea that in their description of the evolutionary process short bursts of change might periodically occur. This they labeled **punctuated equilibrium.** They argued that most species exhibit little or no change throughout most of their evolutionary history (stasis) and that adaptive change (punctuation) is a relatively rare, rapid event, rather than a gradual process. Such change would only occur during speciation. The genetic foundations for punctuated equilibrium have been elusive, and most evolutionary biologists now accept that the rates of phyletic gradualism may vary substantially, thus eliminating the need to postulate a new model of evolutionary change (Figure 4–16).

macroevolution–large-scale change in gene frequencies or other biological traits in a species or higher level taxonomic grouping, generally over a relatively long period of time.

phyletic gradualism–term coined by Stephen J. Gould to characterize Darwin's idea of evolutionary rate; slow, gradual change over long periods of time.

quantum evolution–stepwise evolutionary change.

punctuated equilibrium–term coined by Stephen J. Gould and Niles Eldredge to characterize evolution typified by long periods of little or no change (stasis), interrupted by bursts of rapid change (punctuational events).

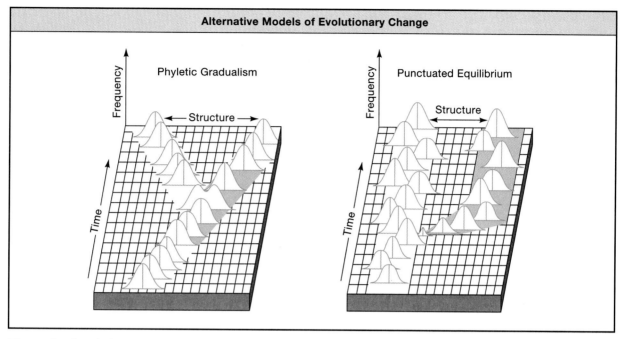

Figure 4–16 • Phyletic gradualism versus punctuated equilibrium: a plot of morphological change against time. (From Verba, 1980)

EVOLUTION OF BEHAVIOR

Behavior is an important part of species' adaptation. It is an integral part of a species' biology and closely bound to its genetic endowment. Although Darwin is most remembered for observing physical characteristics in his formulation of natural selection, he is also responsible for placing animal behavior in an evolutionary context. In his book, *The Expression of the Emotions in Man and Animals* (1872:12), Darwin wrote "[h]e who admits on general grounds that the structure and habits of all animals have been gradually evolved, will look at the whole subject of Expression [behavior] in a new and interesting light." Darwin showed that there were continuities between animal and human behavior, implying a common inherited basis. He concluded that behavioral traits as well as physical traits would be subject to evolution.

Behavior can be defined as patterns of activity through time. This definition allows scientists to measure and compare behavior between individuals in different species. Understanding how animals interact in social groups is also an important aspect of the study of behavior, one that has received widespread attention by researchers. Because humans and most other primates are highly social species, this latter work is important to anthropologists.

sexual selection–selection within a species based on mate choice or competition within the species, usually between males.

sexual dimorphism–presence of two distinctly different forms of male and female individuals in a species.

Sexual Selection

Charles Darwin in his second major book, *The Descent of Man and Selection with Respect to Sex* (1871), elaborated on the concept of **sexual selection.** Sexual selection is based on two levels of selection. The first is competition for mates, occurring among adult members of each sex, in other words male versus male, and female versus female. The second is based on mate choice. In most vertebrates it is generally the female who is more selective, choosing whomever she considers the best available male.

Darwin noted that sexual selection can result in the evolution of two sexes, the adults, who can differ from one another substantially in their external morphology, a condition known as **sexual dimorphism** (Latin, meaning "two-bodied") (Figure 4–17). Sexually dimorphic secondary sex characteristics may be simultaneously threatening to rivals as well as attractive to potential mates. Darwin also noted the paradoxical situation in which characteristics that are advantageous in competition with one's rival may be very disadvantageous when it comes to the basic issues of survival. For example, male–male aggression, which occurs during the mating season in many species of prosimian primates, such as lemurs (Figure 4–18), often results in the severe wounding of both contestants. But because the chance, however small, of a male's mating with a receptive female is overpowering, virtually all of the males engage in this sort of combat. Darwin drew attention to these facts and thereby distinguished sexual selection from natural selection. Larger body size and elaborate coloration of the pelage usually differentiate male from female morphologies in primates as well as in many other kinds of animals, because much of male–male competition depends upon aggressive display.

As Helena Cronin (1992:286) describes the situation:

> If you were asked to invent an irksome challenge to Darwinian theory, you could get a long way with a peacock's tail. And if you were asked to think up a solution to the challenge that would disconcert Darwinians, you would

Figure 4–17 • Sexual dimorphism in mandrills and in human beings.

Figure 4–18 • Ring-tailed lemur males fighting during the mating season.

need to go no further than Charles Darwin's own theory of sexual selection . . . (Natural selection) should abhor the peacock's tail—gaudy, ornamental, a burden to its bearer. Darwin took the view that natural selection would indeed frown upon such flamboyance. It had been concocted, he decided, by female preference.

Thus, the "good taste" theory of female choice was born; females choose their mates on aesthetic grounds; male ornamentation developed to charm the females and "for no other purpose" (Darwin, 1871: 92). Reactions to this idea developed into two different viewpoints. First was the idea that sexual selection was, in reality, unimportant and that gaudy ornamentation could be explained in terms of natural selection, having significance in warning, territorial or threat display. In the 1930s, Julian Huxley, an eminent population geneticist, declared that Darwin had put "too much weight to the view that bright colors and other conspicuous characters must have a sexual function" (Huxley, 1938:1), a view later echoed by Ernst Mayr in the 1960s.

The second viewpoint announced the arrival of "good sense" female choice. In this case females choose their mates on the basis of male vigor, good health, and territory size; in other words, these were sensible choices to make. Cronin (1992:288) describes this situation as "an arms race within a species . . . that male embellishment can act as an indicator of sensible qualities . . . [is] one route to ornamental escalation [that] immediately offers itself." The fact that one embellishment is chosen over another is arbitrary. The characteristic, itself, is unimportant. What is important is that at one time a preference for some characteristic was made and it became reinforced and elaborated in a positive feedback loop. Once preference for, let us say, gaudy colored tails was established, then it was "good sense" for females to continue to make choices for mates on that basis as all other females would be

ethology–naturalistic study of animal behavior and its evolution.

doing the same. On the other hand, such choice may ultimately escalate, becoming a nearly unstoppable, and in many ways a "nonsensical," burden to its possessor.

Sexual selection can lead both to the evolution of behavioral responses, or strategies, and to physical traits. The female reproductive strategy has the primary goal of protecting her offspring, and may include prolonging the period of sexual receptivity, aggression against competitors, which may involve the harassment and killing of the offspring of others, and the suppression of sexual receptivity in subordinate females. Females may also exhibit direct competition for resources necessary for producing and nurturing their offspring, and for attracting the highest ranking males that they can.

Males, on the other hand, may compete through a variety of behaviors that include guarding of territory, dominating other animals, and guarding of females. Other responses, such as "nuptial feeding," bringing food to sexually receptive females, may be part of a reproductive strategy important in the evolution of our own lineage (Parker, 1989).

Trivers (1972) has argued that differences in male and female reproductive strategies may be accounted for by the investment each parent makes in their offspring. Females usually invest more of their time and energy in a fewer number of offspring and are more selective in their choice of mates. Males, on the contrary, increase their reproductive success by producing more offspring by mating with as many females as they can.

Ethology

Scientists have realized that behavior evolves to allow a species to adapt effectively to a particular ecological niche. To study behavioral adaptations of a particular species research must be done on the animal in its natural habitat, not in the convenient, artificial environment of the laboratory or zoo. The study of behavior that incorporates these quantitative, comparative, evolutionary and naturalistic approaches is termed **ethology.** Ethology is the biological study of animal behavior that deals with species-specific or genetically linked behavior (Lorenz, 1965). Ethologists recognize the value of observing behavior in its entirety within an environmental context, because only under these circumstances can the evolution of behavior patterns be fully comprehended (Eibl-Eibesfeldt, 1989).

A species' characteristic physical features develop within certain limits, through an interaction of the genotype with the environment. In a similar manner, a species' behavior—how individuals acquire food, how they interact with the members of the species, how they avoid danger, how they reproduce, and how they raise their young—is also a result of genetic development within a range of appropriate environments. As the ethologist Konrad Lorenz (1970: xii; Figure 4–19) has

Figure 4–19 • Konrad Lorenz and his geese.

noted, "behavior patterns are just as conservatively and reliably characters of species as are the forms of bones, teeth, or any other bodily structures." However, the scientific study of behavior and its evolution is a relatively new field, and many of the interactions of behavior, genetics, and environment are yet to be investigated.

Ethology as a field began with Darwin, who first treated behavior in the same evolutionary context as anatomical structure and physiology. He stated (1874:350), "that the chief expressive actions, exhibited by man and the lower animals, are now innate or inherited,—that is, have not been learnt by the individual,—is admitted by every one." Although this tenet may have been generally accepted during Darwin's time, the rise of experimental psychology and ethnology with their emphases on learned behavior did not allow ethology to progress until well into the twentieth century.

Much of human ethology deals with the nonverbal, nonlearned and noncultural behavior shared with other animals. Anthropologist Sherwood Washburn (1980:273) has suggested that "human ethology might be defined as the science that pretends humans cannot speak." Although he intended it as a critique, because much of human behavior *is* mediated, expressed, and even caused by linguistic cues, it is an apt description of a science that intends to study human behavior within an evolutionary context. To understand the roots of human behavior, one must look at the nonverbal behavioral commonalities that humans share with the animal world.

Ethologists seek to establish a behavioral profile or **ethogram** of a species—a catalogue of all the behavior patterns of an animal. In practice this is difficult. What is a "behavior pattern?" What are the basic units of behavior to be catalogued? If ethology is indeed a comparative science, what behaviors could be compared from one species to another? The first answer to these queries is behavior that is closely tied to genetics.

Fixed Action Patterns

The ethologists Konrad Lorenz and Niko Tinbergen discovered in 1938 that animal species have what they termed "inherited coordination." In more recent literature, **fixed action pattern** (FAP) has replaced the earlier term. Fixed action patterns are behaviors that (1) are *form-constant*—each instance that they are expressed, the same muscles contract and the animal moves in the same sequence; (2) appear spontaneously during development, requiring no learning; (3) are characteristic of all members of the species; (4) cannot be unlearned; and (5) are released or caused by a particular stimulus, external environmental condition or internal physiological environment of the animal. Numerous cases of FAP's are now known from observations of insects, birds, fish, and other vertebrates (Figure 4–20).

ethogram–the behavioral repertoire characteristic of a species.
fixed action pattern–innate, form-constant behavioral patterns released by certain key stimuli characteristic of all members of a species.

Figure 4–20 • Fixed action patterns can be observed in a chameleon's unerring tongue capture of a flying insect; in a mother wren's placing of food in the open mouths of her nestlings; and in the vocal alarm calls of a ring-tailed lemur group, elicited by aerial movement of a bird of prey.

A curious attribute of the FAP is that, once started, an FAP must complete execution, in computer-like fashion, regardless of any further environmental information. A greylag goose mother, for example, once she has seen a loose egg away from the nest and has gone to retrieve it, will always make the same beak movements to roll the egg back to the nest even if an ethologist surreptitiously takes the egg away before the goose gets to it! Because an egg almost never disappears from under the nose of a goose under normal circumstances, natural selection has produced this FAP in the species and it functions quite successfully.

The disadvantage to FAP for solving behavioral problems is that they lack flexibility. An FAP may be ineffective as a behavioral strategy when a species is confronted with changing environmental conditions. Undoubtedly, this is one of the strong selective reasons for behavioral evolution leading to a preponderance of learned behavioral responses in mammals. Human fixed action patterns are discussed in Chapter 12.

 SUMMARY

Species are genetically distinct populations reproductively isolated from other species. By definition viable offspring cannot be produced from matings between individuals of two species. Species can be geographically subdivided into smaller breeding units called demes. Differences in allele frequencies between populations may be the result of a number of evolutionary processes such as selective mating practices, random genetic drift, and migrations, as well as natural selection. Changes in allele frequencies in a single population over time is evolution and these can be determined from the Hardy-Weinberg equation. This equation states that if none of the evolutionary processes are operating on any given chromosomal locus, then whatever the allele frequencies are at that locus at that moment they will remain the same until affected by some process later on. Allele frequency stability is called population equilibrium, which means that at that locus no evolution is taking place. The assumptions for population equilibrium are: random mating practices are in effect, new mutations do not exceed the loss of existing ones, no population movements have occurred, and that the population number is large enough to discount accidental or chance factors from playing a role in allele frequency shifts. Finally natural selection must be ruled out in that no single genotype is preferred over any other. The example of sickle-cell anemia was offered to show how Hardy-Weinberg equilibrium was disturbed by natural selection favoring a heterozygote combination of hemoglobin alleles in the presence of malaria.

Neutral mutations are those that pass through the selective filter that deleterious or advantageous mutations must face. As neutral mutations may exist at any locus there is a chance that they can become the predominant allele and, subsequently, fixed in a population. Fixation by chance is always a slower process than fixation by natural selection. Inbreeding, the result of selective mating, and genetic drift both act to increase homozygosity, which decreases variability in the gene pool.

Natural selection is a process by which a population over time becomes better adapted to its environment. Natural selection is based on individual fitness, which is a measure of reproductive success that is, in turn, related to a specified environment. Directional selection is selection favoring a particular genotype as illustrated in the example of the English peppered moth. Balanced selection favors the heterozygote genotype as shown in the example of sickle-cell anemia. Microevolution is genetic change over time that occurs within a single species. Macroevolutionary change is change over longer periods of time and involves the formation of new species from ancestral ones. New species arise from macroevolutionary change either by phyletic gradualism, the process originally conceptualized by Charles Darwin, or by punctuated equilibrium, a process most recently championed by Stephen J. Gould.

Specific behaviors as well as specific morphologies can be favored by natural selection. Darwin demonstrated the possibility of behavioral continuity between animals and humans, and provided the model of sexual selection to account for certain kinds of sexually dimorphic behavioral as well as morphological patterns. Competition for mates involving specific reproductive strategies play an important role in sexual selection theory. Ethology is defined as the study of animal behavior that is programmed genetically. The fixed action pattern is the simplest kind of genetically programmed behavior that appears usually without much modification or flexibility as a result of specific stimuli perceived by the animal. Although the vast majority of mammalian behavior is learned after birth, the study of fixed action patterns, when they can be identified, provides some measure of the genetic control of behavior.

CRITICAL-THINKING QUESTIONS

1. What are reproductive isolating mechanisms?
2. What are the assumptions of the Hardy-Weinberg equilibrium model?
3. Pick one example of the Hardy-Weinberg equilibrium that has been covered in this chapter and explain it.
4. Define macroevolution and microevolution; how do they affect speciation?
5. How has sexual selection affected individual morphology?
6. Describe the five criteria that are used in determining fixed action patterns.

 SUGGESTED READINGS

Dobzhansky, T. 1971. *Genetics of the Evolutionary Process*. New York: Columbia University Press. A review of the forces of natural selection by a pioneering geneticist.

Eibl-Eibesfeldt, I. 1989. *Human Ethology*. New York: Aldine De Gruyter. A text on the evolutionary aspects of human behavior.

Mayr, Ernst, and W. B. Provine (eds.). 1980. *The Evolutionary Synthesis: Perspectives on the Unification of Biology*. Cambridge: Harvard Univ. Press. Essays on the synthesis of genetics and organismal biology.

Provine, William B. 1986. *Evolution: Selected Papers by Sewall Wright*. Chicago: University of Chicago Press. A compendium of articles and reviews by one of the major contributors to the new evolutionary synthesis.

Simpson, George Gaylord. 1953. *The Major Features of Evolution*. New York: Columbia University Press. Still a classic presentation of the forces of evolution and how paleontology relates to evolutionary science.

Smith, John Maynard. 1978. *The Evolution of Sex*. Cambridge: Cambridge University Press. A general discussion of the evolution of sexual reproduction.

———. 1993. *The Theory of Evolution*. Cambridge: Cambridge University Press. A recent overview of current evolutionary thought by one of the major living evolutionists.

Stages of Vertebrate Evolution

Homologous Structures

Clues from Morphology,
   Embryology,
   and Paleontology

Phylum Chordata

The First Vertebrates:
   Our Fish Heritage
The Evolution of a Bony
   Skeleton
Early Life in Fresh Water
Evolution of Biting Jaws
Evolution of Limbs and Lungs

First Forays onto Dry Land:
   The Amphibians

Reptiles Conquer the Land
Adaptive Radiation of the
   Reptiles
The Evolution of Skull, Teeth,
   and Limbs

Mammals Evolve and Radiate
New Reproductive Strategies
Homeothermy
Enlarged Brain and Related
   Structures

The Human Brain
   in Evolutionary
   Perspective
The R-Complex
The Limbic System
The Neocortex

Mammals and Adaptive
   Radiation

Understanding Human
   Morphology

Summary

Critical-Thinking Questions

Suggested Readings

Humans are animals, just one of many other species that inhabit the planet. Some of us may still cling to the notion that we as a species are unique and apart from nature. But while it is true that we are unique in the same way that every other species is unique in its own way, we are indisputably connected to the rest of nature as well. We humans are intimately linked to the natural world by a network of ecological relationships with our environment and with living species today, as well as by a unique and unbroken series of ancestors extending back to the primordial seas, to the beginnings of life itself (Figure 5–1). We share a series of ancestors with other species on earth, with the most dissimilar being the most remote in time and the most similar being the most recent in time. The very early stages of human evolution, when human ancestors could be called fish, amphibians, reptiles, and primitive mammals, constitute the subject of this chapter. How do we trace this ancestry?

HOMOLOGOUS STRUCTURES

Certainly there are no tombstones marking the graves of our long-lost mammal-like reptile forebears and no family genealogies of generations of ancestral amphibians with which we can piece together our early family tree. Instead, we study anatomical characteristics of living and fossil animals in a rigorous, comparative way to discover ancestor–descendent relationships. Studies of molecular evolution also provide important data on relationships between animal species and on when they shared ancestors in the past, but only comparative anatomy and paleontology can fill in what the actual ancestral species may have looked like.

All anatomical traits that scientists use for studying the comparative evolutionary relationships of animals must be based on a common genetic groundplan. In other words, they must be **homologous.** Evolutionary scientists determine whether structures are homologous by tracing their origins, both through the fossil record and through the embryological history of structures in modern species. Our third finger and fingernail, for example, are homologous to the foreleg and hoof of the modern horse. Horses have a documented loss of the side toes through evolution whereas humans have retained the more primitive five-fingered hand. Some similar morphological features are not, how-

homologous–similar because of common descent or common inheritance.

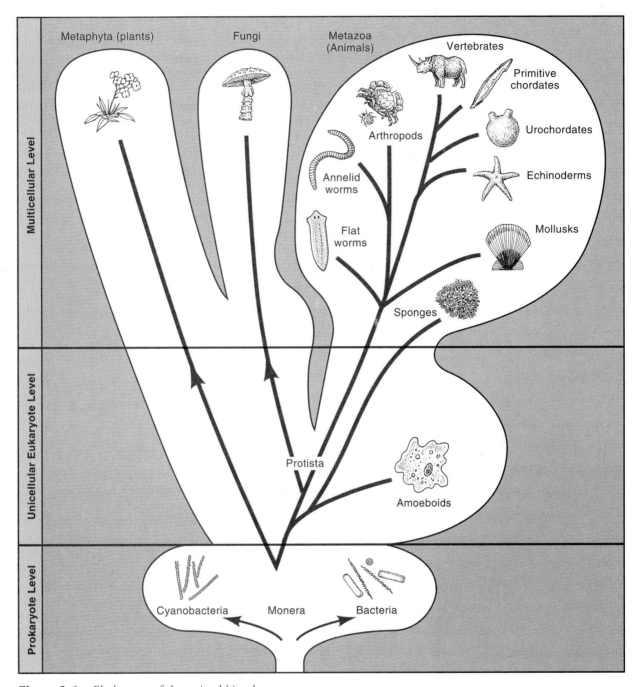

Figure 5–1 • Phylogeny of the animal kingdom.

ever, homologous. The wings of birds and bats, for example, are not homologous. Bird wings developed from and are supported by the first finger of the hand skeleton and bat wings are supported by the fourth finger. Birds and bats evolved independently from flightless wingless ancestors. The fact that both groups have wings is not indicative of their phylogenetic relationships. Nonhomologous structures that are similar in external appearance but have evolved from different sources, like bird and bat wings, are called **analogous** structures.

Anatomical structures, such as limbs or eyes, are formed by proliferations of cells that have become specialized by evolution to perform certain functions in the body. As we have seen in the preceding three chapters, individual cells of all eukaryotic organisms function and reproduce in the same way; that is, all eukaryotic organisms are alike on a cellular level. As we narrow our focus successively on the taxonomic groups to which the human species belongs, we see more and more commonalities in higher levels of cellular organization, in how the cells come together to form structures and perform functions. In this chapter we descend in human taxonomy through the taxonomic levels of phylum (Chordata), subphylum (Vertebrata), and class (Mammalia), and in geological time from the Ordovician Period (500 million years ago) to the beginning of the Cenozoic Era (70 million years ago).

CLUES FROM MORPHOLOGY, EMBRYOLOGY, AND PALEONTOLOGY

When cells of similar type proliferate they form **tissues,** groupings of cells of the same type, such as bone or muscle, that we can see with the naked eye. The morphology of tissues provides one of the most important, and traditionally the only, basis for taxonomic classification and evolutionary study of animal species. Although it is difficult to exactly reconstruct what an animal looked like while it was alive from its bony remains, a great deal can be determined by comparing bones of unknown origin to bones that are known to belong to specific animals. Through such comparisons morphological patterns can be deduced by studying the origin and insertion (the attachment areas) of muscles, which leave their mark on bone in the form of lines or protuberances, and by the shape of the bone itself, which may be reflective of the kind of locomotor behavior that particular animals exhibit. Long gracile limb bones, for example, in primates are reflective of a fast, leaping arboreal form of locomotion. In modern classification genetics and behavioral characteristics can also be used. Fossils provide paleontological evidence of change through time. With fossils the evolutionary history of animals can be reconstructed by studying and interpreting the changes in homologous structures. In this chapter we will discuss the morphological basis for understanding human evolution.

analogous–similar because of adaptation for similar functions.

tissue–literally meaning "woven;" in anatomy referring to an aggregate of cells of the same type, which form a structural unit of the body.

One approach to this study is based on what the German naturalist Ernst Haeckel (1834–1919) first articulated as the "law" that *ontogeny recapitulates phylogeny,* or that growth and development mirrors evolutionary history. Generally speaking, developmental stages of the **embryo,** the early stages of an individual's development, do show similarity to major evolutionary steps through which the species passed. For example, during an early phase in embryological development, dogs, pigs, and humans resemble a fish in form and shape. They will have slits in the head, similar to the gill slits of a fish. These structures then develop into other different structures in the mature fetus. This clear developmental sequence of homologous structures, and the fact that it is shared by dogs, pigs, and humans are strong testimony to the ancient fish ancestry of all three species.

However, Haeckel's law is only a guide, not an unfailing indication, of evolutionary descent. In living animals selection may alter and even eliminate certain developmental stages so that the developing embryo may not replicate exactly the evolutionary stages of its species' ancestors, but it may provide important clues to those stages. This embryological view into the past is possible because new species evolving from more primitive forms start out with the adaptations (and their attendant developmental sequence) evolved in their ancestors and use these as the bases from which their novel adaptations develop. We thus can use embryology, comparative anatomy, and paleontology to piece together the major stages of morphological evolution leading to the primates.

Although biological anthropology focuses on primates in general and hominids specifically, it is important to realize that there is little in the paleontological record to support an *anthropocentric* (Greek, meaning "human-centered") view of evolution. Many animal groups, now extinct like the dinosaurs, were larger, fleeter, more numerous, and ecologically dominant for much longer periods of time than hominids have been in existence. More often than not, ancestral hominids were far from the dominant members of the faunas of which they formed a part. The mistaken view that evolution has been a steady progression leading without divergence to culminate in our own species is termed **orthogenesis** (Greek, meaning "straight beginning"). To the contrary, the human morphological heritage attests to the long and frequently tortuous chain of evolutionary events that has led to our being here now.

embryo—the earliest stages of development, from fertilized egg to the differentiation of most of the major structures and organs. In humans the embryonic period is the first three months of development. At the beginning of the fourth month, the embryo is termed a fetus, and enters a phase primarily of growth.

orthogenesis—mistaken view of evolutionary change always proceeding in a "straight-line," directed course.

PHYLUM CHORDATA

As discussed in Chapter 2, the first actively moving organisms, animals, appeared in the earth's seas some time before 700 million years ago. Because these animals' bodies were soft, their remains were easily

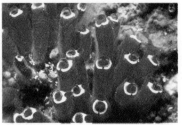

Figure 5–2 • The adult sea squirt (right) is a sedentary animal living attached to the sea floor. Its larval stage (left), however, is free swimming and possesses the defining traits of the Phylum Chordata. Evolutionary differentiation of the chordates likely took place when larval prechordate forms like the sea squirt became able to reproduce (pedogenesis).

destroyed before they could become fossilized. The indications of animal life from this time consist of burrow trails left in the mud of shallow sea floors. Among the animals that made these tracks were the common ancestors of all other living and extinct animal phyla (Figure 2–21). The first **chordates** (see also Chapter 2) must have evolved in the late Archean Era, about 580 million years ago, but the fossil record of this very ancient time is of little help in deciphering chordate beginnings.

Chordates are animals with a stiffened rod of **cartilage** running down the middle of their backs called the *notochord* (Greek, meaning "back string"). They also have nearby a *dorsal nerve cord* in their backs, and a series of *branchial arches* ("gill" arches or the walls of tissue that separate gill clefts or slits). These characteristics are not necessarily found in adult chordates but they do occur at some stage of an individual's development. We are chordates and our most basic patterns of morphological organization have come down to us from our ancient chordate ancestors.

However, in the late Archean Era the dominant animal groups were nonchordates that had evolved the first skeletal elements. These were body coverings with a protective function, probably for defense against attack by predators or worms. Hard parts external to the body cavity, known as the **exoskeleton** (Latin, meaning "outside bony framework"), served as an anchor for muscles as well. Although an exoskeleton is an efficient adaptation for powerful movement, which we can observe today in such living arthropods as insects and crabs, it limits the size of a species. As the animal grows it must "molt," split out of its old exoskeleton and grow another one. If an arthropod is greater in size than a lobster or a large crab, its body cannot retain its integrity during the molting period when there is no support for internal structures.

Other groups, including the ancestors of chordates, did not evolve hard outside coverings. Instead, these prechordates were dome-shaped, soft-bodied animals living attached to the bottom of shallow seas (Figure 5–2). They fed on micro-organisms, which they filtered out

chordates–animals with a notochord and a dorsal nerve cord.

cartilage–a supporting tissue more elastic and flexible than bone; e.g., the "gristle" in meat.

exoskeleton–a hard and inflexible outer covering of the body of invertebrate animals, such as insects and crustaceans.

of the water. Embryological and life-cycle studies of the living sea squirt, which in many ways is similar to these early prechordates, has suggested how our phylum arose.

Although the adult sea squirt is an immobile species that stays attached to the shallow sea bed, its immature form is an active swimmer. This swimming adaptation serves to disperse the population so that at maturity the adults will establish themselves in favorable locations where they settle down and attach to the bottom of the sea. In the swimming stage, the sea squirt has clearly defined head and tail regions, and the tail has a notochord running through it, like chordates and unlike the adult sea squirt. The notochord has zigzag, chevron-shaped muscles attached to it that bend the body from side to side in motions that the animal uses to swim through the water. A nerve cord on the dorsal (back) side of the notochord transmits impulses that activate these muscles. All these immature sea squirt traits are found in adult chordates. However, because the adult sea squirt lacks a notochord, it is classified in a different phylum from chordates, the Phylum Urochordata.

Evolutionary biologists believe that urochordates were the ancestors of chordates. Using the process of **pedogenesis** (Greek, meaning "child origin"), by which forms with immature morphology are able to reproduce, juvenile prechordates gave rise to adult free-swimming chordates. A good living analog to this early ancestor of later chordates is the lancelet, a small gill-feeding and gill-breathing species living in shallow marine environments. The lancelet is an active swimmer, but it has no paired fins or limbs, no jaws, no bones or cartilage, no brain, no ears, and no organs of smell. These adaptations came about in more advanced chordates, the fish.

As chordates, we share at some phase of our development all of the following characteristics with other members of the phylum:

- a solid notochord
- a dorsal nerve chord
- a one or more pairs of branchial or pharyngeal clefts

We share other characteristics with other chordates and with some non-chordates: *bilateral symmetry*—similar right and left sides of the body; *cephalization*—specialization of a head region; a tail at some stage of development; a true *endoskeleton*—a bony or cartilaginous framework overlain by muscle in the body; *segmentation of the body*—similar structural units throughout part or all of the body; and a three-layered structure of *ectoderm, mesoderm, and endoderm* (Latin, meaning "outside," "middle," and "inside skin" during development).

Humans have now lost the solid notochord, but its remnants persist as the semiliquid *nucleus pulposus* (Latin, meaning "pulpy center") of the intervertebral discs of our backbones (Figure 5–3). When we have a "slipped disc" it is this evolutionarily ancient structure that oozes out

pedogenesis—evolution of "child-like" form in adult animals.

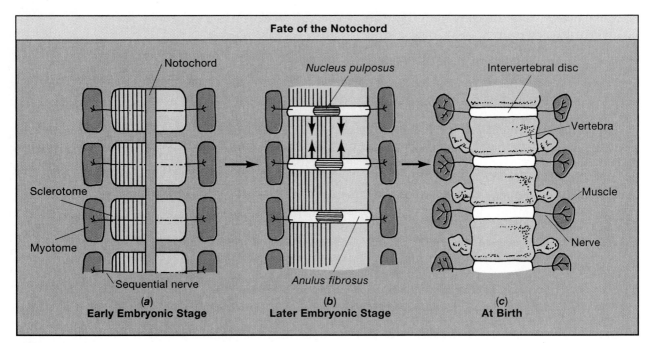

Figure 5–3 • The embryological fate of the human notochord. Early in development (*a*) the human embryo has a clear notochord, like all other chordates, surrounded by mesodermal tissue. At a later stage of development (*b*) the notochord degenerates to form the *nucleus pulposus* of our intervertebral discs, and by the time of birth (*c*) bony vertebrae are formed with the discs in between.

to press against a spinal nerve and causes pain. The early chordate dorsal nerve cord has become greatly enlarged and specialized to become our spinal cord. Branchial clefts, homologous to gill slits in fish, are present in the developing human embryo (Figure 5–4), but they become substantially modified in the mature fetal condition. The auditory ("eustachian") tube (running between the throat and the middle ear) and the ear canal (running between the middle ear and the outside of the head) form the remnants of the cleft between our first and second branchial arches, the tissue divisions between the clefts. That is why we "pop our ears" when undergoing changes in altitude, and hear through a canal originally evolved by our ancient ancestors to filter microorganisms out of sea water. Figure 5–4 shows what happens to the other branchial clefts and arches during embryological development.

We retain the bilateral symmetry that separates us from the *radially symmetrical* (able to be cut up into equal-sized parts from a central point fanning outward) starfish group (the coelenterates) and the differentiation of head region and the internal skeleton of our early chordate ancestors. Much of body segmentation has been lost, but our vertebrae, ribs, sensory nerve distribution, and patterns of certain muscles, such as *rectus abdominis* (Figure 5–5), show this heritage. Furthermore, we have a tail until the eighth week of embryonic development.

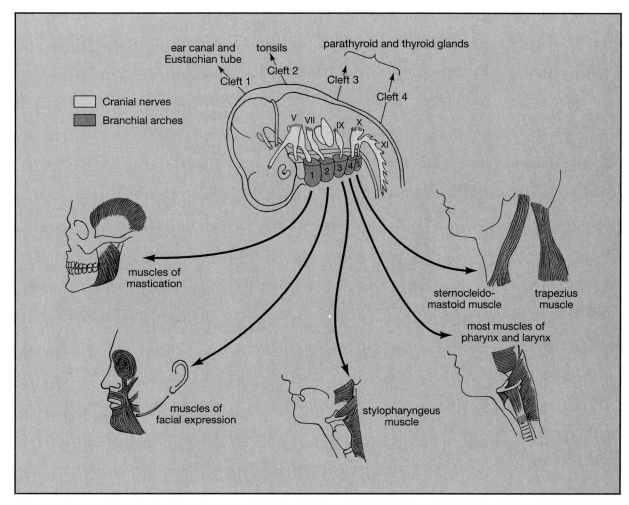

Figure 5–4 • Adult development of cranial musculature from the embryonic branchial arches.

THE FIRST VERTEBRATES: OUR FISH HERITAGE

When environmental conditions change so significantly that major ecological niches are opened up, then evolution proceeds to rapidly fill those niches. "Fanning out" of species in *adaptive radiations,* resulting in occupation of new niches and the formation of new species (see Chapter 1), have occurred numerous times throughout the history of life. They seem to follow periods of significant environmental change and large-scale extinctions. Adaptive radiations may also be related to new adaptations that appear in a species. This chapter will describe several cases of adaptive radiations that are relevant to human evolution.

Near the beginning of the Paleozoic Era, the so-named "Age of Fish," (some 570 million years ago) there was a major adaptive radiation of

Figure 5–5 • Although much of the human body's segmentation has been lost over the course of evolution, our bodies still show some segmentation and bilateral symmetry.

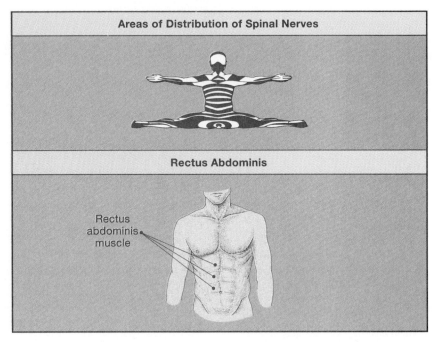

animals. This explosion of new forms may have been the result of increasingly high levels of oxygen in the environment. More oxygen in the water created new ecological niches that could be exploited by new, more active animal species with higher metabolisms. Gill-feeding, gill-breathing, free-swimming chordates appeared at this time, about 550 million years ago. They were the ancestors of the vertebrates.

The first **vertebrates** (animals that have "vertebrae" or backbone segments) in the fossil record are very primitive, small fish. They are called **agnathans** (Greek, meaning "without jaws"). They fed on the bottom of shallow bodies of fresh water through a mouth unsupported by bone or cartilage, filtering micro-organisms and extracting oxygen from the water taken in and expelled through their gills. Because they possessed a series of bony vertebrae articulated into a backbone, they are the earliest animals that we can consider members of the Subphylum Vertebrata. Vertebrates are chordate animals that share the following characteristics (Smith, 1960; Figure 5–6):

- a bony vertebral column
- a cranium
- a brain of three primary parts, or vesicles
- olfactory organs, for sense of smell
- true eyes
- a true skin of dermis and epidermis
- details of internal organs (heart, kidney, liver, pancreas, ear, and pharynx)
- details of reproduction

vertebrates—animals with backbones and segmented body plans.

agnathans—primitive, "jawless" fish.

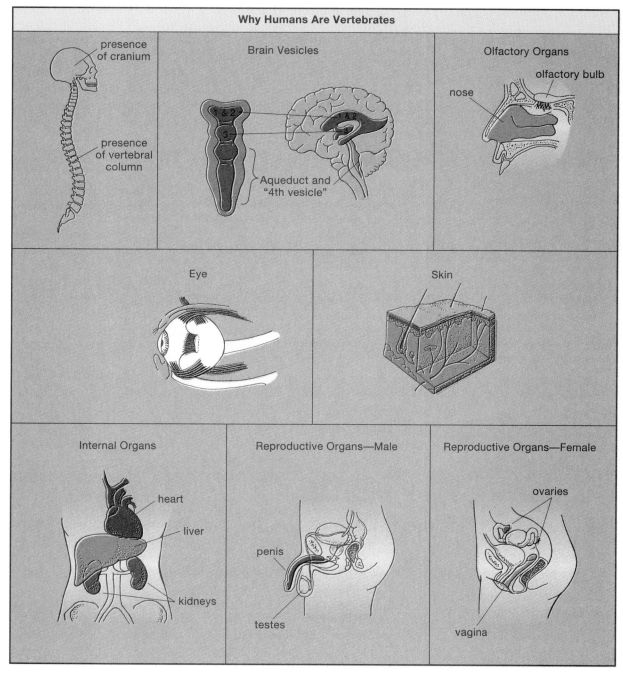

Why Humans Are Vertebrates

Figure 5–6 • A summary diagram of vertebrate traits.

The evolution of these characteristics has been reconstructed partly through the use of embryology and partly through the use of paleontology. The co-occurrence of these features is found first among small agnathan fish of the Silurian Period (430 to 390 million years ago). The morphology of these earliest vertebrates forms the ground plan for the evolutionary modifications that characterize the many different groups of backboned animals. To understand our own anatomy, we must understand the anatomy of our early vertebrate ancestors.

The Evolution of a Bony Skeleton

Why did ostracoderms evolve skeletons of bone and cartilage? One likely explanation is that a rigid backbone provided a frame firmer than the primitive notochord for swimming movements. Skeletal support also allowed the attainment of large body size, which was advantageous in avoiding predation: the larger an animal, the fewer the predators that can eat it.

The bones in our bodies are divisible into two categories: **cartilage bone** and **membrane bone,** depending on how they ossify, or turn into bone. We have inherited both types from our ostracoderm ancestors. Vertebrae and most other *postcranial* (Latin, meaning "behind the head") bones are cartilage bones because they develop from a cartilage base, with bone cells replacing the cartilage cells during bone formation. Growth of cartilage bones takes place at lines of growth called *epiphyses.* In this way vertebrates increase in size as they grow while the skeleton continues to support the body. Membrane bone, on the other hand, lacks epiphyses and instead develops within a net-like membrane. Membrane bone forms from gradual replacement by bone cells within this sheet of mesodermal tissue.

Membrane bones first evolved in the ostracoderms as head armor, most likely to protect them from attacks by predators. Their enemies were likely giant, six-foot, fresh-water scorpions with pincers almost a foot long. By contrast, our ancestors during the Silurian were a mere six inches in length. Membrane bones in the head provide the foundation for the top part of the cranium in all vertebrates. The bones forming the part of our skull that holds the brain, the **neurocranium** (Latin, meaning "brain skull") are membrane bones (see Chapter 2).

The ostracoderms possessed an improved sensory apparatus compared to their chordate ancestors. They had brains that, though tiny by comparison with those of modern fish, had three separate parts, or *vesicles,* the possession of which is a common trait of all more complex vertebrate brains. They had true eyes, not only sensitive to light but able to discern form and movement. They also had a sense of smell. This increased efficiency in sensing environmental stimuli and processing this information probably aided them in obtaining food and avoiding predators.

cartilage bone–bone formed by development from cartilage and growth at epiphyses, characteristic of vertebrate limb bones.

membrane bone–bone formed by development from a connective tissue membrane, characteristic of vertebrate skull bones.

neurocranium–that part of the skull holding the brain.

Early Life in Fresh Water

A major change in the environment occurred between the early chordates and the ostracoderms. Whereas the chordates were sea dwellers, the ostracoderms became adapted to life on the bottom of fresh-water ponds, rivers, or lakes. We know this partly from the physiology of another part of our heritage from the earliest vertebrates—the kidney.

When the first vertebrates moved to a fresh-water environment during the Ordovician Period, their systems were still adapted to ocean salinity. The fresh-water environment did not readily provide the salts that had been obtained easily from sea water. Salts entered the body at irregular intervals and in unpredictable quantities, mainly from food, leading to a potentially dangerous excess or lack of salt in the animal's system at any one time. Therefore in these early fresh-water vertebrates, the kidneys had to take on the function of maintaining a balance of salt-water-adapted internal systems within their new fresh-water environment. Some amount of salt was necessary to ensure the proper functioning of the body. However, when excess salt entered the system, the kidney reacted to it as a poisonous substance to be removed from the blood and excreted from the body. The kidney used large quantities of fresh water to "flush out" excess salts from the internal environment. Because fresh-water was the medium in which the animal lived, the kidney was never lacking in enough liquid to accomplish this task.

Interestingly, the concentration of salts in our bodies closely corresponds with that estimated for the Ordovician seas, when we last shared a common marine ancestor with the lancelet and other chordates. Salt content of the oceans has slowly increased over the millenia because of erosion from the land and dissolution of salt minerals from terrestrial rocks. Because our ancestors left the sea to live in fresh water when its salinity was less than it is today, we cannot exist in equilibrium with modern sea water. This fact is graphically illustrated by shipwrecked sailors who, when overcome by thirst, drink sea water and die of dehydration much more quickly than if they drink nothing at all. This is because our "fresh-water" kidney is adapted to excreting excess salts with water. If there is too much salt in the body, the kidneys pump out all the body's remaining water in the attempt to get rid of it. Our vertebrate relatives, such as modern fish, which have reinvaded the seas, have evolved special mechanisms—salt glands, for example—to extract excess salts that enter their bodies from surrounding sea water.

Evolution of Biting Jaws

The agnathans were jawless fish. We must look to the next stage of our vertebrate heritage to understand the fascinating story behind the evolution of our own jaws and teeth. Fish with biting jaws, called **placoderms** (Latin, meaning "plate-skinned"), first appeared in the Devon-

placoderms—early fish with biting jaws.

ian Period, about 400 million years ago. How and why did their jaws evolve?

The upper and lower jaws of placoderms evolved from the first two **branchial arches.** This development is apparent from the earliest Devonian shark fossils and from the embryology of living vertebrates. The earliest placoderms (and their descendents, the modern sharks) have the upper jaw still separate from the cranium, whereas later more advanced vertebrates have it firmly attached. Our skull is a welding together of the neurocranium and the part derived from the branchial arches, the **splanchnocranium.** Strangely, our teeth do not come from the branchial arches. Embryology shows that they are derived from ectodermal tissue instead, that is, from the hardened parts of the skin surrounding the mouth. The evolution of biting jaws and sharp teeth signal that placoderms had become predatory, feeding on other fish and invertebrates. Predation allows a species to take advantage of "prepackaged" food of higher quality (other animals) but in smaller quantities, rather than eating widely scattered, lower quality but usually more abundant food (such as plant food) in larger quantities. It also creates changes in body shape. For example, to prevent placoderms from turning in the water, pairs of laterally placed fins evolved from flaps of skin and muscle from the body wall. Two pairs of fins, one in front and one behind, constituted the preadaptation that later fish were to employ to conquer the land. These fins evolved into limbs.

Evolution of Limbs and Lungs

During the Devonian Period (390–340 million years ago), the first modern fish evolved. They are called the lobe-finned fish, the **sarcopterygians** (Greek, meaning "fleshy appendage"). They had, as their name implies, thick and fleshy lateral fins (Figure 5–7), which were inefficient by the standards of modern, streamlined fish, but were an effective and important part of their adaptation to a fresh water environment.

Lobe-finned fish were mainly fresh-water species. Some lived in ponds and streams subjected to periodic drought, a situation common in semi-arid parts of the tropics today. Their stout back and front fins consisting of heavy bone allowed them to support their bodies on land and to slither from a drying pond to one with more water. The anatomy of these types of fish form the basic plan on which all later land vertebrate limbs evolved.

As part of the adaptation to periodic drought, lobe-finned fish evolved an *air bladder,* an outpocketing of the pharynx into which air was gulped. The air bladder extracted oxygen from the air, and allowed the fish to make the overland trek necessary for it to reach its normal environment, water. With relatively little modification in basic plan, the lobe-fin lung became the air-breathing lung of the land vertebrates. This primitive air bladder assumed another use entirely in the successful descendents of the early sarcopterygians, the ray-finned fish

branchial arches–the tissue in between the gill slits in the embryos of vertebrates.

splanchnocranium–that part of the skull holding the mouth and jaws.

sarcopterygians–lobe-finned fish who were capable of supporting their bodies on land by the use of stout fins.

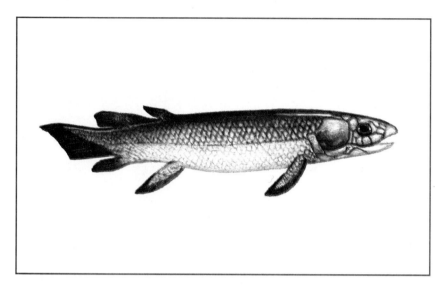

Figure 5–7 • Side view of a sarcopterygian fish.

(our familiar trout, bass, and flounder). Here it became a gas-filled pouch used to vary the density of the fish's body, and thus to control its depth in water.

The adaptations of the lobe-finned fish represent the first important steps away from a watery life. For sarcopterygians, their adaptation was one ensuring continuity of life in the water. Nevertheless, it was a compromise between water and land habitation, out of which evolution later produced more effective adaptations to both. The sarcopterygians eventually went extinct (except for one known surviving marine species, the coelacanth). Now that we have shown how much of our basic body plan we owe to our fish ancestors, we turn our interest to the progressive refinements in adaptation to terrestrial life that we see in amphibians and reptiles, the descendents of the lobe-finned fish.

FIRST FORAYS ONTO DRY LAND: THE AMPHIBIANS

The Class **Amphibia** (Greek, meaning "dual life") comprises vertebrates that are essentially land-living fish, inexorably tied to water because of their mode of reproduction. Amphibians lay eggs in water and their larvae are swimming, gill-breathing forms that die if exposed to air. Modern day amphibians, such as frogs and salamanders, show this type of reproduction. Only in the adult stage do stout limbs develop that are capable of supporting the animal's body on land. Still, most amphibians today live in habitats close to water because their breeding pattern requires it, and commonly their skins must be moist as they are subject to rapid water loss by evaporation. Our knowledge of the fossil record suggests that the earliest amphibians in the Denovian Period, the first land vertebrates, also lived in wet, swampy forests (Figure 5–8).

Amphibia—class of vertebrates that includes frogs, salamanders, and extinct species living much of their lives on land but whose reproduction remains tied to water.

Figure 5–8 • Reconstruction of the Devonian paleoenvironment and a labyrinthodont amphibian (*Ichthyostega*) from the late Devonian of Greenland.

The best known of these early amphibians are the **labyrinthodonts** (Latin, meaning "labyrinthine [very complex] tooth"), animals superficially similar to crocodiles but much more primitive (Figure 5–8). Their heads were covered by armor and most of their internal organs were similarly fish-like. They lived in the swamp forests of the Carboniferous Period (340–270 million years ago), from which much of the world's coal-bearing deposits were formed. The labyrinthodonts were predators and hunted fish in nearby waters.

The limbs of the labyrinthodonts show the greatest departure from the structure of their fish ancestors. The proximal elements (bones nearer the body) of both front and back limbs are single (the humerus and femur, respectively), and the distal elements (bones farther from the body) are paired (the radius and ulna, and tibia and fibula, respectively; see Figure 5–9 and Appendix A). There are small blocky bones making up the hand and foot skeletons, and five digits on each. We share this primitive skeletal arrangement and associated musculature with the labyrinthodonts and with all land vertebrates. In fact, primate limbs, especially the forelimbs, are more like the primitive amphibian limbs than are those of most other vertebrate groups. Compare your hand with that of a salamander, then compare it with that of a horse.

The early amphibians also differed from their fish ancestors by their acquisition of a true ear mechanism. Fish detect vibrations in the water through their skull bones with a sensory apparatus similar to our inner ear. The amphibians developed the ear drum, a membrane of skin stretched over the first gill slit, to pick up vibrations in the air. A bone of the jaw (the hyomandibular) became attached to the ear drum and

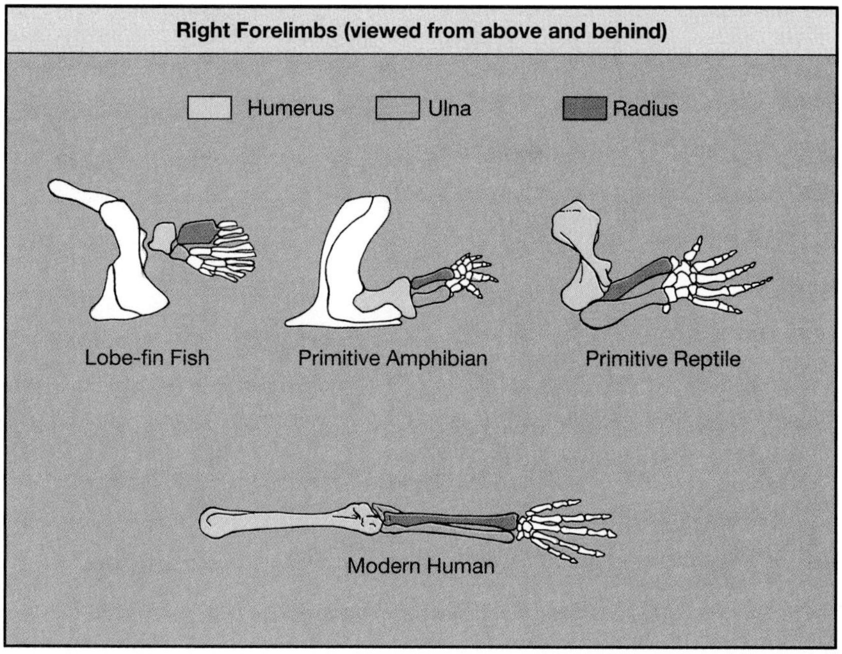

labyrinthodonts—extinct, predatory amphibians of the Carboniferous Period some of whom were ancestral to the first reptiles.

Right Forelimbs (viewed from above and behind)

☐ Humerus   ☐ Ulna   ■ Radius

Lobe-fin Fish   Primitive Amphibian   Primitive Reptile

Modern Human

Figure 5–9 • Comparison of forelimb bones to show homologies from lobe-fins through amphibians and reptiles to mammals (modern humans).

Figure 5–10 • Comparison of vertebrate ear regions to show origins of mammalian middle ear bones.

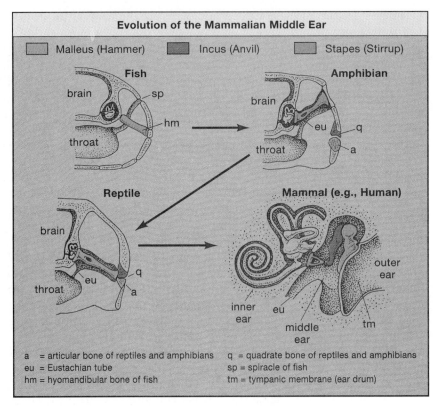

Evolution of the Mammalian Middle Ear

Malleus (Hammer)   Incus (Anvil)   Stapes (Stirrup)

a   = articular bone of reptiles and amphibians   q = quadrate bone of reptiles and amphibians
eu = Eustachian tube   sp = spiracle of fish
hm = hyomandibular bone of fish   tm = tympanic membrane (ear drum)

transmitted the vibrations to the inner ear. This jaw bone has become the stirrup bone (stapes) found in our own middle ear (Figure 5–10).

By the end of the Carboniferous Period, the large amphibians had decreased in numbers. By the Triassic Period, only small species related to frogs and salamanders survived. Today's amphibians form a relatively insignificant part of vertebrate diversity, and they are substantially changed from their early ancestors. Coincident with the demise of the early amphibians was the ascendency of the reptiles, a group much better adapted to full terrestrial life.

REPTILES CONQUER THE LAND

Why did land life evolve? As we have seen, the process was initiated by the need of water-living animals to move overland from a drying body of water to one which could sustain them. But what selective forces would have acted to create the reptiles, who for the most part are fully terrestrial? The answer lies in the paleoecology of the Paleozoic Era (570–220 million years ago).

At the onset of the reptiles, in the Carboniferous Period, the waters were teeming with life while the land was relatively unpopulated. Amphibian eggs and larvae became subjected to new difficulties in their aqueous environment, because as living forms diversified and grew in numbers, more and more species preyed on defenseless eggs and larvae. As we have seen, the Paleozoic Era was a time of marked seasonal droughts, when ponds and streams could dry up completely, killing all the eggs and larvae living in them. Even if eggs survived to maturity and larvae escaped predation, competition for food in the water environment was intense.

These problems were solved for reptiles with the evolution of the **amniote egg,** which was laid and hatched on land. Reptile offspring thus had a much higher chance of survival and were favored by natural selection. Although the earliest reptiles still lived close to water and preyed on water-living species as their amphibian ancestors had done, the land-laid egg eliminated the need for reproduction in water, and thereby served as one important preadaptation that led to the adaptive radiation of land vertebrates.

The amniote egg takes its name from an inside membrane, the *amnion,* that surrounds and protects the developing embryo (Figure 5–11). It has an analogous function to the entire egg of amphibians. In amphibians, the developing embryo receives oxygen and food, and releases wastes, through the egg wall, in direct connection with the surrounding water. The water also protects the embryo from mechanical injury. Because reptilian eggs are laid outside water, four additional structures have evolved to carry out these functions: (1) the *shell* provides the interface between the dry air and the wet ancestral amphibian environment, as well as protects the egg from breakage; (2) the *chorion* is a membrane just inside the shell that takes in oxygen and gives off carbon dioxide through the shell, which is actually porous (If one immerses the egg of a growing reptile or bird embryo in water, it will drown.); (3) the *allantois* grows from the posterior end of the embryo and forms a sac into which body wastes are deposited; and, (4) the *yolk sac* is attached to the digestive tract of the embryo, providing nourishment throughout its development. Because of the yolk and other structures a single amniote egg is much larger than an amphibian egg.

The first vertebrates to develop the land-egg were the **cotylosaurs** or "stem reptiles," which lived alongside the more abundant amphibian groups in the Carboniferous Period, and survived until the Permian Period (270–220 million years ago) (Figure 5–12). They not only lived in the same swampy environments as their amphibian cousins but probably had very similar lifestyles, as attested to by the similarities in their skeletal structures.

Adaptive Radiation of The Reptiles

From the stem reptiles evolved the wide diversity of more advanced reptiles that characterized the Mesozoic Era (220–70 million years ago), referred to as "the Age of Reptiles": shark-like ichthyosaurs, lizards and snakes, marine plesiosaurs, mammal-like reptiles, dinosaurs, and even-

amniote egg–an egg characteristic of the reptiles that could be laid and developed out of water.

cotylosaurs–"stem reptiles;" the earliest reptiles whose skulls like modern turtles had solid roofs; classified in Subclass Anapsida.

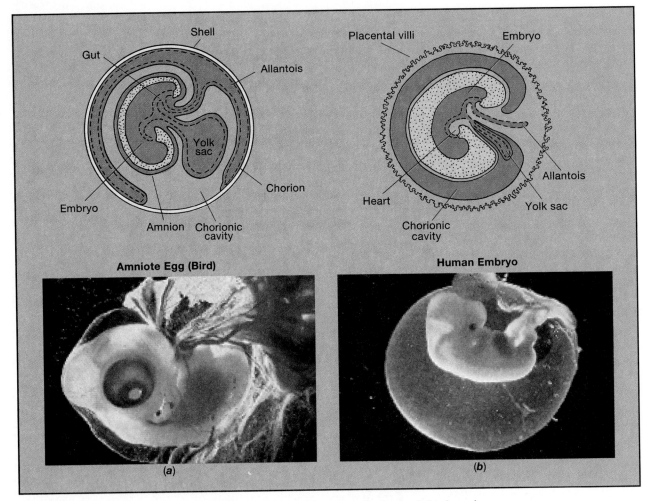

Figure 5–11 • (*a*) The amniote egg structure, inherited from reptiles by both birds and mammals; (*b*) the human embryo with homologous parts labeled.

mammal-like reptiles—reptiles with a skull opening behind the eye (Subclass Synapsida) and with differentiated teeth.

tually birds (Figure 5–12). The **mammal-like reptiles,** described by paleontologist Alfred Romer as appearing to be "an odd cross between a lizard and a dog," lived between the late Carboniferous and the Triassic Periods (290–190 million years ago). They signal some of the major and most fundamental changes in skull and jaw form, teeth, and limbs that separate reptile from mammal (Figure 5–13).

The Evolution of Skull, Teeth, and Limbs

Skull form in the mammal-like reptiles is the key to understanding their ancestral relationship to the mammals (Figure 5–14). The primitive condition is a rounded plate of head armor, as is found in lobe-finned fish, amphibians, and stem reptiles. In order to allow for expansion of the

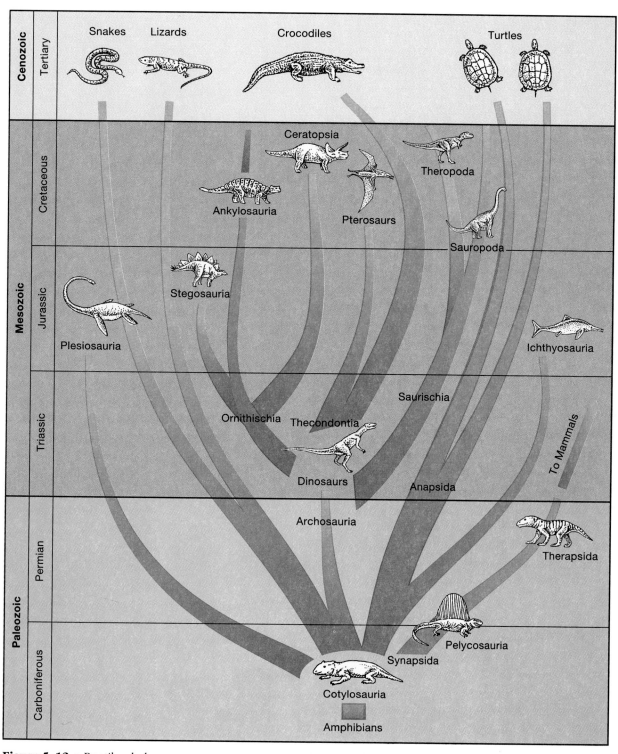

Figure 5–12 • Reptile phylogeny.

Figure 5–13 • Reconstruction of the Permian paleoenvironment and mammal-like reptiles: two *Scylacosaurus* challenging *Dinartamus*.

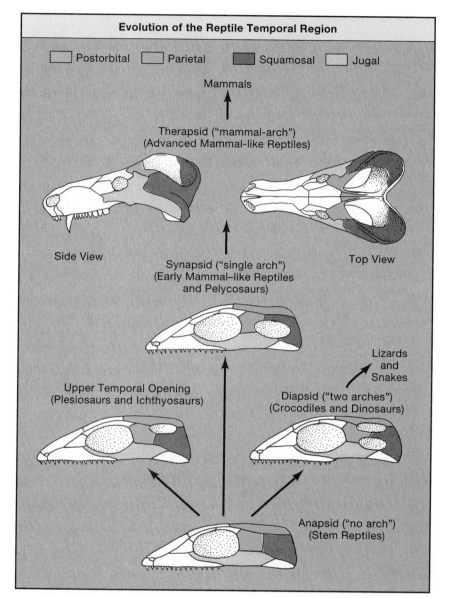

Evolution of the Reptile Temporal Region

☐ Postorbital ☐ Parietal ■ Squamosal ☐ Jugal

Mammals

Therapsid ("mammal-arch")
(Advanced Mammal-like Reptiles)

Side View   Top View

Synapsid ("single arch")
(Early Mammal–like Reptiles
and Pelycosaurs)

Upper Temporal Opening
(Plesiosaurs and Ichthyosaurs)

Lizards
and
Snakes

Diapsid ("two arches")
(Crocodiles and Dinosaurs)

Anapsid ("no arch")
(Stem Reptiles)

Figure 5–14 • Classification of skull form in reptiles is based on the formation of temporal arches. The mammalian temporal region evolved from the therapsid pattern.

contracting temporal muscles during chewing, holes developed in the outside bony head plate of the various reptile lineages. These mammal-like reptiles are called **synapsids** ("single arch") because they exhibit a single hole low in the temporal region and a single arch. The arch becomes more pronounced in the later mammal-like reptiles, the **therapsids** (Latin, meaning "mammal-arch"). It is the homologue of our cheek bone.

The jaws and teeth of the mammal-like reptiles also show progressive features. All the bones of the jaw except the tooth-bearing part, the dentary, were reduced. This is the only bone forming the jaw in mammals. Unlike the more primitive reptiles, which had simple cone-like teeth,

synapsids–mammal-like reptiles characterized by a single temporal arch in their skulls, homologous to the cheek bone or zygomatic arch of mammals.

therapsids–a group of synapsid mammal-like reptiles of The Permian and Triassic periods; ancestral forms to later mammals.

heterodonty–the condition of possessing teeth differentiated for different functions; contrasted with the homodont dentition of many reptiles, such as living crocodiles.

therapsids had teeth of different form and function in different parts of the mouth. They had front *incisors* for cutting and nipping, single *canines* for puncturing, and back teeth for chewing. This condition is a clear precursor to the **heterodonty** ("different teeth") characteristic of mammals.

Limb structure and the mode of walking (locomotion) in the therapsids showed marked advances over those of their ancestors. The limbs grew longer and moved from positions at the side of the body to underneath it. The vertically aligned skeleton of the limb (Figure 5–15) supported the body above the ground, rather than having the body supported by muscular contraction of the limbs alone. When muscles contracted in the limbs, they now acted to propel the animal forward rather than lift it up off the ground—a much more efficient adaptation to terrestrial locomotion. This development allowed the therapsids to become relatively fleet terrestrial predators, the first ancestors in our lineage not entirely dependent on aquatic sources of food.

The mammal-like reptiles were a successful group and speciated into many different niches—herbivorous and carnivorous, large and small (Figure 5–13). During the Triassic Period, however, they largely died out, probably in ecological competition with the very successful dinosaurs. Only a few small and insignificant species survived, scurrying about in the shadows of their ponderous contemporaries. These evolved into the first mammals.

Figure 5–15 • Compared to quadrupedal reptiles, early mammals showed more efficient locomotor adaptations. In mammals, the limbs moved to a position underneath the body and closer to the median plane, resulting in an increase in speed. At the same time, the side-to-side bending motion of reptiles was reduced.

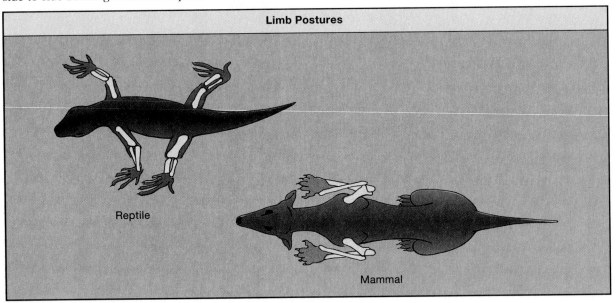

MAMMALS EVOLVE AND RADIATE

We live today in a world replete with many varieties of warm-blooded, large-brained, haired animals that nurse their young: members of the Class Mammalia. Such is the diversity of advanced mammals that it is at first difficult to believe that they are all descended from common ancestral populations that radiated only at the beginning of the Cenozoic Era, "the Age of Mammals," some 70 million years ago. Primates, including our ancestors, are a product of this great adaptive radiation.

A long apprenticeship, however, preceded the age of mammals. In fact, two-thirds of mammalian evolution occurred in the Mesozoic Era, for the first archaic mammals appeared in the Jurassic Period, some 200 million years ago. During much of early mammalian evolution, reptiles were the ecologically dominant life form on earth. During much of this long period the mammalian ancestors of humans were small, rat-sized, insect-eaters that lived primarily in trees and hunted at night (Figure 5–16). Their fossil record is poorly known, but some of their major evolutionary advances can be reconstructed.

The first mammals are identified by their teeth, which, unlike those of the earlier reptiles, possessed a heterodontic pattern. These teeth can be differentiated into incisors, canines, premolars, and molars (Figure 5–17). The molars have a triangular outline with three well-defined cusps. The ridges between the cusps on upper and lower molars slice past each other as the mouth is closed, affording an effective mechanism for cutting up and chewing food. From this basic design all other mammalian chewing teeth have evolved.

New Reproductive Strategies

The earliest mammals may have been egg-laying, as their reptilian ancestors had been. In fact, the two most primitive living mammals, the platypus and the spiny anteater, which live in Australia, bear their young in

Figure 5–16 • Reconstructed view of an early mammal (*Megazostrodon*) from the late Jurassic of North America.

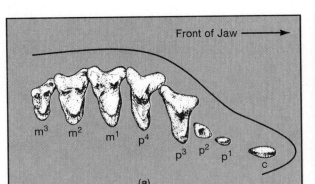
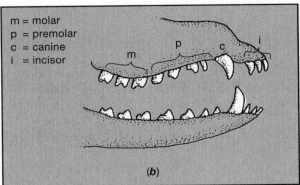

Figure 5–17 • Early mammal heterodont dentition: (*a*) looking up, occlusal view of upper teeth of Cretaceous mammal *Zalambdolestes;* (*b*) generalized reconstruction of an early mammal, showing side view of upper and lower jaw.

this way. But many eggs after being laid are lost to predators, even if they have been well-concealed or if they are guarded by their parents. Because the general history of mammalian (and primate) reproduction is one of greater protection of progeny, in the Mesozoic Era, a new type of reproduction evolved in which young were born alive. Mammal mothers retained the reptile-type egg internally in special structures in their body where the embryo developed. The result was that the egg was better protected, and thus, mammalian offspring survived at higher rates. Because predation was still high on newborn and immature mammals, selection favored offspring who were protected by their parents (or some other adult) until they were capable of making their own way.

During the Cretaceous Period the **marsupials** (Latin, meaning "pouch" [*marsupium*]) and the **placentals** (referring to the membranous structure in the uterus, the *placenta,* that provides prenatal nourishment to the developing embryo and fetus), the two dominant forms of mammals, appeared. Marsupials were the more common of the mammals during the Cretaceous (125–70 million years ago), when the dinosaurs still reigned. They have survived in greatest abundance in Australia and South America, where they have avoided competition with placentals because of the isolation of these two land masses. The marsupials are pouched mammals, two living examples of which are the opossum and the kangaroo. They bear their young in a very immature state of development after a brief period of gestation. The baby then climbs tenuously along the mother's abdomen into the pouch and clasps onto a teat (*mamma,* from which the name of the class derives), where it nurses until ready to emerge fully developed.

Although the marsupials' reproductive adaptation did little more than internalize the reptilian egg and nurture the young externally, the more advanced placental mammals internalized both processes and improved on the method of nurturance of the embryo. The chorion, a membrane that surrounds the embryo, became fused with the wall of the mother's

marsupials–pouched mammals.

placentals–evolved mammals with a very efficient reproductive system, which includes a placenta, a structure that provides the developing embryo with well-oxygenated blood.

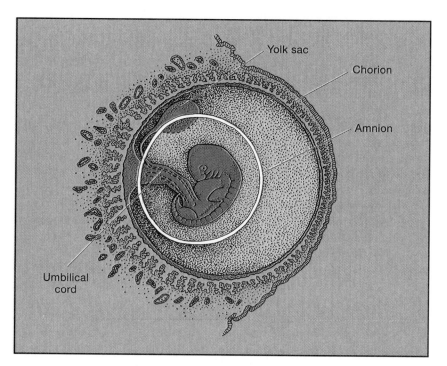

Figure 5–18 • Human embryo at about five weeks, showing umbilical cord attachment to the placenta.

Labels in figure: Yolk sac, Chorion, Amnion, Umbilical cord

uterus, forming the placenta, richly supplied with blood vessels (Figure 5–18). The placenta attaches to the embryo via the *umbilical cord,* carrying oxygen and nutrients to the embryo and carrying wastes away. That placental form of gestation proved ultimately more successful, is evidenced by the placental species' having generally replaced marsupials when they have come face-to-face in ecological competition.

Homeothermy

The Mesozoic mammals physiologically were probably capable of maintaining their internal body temperature at a more constant level than their reptilian ancestors had been able to do. This ability is termed **homeothermy** (Latin, meaning "same heat"), more commonly "warm blooded," and it allowed mammals to be active during relatively cool periods, such as at night. Similar-sized (small) reptiles today are quiescent when they are cold, and must raise their body temperature behaviorally through activities such as sunning themselves. Homeotherms use muscular contraction (in movements and shivering), constriction and dilation of surface blood vessels, sweating, panting, and insulation by hair to maintain body temperature. Not all mammals use all of these methods of heat regulation. For example, higher primates (see Chapter 6) are among the few mammals that sweat, and humans have lost the insulating effect of body hair ("goose bumps" are the physiological vestige of standing our hairs on end in cold situations). Warm-bloodedness allowed a greater range of activities, particularly in hunting and escape

homeothermy–the maintenance of constant body temperature; "warm blooded."

from predators, and especially at night and in cooler seasons of the year in temperate regions. Two other nonmammalian groups independently evolved homeothermy—the birds and at least some of the dinosaurs. Even if the latter lacked many of the physiological modifications of the mammals, the heat conserved in their huge bodies, relative to skin surface area, would have tended to make them facultatively warm blooded.

As part of their more active physiology, mammals evolved a heart and circulatory system that kept oxygenated and deoxygenated blood streams separated, and created greater blood pressure. Because more oxygen and more blood could be delivered to the tissues per unit of time, a higher **metabolic rate** (oxygen consumption and energy production) was possible. The ancestral fish circulation was a simple pumping mechanism, with the *ventricle* pushing blood through two systems of capillaries: first to the gills to pick up oxygen and then to the body to nourish the tissues and pick up waste carbon dioxide. With the advent of the air-breathing lung, a three-chambered heart evolved. The right and left *atria* received blood from the body (deoxygenated blood) and lungs (oxygenated blood), respectively. Blood from the two atria then emptied into the single ventricle, which in turn pumped the blood to both the body and the lungs. This system had the advantage of increasing blood pressure, but the disadvantage of mixing the oxygenated blood and deoxygenated blood in the ventricle. In mammals, as well as in some advanced reptiles and birds, the four-chambered heart evolved in which one side of the heart pumps oxygenated blood and the other deoxygenated blood. Occasionally, human infants are born with incomplete separation of the right and left sides of the heart, a condition recalling the old "mixed" circulation pattern. Because the tissues become oxygen-starved and the babies cannot maintain normal body temperature, they exhibit a noticeable pallor on account of which they are called "blue babies."

Enlarged Brain and Related Structures

The earliest mammals had as one of their major adaptations a significantly enlarged brain for their body size compared to that of the reptiles. The enlargement was not general, but particularly observable in a part of the brain originally concerned with smell, the *cerebrum*. The cerebrum assumed new and expanded functions in the mammals. Sensory information—visual, auditory, taste, and smell—were recorded and remembered in the outside part, the *cerebral cortex*. This increased memory and ability to receive and act upon environmental information with effective behavior became an important component in mammalian adaptation. In Chapter 6, we discuss how this trend intensified in the primates and especially in the apes and ourselves.

Along with changes in the brain, the shape of the skull changed in mammals. The neurocranium expanded to hold the larger brain. A new

metabolic rate–the rate at which energy is expended in all the chemical reactions in an animal's cells and tissues.

design of the head articulating to the vertebral column became perfected in the mammals. Instead of a centrally located bony projection, the *condyle,* on the back of the skull, two condyles developed on both sides of the opening for the spinal cord. This formed a more stable joint and enabled faster, more accurate movements of the head, needed in animals that dispatch prey with their teeth. A *hard palate* evolved to separate the nasal air passages from the oral food passages thus allowing mammals to maintain their oxygen supply while eating. In most reptiles the nostrils open directly into the mouth.

The mammalian jaw, or **mandible,** became a stronger structure, being formed by only a single bone. Greater force could be exerted in biting and chewing. Two of the old reptilian jaw bones assumed a new function in the mammals. They became ear bones: the *malleus* (hammer bone) and the *incus* (anvil bone) of our middle ear (Figure 5–10). The malleus attaches the ear drum to the incus, and the incus connects to the *stapes* (stirrup bone), the third middle ear bone that first evolved in the amphibians. Sound is amplified by this system of bony levers, which constitutes a finely tuned hearing mechanism in the mammals. External "fleshy" ears are a mammalian characteristic. They function to catch and conduct the sound waves to the ear drum.

THE HUMAN BRAIN IN EVOLUTIONARY PERSPECTIVE

Like other parts of our anatomy the brain has been evolutionarily constructed using structures inherited from earlier ancestors. Within our brains we have parts that basically think like our fish, amphibian, reptilian, and mammalian ancestors, although evolution has also undoubtedly acted to change particular details to fit into the functioning of the whole brain.

The phenomenon of "blindsight" is a vivid example of phylogenetically old pathways surviving in the human mind. Research on veterans of World War I by Gordon Holmes in Ireland showed that injuries to the back part of the cerebrum in the occipital lobe resulted in blindspots in the visual field. Much later neurological research (Weiskrantz, et al., 1974) revealed that a patient with an occipital lobe injury causing a visual field blindspot could point accurately to a spot of light shone within the "blind" area of the visual field. The patients were using "unconscious" neural tracts that connect the eyes, subcortical areas of the brain ("below the cortex" of the cerebrum), and the hands. These neural tracts are primitive parts of the brain inherited from early vertebrate ancestors and were in existence long before the evolution of our enlarged cerebral hemispheres. A modern frog uses a similar mechanism to locate and catch a fly with its tongue.

Paul MacLean of the National Institute of Mental Health has shown that the human brain is a three-part **triune brain** (Figure 5–19), each part of which is a legacy of a different stage of development in the hu-

mandible–the lower jaw of mammals, composed of a fusion of the reptile dentary and articular bones.

triune brain–a model devised by Paul MacLean of the workings of the human brain into three broad divisions based on phylogenetic and functional patterns.

R-Complex–the most primitive, "reptilian" part of the "triune brain" model of Paul MacLean; the site of certain ritualistic, stereotypical, and social communication behaviors.

basal ganglia–structures in the forebrain of vertebrates that form part of the R-Complex.

man evolutionary story. These three stages are built on the most ancient "neural chassis"—the spinal cord, mid- and hind-brains–that are inherited from our fish and amphibian ancestors. With these most ancient parts of our brains, we breathe, run our hearts, and have instincts for survival and reproduction. The first part of the triune brain is the reptilian brain.

The R-Complex

The reptiles of 250 million years ago possessed several evolutionary advances in brain function over their amphibian forerunners. The **R-Complex** ("R" standing for reptilian) is in the base of the forebrain of all reptiles, birds and mammals and is made up of several structures, termed **basal ganglia.** A *ganglion* (Greek, meaning "knot" or "swelling") is a concentration of nerve cell connections, identified (Figure 5–19) as the *corpus striatum* (Latin, meaning "striped body"), *olfactostriatum* (Latin, meaning "smell striped part" from its olfactory function), and *globus pallidus* (Latin, meaning "pale sphere"). The R-Complex is rich in concentrations of the protein *dopamine,* the "neural sap" necessary for releasing energy; the neural transmitter *serotonin; cholinesterase,* a protein that helps to transmit signals across synapses; and the opium-like *endorphins.*

Figure 5–19 • View of the "triune brain." (From MacLean, 1990)

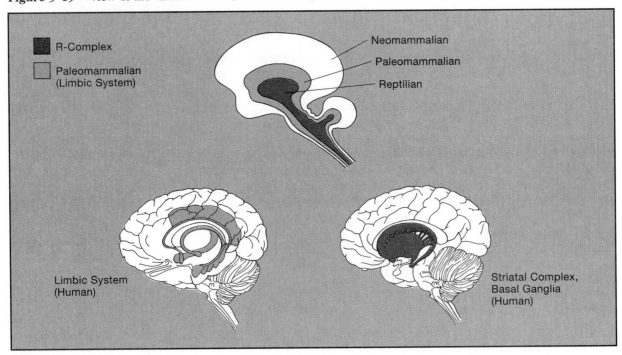

What parts of our thoughts and actions can be traced to this ancient and still functioning part of our brains? What does the R-Complex do? Neurologists believe that the basal ganglia are involved in transmitting or processing signals from the motor cortex to the muscles, because disorders in physical skills result when other, similar ganglia in the midbrain are damaged. But MacLean (1982) has pointed out that destruction by disease or injury of large parts of the R-Complex does not result in motor deficits, nor does electrical stimulation of R-Complex structures result in movement. MacLean has carried out experiments on lizards and monkeys that demonstrate a "basic role in displays used in social communication" for the R-Complex. This part of the brain must also be able to interpret behavioral signals from other animals, and, as a result of this ability, it recognizes other animals as individuals. The R-Complex is active in maintaining social (or "dominance") hierarchies and territories (see Chapter 7), in expressing ritualistic behaviors, and in initiating or mediating aggressive behavior. MacLean (1982:302) listed the following human behaviors as expressions of the R-Complex: ". . . performance of daily routines and subroutines; adherence to fashion (both social and scientific); responses to partial representations whether alive or inanimate; repetitious, obsessive–compulsive acts; slavish conformance to precedent as in legal and other matters and all manner of deception."

It is important to recognize, however, that there exist connecting tracts between the R-Complex and other more evolved parts of the brain in humans and other higher animals. In human behavior therefore neocortical ("learned") input affects the expression of R-Complex output. Not surprisingly, we do not always see exact correspondence between lizard and human display behavior, although the R-Complex is functioning in the same manner in both species' brains. But in some cases, as in a comparison of the stiff-legged agonistic displays of the komodo dragon, mountain gorilla, and World War II German soldier (Figure 5–20), there are remarkable similarities.

The Limbic System

The second part of the triune brain is the **limbic system** (from Latin, meaning "bordering, peripheral"), consisting of the parts of the forebrain surrounding the brainstem and the R-Complex system. There are three main subdivisions of structures making up the limbic system, each, apparently, with a different function. The first area (Figure 5–19) includes the *amygdala* (Greek, meaning "almond"), the *hippocampus* (Greek, meaning a mythological sea creature), the *hypothalamus* (Greek, meaning "below the thalamus"), and the *pituitary* (Latin, meaning "mucussecreting"). This first area of the limbic system is concerned with self- and species-preservation, particularly the activities of fighting, feeding, and self-reproduction. Electrical stimulation of the

limbic system—a mammalian adaptation of the primarily olfactory part of the forebrain, important in sexual and maternal behavior.

Figure 5–20 • Agonistic display in the komodo dragon, mountain gorilla, and human being: a function of the ancient R-Complex? (From Eibl-Eibesfeldt, 1975)

amygdala in cats produces responses of aggressive rage and fear; the hippocampus is important in memory retention.

The second area is called the *septum* and is located in the midline just below the large connecting tract of the brain, the corpus callosum. It is somehow involved in sexual behavior. Both of the first two areas of the limbic system are closely related to the sense of smell, via their neural connection to the olfactory bulbs, the part of the cerebrum that processes smell. Rudimentary homologues of these two limbic areas may also be found in reptiles.

The third section of the limbic system extends through the anterior part of the *thalamus* (Greek, meaning "chamber"), connecting the hypothalamus with the cerebral cortex *cingulate* (Latin, meaning "belt-like") *gyrus*. It has no direct connections with the olfactory part of the brain, and it is not represented in the brains of reptiles. MacLean has postulated that it also has a role in sexual behavior, but it seems uniquely important in maternal behavior and in play. The latter characteristics are behaviors we associate more with mammals than with reptiles.

Much of the influence of the limbic system on behavior derives from the hormonal proteins, which its structures produce. The pituitary gland produces *ACTH* (adrenocorticotrophic hormone), which affects anxiety, attention span, and visual memory.

The Neocortex

The third and most uniquely human part of the triune brain is the **neocortex** (Latin, meaning "new covering"). Human behavior is a function of an expanded mammalian part of the triune brain—the cerebral cortex. This part of the brain is complexly organized, yet there are several principles of its organization that have been discovered.

The **cortical homunculus** (Latin, meaning "little man") was discovered by a British neurologist, John Hughlings Jackson, who in the 1860s researched the behavior of individuals suffering from epilepsy. He discovered that seizures always started with uncontrolled movements of one part of the body. By recording where in the brain an injury occurred, and what part of the body was subsequently affected in the epileptic fit, Hughlings Jackson was able to map out the whole body along a strip of brain tissue. Figure 5–21 shows a refined version of what was termed a "homunculus" because it represents in miniature the human figure. Areas of the body with the greatest area of cortex are represented larger in the homunculus.

Hughlings Jackson had discovered the **motor cortex,** a loop of brain in front of the *central sulcus,* and therefore termed the *pre-central gyrus.* One writer described the motor cortex as "the keyboard of an instrument whose strings are the muscles, which finally play the melody of movement" (Blakemore, 1977:79). There are larger keyboard areas for certain parts of the body, where more finely tuned muscular control is required, such as for the thumbs and lips in humans.

Figure 5–21 • Frontal section of the brain through the pre-central (motor) and post-central (sensory) gyri.

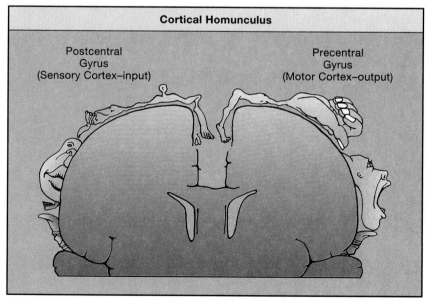

Cortical Homunculus

Postcentral Gyrus (Sensory Cortex–input)

Precentral Gyrus (Motor Cortex–output)

neocortex–the evolutionary "new" part of the cerebral cortex.

cortical homunculus–the localized map of the entire body as represented in the cerebral cortex.

motor cortex–the part of the cerebral cortex located in the precentral gyrus that controls voluntary movements of the body.

Frontiers in Morphological Analysis

By Glenn C. Conroy

Accurate description of anatomical structure is the starting point for paleoanthropological investigations. Over the past several years, we have been adapting two- and three-dimensional computed tomographic (CT) techniques, originally developed for craniofacial surgery, to diverse paleoanthropological investigations. Computed tomography is a branch of radiology, which is the study and analysis of x-ray images of the body. It involves taking many sequentially arranged x-ray "slices" of a part of the body, which are then incorporated by a computer into a three-dimensional image.

The importance of these new technical developments is that, for the first time, they give anthropologists the ability to investigate precious fossils in a noninvasive manner—a way that does not damage the specimens in any way. These new techniques provide high-resolution, geometrically accurate images of previously "hidden" anatomical structures covered by the sedimentary rock ("matrix") preserving the fossil. Researchers compute and display three-dimensional images created from two-dimensional serial CT sections. The resulting computer-generated images can be electronically "dissected" in different planes by making portions of it, and any obstructing matrix, transparent in order to reveal previously hidden morphology.

One interesting example of how this new technology has been used to provide anthropologists with new insights about human evolution is our study of the Taung skull (*Australopithecus africanus*), a 2- to 3-million-year-old fossil hominid from South Africa (see Chapter 10). Over the past half-century the Taung skull has been studied in great detail. However, previous radiographic analyses of the skull have been of limited value because of the dense mineralization and calcified matrix within the skull. For this reason, important structures inside the skull like the developing permanent dentition had never before been clearly visualized, and dental development patterns have been critical in evaluating the growth and maturation of these fossil hominids.

It is well known that modern human children take about twice as long as their closest biological relative, the chimpanzee, to reach maturity. One standard anthropological explanation for the evolution of this "delayed maturation" in humans is that it provided the time necessary for immature individuals to learn complex skills, most notably those relating to tool-making abilities. This extended period of maturation is usually regarded as a major evolutionary advance of humans. The question of just when (and why) this unique developmental pattern emerged in hominid evolution is a critical and, at the moment, contentious one within anthropology. The resolution of this debate has important implications for the way in which the bio-social evolution of our own species is viewed. In light of such controversies, and particularly since the Taung skull is the type specimen of *Australopithecus africanus,* it makes an excellent candidate for a study utilizing CT techniques.

One way of examining the question of "delayed maturation" is by studying patterns of dental development. To do this, we applied our CT techniques to the Taung skull and scanned the entire specimen in contiguous 2 mm thin sections. By manipulating various parameters of the CT scanner, we were able to clearly distinguish mineralized bone, dentine, and enamel from the

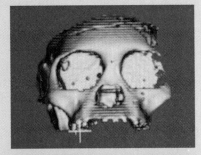

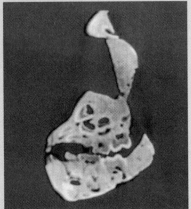

(*Top*) A geometrically accurate three-dimensional image of the Taung skull created from 2-mm thin contiguous CT scans.
(*Bottom*) A 2-mm thin CT scan taken through a parasagittal plane of the skull (at the crosshairs in the top picture) showing the state of calcification of the developing teeth.

surrounding sandstone matrix. These scans showed for the first time the state of development of all the unerupted permanent dentition and many other details of the facial skeleton, thereby allowing more refined inferences to be drawn concerning the developmental patterns of this important specimen.

The critical question in this study was whether the Taung "child" was following a humanlike growth trajectory and therefore about 5 to 7 years old or following a more apelike growth trajectory and therefore perhaps only about 3 to 4 years old. The answer to that question has profound implications for interpreting the evolutionary history of delayed maturation, a uniquely humanlike characteristic. For comparative purposes, a modern human and chimpanzee skull at the same first molar eruption stage as Taung (first molar recently erupted but not yet in functional occlusion) were also scanned in 2 mm serial sections.

The CT data indicated that the dental growth pattern of the Taung "child" was most comparable to a 3- to 4-year-old ape pattern. This difference between apes and humans is manifested in the following way. Humans are distinguished from apes in the eruption timing of the first permanent incisors and first permanent molars. Humans are unique in that these teeth erupt during one relatively brief time span within the growth period (at about 6 years of age). Apes, on the other hand, delay the eruption of permanent first incisors for about two years after first molar eruption. Thus, at first molar eruption stage in apes: 1) there is usually little or no resorption of deciduous incisor roots; 2) the permanent incisors are usually still low in their alveolar crypts; and 3) the permanent incisors have little, if any, root development. The Taung dentition clearly reflected the apelike condition.

Our studies find no dental development evidence for "delayed maturation" in the early hominid fossil record. We conclude, therefore, that any behavioral theory that attempts to link the origins of a long childhood dependency period with the time necessary for the skills associated with toolmaking to be developed in the young cannot be documented in the African fossil record. This would also imply that the assumed association between prolonged childhood dependency and other behaviors often associated with the advent of toolmaking such as cooperative hunting, food sharing, home bases, and sexual division of labor [see Chapter 12] is also suspect.

Additional Readings

Conroy, Glenn and M.W. Vannier. 1987. "Dental maturation of the Taung skull by computed tomography." *Nature* 329:625–627.

Conroy, Glenn. 1987. "Alleged synapomorphy of I1/M1 eruption patterns in robust australopithecines and *Homo*: Evidence from high-resolution computed tomography." *Amer. J. Phys. Anthrop.* 75:487–492.

Conroy, Glenn, M.W. Vannier and P.V. Tobias. 1990. "Endocranial features of *Australopithecus africanus* revealed by 2 and 3-D computed tomography." *Science* 247:838–841.

Conroy, Glenn and M.W. Vannier. 1991. "Dental development in South African australopithecines, Part I: Problems of pattern and chronology." *Amer. J. Phys. Anthrop.* 86:121–136.

Conroy, Glenn and M.W. Vannier. 1991. "Dental development in South African australopithecines, Part II: Dental stage assessment." *Amer. J. Phys. Anthrop.* 86:137–156.

Conroy, Glenn and K. Kuykendall. 199_. "Paleopediatrics: or when did human infants really become human?" *Amer. J. Phys. Anthropol.* 98: 121–131.

Paleoanthropologist and primate morphologist Glenn C. Conroy is Professor in the Department of Anatomy and Anthropology at Washington University Medical School, St. Louis. He is the author of the forthcoming Reconstructing Human Origins: A Modern Synthesis *(New York: W.W. Norton).*

Other researchers discovered that a similar "sensory homunculus" was present directly behind the central sulcus, and thus it was named the *post-central gyrus*. This area is the **sensory cortex**. Sensations from the skin of touch, heat, cold, and pain are perceived in the brain in a clearly organized pattern (Figure 5–21). As in the motor cortex, the proportion of cortical area allotted for sensations correlates with the importance of particular sensations in the animal's adaptation. Human brains have a very large sensory area for the hands, as do most primates, whereas dogs, for example, have larger sensory areas for perceiving touch on the nose.

Understanding the structure and function of the human brain is one of the most challenging frontiers for modern science. The model of the triune brain is one way to understand some very complex structures in an evolutionary framework. The model will certainly need to be modified as new discoveries are made.

MAMMALS AND ADAPTIVE RADIATION

The evolution of diverse mammals during the Cenozoic Era is another example of an adaptive radiation. Since their origin, mammals have diversified into a number of habitats. Changes in the limbs have been of primary importance in the mammalian adaptive pattern (Figure 5–22), and in the different groups of mammals they formed the basis for adaptations to different ways of life. The process of moving the front and hind limbs under the body, begun in the therapsids, was completed. The toe joints were reduced to three in all digits *except* the first (the thumb or *pollex,* and the big toe or *hallux*), where there are two joints—the same pattern that we possess. In the earliest mammals the first digits were stouter and more divergent from the other toes than in the reptiles. This suggests that the former used their hands and feet for grasping and climbing, and perhaps for catching prey.

The most primitive living order of placental mammals is the **Insectivora,** composed of small, usually forest-dwelling animals with high metabolisms, such as tree shrews (Figure 5–23). They are probably very similar to the ancestors of all placental mammals in the Cretaceous Period. Although their name implies that they were mainly insect eaters, they also probably supplemented their diets with other high-quality, energy-rich foods such as tree gum, certain fruits, and other small animals. Using modern shrews as an analog, our Mesozoic ancestors were likely very small, voracious, and nocturnal animals. Our earliest primate ancestors constituted one of the first stems off this basic mammalian trunk.

Excepting the insectivores, primates, and rodents (rats, squirrels, and their kin), which have in the most part remained morphologically primitive, the other placental mammals have radiated into a large number

sensory cortex–the part of the cerebral cortex located in the postcentral gyrus that senses touch, temperature, and pain on all parts of the body.

Insectivora–order of insect-eating mammals that includes shrews and tree shrews; similar to early Mesozoic mammals.

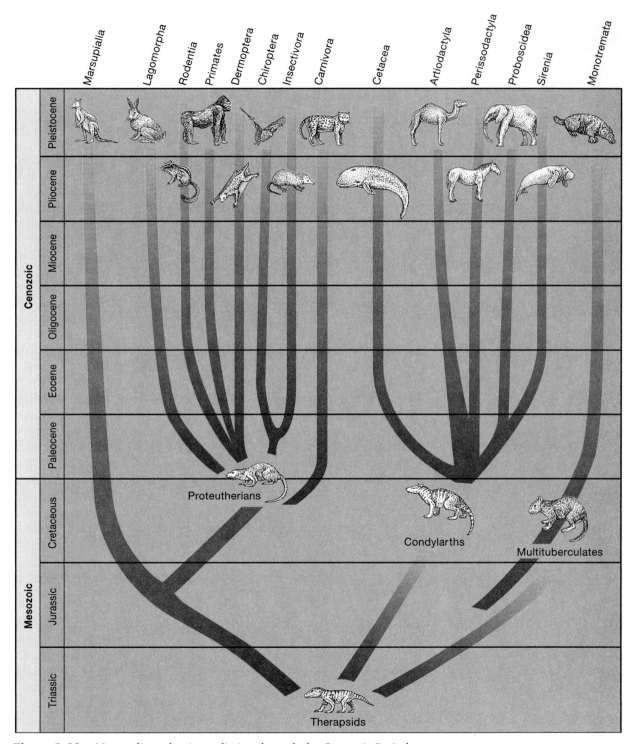

Figure 5–22 • Mammalian adaptive radiation through the Cenozoic Period.

Figure 5–23 • Tree shrew.

Figure 5–24 • Flying lemur or colugo, *Cynocephalus volans,* whose order, Dermoptera, is closely related to the insectivores and primates.

bunodont–referring to low-crowned cheek teeth.

omnivorous–having broad choice in dietary requirements.

hypsodont–referring to high-crowned cheek teeth.

of ecological niches, that is, particular morphological and behavioral specializations for specific habitats (Figure 5–22). The first of these radiations came about in the Paleocene Epoch, beginning about 70 million years ago. In simplified terms, we can categorize the Cenozoic radiation of mammals into five major adaptive zones: aerial, aquatic, fossorial, arboreal, and cursorial.

Bats and some other small gliding mammals (the dermopterans), such as flying squirrels and flying "lemurs," constitute the only members of the aerial radiation. Biochemical studies, and more recently fossil discoveries, indicate that the dermopterans (Figure 5–24), may be closely related to the primate stem (see Chapter 6). Mammals have also adapted to marine niches. This group includes the whales and porpoises, along with the sea cows and carnivorous seals and otters. Fossorial mammals are burrowers, such as moles and aardvarks. The arboreal mammals are evolutionarily the most conservative of the entire class, and our own order, Primates, is the most arboreal of the mammals. Cursorial, or running, mammals are by far the largest ray of the adaptive radiation of Cenozoic mammals. Foremost among the cursorial mammals are the hoofed mammals: the odd-toed *perissodactyls* (horses and rhinoceroses) and even-toed *artiodactyls* (pigs, antelopes, deer, hippopotamuses, and giraffes), and the carnivores. In primates, the patas monkey has adapted to a fast terrestrial running niche, and human bipedalism seems to be adapted more for long-distance locomotion than for speed (see Chapter 10).

The five-fold classification of broad locomotory adaptive zones of mammals cuts across taxonomic boundaries and it lumps together animals that may differ significantly in other important ways. For example, pigs are put into the cursorial category but their dietary requirements are quite different from most of their fellow artiodactyls. Most pig species have low-crowned or **bunodont** (Latin, meaning "low tooth") molar teeth, which allow them to crush and grind the food that makes up their **omnivorous** (eating everything) diet. Many other artiodactyls have high-crowned **hypsodont** (Latin, meaning "high tooth") teeth adapted to slicing up grasses and resisting the abrasion that results (Figure 5–25).

Research on the dietary adaptations of fossil mammal species provides some of the most important information on their behavior. Scanning electron microscopy of the wear on fossil teeth is one such area of study. Using this technology, Alan Walker of Pennsylvania State University was able to determine the general dietary preferences of a number of fossil mammals. Grazing animals have many deep parallel scratches resulting from the small particles of silica in grass, whereas browsing animals have a more random pattern of shallower scratches. Omnivorous species such as most primates and pigs have pits and gouges in their molar teeth resulting from their crushing of food and, accidentally, particles of sand.

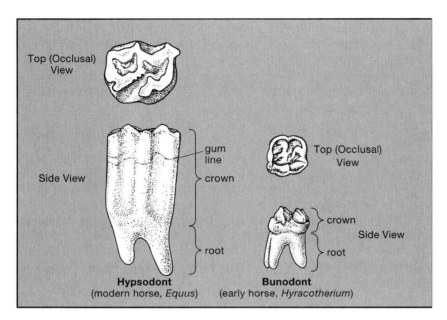

Top (Occlusal) View

Side View

gum line

crown

root

Hypsodont
(modern horse, *Equus*)

Top (Occlusal) View

crown

Side View

root

Bunodont
(early horse, *Hyracotherium*)

Figure 5–25 • Occlusal and side views of a molar of a modern horse, *Equus* (left), compared with a molar of the early horse, *Hyracotherium* (right).

UNDERSTANDING HUMAN MORPHOLOGY

The vertebrates, and particularly the mammals, provide an essential background for understanding human evolution. The human body is a mosaic of many anatomical structures and physiological mechanisms derived from ancestors at many stages in a long evolutionary development. Humans, like any other animal, are evolved organisms, not a patchwork of evolved pieces. At each stage those pieces or traits were important parts of the species' adaptation to its environment. Clearly, there was no orthogenetic, or predetermined, trend toward the human condition. This common misconception results partly from our anthropocentric focus on the human species, and partly from a lack of appreciation of the adaptations of past species in and of themselves. The story of our early pre-primate evolution, with all its twists and turns, is a much more complicated and, indeed, exciting one than a simple plodding progression towards ourselves.

Many of the main adaptive grades (roughly a stage in evolutionary development) in our vertebrate heritage have been recognized for some time, having been discovered by several generations of comparative anatomists, embryologists, and paleontologists. Yet, nonprimate data continue to provide important contributions to our understanding of human evolution. A number of biological anthropologists and evolutionary biologists are working with nonprimate vertebrate data to solve anthropological problems. These contributions are coming today primarily from functional morphology, in which comparative data from other vertebrates are essential to the interpretation of hominid behavioral capabilities. Vertebrate paleontology is also providing important information on the context of human evolution: the environmental conditions, regional connections, and ages of fossil faunas that tell us about the world of our ancestors.

The human body is not a well-designed machine unique unto itself. Each part has a long history of evolutionary change behind it. A biomechanical engineer starting from scratch, for example, would almost certainly not design the human foot the same way that evolution has. It is therefore important in human anatomy, and its practical applications in medicine, to appreciate the evolution and development of structures as well as their present functional configurations. Comparative anatomical, paleontological, embryological, and biochemical data provide compelling evidence of human beings' connections with and evolutionary differentiation within the animal world. Regardless of how dramatic the later developments of human evolution may seem to be, their bases lie in the adaptations inherited from our chordate and vertebrate ancestors.

 SUMMARY

We can trace the ancestry of humans through the vertebrates by using data from comparative anatomy, embryology, and paleontology. Contrary to an anthropocentric view of evolution, humans and their ancestors were until quite recently minor components of life on earth. The evolution of backboned animals or vertebrates proceeded through a series of ancestral stages many of which are represented by living forms today. By a process known as pedogenesis chordates arose, which were capable of a free-swimming form of locomotion. Early fish evolved skeletons of cartilage and bone, which allowed the increase in animal body size. The development of biting jaws among the placoderm fish was an adaptation to a predatory way of life. Land vertebrates evolved from lobe-finned fishes that possessed air bladders and were capable of limited movement on land. By developing the drought-resistant amniote egg, early reptiles evolved during the Carboniferous Period as animals free from life in the water. Mammal-like reptiles evolved many features of the skull, jaws, teeth, and limbs characteristic of the later mammals. Early mammals differentiated from the reptiles in their adaptations (a) to maintaining a constant internal body temperature (homeothermy), (b) to giving birth to live young, and (c) to possessing a considerably larger brain, consisting of the new additions of the limbic system and the neocortex. The adaptive radiation of mammals into five major zones began about 70 million years ago from ancestors similar to the insectivores of today. Later primate and human evolution is best understood with this backdrop of the whole of vertebrate evolution, because the nonhuman primate and the human body represent mosaics of many anatomical structures and physiological mechanisms that appeared in various stages of the evolutionary development of our vertebrate ancestors.

 ## CRITICAL-THINKING QUESTIONS

1. Define and give examples of homologous and analogous structures.
2. Discuss "our fish heritage," and the role it played in the evolution of vertebrates.
3. Explain the development of the different bone types found in the human body.
4. What are the primary characteristics that set off the Class Mammalia from all other classes of animals?
5. Briefly discuss the role homeothermy played in mammalian evolution.
6. Describe the functions of the limbic system and how they relate to the "triune brain."

 ## SUGGESTED READINGS

Cartmill, M., W. Hylander, and J. Shafland. 1987. *Human Structure*. Cambridge: Harvard Univ. Press. An evolutionary perspective on human anatomy. Detailed but understandable.

Falk, Dean. 1992. *Brain Dance*. New York: Morrow. A popular account of the human brain and its evolution.

Hildebrand, M. 1974. *Analysis of Vertebrate Structure*. New York: Wiley. A good general introduction to comparative anatomy of vertebrates.

MacLean, Paul. 1989. *The Triune Brain*. New York: Academic. A detailed discussion of MacLean's theory of the triune brain. Comprehensive.

Romer, Alfred S. 1971. *Vertebrate Paleontology*. Chicago: Univ. Chicago Press. A venerable but still very useful overview of the evolution of the vertebrates.

Savage, R.J.G. 1991. *Mammalian Evolution*. New York: Longmans. A well-illustrated general introduction to the evolution of the mammals.

Introduction to Primates: Origins and Evolution

What Is a Primate?
Suborders of Primates
Insectivore Ancestry
  of Primates

**The First Primate Radiation:
  Plesiadapiforms**

**The Second Primate
  Radiation: Prosimians**

**Behavior and Social
  Organization of Prosimians**

**The Third Primate Radiation:
  Anthropoids**

**Origins and Evolution
  of the Monkeys**
New World Monkeys
Old World Monkeys

Summary

Critical-Thinking Questions

Suggested Readings

With the evolution of flowering plants, including trees, in the latter part of the Mesozoic Era, forests became complex environments. There were more niches available for exploitation. One group of mammals radiated to fill the new tree-living niches. These were small creatures who climbed in the trees by grasping. They are called primates.

WHAT IS A PRIMATE?

The term **primates** was coined by Linnaeus in 1758 to name the order of mammals which includes the monkeys, apes, and humans. In this taxonomic category, Linnaeus included the known apes and monkeys, as well as what are now recognized as the nonprimate groups of bats, sloths, and even some mythological humans. Primate comes from the Latin *primas,* meaning "of the first rank." Linnaeus considered the order that contained humans to be first among the animals. But *primas* is also the root of "primitive." This latter meaning, although probably not intended by Linnaeus, is quite accurate as a description of the order. Not only are the primates one of the first mammalian groups to appear in the fossil record but, as a group, they are one of the least specialized in terms of their morphological and dietary adaptations.

Primate species are numerous throughout the Old and New Worlds, from Africa and Asia to South and Central America (Figure 6–1). Almost all of the primates are tree living or *arboreal,* one of the main exceptions being humans. As a group they are subdivided into two major taxonomic groups. The **prosimians** (Latin, meaning "before monkeys") are the most primitive of living primates, that is, they retain many characteristics of their earliest ancestors. Most species of prosimians are small, solitary, and active only at night. **Anthropoids** (Greek, for "human-like"), often called the "higher primates," include the monkeys, apes, and humans. They share derived characteristics ("apomorphies") that distinguish them from their earliest primate ancestors. As a group anthropoids are generally larger in body size and are organized into social groups that are active during the day (Figure 6–2).

The anatomist Sir Wilfred Le Gros Clark (1964) set out a number of trends that typify most, if not all, primates.

1. Primates tend to have a well-developed *visual sense,* which includes good depth perception. The latter ability is correlated with over-

primates–the order of mammals that includes living and extinct monkeys, apes, and humans, as well as more primitive taxa.

prosimians–primates typified by small body size and frequently nocturnal adapations in the living forms.

anthropoids–"higher" primates, including the monkeys, apes, and humans.

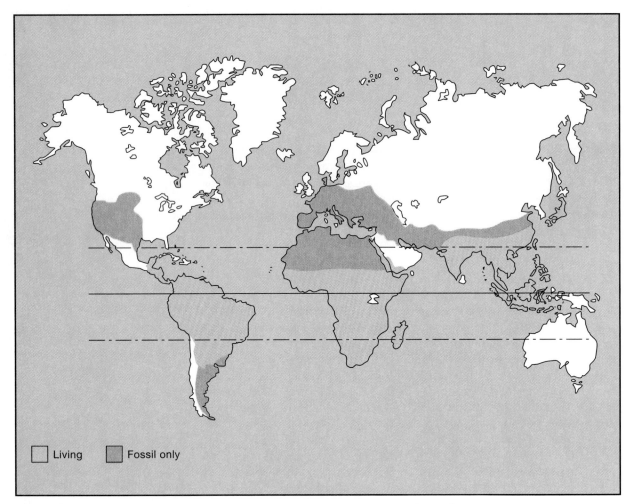

Figure 6–1 • World distribution of nonhuman primates. Living primates are basically tropical to subtropical, as indicated by the area bounded by the broken lines on either side of the equator. Fossil primates are found in regions of the world that were once tropical.

stereoscopic vision–the ability to perceive depth by virtue of the fact that the fields of vision of each eye partially overlap, thus giving the brain information sufficient to reconstruct an accurate impression of depth or distance.

lapping fields of vision for each eye (binocular vision) which, when integrated in the brain, yield a perception of three dimensions, **stereoscopic vision** (see Figure 6–3). Primates have eyes that face forward near the front of their head, a condition known as *orbital frontality*. Orbital frontality may have evolved in response to animals' living in the trees and requiring good depth perception in leaping from branch to branch (the traditional interpretation; LeGros Clark, 1970) or as a result of an adaptation to preying on smaller animals, which also requires forward-facing eyes in order to focus on prey (Cartmill, 1974; see Frontiers box, page 192). Prosimians show less orbital frontality than do anthropoids.

Figure 6–2 • Prosimians and anthropoids compared.

Figure 6–3 • Diagrammatic view of stereoscopic vision with overlapping visual fields. Half of the fibers (from the medial side) of the optic nerve cross to the opposite side in the optic chiasm, thus giving each side of the brain information from a wide range of the visual field. This information is processed into a three-dimensional picture in the cerebral visual cortex.

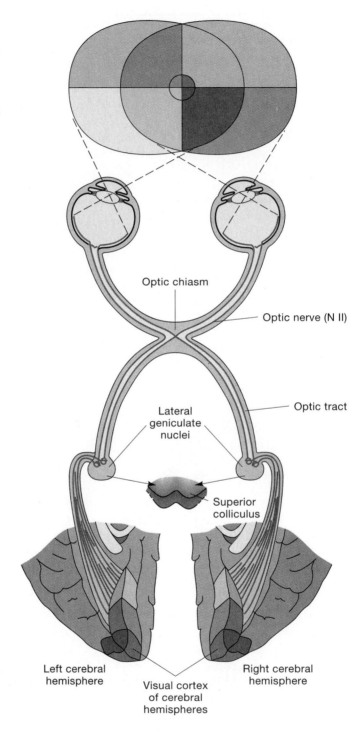

2. *Color vision.* The ability to see and discriminate a wide range of the color spectrum is another characteristic of all primates except the nocturnal prosimians. Color vision in primates may have arisen by selection for a fruit-eating diet that included the ability to determine the ripeness and edibility of particular food.

3. Primates in general have *larger brains* for their body sizes than do other mammals (Table 6–1). This is particularly true for anthropoids, and among them especially true of the apes and humans. The trend for increased brain size, that relates in a general way to increased intelligence, may have been initiated in primates by a predatory lifestyle requiring adaptability in outsmarting and capturing prey (Cartmill, 1982). It may have been further developed in higher primates for reasons of increased and more complex social adaptations to life in well-integrated groups. In any case, human ancestors underwent extensive brain development due to their increasing reliance on a peculiar social adaptation of learned behavior, known as *culture.*

4. *Increased parental investment in offspring.* Primates show a tendency to give birth to fewer offspring than do many other mammals. In ecological terms this is known as a "K-selection" strategy (see Chapter 4). There is a greater degree of parental investment in looking after offspring, throughout the relatively longer period of infant dependency after birth. As a consequence infant mortality is generally low. Primates are quite distinct from such "r-selected" species as rats or rabbits, which produce large litters of offspring, that usually suffer a high mortality rate. Aspects of primate anatomy and physiology reflect this reproductive strategy. Almost all primates have only two breasts for suckling infants whereas other mammals have a series of nipples.

5. The period of development of the primate fetus, *gestation,* increases from prosimians to anthropoids.

6. Primates show a diversity of modes of locomotion. Figure 6–4 is a classification of the various types of locomotion seen in primates today (Napier and Napier, 1965). The earliest primates probably were arboreal quadrupeds, somewhat similar to but less specialized than modern prosimian **vertical clinging and leaping** forms. Vertical clinging and leaping is a type of locomotion typified by grasping a vertical tree trunk with the hands and feet encircling the trunk, and then jumping to another such perch. Prosimians thus possess hands and feet capable of grasping. Some of the traits associated with these adaptations for locomotion are an *opposable thumb and big toe,* capable of being flexed or "opposed" against the other digits, *flat nails* instead of claws to support sensitive finger and toe tips, *finger-print ridge patterns* to increase friction in grip, and relatively *short fore- and hindlimbs* of nearly equal length, a generalized mammal trait (Figure 6–2). Body size increased in a number of descendant primate groups and new locomotor adaptations appeared: (a) forelimbs increased in length in arm-swingers which facilitated speed and reach in the trees; (b) fore- and hindlimb

vertical clinging and leaping—the method of locomotion characteristic of many living prosimians, and inferred to have been a method of locomotion in some early primates.

Table 6–1 • Brain Weights, Body Weights, and Encephalization Quotients in Extinct and Living Primates

Taxon	Body Weight (g)	Brain Weight (g)	Martin EQ[1]	Jerison EQ[2]
Australopithecus afarensis	50,900	415	1.87	2.44
Australopithecus africanus	45,500	442	2.16	2.79
Australopithecus boisei	46,100	515	2.50	3.22
Australopithecus robustus	47,700	530	2.50	3.24
Homo habilis	40,500	631	3.38	4.31
Homo erectus	58,600	826	3.34	4.40
Homo sapiens	44,000	1,250	6.28	8.07
Gorilla gorilla	126,500	506	1.14	1.61
Hylobates	6,521	112	2.40	2.60
Pan troglodytes	36,350	410	2.38	3.01
Pongo pygmaeus	53,000	413	1.80	2.36
Cercocebus	7,433	108	2.09	2.29
Cercopithecus	4,245	66	1.96	2.05
Colobus	8,729	74	1.27	1.41
Erythrocebus	7,800	107	1.99	2.19
Macaca	7,280	90	1.78	1.95
Nasalis	15,100	94	1.07	1.24
Papio	17,043	168	1.74	2.05
Presbytis	8,861	83	1.42	1.61
Theropithecus	17,050	132	1.36	1.61
Alouatta	6,667	57	1.19	1.29
Aotus	960	18	1.67	1.52
Ateles	6,800	111	2.29	2.49
Brachyteles	9,500	120	1.93	2.17
Calicebus	1,088	21	1.73	1.59
Cebus	2,733	78	3.25	3.25
Chiropotes	3,000	58	2.25	2.27
Lagothrix	6,300	96	2.12	2.29
Pithecia	1,500	32	2.08	1.97
Saimiri	665	25	3.04	2.68

[1]$\text{Log}_{10}(\text{BrW}) = 0.761\text{Log}_{10}(\text{BoW}) + 1.77$ (following Martin, 1983).
[2]$\text{log}_{10}(\text{BrW}) = 0.671\text{Log}_{10}(\text{BoW}) + 2.08$ (following Jerison, 1973).

From Aiello and Dean (1990).

Figure 6–4 • Primate locomotor categories.

Figure 6–5 • Primate skull and dentition showing molar crown structure for archaic primates and anthropoids.
(Refer to appendix 1 for definitions of dental terminology.)

cingulum–a "belt," (latin) in the dentition a raised ridge of enamel encircling a tooth crown.

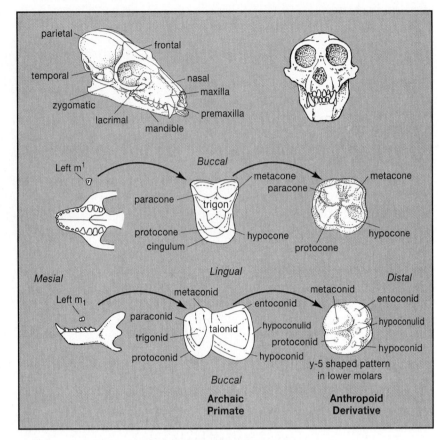

lengths increased in ground-running primates which increased stride length and speed; and (c) lower limb length increased in the human lineage which allowed greater stride length in a virtually unique form of terrestrial locomotion, bipedal walking (Figure 6–4).

7. *Low-crowned molar and premolar teeth* adapted to grinding and crushing food, as opposed to slicing, cutting, and piercing food. Primates have been described as an "order of omnivores" (Harding and Teleki, 1981), and indeed the basic primate dietary adaptation seems to cover a wide range. Animal protein in the form of insects and small vertebrates probably made up a large part of early primate diet, along with fruit and other types of vegetation. Later and generally larger primates have evolved adaptations that emphasize one of several components of this basic dietary adaptation. The dentitions of primates clearly correlate to their diets. In general, primate teeth (Figure 6–5) show some degree of flat, rounded (bunodont) structure in their molar teeth, which indicates their function in crushing and chewing food. Bunodonty is very well developed among the apes and humans. In contrast, monkeys tend to have shearing crests or *lophs* on their molars, adapted for cutting tough plant food.

8. Primates are generally *tropical* animals. However, the Japanese macaque has been able to extend its range into cold regions and has an adaptation that includes heavy fur; *Homo sapiens* has extended its range by means of culture.

9. Most primates are *active in the daytime (diurnal)*. This is understandable from the standpoint of the primate emphasis on the sense of sight. Food is located, predators are avoided, and movement is effected by visual referents. Most primates nest for the night in a secure location. Only a few primates are nocturnal, such as the mainland African and Asian prosimians (galagos and lorises) and the South American owl monkey (*Aotus*).

Suborders of Primates

Although the basic division among the living primates is that between prosimians and anthropoids, there is a third suborder of extinct, primitive primates, the plesiadapiforms, which we will discuss below. Within the Suborder Prosimii are found the Infraorders Adapiformes, containing most of the prosimians, and Tarsiiformes, containing only one living form, the tarsier. Within the anthropoid suborder are found the platyrrhine infraorder, containing the New World monkeys, and the catarrhine suborder, containing the Old World monkeys, and the hominoids: the apes and humans (Figure 6–6; Appendix 3).

A taxonomic problem, however, exists regarding the placement of the tarsiers within the Order Primates. The tarsiers and their fossil antecedents shared a more recent common ancestor with the higher primates (anthropoids) than with their prosimian relatives (lemurs, lorises,

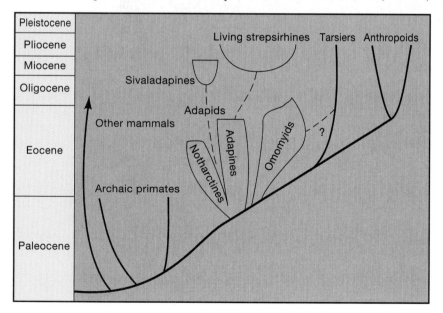

Figure 6–6 • Primate phylogeny.

and related fossil forms) (Figure 6–6). Yet they are usually grouped with the prosimians (Fleagle, 1989) because they lack many of the specializations of the anthropoid grade. Classifications based at least in part on grades of organization, such as the Suborder Prosimii, are termed *gradistic*; the Suborder Prosimii is used in this book.

Figure 6–7 • The "archontans": tree shrews, bats, dermopterans, and primates.

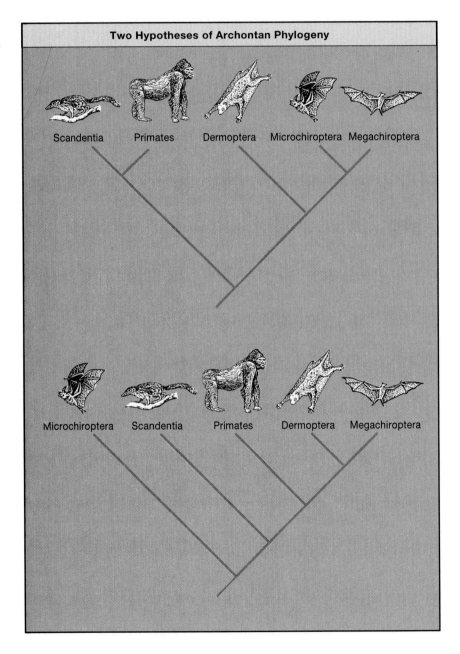

Insectivore Ancestry of Primates

Among the mammals, primates likely share a common ancestor with tree shrews (insectivores, sometimes put into their own order, Scandentia), flying lemurs (dermopterans), and, more distantly, two orders of bats (microchiropterans and megachiropterans) (Figure 6–7). William King Gregory (1910) referred to this grouping taxonomically as the "Archonta."

An animal known from the badlands of Montana 67 million years ago, about the size of a small rat, has some of the dental characteristics that may relate it to the base of the archontan lineage. It was named *Purgatorius* (from the locality of Purgatory Hill, Montana) by Van Valen and Sloan (1965). Although its dental formula is primitive, with three incisors and four premolars, it has an enlarged central incisor, like later primates, and several characters indicate a greater crushing function of its teeth. Its last premolar is flattened and more adapted to a crushing, molar-like function, its last molar is elongated for greater surface area, again for greater chewing/crushing function, and its molars have low relief. *Purgatorius* is so primitive that it might be better placed within the Insectivora than in the Primates. Nevertheless, the genus seems representative of the mammalian populations closest to the origin of the primates. Modern tree shrews may be very similar in morphological structure to *Purgatorius*.

THE FIRST PRIMATE RADIATION: PLESIADAPIFORMS

The significant changes in the earth's environment, fauna, and flora that occurred at the boundary of the Mesozoic and Cenozoic Eras are currently a subject of considerable debate. Flowering plants, characterized by a covered seed coat, had first appeared in the Cretaceous Period at the end of the Mesozoic. They diversified to form forests of greater complexity, opening up new niches for animal life. Among the faunal changes the most noticeable is the disappearance of the dinosaurs, large and small, by the end of the Cretaceous Period, 65 million years ago. This mass extinction may have been quite sudden, perhaps caused by meteoritic impact(s) with the earth, or more gradual, caused by significant temperature and climatic change over several millions of years. In whatever manner it occurred, the extinction of the dinosaurs also left many ecological niches vacant that were, subsequently, reoccupied by the birds and mammals.

During the Paleocene and Eocene, birds evolved into many of the largest animals in the world's faunas. There were no mammals, on the other hand, larger than a medium-sized dog. Among the successful members of the early mammals were the archaic primates, the **plesiadapiforms** (Figure 6–8). The term comes from the Greek word *plesi-*

plesiadapiforms—archaic primates of the Paleocene and Early Eocene Epochs.

Figure 6–8 • Reconstruction of plesiadapiforms and their environment, the Late Paleocene of North America. Left, *Ignacius frugivorus*; foreground, two individuals of *Plesiadapis rex*; right, *Picrodus silberlingi*.

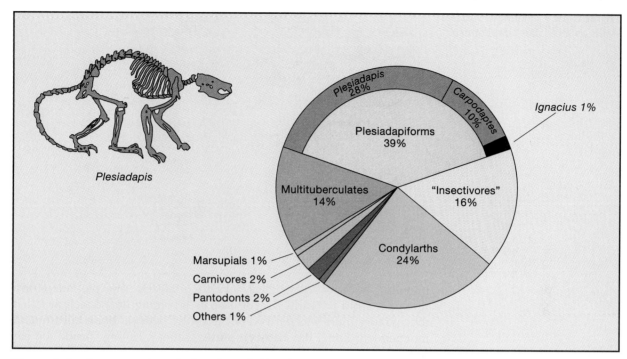

Plesiadapis

Figure 6–9 • Reconstruction of *Plesiadapis* (left); relative abundance of plesiadapiforms in relation to other Paleocene mammals (right).

meaning "like" and *Adapis,* the first fossil primate to be named (by Cuvier in 1821), originally thought to be an ungulate ancestor and named for the ancient Egyptian bull god Apis—thus *ad* (Greek, meaning "toward") Apis.

The plesiadapiforms were among the most common animals in the Paleocene and early Eocene Epoch sites of North America and Europe some 50 to 65 million years ago (Figure 6–9). Over 60 species in 30 genera are known (Rose and Fleagle, 1981). They lived in environments of dense lowland forests along rivers, lakes, swamps, and at the edge of the midcontinental sea that divided eastern and western North America. Comparable environments are to be found today in Southeast Asia and subtropical parts of the southeastern United States.

The primitive plesiadapiforms (Figure 6–10) have two incisors, one fewer than *Purgatorius,* and in this respect they resemble all other living and fossil primates. Plesiadapiforms have a unique configuration on the enamel of their upper molars called the "*Nannopithex*-fold," a characteristic groove on their heel-bone indicating strong flexor muscles for the toes, and a bony covering of the middle ear region, the **auditory bulla** (Latin, meaning "enlargement in the ear region"), until recently generally believed to have been derived from the **petrosal** bone of the skull. The petrosal bone gets its name from Latin for "rock" because of its dense, rock-like consistency. It is now part of the temporal

auditory bulla—the bony covering of the middle and inner ear structures in primates.

petrosal—a part of the temporal bone in the modern human skull; a separate bone in early primates.

Figure 6–10 • Dentitions and skulls of some plesiadapiforms.

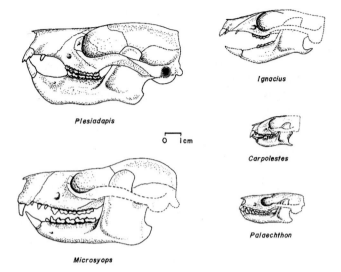

bone in humans. Kay et al. (1990) analyzed the plesiadapiform *Ignacius,* from an early Eocene site in Wyoming and concluded that the auditory bulla was derived not from the petrosal bone but from an independent bone, the **entotympanic** (Latin, meaning "inside the ear drum"). These authors prefer to remove the plesiadapiforms from Primates altogether, putting them instead in the dermopterans, or flying lemurs. Other authorities keep them within the Primates because of their other similarities, a course followed here.

There are two superfamilies of plesiadapiform primates: the **paromomyoids** (Greek, *par-* meaning "near," *Omomys* meaning "raw meat eating" and "molar," an early primate named by Leidy in 1869, and incorrectly thought by him to be an early carnivore), and the **plesiadapoids.** Both groups were part of a placental mammalian radiation into arboreal niches of which megabats ("flying foxes") and dermopterans ("flying lemurs") were also a part (Pettigrew et al., 1989). Recent work on new postcranial fossils (Beard, 1989, 1990) has shown that the paromomyoids were a group whose primary locomotor behavior was that of gliding, similar to the modern flying lemurs. Evidence for this is the elongated intermediate phalanges seen in the paromomyoid *Phenacolemur* indicating that this species had a membrane (a "*patagium*") that could be used for gliding (Beard, 1990).

The plesiadapoids are the more generalized of these archaic primates, and they may represent the ancestral group from which later primates arose. They lack the postcranial adaptations to gliding seen in the paromomyoids. Both pairs of their central incisors, upper and lower, are enlarged, and the uppers have a characteristic three-pronged mitten shape. Like later primates, the plesiadapoids had a forearm that could easily supinate and pronate the forearm (see Appendix 1), and their ankle-joint articulations allow a wide degree of movement seen in living animals adapted to a climbing life in the trees.

entotympanic–a separate bone of early primate ancestors that according to some workers accounts for the morphological origin of the auditory bulla.

paromomyoids–plesiadapiform primates that had gliding adaptations.

plesiadapoids–plesiadapiform primates that were generalized archaic primates and may have been ancestral to later primates.

During the Eocene the plesiadapiforms underwent significant decline and by the end of the Eocene Epoch they were extinct. Their demise is most likely explained by the presence of more specialized small mammals who evolved adaptations that were successful in exploiting the archaic primate niches. Rodents, who continuously grow front teeth used for gnawing, likely out-competed many of the plesiadapiform primates. Other groups that may have competed with the plesiadapiforms were the bats, the dermopterans, as well as their own relatives, the prosimian primates.

THE SECOND PRIMATE RADIATION: PROSIMIANS

The end of the Paleocene Epoch marked a period of global warming that caused greater rainfall and higher temperatures over much of the earth (Figure 6–11). The area around London, England, for example, which was near its present latitude, was vegetated by lowland tropical forest. Similar evergreen tropical forests extended over much of Africa, North America, and Eurasia at this time (Stanley, 1990). The spread of tropical forests and warm temperatures facilitated the spread and adaptive radiation of primates into new areas. Faunal interchange between North America and Eurasia was possible because of a landbridge across what is now the Bering Strait. However, since continental drift had not yet brought South America into contact with North America, this region lacks a prosimian fossil record.

The Eocene Epoch, beginning some 58 million years ago, was a period of worldwide expansion of the early primates. These were prosimians, and they possessed such distinguishing characteristics as a postorbital bar completing the lateral or outside ring of bone around the eye socket; a thumb that diverged from the other digits, allowing opposability and grasping; and nails, rather than claws, on their digits.

Primates may have first diversified in Africa and spread northward as climates warmed at the Paleocene/Eocene boundary (Gingerich, 1990). In Morocco, North Africa, there is evidence of the evolutionary split between the lines leading to the modern lemurs and lorises, also known as strepsirhines (Greek, meaning "twisted nose") on the one hand, and those leading to the group including tarsiers and anthropoids, also known as haplorhines (Greek, meaning "single nose") on the other. These two lineages are represented in the fossil record by the lemur-like **adapids** (Figure 6–12), animals larger than their plesiadapiform predecessors and about the size of the modern Malagasy lemurs, and the early tarsier-like prosimians, the **omomyids.** One of the earliest of the tarsier-like omomyids, named *Altiatlasius,* is dated to about 60 million years ago (Sige et al., 1990). *Altiatlasius* was about the size of a mouse lemur or a galago (50 to 100 grams). Both adapids and omomyids had the elongated limbs characteristic of today's clinging and leaping species, although in other respects they are much more

adapids—lemur-like prosimians, among the earliest strepsirhines.

omomyids—tarsier-like prosimians, among the earliest haplorhines.

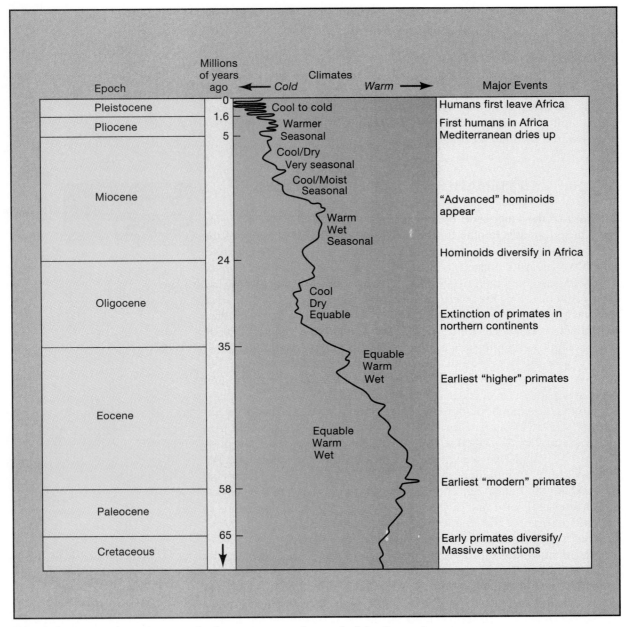

Figure 6–11 • Geological time and paleoenvironmental record of the Cenozoic.

primitive. The common ancestral population of these two Paleo-Eocene prosimian lineages likely lies among the plesiadapoids.

The pulse of climatic cooling at the end of the early Eocene, coupled with mountain formation in western North America and Europe, made for diversifying environments over the ranges of prosimians. The Eocene primates of North America and Europe evolved in their own distinctive ways. North American Eocene sites seem to record a greater diversity of omomyids whereas European sites show a greater diversity of adapids. Though the prosimians have left a trail of their evolutionary history with scattered fossils through the Eocene and into the Pleistocene, prosimian dominance was well on the wane by the beginning of the Oligocene, some 37 million years ago. They disappeared from the fossil record in North America during this period.

The living prosimians are relics of what was once a widely distributed and ecologically diverse group. Today, in the mainland areas of Southeast Asia and tropical Africa, the prosimians have been displaced from the daytime world by the anthropoids, as a result of competition for natural resources. With the exception of the isolated case of Madagascar, a large island off the southeast coast of Africa, now only nocturnal prosimian species survive.

In Africa and Southeast Asia, prosimians range into tropical woodlands, deciduous forests and rain forests. In addition, the largely diurnal lemuroid groups live in the dry spiny forests and the rain forests of Madagascar (Figure 6–13). Three species of bush babies ("galagos") are found in habitats throughout the forests of central to southern Africa. Two additional prosimians in the lorisid family, the potto (*Perodicticus*) and the angwantibo (*Arctocebus*), live together with the galago over much of their forested range. In Asia the nocturnal prosimians include the slender loris (*Loris*) and the slow loris (*Nycticebus*), as well as the leaping form, the tarsier.

Napier and Walker (1967) described prosimian locomotion as primarily a form of vertical clinging and leaping (Figure 6–14). Among the prosimians exist the extremes in locomotor speed. The tarsier and galago are "vertical-clinger-and-leapers," moving by rapid jumping and clinging to branches, while the potto and slow loris move, as the latter's name implies, at a casual pace with caution along the branches. The limb skeleton of each reflects their locomotor capabilities. The tarsier, perhaps the most dramatic jumper, has extremely elongated hindlimbs. The lower portion of the hindlimb has a largely fused tibia and fibula. This adaptation increases the stability of the lower limb and at the same time adds greater strength to withstand compressive shock in landing after long jumps. Two of the tarsier's tarsal (foot) bones, the heel bone or *calcaneus* and ankle bone or *talus,* are also elongated. This elongation of tarsal bones provides greater leverage in jumping and gives the tarsier its name.

The functional analysis of the postcrania suggests that the early Miocene lorisids moved in a more general manner compared to recent lorisids, leaping, climbing, moving quadrupedally, and perhaps at times hanging below branches in some form of suspensory movement (Gebo, 1989). The fossil record shows us that the modern, rapid galago-like locomotor behavior, characterized by long foot bones and specializations in the ankle, did not appear much before the Pleistocene.

Figure 6–12 • Reconstruction of the Eocene adapid *Notharctus* from North America.

Figure 6–13 • Ringed-tailed lemur in native habitat in Madagascar.

Figure 6–14 • Vertical clinging and leaping in prosimians.

BEHAVIOR AND SOCIAL ORGANIZATION OF PROSIMIANS

The study of living prosimians began with field investigations of the lemurs of Madagascar by Jean-Jacques Petter in 1956. Other early studies were reported by Alison Jolly (1966) and by P. Charles-Dominique (1977). Since that time further studies have brought to light the unique adaptations and behavior of these primates.

Charles-Dominique (1977) noted that "all lemurs are social, even those which are not particularly gregarious." He thus dispelled the myth that the majority of nocturnal African and Asian primates, as well as the nocturnal dwarf lemur and aye-aye on the island of Madagascar, led solitary lives, seldom interacting with other individuals except for purposes of mating.

Although it is generally true that the males and females of these nocturnal species avoid contact with one another except during the breeding season, their successful reproduction depends upon the continuing knowledge of one other's whereabouts. This knowledge is imparted by scent marking such as the urine or fecal marking, commonly practiced by most prosimians throughout their individual home ranges—that space which a group of animals occupies all through the year. Other prosimians possess glands on the neck and chest from which the males deposit scent on branches as well as on nearby females. Pair-bonding is reinforced by tactile signals such as grooming and side-by-side contact, both of which increase in frequency as the annual breeding season approaches. Even during the solitary foraging of the nocturnal prosimians these animals maintain a network of social interactions through scent markings and vocal calling and, at times, direct contact.

The adult female of each species generally occupies a distinct home range. During the day female lorises often sleep alone or with those immature offspring that remain with them. The galagos forage alone at night in overlapping home ranges but females often sleep in groups of two or three, with their young. Males of all these species usually forage and sleep by themselves. The home ranges of one or more of the females overlap with that of a single male. The male keeps constant vigilance throughout his range, periodically visiting females and mating with those who are in estrus. Young males, in order to find a spot devoid of another "central" male, may travel substantial distances from their natal home ranges to establish themselves. Females, on the other hand, usually remain near the area of their birth throughout their life. Perhaps in order to ensure a space for their young daughters, potto mothers sometimes leave their established home ranges to their daughters and move to new ranges close-by (Charles-Dominique, 1977).

The day-active (diurnal) prosimians are found only on Madagascar, where they have avoided ecological competition with the higher primates. Diurnal prosimians are gregarious in their social behavior. Of these Madagascar prosimians the best studied have been the ring-tailed lemur (*Lemur catta*) (Figure 6–13) and the sifaka (*Propithecus*).

The ring-tailed lemurs form social groups numbering between 5 and 22 animals of all ages and sexes. The core of the group consists of females and their young with the several adult males spatially peripheral to the core. Adult males often transfer between groups and will aggregate temporarily into all-male groups. Lemur home ranges may be exclusively utilized by a single group or they may overlap with other groups which mutually avoid one another by adjusting to the others' foraging patterns and times.

Dominance interactions are displayed by both the adult males and females of the troop. In lemurs, however, it is the adult females who are dominant over the males, and, as in most other primate social units, the female dominance hierarchy is generally more stable than that of the males. Agonistic (or aggressive) behavior between the males is common, but only during the mating season do these aggressive interactions result in physical injury. During the breeding season the male dominance hierarchy breaks down and the males interact in a free-for-all for sexual access to the estrous females.

Among the Indriidae, the sifaka social group consists of adult males and females but group size tends to be smaller, ranging between 2 and 12 animals. Some sifakas occupy the drier spiny forests of southern Madagascar and establish and defend their home ranges, called *territories,* with ritualized aggression towards other groups, aggression that seldom results in actual physical violence. In other areas of Madagascar, however, sifakas show no defense behavior when their home

FRONTIERS

Predation, Feeding Strategies, and Primate Origins

by Matt Cartmill

Several new accounts of primate origins have been put forward to fill the vacuum left by the collapse of W.E. Le Gros Clark's (1934, 1959) classical synthesis. Until recently, the main contenders were the conflicting stories offered in various versions over the past two decades by Frederick S. Szalay (1972) and myself (Cartmill, 1974, 1982). Szalay's account offered to explain primate origins in terms of the synapomorphies (shared derived features) of modern and archaic primates, whereas my explanations centered on the traits peculiar to "primates of modern aspect." Both of these accounts are now being challenged by new findings and interpretations.

In Szalay's view, primates evolved from a tree-shrewlike arboreal "archontan" ancestor through a shift to a more herbivorous diet. He inferred this shift from various specialized features of molar morphology, including lower cusps and broader crushing surfaces, that are shared by archaic and modern primates. Szalay has argued that *Plesiadapis* and other archaic primates may have had somewhat divergent and thumblike first toes, but he thinks that perfected grasping extremities and flattened nails first appeared in the ancestral "euprimates" (modern or non-archaic primates) as adaptations for a more acrobatic, grasp-leaping form of locomotion.

I arrived at a very different account of euprimate origins by studying non-primate mammals that live in trees. Most of these tree-dwellers do not look much like euprimates. Their organs of smell are well developed, and almost all of them have sharp, sturdy claws. Many of them—for example, squirrels—have eyes that face more or less sideways. Nevertheless, they have no difficulty running around and feeding in trees. From these facts I concluded that arboreal life does not automatically select for primatelike features, and that some additional factor must have been responsible for producing the distinctive characteristics of euprimates.

The forward-facing eyes of primates had been explained by Le Gros Clark as an adaptation for stereoscopic vision, particularly for the accurate judging of distance and direction in arboreal acrobatics. I rejected this analysis. It seemed to me that shoving the eyes together in the middle of the face would enlarge the field of stereoscopic vision but decrease parallax (the separation between the two eyes and the amount of difference between the pictures they see), thus reducing the distance at which stereoscopic vision can work. Optic convergence, I argued, must have evolved in animals that needed a wide field of stereoscopic vision at close range.

Marked optic convergence is also seen in cats and many other predators that rely on vision in tracking and nabbing their prey. Noting the predatory habits of small prosimian primates such as tarsiers and lorises, which track insect prey by sight and seize them in their hands, I interpreted optic convergence as a hunting adaptation in the ancestral primates as well.

Grasping extremities and claw loss, I suggested, had also originated as predatory adaptations, facilitating stealthy locomotion among the slender twigs of the forest canopy and undergrowth where insects are most abundant and where sharp claws, which help in climbing thick trunks, are of little use. I saw olfactory reduction as a side effect of the shoving-together of the two eye sockets, which necessarily constricts the space available for the organs of smell and their connections to the brain. All these distinctive euprimate traits, I concluded, could be explained in this way as adaptations for an ancestral habit of "visually directed predation," and I urged that *Plesiadapis* and other archaic primates, which showed no signs of such adaptations, be removed from the primate order.

But not all visually oriented predators have eyes that point in the same direction: cats, tarsiers, and owls do; mongooses, tree shrews, and robins do not. To support my theory of optic convergence in the ancestral primates, some other factor must be involved. John Allman (1977) suggested that it was the nocturnal habits of certain predators that further explained the adaptation of optical convergence. Nocturnal predators, such as owls and cats, have eyes in which the lens focuses the image in the center of the visual field, whereas diurnal predators with plenty of bright light do not require the same visual acuity to bring prey into focus. Early primates thus fit the nocturnal predator pattern and not the more walleyed, diurnal adaptation with a more panoramic view.

Robert Sussman (1991) has put forward an alternative to my theory that posits the central adaptation of fruit-eating in the earliest primates. The visual and grasping adaptations of the early primates Sussman sees as adaptations to feeding at the ends of branches, and he suggests that the radiation of the early primates may have been a side effect of great diversification of flowering plants at the end of the Eocene Epoch (Sussman and Raven, 1978). However, as I have pointed out, the known teeth of the earliest primates do not suggest fruit-eating, and Sussman's theory also does not explain the characteristic visual specializations of the primates. It would make sense for a visually predatory animal to have a wide range of sharp stereoscopic vision directly in front of it, whereas such specializations are not obviously needed when the prey is a banana.

Tab Rasmussen (1990) suggested a new hypothesis that incorporates some of both Sussman's and my ideas. Finding that a South American primatelike opossum eats both fruit and insect prey, Rasmussen suggests that early primates may have climbed out into the terminal branches in search of fruit (as Sussman thinks), and developed their visual peculiarities to help them catch the insects that they encountered there (as my theory implies).

Continuing research on the comparative behavior and adaptations of other tree-living mammals will help to sort out and test the explanations that have been offered for the evolution of grasping feet and flattened nails in the first primates. It would also help if we knew something about the order in which the various primate peculiarities were acquired. If the first primates had grasping feet and blunt teeth adapted for eating fruit, but retained small, divergent orbits like those of *Plesiadapis,* Rasmussen's account would gain added plausibility. If they had convergent orbits and the sharp, slicing molar teeth of insect-eaters, that would support my ideas. The oldest fossil primates we know of at present resemble modern primates in both their foot bones and their eye sockets, and so they do not help to answer this question. We can only hope that new fossil finds will help us to tease apart the various strands of the primate story, and give us some clearer insights into the evolutionary causes behind the origin of the primate order to which we belong.

Additional Reading

Allman, J. 1977. "Evolution of the visual system in the early primates." *Progress in Psychobiology and Physiological Psychology* 7:1–53.

Cartmill, M. 1974. "Rethinking primate origins." *Science* 184:436–443.

———1982. "Basic primatology and prosimian evolution." In F. Spencer, ed. *A History of American Physical Anthropology, 1930–1980.* New York: Academic Press, pp. 147–186

Clark, W.E. Le Gros. 1934. *Early Forerunners of Man.* Baltimore: William Wood.

———1959. The Antecedents of Man. Edinburgh: Edinburgh University Press.

Rasmussen, D.T. 1990. "Primate origins: Lessons from a neotropical marsupial." *American Journal of Primatology* 22:263–277.

Sussman, R.W. 1991. "Primate origins and the evolution of angiosperms." *American Journal of Primatology* 23: 209–223.

Sussman, R.W. and P.H. Raven. 1978. "Pollination by lemurs and marsupials: An archaic coevolutionary system." *Science* 200:731–736.

Szalay, F.S. 1972. "Paleobiology of the earliest primates." In R.H. Tuttle, ed. *The Functional and Evolutionary Biology of Primates.* Chicago: Aldine, pp. 3–35.

Matt Cartmill is Professor of Biological Anthropology and Anatomy at Duke University. He is past editor of the American Journal of Physical Anthropology *and the author of* A View to a Death in the Morning: Hunting and Nature through History *(Cambridge, MA: Harvard University Press, 1994).*

ranges overlap. As with the lemurs male social dominance hierarchy disappears during the annual breeding season.

The indri exhibit a particularly interesting social organization which is similar to the organization of the marmosets, small monkeys of South America. It was first believed that the indri had monogamous social groups consisting of only adult males and females and their immature young. Additionally these pair-bonded groups displayed territorial aggression towards other groups. More recent studies show, however, that the indri form groups which may include other siblings and unrelated younger males (Richard, 1985:296). How these additional individuals function in the indri group is as yet unknown. It may be, however, that as in the marmosets, these hangers-on are put to work baby-sitting troop newborns. Although the prosimians are anatomically more primitive than the monkeys and apes, they do display many similar behavioral patterns that parallel those observed in their more advanced cousins, the anthropoids.

THE THIRD PRIMATE RADIATION: ANTHROPOIDS

The latter half of the Eocene Epoch to the beginning of the Oligocene Epoch (35 to 47 million years ago) was a period of global cooling and of increasingly open, less forested habitats. Faunas worldwide changed to include more browsing and terrestrial forms (Stanley, 1990). Anthropoids appear suddenly in the Late Eocene–Early Oligocene sediments of Africa, and possibly South East Asia, without any obvious antecedents. Paleontologist Glenn Conroy believes that:

> In fact any dogmatic interpretation of the Prosimian–Anthropoid transition goes far beyond what the fossil evidence warrants at this stage. (Conroy, 1990)

The earliest fossil record of possible anthropoids comes from Late Eocene deposits in Burma. Specimens have been attributed to two species (*Pondaungia cotteri* and *Amphipithecus mogaungensis*) which show the anthropoid-like characteristics of deep mandible and low-crowned molars. But because the specimens are so fragmentary, experts disagree on whether they represent the first anthropoids or just large prosimians.

The first undisputed anthropoid is the recently discovered *Catopithecus browni* (Figure 6–15) from the Fayum Depression of northern Egypt (Simons, 1990). It dates from below or near the Eocene–Oligocene boundary, some 37 million years ago. The skull and mandible of this species show a dental formula of 2.1.2.3, the condition of Old World monkeys and apes, presence of a postorbital bar, a fused frontal bone in the midline, and likely a fused mandible in the midline. All these are higher primate characteristics, which indicate that the

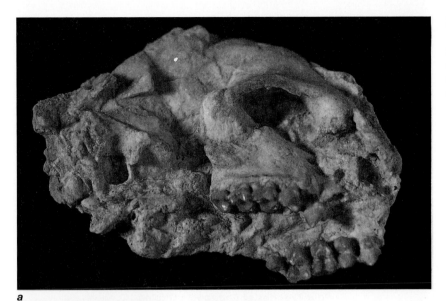

a

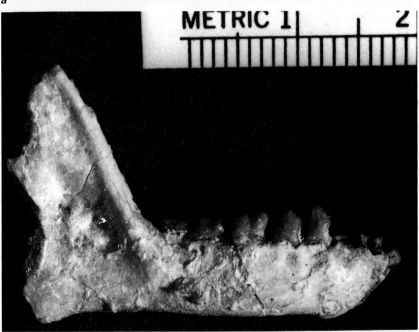

b

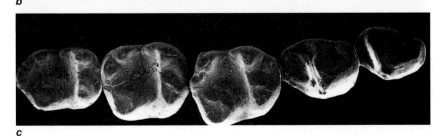

c

Figure 6–15 • *Catopithecus browni,* the first undisputed anthropoid: (*a*) skull and mandible; (*b*) lower dentition, buccal view; (*c*) lower dentition, occlusal view.

ectotympanic bone–a separate bone covering the ear canal.

species is definitely an anthropoid, but details of the teeth and ear region (absence of a tubular **ectotympanic bone**), have led Simons (1990) to suggest that *Catopithecus browni* is descended from adapoids rather than omomyoids, an opinion that is different from that now held by many specialists (Figure 6–16).

The Fayum is a low-lying desert region of the northernmost Egyptian Sahara and it is the primary spot on earth to have provided a window on the period when the first anthropoids arose. The fossil-bearing sections of the Fayum date from the late Eocene to middle Oligocene Epoch, between approximately 31 and 37 million years ago (Figure 6–17). First discovered in the late nineteenth century and investigated by teams from the Natural History Museum (London), and American

Figure 6–16 • Different views on the phylogenetic relationships between the fossil prosimians and later anthropoids.

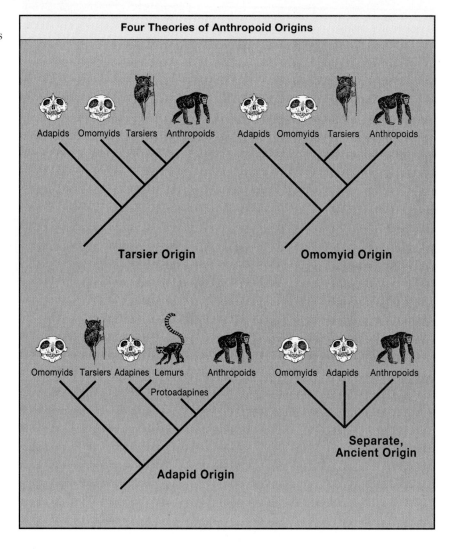

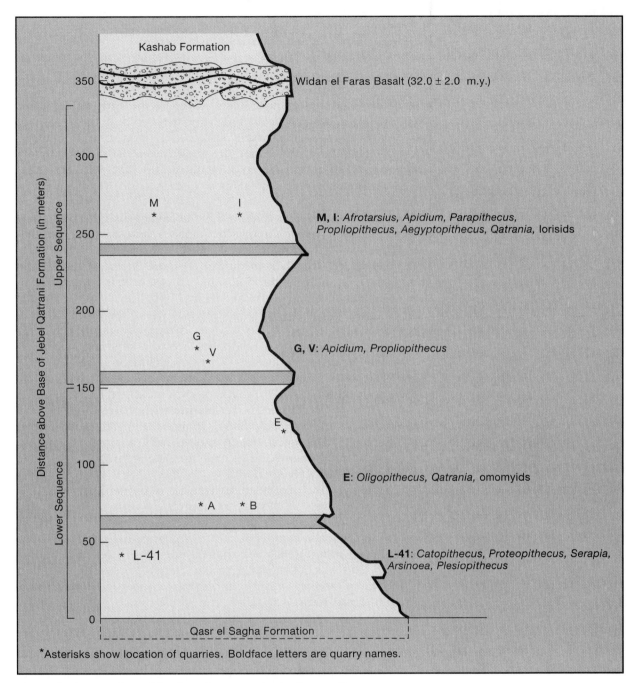

Figure 6–17 • Geological levels and primates in the Fayum, Egypt.

Museum of Natural History, the site has been under study since 1961 by Elwyn Simons's team based at Duke University.

The environmental setting at the Fayum (Figure 6–18) has been reconstructed through painstaking geological and paleontological work by Bown and Kraus (1982). The fossil plants preserved at the Fayum provide an important glimpse at the world of the early anthropoids. Mangrove trees, which live in low-lying swamps near the sea, large broad-leaved trees characteristic of dense rain forest, and climbing, vine-like plants known as lianes, are abundant in the identified plant assemblage. Well-developed soils in the Fayum deposits show that there was abundant rainfall, in marked contrast to the desert conditions found today.

The Oligocene primates that lived in the Fayum shared it with many large and small mammals. Among the primates there are the parapithecids (*Apidium* and *Parapithecus*), small anthropoid primates only slightly advanced over their prosimian relatives, that were more common than the primitive anthropoids. In fact, *Apidium* is the most common small animal found in the middle and upper levels at the Fayum.

In the early levels of the Fayum, the smallest of the Fayum anthropoids, known as *Oligopithecus savagei,* is morphologically similar to and related to *Catopithecus.* It was the size of a large marmoset, approximately 20 to 35 centimeters (8.5 to 15 inches) in head and body length. The species is not well known, but Simons (1972), Kay (1977), and Fleagle and Kay (1987) consider it most closely allied with and a possible ancestor for the later, larger **propliopithecoids** in the Fayum, *Aegyptopithecus* and *Propliopithecus.* On the other hand, Szalay (1970) and Delson (1977) suggest that it was actually a more generalized species, not a propliopithecoid or early ape-like anthropoid itself, and should be included with *Apidium.*

There are two, and possibly more, species of propliopithecoids preserved in later levels at the Fayum. *Aegyptopithecus zeuxis* was the largest species (Figure 6–19), the size of a modern gibbon. It was thus about 40 to 65 centimeters (1.5 to 2 ft.) in combined head and body length. *Propliopithecus* has two named species, *P. haeckeli* and *P. markgrafi,* and was substantially smaller, about the size of a modern African swamp monkey or talapoin. *Aegyptopithecus* and *Propliopithecus* had a dental formula for each side of the mouth of two incisors, one canine, two premolars, and three molars, shown as:

$$\frac{2.1.2.3.}{2.1.2.3.}$$

propliopithecoids–anthropoid (catarrhine) primates from the Oligocene of Egypt, sometimes considered the earliest hominoids.

This is the same dental formula as all living apes and Old World monkeys, and it distinguishes *Aegyptopithecus* and *Propliopithecus* (and *Catopithecus*) from the contemporary parapithecids, which have three premolars.

Figure 6–18 • The environmental setting and vertebrate fauna from the Fayum, Egypt, Early Oligocene. A group of *Aegyptopithecus zeuxis* is in the foreground, and 2 individuals of *Apidium* are in the background. The large horned *Arsinotherium* (left) and elephant-like *Phiomia* (right) share the riverbank with a primitive crocodilid.

Figure 6–19 • Reconstruction (left) and skull and mandible (right) of *Aegyptopithecus zeuxis*.

Aegyptopithecus shows a significant amount of sexual dimorphism, with the males about a quarter larger than the females. Using modern primates as a guide, this degree of sexual dimorphism suggests that the mating structure of these early anthropoids was a single-male group with several females and offspring. Other possible correlates of behavior, such as territoriality, are as yet unknown.

ORIGINS AND EVOLUTION OF THE MONKEYS

The evolutionary origins of the monkeys involves the split between the primate infraorders of **platyrrhines** (Greek, meaning "flat-nosed") and **catarrhines** (Greek, meaning "downward nose"). New World monkeys, which have noses with laterally facing nostrils, belong uniquely to the former group, and Old World monkeys belong to the latter, along with apes and humans.

The origins of the Old World monkeys has not been controversial because generally acknowledged ancestral forms from the Oligocene exist in Africa. But the evolutionary origin of the New World monkeys has been problematical. There are no fossil primates known at all from South America during the Paleocene or Eocene Epochs, when open sea separated it from North America, which was teeming with prosimians (omomyoids and adapoids). By the beginning of the Cenozoic, South America was also separated from Africa by a substantial expanse of Atlantic Ocean.

Monkeys appear suddenly in the fossil record of South America, in the late Oligocene. The **cebid** genus *Branisella* occurs at the Bolivian site of Salla with a potassium-argon date of approximately 26 million years ago (MacFadden, 1985) (Figure 6–20). The fact that monkeys ap-

platyrrhines–New World monkeys.

catarrhines–Old World monkeys, apes, and humans.

cebid–New World monkeys excluding marmosets and tamarins.

pear full-blown in South America with no apparent ancestral source in South America indicates that they migrated from elsewhere. Opinions on the origin of the platyrrhine monkeys have been divided between those favoring an evolutionary origin from North American prosimian ancestors (Gingerich, 1980; Rosenberger, 1986) and those favoring an African origin (Hoffstetter, 1972; Fleagle and Kay, 1987). Dispersal from North America would have been across the strait of Panama or the Caribbean Sea, but there are no good North American candidates for direct ancestors of New World monkeys in the Eocene and no North American Oligocene monkey fossil record at all. Dispersal from Africa might seem less likely because it would have required transport of monkey ancestors across the South Atlantic Ocean, estimated to have been some 200 kilometers wide in the Oligocene (Tarling, 1981) (Figure 6–21), but this apparently unlikely event is probably what happened.

Parapithecids as known from the Fayum appear to be more primitive than either catarrhine or platyrrhine anthropoids (Fleagle and Kay, 1987), and they may be good candidates for the ancestral populations of the New World monkeys. Both parapithecids and New World monkeys have three premolars, a major distinction from the catarrhines, which all have only two. The age of the earliest *Parapithecus*-bearing levels in the Fayum is dated to 31 million years ago (Fleagle et al., 1986), thus predating the earliest monkey-bearing fossil sites in South America. The data strongly suggest that platyrrhines had an African origin and dispersed to South America by rafting on floating mats of vegetation across the open ocean. In modern times, large rafts of vegetation, some large enough to support standing mid-sized trees, are known to

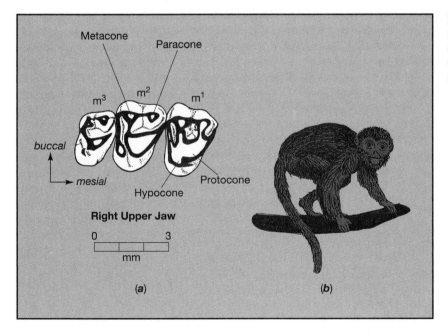

Figure 6–20 • Fossil New World monkey *Branisella:* (*a*) upper dentition (right first, second, and third molars); and (*b*) a reconstructed view.

Figure 6–21 •Hypothetical possible routes of dispersal of the ancestors of the New World monkeys from Africa and North America, respectively.

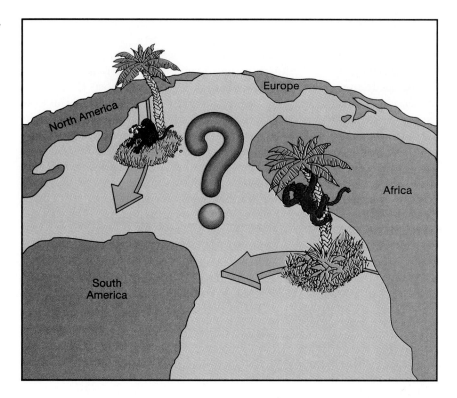

break off from river banks of large tropical rivers and drift out to sea. Such a raft emanating from perhaps the Zaire or Niger Rivers of western Africa may have launched primates on their new evolutionary career once they reached South America. The idea of an African origin for South American monkeys is additionally supported when we look at other mammalian species. For example, the close evolutionary relationships observed between African fossil porcupines and the South American guinea pigs (Hofstetter, 1972) make it likely that these animals, too, were transported across the ocean from Africa to South America.

New World Monkeys

The French naturalist Buffon (1767) was the first to recognize the primates of the New World and differentiate them from those better known monkeys and apes in the Old World. He based his early, simple classification primarily on their external morphological features, of which the three most visible characteristics were an absence of cheek pouches and ischial callosities, and more widely spaced nostrils (Figure 6–22).

Later in the nineteenth century the discovery of the **callitrichids,** marmosets and tamarins, distinguished by the lack of the prehensile tail common to a number of other New World primates, the lack of third molars, their tritubercular (three-cusped) morphology of the upper molars, and also by the presence of claws. These claws function in

callitrichids–marmosets and tamarins.

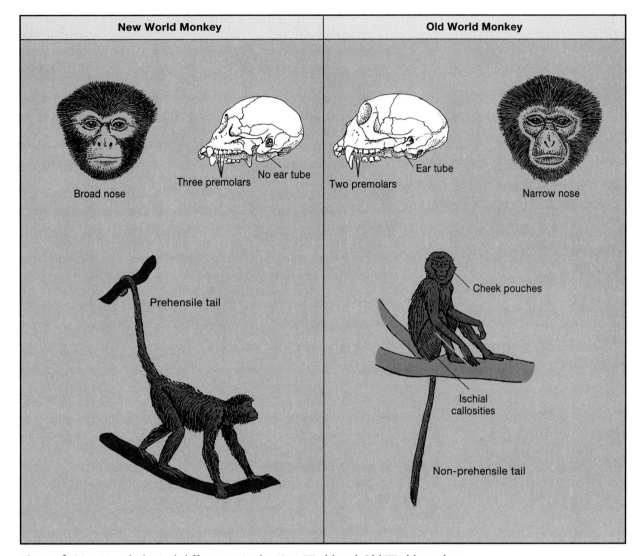

New World Monkey	Old World Monkey

Broad nose

Three premolars   No ear tube

Prehensile tail

Two premolars   Ear tube

Narrow nose

Cheek pouches

Ischial callosities

Non-prehensile tail

Figure 6–22 • Morphological differences in the New World and Old World monkeys.

much the same way as do those of rodents for example, opening up the possibilities for very small animals to vertically ascend and descend large trees, and to engage in cling-and-leap locomotion.

The modern species of New World primates are all arboreal and with one exception, the night or owl monkeys (*Aotus*), are diurnal. They range as far north as the Yucatán in Mexico and as far south as the southernmost expansion of the tropical rainforests of South America. Of the 16 genera and 46 species of New World primates all but two genera with ten species occur within the reaches of the Amazonian rainforest basin.

Figure 6–23 • The spider monkey.

Quadrupedalism and leaping found among the New World primates appear to represent the earliest arboreal locomotor adaptation in the evolution of this group (Gebo, 1989). The fossil remains of early New World primates show a widened foot, a lengthened great toe for purposes of grasping, and an increased mobility of the limb joints. This pattern was later modified by the atelines, such as the spider monkey (Figure 6–23), which developed tail-assisted suspensory movement including a greater mobility in the upper limb which makes them almost as agile as the aerially acrobatic gibbons. These adaptations allowed them to carry out an arm-swinging form of locomotion paralleling, though not precisely analogous to, true brachiation (Jungers and Stern, 1980).

On the other end of the spectrum, the marmosets and tamarins and the night monkey have only a minor ability in arm-swinging. These animals are generally quadrupedal, using a squirrel-like gait, and confine their locomotor activities to larger tree limbs. Midway between the smaller marmosets and the tail-assisted brachiators are a third group of fairly acrobatic species such as *Lagothrix* (the woolly monkey) and *Alouatta* (the howling monkey), which occupy the smaller branches in the forest canopy.

Old World Monkeys

The earliest fossil record of Old World monkeys is a species found on the eastern shore and nearby islands of Lake Victoria, Kenya, known as *Victoriapithecus maccinnesi*. It shows the double-crested pattern of the lower molars (bilophodonty) that characterizes Old World monkeys. It dates from the early Miocene, some 18 to 20 million years ago. Of almost comparable, but likely middle Miocene, age is a North African species, *Prohylobates tandyi*.

Monkeys are scarce in comparison to apes in the earliest fossil sites in which they are known. This is quite the opposite of the modern situation in which apes are rare in terms of both population numbers and species diversity. Modern day monkeys have likely taken over many of the ecological niches occupied in the Miocene by the numerous species of small-bodied apes.

The superfamily of Old World monkeys, **Cercopithecoidea,** is made up of a large number of species whose appearance differs widely. The living cercopithecoids are generally classified within one family, but are divided into two subfamily groups: the **cercopithecines,** the baboons, macaques, and relatives; and the **colobines,** the leaf-eating monkeys. Among many species and even within subspecies remarkable variety in coat coloration and hair patterns have evolved, paralleled only among the New World marmosets. In other morphological characteristics, however, the cercopithecoids have few divergent specializations compared to the prosimians, the New World monkeys, or the hominoids (Figure 6–24). Size differences are not as great as those found in the other primate groups: the smallest cercopithecoid,

Cercopithecoidea—Old World monkeys.

cercopithecines—Old World monkeys with generally omnivorous or graminivorous diets, frequently ground-living, and sometimes lacking tails.

colobines—leaf-eating monkeys, mostly arboreal.

the talapoin, weighs about 1.2 kilograms, and the largest, the mandrill, weighs about 30 kilograms. As Schultz (1970) said:

> . . . (C)atarrhine monkeys have remained a more tightly-knit clan than have the platyrrhines or the hominoids because they have acquired fewer and more moderate specializations in most of their bodily characters as well as in their basic mode of locomotion. This is of particular interest in view of the fact that the catarrhine monkeys have probably existed for at least as long as the hominoids, have a wider distribution and contain types which are more adaptable to different environments and climates than any other non-human primates.

The Old World monkeys are basic quadrupedal animals showing few locomotor specializations with the exception of the relative elongation of the hindlimb as seen in the colobines, the specialized leapers in this group. Primate quadrupedalism in general has been much less studied than the more exotic types of locomotion such as leaping or brachiation. Quadrupedal locomotion does vary, however. Within one genus, *Cercopithecus,* Ashton and Oxnard (1969) noted that some species preferred quadrupedal walking and running on larger branches while other species used the smaller branches more frequently in acrobatic leaping. Other genera show the same diversity and new field studies have modified our knowledge of how primates move about in

Figure 6–24 • Skeleton of an Old World monkey (baboon, genus *Papio*).

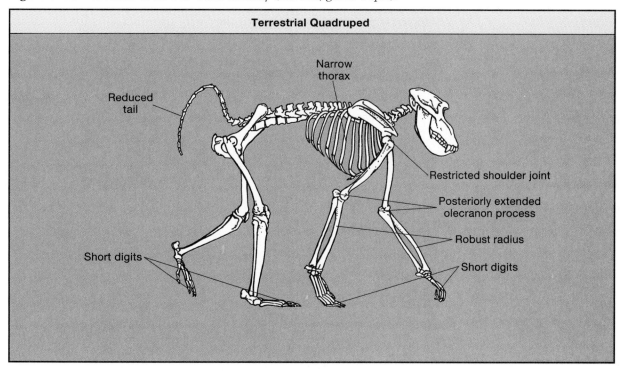

the trees and how much time they spend moving arboreally or terrestrially.

In the Old World monkeys leaping is less developed than in the prosimians. Their leaps have a downward direction, spread-eagle, midair posture and a crash-like mode of landing. In the trunk skeleton many leaping forms have a shortened robust lumbar region distinct from the slighter thoracic vertebral region. In addition to leaping, Old World monkeys also show some inclination towards side-raised upper-limb positioning as seen the New World primates and the apes. The shoulder blades of all the Old World monkeys lie at the sides of their relatively narrow chests and, as a consequence, their collar bones have remained proportionately short. In the lower trunk the pelves are quite similar. The ilium forming the blade of the pelvis is long and narrow in a cranial-caudal direction, and the pubic bones are rounded which allows for a birth canal which is slightly larger in size than the usual head diameter of a newborn.

Limb proportions, as measured by the *intermembral index* (the length of the forelimb divided by the length of the hindlimb $\times$ 100), differs far less in the Old World monkeys than in other primate groups (Table 6–2). The active arm swingers—the Asiatic gibbons and the larger-bodied orangutans—show the longest relative arm lengths. The longest relative leg lengths belong to the bipeds and the leaping Asiatic tarsiers and Madagascar sifakas. In the hands and feet the Old World monkeys are also relatively unspecialized and do not show the opposible capability as seen in many prosimians. Old World monkeys do not possess prehensile tails though they may use their tails for balancing and perhaps in assisting in vertical climbing. Tail length varies consid-

Table 6 – 2 • Intermembral Indexes of Anthropoids

Taxon	Average	Range
Australopithecus[1]	89	?
Homo (Human)[2]	70	64–78
Pan (Chimpanzee)[3]	110	102–114
Gorilla (Gorilla)[3]	116	110–125
Pongo (Orangutan)[3]	144	135–150
Hylobates (Gibbon)[3]	129	121–138
Proconsul[4]	95	?
Oreopithecus[4]	120	?
Pliopithecus[4]	95	?
Papio (Baboon)[3]	95	92–100

[1]Data from Robinson (1972).
[2]Data from Campbell (1974).
[3]Data from Napier and Napier (1967).
[4]Data from Rose (1993).

erably among species in the Old World monkeys. Whereas tail length can be more than twice the length of the trunk in some adult colobines it can also be quite short, as seen in several species of *Macaca,* most notably the stump-tailed macaque (*M. arctoides*).

In most species males are generally significantly larger in body size than females. In the terrestrial baboons they are often twice the size of females. Certain Old World monkeys exhibit sexual differences in such features as the shape of the ischial callosities on which both males and females sit or sleep during the night, the size of the cheek pads (as in the drills), and the size of the nose (as in differences in the large nose of the proboscis monkey, *Nasalis)* (Figure 6–25). No such comparable sexual dimorphism can be seen in the living New World monkeys or Old World prosimians.

The skull of Old World monkeys shows proportions different from those seen in most other primates. The most striking differences appear in the relative length and protrusion of the jaws, the extreme of which is seen in baboons. Jaw prognathism is the result of the large size of the canine teeth and first lower premolar, which are significantly sexually dimorphic in all but the smallest Old World monkeys. The dentition of the Old World monkeys (as well as the apes and humans) shows the typical dental formula 2.1.2.3. Old World monkeys, however, as we have seen, have the two-ridged, bilophodont molar cusp pattern which

Figure 6–25 • Sexual dimorphism in cercopithecoids: *Nasalis,* the proboscis monkey.

serves to differentiate them from the bunodont molar pattern of the hominoids.

The Colobinae form a group distinct from the Cercopithecinae, characterized by a number of morphological adaptations for a predominantly leaf-eating (folivorous) diet. Additional morphological features which distinguish them from the cercopithecines are related to locomotor specializations in leaping and arboreal suspension. Colobines are more capable of greater forelimb abduction including shoulder rotation with the elbow joint fully extended. This larger range of forelimb movement allows them to sit on branches and from overhead pull down smaller twigs containing food (Tuttle, 1975). They also often use their forelimbs and hands to grasp overhanging limbs in order to steady themselves (Morbeck, 1979).

The subfamily of colobines is divided into two subgroups, the colobus monkeys of Africa and the Asian leaf monkeys or langurs. Although there are a few studies of the African species, *Colobus guereza* and *C. badius,* most work on the social behavior and locomotion has focused on one of the Asian species, the common langur *Presbytis entellus.* In contrast to other colobines, common langurs extend from the foothills of the Himalayas with its seasonal snow fall, to the semidesert areas of Ragastan, in northwest India to the tropical forests of South India. The southernmost part of their range overlaps with that of the Nilgiri langur, *P. johnii,* a species confined to the dense and continuous mountain forests of the Western Ghats of southwest India.

 SUMMARY

True primates originated during the Paleocene as tropical animals who evolved hands and feet for grasping as a form of locomotion in newly available arboreal niches. As a way of catching prey as well as locomoting rapidly in the trees they developed stereoscopic vision and, in many forms, color vision. These and other characteristics set primates off as a group from other closely related mammals such as the bats, insectivores and "flying lemurs." The ancestry of the primates is perhaps most closely related to that of the insectivores who today are represented by one common form: the tree shrew of southeast Asia, once thought to be a primate itself. An omnivorous diet, as it is reflected in bunodont cusp morphology, distinguished the earliest or archaic primates, including the well known plesiadapiforms, from these other mammals. The evolution of the archaic primates was followed by a series of three major adaptive radiations which characterized the evolution of the early prosimian-like primates through the evolution of the higher primates or anthropoids. During the first radiation which occurred during the Paleocene and Eocene the plesiadapiforms diversified. The second radiation, which began at the end of the Paleocene, produced the arboreal prosimians, the ancestors of the living lemurs, galagos, and tarsiers. The third radiation occurred in the Oligo-cene during which anthropoid primates appeared and spread out of Africa. In South America primates, the platyrrhines, diversified as ancestral forms to all of the modern New World monkeys who possess both unique (as in the prehensile tail) and parallel characteristics (as in larger brains) with monkeys who evolved contemporaneously elsewhere in the Old World. This chapter examined the questions of primate origins and evolutionary history and discussed the specific anatomical adaptations which primates made to their respective niches. Geographic changes in the distribution of primates are related to continental drift and to changing climatic and ecological conditions worldwide.

 ## CRITICAL-THINKING QUESTIONS

1. What is a primate?
2. Describe the general characteristics of plesiadapiforms.
3. Briefly discuss the behavior and social organization of the prosimians.
4. What are the anatomical differences that distinguish anthropoids from prosimians?
5. Discuss the differences between nocturnal and diurnal primates.
6. Compare and contrast Old World and New World monkeys.

 ## SUGGESTED READINGS

Ankel-Simons, F. 1983. *A Survey of Living Primates and their Anatomy.* New York: Macmillan Publishing. An introduction to the diversity of living primates and their adaptations.

Conroy, G. 1990. *Primate Evolution.* New York: W.W. Norton. A general text on primate evolution and morphology.

Fleagle, J. 1988. *Primate Adaptation and Evolution.* New York: Academic Press. A general text on primate evolution and morphology.

Fleagle, J. and A. Rosenberger. 1990. *The Platyrrhine Fossil Record.* New York: Academic Press. A review of the fossil record of the New World monkeys.

Szalay, F. and E. Delson. 1979. *Evolutionary History of the Primates.* New York: Academic Press. A detailed treatment of primate evolution for the advanced student.

Primates: Patterns in Social Behavior

History of Field Studies

Advantages of Group Living

Development of Behavioral Modeling
Causes of Behavior

Male and Female Reproductive Strategies
Female Behavior
Seasonality and Behavior
Male Strategies and Behavior
Female Strategies

Primate Foraging and Feeding

Primate Defenses Against Predation

Communication in Nonhuman Primates

Aggression and Dominance Interactions

Birth and the Mother–Infant Bond

Learning as Adaptation to Sociality

Summary

Critical-Thinking Questions

Suggested Readings

hapter 6 examined primate evolution by looking at the fossil record and the morphological adaptations of modern primates. This chapter explores aspects of the **social behavior** of the anthropoids, the monkeys and apes. Such studies of modern primates, both in the wild and under laboratory situations, are instructive in two broad areas. First, in a general sense behavior is ecologically constrained (Figure 7–1); thus, behavior is adapted to ecology, and variations in behavior patterns can be explained by how a species exploits its natural resources. Survival or life history strategies of a species must be successful in its environment if an animal is to eat, mate, and avoid predators. Second, the study of behavior sheds light on evolutionary problems. Behaviors which are found to be universal among modern primates provide us with some clues as to the kinds of behaviors that our ancestors may have practiced. With such clues we can develop models of ancestral behaviors. For example, theories about the origin in ancestral hominids of habitual terrestrial bipedalism have as support specific behavior patterns observed in modern nonhuman primates, such as upright stances that accompany aggressive displays (Jablonski et al., 1993). The social behavior of modern prosimians, discussed in the last chapter, provides us with information on those basic primate behavioral adaptations from which the more complex behaviors of the higher primates have evolved. We turn our attention in this chapter to social behavior of the anthropoids.

social behavior–actions and interactions of animals within groups.

field studies–in primatology, studies of species in their natural habitat, uninfluenced or influenced to a minor degree by interactions with humans.

semi-free-ranging studies–in primatology, the study of primate groups that are in some way affected by or are dependent on humans, yet live more or less "normal" social lives.

laboratory studies–in primatology, controlled studies of captive primates.

HISTORY OF FIELD STUDIES

The first review of the literature on the social behavior of higher primates was undertaken by Yerkes and Yerkes in 1929. Up to that time not a single field report on primates—apes, monkeys or prosimians—had been published. Perhaps the first study of a primate species done in the wild was C. R. Carpenter's work on the howler monkeys of Barro Colorado Island, Panama, in 1934. Since then **field studies, semi-free-ranging studies** and **laboratory studies** on primates of both the Old and the New Worlds have expanded dramatically. Most of this growth dates from about the middle 1950s. Interest in general social behavior of a wide variety of primate species was followed by more specific studies on communication, mother–infant behavior, matrilineal kinship, and dominance, as well as the relationships of behavior to ecology.

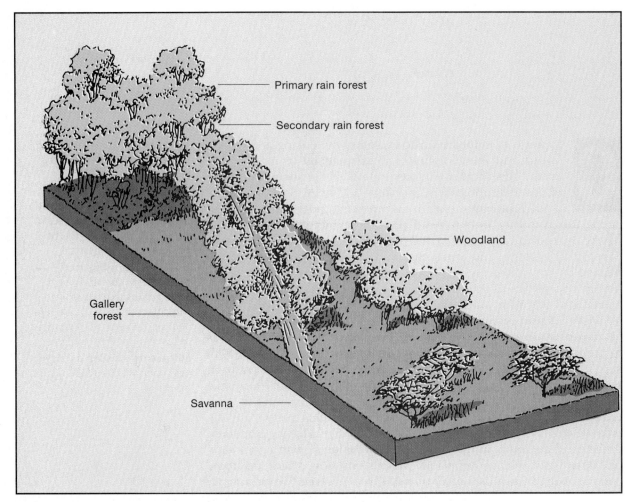

Figure 7–1 • Diversity of primate habitats.

Long-term studies (more than one year in length) have been undertaken on genealogical relationships and life histories of animals of such species as the common chimpanzee (Goodall), gorillas (Fossey), savanna baboon (Strum), orangutan (Galdikas) and the Japanese macaques (beginning with Itani).

In the late 1950s, K.R.L. Hall studied the chacma baboons of South Africa; Sherwood Washburn and Irvin DeVore studied the yellow and olive baboons of the Serengeti Plains in Kenya (Figure 7–2); Hans Kummer and Fred Kurt studied the desert baboons (*Papio hamadryas* of Ethiopia); and Phyllis Jay Dolhinow studied the langurs of North India. During the 1970s, studies on almost every genus and most species followed, all of which have increased our awareness and concern for those conservation measures that might help stem the alarming trend

Figure 7–2 • Irven DeVore in Nairobi National Park.

of habitat destruction, which threatens the survival of many species throughout the world (Southwick and Smith, 1986).

ADVANTAGES OF GROUP LIVING

One of the most important primate characteristics is sociality, the fact that we are social. In primates social behavior is organized around the continuous interactions of a group of animals. Some members of the group may continue to interact with certain other members throughout their life span. Long term interactions, such as those seen between a mother and her offspring, support group cohesiveness and make social living possible. Because group living demands complicated social interactions, each animal must spend a substantial amount of time learning about other animals and the roles they play. The individual's ability to recognize other individuals and act according to what they know about them based on past experience forms the basis for group interaction. Primate group living on a year-to-year basis also demands a great measure of social control over each individual's actions, as individual deviant behavior, for the most part, must be constrained if the group is to survive as a unit.

All animal species that interact among themselves on an ongoing basis share the same advantages and costs of group living (Figure 7–3). Perhaps the first advantage is that social living sets the stage for **observational learning** by individuals and, thereby, reduces the necessity of novel experimentation by any single animal. Knowledge of group traditions and the adaptive solutions to recurring problems allow an animal to learn how to survive within its ecological setting. In this regard the advantage of sociality is that such information is transmitted

observational learning–learning by seeing and hearing.

Figure 7–3 • Costs and benefits of diurnality and nocturnality for two species of New World monkeys, the dusky titi monkey (top, left) and the owl monkey (bottom, right).

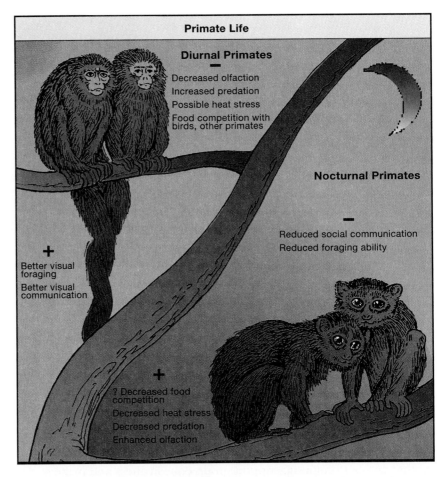

more easily among animals living in a group. Through the socialization process the group makes available to its members more knowledge than a single individual could acquire in its own lifetime.

A second advantage of social behavior is that it increases the possibility of resistance to diseases and parasites. During the evolution of the primates measurable genetic differences have accumulated as resistance to various diseases. Not surprisingly the development over time of such resistance is less likely among solitary animals than among those animals who are social.

A third advantage is that social behavior functions to increase the reproductive fitness of group members. Generally, group living is organized by a dominance hierarchy in which all members are ranked according to various criteria. This hierarchical structure of groups may result in reduced reproductive fitness of subordinate members relative to fitness in individuals of higher dominance rank. But even a subordinate, group-living individual probably has a higher fitness, because of the availability of mates, than do individuals living a solitary existence (Figure 7–4).

Figure 7–4 • Troop of savanna baboons.

Furthermore, social groups are more efficient in finding food resources, as foraging becomes more effective with larger numbers of individuals looking for food. For females an additional benefit of social groups is the reduced chance of **infanticide** of their offspring by nongroup males, as group females and their young are often afforded protection from attack by resident males.

These benefits must be weighed against the costs of social group living: (1) a reduced fecundity (reproductive output) of individuals, due to stress of ongoing social interactions (Dunbar, 1989) which balances against increased reproductive fitness due to the increased number of potential mates in a social group; (2) greater competition for food, which increases as the size of the group increases, but which also balances against a higher likelihood of finding food in the first place due to an increase in foragers; and (3) an increase in the possibility of killing of infants of those females who shift their residency from one group to another or, on the other hand, whose resident males transfer out of the group; however, there are lower frequencies of infanticide for those females whose group remains stable and whose social history is known to the resident males; and (4) an increase in the immediate spread of disease or parasites due to the close proximity of group members; this balances with the long-term advantage group-living, sexually reproducing organisms have towards acquiring resistance to disease and parasites.

infanticide–killing of infants.

DEVELOPMENT OF BEHAVIORAL MODELING

As information from numerous field studies accumulated, syntheses or models of behavior were needed to explain various patterns of primate social organization (Figure 7–5). Variations in social patterns had to be

Figure 7–5 • Common types of primate social groups. Social groupings vary from monogamous partnerships, as observed in gibbons, to opportunistically mating multi-male, multi-female troops, as seen in the baboons and macaques. Single-male units vary from the noyau pattern of the orangutans, to one-male troops, as observed in the south Indian langurs, to the single-male harems that are the smaller foraging-mating units of the larger aggregate of hamadryas baboons. The most fluid type of social grouping is the fission-fusion societies of the chimpanzees.

demographic—relating to the age composition, proportions of the sexes, size, and other statistical parameters of a population.

integrated with the ecological and **demographic** data being simultaneously collected by field workers.

Some of the first attempts to synthesize primate behavioral data borrowed theory from ethological studies of other animals, mainly birds and the social insects. One of ethology's pioneers was Konrad Lorenz.

His efforts focused attention on **stereotypic** (species-specific) aspects of behavior that clearly reflected evolutionary or phylogenetic patterns. The complex social behavior of mammals, and primates in particular, remained mostly outside this field of study. The primary reason was that species-specific behaviors, which are primarily genetically programmed, were considered to be relatively minor components of the total behavior patterns of these species. Variations in social behavior were not considered significant because either the ethologist was concerned with innate behaviors, or prior to the 1960s, behavioral variation within the species was thought to have little evolutionary or adaptive importance.

During the middle 1960s new theoretical perspectives emerged through the efforts of William Hamilton, George Williams, and J. Maynard Smith. From these perspectives evolved the concepts of **inclusive fitness.** Inclusive fitness is the sum of an individual's reproductive success and that of its relatives in proportion to their shared genes. It involves the success of individual strategies of game playing and optimality, game playing referring to how specific behavior patterns develop that maximize an individual's reproductive success, and optimality referring to alternative behaviors available to an individual. Along with this body of work, Dawkins (1976) developed the model of the "selfish gene," which argued that the basic unit of selection was the gene and not the individual. These replaced the earlier ethological views with notions that animal behavior is flexibly opportunistic and designed to maximize reproductive fitness through various strategies of self-interest.

These ideas were incorporated in a new field in animal behavior called **sociobiology** (Wilson, 1975). Sociobiology turned its attention on behavioral adaptation most important to an animal's reproductive strategies. It argued that the evolution of sociality must be explained at the level of reproductive costs and benefits to the individual (Alexander, 1974). Behavioral variation especially between the sexes, rather than being ignored, became the focus of evolutionary significance, and behavioral decisions were viewed with regard to the influence played by current social and ecological variables. Within the scope of reproductive strategies the primary interest was on concerns involving *sex-ratio manipulation* (how to alter the number of males or females produced in relation to environmental demand); *parental investment* (how much time and energy should be spent on any given offspring); and *parent–offspring conflict.*

The second field of interest to arise from the ethological perspective is behavioral ecology or **socioecology** (Figure 7–6), which looked at ways in which the nonsocial environmental variables, such as the availability of food or the threat of predators, could determine or constrain behavior. Whereas sociobiology measures genotypic success, based on gene propagation or spread, socioecology measures phenotypic success, that is, how successful animals are at food acquisition, re-

stereotypic–referring to repetitive behavior reproduced without significant variation.

inclusive fitness–the relative reproductive potential of an individual within a group of related individuals in a population.

sociobiology–evolutionary study of social behavior emphasizing relative reproductive rates of success of individuals within a population.

socioecology–evolutionary study of social behavior emphasizing the adaptation of species to their environment and ecological conditions.

Figure 7–6 • Factors involved in socioecological analysis. Primate social structure observed in the field is ultimately related to evolutionary history (phylogeny), then to development (ontogeny), and finally to environmental condition (ecology). (*From Milestones in Human Evolution* by H.D. Stecklis, Waveland Press, 1993)

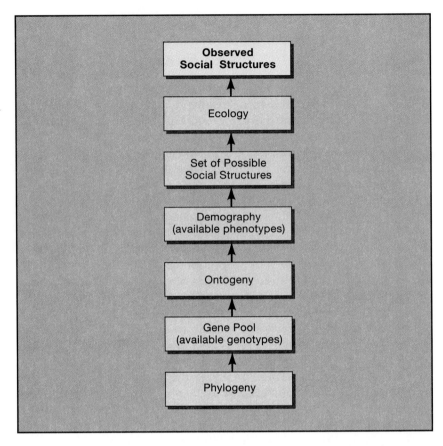

source defense, and mating (Wrangham, 1987; Terborgh and Jansen, 1986; Isbell, 1991).

Causes of Behavior

The question of why individuals perform specific behaviors in a given situation requires answers at different levels of understanding. Evolutionary biologists have separated the causes of individual behavior into two main types, proximate and ultimate. Proximate behavior refers to causes that are directly linked with physiological, neural, or hormonal factors. For example, the expression of aggression may be directly related to stimulation in the part of the brain that causes rage. In primates, however, aggressive behavior is usually modified by further proximate mechanisms, that is, by the effect of social group size and individual dominance rank. Ultimate behavior refers to evolutionary origins. For example, natural selection is the ultimate cause of aggressive behaviors, favoring them as part of the overall defense and reproductive strategies of males and females.

The study of proximate mechanisms, that is, attributing behavior solely to the workings of genes, has been considered by many social scientists to be inappropriately **reductionistic** or too **deterministic** to be of use in understanding causes of primate behavior. Reductionistic implies that all behavior can be explained by the actions of only a few variables; deterministic implies that all behavior is caused by these same variables and can be modified in only insignificant ways. Other mammalian biologists, however, are concerned that biology is too often ignored by those who study behavior. This sentiment was recently expressed by Goldsmith (1991):

> Biological "reductionism" can be used to trivialize evolutionary biology in an effort to keep it at arm's length, but this is an unworthy goal. The social sciences will have matured only when they are firmly grounded in, and consistent with, the rest of our understanding of nature. In this enterprise, biology and the social sciences should work together . . . .

In an attempt to reconcile the notion of behavioral flexibility with that of biological determinism in studying primate behavior, biological anthropologists develop models in which social and environmental factors play key roles in determining behavior within a context of genetic and physiologic influences. All of the elements of genetics, ecology, sociality, and learning are used in explaining behavior. We will now look at specific aspects of behavior, beginning with those that have formed the cornerstones of sociobiology: male and female reproductive strategies.

MALE AND FEMALE REPRODUCTIVE STRATEGIES

Central to the theories of vertebrate social organization today is the consideration of male and female reproductive strategies. The social structure and organization for any species relates to the interplay between male and female reproductive interests which unfold under unique ecological and demographic circumstances. Female behavior and, consequently, female social organization, relate to habitat characteristics, that is, where females find food and safety. Male behavior, on the other hand, relates to their ability to improve reproductive access to females. Because of this we would predict that male social organization is primarily correlated with the distribution of females but that it may also vary according to the demands of the environment.

reductionistic—referring to explanations or hypotheses that explain phenomena in terms of only one or two correlated factors or variables.

deterministic—referring to explanations or hypotheses that explain phenomena as caused by only one or two factors or variables.

social bond—linkage or tendency to associate between one or more individuals in a group.

Female Behavior

Although Zuckerman (1932) was convinced that the primary reason for the nonhuman primate year-round **social bond** was sexual attraction, most subsequent studies have shown that sexual behavior for any single individual is quite limited over the period of one year. Field work also points up another interesting characteristic of social organization

estrus–the period of maximum sexual receptivity.

ovulate–release of a mature egg cell from the female's ovary after which time it can be fertilized by a male sperm cell.

in that matings between close matrilineal relatives (especially between sons and mothers) are almost totally absent. Females have multiple mating partners, if they are available, and they often show a preference for mating with unfamiliar males. Between their selective mating patterns as well as through dispersal from one troop into another the problems of inbreeding are avoided and genetic heterogeneity within groups is maintained.

Because breeding patterns of many nonhuman primates were observed by early field workers to be seasonal the female reproductive cycle was termed **estrus**, the term that gave rise to the celebration of the season of fertility and rebirth that Christianity celebrates as Easter. A common example of estrus is the domestic dog or cat in "heat." It is during this period that females are most willing to mate with a male and in most mammalian species it is the only time in their reproductive cycles that they actually do mate. Biologically speaking, estrus is that part of the mammalian reproductive cycle when females **ovulate** (Figure 7–7).

Hormonal change related to ovulation in many species leads to specific external physiological and behavioral changes. Just before the release of the egg from the ovary into the fallopian tube, increases in estrogen and testosterone, and physiological changes occurring as a re-

Figure 7–7 • Mammalian reproductive cycle. Ovulation occurs during the period of estrus. (From *Primates in Nature* by Richard. Copyright © 1985 by Freeman and Company. Used with permission.)

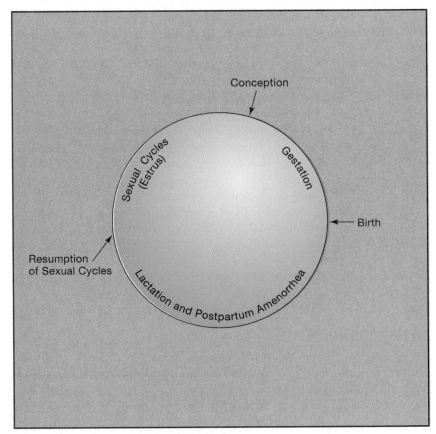

sponse to the elevation of these hormones, may produce other external signals of ovulation: (1) visual signals, (2) olfactory signals, and (3) behavioral signals. **Pheromones** (Greek, meaning "carriers" [of scent messages]) as well as a scent in urine have the effect of signaling receptivity to males. In some primate species, females also have a specialized **perineal** skin which reacts to ovarian **steroids** by swelling and reddening beginning a few days before ovulation, and lasting a few days afterward. This sort of reproductive signaling was remarked upon in 1876 by Charles Darwin, who concluded that the swelling of the perineum functioned as an attractant to males. Among species whose females do exhibit perineal swelling, including baboons (Figure 7–8), many other Old World monkeys, as well as the common chimpanzee, copulations become much more frequent as the size of the perineal area increases. During the period of maximum swelling, as male arousal becomes more intense, ejaculations are also more frequent. Recent experiments have pointed out that the swollen perineum by itself, independent of any smell-detected vaginal secretions, is the important arousing stimulus affecting male sexual behavior. On the other hand, female cotton-top tamarins seem to exhibit no other cue of ovulation except olfactory ones (Ziegler et al., 1993).

Although the term estrus may accurately describe sexual cycling in other mammals and in the prosimians it is not altogether accurate in describing the reproductive cycle of all monkeys and apes (Loy, 1987). Prosimians are more similar in their reproductive behavior to other mammals in that their reproductive activity is exclusively tied to ovulation and is rarely observed during other phases of the cycle. Some species of the higher primates do breed seasonally and may also restrict their entire sexual activity to this one period during the year. However, there are numerous exceptions to this rule. Some spec-

pheromones–hormones that produce their effect by the sense of smell.

perineal–relating to the area between the anus and the external genitalia, the perineum.

steroids–family of chemical substances that includes many hormones, constituents of the body, and Vitamin D.

Figure 7–8 • Swollen perineal region of female baboon in estrus.

ies have breeding seasons but continue sexual activity throughout the year. The crab-eating macaque (*Macaca fascicularis*), of Southeast Asia, for example, breeds year round, and copulates throughout the female's reproductive cycle and during her pregnancy.

In primates there is not necessarily a simple cause-and-effect relationship between hormones and sexual behavior. Gorden and Bernstein (1973) showed that, when male rhesus macaques are removed from their normal heterosexual groups, they fail to show any sexual activity at all, even during a mating season when they would normally associate with receptive females. These studies show that primates differ from other mammalian species in that hormonal influences on both sexes act on the brain's motivational systems rather than directly on the specific motor activity of a species' sexual behavior patterns. Consequently, sexual behaviors in the higher primates are more affected by context and other external factors.

The estrus cycle is the same reproductive cycle as that of human females but with a number of important differences. The first difference is that human females show very little indication of ovulation. In humans, ovulation may be detected by a slight rise in body temperature as measured by thermometer, by testing for a change in levels of hormones, and by, perhaps, subtle changes or shifts in some behavior patterns. On the other hand, the end of the reproductive cycle or **menstruation,** which occurs if the female fails to become pregnant, is quite obvious by the copious discharge of blood and tissue of the built-up uterine lining. In humans, as ovulation is subtle and menstruation is not, the human reproductive cycle has been labeled the menstrual cycle. The second important difference lies in the area of sexual activity, which for humans as well as for many of the monkeys and apes, is ongoing and continual throughout the entire reproductive cycle including pregnancy and **lactation** (breastfeeding) phases.

Seasonality and Behavior

Given the large differences in primate life history strategies and the complexity of ecological relationships, biological anthropologists have not been able to clearly tie environmental variables to the timing of reproductive events among all primate species. Nevertheless, it is obvious that some breeding seasons are environmentally related (Table 7–1). Because seasonal reproduction is part of the reproductive strategies of some species, natural selection may favor individuals who time their births to coincide with optimal environmental conditions, guaranteeing a better chance for survival of both offspring and mother. For example, among yellow baboons it appears that those young baboons who are born late in the season relative to other infants are at some disadvantage. About 30% of these late-comers die during their first two years of life. Possibly, because of the timing of their births, limited resources may ultimately affect their survival.

menstruation–monthly, cyclic shedding of the lining of the uterus by nonpregnant female primates, particularly noticeable in humans.

lactation–in mammals the period of production of milk following birth of offspring, during which offspring are suckled by the mother.

Table 7–1 • Primate Species and Birth Seasons

Species and Source	Number of Births and Newborns	Mating	Births
Japanese Macaque (Mizuhara)	545	Copulations restricted to season from Oct. to April. Peak frequency in Jan. and Feb.	99% of births during May to Sept. 1% April and Oct. No births ever reported mid-Oct. to mid-April.
Rhesus Macaque (Koford)	237	Copulations restricted to distinct period beginning in July and ending in Jan.	Most births restricted to period from Jan. to June. 75% in March and April. No births Aug. to Jan. (1 on Dec. 29).
Rhesus Macaque (Southwick, Beg, and Siddiqi)	217	Copulations observed in all months of study except March. Greatest frequency of sexual behavior from Oct. to Dec.	Births and young observed March to June and a few in Sept. From Nov. to March observed 2092 females, none with newborn infants.
Bonnet Macaque (Simonds)	10+	Copulations observed throughout year. Peak observed in Oct. and Nov. Probably high in Sept. as well.	Births occur mainly from late Jan. to late April. A few in June and July. No dark-phase infants observed Sept. to mid-Jan.
Indian Langur (Jay)			
Abujhmar Hills	6	Copulations rarely observed.	No seasonal clustering of births noted.
Raipur-Nagpur Road	33		A few births Jan. to March. Many newborns in April. No newborns in Nov. or Dec.
Lucknow District	10	Copulations observed in all 4 months of study (Dec. to April).	Births and newborn infants observed in March and April.
Hamadryas Baboon (Kummer)		Copulations observed throughout observation period (Feb. to Nov.). Sharp increase of swelling in females and of copulations in May; peak in June.	Births observed throughout study. Greatest number of dark infants from May to Aug.
Kenya Baboon			
(DeVore)	11	Copulations noted all months but fewer in Sept. to Dec.	Observed 1 birth from March to Sept.; 10 births Sept. to Jan.
(Washburn)	80	A few copulations observed each day of study.	Counted twice as many newborn infants in Oct. as in Sept.
Chacma Baboon (Hall)		Copulations noted all months. March/April frequency more than twice that of Sept. to Nov.	No clustering of births noted.
Mountain Gorilla (Schaller)	54	Copulations rarely observed.	Births observed throughout year.
Chimpanzee			
(V. and F. Reynolds)		Copulations rarely observed.	Mothers and young observed in all months of study.
(Goodall)		Copulations observed almost daily in Sept., Oct., and rarely in other months. Females with sexual swelling observed at all times of the year.	Small infants observed in April, June, Sept., and Oct.

From Lancaster and Lee (1965).

predation rate–frequency of killing and eating of individuals of a prey species by one or several predator species.

androgen–any of a class of hormones that stimulates activity of the male sex organs or promotes development of male sex characteristics.

testosterone–the hormone produced by the testis that initiates and then maintains male secondary sex characteristics.

Where yearly variation in temperature is small and the **predation rate** on both parent and young is low, seasonal availability of food is generally the most important variable to explain the timing of births. For *Cercopithecus* monkeys food apparently is the primary determinant of when a female should give birth, and rainfall, through its effect on the food supply, plays the major indirect role. In regard to food, however, it is not so much what the mother eats as it is what is available to those young who are newly weaned. Their diet at this critical time may be the most important causative factor in birth seasonality.

Male Strategies and Behavior

Whereas females in many nonhuman primate species exhibit seasonal reproductive behavior, seasonal changes in male **androgen** levels is less well understood, but it is apparent that in many nonhuman primate species they also vary. The influence, for example, of female receptivity on male cyclically has been documented for squirrel monkeys (Dumond and Hutchinson, 1967). During the mating season plasma **testosterone** levels in adult males are considerably higher than at other times of the year, accounting for distinct birth peaks (Figure 7–9).

In contrast to those species that show a restricted breeding season, others such as the stumptail macaque, found in Southeast Asia, breed all year long, and testosterone levels do not show a seasonal pattern. The stumptail macaque might well be the "sexiest" primate on record with an ejaculation rate for one male of 59 times during a 6-hour period. Observed rates for other macaque species occur at less than 10 times per day (Nienwenhayen et al., 1988).

Figure 7–9 • Seasonality of matings and births observed in the squirrel monkey. (From Dumond, 1967)

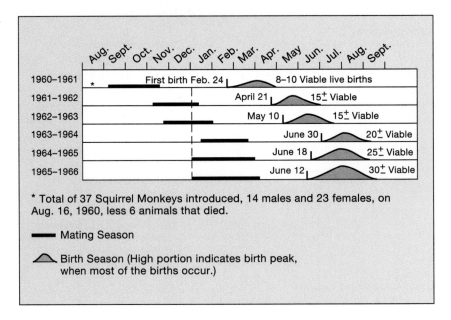

Carpenter (1942) studied rhesus monkeys colonized on Cayo Santiago Island near Puerto Rico (Figure 7–10). On the basis of his observations he hypothesized that the number of females with which any male mated was directly proportional to the individual male's dominance rank. However, more recent studies have shown that male rank and copulatory frequency are not significantly interrelated. Copulation frequency of young low-ranking males is usually underestimated because as part of these individuals' reproductive strategies they often conceal themselves from the view of others, knowing that dominant males will usually disrupt their copulation attempts if they can see them.

In young males, copulatory frequency rises sharply between the sixth and twelfth months prior to the descent of their testicles, which occurs as the males reach sexual maturity. Up to this point and a few months beyond, young males attempt mating with willing females openly in view of other group members without interruption from other adults. Starting about a year following testicular descent, however, this sexual freedom for the most part ends because of increasing intolerance of these males by fully adult males, as well as by females. It is this growing intolerance of the presence of the young adult males which in many cases ultimately forces them to the periphery of the group and then their ultimate immigration into nearby all-male or other heterosexual groups.

Figure 7–10 • Cayo Santiago Island, Puerto Rico.

Although paternity will always be to some extent uncertain in **multi-male groups,** males who have mated and then remain in the group during the birth of infants are usually assumed in field studies by primatologists to be the fathers. These males also associate with newborns far more than do other more transient males. From the point of view of the infant, "paternal" protection often prevents harassment and aggression by other males or females. From the protector's point of view, it may serve to either develop or further social relations with the infant's mother. Such nonkin alliances or "friendships" often develop in this way and are maintained for long periods of time.

Adult male–infant behavior may work in another direction to benefit the adult male. Sometimes males "kidnap" infants temporarily to use as buffers or "shields" in **agonistic** encounters with other males. In baboons a very common three-way interaction has an adult male holding or carrying an infant while accompanied by another adult male (Figure 7–11). In this manner potential aggression between these males is often thwarted.

Male parentage is more easily determined in species that are (at least serially) **monogamous,** and in which males make regular contributions to the care of offspring. In the New World monkeys—among the marmosets, tamarins, titis, and the owl monkeys—males usually do most of the infant carrying and return infants to their mothers only for feeding. Fathers, with the help of previously born juveniles and in some cases even unrelated subdominant males, carry infants on their backs, share food after the infants are weaned, and play with, as well

multi-male groups–a pattern of social organization, in primates where several adult males live together in the same group.

agonistic–in ethology, referring to behavior that appears in aggressive encounters.

monogamous–referring to one male–one female pair bonding.

Figure 7–11 • Use of an infant as a shield in a potentially agonistic encounter among baboons.

Figure 7–12 • New World monkey, *Callimico;* father carries single infant.

as protect, infants from predators and other dangers (Figure 7–12). Fathers, however, will get out of "baby-sitting" if they can and will relieve themselves of the chore if they have available helpers (McGrew, 1988). In the marmosets and tamarins, one primary function of paternal care is to aid the mother in carrying multiple offspring, as twinning (producing twins) is common rather than the exception for this group. Among the Old World anthropoids males do not habitually carry infants. In single-male, multi-female **harem species** such as the hamadryas and gelada baboons, males may adopt prepubescent females, carry them about and protect them much as their mothers would do and, ultimately, when they become adults incorporate them into the "harem."

Under certain circumstances adult males may kill infants (Hausfater and Hrdy, 1984). Numerous reports have shown that the most common instance of infanticide occurs when an unfamiliar male immigrates into a troop and by challenge usurps the position of the resident dominant male. Such behavior, noted especially for the common langur of South India, often occurs when the new male has established his position of dominance in the group, at which point he may systematically kill young infants belonging to the group's resident females. Sarah Hrdy's study in 1970 revealed that on the average, every 27 months, a female langur's infant was killed in this manner. One apparent result of this behavior is that females soon after the death of their offspring begin to ovulate and become sexually receptive. Langur infanticide is explained as part of a male's reproductive strategy that brings females into estrus and thus ensures his paternity for the next round of infant births.

Other examples of infanticide have been observed among baboons, red colobus monkeys, silver leaf monkeys, and the New World red howler monkeys. In these cases infanticidal males were **natal residents** of the troop. Apparently the trigger for this sort of behavior was the male's rise to higher dominance status.

Female Strategies

Hrdy has further shown that females are not passive objects of males' reproductive strategy. In order to avoid male infanticide, instead of relying on the single best male as a mate choice, females, even when pregnant, will often engage in sex with numerous males. Hrdy theorized that females use **promiscuity** to confuse paternity and she believes that mating with many males increases the number of males who might befriend her. In this way a female can muster support for herself and her infant from more than one male and at the same time deflect future attacks by them.

In some species, however, females can reduce the risk of aggression by forming longterm breeding relationships with one male. Van Schaik and Dunbar (1990) believe that monogamous relationships are best explained by the service the male provides against infanticide by other males. They cite studies on the incidence of infanticide in gorillas (Watts, 1985, 1989), showing that in 8 out of the 11 observed cases of male infanticide a mother and her infant were attacked when they were unaccompanied by a mature male. Perhaps for this reason females live in some form of social groups to reduce the possibility of infanticide.

Both birth seasonality in addition to the **inter-birth interval** may play a role in infant survivability. For example, in rhesus monkeys there appears to be an earlier onset of maturation, somewhere between four to five years, versus five to six years for the Japanese macaque. Rhesus monkeys also show a shorter inter-birth interval of 14.3 ± 5.5 months as compared with 18.0 ± 6.6 months for Japanese monkeys. The slower reproductive rate for the Japanese monkeys might be favored because of the harsh winters these animals experience, and females with a reduced reproductive rate may have a better opportunity to care for their infants for longer periods of time.

The **dominance rank** of the mothers also appears to be an important variable in the survival of her offspring (giving birth seldom increases a mother's social dominance). One way dominant females can affect the reproductive success of their low-ranking competitors is by harassing them during copulation. In langur monkeys, for example, rank plays some role in the frequency of harassment: females disrupted only 50% of the copulations that involved the top three adult females in a troop; in contrast, females disrupted almost 96% of those copulations involving the three lowest ranking females. Dunbar (1986) demonstrated with gelada baboons that social stress caused by dominant females harassing subordinate females limited the latter's reproductive success, quite probably, by suppressing ovulation. Higher ranking females often threaten, chase and perhaps bite low-ranking females more frequently when these females showed estrous behavior.

In spider monkeys composition of adult animals in the group shows a heavily biased sex ratio of about 3 to 1 favoring females over males.

harem species—in primatology, species characterized by social groupings of one dominant male and a number of females and their young.

natal residents—residents of a group born there.

promiscuity—sexual relations with a number of partners.

inter-birth interval—the period of time between births.

dominance rank—the relative hierarchical position of an individual in a social group.

Figure 7–13 • A chimpanzee foraging and feeding.

Through as yet unknown mechanisms, dominance rank also plays some role in the timing and sex determination of a newborn. Low-ranking females have a much longer birth interval than do high-ranking ones, about 36 months as compared to 29 months, and they almost exclusively give birth to daughters, whereas high ranking females produce most of the sons. By chance alone the ratio of males to females at birth should be about 50:50. The skewed birth ratio, which is correlated heavily with maternal rank, presupposes some postconception mechanism which results in a differential male mortality *in utero*.

After the birth of the infant aggressive harassment by adult high ranking females further reduces the chance of survival of young males. Their attacks resulting in some injury on the immature males are about 1.7 times more likely to occur than they are on the young females (Chapman et al., 1989). One explanation is that under the conditions of intense resource competition it may be advantageous for adult females somehow negatively to affect the production and survival of male offspring of other females in order to decrease competition later on for their sons. The consequences of these behaviors give an additional advantage to sons of higher ranking females, who are likely to be competitively superior to the sons of lower-ranking females anyway.

PRIMATE FORAGING AND FEEDING

A group's **foraging strategies** must be modified to accommodate the number of animals in a social group who feed on relatively concentrated food sources (or patches) (Figure 7–13). Having to compete among themselves for food may give rise to higher frequencies of dominance interactions, and the resultant increase in social friction may be considered as one cost of social group living. Alexander (1974), who proposed that predator pressure was the primary determining factor for sociality, believed that intragroup competition in foraging was a cost of group living. When too many animals feed in the same area at the same time, they tend to reduce foraging efficiency by depleting available resources. To solve these problems there must be some optimal group size for which foraging efficiency is maximized. Optimal group size, however, may vary from group to group, species to species, and year to year (Figure 7–14).

When food sources are scarce (or patchy) and the geographical location of these patches and their annual productivity are more or less unpredictable, an increased number of foragers may be advantageous, because it increases the group's chance of finding food in shorter periods of time (Ward and Zahavi, 1973; Clutton-Brock and Harvey, 1977; Rodman, 1988; Isbell, 1991). As an example, often when a few chimpanzees locate a particularly coveted food, those making the discovery

foraging strategies—behavior patterns which result in the discovery and procurement of food.

Figure 7–14 • Foraging unit, the gelada baboon harem.

hoot loudly as a signal for others to join them, which they often did. Sharing of information on preferred food sources among group members is clearly of benefit.

The ideas discussed above have been more formally organized into what has become known as **optimal foraging theory.** Here optimal behavior will develop when returns and benefits are maximized in relation to costs and risks within the context of resource availability and socioecological factors. As Robinson (1986) has shown from his field studies of the wedge-capped capuchin, a New World monkey, foraging groups do possess considerable knowledge of the resources in their

Table 7–2 • Group Size, Intergroup Displacement Rank, and the Use of Space in the Wedge-Capped Capuchin Monkey

Intergroup Displacement Rank	Average Group Size[1]
1	30+
2	30+
3	26.0
4	21.3
5	22.5
6	14.3
7	20.5
8	8.2
9	13.0
10	13.2

[1]A major selective advantage to living in a large group is the ability to displace smaller groups at fruit trees, compensating for the increased within-group competition at food resources.

From Robinson (1986).

optimal foraging theory–a predictive theory based on food-getting behavior selected to balance a group's needs to find food against the costs of getting it.

home range–the area that a group or population inhabits and ranges over, the boundaries of which, unlike a territory, are not defended.

home ranges and utilize this knowledge effectively to find seasonal fruit. The capuchin's large home range ensures that some fruiting species is available throughout most of the year and, because the home ranges overlap extensively, inter-group competition makes social living and large group size the practical solution to their feeding problems (Wrangham, 1980, 1983; Rodman, 1988) (Table 7–2).

PRIMATE DEFENSES AGAINST PREDATION

Whereas a solitary animal must depend solely on its own ability to detect a predator, group living in primates almost always ensures early detection of a predator by many animals (Hamilton, 1971) and the sub-

Figure 7–15 • The distribution of the various subspecies of savanna baboon. From *Primates in Nature* by Richard. Copyright © 1985 by Freeman and Company. Used by permission.

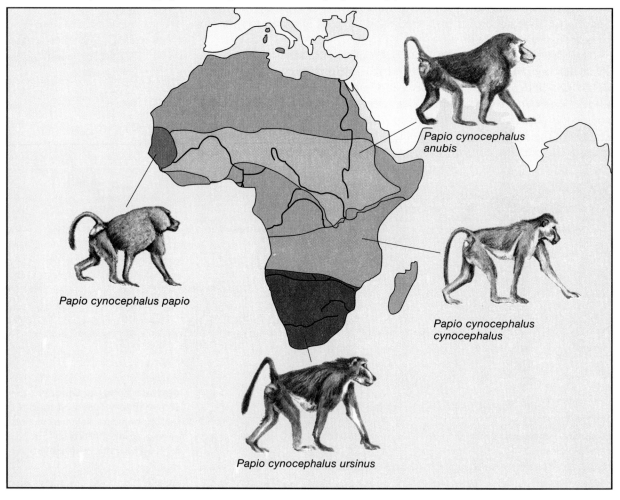

sequent emission of a warning signal, thereby reducing each member's chance of being attacked. A number of species have elaborated on this defense strategy and, in addition to warnings, have developed some form of cooperative defense against the predator. The African savanna baboon (Figure 7–15) may use cooperative adult male threat behavior to ward off predators (Washburn, 1983:17). Adult males typically show greater peripherality, especially the most dominant ones, and are usually the first animals to confront a predator. In a similar fashion the juveniles and females often form the center of the group (Figure 7–16). Japanese macaques, and the more arboreal mangabeys, often use this spatial patterning which Itani (1954) described as the duplicate concentric circle pattern of social organization. The argument is that the peripheral, more self-sufficient adult males are better able to defend themselves against predators and at the same time ward potential danger away from the other more defenseless members of the group. Of course, adult male peripherality has one advantage for the males in that these individuals will be the first to discover and exploit new food resources with less competition from other members of the troop.

The potential effect of predation on the survival of solitary males may help explain why multimale associations persist in seasonally breeding species. Van Schaik (1983), following Alexander (1974), believes that predation avoidance offered the only universal selective advantage of group living. They believe that predation is what sets the lower limit for group size, whereas intragroup feeding competition is what sets the upper limit. Broad generalizations about the relative influence of predation pressure on primate social organization, however, may be difficult to prove. The Boeschs' (1991) study on chimpanzees

Figure 7–16 • Positioning of baboon troop members during foraging. Adult males tend to lead and follow up the main group.

show the difficulties in observation intended to actually determine who predates on whom and in what frequency.

COMMUNICATION IN NONHUMAN PRIMATES

Considering that nonhuman primates have no spoken language in the human sense, they communicate a great deal. In order to live together peacefully year after year animals must communicate their needs and emotions by means of various signals. **Communication** usually results in cooperative action of a give-and-take nature. Communication is necessary to all primates, even the less gregarious ones, for purposes of reproduction at least. For the more highly social primates, precise communication of emotional states and information about the environment is critical to social life. As a result, primates have developed elaborate communication systems, ones that incorporate both specific anatomical structures and specific types of signals which vary, depending upon the environmental situation. For instance, high canopy forest monkeys often rely on discrete vocalizations, because individual animals cannot usually see each other in the dense foliage. By contrast, savanna baboons, who are almost always in sight of one another, usually rely on visual or postural cues to communicate their intent.

One trend in primate communication has been to reduce the emphasis on signals based on olfaction (sense of smell) and to increase those based on vision. This change is understandable considering the importance of vision to arboreal locomotion in all primate species. The Old World monkeys and apes rely on visual means in communication and use a more expanded array of facial gesturing and expression than do their New World and prosimian cousins. The expansion of visual signaling in all Old World species, including humans, is in part related to a more elaborate and complex facial musculature (Figure 7–17).

Being able to describe past or future action is still a prerogative of human language, yet in other ways humans and nonhumans communicate similarly. Most primate species communicate using a number of different signals or modes. For example, vocalizations, facial gestures, postures, and touch may all be incorporated in a single message and often simultaneously. For some species signals are discrete from one another to avoid ambiguity. Vervet monkeys use distant vocal calls to distinguish between snake and bird predators. Many primates also have the ability to intergrade their messages to relay subtle changes in their emotional state during an interaction. For that reason, most expressions of dominance involve signals that intergrade.

The early studies of primate communications systems initially showed that primates only communicate about their emotional state and that they could relay little information about objects or events around. Steklis (1985:159) in reappraising this notion stated:

communication–transmittal of information by sensory means.

Figure 7–17 • Facial expression in *Cercopithecus*.

One might expect that intelligent, long-lived primates who spend most of their lives in close proximity to relatives and fellow group members would readily learn to associate individual vocal characteristics with other attributes of social relevance.

Indeed, more recent studies involving the recording of individual vocalizations and their subsequent playback to the animals have revealed a much greater complexity in the kinds of information relayed. These studies have shown that apes as well as monkeys produce variable vocal signals that can give information about the sender's sex, the kinship group to which the sender belongs, and the sender's social status. For example, wild forest mangabeys respond selectively to the long distance calls of adult males from outside their group. Presumably group members' responses to these vocalizations are based on their past experience with the individuals making the calls.

Within the vocal repertoire of many species calls may be age–sex specific. The colobine genus *Presbytis* uses between 18 to 21 discrete vocalizations, out of which four calls are used exclusively by adult males and one call is used by adult females. In *Presbytis* alarm calls of adult females and juveniles of both sexes differ in structure from the harsh bark of adult males. Similar findings were also made for the golden monkey (*Rhinopithecus roxellena*). On the other hand, Marler (1973) found certain structural similarities in the alarm calls of many sympatric species (those living in the same habitat) who were endangered by the same predators, indicating how minimizing the difference of specific vocalizations that function solely as alarm signals could mutually benefit different species.

FRONTIERS

Insights From Field Primatology

by Linda D. Wolfe

Field primatology, that is, the study of the alloprimates (primates other than ourselves) in their natural environment, encompasses social behavior, sexual behavior, demography, activity budgets, foraging and ranging strategies, and the environmental factors that impinge on the lives of the alloprimates. In order for researchers to view the full range of adaptations and social behaviors, species must be studied in their natural habitats. Because primates are long-lived, that is, individuals live past twenty years of age, long-term field studies produce the most valuable insights into behavior. Field primatologists have been amazingly productive in the last fifty years. There are now field reports on the alloprimates from all major taxonomic groups [see Appendix 3], and the research continues.

Much of what we know about the behaviors of the alloprimates comes under the rubric of primate ecology and primate socioecology. Primate ecology involves a field study of ecological adaptations of a particular group of free-ranging primates. During the field study, a primatologist collects and analyzes data on foraging and ranging patterns (where the group goes and where it eats), specific foods ingested, activity budgets (how the group spends its time during the day), polyspecific relationships (how the alloprimates relate to other species), and the group composition (the individual primates making up the group). Primates are omnivores in

the sense that they consume fruit, leaves, seeds, flowers, gum, insects, and in some cases, meat. Fig, tamarind, acacia, and palm nut trees are among the most important food sources for primates. There is also evidence that at least chimpanzees deliberately eat plants for their medicinal effects (Jisaka et al., 1992). Alloprimates learn to avoid eating plants with high levels of toxins. Research has shown that colobine monkeys (who are leaf eaters) are generally more tolerant of plant toxins than are cercopithecines (fruit and insect eaters), and the cercopithecoids as a group are more tolerant than the hominoids (Jolly, 1985).

Almost since the inception of field primatology in the 1930s there has been interest in primate socioecology, which is the study of the relationship between primate social systems and the environment through comparative studies (Richard, 1985). The literature on primate socioecology includes both large-scale studies that use multiple variables from field studies to link social systems and the environment, and smaller-scale studies in which the adaptations of members of one species living in different environments are compared. An example of the latter is Mitani's (1992) study of the western lowland gorilla in the northern tropical forest of the People's Republic of the Congo, an area that has not been disturbed by human occupation. Mitani indicates that gorillas in this area have a fission-fusion type of social system rather than the uni-male grouping usually reported for gorillas. He suggests that if gorillas do indeed have a fission-fusion social system in this area, it is related to the patchy distribution of fruit consumed by the gorillas.

A number of researchers have attempted to demonstrate a relationship between primate social systems and the environment (Crook and Gartlan, 1966; Eisenberg et al., 1972; Clutton-Brock and Harvey, 1977; and Wrangham, 1980). None of these attempts has proved entirely satisfactory because evolutionary history (phylogeny) or random changes in the behavior of a species may be more important than current environmental factors in determining present-day social systems. The phylogeny-versus-ecology debate is ongoing and will not be resolved any time soon. Further complicating the issue is Rowell's (1993) suggestion that alloprimates do not perceive a social system and that analyzing their social behavior with this theoretical construct is not productive. Dunbar (1992) has recently made the suggestion that brain size (neocortical volume), not environmental variables, most accurately predicts primate group size. Finally, there is considerable individual variation in behavior and in behavioral traditions in different troops, which can make cross-species comparative studies difficult. When carrying out a comparative primate research project, the researcher needs access to all of the data on the species being compared and must take that variability into account.

Field primatologists have also been interested in sexual behavior. Alloprimate sexual behavior is similar to that of other mammals, involving the practicing of adult behavior by juveniles, and after puberty the emergence of adult courtship behavior and approach patterns. However, estrus in higher primates has been found to be different from that among nonprimate mammals. In general, a female mammal in estrus is receptive to a male, and sexual behavior is associated with ovulation. In primates, females are continuously receptive and proceptive behavior may or may not correlate with ovulation. Mating appears to be more closely associated with ovulation in those species which have a midcycle swelling of the genital area than in those species which lack the "sex swelling." There is evidence that humans follow the higher primate pattern of increased sexual activity in midcycle (Matteo and Rissman, 1984).

The study of the structure, function, and meaning of alloprimate vocalizations is a burgeoning field of inquiry by field primatologists. It was once believed that alloprimate vocalizations were emotional statements that lacked actual referents. However, it is now evident that vocalizations can and do have specific referents. Cheney and Seyfarth (1990) in a classic study have shown that vervet monkeys have three different alarm calls corresponding to their three main predators—leopards, snakes, and martial eagles. Each of the alarm calls demonstrates that monkeys can associate a vocalization with a specific danger in their environment and react appropriately. In another study Gouzoules et al. (1984) demonstrated that screams given by juvenile rhesus monkeys when in contact with higher-ranking opponents elicited stronger behavioral responses from their mothers than did screams emitted during contact with kin.

There is a growing debate among field primatologists as to whether primates other than humans have culture (McGrew, 1992). It is evident that there are behavioral traditions, such as potato-washing (Kawamura, 1959) and branch-shaking displays (Wolfe,

1981) among Japanese macaques, and tool-use and grooming postures among chimpanzees (McGrew, 1992), which may vary from group to group within the same species. If culture is behaviorally based and defined as learned, shared behaviors that are passed on from one generation to the next, then we would have to say that the alloprimates have culture. If, on the other hand, culture is based on symbols, and defined as the rules in the mind used to generate behavior, then it would seem evident that other primates do not possess culture. The resolution of the issue of alloprimate culture will ultimately depend on greater communication between cultural anthropologists and primatologists, and a consensus on the definition of culture.

References

Cheney, D.L. and B.M. Seyfarth. 1990. *How Monkeys See the World*. Chicago: University of Chicago Press.

Clutton-Brock, T.H. and P.H. Harvey. 1977. "Primate ecology and social organization." *Journal of Zoology* 183: 1–39.

Crook, J.H. and J.S. Gartlan. 1966. "Evolution of primate societies." *Nature* 210:1200–1203.

Dunbar, R.I.M. 1992. "Neocortex size as a constraint on group size in primates." *Journal of Human Evolution* 20:469–93.

Eisenberg, J.F., N.A. Muckenhirn, and R. Rudran. 1972. "The relation between ecology and social structure in primates." *Science* 176:863–874.

Gouzoules, S., H. Gouzoules, and P. Marler. 1984. "Rhesus monkey (*Macaca mulatta*) screams: Representational signalling in the recruitment of agonistic aid." *Animal Behavior* 32:182–93.

Josaka, M., M. Kawanaka, H. Sugiyama, K. Takegawa, M.A. Huffman, H. Ohigashi, and K. Koshimizu. 1992. "Antischistosomal activities of sesquiterpene lactones and steroid glucosides from Vernonia amygdalina, possibly used by wild chimpanzees against parasite-related diseases." *Bioscience, Biotechnology and Biochemistry* 56:845–846.

Jolly, A. 1985. *The Evolution of Primate Behavior*. New York: Macmillan.

Kawamura, S. 1959. "The process of sub-culture propagation among Japanese macaques." *Primates* 2:43–60.

McGrew, W.C. 1992. *Chimpanzee Material Culture*. Cambridge: Cambridge University Press.

Matteo, S. and E.F. Rissman. 1984. "Increased sexual activity during the midcycle portion of the human menstrual cycle." *Hormones and Behavior* 18:249–255.

Mitani, M. 1992. "Preliminary results of the studies on wild western lowland gorillas and other sympatric diurnal primates in the Ndoki Forest, northern Congo." In Itoigawa, et al., eds., *Topics in Primatology, Volume 2*. Tokyo: University of Tokyo Press, pp. 215–24.

Richard, A. 1985. *Primates in Nature*. New York: W.H. Freeman.

Rowell, T.E. 1993. "Reification of social systems." *Evolutionary Anthropology* 2:135–37.

Wolfe, L.D. 1981. "Display behavior of three troops of Japanese monkeys." *Primates* 22:24–32.

Wrangham, R.W. 1980. "An ecological model of female-bonded primate groups." *Behavior* 75:262-300.

Linda D. Wolfe is Professor and Chair of Anthropology at East Carolina University. She has conducted extensive primatological field research in Asia.

aggressive–tending toward or threatening physical injury.

Expanding these notions in terms of the origin of human language, Seyfarth, Cheney, and Marler (1980) have suggested that the simplest sort of "representational" signaling such as the alarm calls of vervet monkeys which distinguish specific predators, provides a considerable selective advantage, and, therefore, an adaptive advantage to individuals who use it. Success in alarm call signaling might support the further development of this ability into many other social situations such as feeding behavior where specific food sources could be identified. Studies of the titi monkeys of South America have further blurred the distinction between the communications of the nonhuman primates and human language: these primates have been known to repeat calls to form what might be considered phrases and combine them in sequence, mimicking the elementary rules of syntax.

AGGRESSION AND DOMINANCE INTERACTIONS

One of the major functions of communication in group-living animals is to provide group cohesion. Primatologists have looked at the ways primates maintain group cohesion in spite of infrequent **aggressive** acts by members within the group itself (Figure 7–18). These studies have shown that primates resolve most of their conflicts through a series of reconciliation behaviors, which usually follow some aggressive act, by seeking out one's former opponent and attempting to repair whatever damage had been done to the relationship. Kinship plays an important role, as studies have shown that two opponents are much more likely to reconcile if they are matrilineal kin than if they are unrelated. For most primates kinship functions as a major feature of intragroup behavior, and is useful in explaining many patterns of grooming, dominance, and aggression. Some species of primates have specific gestures and social displays to accomplish a reconciliation such as lip smacking (Figure 7–19) and presenting, commonly observed

Figure 7–18 • Primate aggressive interaction between two subadult male gorillas.

in baboons and macaques. Other species such as patas monkeys and some species of *Cercopithecus* use adjustments in proximity to one another to accomplish the same end.

In many cases, rather than patching up a relationship, some nonhuman primates exhibit behaviors aimed at preventing aggression in the first place. Peripherality that adult males often maintain to the center of the group is an extremely good way to do this. But when males cannot avoid interacting, they may display behaviors to help maintain peaceful co-existence (Dohlinow and Taff, 1993). Male–male mounting behaviors, for example, may function in this manner. Because observations show that a significant number of these mounts are made by subordinate individuals over animals more dominant than themselves, this behavior cannot be explained in terms of an expression of higher dominance rank. Mountings of this type frequently occur before friendly relations are established between two individuals, in which case, they may function cohesively by promoting nonaggressive social contact. **Grooming behavior** also prevents aggression and at the same time helps maintain group solidarity. In fact, grooming is a good example of a behavior pattern which serves a multitude of social functions. From a hygienic point of view grooming is necessary for the maintenance of good health, because ticks, lice, and other ectoparasites infest many species and grooming generally concentrates on those regions of the body that are difficult to get at by oneself. Also grooming may be traded for sexual access, for proximity to a mother with a new infant, or for forming an alliance with another animal for assistance in future aggression with a third party. Mothers spend a good deal of time grooming their infants, although as their offspring mature, mother monkeys tend to groom them less, and sons less than daughters.

The patterns of dominance based on the rank of the adult males and females organize most of the social interactions in the nonhuman primate group. Dominance rank is established and maintained by aggressive interactions, yet aggressive behavior is usually not disruptive to social order. In fact, because aggression is most often based on threat rather than actual fighting it functions positively to maintain social integration and group cohesion. Although the biological elements of aggression are similar in most nonhuman primates, the pattern and degree of the development of aggressive behavior differs between species and within species in different habitats.

The expression of dominance occurs in many ways. One individual may displace another in a favored resting place or an individual, usually high-ranking individuals (males as well as females), may purposefully break up disputes even at the physical risk of intervening so as to restore peace within the group. Interference behavior of this sort may be a defense of self-interest in that an interfering animal might be supporting kin, a friend, or a potential sex partner. Finally, interference interactions may have the continuing function of improving (or at least monitoring) one's dominance position.

Figure 7–19 • Primate appeasement behavior in chimpanzees.

grooming behavior—slow systematic picking through the hair of another individual to remove foreign matter; important in primate social interactions.

Female dominance rank relationships are generally more stable and continue over longer periods, because females usually do not emigrate from their natal troops and males often do. Until puberty both males and females, even fostered infants, assume the rank of their real or foster mothers. If a mother dies while her daughter is still a juvenile, the daughter's rank may be reduced, although one study showed that about 55% of these orphaned daughters inherited the rank of their mothers. Apparently, the most important factor that determines a daughter's rank is the memory others have of those dominance relations that existed while her mother was still alive. On the other hand, some females from an early age can significantly elevate their rank through their associations with older males and females (Small, 1989).

Unlike the females, the males of most primate species who are at or near the age of puberty often emigrate from their natal group (Pusey and Parker, 1987). Field data indicate that the numbers of males that actually move from group to group ranges from a low of 30% to as many as almost every male in the group. Because young males often migrate from their natal troops at puberty, and later in life older males may also move from group to group, male dominance hierarchies tend to be unstable over time. Many different males may at one time or another reach the highest position in the group's dominance hierarchy, but sooner or later each one of them will ultimately be replaced by younger individuals. Factors other then current dominance rank that affect the behavior and social interactions of adult males include their age, physical strength, residence time, and previous mating successes.

BIRTH AND THE MOTHER–INFANT BOND

All mammalian mothers nurse, protect, and care for their young during lactation. However, the duration and intensity of the mother–infant relationship varies considerably. Among mammals, with the exception perhaps of elephants, the primate (including human) mother–infant bond seems to be the most intense and long lasting.

Primates are usually born during the night or in the early morning hours before the group begins to wander in search of food. Births at night have the advantage of allowing some time for recovery for both the mother and newborn before the group's social life resumes its daily pace. Within hours after birth the new mother and her infant must be able to move away from the sleeping area with the group in search of food, and the young infant must be able to cling to its mother's hair with little or no assistance. An adult male may linger behind the group to assist the new mother or thwart aggression from others but this often depends upon the mother's earlier "friendships" or her kin relationships. The group as a whole rarely modifies its behavior to suit a new mother.

During the first few months of an infant's life it remains in close proximity to its mother and while traveling the mother transports the infant under her belly in a **ventro-ventral position.** Infant monkeys attract attention in the social group, and in the first few weeks after birth mothers may react differently to the more frequent social contacts they have with other members of their group. Some mothers appear to be very responsive to other individuals' curiosity about their newborn; others are quite restrictive and intolerant of other animals' presence. Nonlactating females may "kidnap" an infant for a period of time if they can. However, this "aunt" behavior of caring for and holding the infant may, for a short time, help the real mother. It is certainly a way by which younger females learn about infant care before they have off-spring of their own. In contrast to earlier views we now know that much of the increased interaction which occurs between new mothers and other group members is antagonistic rather than friendly. New mothers often direct aggression towards juveniles and experience more aggression from adult males than they do when they are not pregnant or lactating.

If a mother dies other females in many species may adopt the or-phaned infant. Observations of adult females adopting infants have been made on both New and Old World monkeys and apes. Parental care that can be given by other females to older infants may afford them some protection against the aggressive behavior of other animals. However, when an infant who is still dependent upon its mother's milk is orphaned, the adopter must be either a female who is lactating or one capable of it. Often an adopter is kin. Lynn Fairbanks (1988) demonstrated that even grandmothers form affiliative relationships with their grandinfants, though the intensity of this relationship varies considerably with the dominance rank of the grandmother. High-rank-ing grandmothers associated with their grandinfants more often, as-sisted them by providing social support and protection and groomed them more frequently than did lower ranking grandmothers. According to Fairbanks, grandmothers are generally effective in contributing to the reproductive success of their daughters by assisting them in pro-tecting the offspring.

The psychologist Harry Harlow demonstrated in his early experi-ments on bond formation and "love" in monkeys that an infant's cling-ing plays a vital role in its development (Figure 7–20). In fact, if the in-fant becomes agitated or frightened for some reason, body-to-body contact is more important to it than is nursing. The mother is a safe se-cure home base from which the infant launches its exploration of its environment, learning to associate its mother's reactions to and ten-sions with specific individuals and later with specific situations while clinging to her.

The social development of a young primate is not always a continu-ous process. In fact, its social development passes through a series of

Figure 7–20 • Harlow's experi-ments on primate mother–infant interaction.

ventro-ventral position—two individuals facing each other with bodies in contact.

discrete phases. Each successive phase is linked by transitional steps in which relationships may change considerably. The sex of the infant appears to be a crucial variable during these transitions. In most species sex differences during the infancy and juvenile period show a mixture of behavioral patterns that resemble those of the adults together with those that are specific to the particular demands of the earlier stage. For example, juveniles may regularly incorporate in their vocalization a mixture of signals, some typically infantile as well as some common to adults.

During the transitional phase from infancy to the juvenile stage, young males transfer much of their affiliative behavior away from their mother towards others, usually adult males. Loy (1992) notes this especially in his studies of patas monkeys. The juvenile's successes in achieving a friendly bond with the adults will be limited primarily by the youngster's own rank relative to that of its choice of older friends, the interest or behavioral reciprocity its friends might have in them, and finally any kin relationship the young males might have to a "friend" (Smuts, 1987). If bonds with high-ranking males can be made, the young male's chance of being forced out of the group later is diminished. Female yearlings, on the other hand, usually maintain their close association with their mothers, their kin, and friends.

LEARNING AS ADAPTATION TO SOCIALITY

Primates have the ability to **learn** a great number of things. Consequently, they require more developmental time for learning than any other group of mammal, and so it is not surprising that the two most important ingredients for learning, one's mother and interactive play, form a substantial part of a primate's lifetime of experiences. In the previous discussions of feeding, reproduction, and defense behavior situational responses are easily learned within the context of the group and the affectional bonds and stability which the group affords.

The ability to learn can be explained in part by the expansion of that part of the brain known as the neocortex (Chapter 5). Primates have a large brain-to-body weight ratio. But bigger brains are only part of the answer. We have to be motivated to learn, and effective learning requires strong motivation. Psychiatrist David Hamburg has explained the primate learning process as being an emotionally pleasurable experience. Natural selection has endowed that part of the brain that moderates pleasurable responses, the limbic system, with the ability to motivate individuals to do what they have to do in order to survive. This system makes it pleasurable to form social bonds and, thus, makes it easy to learn them. In laboratory situations, for instance, infant monkeys will establish contact relationships with their mothers regardless of the treatment the infants may receive from them.

learn–remember information or experience and retain for use in future behavior.

Early primate learning is **imitative** usually of its mother's reactions or actions to individuals or objects. Typically these concern the appropriate foods to eat and where they can be found, where to sleep and where to find water, and what animals can be approached and what animals should be avoided. However, the major part of a young primate's education is not the simple facts about its physical environment but learning to live successfully with other members of its group. Depending on the species, the infant increases its independence from its mother after a time and the usually gradual process of separation called weaning begins. As weaning progresses the mother may refuse her infant the nipple and refuse to carry her infant. Nevertheless, through this transitional stage the infant continues to be influenced by its mother, most importantly by her personality and social position (rank). As infants become older they leave their mothers for longer periods of time, widening their explorations and increasing their social relationships usually through play with other age-mates, but frequently through interactions with older adults.

An important component of learning in the young primate is **play** (Figure 7–21). Play is not a frivolous activity, but a behavior pattern that is practiced for skill acquisition and problem solving in adult life. Play provides the secure, largely carefree environment and the emotional motivation needed to sustain an individual's attention to a specific object or activity. Play is pleasurable and, because it involves a seemingly endless series of imitations, repetitions and experimental variations supervised by adult animals, young animals are seldom hurt.

Initially, as young primates leave their mother for periods of time their play is solitary and it consists primarily of locomotion explo-

imitative—relating to information gained through observing other individuals and not through one's own experience.

play—behavior that is not directed toward any clearly defined end result such as food getting, and which is frequently characteristic of young mammals.

Figure 7–21 • Young bonnet macaques at play. (From Paul Simonds)

rations, which ultimately become explorations of their environment. Because primates are extremely curious animals, over time their play helps them explore and become familiar with the entire area over which their group wanders. However, for exploratory play to remain interesting it must have some constantly changing element. But there are only so many trees to climb and so many ways to climb them and considering how much time a young primate spends in play, the environment's novelty soon disappears.

Social play then becomes the logical continuation of the process. Peers are perfect play subjects. They are familiar and secure; they are mobile and not always predictable. Hence, peers are endlessly interesting. Whereas observers readily see the importance of social play for learning the basic social skills needed in adult life, this probably is not the reason young primates, in fact, play. Most likely it is because it is more emotionally pleasurable and, therefore, more "fun" to play with one another than with a twig. Once again, natural selection has produced a situation in which the critical learning necessary for an individual's survival is made easy and enjoyable. Under these circumstances new information is rapidly assimilated into an individual's body of knowledge.

In humans the learning system works in the same way. Most of our effective learning is done under circumstances that are enjoyable as well as nonstressful. S. L. Washburn (1993) has pointed out that school environments may work against our biology and effective learning because our motivations to do well in school are usually based on emotions other than pleasure, such as fear of negative consequences if we do poorly.

In order to play socially the young primate must be social; that means it must make adjustments in its own behavior so that it can get along with others. Play allows the young animal to learn from its experiences which behaviors are acceptable and which are not. This knowledge, which is a necessary pre-condition of social acceptance as a playmate, is later important to the adult membership in the group. In this sense social play serves as a model of later adult social interactions. For example, the social skills required in juvenile play fighting are the same as those required in adult real fighting if either is to be successful. An individual must be able to rapidly and correctly appraise a situation and through effective communication use this information to its advantage. This development of effective communication is the basis of all adult interaction. Fortunately, play has an advantage: while using all these social skills it allows the players to make mistakes, misinterpret intent, and communicate ineffectively without suffering serious punishment. In contrast, generally speaking, adults making these kinds of errors must pay for them.

However, there is danger in play because young animals are less attentive to external events and, because of the commotion they create they may attract predators. Hausfater (1976) observed play groups of African vervet monkeys that typically occurred at some distance from the adults. Juveniles of this species were often stalked and successfully killed and eaten by adult baboons. The adults of other species may exhibit more vigilant behavior while their young are engaged in play. Squirrel monkey mothers, for example, respond quickly to the alarm calls of their close associates, the capuchins. Although loud vigorous play may provoke the curiosity of a predator, it also seems to alert the adults that play is going on and, perhaps, because of this, juvenile vocalizations stimulate greater vigilance in predator detection by the adults.

 ## SUMMARY

One of the most important behavioral characteristics of anthropoid primates is that they live in year-round social groups. From studies of primates in the wild we have come to understand many of the reasons for variability in the social organization and behavior that have been observed. Whereas the earlier field studies focused on the daily activities of members of a single group, more recent studies have concentrated on the ecological variables affecting primate societies and the life history or survival strategies that animals have developed in response to the surrounding environment. Two levels of explanation are useful in understanding behavior patterns: proximate explanations concern an animal's immediate motivation for behavior and ultimate explanations look at the evolutionary significance of such behavior. Within the context of the group primates have evolved solutions to problems involving reproduction, predation, and feeding. Life history strategies are the resulting behavioral responses of social animals to these problems.

In an attempt to explain primate social behavior the first question that needs to be asked is, "Why are primates social at all?" Answers to the question involve analysis of the costs and benefits of social group living. Some of the costs are loss of individual freedom of behavior in exchange for group cohesiveness; increased competition for a limited food supply, and, possibly, increased stress due to on-going social interactions. The benefits include increases in reproductive fitness because of the greater availability of mates; improved mechanisms for predator avoidance because of the number of individuals on watch for predators; and enhanced efficiency in feeding because of the increased number of foragers seeking available food.

Primatologists have borrowed from studies of other animal species in their attempts to synthesize primate behavioral data. The ethological perspective focused on phylogenetic aspects of behavior, those which are more controlled by the genetics of the species. Sociobiological analysis looked at an individual's reproductive strategies, and socioecology looked at ways in which animals were successful in finding food and in defending themselves and their resources from attack by other animals.

Although genetics, natural selection, and evolution can explain a great deal of what occurs behaviorally in a primate social unit, primates, more so than perhaps any other group of mammals, depend on their ability to learn through social interaction how to develop those behaviors patterns that will prove to be successful in adult life. For the learning process to be effective, substantial amounts of time must be spent during the early phase of a primate's life in playing, developing skills, and establishing new relationships. This ability to learn, coupled with the ability to adapt to a wide range of ecological habitats has made the Old and New World monkeys successful life forms among animals on earth.

 ## CRITICAL-THINKING QUESTIONS

1. Why is group living advantageous for primates?
2. Compare and contrast male and female reproductive strategies.
3. Discuss some of the commonalties between nonhuman primate communication and human communication.
4. Why is it important that there be a strong mother-infant bond in primates?
5. How does play influence learning in a young primate?
6. What important functions do grooming behaviors accomplish?

 ## SUGGESTED READINGS

Bramblett, C. 1994. *Patterns of Primate Behavior.* Prospect Heights, Ill.: Waveland Press. A good treatment of primatological field work and deductions arising from it.

deWaal, F. 1989. *Peacemaking Among Primates.* Cambridge: Harvard University Press. A readable account of primatologist Frances deWaal's research among the bonobos of central Zaire.

Loy, J. D. and C. B. Peters (eds.). 1991. *Understanding Behavior. What Primate Studies Tell Us About Human Behavior.* New York: Oxford University Press. An edited volume that emphasizes the "primateness" of human behavior, especially the social and ecological aspects of that behavior.

Mason, W. A. and S. P. Mendoza (eds.). 1993. *Primate Social Conflict.* Ithaca, N.Y.: State University Press. A book on causes and resolution of conflict among primates, with lessons for humans.

Quiatt, D. and V. Reynolds. 1993. *Primate Behaviour: Information, Social Knowledge, and the Evolution of Culture.* Cambridge: Cambridge University Press. A book that looks at the continuity of nonhuman primate behavior to human cultural behavior within society.

Small, Meredith. 1993. *Female Choices: Sexual Behavior of Female Primates.* Ithaca, N.Y.: Cornell University Press. A primatological study from a female perspective, looking at what strategies evolution has produced for choice of mates in female primates.

Smuts, B. B., R. L. Cheney, R. M. Seyforth, R. W. Wrangham, and T. T. Struhsaker. (eds.). 1987. *Primate Societies.* Chicago: The University of Chicago Press. An edited volume for advanced students dealing with theoretical issues of primate behavior and adaptation.

Strum, S. C. 1987. *Almost Human. A Journey into the World of Baboons.* New York: Norton. An introduction to the study of baboons by primatologist Shirley Strum based on her long-term studies in western Kenya.

The Florescence and Decline of the Hominoids

Introduction to the Hominoids

The Apes
What Is an Ape?

Anatomy of a Climbing Heritage

Proconsulids: The Earliest Hominoids

Hominoids with Thick Molar Enamel Appear

Ape Evolution in Eurasia

Evolutionary Relationships of Hominoids

Summary

Critical-Thinking Questions

Suggested Readings

INTRODUCTION TO THE HOMINOIDS

Hominoids (Latin, meaning "like humans") are members of the zoological Superfamily Hominoidea, which includes early apes, modern apes, and humans. The first apes, distinct from their Oligocene catarrhine ancestors (Chapter 6), appear in the fossil record of the Miocene Epoch some 20 million years ago. These early apes and the other hominoids are characterized by a unique mode of locomotion. They are able to climb about vertically in the trees much more dextrously than their ancestors. Some of the later apes came to suspend themselves by their arms from tree branches and to even swing from branch to branch. The importance of the arms in locomotion led to hominoids sometimes being referred to as "brachiators" (Latin, meaning "arm") (Figure 8–1).

Hominoids first appear in Africa in dense lowland forested environments (Figure 8–2). By the middle Miocene, about 15 million years or so ago, apes expanded from Africa into Europe and Asia (Figure 8–3). This period of expansion is a time when forests and dense woodlands connected Africa and Asia. But as hominoids expanded their ranges they came into contact with an increasing diversity of environments. By 10 to 14 million years ago there were fewer species of apes, but they were found throughout Africa and Eurasia. By about 5 million years ago most of these species had become extinct with only a few forms surviving to the present day (Figure 8–4).

The late Miocene marks the end of the radiation of apes. What remained were the ancestors of the living gibbons, orangutan, and the common ancestor of humans, chimpanzees, and gorillas. Monkeys, however, were expanding in number of species and diversity, just as the apes were declining. It is likely that there was broad ecological competition between the Old World monkeys and apes. Monkeys prevailed and in most niches outcompeted ancestral apes.

The hypothesis of monkey–ape competition in the late Miocene may explain today why we have five separate hominoid adaptations, all radically different from one another, and from their more "monkey-like" ancestors. Today among the hominoids there is a small-bodied suspensory locomotor, the gibbon; a large-bodied **knuckle-walking** terrestrial form, the gorilla; a smaller knuckle-walking terrestrial form, the chimpanzee; a large-bodied arboreal and terrestrial **fist-walking** form, the orangutan (Bornean, meaning old man of forest); and a bipedal terrestrial form, the hominids (Figure 8–5).

Figure 8–1 • View of a gibbon brachiating.

hominoids—modern apes, modern humans, and their immediate ancestors.

knuckle-walking—a terrestrial quadrupedal form of locomotion characteristic of chimpanzees and gorillas involving the placement of the flexed second phalanges instead of the palms on the ground for support.

fist-walking—a terrestrial quadrupedal form of locomotion characteristic of orangutans involving the placement of the flexed first phalanges instead of the palms on the ground for support; similar in function but probably not homologous to knuckle-walking.

247

Figure 8–2 • Reconstruction of an Early Miocene environment in eastern Africa. A female with infant and subadult male of *Proconsul africanus* avoid a common predator while an individual *Dendropithecus macinnesi* (above, right) looks on.

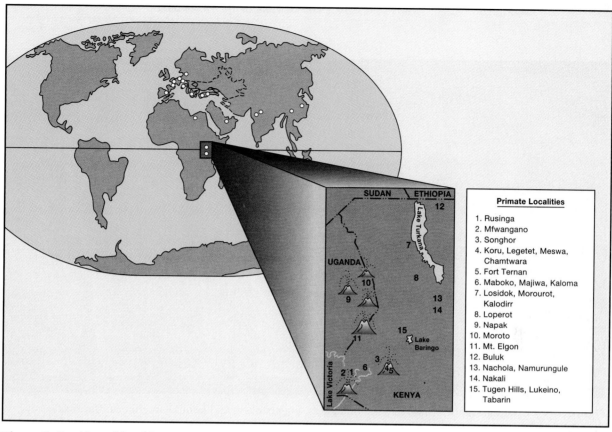

Figure 8–3 • Map of fossil hominoid sites for the Miocene epoch.

Primate Localities

1. Rusinga
2. Mfwangano
3. Songhor
4. Koru, Legetet, Meswa, Chamtwara
5. Fort Ternan
6. Maboko, Majiwa, Kaloma
7. Losidok, Morourot, Kalodirr
8. Loperot
9. Napak
10. Moroto
11. Mt. Elgon
12. Buluk
13. Nachola, Namurungule
14. Nakali
15. Tugen Hills, Lukeino, Tabarin

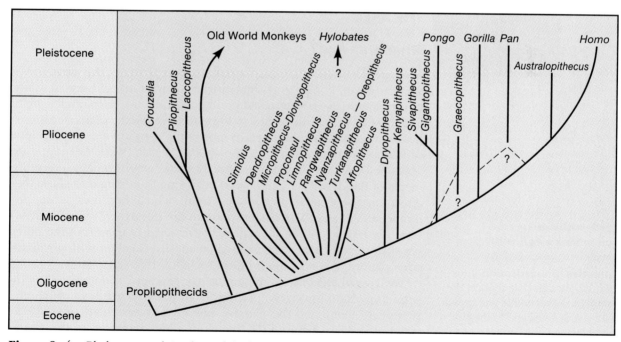

Figure 8–4 • Phylogeny and timeline of the hominoids.

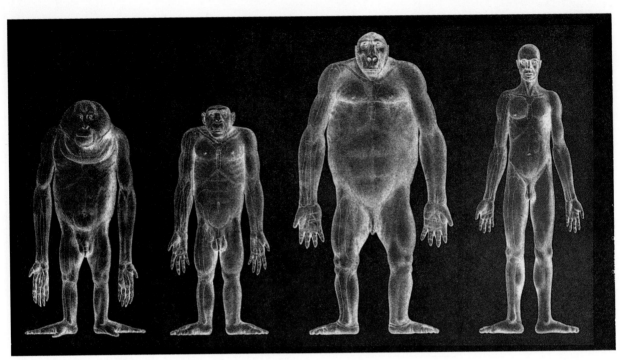

Figure 8–5 • Extant great apes (from left, the orangutan, chimpanzee, and gorilla) and human (far right). (After Adolf Schultz, 1933)

THE APES

What Is an Ape?

Apes are generally larger than monkeys, and as adults, the great apes—the orangutan, gorilla, and chimpanzee—exhibit marked sexual dimorphism (Figure 8–6). In terms of cranial anatomy the Hominoidea are all largely similar at birth (Schultz, 1924; Biegert, 1963). Characteristics of postnatal infant morphology are mostly the result of the requirements of brain size and housing for the special senses (sight, hearing, taste, and smell). As the dentition erupts, however, the mechanical requirements of the developing teeth and enclosing bone begin to show their effect on the cranial anatomy, a trend which becomes more pronounced with age. With the eruption of the permanent canines, a substantially larger tooth in the males, the patterns of growth of the different skull regions begin to change dramatically, finally resulting with the adult pattern of sexual dimorphism (Schultz, 1969).

The cranial anatomy of the gorilla, for example, is dominated by the large upper and lower canines, the large **prognathic** jaws which give support to them, and the massive **muscles of mastication** which attach to the jaws (Figure 8–7). The skull itself is covered by the *tempo-*

prognathism—forward-protruding jaws (maxilla plus mandible) or lower face.

muscles of mastication—four paired muscles that connect the skull to the mandible and move the jaw upward and to the sides in chewing.

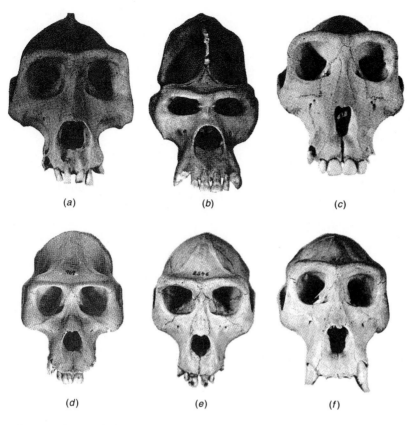

(a)   (b)   (c)

(d)   (e)   (f)

Figure 8–6 • Ape sexual dimorphism in skulls of gorillas: (*a*), (*b*), (*c*), and (*f*) are male skulls; (*d*) and (*e*) are female.

ralis muscles and the *masseter* muscles in the cheek region. As gorillas mature, the left and right *temporalis* muscles meet at the top of the skull and attach to it producing a bony **sagittal crest,** the largest of its size in any primate.

When moving on the ground apes do not run with their hands *palmigrade* (flat on the ground), but either knuckle-walk, like chimps and gorillas, fist-walk, like orangutans, or walk on two legs, like gibbons and people. In the upper torso the distinctive anatomy of knuckle-walking seen in the African apes was recognized and described as early as the late 1800s (Schultz, 1936) and it was argued that the two African apes were phylogenetically more closely related, to the exclusion of the orangutan (Keith, 1915; Weinert, 1932; Andrews, 1987). This observation was based primarily on the fact that in the hand skeletons of humans and African apes the primitive *os centrale* (Latin, meaning "central bone") in the wrist fuses with the *scaphoid* (Greek, meaning "ship-like," in reference to its shape) (Figure 8–8).

Apes also differ from monkeys in a number of other significant traits (Figure 8–9). Primary among these is their ability to raise their arms above their heads, as we do when we do chin-ups or hold on to a strap while standing on a bus. Apes raise their arms when they hang by their

sagittal crest–a bony crest running along the length of the top of the skull, formed by the attachment areas of the temporalis muscles from opposite sides.

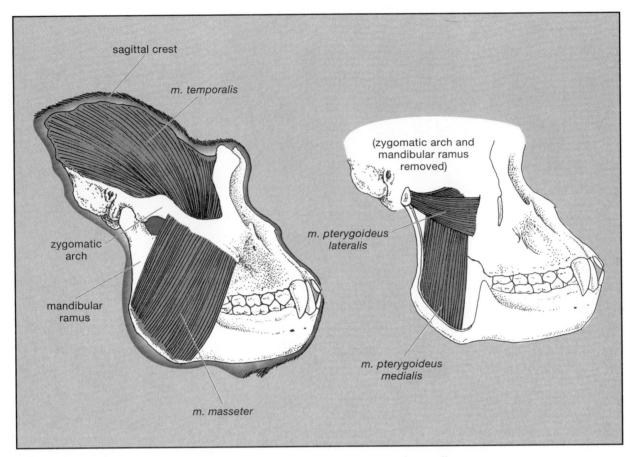

Figure 8–7 • Muscles of mastication and associated cranial structures in the gorilla.

arms from tree limbs or climb in trees. There are a number of specific anatomical differences that separate apes from monkeys for this trait. These include a *broader sternum and thorax* (chest), a *short lumbar vertebral region* (lower back), a *forelimb capable of full extension,* and a *large, strong hallux* (thumb). Apes also all *lack tails,* have *larger brains* than monkeys, both in absolute terms and relative to their body size, and have *bunodont molar teeth* with lower and more rounded cusps (Figure 8–10).

Although all apes are capable of a wide range of arm movement, "arm-swinging" or brachiation is characteristic of those aerial acrobats, the gibbons and siamangs, whose genus name, *Hylobates,* means "forest walker." Slower climbing and hanging are characteristic of the great apes, when they are in trees, which is less frequent than in gibbons. The forelimb and shoulder movements involved in ape-like climbing are correlated with particular anatomical characteristics, the details

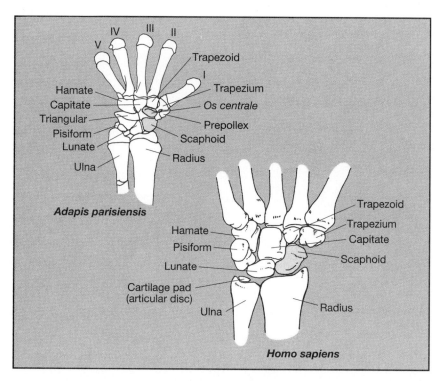

Figure 8–8 • The hand skeleton of *Homo sapiens,* showing the *os centrale* fused with the scaphoid, as compared to the hand skeleton of *Adapis parisiensis,* an Eocene prosimian, in whom the *os centrale* is a separate wrist bone. Humans and the African apes share this characteristic, which is not shared with the orangutan.

of which help to define apes (Keith, 1896; Schultz, 1936). Washburn (1963) stressed the importance of the ape's ability to hang with one hand, grasping a branch while feeding with the other hand. He realized that the ape's locomotion was in reality an arboreal feeding adaptation: its adaptive advantage is obtaining food in trees (primarily fruit) from the ends and the tips of branches. Knowledge of tropical forest ecology shows that the best and sometimes the only digestible foods in a tree are at the edges (Figure 8–11). These include fruits, nuts, flowers, and, perhaps on a more regular basis, new leaves, that is leaves whose internal chemistry has not yet built up the defense systems that make most mature leaves indigestible to the average vegetarian.

As we have already seen, the Colobinae or leaf-eating monkeys met and solved the problem of obtaining food in the trees in a different way from the brachiators. Colobines evolved a specialized stomach/lower intestine complex which could digest those types of vegetation, such as mature leaves, that are hard or impossible for other animals to eat. They thus managed to avoid competing for the same foods (fruits) with apes while living in the same habitat.

Traditionally, all the living apes were grouped together in the family Pongidae, although a number of authors preferred a taxonomic system that split the Southeast Asian gibbons and siamangs into a separate family, the Hylobatidae (Le Gros Clark, 1960). Likewise, some researchers include both the gorilla and chimpanzee within their own family, Panidae, separate from the Asian Pongidae. Included in this

Figure 8–9 • How an ape differs from a monkey.

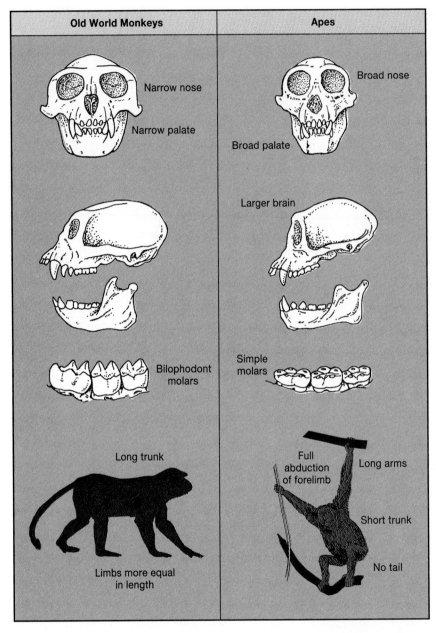

Old World Monkeys	Apes
Narrow nose	Broad nose
Narrow palate	Broad palate
	Larger brain
Bilophodont molars	Simple molars
Long trunk	Full abduction of forelimb
	Long arms
	Short trunk
Limbs more equal in length	No tail

bonobo *(Pan paniscus)*—a species of chimpanzee distinct from the common chimpanzee, *Pan troglodytes,* and living in a different, nonoverlapping range—the Central Zaire forest basin; also termed the "pygmy chimpanzee" but its differences from the common chimp are more in terms of morphology and shape than size.

group but described more recently (in 1929) is the smaller West African **bonobo** or pygmy chimpanzee, *Pan paniscus.* Newer molecular results consistently show the chimpanzees and gorilla to be at least as distinct as are humans, and for this reason they are taxonomically classified in their own families here—Panidae for chimpanzees and Gorillidae for gorillas (see Appendix 3). This leaves within the family Pongidae only the orangutan (Bornean, meaning "old man of the forest"), now found only on the Indonesian islands of Borneo and Sumatra. The molecular

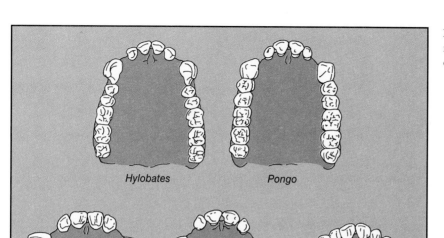

Figure 8–10 • Modern hominoid dentition showing bunodont molar structure.

Hylobates

Pongo

Pan

Gorilla

Homo

* Figure not drawn to scale.

evidence places the orangutan closer to the African apes than to the gibbons (Figure 8–12). Both the molecular and fossil evidence, however, agree in showing that the orangutan has a long separate history from its African cousins, the chimpanzee, gorilla, and people.

Figure 8–11 • A gibbon reaches for food at the periphery of a tree.

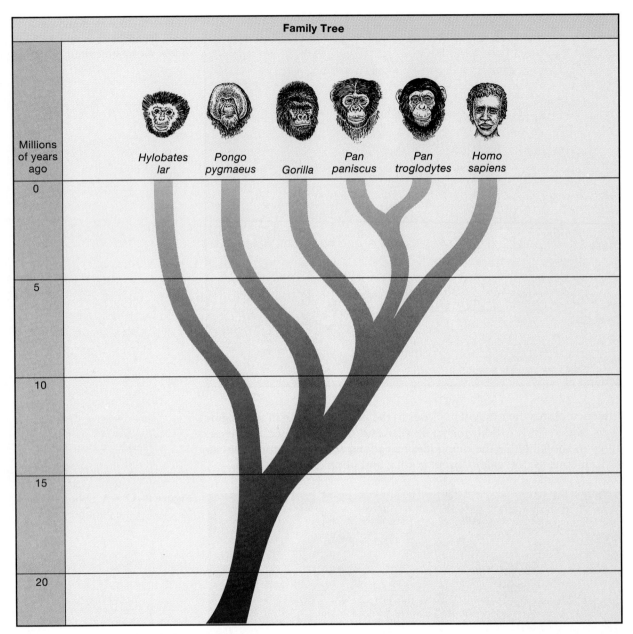

Figure 8–12 • Molecular phylogeny of the apes.

Apes today are generally found in tropical rainforests from sea level to heights of 4,000 meters above sea level in the Virunga Volcanoes of Zaire, Uganda, and Rwanda, where the remnants of the mountain gorilla make their home. The apes have fared poorly at the hands of fate and humans. Few in number and pushed to the limits of their environmental resources, the living apes face a dismal future today in the wild.

On a sliding scale of evolutionary success in the primates, apes rate near the bottom, barely holding their own. The seriously threatened condition of the living apes makes it important not only that we study them in the wild while there is still time, but also that primate conservation efforts go hand in hand with scientific study of the species.

ANATOMY OF A CLIMBING HERITAGE

The hominoids all share similar anatomy of the forelimb, shoulder, and upper back, traits that trace back to their arboreal climbing heritage. Members of the human lineage as well share this anatomical structure, a similarity recognized as far back as Tyson (1699) although he used it to infer that the then-unknown chimpanzee was bipedal in its natural state. This early observation lent additional support to the theory that

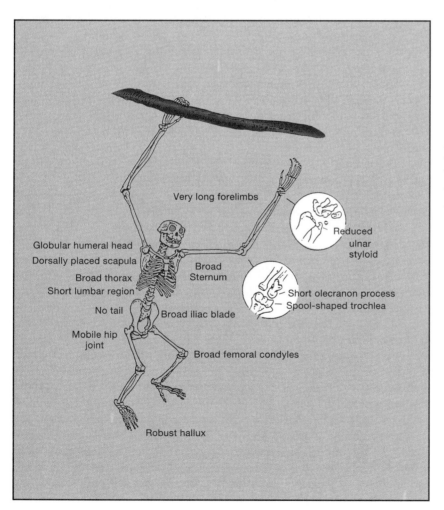

Figure 8–13 • Anatomy of climbing: loss of ulnar articulation with the carpals, reduced olecranon process at the elbow, and change in position of the scapula; broadening of the thorax, elongation of the clavicle, and change in the shape of the shoulder joint; strengthened deltoid and other muscles of abduction; shift from strength of triceps in quadrupeds to biceps in brachiators.

Figure 8–14 • Bipedal locomotion by the gibbon when on the ground.

Figure 8–15 • Fist-walking by an orangutan.

apes and humans are more closely related to each other than to any other primate group. The evolutionary origins of climbing morphology are not yet fully documented in the fossil record. The Miocene apes could climb but their locomotor pattern was apparently more that of monkeys. By the Pliocene and early Pleistocene an early form of the hominid *Australopithecus* (see Chapter 10) showed all of the anatomical characteristics of a climbing heritage, although it was clearly also adapted to a bipedal mode of locomotion. Some Miocene apes must surely have shared the same brachiation anatomical characteristics with *Australopithecus,* but we have, as yet, no fossils to show it.

In the hominoids the anatomical adaptations made for climbing and suspensory locomotion are shown in Figure 8–13. These include changes that increased rotational movement at the wrist joint, permitting a 180 degree *pronation* (turning the hand into a palm-down or "prone" position); at the elbow joint, allowing for 180 degree *extension* ("unbending the elbow"); and at the shoulder joint, permitting full *abduction* of the forelimb (lifting the arm away from the body and over the head; see Appendix 1). Effectively, these changes allow hominoids to raise their forelimbs over their heads while maintaining a vertical posture.

In addition to changes in the forelimb and related skeleton, the hand was modified by the evolutionary process towards the development of a curved hook-like arrangement of the *metacarpals* and *phalanges* (Appendix 1), solving a potential problem of hand fatigue for an animal hanging for a period of time in one spot. Of all of the climbing adaptations that humans share with the apes the hook-shaped hand was not retained, the human hand developing in the direction of finer motor coordination and precise gripping ability.

Brachiation as a morphological adaptation for arboreal locomotion has seen its greatest efficiency in the small-bodied Asian apes: the gibbons and siamangs. In fact, Napier and Napier (1967) describe these forms as the *true brachiators,* as opposed to the great apes which they describe as *modified brachiators.* Movement through the trees in these two forms is rapid because of the greater elongation of the forelimbs and fingers of the hands, with the exception of the shortened thumb that apparently functions to increase the breadth of the grasping hand in vertical climbing, an important additional gibbon locomotor component. On the ground and in the trees gibbons and siamangs are also unique in that both occasionally adopt bipedal posture in locomotion (Figure 8–14). The other apes move much more carefully (and slowly) due to their larger size. They usually support their weight with the use of their hindlimbs while in the trees. On the ground these animals generally move quadrupedally, though bipedal locomotion is sometimes seen.

The orangutan (*Pongo pygmaeus*) often travels arboreally, but generally climbs rather than swings along branches to make forward progress. The brachiating anatomy that we have described for gibbons and siamangs is much the same for the orangutan, size being the limiting factor to rapid arboreal locomotion. Infant and juvenile orangutans are much more mobile than the adults both in the trees and on the ground. On the ground orangs move quadrupedally in a more upright posture than seen in monkeys because of the longer length of the forelimbs relative to the hindlimbs.

Among the the large apes, only the orang's quadrupedal locomotion is usually accomplished with the fists in a clenched position (Figure 8–15), although they have occasionally been observed to use a palm-down stance like monkeys. The African apes almost invariably use a unique rigid hand posture already described as knuckle-walking (Figure 8–16). Due to the similarity in hand structure and probably the result of relatively infrequent terrestrial locomotion, the orangs sometimes also mimic the knuckle-walking posture.

The ancestry of the living apes is far from clear because their fossil records are quite sparse or nonexistent. This paucity of fossils that can be directly connected to modern apes is possibly due to the fact that these species probably lived in dense tropical forest. Upon death, the acidic forest floor would act to chemically erode their skeletal remains, and thus destroy all potential fossils. But equally important is the fact that forests today still cover most of the forest refuge areas of the past, making paleontological investigation of these important areas difficult. When we have found geological levels containing fossils, even forest-living animals of the past have been discovered.

Figure 8–16 • Knuckle-walking in the gorilla.

PROCONSULIDS: THE EARLIEST HOMINOIDS

The Miocene Epoch, extending in time from 23 to 5 million years ago, was a time of a great adaptive radiation of apes. In the Early Miocene, dating from approximately 23 to 18 million years ago, at least 15 species have been recognized which are assigned to 11 genera. They range in size from the diminutive, cat-sized *Micropithecus* (3.5 kg), to the large *Afropithecus,* the size of a female gorilla (50 kg). These apes are known as **proconsulids** ("pro" meaning before and "Consul," a well-known chimpanzee in the London zoo in the 1940s), and they show a diversity of locomotor types, dietary adaptations, and body sizes (Figure 8–17).

The proconsulids share a number of dental characteristics, forming a *monophyletic group:* they evolved in a single adaptive radiation from a single source population of prehominoids, most likely the propliopithecoids (see Chapter 6). Among the morphological traits that herald this change are upper molars of squarish shape with a distinctive belt of raised enamel on the tongue side (the lingual **cingulum**); lower molars with a broad posterior basin (the talonid basin) surrounded by five prism-like cusps (forming a so-called **Y-5 pattern**); and a strongly de-

proconsulids—Early to Middle Miocene catarrhines or primitive apes from Africa ranging in size from a small monkey to gorilla-sized.

cingulum—a "belt" (from Latin), connoting in the dentition a raised ridge of enamel encircling a tooth crown.

Y-5 pattern—a pattern in the lower molars of five distinct cusps, separated by a backward (distally) facing Y-shaped groove; characteristic of hominoids.

FRONTIERS

Miocene Apes and Modern Hominoids

by David R. Begun

The results of the last twenty years of research in Miocene hominoids has produced some dramatic changes in interpretations of hominoid evolution. Hominoid evolution is much more complicated than was once thought; at least 25 different genera from between about 20 to 6 million years ago are now known. This increase in recognized hominoid diversity may prompt cries of "splitting," but in fact is more in line with the known diversity of primates in other superfamilies, such as Old World Monkeys (Cercopithecoidea) or New World Monkeys (Ceboidea). Living hominoids are but a mere shadow of the former diversity of this group.

The earliest well-documented Miocene hominoid is *Proconsul,* who dwelled in Kenya and Uganda up to about 20 million years ago. Many fossil hominoids are known from these sites, including species of *Proconsul, Rangwapithecus,* and other smaller forms of very unclear evolutionary affinities. Most are probably related to *Proconsul,* but some, like *Dendropithecus,* may represent a different kind of hominoid, or may not be a hominoid at all. It may be that *Proconsul* was already somewhat specialized in its own direction and is not directly related to modern forms, but the common ancestor of modern hominoids must have been very similar to *Proconsul.*

Contemporary with the latest specimens of *Proconsul* are the enigmatic hominoids, *Afropithecus, Turkana-*

pithecus, and *Simiolus.* These forms are known from sites in northern Kenya, and a fragmentary mandible from Saudi Arabia, originally attributed to *Heliopithecus,* may also be *Afropithecus.* Although contemporary with *Proconsul,* these three species are very different in their cranial anatomy from other early Miocene forms, which makes their correct placement among the hominoids very difficult. *Simiolus* is a very small form with unusual cresty teeth and a primitive postcranial skeleton. *Turkanapithecus* is close in size to the smallest species of *Proconsul* but has a more projecting midface and nose region. *Afropithecus* is closest in size to the largest species of *Proconsul* but has a distinctive cranial morphology, with a mixture of features resembling the primitive *Aegyptopithecus* and *Proconsul.* More fossil material is needed to resolve the enigmatic relations of these relatively newly described Miocene hominoids.

The middle Miocene lasted from about 16.5 to about 11.5 million years ago. The Kenyan site of Maboko, dating to abut 15 million years ago, preserves a new type of hominoid with thick molar enamel, known as *Kenyapithecus,* first described from the somewhat younger site of Fort Ternan, also in western Kenya. *Kenyapithecus* is more advanced than early Miocene hominoids in molar morphology but retains many primitive features also found in *Proconsul.* However, certain characteristics of the shoulder joint in *Kenyapithecus,* combined with its thickly enamelled molars, suggests a greater dependence on terrestrial sources of food, which tend to contain more grit and therefore tend to wear teeth more rapidly. More will be known about the cranial

and postcranial anatomy of *Kenyapithecus* when a large sample from the Nachola area of northern Kenya is analyzed. Dentally and postcranially similar hominoids are also known from the middle Miocene in Europe and Turkey. These forms, called *Griphopithecus,* may, together with *Kenyapithecus,* be the earliest members of the lineage that includes the living great apes and humans. However, the precise placement of this group of hominoids represents a major puzzle in hominoid evolutionary studies. *Griphopithecus* and *Kenyapithecus* have molars and premolars that look more like those of modern great apes than do those of early Miocene forms or those of hylobatids (gibbons and their relatives). Yet hylobatids and all late Miocene hominoids have postcranial attributes in common with great apes, all of which reflect the importance of suspensory postures in the trees. So there is conflict between the evidence for the limbs and the evidence of the teeth.

By the end of the middle Miocene and into the late Miocene, modern great ape anatomy becomes evident. Two forms appear at nearly the same time—*Sivapithecus* in South Asia (India and Pakistan) and *Dryopithecus* in Europe. The sample of *Sivapithecus* was formerly divided into several different forms but is now universally accepted as two genera, *Gigantopithecus* for a small number of large-to-gigantic specimens and *Sivapithecus* for the vast majority of the material. It was the discovery of a remarkably complete face, GSP 15000 [see Figure 8–19], more than any other development, that convinced most paleoanthropologists that *Sivapithecus* was not a "dryopithecine" but an early member of the lineage of the orang. With the publication of GSP 15000 it became widely accepted that *Sivapithecus* (now including *Ramapithecus*) was a close relative of the orang, and had nothing to do with the origins of the human lineage.

The interpretation of *Dryopithecus* has also changed considerably due to new discoveries. Three partial crania and large numbers of jaws, teeth, and limb bones from various sites in Europe show that *Dryopithecus* has characteristics only found in African apes and humans, and one other Miocene hominoid, *Ouranopithecus,* from the late Miocene of Greece. *Ouranopithecus* is much larger than *Dryopithecus* and has many of the same features found in *Dryopithecus* but in exaggerated form. The Greek form also has many unique features of the face and teeth, and even shares a few traits, such as extremely thick enamel and very small canines, with early humans. However, for a number of reasons, it appears more likely that the similarities to australopithecines (see Chapter 9) occur convergently, that is, they were acquired independently. The new interpretation that links *Dryopithecus* and *Ouranopithecus* from Europe, rather than Asian *Sivapithecus,* more closely to African apes and humans, is almost exactly the opposite of the interpretation of these genera 25 years ago.

A major conclusion from recent research in Miocene hominoids concerns our understanding of the relations among living hominoids and the place humans occupy among them.

There is now widespread agreement among morphologists and molecular systematists that humans are more closely related to African apes than either is to orangs. Furthermore, it is also becoming apparent that humans and African apes are very closely related to one another, such that the precise order in which each diverged from their common ancestor is very unclear. Molecular systematists have been saying with increased frequency that humans and chimps are most closely related, though many continue to hold that it is just too close to call. Most paleoanthropologists who focus on morphology believe that chimps and gorillas are the closest, citing such specializations as knuckle-walking and thinly enamelled teeth. But the significance of these characteristics is not so clear-cut. Enamel thickness is a poor indicator of evolutionary relationships because it changes so often in response to dietary requirements. Knuckle-walking, which is unique among living forms to African apes, is commonly considered to be a recent specialization of the African apes. A more controversial, but in my mind more likely, view is that knuckle-walking characterized our ancestors too. After all, humans do share unusual features of the hand and wrist only with African apes, such as fewer wrist bones, more stability of the joints of the wrist, and shorter hand and finger bones. One real possibility is that humans retain these characteristics because we evolved from a knuckle-walker that needed

them to ensure wrist and hand stability while walking on the knuckles. When humans shifted to two feet we may have lost many features still found in knuckle-walkers, while other characteristics were suitable to the tasks important to early bipeds, such as enhanced manipulation, and were thus retained.

Additional Reading

Andrews, Peter. 1992. "Evolution and environment in the Hominoidea." *Nature* 360:641–46.

Begun, David R. 1992. "Phyletic diversity and locomotion in primitive European hominoids." *American Journal of Physical Anthropology* 87:311–40.

Pilbeam, David R. 1982. "New hominoid skull material from the Miocene of Pakistan." *Nature* 295:232–34.

Rose, Michael D. 1983. "Miocene hominoid postcranial morphology: Monkey-like, ape-like, neither, or both?" In *New Interpretations of Ape and Human Ancestry,* eds. Ciochon, R.L., and R.S. Corruccini. New York: Plenum, pp. 405–17.

Walker, Alan, and Mark R. Teaford. 1989. "The hunt for *Proconsul.*" *Scientific American* 260:76–82.

David R. Begun is Professor of Anthropology at the University of Toronto. He studies hominoid morphology and evolution, especially that of the European Miocene.

Figure 8–17 • Range of *Proconsul* size and adaptations.

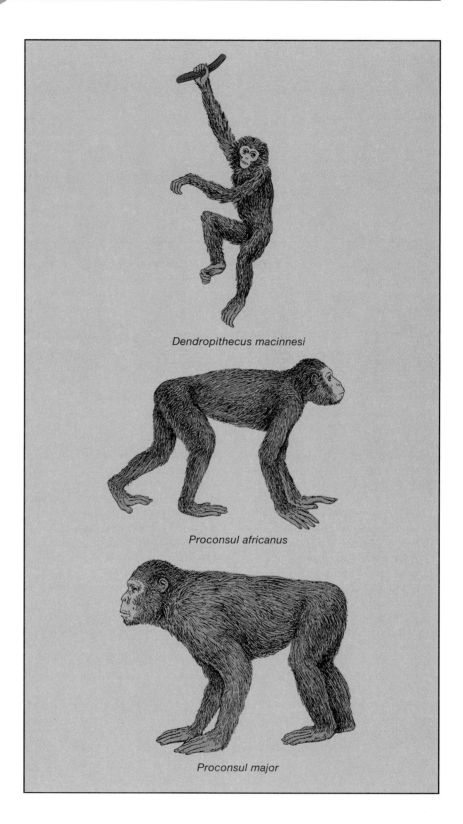

veloped last cusp on the lower molars (the hypoconulid) (Figure 8–10 and Appendix 1).

The proconsulids share many primitive catarrhine cranial traits with the Old World monkeys, the cercopithecoids. These include a tubular ectotympanic extending out from the bulla in the ear region. The relative size of the brain compared to overall body size also seems to be similar between the proconsulids and the living Old World monkeys.

Proconsulid postcranial anatomy shows few similarities to those of the living hominoids, appearing more primitive and most similar to that of the living New World monkeys (Figure 8–18). There is a range of adaptations within this general pattern: suspensory species (similar to the modern spider monkey) such as *Dendropithecus macinnesi,* the gibbon-like species of *Limnopithecus* and *Simiolus,* and a terrestrial quadruped, *Proconsul nyanzae.* The proconsulids show considerable sexual dimorphism in body size, according to a study of their canine size (Kelley, 1987).

Two new species of early to middle Miocene East African apes that may or may not belong with the other proconsulids were discovered at the 16 million-year-old site of Kalodirr, in northern Kenya and named *Afropithecus* and *Turkanapithecus* (Leakey and Leakey, 1986).

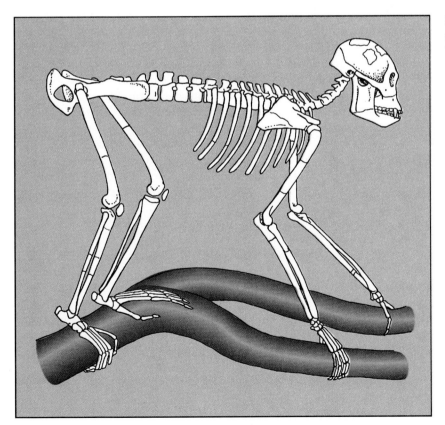

Figure 8–18 • Skeletal reconstruction of *Proconsul.* (After Alan Walker)

Afropithecus, a large hominoid the size of a female gorilla, had a long and narrow face with large canines and incisors. It is also likely represented at sites in Uganda and Saudi Arabia. Despite some superficial similarities to the modern gorilla, the brain in *Afropithecus* was relatively small and less convoluted than in modern African apes, and the nasal opening was small, like Old World monkeys, so it is unlikely that this ape had any direct ancestral relationship to living species. Only further discoveries will assist in confirming this assessment. *Turkanapithecus* was a smaller, medium-sized hominoid with a relatively broader face than *Afropithecus.* Its unusual, long upper molars with numerous extra cusps make assessments of its phylogenetic connections unclear, but it is also unlikely to have had any close relationships to modern apes.

The teeth of the proconsulids indicate that they had a range of dietary adaptations, from primarily frugivory, indicated by low rounded molar cusps, to folivory, indicated by a greater development of molar shearing crests and cusps. There also seems to have been a number of paleoecological contexts in which the proconsulids lived. The gibbon-like *Limnopithecus* and *Micropithecus,* the unique leaf-eating ape *Nyanzapithecus* (Swahili *nyanza,* meaning "lake" and *pithecus,* Greek, meaning "ape"), and the poorly known but probably gorilla-like *Proconsul major* lived in rain forest environments. Localities that seem to record more dry forest habitats have yielded *Dendropithecus, Proconsul africanus,* and *Proconsul nyanzae.*

Our understanding of the evolutionary relationships of the proconsulids has undergone a revolution in recent years. Simons and Pilbeam (1965) believed that there was a straightforward phylogenetic connection between Miocene forms and living species. *Proconsul africanus* was hypothesized to be ancestral to the chimpanzee, *Proconsul major* to the gorilla, possibly *Sivapithecus indicus* to the orangutan, and *Ramapithecus* to hominids. Greenfield (1980) termed this hypothesis the **Early Divergence Hypothesis,** which stated that the branching of the lineages leading to the modern apes occurred prior to the Early Miocene.

The sivapithecids, especially the genus *Ramapithecus* (now included within the genus *Sivapithecus*), were thought for a number of years to be close to or on the direct lineage leading to hominids. Developments in two areas of biological anthropology, however, changed general opinion regarding the phylogenetic position of *Sivapithecus* and its kin. Biomolecular studies indicated that humans were derived from a common ancestor with African apes only relatively recently. According to two of the earliest workers, this date of divergence was only some 4 to 6 million years ago (Sarich and Wilson, 1967). A hominoid dating from some 13 to 8 million years ago therefore could not be a unique hominid ancestor because the lineage had not branched off independently by that time. The result of the eventual acceptance of the

Early Divergence Hypothesis—hypothesis that there was an ancient evolutionary split (more than 15 million years ago) of African apes and humans from a common ancestor.

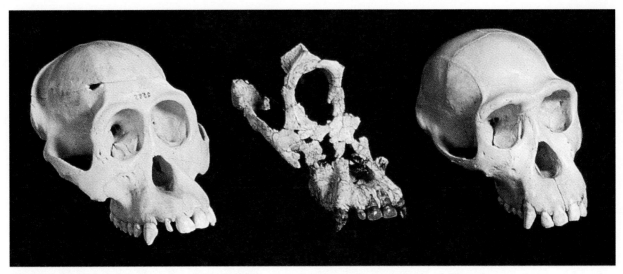

Figure 8–19 • Face of *Sivapithecus* (GSP 15000, center) compared to orangutan (left) and chimpanzee (right).

molecular interpretation of late divergence of hominids from apes was the rejection of *Sivapithecus* as a hominid ancestor.

Discoveries of more complete remains as well as of many new taxa of fossil apes in the Miocene of Africa and Eurasia also began to cast doubt on this simple, straighforward interpretation. A relatively complete fossil facial skeleton of *Sivapithecus* (Figure 8–19), discovered in Pakistan, showed that this taxon (including *Ramapithecus*) shared many anatomical characteristics with the orangutan. This realization removed the best candidate for a Miocene ape uniquely ancestral to the hominid lineage and thus argued strongly against the Early Divergence Hypothesis (Pilbeam et al., 1977). The discovery that there was a high degree of parallelism among Miocene hominoids in body size also made the Early Divergence Hypothesis difficult to support. For example, large body size seems to have evolved in at least four different lineages, *Afropithecus* and probably *Proconsul major* in Africa, and *Sivapithecus parvada* and *Gigantopithecus* in Asia. Similarly there was a diversity of small-bodied apes. In the postcranial skeleton *Proconsul africanus* was shown to resemble modern hominoids in some ways, but yet it retained a primitive, monkey-like articulation between its ulna and hand bones. This finding indicated that it did not possess the fundamental limb structure of modern apes and thus was not an appropriate choice for a last common ancestor of any of the living species of hominoids.

The Early Divergence Hypothesis has thus been replaced with the **Late Divergence Hypothesis,** a term also coined by Greenfield (1980). Both fossil evidence and molecular evidence played important roles in the acceptance of this hypothesis. The Late Divergence Hypothesis holds that hominids, the African great apes (panids and gorillids) and their fossil ancestors, and the Asian great ape (pongids) and

Late Divergence Hypothesis— hypothesis that there was a recent evolutionary split (5 to less than 15 million years ago) of the African apes and humans from a common ancestor.

Figure 8–20 • Early Divergence Hypothesis (top) compared to the Late Divergence Hypothesis (below).

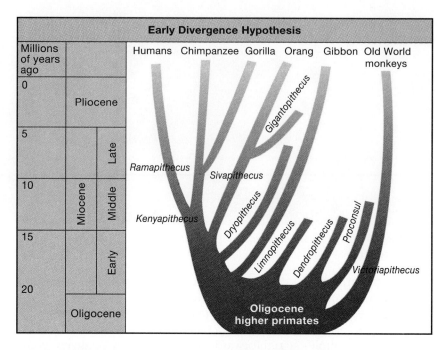

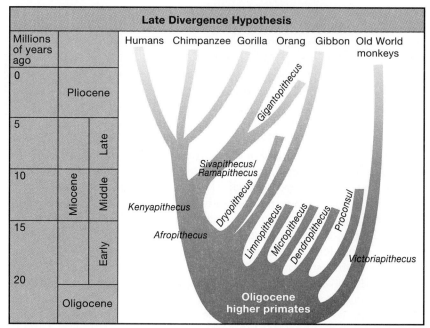

its fossil ancestors, shared an ancestor in the middle Miocene, not later than 13 million years ago (Figure 8–20).

HOMINOIDS WITH THICK MOLAR ENAMEL APPEAR

Appearing in the middle Miocene were hominoids that for the first time had molar teeth with thick enamel (Figure 8–21). This represented an adaptation most likely for the biting and crushing of hard foods. Species inhabiting dry forest, savanna, and woodland in Africa, known as *Kenyapithecus,* are characteristic of these hominoids. For a number of years during the 1960s to 1980s these hominoids were considered by many workers in the field to represent the ancestral hominids. Among the traits used for this deduction were *thick molar enamel,* a *more orthognathous,* or "straight-faced" profile of the subnasal region and midline of the mandible, and somewhat *reduced canine size* compared to that of most other apes. *Kenyapithecus* is a medium-sized ape known from primarily dental and jaw remains. Current opinion of its thick molar enamel, robust mandible, and large upper premolars suggests a possible relationship to the last common ancestor of great **apes** and hominids, but not uniquely to the latter (Fleagle, 1988:371–2). *Kenyapithecus* has a humerus that has been interpreted by Benefit and McCrossin (1993) to

Figure 8–21 • Evolution of thickness and rate of formation of molar enamel thickness in hominoids.

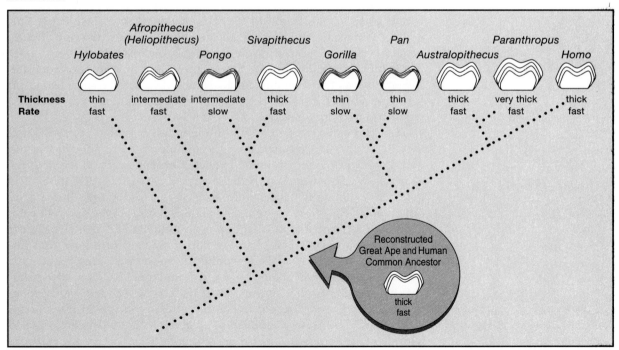

suggest at least partial terrestrial locomotion and to indicate a lack of specializations associated with modern apes. It has been discovered at the Kenyan sites of Maboko (ca. 15 million years ago), Fort Ternan (13–14 million years ago), Samburu Hills (9 million years ago), and possibly at a few other Miocene sites where fragmentary remains are known.

The fossil record of African apes after the middle to late Miocene is a blank except for a possible gorilla-like fossil canine tooth recently reported by Pickford et al. (1988) from the Pliocene deposits of the Western Rift Valley of Uganda. Interestingly, there are no fossil apes in the Pliocene hominid sites of eastern or southern Africa, implying that these areas were either isolated by corridors of open vegetation from the forests of Central and West Africa, or were themsleves too arid and unforested to have served as appropriate ape habitats. Future paleontological work in Central and West Africa may assist our understanding of the history of modern ape habitats and their fossil record.

APE EVOLUTION IN EURASIA

Eurasian hominoids appear in the fossil record for the first time at about 17 million years ago, having migrated from Africa. The lesser apes, the gibbons and siamangs, do not have a well-documented fossil record, but it now seems likely that the diminutive ape from the Late Miocene of China, *Dionysopithecus,* may be an ancestor to the modern hylobatids. There are two large groups of nonhylobatian Eurasian apes, the aforementioned sivapithecids, named by Pilgrim (1911) for the Hindu god *Siva* and *pithecus* (Greek, meaning "ape"), which are limited to the Asian Middle to Late Miocene, and the **dryopithecids,** named by Lartet (1856) from *dryo-* (Greek, meaning "oak") and *pithecus,* which are limited to the European Middle to Late Miocene. Like *Kenyapithecus* the sivapithecids had thick, fast-developing enamel on their molar teeth. Their paleoenvironmental context was a mixed woodland and dry forest.

The dryopithecids are a group of hominoids with thin molar enamel; they lived only in Europe during the middle and late Miocene, at the end of which time they became extinct. *Dryopithecus* was the first fossil hominoid discovered, in the Paris Basin of France (Lartet, 1856). The genus and subfamily names were applied to a wide range of Miocene hominoids (e.g. Gregory and Hellman, 1926; Simons and Pilbeam, 1965), but as more fossil evidence has accumulated it has become clear that this group was a late-surviving thin-enameled form limited to Europe at the same time as the sivapithecids were flourishing to the east. Recent evidence from Spain suggested to Begun (1992) that dryopithecids had facial anatomy similar to the modern African apes and probably shared a more recent common ancestry with African hominoids than with Asian sivapithecids (Figure 8–22). A Greek Middle to late Miocene hominoid known as *Graecopithecus* or *Ouranopithecus*

dryopithecid—family of apes known from the Middle Miocene of Europe.

shows some of these same characteristics of the face and has also been linked with the African rather than the Asian hominoids. But both of these suggestions have been contested on anatomical grounds, and the geographical and temporal placement of the specimens make a hypothesis of close African and European hominoid affinities hard to support. Most likely the middle to late Miocene European hominoids represent a separate radiation of apes that became progressively cut off from the forests of Africa and Asia as the Miocene Epoch drew to a close.

Europe was also home to two other descendents of Early Miocene proconsulids. The **pliopithecids** (Greek, meaning "lesser ape") were small-bodied, forest-living, climbing and suspensory hominoids frequently found associated with *Dryopithecus*. Although they were gibbon-like in their adaptations, details of their teeth and cranial anatomy are much too primitive to indicate a close relationship with modern gibbons.

Oreopithecus (Greek, meaning "forest ape") has been an enigmatic primate first discovered at an 8 million-year-old site, Mount Bamboli,

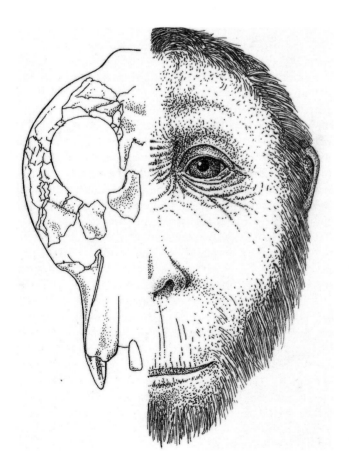

Figure 8–22 • Dryopithecid facial anatomy. (After David Begun)

pliopithecid—medium-sized, folivorous apes known from the Middle-Late Miocene of Eurasia.

Oreopithecus—unusual Middle-late Miocene European fossil ape showing suspensory adaptations in its post-crania but possessing teeth unlike other fossil or living apes.

Figure 8–23 • *Oreopithecus*. Reconstructed skull, skeleton in suspensory habitus, and how the animal may have appeared in life.

in Italy. It lived in a swamp forest and probably seldom came down out of the trees. *Oreopithecus* was unique in its postcranial anatomy. It possessed a broad thorax, short lumbar region of the vertebral column, long forelimbs, and short hind limbs. In comparison to the rest of the Miocene hominoids, this enigmatic primate shows the clearest early adaptations for suspensory, "forelimb-dominated" locomotion. In its locomotor adaptation it is most similar to the modern orangutan. On the other hand, its very different molar teeth indicate that it had no close genetic connection to any modern hominoids (Figure 8–23). Recent work by Harrison (1986) indicates that the family Oreopithecidae had an African origin through the Middle Miocene genus *Nyanzapithecus,* which in turn probably arose from the proconsulid *Rangwapithecus.*

EVOLUTIONARY RELATIONSHIPS OF HOMINOIDS

The biomolecular evidence argues for four major cladistic events in hominoid evolution. First is the separation of the gibbon and its relatives from the line leading to the great apes and hominids. Second is the subsequent divergence of the orangutan from the lineage leading to the African apes and hominids. Third is the split of the gorilla from hominids and *Pan.* Fourth is the split of the hominid and chimpanzee lineages.

The molecular data argue for a single evolutionary divergence of hominoids, with a separation from the cercopithecoids some 20 million years ago. The lineage leading to the modern gibbons is the first split detected in the evolution of living hominoids. This lineage diverged from the common great ape-hominid line between 12 to 15 million years ago (Figure 8–24). *Dionysopithecus,* known in the Late Miocene of China, suggests the presence of this lineage in the fossil record (Figure 8–4) although the available fossil evidence is not conclusive regarding this relationship (Fleagle, 1988:372).

The origin of the modern orangutan (node A in Figure 8–24) has direct bearing on the relationship of *Homo* vis-a-vis the living great apes. The traditional grouping of all the great apes as one family, Pongidae, as distinct from Hominidae, is not supported by the molecular evidence. There is now overwhelming evidence that there is a common lineage leading to the African apes and *Homo,* with *Pongo* as a sister group to this clade. The divergence of *Pongo* occurred, according to molecular estimates, between 10 to 13 million years ago. This corresponds with the known range of *Sivapithecus* in the fossil record (Andrews and Cronin, 1982).

The common panid-gorillid-hominid lineage existed for some time before molecular studies show that the gorilla lineage split off from it around 9 to 12 million years ago (Caccione and Powell, 1989). Hominid and chimp lineages, according to the molecular data, diverged between 5 to 8 million years ago (Cronin, 1983). Earlier data were unable to separate the times of divergence of the gorilla and the chimpanzee lineages

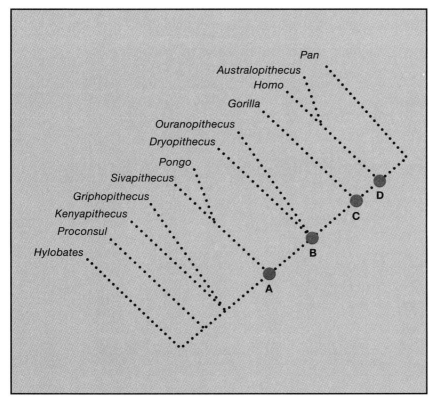

Figure 8–24 • Monophyletic clustering of the hominoids. This phylogenetic hypothesis incorporates fossil and molecular data. Nodes represent the following divergences: A, orangutan; B, European hominoids; C, gorilla; and D, chimpanzee-hominid.

(e.g. Sarich and Wilson, 1967), and some authorities are still unconvinced by the molecular evidence that indicates an earlier split of the gorilla lineage. Confirmatory fossil evidence for the evolutionary histories of the modern chimp and gorilla lineages is virtually nonexistent.

The question of the chimpanzee-human divergence time has been one of the most controversial of points in modern biological anthropology. It has been known for some years how close the genetic relationships are between apes and humans (Goodman, 1961, 1962, 1969a, 1969b; Hafleigh and Williams, 1966). These data include information from DNA studies, **globin** sequences, **fibrinopeptide** sequences, immunology, and electrophoretic studies (Table 8–1). Besides cladistic information, these data have yielded estimates of the time of divergence of humans and the African apes on the order of 4 to 8 million years ago (King, 1973).

The data in Table 8–1 show the sequences of fibrinopeptides A and B, a total of 30 residues, are identical for human, chimpanzee, and gorilla. An extensive number of alpha, beta, gamma, and delta chain hemoglobin sequences are available from various species of primates (Goodman et al., 1971; Boyer et al., 1971). Humans differ from chimpanzees in only one amino acid substitution in the delta chain (De Jong, 1971a, 1971b). Humans and chimpanzees both differ from gorilla by one alpha and beta chain substitution. An analysis of the available myoglobin data yields similar results (Romero-Herrera et al., 1973). Humans and chimpanzees differ by one amino acid. The sequence data

Table 8–1 • Differences in Amino Acid Sequences of Human and Chimpanzee Polypeptides

Protein	Amino Acid Differences
Fibrinopeptides A and B	0
Cytochrome C	0
Lysozyme 1	0[1]
Hemoglobin (alpha)	0
Hemoglobin (beta)	0
Hemoglobin (A gamma)	0
Hemoglobin (G gamma)	0
Hemoglobin (delta)	1
Myoglobin	1
Carbonic anhydrase 1	3[1]
Serum albumin	6[1]
Transferrin 1	8[1]
Total	19

[1]These proteins have been compared immunologically; the remainder, have been compared by direct amino acid sequencing.

Adapted from King and Wilson (1975).

globin–protein of hemoglobin which comprises red blood cells.

fibrinopeptide–blood protein related to blood clotting.

are all concordant in showing that humans and chimpanzees are extremely closely related at the protein level. Out of the 430 amino acid sequences from alpha and beta hemoglobin, myoglobin, and fibrinopeptides, humans and chimpanzees differ by only one substitution.

It has also become possible to measure genetic difference by **nucleic acid hybridization,** and data are now available on several primate species (Kohne, 1970; Kohne et al., 1972; Hoyer et al., 1972; Sibley and Ahlquist, 1987; Sibley, Comstock, and Ahlquist, 1990). This technique uses "nonrepeated" DNA sequences of two species, and compares the temperature required to break apart hybrid DNA (for example, chimpanzee-human hybrid DNA) from the temperature required to break apart nonhybrid DNA of either species. With this technique researchers have estimated that human-chimpanzee hybrid DNA dissociates at a temperature of between 0.7°C and 1.5°C lower than the dissociation temperature of recombined human DNA (Kohne, 1970; Kohne et al., 1972, Hoyer et al., 1972).

Although the absolute values of the dissociation temperature (T_m) of human and chimpanzee are certainly different, what is important is the relative difference. For example, if we measure the human-capuchin monkey difference at 10.5°C (as representative of a platyrrhine-catarrhine distance) and use 35 million years as the time of separation of the two infraorders, then the human-chimpanzee difference of 1.5°C translates to about a 5 million year divergence time. Similarly a difference of 6.3°C between human and green monkey translates to a time of separation of 21 millon years, and the human-gibbon difference of 3.5°C translates to a divergence estimate of 11.7 million years. All are in excellent agreement with the time of divergence calculated using the immunological data.

Work on DNA hybridization by Sibley and Ahlquist (1987, 1990) and others has suggested that humans and chimpanzees share a common lineage to the exclusion of the gorilla, which would have diverged earlier (Table 8–2). They have estimated a date for this divergence of about 8 million years ago. Although some subsequent studies (Caccone and Powell, 1989; Williams and Goodman, 1989; Spuhler, 1989) have supported this cladistic arrangement, other studies (Bianchi et al., 1985; Smouse and Li, 1987; Templeton, 1985, 1986) have not. There has been debate regarding the techniques of analysis (e.g. Marks et al., 1988) and how they may have skewed results, but it also seems likely that different molecules evolved at different rates, as would be expected statistically, and that this factor may also contribute to the lack of resolution of the sequence of African ape and hominid cladogenetic events (Holmquist et al., 1988). This problem certainly ranks as one of the most intriguing currently facing hominid evolutionary studies.

An integrated biomolecular and paleontological perspective argues increasingly for an entirely African origin for the common ancestral hominid-panid-gorillid and hominid-panid lineages. These lineages may have diverged at about 9 to 11 million years ago and 5 to 8 million

nucleic acid hybridization– method of assessing genetic relationships by splitting and then "re-annealing" strands of DNA from different species.

Table 8–2 • DNA Hybridization[1]

	Pp	Pt	Hs	Gg	Po	Hy	Hl
Pan paniscus (Pygmy chimpanzee)							
Pan troglodytes (Common chimpanzee)	0.69						
Homo sapiens (Human)	1.64	1.63					
Gorilla gorilla (Gorilla)	2.37	2.21	2.27				
Pongo pygmaeus (Orangutan)	3.56	3.58	3.60	3.55			
Hylobates syndactylus (Siamang gibbon)	4.20	5.13	4.70	4.54	4.93		
Hylobates lar (Lar gibbon)	5.00	4.76	4.78	4.75	4.74	1.95	
Papio hamadryas (Hamadryas baboon)	6.97	7.34	7.33	7.08	7.49		7.10

$$\triangle T_{50}H^2$$

7 6 5 4 3 2 1 0

DNA hybrid dissociation temperature scale

Pygmy Chimpanzee
$\triangle = 0.7$
Common Chimpanzee
$\triangle = 1.6$
Human
$\triangle = 2.3$
Gorilla
$\triangle = 3.6$
Orangutan
$\triangle = 4.8$
Gibbons
$\triangle = 7.3$
Old World Monkeys

[1] Differences between the average value of each paired species' DNA melting temperature and the melting temperature of the hybrid DNA. Thermal stability of DNA is measured by the temperature at which 50% of the DNA is dissociated into single strands ΔT_{50}. From this data, a phylogeny of the hominoids is derived. From Sibley and Ahlquist (1987).
[2] Phylogeny of the hominoid primates as determined by average linkage clustering of $\Delta T_{50}H$ values derived from DNA-DNA hybridization.

years ago, respectively. These postulated separation dates, that have yet to be documented in the fossil record, are close to the dates of significant Late Middle Miocene global cooling (11 to 14 million years ago); the formation of the Western Rift Valley in Central Africa (ca. 8 million years ago); and the "Messinian Event," the drying up of the Mediterranean Sea, between about 6.2 and 5 million years ago (Boaz, 1993). These climatic events may be important in the evolutionary origins of the various hominoid lineages (Figure 8–25).

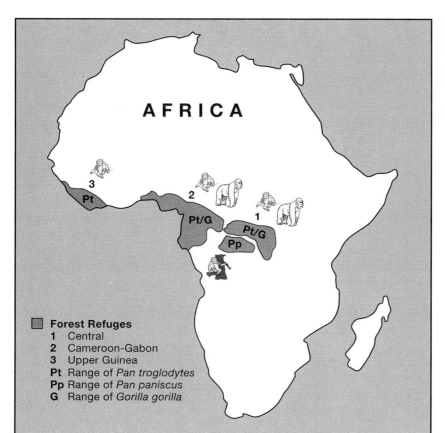

Figure 8–25 • Modern African forest refuges and the distribution of chimpanzees and gorillas may be a direct result of the partitioning of forests related to the "Messinian Event" of 5 to 6 million years ago.

Molecular work further reveals genetic differentiation within the modern *Pan* species into the bonobo (*Pan paniscus*) and the common chimp (*Pan troglodytes*) who shared a common ancestor about 2 million years ago. The living populations of the gorilla are somewhat less divergent genetically and may have separated into western and eastern populations about 1 million years ago.

 ## SUMMARY

The earliest members of the hominoid group appeared in Africa during the Early Miocene more than 20 million years ago. These fossil forms, known as proconsulids, differed from fossil monkeys at that time in molar cusp morphology (the hominoids shared a Y-5 pattern), in locomotor abilities (the hominoids were more dexterous climbers), and, in some later forms, unique patterns of locomotion (such as brachiation and knuckle-walking). Hominoids spread throughout the Old World by 15 million years ago. In Europe they appeared as the dryopithecids, and in Asia as the sivapithecids, in addition to a number of smaller species who were possibly ancestral to the modern gibbons. By 5 million years ago most of these early species had become extinct, possibly because of unsuccessful competition with a growing number of monkey species.

Brachiation is a form of arboreal locomotion and involves specific anatomical changes in the upper torso and forelimb. These changes permitted hominoids a much greater degree of rotational freedom and use of the forelimb in climbing and feeding activities. Brachiation also involved a loss of the tail.

The four surviving hominoid groups, the lesser apes or hylobatids, and the great apes—gorillas (gorillids), chimpanzees (panids), and the orangutans (pongids)—have limited distribution today in tropical rainforests of Africa and Southeast Asia.

Molecular studies of living apes have changed our ideas about their phylogenetic relationships with the miocene forms. We once considered middle Miocene species such as *Ramapithecus* and *Kenyapithecus* to be contenders for direct human (hominid) ancestry. *Ramapithecus,* now taxonomically included with *Sivapithecus,* is believed related to if not ancestral to the orangutan, and not to humans. The Early Divergence Hypothesis predicted independent lineages for the modern apes and humans to extend back over 15 million years. Molecular studies involving such techniques as electrophoresis, immunology, protein sequencing, and DNA hybridization, as well a more complete fossil record now support a Late Divergence Hypothesis and a more recent date for a point of common ancestry of the chimpanzees and humans, with an earlier split of this group from gorillas.

 ## CRITICAL-THINKING QUESTIONS

1. What morphological characteristics distinguish a hominoid from a monkey?
2. Why was it important for hominoids to evolve arboreal capabilities different from those of monkeys? Explain.
3. Who was *Proconsul;* why was *Proconsul* important to the human lineage?
4. Compare and contrast three of the Miocene apes.
5. Discuss the four main cladistic events in hominoid evolution.
6. What can cusp patterns and tooth enamel thickness of Miocene apes tell us about the environment at that time?

 ## SUGGESTED READINGS

Conroy, Glenn. 1990. *Primate Evolution.* New York: Norton. A general discussion of the anatomical trends and paleontological histories of the major primate groups.

Fleagle, John. 1988. *Primate Adaptation and Evolution*. Academic Press, New York. An excellent overview of primate evolution.

Hill, W. C. Osman. 1972. *Evolutionary Biology of the Primates*. New York: Academic Press. An abbreviated version of Hill's multi-volumed Primates, summarizing much information of anatomy, evolution, and distributions of primates.

Schultz, Adolf. 1969. *The Life of Primates*. New York: Universe. Still a good introduction to non-human primates, especially apes, by one of the great primate anatomists.

Simons, Elwyn. 1972. *Primate Evolution*. New York: Macmillan. A classic by one of the great primate paleontologists. Still a good introduction.

Wolfheim, Jaclyn H. 1983. *Primates of the World: Distribution, Abundance, and Conservation*. A comprehensive compilation of the primate species throughout the world.

Evolution of Hominoid Behavior

The Lesser Apes: The Gibbons and Siamangs

The Great Apes
The Orangutan
The Gorilla
The Chimpanzee
The Bonobo or Pygmy Chimpanzee

Human Social Behavior
Human Fixed Action Patterns
Other "Innate" Behaviors
Human Sociobiology
Human Behavioral Ecology
Culture and Biology
Future Prospects

Summary

Critical-Thinking Questions

Suggested Readings

Genetically the living apes are our closest relatives. Studies in the field and laboratory have shown that this is true behaviorally as well. This makes studies of the social behavior of apes important in terms both of increasing our knowledge of the genetic basis of behavior and of developing models for understanding human evolution. This chapter will review ape social behavior and show how a behavioral continuum model is useful to an understanding of human behavior. The chapter concludes with a discussion of the genetic underpinnings of human behavior within the context of human culture.

There is no single pattern of social organization among the hominoids (Figure 9–1). From field observations, patterns of behavior among the apes are considerably more complex than those observed in the monkeys, and in some cases, they are also unpredictable. Long-term field studies on the best known of the apes, the chimpanzees, have shown how complex this behavior can become as patterns emerge and change with varying environmental or social conditions. For example, Jane Goodall reports from her field station at the Gombe Stream Reserve in Tanzania, East Africa, cannibalism and group warfare as bizarre patterns of behavior never observed in her previous 20 or so years of studying these animals.

The geographical and ecological distribution of the living apes is much more limited than in the past. Today, the five ape groups survive almost exclusively in tropical rain forests in Africa and Asia. Only the African chimpanzee has extended its range into the drier savanna habitats (Figure 9–2).

THE LESSER APES: THE GIBBONS AND SIAMANGS

Of all of the apes, the gibbons and siamangs are the least well known behaviorally in the wild. The smaller of these two apes, the gibbons, of which four species and up to nine subspecies form the taxonomic group, range in the north from Southern China throughout Southeast Asia into the islands of Melanesia. Siamangs, found only in the Malay peninsula and on the island of Sumatra, consist of the single species, *syndactylus* (Figure 9–3). Clarence Ray Carpenter (1940), a pioneer primate field worker, studied the gibbon in Malaysia in one of the first sys-

Social Organization Among Various Primates

Bonobo

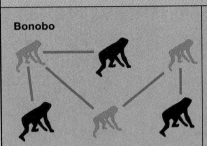

Bonobo communities are peace-loving and generally egalitarian. The strongest social bonds (blue) are those among females (green), although females also bond with males. The status of a male (purple) depends on the position of his mother, to whom he remains closely bonded for her entire life.

Chimpanzee

In chimpanzee groups, the strongest bonds are established among the males in order to hunt and protect their shared territory. The females live in overlapping home ranges within this territory but are not strongly bonded to other females or to any one male.

Gibbon

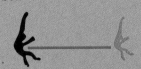

Gibbons-establish monogamous, egalitarian relations, and one couple will maintain a territory to the exclusion of other pairs.

Human

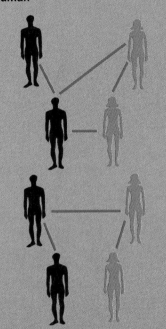

Human society is the most diverse among the primates. Males unite for cooperative ventures, whereas females also bond with those of their own sex. Monogamy, polygamy and polyandry are all in evidence.

Gorilla

The social organization of gorillas provides a clear example of polygamy. Usually a single male maintains a range for his family unit, which contains several females. The strongest bonds are those between the male and his females.

Orangutan

Orangutans live solitary lives with little bonding in evidence. Male orangutans are intolerant of one another. In his prime, a single male establishes a large territory, within which live several females. Each female has her own, separate, home range.

Figure 9–1 • Studies of the behavioral organization of the living apes and humans have provided a good deal of insight about traits that our ancestors may have possessed. This information has enabled us to develop different hypotheses that we can test about behavioral evolution.

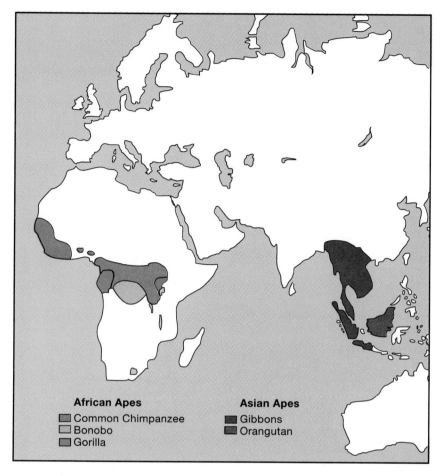

Figure 9–2 • Geographic distribution of the living apes.

African Apes
◾ Common Chimpanzee
☐ Bonobo
◾ Gorilla

Asian Apes
◾ Gibbons
◾ Orangutan

tematic field studies. In his four-month study in 1937 he observed that adult gibbons lived as monogamous pairs, joined by up to four offspring ranging in age from infants to subadults, and together they occupy space described by Carpenter as a "territory." In ethological terms a territory is the home range which is defended by the social group against encroachment by other groups of the same and (perhaps) other species. The observations of a lifelong pair bond between adult males and females and the unique territorial behaviors of gibbons, which are characteristically accompanied by loud vocalizations that usually occur as a morning activity, was later confirmed in a longer field study by John Ellefson (1968). Gibbons also were the subject of a recent book, *The Gibbons of Siberut* (Whitten, 1982), where they were studied on an island off the west coast of Sumatra.

In the wild, gibbon groups range over areas in size between 20 to 40 *hectares* (unit of area measure equal to 10,000 square meters) and feed on a wide variety of food objects, ranging from small birds to fruit, the latter of which is about 80% of their diet. Of the four ape groups the

Figure 9–3 • Distribution and taxonomy of gibbons, genus *Hylobates*. Distributions are labelled by subspecies. (From *Primates in Nature* by Richard. Copyright © 1985 by Freeman and Company. Used with permission.)

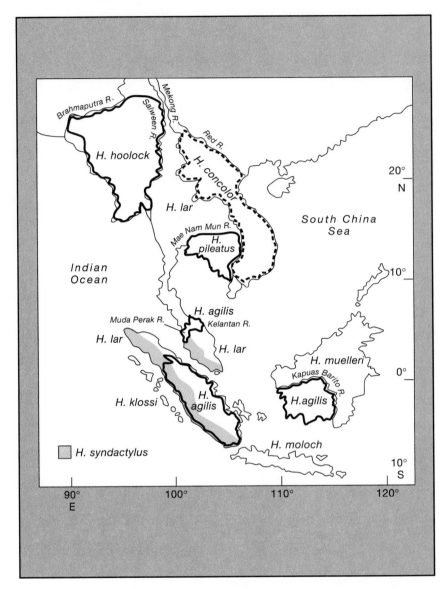

gibbons are the only ones who do not build sleeping nests for their night's rest. They sleep sitting in an upright position on their ischial callosities in the forks of trees, in much the same fashion as do the Old World monkeys.

The species-specific nature of the gibbons' **call** helps not only to maintain territorial organization among neighboring families but also to attract females to unmated males. The absence of morning duets will tell another gibbon group that the caller is a solitary animal. Because of the nature of the call (the female call usually being the longer of the two) other gibbons can determine the sex of the caller. Frequently, perhaps on a daily basis, two gibbon groups will go to a territorial border

call–loud vocalization emitted for purposes of social communication.

area and make contact in response to the morning calls. The interaction that ensues consists of threats and displays along with spectacular acrobatics by the males. The intensity of this behavior varies, depending upon the circumstances. A valuable resource, such as fruiting food trees, for instance, motivates individuals to a direct attack without first vocally warning or threatening the intruders. In such cases, the females may enter into the fray in order to give support to their partners.

Partially because sexual dimorphism in the gibbon is small (about 13% difference in size between male and female), males and females are equally dominant. Either member of the pair is able to initiate action and either can displace the other. As Ellefson reports, gibbons are intolerant of not only the presence of other gibbon groups and other species while they feed, but of the presence of each other as well. Norikoshi (1986) has observed that siamangs, the larger cousin of the gibbon, often threaten and harass nearby younger orangutans and macaque monkeys attempting to feed with them in preferred fruiting trees.

Birth intervals in gibbons have been estimated to be between two to three-and-one-half years. When the young gibbons and siamangs mature, with luck, they form new pair-units. As juveniles reach the age of two years or so they experience the same sort of parental intolerance for their presence as do other non-related gibbons. By the time the individual is about four years of age it may be attacked severely if it wanders in too closely while its parents are feeding. Eventually the young gibbons are driven off to the boundaries of their territory and begin to move independently of their birth group, establishing their own home range. Gradually, by initiating their own morning calls, solitary males and females will attract each other and a new monogamous pair bond will develop. The newly mated pair is now established apparently for life. Occasionally, all-male or all-female groups form for periods of time, perhaps occasioned by the death of pair members or the temporary unavailability of suitable mates. Carpenter reported that the all-male units he observed contained three males ranging from old to young in age. The one all-female unit that was observed contained two individuals, a young female and an old one. The duration of such social groups over time is not known. Similar observations have been made on the siamangs (Chivers, 1974).

THE GREAT APES

The Orangutan

Thomas Huxley (1863) was one of the first to point out that the orangutan is less similar to humans morphologically than are the gorilla or chimpanzee. Ernst Haeckel (1896), on the other hand, ventured to suggest that the orang showed closer evolutionary ties with humans be-

laryngeal sacs–outpocketings at the sides of the voice box (larynx) used as resonating chambers in certain primates; remnants of the laryngeal sacs can be seen in human individuals who, like trumpet players and glassblowers, create high air pressure in their throats.

sternal glands–glands located near the sternum or breast bone.

cause of some similarities in brain morphology. Today most researchers believe that there is a closer phylogenetic link between chimpanzee, gorilla, and humans, but there is, at least, one dissenting opinion (Schwartz, 1987).

In 1967, David Horr initiated the first long-term study of the orangs in Borneo. Later Mackinnon, Rodman, Galdikas, and Mitani also worked in the same general study areas. Additionally Rijksen and Schurmann observed orangs at the site of Ketambe in Western Sumatra. It is apparent from the fossil evidence that the distribution of the orangs during much of the Pleistocene Epoch was much more extensive than today. Orangs ranged widely in East and Southeast Asia as well as in the tropical rain forests of Sumatra and Borneo, where they are now exclusively found. Orangutans are the largest living arboreal mammals, with males weighing as much as 83 kilograms. Females weigh about half the males' weight, approximately 37 kilograms on the average. The extreme differences in body form between adult male and female orangs is comparable to that seen in gorillas and baboons (Figure 9–4). At full maturity one striking characteristic of the male is the large cheek pads of subcutaneous (Latin, meaning "under the skin") tissue located between the eyes and the ears. The exact function of the cheek pads is unknown but appears to be related in some fashion to full maturity and dominance rank. The appearance and development of these pads may be retarded in younger males if older and more dominant adult males are present. Adult males also possess large **laryngeal sacs** that are inflatable, producing their characteristic "long call," the function of which is likely to keep groups spaced apart. Orangs also possess a unique set of **sternal glands** on their chest which may function in territorial marking.

In postcranial structure orangs have a very mobile hip joint and a more fully opposable big toe than is found in the African apes. This

Figure 9–4 • Male and female orangutans.

may be due to the fact that the orang is generally more arboreal in its habitat use than the relatively terrestrial chimpanzee and gorilla. Field studies have shown that the adult female orangs travel nearly exclusively through the middle layers of the forest canopy. Adult males on the other hand, while also arboreal, are known to come down to the ground when they travel over long distances. In both cases arboreal and terrestrial modes of locomotion are slow going. The orang's selection of habitat use may in part depend upon avoidance of danger from predators. On Borneo, where tigers are absent, orangs are much more terrestrial than in Sumatra, where tigers have been observed in orang home ranges (Galdikas, 1978).

Orangs are the least gregarious of all the diurnal primates studied so far. The primary units consist of solitary males, solitary subadults and adult females, with their young offspring. Larger units occasionally occur when two or more primary units aggregate at a common food source, engage in social play (usually involving subadults) or form consort units for reproductive purposes. Social interactions in orangutans tend to increase as preferred fruit trees come into season and produce a temporary abundance of concentrated food. This also increases the chance that nonresidents, who are usually not observed in the vicinity, will also come into the area to feed.

Despite a temporary concentration of many orangutans in a single area, social interactions in the form of play takes place almost exclusively between immature individuals and the infants of adult females. Generally speaking adult males do not tolerate one another. Encounters between adult males when they do occur are usually aggressive, and chases and physical fights are common. Physical confrontation, however, between the males may be mediated by natural avoidance, the result of the long call given exclusively by the full grown adults. On the other hand, with the exception of a subadult attempting to copulate with an adult female, adult males tolerate subadult males, and subadult males are rarely aggressive toward each other. The establishment of a permanent home range is one of the prerogatives of dominance. Lower ranking males are generally transient.

Interactions among adult female orangs are also relatively rare but generally amicable. Adolescent females are the most sociable of all of the age-sex classes and they remain so generally until the birth of their first offspring.

The home range of adult females lies anywhere between 1.5 to 6 square kilometers. Adult females occupy overlapping ranges located within the larger adult male ranges. No study, so far, has produced a reliable estimate of the males' home range size due primarily to the complexity of factors that contribute to their pattern of ranging and disposal. The two most important factors are whether local females are receptive to the male's sexual advances, and the availability of preferred food sources. Male residency is generally not permanent because regularly observed males often leave particular areas when resident females give birth. Field researchers report that males often stay away for up to several years, returning only when the particular female begins her sexual cycling.

Unlike chimpanzees female orangs show no external signs of ovulation, but they do develop pale labial swelling during their pregnancy. Orangutans in mating tend to be promiscuous, even though one dominant male's home range tends to overlap that of several females. The relatively large size of each female's home range in combination with the generally slow locomotion of adults make it difficult for a single male to defend his entire range and maintain exclusive access to "his" females (Rodman, 1984). When the females are cycling, they prefer the company of adult males and often seek them out, among other reasons, for the protection which the adult male affords the females. Unescorted females are prone to being raped by subadult males if the subadults can get away with it and forcibly copulate with them until a larger adult male drives them away. Females who are sexually receptive are more liable to be raped and, accordingly, do what they can to avoid subadult males and resist mating attempts if they come in contact with them.

The interbirth intervals in orangutans seem to be among the longest of any primate species. The minimum interval has been reported by Galdikas to be about five years with an average span of between six or seven years (Table 9–1).

Mothers and their infants are in close association with one another for a number of years. The dispersal of the young away from their mothers begins when the juveniles start to travel and forage independently, spending progressively more time alone in the ensuing years. Occasionally older juveniles will rejoin their mothers for variable periods of time. Young females probably settle in a home range near their mothers whereas male offspring disperse over larger distances competing with other males for residence in areas occupied at the same time by females.

Table 9–1 • Gestation and Interbirth Intervals in Hominoids

Taxon	Gestation Length	Interbirth Interval
Hylobates	210 days[1]	2 years[1]
Pongo	275 days[1]	8 years[2]
Pan	225 days[1]	4.5–7.5 years[2]
Gorilla	251–289 days[1]	4 years[2]
Homo sapiens		
!Kung (Botswana)	266[2]	4–5 years[2]
Hutterites (North America)	266[2]	2 years[2]

[1]Data from Napier and Napier (1967).
[2]Data from Jolly (1985).

Many factors contribute to orangutan social behavior, or lack of it, as it may seem when there is little or no interaction among adults, especially the males, for long periods of time. Certainly the areas where orangs live today have been substantially modified by humans, and because of this, present-day orang ecology may be greatly different from what it was when orangs roamed most of Asia. In Borneo where most of the field studies have been undertaken, the lack of nonhuman predators may also be a contributing factor to orangutan behavior. MacKinnon (1979) astutely noted that in Sumatra where tigers still roam the home range of the orangs, adult males spend a great deal more time with females and their offspring. This behavior no doubt serves to mitigate the tigers' potential threat as a predator.

The Gorilla

The gorilla is distributed discontinuously in Central and West Africa into three subspecies. The western lowland gorilla (*Gorilla gorilla gorilla*) is found in West Africa approximately from the Zaire (Congo) River to Nigeria. The eastern lowland gorilla (*Gorilla gorilla graueri*), a subspecies smaller in numbers, is found only along the western shores of the Central African Western Rift Valley lakes and adjoining forest. The best-studied in terms of social behavior in the wild is the mountain gorilla (*Gorilla gorilla beringei*) which inhabits mountainous rain forest up to 4,000 meters in the Virunga Volcanocs and nearby mountain areas of Zaire, Rwanda, and Uganda.

The gorillas are the largest of all the wild species of primates: the males weighing over 180 kilograms in the wild and up to 300 kilograms

Figure 9–5 • Male and female mountain gorillas in the Virunga mountains, Rwanda.

in captivity; the females weigh about half as much as the males, in the range of 70–115 kilograms (Figure 9–5). The gorilla shares with the other apes the same basic brachiating anatomy of the upper torso, but because of its large size, arm-swinging is not an efficient form of locomotion, and it is hardly practiced except by the very young. Adult gorillas spend most of their time on the ground and, like the chimpanzee, knuckle-walk. Gorillas may often assume a bipedal stance while displaying, chest beating, or charging, a ferocious picture no doubt accounting for earlier travelers' tales describing the "fearsome" gorilla. The display is initiated by the male who begins to vocalize with a low "hoot" that gets louder and faster as the display continues. The male may stand bipedally, running about, throwing vegetation, and slapping his chest, with cupped hands making a violent noise. The sequence may end with the male thumping the ground with one or both palms. Unlike the earlier travelers' tales and movie stereotypes, such as King Kong (Figure 9–6), the gorilla is basically an extremely shy, unobtrusive vegetarian. For obvious reasons of size, gorillas consume on a daily basis large quantities of leaves, shoots, and the pith of trees, which they break apart with their hands and canine teeth.

The earliest field study of the gorilla was attempted by Harold Bingham in 1932. In 1957 Louis Leakey interested two biologists, Rosalie Osborn and Jill Donisthorpe, in observing these shy animals. Neither study was able to directly observe the gorillas for any length of time, but they demonstrated the feasibility of a long-term project. Two years later John Emlen and George Schaller investigated the mountain go-

Figure 9–6 • Hollywood movie creation King Kong.

rilla at a now-famous site of Kabare meadow, Rwanda. A third student, Dian Fossey, again at the urging of Louis Leakey, took up the study after Schaller at Kabare and remained there until her untimely death in 1987. Schaller's book, *The Mountain Gorilla* (1963), and Fossey's book, *Gorillas in the Mist* (1983), are the best accounts of the gorilla's behavior in the wild.

Gorilla social groups differ from those of chimpanzees in that they live in relatively stable units of up to 30 animals consisting of one or more "silver-back" males (those whose hair along the upper back on fully adult males turns a silver or white color), black-backed younger males, females, and their immature young. Recent reports show that gorillas may also form all-male units that may last for at least three years. Younger males who have typically emigrated from their natal groups also travel alone for long periods of time, eventually forming their own bisexual troops by taking one or more young females from other groups (Fossey, 1974). Only in rare cases do adult males migrate between established troops. Gorilla females after the initial formation of a social unit also generally remain in that unit, probably because of mutual attraction to the dominant male. Fossey (1983) reported that in groups that lose their male, usually, presumably, by death, females do not remain together but rapidly disperse into other groups.

Gorillas occupy an average home range size of up to 4,000 hectares that may totally overlap with the range of a neighboring group. Even with extreme overlapping of range and the consequent frequent intergroup contact, gorillas do not appear to be territorial. The daily routine of slow feeding, play, and resting is usually accomplished over an average distance of only one kilometer. The abundance of food makes for a leisurely pace, and the social encounters, too, are conducted in the same relaxed fashion. Both Fossey and Schaller report infrequent dominance behavior among the group's linearly ranked members. The dominant silver-back appears to lead the group in its daily activities without quarrel. Play behavior among the juveniles and subadults, as well as grooming, appear to be relatively infrequent.

Gorillas apparently have no breeding season. Reproductive behavior in the wild, though infrequent, is varied, with observations of not only dorso-ventral mounting but ventro-ventral (face to face) mounting as well (Figure 9–7). Yamagiwa (1987) reports that in the all-male groups he observed that extensive male–male sexual interactions resembling the courtship and mating patterns of the heterosexual troops were common.

The end of the day for a gorilla group finds individuals searching out a suitable spot for retiring for the night. Like chimpanzees, gorillas construct nests of branches and leaves. However, most nests are built low in the forest canopy or, not uncommonly, on the ground. Nests are not revisited and gorillas usually find different sites to sleep in each night.

Figure 9–7 • Copulatory positions assumed by gorillas. (Based on Schaller, 1963; and Dixon, 1981)

The Chimpanzee

The first descriptive anatomy of the chimpanzee, *Pan troglodytes,* was credited to the Dutch anatomist Nicolaas Tulp, who dispelled most of the early half-man/half-beast myths surrounding the chimpanzee in a paper he published in 1641. However, it was not until 1699 when the English anatomist Edward Tyson had the opportunity to dissect a chimpanzee that the correct anatomical relationship to humans was established (Figure 9–8). Schwarz (1934) classified the chimpanzee, *Pan troglodytes,* into three subspecies—*troglodytes, verus,* and *schweinfurthi.* The species name *troglodytes* (Latin, meaning "cave-living") reflected early thinking on the behavior of the chimpanzee based on travelers' tales brought back to Europe. We now know of course that chimpanzees do not live in caves.

Chimpanzees are anatomically similar to gorillas in form but are less massive. The average weight of a male chimpanzee is about 40 kilograms whereas that of the female is less than 30 kilograms (Figure 9–9). Sexual dimorphism between male and female chimpanzees is less than in the gorilla, in terms of overall body size differences, less prognathic (Greek, meaning "forward face") jaws, less massive cheek and temporal muscles, and, consequently, a less pronounced sagittal cresting on the top of the skull.

In postcranial anatomy the limb proportions are much the same as the gorilla's. The morphology of the limbs, however, is much less robust and the digits of the hand and feet are more slender and curved. These differences bear witness to the fact that even adult chimpanzees are generally more active arborealists than gorillas.

Chimpanzees inhabit a broad range across Central and West Africa and they occupy more diverse habitats than gorillas, ranging from tropical rain forests to open dry savanna (Figure 9–10). From the field studies that have been undertaken behavior of the chimpanzee largely depends upon the specific ecological niche that it inhabits. The diet of chimpanzees is opportunistic, though fruit (60%) and leaves (20%) constitute the majority of the food types. Movement from food source to

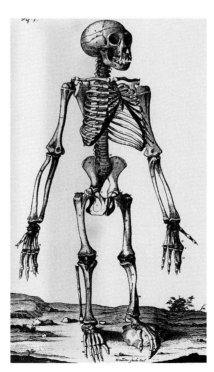

Figure 9–8 • Tyson's chimpanzee.

Figure 9–9 • Male and female chimpanzees.

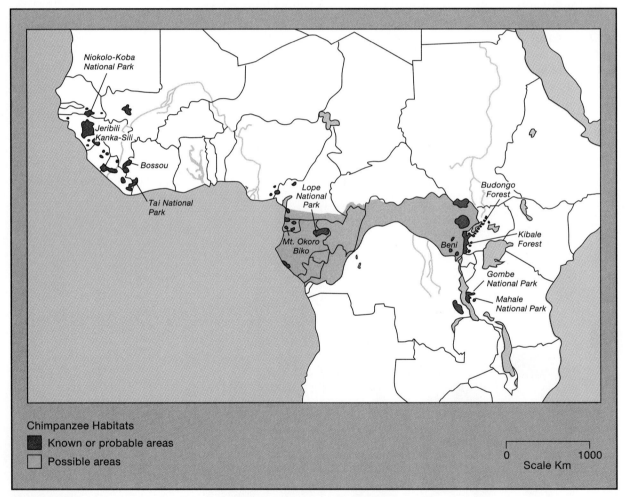

Chimpanzee Habitats

■ Known or probable areas

□ Possible areas

Scale Km
0 _____ 1000

Figure 9–10 • Geographic distribution of the chimpanzee and study sites used by various primatologists.

food source on the ground is generally achieved by quadrupedal knuckle-walking. Arboreal locomotion is accomplished either quadrupedally or by arm-swinging.

European zoo visitors and others quickly discovered that the intelligence of the chimpanzee was remarkable. A suggestion was even made in the nineteenth century that they might be domesticated to replace household servants and common laborers. It was not until 1912 that Wolfgang Kohler undertook the first formal studies attempting to investigate the quantitative differences in intelligence between the chimpanzee and humans. Kohler worked at the primate field station established at Tenerife in the Canary Islands by the Prussian Academy of Sciences. He carried out substantial research on chimpanzee cognitive ability which he published in 1925 as *The Mentality of Apes,* and concluded that "chimpanzees manifest intelligent behavior of the general kind familiar in human beings" (1925:226). Later in 1925, the American psychologist Robert Yerkes established a chimpanzee colony which, after several relocations became the Yerkes Regional Primate Research Center in Atlanta, Georgia. Yerkes, like Kohler, was interested in chimpanzee intelligence but from a developmental point of view. An associate of Yerkes, Winthrop Kellog raised a chimpanzee in his home for nine months along with his son of the same age. Yerkes may also be credited with lending support to the first scientific interest in chimpanzee behavior in the wild. Another Yerkes associate, Henry Nissen, began in 1930 his two-and-one-half month expedition to French Guinea (now Guinea) in search of the elusive chimp.

Long-term field research on the chimpanzee did not effectively begin until the 1960s with the most extensive ongoing study of the chimps at the Gombe Stream Reserve, Tanzania by Jane Goodall. She, too, along with Fossey and Galdikas, was initially sponsored by Louis Leakey. Other field studies on chimpanzees have been undertaken by Junichero Itani, followed by Toshisada Nishida from Japan in the Mahale Mountains, Tanzania; Vernon and Frances Reynolds and then Akira Suzuki who studied the chimps in Uganda's Budongo Forest; Adriaan Kortlandt's work in Zaire; Michael Ghiglieri's observations in the Kibale Forest of Uganda; the Boeschs' work in the Tai Forest of the Ivory Coast, and, finally, the Tutins' studies of chimpanzees in the Lope National Park, Gabon.

Chimpanzees exhibit a **fusion-fission social organization** first described by Badrian and Badrian in 1984, in which individuals are found in groups that are flexible in size and composition. Within many wild groups, small, very temporary subgroups form on the basis of mutual attraction, friendship, and inclination. They forage over a generally loosely defined but familiar home range.

Females tend to show little affection toward each other and spend much of their time alone or with their offspring in extensively overlapping home ranges. Males, in contrast, are much more gregarious and, at least in the Mahale-Gombe troops, at times they cooperate in de-

fusion-fission social organization—social organization based on formation and dissolution of groups.

fending communal territory that includes the feeding areas of several females. The social structure of the community depends upon male––male bonding and males often show affiliative behavior towards one another, such as grooming. Male–male grooming may account for almost 50% of all adult interactions. On the other hand, female cooperative aggression, as well as the frequency of grooming among adult females, is rare. It only accounts for approximately 10% of those interactions. The amount of grooming between adult males and females appears to be directly correlated with mating. Female chimpanzees tend to mate with males who spend substantial amounts of time near them grooming or sharing food. Grooming between mothers and sons becomes more reciprocal with age, but sons tend to groom their mothers more than the reverse. Grooming is also used by all individuals as an exchange for access to infants, for assistance in alliance formation, and in aggressive behavior as a form of tension release or appeasement.

From the field reports at Mahale Mountains and Gombe Stream no male chimpanzees except for a few immatures have been observed to transfer from one community to another. Quite the opposite, female chimpanzees at puberty frequently leave their natal group and transfer to other groups (Goodall, 1983). Consequently, males in a group tend to be more closely genetically related than the females, who may come from many different backgrounds (Tutin and McGinnis, 1981). Females who do transfer typically do so only when they exhibit genital swelling. Nonswelling females who attempt to transfer are frequently attacked, often fatally.

Female chimpanzees exhibit genital swelling during their normal menstrual cycle and also during the early phases of pregnancy. Swelling during pregnancy is also accompanied by typical sexually receptive behavior. When in estrus females are usually seen moving with one or more adult males. Female Mahale chimps have shown that, when more than one cycling female is present in a subgroup, their periods of genital swelling often become synchronized. One mother and daughter pair at Gombe traveled and cycled together and later gave birth within days of each other.

More than 70% of the copulations seen in the wild are opportunistic, involving virtually no competition and allowing free choice for either sex. **Consort relationships** lasting from 3 hours to 50 days, during which a male monopolizes an estrous female, constituted under 25% of recorded copulations (Tutin and McGinnis, 1981).

For females transferring between groups sexual receptivity may help to establish bonds with resident males and to reduce the immediate danger of aggression. Establishing bonds with resident males increases male protection of the female and her offspring, reduces aggressive encounters that might adversely affect females' pregnancies and later may reduce the chance of neonatal infanticide by the males. Male chimpanzees may use a recent history of social–sexual interactions with fe-

consort relationships–pairing off of a female and male for the purposes of mating.

males as determinants of whether to attack or to tolerate females and offspring (Hrdy, 1979). It is noteworthy that all of the victims of male-instigated infanticide at Mahale were male infants. In the one reported incident from Gombe, an attack on a female newborn, the individual was rescued and not eaten (Goodall, 1977). So it appears that male infants are at greater risk than females. Takahata (1989) reports that one mother and five-year-old son transferred together to a neighboring community. A year-and-a-half later the female gave birth to a male offspring who was subsequently killed and eaten by the resident males. After this episode the mother/older son pair and the resident adult males' interactions stabilized and the five-year-old son was regularly observed traveling with the adults for days without his mother.

Foraging subgroups offer another common pattern of social interaction in chimpanzees, and party size is dependent on the abundance of food. Foraging subgroups that find an ample food source will pass this information on by hooting and drumming on trees. In the nonterritorial groups any individual whether of the callers' group or not, may respond to these calls and join this temporary gathering. This congregation, described by Reynolds (1965) as a "carnival," has all the earmarks of one large party. Different individuals would dash about in highly excited nonaggressive displays; then finally settle down for a period of intense social interactions, which included copulations and grooming. These large scale, temporary groups give ample opportunity for individuals to make new friendships and renew old ones and for the young to learn appropriate social behaviors.

Other unique social behaviors recorded for chimpanzees include cooperative hunting of small animals by adult males. They often share the kill among themselves and occasionally with other bystanders who may beg, often gesturing with up-turned palms (Figure 9–11).

Figure 9–11 • Chimpanzee hunting and food sharing in Gombe, Tanzania.

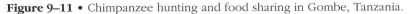

Perhaps the most exciting observations of chimpanzee social behavior are those of tool use. When Goodall's first reports of this behavior reached Louis Leakey, he exclaimed that now the definition of what is human must be substantially changed. Since then tool use in chimpanzees has been reported for most of the groups studied. The most common tool described by Goodall is the termite tunnel probe, which is a carefully prepared stick or blade of grass sufficient in size and length to penetrate a termite mound, inviting the resident termites to attack it (Figure 9–12). The probe is then carefully drawn outward by the chimpanzee and the termites consumed as a tasty dish. Other tools manufactured by chimpanzees include stone and wood hammers used to crack open hard seeds or nuts, and munched up leaves which act as sponges to retrieve water from caches in trees or otherwise inaccessible small pools.

In the area of communication, chimpanzees are the most outspoken of all the apes (Figure 9–13). The remarkable behavior of the chimpanzee, however, led some observers to believe that their capabilities were limitless, only requiring greater effort on the part of the observer to propel these animals to greater feats. During the 1920s and 1930s some behaviorists believed that with sufficient training chimpanzees could be taught to use human language and directly communicate their thoughts to us.

These efforts at teaching chimpanzees to speak ultimately failed primarily because chimpanzees as well as all other nonhuman primates lack the specialized language centers unique to the human neocortex. Efforts were then directed towards teaching chimpanzees, as well as orangutans and gorillas, some form of hand sign or visual cue language

Figure 9–12 • Chimpanzee tool use.

Figure 9–13 • Chimpanzee facial expressions.

(Figure 9–14). In terms of nonspoken communication systems, chimpanzees are generally on a par with humans, and they perhaps excel in some areas. In the wild as part of the normal developmental process, changes in an animal's communication skills take place between the ages of five and eight years. During this period it loses many of its infantile gestures and replaces them with a substantial repertoire of adult gestures. The vast majority of these are learned from interactions with peers and other adults rather than from their mothers (Tomasello et al., 1989). The success of the captive ape nonverbal language studies is partially based on the fact that apes have a large preexisting inventory of signs and gestures, with the capability of learning new ones.

The supposed success of the ape language studies was not without criticism. In a paper published in 1979 Herbert Terrace et al. jolted the entire field of ape language research by reporting work from his own project with a chimpanzee he named Nim. Terrace later revised his earlier position that showed the chimp's ability to acquire both vocabulary and syntax, and now claimed that little evidence existed to support the notion of primitive language skills in apes. He maintained that neither Nim nor the other signing chimpanzees were talking. Rather they were doing tricks or simple mimicking in order to get what they wanted, usually a food reward. Terrace claimed that there was no meaning behind their signs. The Lana project founded by Duane Rumbaugh and Sue Savage-Rumbaugh at the Yerkes Primate Center, however, provided results which contradicted Terrace's position. Rumbaugh designed experiments that utilized a keyboard with over 100 symbols with which the chimp could respond, and these tests seemed to show that the chimp could formulate some basic rules for grammatical order-

Figure 9–14 • Chimpanzee sign language.

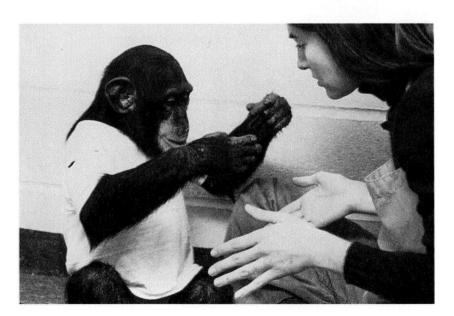

ing of responses. Chimpanzees, it seemed, can learn words spontaneously, and they can use them to refer to things that are not present,
an ability known as "displacement." Rumbaugh claims that they can
learn words from one another and talk to one another of things that the
listener does not know. As Rumbaugh (1985) describes it, "apes are in
the language domain, a behavioral domain that is a continuum, not a
dichotomy" (Table 9–2).

The Bonobo or Pygmy Chimpanzee

There is only one species of pygmy chimpanzee, or bonobo, *Pan
paniscus* (Figure 9–15), which is limited in its distribution to the forests
of central Zaire (Figure 9–2). Its anatomy, possibly because of its
smaller size, is at first glance more similar to humans' than it is to the
common chimpanzee's. This anatomical similarity was first observed by
Harold Coolidge in 1933 when he wrote "it may approach more closely
to the common ancestor of chimpanzees and man than does any living
chimpanzee hitherto discovered and described" (1933:56).

Pan paniscus is not in fact much smaller than *Pan troglodytes,* the
smallest of the subspecies of common chimpanzee, and when skeletal
size differences between the two are compensated for, very few traits
are significantly different (McHenry, 1984). The bonobos, like the other
African apes, are sexually dimorphic in body size; females weigh only
about 75% of what males weigh. In their cranial anatomy, bonobos
have smaller brow ridges, show less prognathism in jaw size, and are
more *pedomorphic* ("childlike") in overall form than is the common
chimpanzee.

Like *Gorilla* and *Pan troglodytes,* pygmy chimpanzees knuckle-walk
as a general mode of locomotion while on the ground and in the trees.
In arboreal locomotion the pygmy chimpanzee appears to be more agile than the common chimpanzee at both arm swinging and climbing,
again due no doubt to its lighter body build.

Pygmy chimpanzees have been studied at two major field sites in
the Lomako forests (Susman, 1984; White, 1986) and at Wamba in
Zaire. Major differences in the social structure and behavior from those
observed for the common chimpanzee have been reported by White
(1986).

In many ways the overall social structure of the pygmy chimpanzee
reflects an adaptation to feeding in large, predictably abundant food
patches. Parties of pygmy chimpanzees consisting of between two
and fifteen individuals and containing individuals of both sexes and
all age classes are generally larger than those of the common chimpanzee. In any party of pygmy chimpanzees one can always find females who are both reproductively active or nursing offspring. Groups
of the common chimpanzee seldom contain both kinds of females in
these different reproductive states. During the more frequent intragroup interactions, various behavioral patterns may be seen, such as

Table 9–2 • Chronology of Studies to Teach Apes Language

Researcher	Year of Study	Subject	Duration of Study	Year Published	Conclusions
Nadia Kohts	1913	Joni (Chimpanzee)	2 1/2 Years	1923	First psychologist to raise an infant chimpanzee. Apparently Joni could understand 50–60 phrases of Russian.
The Kelloggs	1930s	Gua (Chimpanzee)	9 Months	1933	Reacted to English. Understood 95 words or phrases. Gua was raised with Kelloggs' infant son, Donald.
Catherine and Keith Hayes	1947	Vicki (Chimpanzee)	6 1/2 Years	1971	Taught with difficulty to pronounce a few words such as mama and papa. Conclusion was that human speech was very hard for a chimpanzee to master.
Beatrice and Allan Gardner	1966	Washoe (Chimpanzee)	4 1/4 Years	1971	Tested linguistic ability of Washoe using American Sign Language. Proved two-way communication between humans and chimpanzees is possible.
Ann and David Premack	1966	Sarah (Chimpanzee)	1 1/2 Years	1971	Use of plastic symbols in different shapes and sizes to denote words. Language capability comparable to a 2 1/2 year old child was attained.
Roger Fouts	1970	Washoe and 4 other chimpanzees	ongoing	1993	Continued the work of the Gardners. Washoe was observed spontaneously teaching signs to her adopted infant son, Loulis, without human intervention.
Francine Patterson	1971	Koko, Michael (Gorillas)	ongoing	1981	Taught Koko and Michael more than 500 American Sign Language (ASL) signs.
Herbert Terrace	1973	Nim Chimpsky (Chimpanzee)	4 Years	1979	Terrace believed that apes could sign using ASL but with ungrammatical sequence, often unconsciously cued by human trainees.
Keith Laidler	1978	Cody (Orangutan)		1980	Was taught to ask for food vocally along with other simple single-word requests.
Duane Rumbaugh et al.	1970	Lana Project Lana, Sherman and Austin (chimpanzees)	ongoing	1977	Computer controlled, lighted keyboard, translating color-coded symbols into vocabulary.
Duane Rumbaugh and S. Savage-Rumbaugh	1980	Kanzi (pygmy chimpanzee)	ongoing	1994	Learned to use a lexicon board containing 261 symbols by pointing to the desired symbols.
Lynn Miles	1979	Chantek (Orangutan)	7 Years	1990	Duplicated results achieved by chimpanzees. Demonstrated ape-level intelligence. Acquired 127 signs.

the branch-dragging displays by adult males, female-to-female genital rubbing, which appears to be unique among chimpanzees, and heterosexual copulations initiated by either males or females that include both the dorso-ventral and ventro-ventral positions.

Unlike the common chimpanzee, *Pan paniscus* social units revolve around a stable core of females who regularly associate with one another and are characterized by high levels of affiliation (Kuroda, 1980). Friendship bonds between individual males and females appear to be quite strong at times, as demonstrated by two individuals cooperating in obtaining food and even sleeping together in the same nest at night. The more frequently observed sexual behavior of the females apparently has resulted in a strong tie forming between female and male, with the resulting inclination to form much more stable mixed groups. Although male *Pan paniscus* show little affection toward one another, and all-male groups are almost totally absent, the males show little interest in aggressive interactions outside of intergroup interactions or dominance rivalry among themselves.

Figure 9–15 • Male and female bonobos.

One unusual characteristic of the reproductive behavior of the female pygmy chimpanzee is the greater length of time she is receptive within her menstrual cycle. Furthermore, studies demonstrate that the adult female is fully or partially swollen almost all of the time, and this genital swelling continues through much of her pregnancy. Apparently only when the adult female has reached advanced age does she show complete detumescence, perhaps related to menopause.

Pygmy chimpanzees also show some unique features in their communicative skills. As Rumbaugh (1985) reports, some pygmy chimpanzees who were used in the Yerkes ape language studies spontaneously began to use symbols to communicate with people (Figure 9–16). They apparently acquired these symbols by observation. In this

Figure 9–16 • The pygmy chimpanzee, Kanzi, gestures to his human companion.

light, the communicative skills of pygmy chimpanzees may be much more advanced than those of their well-studied cousins, an observation worthy of closer scrutiny.

HUMAN SOCIAL BEHAVIOR

Although understanding human behavior has always been a primary anthropological concern, how to investigate it has been the subject of continuing debate. Most biological anthropologists, primatologists, and ethologists believe that the study of behavior of the nonhuman primates is important as Carpenter (1964:358) argued:

> "The study of the phylogenesis of behavior and social relations on the non-human primate level will facilitate the understanding and control of human activities. This approach is likely to reveal *archaic behavior mechanisms* [italics ours] which are organically functional at the human level."

The paradigm framed in this quote focuses on the biological or genetic basis of behavior. Carpenter's view was that the study of the behavior of the living primates would be useful in reconstructing human behavioral and social evolution, and, consequently, would give us insight into finding solutions to contemporary human problems. Stepping back somewhat from this goal, other behaviorists, while generally agreeing with Carpenter, caution that if we want to study the specifics of behavior (or, for that matter, anatomy and physiology), we will not learn about one species by studying another. Nadler and Phoenix (1991: 152) go on to state, "Nonetheless, if we take a wider, and perhaps more meaningful view, it is possible to learn something about one species that is generally applicable to others."

Although this section of the chapter concerns the biological and evolutionary basis of human behavior, we must temper our remarks and observations. In our search for the evolutionary origins of human social behavior we are reminded of a unique influence on that behavior, that being culture. Culture is part of the modern human environment; it molds behavior and makes an indelible imprint on each one of us. One can argue persuasively that it is the cultural variables that have a much more immediate influence on behavior than do biological variables. For humans, as in any other species, however, biology forms the template upon which behavior is acted out.

Depending on the species under study, the exact contribution that biology or environment makes to behavior varies. For the social insects, for example, there are only a limited number of behaviors that may be elicited by environmental stimuli. For humans, on the other hand, the question of how much biology contributes to overall behavior remains, in large measure, unanswered. At the one extreme, anthropologist Ashley Montagu argued (1968:11) that biology played an almost insignificant role in motivating human behavior:

> (T)here is, in fact, not the slightest evidence for assuming that the alleged "phylogenetically adapted instinctive" behavior of other animals is in any way relevant to the discussion of the motive forces of human behavior. The fact is that with the exception of the instinctoid reactions in infants to sudden withdrawal of support and sudden loud noises, the human being is entirely instinctless.

To Montagu a study of any biological basis of human behavior is pointless, because humans differ from all other animals in their ability to behave without any biological direction at all. This position, we will argue, is an extreme one that few behaviorists believe is accurate.

Throughout this book we have attempted to show humans as part of the natural world, confronting the view that we are a species set apart from it and able to exploit it at whim with little consequence. With this in mind, our review of the biological basis of human behavior returns to an earlier discussion of the concept of the fixed action pattern and the ethological approach to the study of behavior and, with specific examples, will define their roles. We will start with examples of genetically controlled human behaviors and advance to a discussion of more complex behaviors.

Human Fixed Action Patterns

Many of the clearest human examples of **fixed action patterns** (FAPs) come from infants, because learning, culture, and language can be discounted as factors influencing their behavior and because certain form-constant behaviors occur only at certain developmental stages after birth. The behavior of anencephalic infants (lacking cerebral development) during the first two months of life is hardly different from that of normal children, indicating that most early behavior is moderated by the brainstem and lowest parts of the brain.

Certainly mothers and midwives could describe many "instinctual" patterns of behavior in newborns long before these were recognized by behavioral scientists. These neonatal behaviors might include rhythmic searching movements for the mother's nipple, grasping reflexes of the hands and feet which close firmly around an object after tactile stimulation of the infant's palm or sole (Figure 9–17), and paddling reactions if the infant is set into water. Newborn infants show FAPs in the first few days of life when their lips are touched, a stimulus that evokes a rhythmic side-to-side movement of the head. The movement stops when the infant begins to suckle. This is a programmed "search for the nipple" which disappears between six and ten days after birth, when it is replaced by a visual-oriented search. Programmed crying, homologous to the "lost call" of other mammals, occurs in human infants. When the infant is "found," that is it is picked up, the behavior stops.

fixed action patterns—inborn, genetically programmed behaviors that are always released by the same stimuli and always show the same sequence of actions.

Figure 9–17 • Hand and foot-grasping reflexes in response to touch in human infants, examples of fixed action patterns.

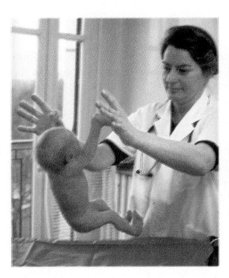 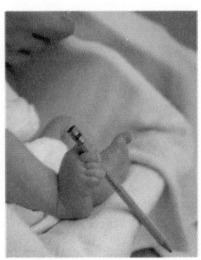

The appearance of these behaviors for developing infants is universal and they are lost after a few weeks or months.

As time goes on, infants continue to react innately to certain other stimuli. For example, until the onset of the second month eye-sized spots painted on a square or round two-dimensional surface invariably evoke smiling in the infant. Up to a point, in fact, this cardboard schematic representation of the human face does a better job eliciting smiling than a completely painted and lifelike face. More recent experiments have shown that it makes no difference whether the pair of dots are parallel or vertical or whether in fact there are three dots instead of two. Only one dot by itself fails to evoke infant smiling. In addition to smiling, laughing also appears to arise innately. Infants at this young stage are not attempting to imitate adult behavior. In fact, laughing by adults often startles an infant, causing distress. As a further example, at an initial stage of language development deaf-born children begin to babble. No doubt the reason many of these behaviors occur can be found by examining the reactions they have on the mothers. Experiments show that mothers, as well as surrogates, react very strongly and positively to infants as the infants start to look at them and as their vision focuses at about four to five weeks. Similarly, laughing reinforces an already very strong mother–infant bond as the child matures. We can see how strong this bond is in primates when we observe how a monkey or ape mother carries a still-born infant around with her for days after delivering her dead offspring.

Some reactions that the infant shows, however, are not exclusively for its mother's benefit. In infants who have had no previous life-threatening experiences a typical fear reaction may be elicited by almost any unfamiliar approaching object. Infants invariably turn their head away and lift their hands protectively. They also exhibit a marked increase in pulse rate.

Some FAP's seen in infants exemplify "evolutionary baggage." They are left over from earlier stages of evolution when they were important for survival. For example, when human infants close their fingers and curl their toes around any object that touches their palms or soles they are probably exhibiting a relic adaptation from clinging onto a hairy mother, especially while nursing.

The development of a child's locomotor abilities mirrors the evolution of human locomotion. Earliest crawling follows the same sequence of limb movements and the same sinuous side-to-side flexing of the back that amphibians and reptiles show when they move. When a child raises its body off the floor in crawling it begins to move like a mammal, with the limbs below the body moved in an alternating sequence. The adoption of the typically human stance of bipedalism still retains the remnant of this alternating sequence of quadrupedal limb movements, seen as we swing our arms in walking.

Adult human fixed action patterns are more difficult to define precisely. Evidence suggests, however, that adult behavior has a stronger biological component than many social scientists might admit. Acoustical releasing stimuli such as crying, sobbing, or calls for help have the effect of alarming us, eliciting negative or fearful responses that can be measured by heart rate increases and irregularity in breathing. Olfactory releasing mechanisms, too, can have very subtle responses. Women who are sexually mature often can distinguish odors such as musk, which are imperceptible by adult males. Women who have lived together in dormitories show a tendency for synchronic menstruation. One female who begins her menstrual cycle triggers similar behaviors in other women who are closely associated with her. It appears, however, that ovulation rather than menstruation is the cause of synchronization and that the cause is the hormonal content of urine, perspiration, and saliva passed directly from one individual to another during grooming or through the exchange of clothing (Russel et al., 1980).

Cross-cultural comparisons provide one indication of shared behavior patterns (Table 9–3). Cultures around the world share characteristics, and individuals within cultures also show consistent forms of behavior. These similarities do not seem to derive from contact between cultures, but result from a common biological and psychological substrate. Some examples of these possible adult human FAPs are flirting behavior (Figure 9–18), and greeting behavior (including a very brief upward "flash" of the eyebrows). A group of infants left on a desert island, if they survived, would theoretically develop all of these cultural attributes *de novo*.

Other "Innate" Behaviors

In addition to FAPs, ethologists have discovered other sorts of "innate" behaviors. One of these is **imprinting,** the formation of a lasting impression during a period of heightened sensitivity to a certain stimulus.

imprinting–the fixation in an individual of a specific stimulus or set of stimuli during a particular period of sensitivity to learning that stimulus.

innate releasing mechanism— a sensory cue that triggers a certain behavior or set of behaviors in an animal.

Table 9–3 • Universal Cross-Cultural Human Behavioral Characteristics

Age-grading	Sports	Vengeance
Cosmology	Divination	Community organization
Food taboos	Hospitality	Ethics
Law	Magic	Kin groups
Ritual	Sexual restrictions	Status differentiation
Symbolization	Incest taboos	Dominance-subordination
Altruism	Defense and/or	Ethnocentrism
Self-sacrifice for others	attachment to territory	Warfare
	Reification and personification	

From Lopreato (1984).

Konrad Lorenz became the "mother" on which a group of goslings became imprinted, because he was the sole mature being around them after their hatching and by acting like a large slow-moving object. On subsequent occasions, he became the **innate releasing mechanism** that initiated the goslings to follow him as their mother. Human imprinting is much less clear-cut and more subject to interpretation.

Mammals in general and humans especially have an added level of complexity in their behavior: "logical," or reasoning, ability residing in the large cerebral hemispheres. This part of the brain often overrides the innate releasing mechanisms of the more primitive brain. This override should not obscure the fact that some part of our brains may be re-

Figure 9–18 • Flirting, the prolonged look, looking away and down, reestablishing brief eye contact, and the slight smile provide an example of an adult human FAP. (Eibl-Eibesfeldt, 1989)

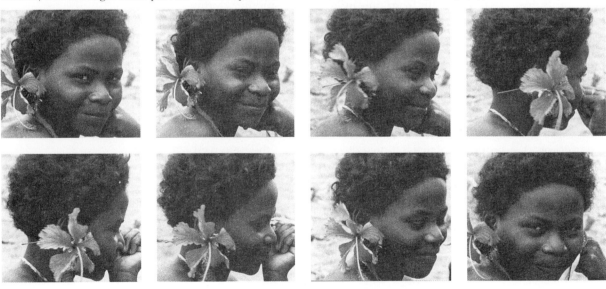

acting to the world in a different manner than our "thinking" brain. The study of human ethology concentrates on important areas in understanding human behavior—including whatever FAPs, innate dispositions to learn, and innate releasing mechanisms we may have inherited from our ancestors, as well as how our brains are affected by this inheritance.

We have good evidence that certain visual and olfactory cues in humans are innate releasing mechanisms for sexual behavior. Bare legs, buttocks, and torsos, especially in poses suggestive of copulatory positions, arouse sexual interest in both males and females (Figure 9–19). These cues are a mainstay of the advertising and entertainment industries. In regards to olfactory cues, women can identify musk odors at lower concentrations than can men, and this threshold varies with the menstrual cycle, being at its lowest point during ovulation. Recently a substance (androstenol) that smells like musk was isolated from human male axillary perspiration. Musk-dominated perfumes that mimic normal human scent are also widely used by both males and females as sexual attractants. Fisher (1992) reports that in parts of Greece and the Balkans, some men during social gatherings place handkerchiefs in their armpits and offer them to the women they invite to dance. According to her sources this act increases the woman's attraction to the man. Fisher speculates that "perhaps ovulatory women become more susceptible to infatuation when they can smell male essence and are unconsciously drawn toward it to maintain menstrual cycling."

Human Sociobiology

A growing number of biologists accept *sociobiology* as a powerful new discipline within which scientists can effectively study the evolution of social behavior in animal species. In comparison to human beings, however, no animal has a spoken language with unlimited possible constructions, nor other aspects of "culture," nor as highly developed and large a cerebral cortex.

How do we relate, then, the findings of sociobiology to human behavior, considering that so much of what we do is apparently learned, affected by personal choice, and subject to change from one situation to the next? E.O. Wilson (1980:296) has suggested three possibilities:

1. Genes merely prescribe the capacity for culture because during hominid evolution natural selection needed an adaptive mechanism which provided additional variability to social behavior—more than was available through genetically programmed behaviors (such as FAPs). Therefore, all human behavior is determined by culture; or
2. Genetic variability affecting behavior has been exhausted, as in (1), but the genotype predisposes humans toward development of certain genetically controlled species-specific behaviors; or

FRONTIERS

Chimpanzee Hunting Behavior and Human Evolution

by Craig B. Stanford

In a forest in Tanzania in East Africa, a group of a dozen chimpanzees is travelling along the forest floor, stopping occasionally to scan the trees overhead for ripe fruit. The group is composed of five adult males, plus several females and their offspring. They come upon a tree holding a group of red colobus monkeys; these are long-tailed leaf-eating monkeys weighing about twenty-five pounds each. This group has twenty-five members. The male chimpanzees scan the colobus group looking for immature animals or mothers carrying small babies. The colobus, meanwhile, have heard the pant-hoot calls of the chimpanzees approaching for the past several minutes and have gathered up their offspring and positioned themselves against a possible attack.

The chimpanzees do indeed attack, the five males—Frodo, Goblin, Freud, Prof, and Wilkie—climbing the larger limbs of the tree. They meet the male colobus, who have descended to counter-attack. In spite of repeated lunges by the chimpanzees against the colobus group, they are turned back by the colobus' aggressive defense; at one point two male colobus even leap onto Frodo's back, trying to bite him as he runs along a tree limb; Frodo scatters the male colobus and manages to pluck a newborn infant off of its mother's belly. Just in front of me a young colobus whom I had watched all morning as it fed on leaves and played with other juveniles attempted to flee the chimpanzees by leaping onto a branch that unfortunately held a male chimpanzee named Atlas. Atlas quickly grabbed the

young colobus and dispatched it with a bite to the skull. Within seconds, an estrous female chimpanzee named Trezia ran up to Atlas and begged for meat. Atlas held the colobus carcass away from her; she then turned and presented her sexual swelling to him, they copulated, and only then did she receive a share of the meat. Others gather around Frodo, begging with extended hands for scraps of meat from the baby colobus' tiny carcass. Frodo offers bits of meat to his allies and to females with whom he has a close relationship; rivals, however, are denied meat. Meanwhile, the other hunters capture the mother of the baby, who has strayed too close in her effort to rescue her now-consumed infant. The mother is grabbed by a young chimpanzee, Pax, and flailed against the tree trunk until nearly dead. The alpha (dominant) male, Wilkie, promptly steals the prey from Pax, however, and a number of females and juveniles crowd around him. An hour later, the last strands of colobus meat, bone, and skin are still being consumed amid occasional outbursts of aggression by individuals who have not received meat .

Two of the most important and intriguing questions in human evolution are when and why meat became an important part of the diet of our ancestors. Physical anthropologists and archaeologists try to answer these questions using a number of techniques. The presence of primitive stone tools in the fossil record tells us that 2.5 million years ago, early hominids were using stone implements to cut the flesh off the bones of large animals that they had either hunted or whose carcasses they had scavenged.[1] The pattern of obtaining and processing meat by more recent people has been studied by examining archaeological sites[2] and also by studying the hunting and meat-eating behavior of modern foraging people, the so-called hunter-gatherers.[3]

Earlier than 2.5 million years ago, however, we know very little about the foods that the early hominids ate or the

role that meat may have played in their diet. We know that the earliest bipedal hominids evolved in Africa about 5 million years ago, and that they shared a common ancestor with modern chimpanzees before that time. Modern people and chimpanzees share an estimated 98.5 percent of the DNA sequence, making them more closely related to each other than either is to any other animal species.[4] Therefore, understanding chimpanzee hunting behavior and ecology may tell us a great deal about the behavior and ecology of those earliest hominids.

After three decades of research on the hunting behavior of chimpanzees at Gombe and elsewhere, we already know a great deal about their predatory patterns. Adult and adolescent males do most of the hunting, making about 90 percent of the kills recorded at Gombe over the past decade. Females also hunt, though more often they receive a share of meat from the male who either captured the meat or stole it from the captor. We know that, although chimpanzees have been recorded to eat more than twenty-five types of vertebrate animals,[5] the most important vertebrate prey species in their diet is the red colobus monkey. At Gombe, red colobus account for more than 80 percent of the prey items eaten. But Gombe chimpanzees do not randomly select the colobus they will kill; infant and juvenile colobus are caught in greater proportion than their availability[6]—75 percent of all colobus killed are immature. Chimpanzees are largely fruit eaters, and meat-eating comprises only about 3 percent of the time they spend eating overall. I estimate that in some years the forty-five chimpanzees of the main study community at Gombe kill and consume more than 1,500 pounds of prey animals of all species. During the peak dry season months, the estimated per capita meat intake is about sixty-five grams of meat per day for each adult chimpanzee. This is far more than most previous estimates of the weight of live animals eaten by chimpanzees. This approaches the meat intake by the members of some human foraging societies in the lean months of the year. Chimpanzee dietary strategies may thus approximate those of human hunter-gatherers to a greater degree than we had imagined.

Whether or not chimpanzee hunters cooperate is a question that has been debated, and the degree of cooperative hunting may differ from one forest to another.[7] In the Taï forest in the Ivory Coast, Christophe Boesch has documented highly cooperative hunting behavior and meat-sharing behavior after a kill that rewards those chimpanzees who participated in the hunt.[8] The highly integrated action by Taï hunters has never been seen at Gombe. In both Gombe and Taï, however, there is a strong positive relationship between the number of hunters and the odds of a successful hunt.[9] This points out the difficulty of interpreting cooperative behavior; even though Gombe hunters do not seem to cooperate, the greater success rate when more hunters are present suggests that some cooperation is occurring. We are still looking for measures of cooperation that can distinguish true cooperation from hunts in which some chimpanzees hunt and others follow along, hoping to capitalize on the efforts of others.

Did early hominids hunt and eat small and medium-sized animals in numbers as large as these? It is quite possible that they did. We know that these earliest hominids were different from chimpanzees in two prominent anatomical features: they had much smaller canine teeth, and they had a lower body adapted for walking on the ground rather than swinging through trees. In spite of lacking the weaponry such as large canine teeth and tree-climbing adaptations that chimpanzees possess, early hominids probably ate a large number of small and medium-sized animals, including monkeys. Chimpanzees do not use their canine teeth to capture adult colobus; rather, they grab the prey and flail it to death on the ground or a tree limb. And once the prey is cornered in an isolated tree crown, group cooperation at driving the monkeys from one hunter to another would have been a quite efficient killing technique.

In addition to the availability of prey in the trees, there were of course small animals and the young of larger animals to catch opportunistically on the ground. Many researchers now believe that the carcasses of dead animals were an important source of meat for early hominids once they had stone tools to use for removing the flesh from the carcass.[10] Wild chimpanzees show little interest in dead animals as a food source, so scavenging may have evolved as an important mode of getting food when hominids began to make and use tools for getting at meat. Before this time, it seems likely that earlier hominids were hunting small mammals as chimpanzee do today, and that the role that hunting played in the early hominids' social lives was probably as complex and political as it is in the social lives of chimpanzees. When we ask when meat became an important part of the human diet, we therefore must look well before the evolutionary split between apes and humans in our own family tree.

Notes

1. Richard Potts, Early Hominid Activities in Olduvai Gorge (New York: Aldine de Gruyter, 1988).

2. Mary C. Stiner and Steven L. Kuhn, "Subsistence, Technology, and Adaptive Variation in Middle Paleolithic Italy," American Anthropologist 94 (1992): 306–39.

3. Hillard Kaplan and Kim R. Hill, "The Evolutionary Ecology of Food Acquisition," in Eric Alden Smith and Bruce Winterhalder, eds., Evolutionary Ecology and Human Behavior (New York: Aldine de Gruyter, 1992), pp. 167–202.

4. Maryann Ruvolo, Todd R. Disotell, Michael W. Allard, W.M. Brown, and R.L. Honeycutt, "Resolution of the African Hominoid Trichotomy by Use of a Mitochondrial Gene Sequence," Proceedings of the National Academy of Science 88 (1991): 1570–74.

5. Richard W. Wrangham and Emily van Zinnicq Bergmann-Riss, "Rates of Predation on Mammals by Gombe Chimpanzees, 1972–1975," Primates 31 (1990): 157–70.

6. Jane Goodall, The Chimpanzees of Gombe: Patterns of Behavior, (Cambridge, MA: Harvard University Press, 1986).

7. Curt Busse, "Do Chimpanzees Hunt Cooperatively?" American Naturalist 112 (1978): 767–70.

8. Christophe Boesch, "Hunting Strategies of Gombe and Taï Chimpanzees," in William C. McGrew, Frans B.M. de Waal, Richard W. Wrangham, and Paul Heltne, eds., Chimpanzee Cultures (Cambridge, MA: Harvard University Press, 1994), pp. 77–92.

9. Craig B. Stanford, Janette Wallis, Eslom Mpongo, and Jane Goodall, "Hunting Decisions in Wild Chimpanzees," Animal Behaviour 131 (1994): 1–20.

10. Henry T. Bunn and Ellen M. Kroll, "Systematic Butchery by Plio/Pleistocene Hominids at Olduvai Gorge, Tanzania," Current Anthropology 27 (1986): 431–52.

Craig B. Stanford is Assoicitae Professor of Anthropology at University of Southern California.

Figure 9–19 • Visual cues in humans are innate releasing mechanisms for sexual behavior. (Eibl-Eibesfeldt, 1989)

3. Genetic variability still exists, and . . . at least some human behavioral traits have a genetic foundation.

Many sociocultural anthropologists would opt for possibility 1. A fuller argument of this position is presented by authors in Montagu (1980). A detailed consideration of human ethology (e.g., Eibl-Eibesfeldt, 1989), however, argues for at least the possibility of point 2 insofar as it suggests that there are human species-specific behaviors. Even point 3 goes only so far to maintain that *some* human behaviors have a genetic foundation. Sociobiologists generally do not maintain the extreme position, sometimes imputed to them, that all human behavior is under direct genetic control. It obviously is not.

As we have learned, sociobiologists have discovered that the degree of relatedness, thus the percentage of shared genes, can affect certain behaviors. This realization explains both the existence of apparently selfless or altruistic behaviors on the one hand and selfishness and interpersonal competition on the other. Humans throughout the world tend to favor their relatives; furthermore, sociobiologists believe that, given the appropriate opportunities, the higher the degree of relationship is, the greater the number of social interactions tends to be. The literature of anthropology is laden with the descriptions of the complex patterns of human kinship systems, and every human language has numerous terms of relatedness of one individual to another. However, before such inquiries become useful, we must determine the extent kinship systems reflect genetic relationships beyond the nuclear family, or whether these systems are only cultural devices for creating alliances that hold little genetic fact. If the common substructure of kinship is rooted in biology, then sociobiological theory could predict behaviors that are based on this linkage. Napoleon Chagnon of the University of California, Santa Barbara, for example, demonstrated that genetic relatedness does play a role in a South American Yąnomamö's life, often explaining the basis on which villages fission and fights between village hosts and guests occur. The costs and benefits of behavior towards kin and nonkin must be factored in, and these are determined by the ecological and social contexts in which action occurs. Kinship systems, at times, do prescribe preferential treatment of in-laws and others who are not closely related.

Sociobiology has also played a significant role in explaining the possible adaptive nature of apparently bizarre behaviors, such as infanticide, cannibalism, rape, and child abuse. Studies in urban societies, for example, suggest alternative frameworks for looking at the occurrences of rape. For example, traditionally rape is viewed as a purely aggressive act without sexual meaning. But rape can be viewed in terms of an alternative reproductive strategy for some men with little likelihood of passing on their genes through other, more stable, relationships. Sociobiology explains to some extent the choice of victim, usually a female in her peak reproductive years, and the nature of the rapist, usually a young male from a low social class with low self-esteem. Such examinations of child abuse, murder, and wife beatings have had similar explanatory successes. Martin Daly and Margo Wilson of McMaster University, Ontario, in their support of sociobiological theory showed that child abuse is, predictably, often at the hands of such individuals as stepfathers, parents with inadequate resources, parents of "defective" children and mothers who experienced a significant separation from their child soon after birth.

Mildred Dickemann (1985) of California State University, Sonoma, prophesied that, although much more refined hypotheses are needed and much better descriptive data at the level of the individual must be gathered, sociobiological theory does hold a promise as an important tool in the study of the human sciences.

Human Behavioral Ecology

Human behavioral ecology has become part of the field of evolutionary ecology. Two important papers by Borgerhoff Mulder (1991) and Smith (1992) have defined this research that views behavior within its ecological context. It shares many of its perspectives with ethology and sociobiology. However, as Smith points out:

> The ethological view of animals enacting "fixed action patterns" was replaced with the view of animals as self-interested strategizers and fitness maximizers—flexible opportunists who could size up any setting they encountered and figure out how to get the most offspring out of it. (Smith, 1992:21)

The field of behavioral ecology has borrowed tools from many disciplines, such as economics and engineering. Thus, decision making under risk and uncertainty, tradeoffs, and **game theory,** to name a few, have become a part of behavioral ecological analysis.

In terms of human behavioral analysis Smith (1992) lists the following topical areas of interest: subsistence strategies, mating ecology, spatial organization, and the ecological determinants of variation in patterns of competition and cooperation. The earliest applications to humans of this theory researched certain hunter–gatherer groups and their spatial organization. These studies looked at the incidence of territoriality in light of projected benefits of exclusive use versus the costs of monitoring and defending that territory (Dyson-Hudson and Smith, 1978). More recent analysis involving subsistence strategies through optimal foraging theory has demonstrated that foragers will make choices that yield the highest feasible rate of return (in energy) from their foraging efforts (in time). Studies of the Ache Indians of Paraguay have shown, for example, that changes in technology to hunting with shotguns from hunting with bows and arrows predictably altered the

game theory—the analysis of win-loss combinations in any competitive relationship in order to determine strategy or to predict outcomes of the competition.

expected return rates for certain prey species (Hill et al., 1987). This simplified picture is complicated with the fact that in humans, unlike other species of animals, prey choice may be ranked in multiple dimensions beyond simple nutritional values. Human cultural values may rank certain prey higher in accordance with their material value (ivory, pelts, etc.) and social value (i.e. prestige). Also gender differences in foraging strategies must be taken into account.

In terms of reproductive strategies, behavioral ecological analysts look at such topics as maturation rates, age at first and last reproduction and senescence, birth spacing, offspring sex ratios, and those ecological determinants of variation in mating systems involving monogamy, polygyny, and polyandry. It is in this area that human behavioral ecology most clearly overlaps with sociobiological interests. Early research efforts involved investigations of South African Kalahari !Kung San birth spacing and the idea of self-regulation of fertility. The average birth interval of !Kung mothers is about four years. Lee (1980), who studied these people, argued that the wide birth spacing among foraging !Kung was an adaptation that benefited the mothers by reducing their work effort in terms of transporting and feeding children. Later Blurton-Jones (1987) showed that offspring survival was maximized by 48 month interbirth intervals. Comparisons with another foraging population, the Hadza, living on the East African savanna, however, provided quite different data from that of the !Kung. Hadza mothers carry their infants less, allow them to forage independently for their own food, and show a significantly higher fertility. These differences seem to stem from the fact that the !Kung live in an area where the relatively flat land surface provides for poor distance visibility and a lowered concentration of plant foods for collection. Both of these factors contribute to the !Kung's greater parental vigilance and care per child and, consequently, the increased spacing between births.

As Smith reflects, thus far human behavioral ecologists have designed their research efforts to ask and answer simple questions only to discover that this research involves complex social interactions. A simple matter of prey choice turns out to be connected to gender roles and mating strategies as well as a decision as to who hunts and who stays in camp to reap the benefits brought back by the hunters; optimal birth spacing is interconnected with divisions of labor, parent–offspring relations and perceived investment. Smith concludes with a warning that it will be difficult to look at ecological adaptations in any social species, especially humans, without considering social processes and cultural transmission.

Culture and Biology

It is apparent from studies on the learning process that the kinds of things which humans do are learned easily. If a genetic basis exists for behavior and culture, it must lie somewhere within the area of ease of

ethnocentrism–the pervasive belief present in all cultures that tends to lead individuals within a culture to view their own culture as superior to all others.

Figure 9–20 • A World Cup soccer game. Lorenz suggested that national sports might be a harmless substitute for war.

learning those behaviors that at some point in our history were adaptive to us. This may explain why humans find it so difficult to live within large groups in urban environments where, for example, kinship usually does not guide social interaction and economic exchange. Modern urban life presents additional problems because individuals may be required to act within a number of ambiguous social situations, rather than within one that is more typical of traditional societies. Individuals may belong to many different groups and within each one attain different statuses. Members of urban societies may face clashing status cues, and the human mind did not evolve to cope with such situations.

Some aspects of our behavior have been looked upon by social scientists as inappropriate and undesirable. Aggression, **ethnocentrism,** territoriality, and dominance might join the list of human behavior patterns that may appear at times to be dysfunctional and at odds with modern societal goals of establishing amicable relations among all of the world's societies. However, as aggression appears to be a fundamental characteristic of nearly all animal life, especially in social species, it must have a substantial heritable component. Lorenz (1966) in his book, *On Aggression,* looked at the ways aggression functioned to maximize fitness and identified its role in the adaptive strategy of all species. In the nonhuman primates aggressive behavior often leads to the establishment of rank or dominance, which, in turn, provides societal stability to the relationships between individuals. Aggressive behavior is limited, because high ranking individuals assume a leadership function and are not frequently challenged and because subordinates accept, at least for a time, the dominant animal's social rank.

Human aggression probably functioned much the same in the past. Lorenz believed that organized group aggression served a valuable function for defense and territorial spacing in early hominid societies. He once suggested that organized national sports is one harmless way for modern-day humans to release these phylogenetically ancient behaviors (Figure 9–20). In recent years, however, the violence that has accompanied many sports, such as soccer, has removed even these events from the category of "harmless."

Aggressive behavior is ethologically closely related to the fear response. A "fear-of-stranger" response develops in even congenitally deaf and blind children who have never experienced any aggressive encounters with strangers. Eibl-Eibesfeldt (1975) has suggested that the concept of "enemy" develops according to the pattern "familiar = friend; unfamiliar (stranger) = enemy."

Humans are not unlike other animals in exhibiting distinct territorial behavior. Even in some hunter and gatherer groups that are said to be "nonterritorial" numerous aggressive behaviors have been reported between members of different groups (Eibl-Eibesfeldt, 1972). Territoriality and the maintenance of individual space are similar phenomena. Although the exact parameters are culturally defined, we do maintain specific distances between one another. Children develop an awareness of culturally determined appropriate individual distance at about the same time they develop an understanding of property (Ploog, 1964).

Some aspects of modern life are simply recurrent patterns of behavior that were adaptively useful to our ancestors. For example, the phenomenon of urban street gangs may be viewed as a completely natural reaction to the unnatural urban setting. The system of "blood brotherhood," with its rites of passage, stake-out of specific territory, and "warfare" between rival gangs (Figure 9–21), must certainly mimic the situation of our ancestors who lived in small groups only a few thousand years ago.

Recent research (1988) on the evolutionary explanations for human aggression and violence was conducted by evolutionary psychologists Daly and Wilson, in an attempt to link aggressive behavior to particular biological markers. This, as well as other work, has shown that there is a correlation between low levels of the hormone (neurotransmitter) serotonin and individuals who are prone to violence. As with the nonhuman primates, aggression, or the threat of it, often leads to higher status, and, predictably, in many cases to increased reproductive success. Human males compete for status through whatever means are available to them. Urban street gang members often use violence, or a credible threat, to maintain their reputations. This research, however, does not support the notion that certain individuals are prone to violence because they are born with low levels of serotonin. Rather research on the nonhuman primates demonstrates that serotonin levels can be raised or lowered by environmental stimuli and that there may be an evolutionary explanation for this.

Figure 9–21 • A modern urban street gang.

Michael McGuire of the University of California, Los Angeles, in his study of vervet monkeys has shown that the highest ranking males in a troop have the highest serotonin levels. Low ranking males show the lowest levels, and also tend to be more implusively aggressive. These studies suggest that serotonin levels increase with an increase in individual dominance rank, and once high rank is achieved high levels of serotonin function to maintain, in the case of monkeys, self-confidence, or, in the case of humans, high self-esteem. To some researchers serotonin levels function to regulate self-confidence depending upon feedback from others. It is thought that variable self-confidence may be adaptive in preparing an individual to deal with the level of social status that can be achieved. High levels of serotonin assist in the maintenance of high social status; low levels are likely to discourage an individual from conspicuously challenging others of higher statuses than themselves for fear of punishment. The hypothesis explains observed behavior in low ranking monkeys whose rage centers in the brain were stimultated through implanted electrodes. These monkeys, rather than attacking other monkeys as higher ranking males under the same circumstances would do, would cower by themselves in some remote corner of their laboratory cage. Although the low ranking monkeys knew the consequences of any aggressive action on their part towards dominant animals, they were also clearly not motivated to attack.

On the other hand, what is the significance of the correlation between low levels of serotonin and implusive behavior? For low-ranking individuals who find themselves in a situation where the existing social system is not providing adequate rewards, individuals, if they can do so, tend to circumvent the rules. Low-dominance monkeys in their attempts to mate with females often do so surreptitiously, hiding from the view of dominant males. In the absence of legitimate ways to achieve status individuals use illegitimate means and risk-taking increases. Although this behavior increases the risk of personal harm, it may also increase an individual's reproductive fitness, for example, if the low-dominance monkey is successful in thwarting the attempts of dominant males to keep him from mating. It seems, therefore, that low serotonin levels are adaptive in the sense that they prepare individuals to take risks and evade the rules. As in the case with humans, this evolutionary explanation suggests that the way to reduce urban violence would be to develop nonviolent means for young men to achieve social status and the means and motivations that would encourage these youth to use them.

Future Prospects

No matter what the sequence of events that brought together the behaviors of modern humans, anthropology has offered many useful perspectives towards an understanding of human nature. As we have seen, the behaviors that were thought to make humans unique from the rest of the animal world, such as tool use, cognitive thought, and language are, at least, in part shared with other primates. Anthropology has brought us, thus far, towards the realization that we humans with all our advanced technological skill still bear the stamp of our earlier history. As we learn more about ourselves, this fact becomes even more obvious. Distinctions created between ourselves and the rest of the animal world continue to fall as research progresses. The intellectual capacity of the great apes, just as we think we have reached an understanding of its limits, continues to amaze us. Recent experiments involving the bonobo chimpanzee, Kanzi, showed that even stone tool-making was not outside the range of possibility for these apes. While we continue to dream with a mind only recently evolved, within it lies a heritage which is still mostly unexplored, mostly misunderstood, and, until quite recently, mostly ignored as a matter of scientific investigation. The promise of anthropology has been to change all that.

 ## SUMMARY

The living apes consist of two groups: the lesser apes, the gibbons, and siamangs from many parts of Southeast Asia; and the great apes, the orangutan from Borneo and Sumatra, and the gorilla, chimpanzee, and pygmy chimpanzee from central Africa. Adult gibbons and siamangs form a mated pair type of social organization, defend their home range and react aggressively towards other adult pairs and their own offspring once these have reached the age of about two years. Formation of new mated pairs occurs as solitary animals encounter one another.

Unlike gibbons and siamangs, the great apes, led by the gorilla exhibit various degrees of sexual dimorphism. The larger orangutan adult males defend extensive home ranges that overlap with the smaller ranges of a number of adult females. Female orangutan social organization is usually limited to interactions with close female kin, a mother's younger offspring, and, on occasion, when a female is sexually receptive, an adult male.

Gorillas form stable groups consisting of one or more older "silverback" males, some younger "black-backed" males, females, and their young. Groups consisting of adult males only and solitary males are also observed. Heterosexual groups apparently remain together because of the attraction to the adult "silver-back" and often dissolve upon the death of that individual. The adult male chest-beating display is a common pattern of intimidating behavior.

Chimpanzees display a fisson-fusion pattern of social organization where members of a community interact with others on an on-demand basis. Mothers with newborns frequently associate with one another; females in estrus are usually found with adult males. Although female kinship relations are an important component in understanding social interactions, like males in many primate species, female chimpanzees usually emigrate from their birth group. Chimpanzees have been observed in unique behavior patterns of tool use and cooperative hunting.

Pygmy chimpanzees exhibit similar patterns of social organization and behavior as do common chimpanzees, except that there is a higher degree of female affiliation and lower levels of male intratroop display and aggression among members of the pygmy chimpanzee social groups studied. Sexual behavior is also more frequently observed and this may account for the appearance of stronger, longer lasting bonds established between males and females, and, consequently, much more stable mixed groups.

Nonverbal language skill studies with the great apes show all species capable of learning and using symbols, signs and gestures. Some chimpanzees have even learned signs from other chimpanzees, and have then used them to communicate among themselves.

Studies of the apes holds promise in increasing our understanding of early human behavior patterns, and in the evolution of those patterns towards the modern human condition. Human behavior forms a continuum with ape behavior and biologists recognize that many similarities in the behavior of apes and humans is the result of commonly shared genes. Tool use, hunting and gathering practices, and bipedal locomotion are aspects common to modern humans, and are also shared homologous behaviors with the apes. In the development of models of ancestral behaviors ongoing field and laboratory research on the apes will continue to provide enlightenment.

The most clearly recognizable human behaviors that bear the genetic stamp are fixed action patterns of infants. Whereas culture provides the framework for almost all human interactions, biology forms the template that, in many ways, limits human behavioral plasticity. Human sociobiology and human behavioral ecology have the potential to be two useful tools in looking at the interface of biology and culture.

 CRITICAL-THINKING QUESTIONS

1. What does the sexual dimorphism of gibbons tell scientists about mating behavior?
2. Briefly discuss three main aspects of orangutan behavior.
3. Compare mating strategies of all the great apes.
4. Is the study of the nonhuman primates a valid way to learn about human behavior? Why, or why not?
5. Explain how sociobiology has been used to explain deviant behavior; give an example.
6. How does aggression function as an adaptive strategy?

SUGGESTED READINGS

Krebs, J. R. and N. B. Davies (eds.). 1991. *Behavioral Ecology: An Evolutionary Approach*. (3rd. ed.). Oxford: Blackwell Press. Text discusses natural selection, life histories, exploitation of resources, sexual selection, reproductive strategies, cooperation, and conflict as it pertains to animal behavior, ecology, and evolutionary aspects.

Durham, W. H. 1991. *Coevolution: Genes, Culture, and Human Diversity*. Stanford: Stanford University Press. Text proposes an evolutionary theory of cultural change and uses that theory to examine the range of relationships between genes and culture in human population.

Eibl-Eibesfeldt, I. 1989. *Human Ethology*. Hawthorne, N.Y.: Aldine de Gruyter. Text discusses the basic concepts and methodology of ethological studies as they apply to humans. Provides specific examples and offers ethological contributions to the understanding of such topics as aesthetics and ethics.

Goldsmith, T. H. 1991. *The Biological Roots of Human Nature. Forging Links Between Evolution and Behavior*. New York: Oxford University Press. Chapters in this lively text discuss evolutionary theory since Darwin, proximate and ultimate causes in biology, life history strategies, the "myth" of biological determinism, free will, and language as well as review the role of animals as decision makers; coevolution of biology and culture and sociobiology and cultural materialism.

Goodall, J. 1986. *The Chimpanzees of Gombe*. Cambridge: Harvard University Press. In-depth study recounting 25 years of research among the wild chimpanzees of the Gombe Stream Reserve, Tanzania. Exhaustive descriptions of various aspects of chimpanzee behavior, including tool use and warfare.

Maple, T. L. 1980. *Orangutan Behavior*. New York: Van Nostrand Reinhold. Integrates the captive and field literature on the orangutan, taking into account its natural history and range of behavioral patterns. Emphasizes the problems of captive management, husbandry, and conservation of this endangered species.

Savage-Rumbaugh, S. and R. Lewin. 1994. *Kanzi, the Ape at the Brink of the Human Mind*. New York: John Wiley and Sons. Personal narrative of ape language studies by an eminent researcher in the field, focusing on the linguistic and manipulative abilities of the bonobo chimpanzee, Kanzi.

Schwartz, J. 1987. *The Red Ape and Human Origins*. Boston: Houghton-Mifflin. Text discusses discovery of fossil evidence that places the orangutan as a central figure in major evolutionary debates, challenging the strong African ape-human connection.

Australopithecines

Definition of Hominidae

The Earliest Hominids

What the Earliest Hominid Looked Like

Taphonomy and Hominid Paleoecology

The Australopithecines
Australopithecus africanus
Further Discoveries of the Australopithecines
The Subfamily Becomes Defined
Interpretation of the Evolutionary History
Australopithecine Phylogeny

Hominid Morphology and Behavior

Australopithecine Paleoecology and Behavior

Robust Australopithecines

Summary

Critical-Thinking Questions

Suggested Readings

Understanding the origin of the hominid family is one of the most active areas of current investigation in human evolution. As paleoanthropologists have discovered successively older and more primitive fossil remains of hominids, the definition of the Family **Hominidae** and its distinction from apes have had to be constantly reassessed. Past definitions of hominid have been based primarily on characteristics of *Homo sapiens,* our own species, which is the best known member of the family. The fossil record now presents to us several species of hominids that, in varying degrees, are unlike modern humans. Where to draw the line between human and ape has had to be spelled out in much more detail.

DEFINITION OF HOMINIDAE

The Greeks defined people in the natural world as "featherless bipeds." The term "biped" split people off from all four-footed animals, and "featherless" removed people from the largest category of bipedal animals, the birds. But such living animals as the kangaroo, gerbil, and gibbon and such fossil animals as the *Tyrannosaurus,* pterodactyl, and an Eocene bipedal insectivore also fall into this category. As discussed in Chapter 1, some authors, such as Delson and Szalay (1979:460–62), consider the term "Hominidae" to include all the living apes and humans. The term is used here (Appendix 3) in its more generally accepted sense of bipedal hominoids closely related to modern humans.

The British anatomist Sir Wilfrid E. Le Gros Clark provided (1964) what has been the most widely accepted definition of Hominidae (Table 10–1). Hominidae, or hominids, are relatively *large-brained* and *bipedal* members of the Order Primates. They have *orthognathous facial skeletons* that protrude less than those of apes and *canine teeth reduced* in size in relation to their other teeth, compared to those of apes. However, as more primitive hominid fossils have become known, some of these distinctions have become less absolute. The earliest hominids now known show characteristics only slightly more advanced than those of apes. Nevertheless, these early hominids were well-adapted bipeds, notwithstanding significant climbing abilities, and bipedalism still serves as the most useful distinguishing characteristic of the family.

Hominidae–the zoological family in which humans and their more recent fossil antecedents are classified; bipedal hominoids with increased brain-to-body-size ratio.

Table 10–1 • Characteristics Defining the Family Hominidae

Skeletal adaptations to erect bipedalism, especially proportionate lengthening of lower extremity and changes in proportions and morphological details of the pelvis, femur, and foot skeleton

A well-developed pollex (thumb)

Loss of opposability of hallux (big toe)

Increasing flexion of basicranium with increasing cranial height

Forward positioning of occipital condyles

Restricted nuchal area on occipital bone for attachment of posterior neck muscles

A strongly developed pyramid-shaped mastoid process of the temporal bone

Reduced forward projection of the face in the area below the nose opening and fusion of premaxilla bone

Canines spatulate in form, showing little or no interlocking, and lacking sexual dimorphism

No diastemata (gaps) in the tooth row related to the canine teeth

First lower premolars bicuspid and nonsectorial (non-shearing)

Tooth wear largely even and horizontal on the crowns

Dental arcade evenly rounded

In later stages of evolution reduction in size of the molar teeth

Accelerated replacement of deciduous teeth in relation to the eruption of the permanent molars

"Molarization" of the first deciduous molar

In later stages of evolution, marked and rapid expansion of cranial capacity, associated with reduction in the size of the jaws and in the attachment areas for the muscles of mastication, and with presence of a mental eminence (chin)

From Le Gros Clark (1964).

THE EARLIEST HOMINIDS

Despite intensive searching for more than a hundred years, fossils that document the common ancestor of the ape-human clade have eluded discovery. The hominoid fossils in this time period are fragmentary and pre-date the earliest known definitive hominids (Table 10–2). The sites from which these fossils come are in Africa and date between 5 million to 11 million years ago.

An isolated upper molar tooth from Ngorora, Kenya, is the earliest possible fossil evidence for hominids in Africa. It is dated to about 11 million years ago. The specimen is similar to that of a modern chimpanzee except that it is larger and likely has a thick enamel capping on the crown of the tooth. Both of these characteristics differentiate the tooth from that of modern African apes, and, in this respect, the tooth resembles the teeth of modern humans. However, because thick enamel is a primitive characteristic for the great-ape–hominid ancestor, as we saw in Chapter 8, it does not confer definitive hominid status on

Table 10-2 • Major Fossils Attributed to Australopithecines

Taxon	Locality	Specimen Number	Body Part	Geological Age
Ardipithecus ramidus	Middle Awash, Ethiopia		Dentition, isolated skull fragments, and postcrania	4.3–4.4 million years
Australopithecus afarensis	Laetoli, Tanzania	LH (Laetoli Hominid) 4	Mandible with teeth	3.6–3.8 million years
	Hadar, Ethiopia	AL (Afar Locality) 288-1 ("Lucy")	Partial skeleton	3.2–3.4 million years
		AL 333 various ("The First Family")	Various cranial, postcrania, and dental specimens of some 14 individuals	
Australopithecus africanus	Taung, South Africa	Taung 1 ("The Taung Child")	Complete skull and mandible with teeth	circa 2.5 million years
	Sterkfontein, South Africa	STS (Sterkfontein Type Site) 5 ("Mrs. Ples")	Skull lacking teeth	circa 3.0 million years
Australopithecus aethiopicus [also considered *A. boisei*]	Omo, Ethiopia	Omo 18-67-18	Mandible with tooth roots	2.8 million years
	West Turkana, Kenya	KNM WT (Kenya National Museum, West Turkana) 17000 ("The Black Skull")	Skull lacking teeth	2.5 million years
Australopithecus [or *Paranthropus*] *boisei*	Olduvai Gorge, Tanzania	OH (Olduvai Hominid) 5 ("Nutcracker Man" or "Dear Boy")	Complete skull with teeth	1.8 million years
	East Turkana, Kenya	KNM ER (Kenya National Museum, East Rudolf) 406	Skull lacking teeth	1.9 million years
Australopithecus [or *Paranthropus*] *robustus*	Swartkrans, South Africa	SK 47	Skull with partial dentition	circa 2.0 million years
	Drimolen, South Africa			

the Ngorora specimen. Without associated postcranial bones it is impossible to determine the body size of the Ngorora hominoid, and thus decide whether its molar teeth were relatively enlarged, as in hominids. A second hominoid specimen found at Ngorora is a premolar that Hill and Ward (1988) have suggested represents the last surviving *Proconsul*. The Ngorora molar, however, belonged to a different species of hominoid. It also differs from the gorilla-like Samburu Hills hominoid, being at least one million years younger. It may represent the earliest hominid or, more likely, it may be one of several still poorly known Late Miocene East African species of apes. Another isolated molar tooth, also from Kenya, comes from the site of Lukeino, dated to about 6 million years ago. In overall appearance it is also chimpanzee-like, but for the same reasons as for the Ngorora specimen its affinities are difficult to determine with certainty.

The earliest fossil evidence generally accepted for Hominidae is the *Lothagam* mandible (Figure 10–1), dated at somewhat more than 5.5 million years ago. This specimen consists of a right portion of a jaw with the first molar and the root of the last premolar preserved. The thickness of the mandible and the squared shape of the molar, as well as a number of morphological details, show that this specimen was similar to those of later hominids and significantly different from those of apes. A second jaw discovered at Tabarin, Kenya, and dating to about 5.0 million years ago, confirms that hominids were present in East Africa by the end of the Miocene Epoch.

The earliest fossil evidence for Hominidae, the definition of which ironically is based on a postcranial locomotor adaptation, bipedalism, then consists of dental and mandibular remains. There is no clear indi-

Figure 10–1 • The Lothagam mandible, Baringo Basin, Kenya, the earliest clear example of Hominidae in the fossil record.

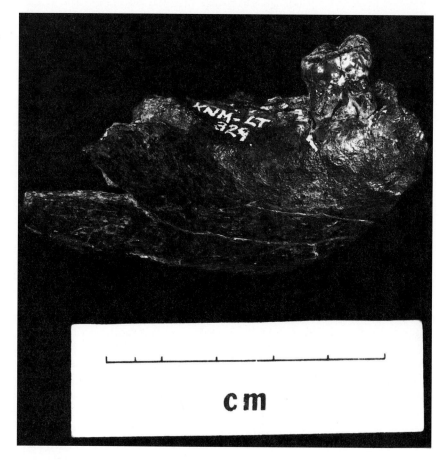

cation of whether the Lothagam and Tabarin hominids were in fact bipeds, since relevant portions of the postcranial skeleton, especially lower limb bones, are lacking.

The earliest possible lower limb bone that may be hominid is the end of a fibula, the outer bone of the lower leg from the Libyan fossil locality of Sahabi, dated at 5 to 6 million years ago. The specimen shows the stout shaft and reduced fibular head seen also in humans. A femur fragment from the northern Ethiopian site of Middle Awash, dated at less than 4 million years ago, is clearly hominid in its long, straight neck and small greater trochanter (Appendix 1). The straightness of the head, neck, and shaft indicates that weight was transferred in a more or less vertical manner, as expected in a biped.

WHAT THE EARLIEST HOMINID LOOKED LIKE

When paleoanthropological research succeeds in uncovering remains of hominids more primitive than are currently known, what sort of creature will they reveal? Equally intriguing is the question of what the common African ape-hominid ancestor was like.

Many quite imaginative scenarios for hominid divergence from the rest of the primates have been proposed during the last century of investigation, but hypotheses have become more and more constrained as the fossil and molecular data bases have increased in size. Majority opinion among experts supports an African origin from a common *Pan-Gorilla*-hominid ancestor. The history of this hypothesis goes back to Darwin and Huxley. Schwartz and a few others, however, have held to the minority opinion of an Asian origin for hominids and a close evolutionary relationship between hominids and the orangutan, the Asian great ape.

If hominids share a common ancestor with chimps and gorillas, which of the three is the least changed from the common ancestor and which is the most derived? Comparing only the living species of *Homo, Pan,* and *Gorilla,* the answer to this question has seemed to be that humans are the most derived and that chimps and gorillas are the most primitive, because they are more similar to each other than to people. The deduction follows, therefore, that our common ancestor would have been a knuckle-walking, ape-like form (Washburn and Moore, 1960). Zihlman et al. (1978) suggested that the common ancestor would have been very similar to a small chimp, specifically the pygmy chimpanzee or bonobo, *Pan paniscus.*

With the extension of the hominid fossil record back to more than four million years ago and with greatly expanded morphological and molecular studies, this situation has now changed. DNA analyses indicate that humans and chimps share a more recent common ancestor than either do with gorillas (Sibley et al., 1990). If true, this implies that many of the traits common in chimps and gorillas, including possibly knuckle-walking, are parallelisms, and not primitive at all. Studies of tooth enamel by Martin have shown that the thick molar enamel of hominids is the primitive condition and that chimps and gorillas have secondarily thinned enamel on the top surfaces of their molars. The thin enamel of African apes, then, is not a characteristic that allies them with thin-enameled Miocene apes. Finally the fossil record of hominids now shows that the earliest known representatives of the lineage were bipedal and small-bodied, about the size of a baboon (Hill and Ward, 1988; Boaz, 1988).

These new observations have cast doubt on the traditional ideas of a chimp-like, ape-human common ancestor. Tuttle (1975) has suggested that the common ancestor would have been more gibbon-like than chimp-like, in keeping with his findings that there are no anatomical remnants of a knuckle-walking heritage in the modern human hand and forelimb. Boaz (1993) suggested that the common ancestor would likely have been a small-bodied, thick-enameled, and perhaps primitively bipedal form, from which chimps and gorillas independently evolved larger body size, thin molar enamel, and a knuckle-walking adaptation. Further research will be needed to resolve this question.

TAPHONOMY AND HOMINID PALEOECOLOGY

It has been said that paleoanthropology is a unique scientific discipline in that its practitioners likely outnumber the scientific specimens available for study. Each fossil specimen, especially those found early in the hominid fossil record, is routinely subjected to rigorous description and analysis by a number of investigators. Yet basic problems in understanding the nature of the morphology and the amount of variability in anatomical structures persist because the fossil record of hominids is still relatively poor, both in terms of numbers of specimens and in the state of preservation of the specimens that are available. Many important issues in hominid evolutionary studies could be resolved simply with a larger repertoire of fossil remains, yet these are extremely elusive. Why should this be so? After all, many dinosaurs that lived many millions of years before hominids are known in much greater detail than are our closest hominid ancestors and hominoid relatives.

Several reasons account for hominids and their relatives being rare in the fossil record. Some of these reasons are *taphonomic* (Greek, *taphos* meaning burial and -*nomy* meaning law), that is, they relate to the conditions under which bones were deposited in a fossil site; and some are *paleoecological,* that is, they relate to aspects of the species' adaptations that affected whether their fossils were preserved or not. **Taphonomy** is the paleontological study of how bones become buried and preserved as fossils. Perhaps the largest taphonomic factor accounting for the rarity of hominid fossils is that hominids, especially early in the record, were small animals. All the various destructive

taphonomy—the paleontological study of burial processes leading to the formation and preservation of fossils.

forces of erosion, weathering, and scavenging by other animals, therefore, affected the hominid bones much more so than the bones of larger animals, such as horses or giraffes.

Paleoecological aspects of this problem relate to the probability that hominids were not common animals in the environment. They were K-selected (Chapter 4), relatively rare animals that had large home ranges (Boaz, 1979a). They were, therefore, unlike r-selected prey species, such as antelopes, that were common in the environment and thus contributed their bones to the fossil record in proportion to their population numbers. The hominid fossil record is more similar in this regard to that of some of the larger carnivores, such as lions, leopards, and canids (dogs). At Omo, Ethiopia, early hominid fossils, usually single teeth, are approximately 1% of the mammalian fossil record recovered in excavations and fossil surveys of surface exposures (Boaz, 1985).

Finally, there is the problem of **collector bias.** Paleontologists in the past have not always been interested in or aware of the smaller animals at their sites. Fossils of elephants, hippos, rhinos, antelopes, giraffes, and even pigs are larger, more "impressive," and easier to spot in the field. Paleontologists now focus on the smaller elements of fossil faunas, the smallest members of which are termed **microfauna.** These smaller fossils are particularly important in recovering information about ancient environmental conditions as they are usually more sensitive to changing conditions than are larger animals.

collector bias–the selection that an individual makes in assembling a collection of specimens, which can vary from one individual to another.

microfauna–the smallest members of a fauna, usually used in paleoanthropological research to refer to small mammals, such as rodents, insectivores, and prosimian primates.

australopithecine–subfamily of the Hominidae containing the most primitive species within the family; characterized by relatively small crania, large cheek teeth, and according to some researchers enhanced climbing capabilities.

hominine–subfamily of the Hominidae containing the members sharing derived characters with modern humans; characterized by relatively large brains, small dentitions, and fully modern postcranial adaptations.

THE AUSTRALOPITHECINES

Australopithecine refers to the subfamily of hominids, the Australopithecinae (see Appendix 3). It is used as an inclusive term for species of hominids which are more primitive than members of the genus *Homo,* which can be termed **hominines,** from the subfamily term, Homininae. Australopithecines have sometimes been referred to as "ape-men" or "man-apes" (Le Gros Clark, 1967), allusions to their transitional position between humans and apes. They are characterized as a group, and set apart from humans, by their *small cranial capacity,* a *protruding facial profile,* a somewhat *larger overall dentition,* and *different hip and lower limb structure.* In contrast to great apes, the australopithecines were *bipedal,* possessed *smaller and functionally different canine and premolar teeth,* and showed many anatomical details of the skull and face that ally them with more advanced hominids.

Australopithecus africanus

Controversy surrounded the original australopithecine find, a skull of a juvenile hominid from a cave site quarried for lime in northern South Africa known as Taung, meaning "place of the lion" in the Tswana lan-

Figure 10–2 • Raymond Dart and frontal view of the Taung skull, type of *Australopithecus africanus.*

***Australopithecus africanus*—**the first species of *Australopithecus* to be named, based on the type of the Taung child; characterized by "harmonious dentition" and relatively "gracile" skull morphology, the species dates to between about 3 and 2.5 million years ago; represented at other sites in South Africa, and probably also in East Africa.

guage (Figure 10–2). Nevertheless, the discovery is a singularly important event in the history of human evolutionary studies because it brought to light a totally unknown, though not unexpected, primeval state of human existence.

The specimen was blasted out of a lime deposit by a quarryman with the Northern Lime Company. He immediately recognized that it was not that of a baboon, the skulls of which he had come across in the same manner. He speculated that it belonged to a fossil bushman, possibly an ancestor of the San people who still inhabit the region. The specimen, still imbedded in a large chunk of rock, made its way to Johannesburg and to Raymond Dart, an Assistant Professor in the Anatomy Department of the University of the Witwatersrand Medical School. Primarily interested in the evolution of the human brain he became involved with paleoanthropology when it came to his attention that fossil primate skulls were being turned up in the course of quarrying in South Africa. He broke away from the final preparations of hosting his daughter's wedding to receive and examine the shipment of rock-imbedded bones arriving from Taung. His excitement was warranted, because the specimen turned out to be the first of many australopithecines to be discovered.

Dart described the new specimen soon after its discovery in the February 7, 1925, issue of *Nature,* the British scientific journal. In the article he suggested that the *Taung child,* as it came to be known, represented "an extinct race of apes intermediate between living anthropoids and man," a "missing link," to use T.H. Huxley's now famous term. Dart named it a new genus and species, ***Australopithecus africanus.***

The name itself, translating as "southern ape from Africa," first stirred debate. A geologist from Oxford wrote that the term was a barbarism, mixing both Latin ("*australo-*") and Greek ("*-pithecus*") roots in the generic name. This was merely literary criticism because taxonomic names serve the function of scientific labels for species of animals and plants, and therefore do not necessarily have to be classically or grammatically correct. Nevertheless, Dart responded that even though *pithecus* was a Greek word, several Latin writers, among them Virgil and Cicero, had used the term.

The real contention, however, lay in Dart's claim of human ancestry for the Taung child. Sir Arthur Keith, perhaps the most highly respected British paleoanthropologist of the day, branded Dart's assessment as "preposterous" in a letter to *Nature* in 1925, after having seen an exhibition including a cast of the specimen in London. He considered that the skull showed the essential anatomical features of an ape, with the possible exception of its smaller front teeth. The dating of the find was unclear and Keith suggested that *Australopithecus* may have been contemporaneous with the advanced "Rhodesian Man" (a *Homo sapiens* fossil from Kabwe, Zambia) (see Chapter 11), a fossil hominid known from a locality some miles to the north of Taung. If this suggestion were true, it would have precluded Taung from human ancestry by showing it to be merely a primitive holdover, living alongside essentially modern humans. The date of the Taung specimen, however, was later shown to be quite a bit earlier than that of the Zambian specimen. Robert Broom, a South African physician and paleontologist, began a study of the fossil vertebrates from the Taung cave in 1937 and established, on the basis of the evolutionary stages of the fossil mammals contained in the cave deposits, that the date had to be earliest Pleistocene or late Pliocene, circa 1.8 to 3 million years old. It is also important to recognize that the infamous Piltdown forgery (see Chapter 11), indicating an enlarged brain and primitive ape-like dentition in an early hominid (opposite to the condition seen in *Australopithecus*) was accepted by Keith and many anthropologists in 1925.

The dating of the Taung site has been a source of continuing controversy. Geological studies (Vogel, 1985; Partridge, 1986) have suggested a date for Taung of only about 1 million years ago. Studies of the monkey fossils at Taung (Delson, 1988), however, suggest a correlation with Sterkfontein (the Member 4 level), closer to 2.5 million years ago, and this date seems to accord well with most current assessments.

Further Discoveries of the Australopithecines

After Dart's original 1924 find, and the inevitable taxonomic problems associated with a juvenile type specimen (the fossil upon which a taxonomic name is based), there was much interest in recovering more australopithecine remains, this time of adults. A number of anatomists had pointed out that juveniles of many higher primates can closely resemble one another, whereas the adult forms are quite divergent.

Robert Broom (1867–1951) undertook in 1936 an exploration of the fossiliferous region of northern South Africa, the Transvaal. The fossils here are found in **breccia,** a geological term used to describe the variably sized rock formed from the debris falling into a vertical cave opening (Figure 10–3). Broom's expressed purpose was to find adult australopithecine fossils and in this manner confirm their hominid status.

Broom's techniques were essentially the same as those of the quarrymen who worked in the area, blasting with dynamite. This did not allow a precise mapping of the location of the finds, but it was successful in recovering fossils. Broom managed to find four bone-bearing cave sites, in addition to Taung, which did indeed yield remains of adult australopithecines, including a complete skull from a site known as Sterkfontein (from the Afrikaans language for "strong spring") (Figure 10–4). These sites have continued to yield fossil bones to the present day.

Partly as a result of the early hominid discoveries in South Africa, Louis Leakey, an anthropologist trained at Cambridge University, became interested in the exploration for hominid fossils in East Africa. The son of missionary parents, Leakey grew up in Kenya, and with his

breccia–from Italian, meaning "broken;" a geological term used to refer to the sediment found in cave deposits composed from rock fragments of widely varying sizes cemented together.

Figure 10–3 • Reconstructed geological history of the Swartkrans cave site by C.K. Brain. Percolating water creates solution cavities in the dolomite bedrock. Over time these cavities are filled with a type of sediment known as "breccia," a combination of above-ground sediments and pieces of dolomite. Fossil bones are also incorporated in breccia.

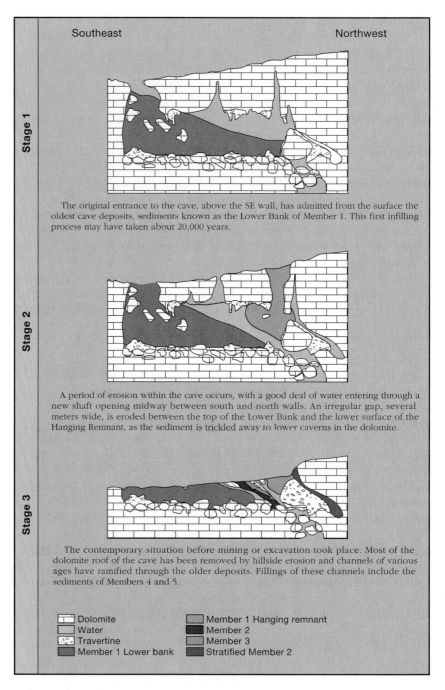

Stage 1

Southeast   Northwest

The original entrance to the cave, above the SE wall, has admitted from the surface the oldest cave deposits, sediments known as the Lower Bank of Member 1. This first infilling process may have taken about 20,000 years.

Stage 2

A period of erosion within the cave occurs, with a good deal of water entering through a new shaft opening midway between south and north walls. An irregular gap, several meters wide, is eroded between the top of the Lower Bank and the lower surface of the Hanging Remnant, as the sediment is trickled away to lower caverns in the dolomite.

Stage 3

The contemporary situation before mining or excavation took place. Most of the dolomite roof of the cave has been removed by hillside erosion and channels of various ages have ramified through the older deposits. Fillings of these channels include the sediments of Members 4 and 5.

Dolomite
Water
Travertine
Member 1 Lower bank
Member 1 Hanging remnant
Member 2
Member 3
Stratified Member 2

Olduvai Gorge–a site in northern Tanzania, yielding remains of robust australopithecines and early *Homo*.

wife, archaeologist Mary Leakey, undertook fieldwork at the now-famous site of **Olduvai Gorge,** Tanzania (then Tanganyika) beginning in 1931. The Leakeys were mostly unsuccessful in discovering early hominids until 1959, twenty-eight years after they had begun their work, when Mary Leakey found a complete australopithecine skull. Earlier,

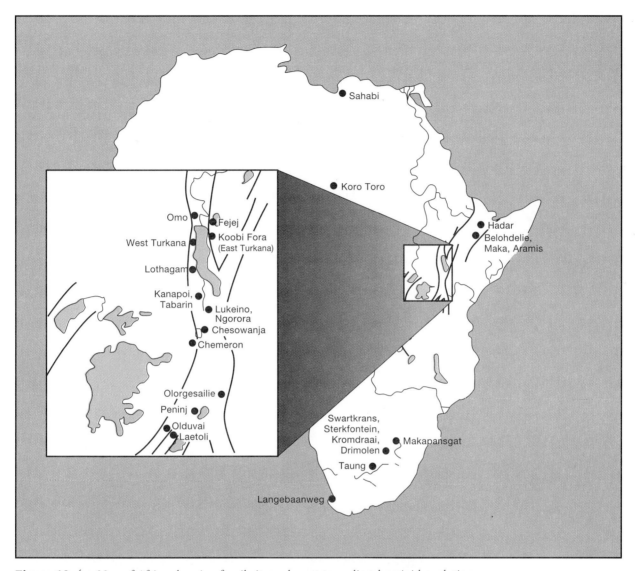

Figure 10–4 • Map of Africa showing fossil sites relevant to earliest hominid evolution.

however, in 1935, Louis Leakey recovered a lower canine tooth at the site of **Laetoli,** just to the south of Olduvai. This specimen sat in a museum tray in London until 1979, when it was recognized as the first discovery of an australopithecine from East Africa. Laetoli became known through the discovery by a German team of a hominid upper jaw and single tooth in 1939. But until the locality was intensively collected by a team directed by Mary Leakey between 1974 and 1979, its importance was not recognized. Twenty-four australopithecine fossils, as well as two trails of hominid footprints, are now known from this site.

Laetoli–a site in northern Tanzania, south of Olduvai Gorge, where hominids were first found in the 1930s and again in the 1970s; dated to between 3.6 and 3.8 million years ago.

Omo–a site in southern Ethiopia along the lower Omo River, with numerous hominids dating from about 3.4 to 1.0 million years ago.

Lake Turkana–hominid sites on both the east and west sides of Lake Turkana (formerly Lake Rudolf), closely associated with Omo and dating to between 4.0 and 1.4 million years ago.

Hadar–hominid site in northern Ethiopia dating to between 3.0 and 3.4 million years ago.

During the 1960s and 1970s eastern Africa became an increasingly active area of paleoanthropological research, and the results have greatly increased our knowledge of the australopithecines, as well as of other stages of hominid evolution. The Lake Turkana Basin (Figure 10–4) contains the australopithecine sites of **Omo,** East and West **Lake Turkana,** and the recently discovered site of Fejej. Paleontological studies aimed at discovering early hominids were first pioneered here in 1932 by Camille Arambourg of the Museum d'Histoire Naturelle, Paris, who thirty-five years later, found an australopithecine mandible, the first of many hominid specimens now known from Omo. F. Clark Howell of the University of California, Berkeley, and Yves Coppens, of the Musée de l'Homme, Paris, continued to work until 1975 at Omo, where 238 fossil specimens have been discovered. Richard Leakey of the Kenya National Museum and Glynn Isaac, then of the University of California, Berkeley, began collecting fossils and stone artifacts east of Lake Turkana near Koobi Fora in Kenya. The Koobi Fora Research Project has recovered some of the best preserved specimens of australo-pithecines and early *Homo* now known. Work on the western side of Lake Turkana by Richard Leakey, Alan Walker, and Frank Brown has re-sulted in the discovery of the australopithecine "Black Skull" as well as a nearly complete *Homo erectus* skeleton (see Chapter 11).

One of the most important eastern African sites for early australo-pithecines (*Australopithecus afarensis*) is at **Hadar,** in the Afar Triangle (Figure 10–5), northern Ethiopia. Hadar was explored by French geolo-gist Maurice Taieb in the late 1960s, and fossil collecting and excava-tions were started there in 1973 by American paleoanthropologist

Figure 10–5 • View of the Hadar Formation.

Donald Johanson. Together with Laetoli, Hadar has given paleoanthropologists their best glimpse of the early australopithecines in eastern Africa at time periods earlier than at the South African sites of Sterkfontein, Makapansgat, and Taung.

The Subfamily Becomes Defined

In Dart's original paper he proposed that a new zoological family, Homo-simiadae (Latin, meaning "human-ape"), be created for its single contained species, *Australopithecus africanus*. It was later pointed out that, according to the International Rules of Zoological Nomenclature, a family name must come from a generic name of one of the species within it. After anatomical studies by William King Gregory of the American Museum of Natural History and Sir Wilfrid Le Gros Clark of Oxford University in the 1940s, the Taung specimen and other South African australopithecines were generally considered to be *bona fide* members of the Family Hominidae. These South African near-humans, however, were different and warranted some distinction from the genus *Homo*. For this reason they were placed in their own subfamily, the Australopithecinae, to be distinguished from the more advanced members of the family, placed in the subfamily Homininae.

Many paleoanthropologists consider there to be two types of australopithecines: a "gracile" species with a more lightly built skull, termed *Australopithecus africanus* (the earlier East African *A. afarensis* is sometimes included in this category), and a "robust" form with a more heavily built skull, known in South Africa as *Australopithecus robustus,* or in eastern Africa as *A. boisei* (Figure 10–6). Most of the anatomical differences between the two australopithecines are related to the very large cheek teeth of the robust australopithecines and the chewing anatomy associated with this adaptation. The gracile forms, by most reckonings, occur earlier in time than the robusts and are considered by most paleoanthropologists to be ancestral, in a broad sense, to the genus *Homo.*

Stone tools have never been clearly associated with fossil remains of the gracile australopithecines. Artifacts are lacking at Laetoli, the early portions of the Omo sequence, the early, hominid-bearing levels at Hadar, Makapansgat, Sterkfontein, and Taung. It thus appears unlikely that gracile australopithecines made and used stone tools.

Dart originally suggested that bone fragments found in Makapansgat were in fact tools that australopithecines had used to kill, dismember, and eat animal prey. Dart named the *osteodontokeratic* tool culture on the basis of this evidence, because the supposed tools consisted of bone (*osteo-*), tooth (*-donto-*) and horn (*-keratic*). Recent research has shown that much of the damage on fossil bones can be attributed to chewing by hyenas and other carnivores, but some wear and breakage on fossils from the cave of Swartkrans have been ascribed anew

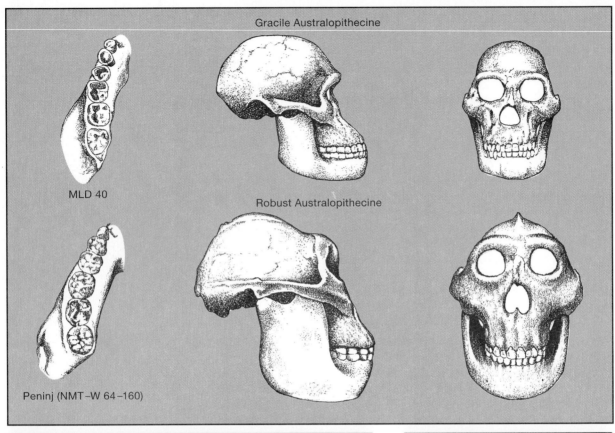

Gracile Australopithecine

MLD 40

Robust Australopithecine

Peninj (NMT–W 64–160)

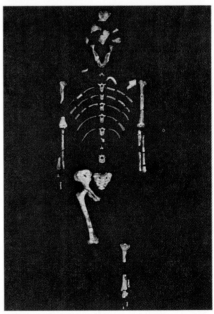

Figure 10–6 • Line drawing (top) shows lower dentition, crania, and mandibles of gracile *Australopithecus africanus* compared to the robust *Australopithecus boisei*. (*A. africanus* drawing based on Sts 5 from Sterkfontein, South Africa; *A. boisei* based on OH5 from Olduvai, Tanzania.) Lower left: the most complete skull of *A. afarensis* (AL444-2) from Hadar, Ethiopia. Lower right: the partial skeleton of *A. afarensis* (AL288-1, known as "Lucy") from Hadar.

by C.K. Brain to hominid activity. It thus appears that australopithecines may have been tool makers, although their use of stone for this purpose remains improbable or at least not likely on current evidence.

An early belief that fire had been utilized at the australopithecine stage prompted Dart to name one specimen *Australopithecus prometheus,* after the figure in Greek mythology who brought fire to earth. K.P. Oakley of the British Museum later demonstrated that what Dart had taken to be carbon and thus the remains of fire at Makapansgat was actually a naturally formed manganese oxide deposit.

Interpretation of the Evolutionary History

The evolutionary origin of *Australopithecus* is a tantalizing question that has so far remained unsolved, despite recent discoveries dating up to more than 5 million years ago. Evolutionary relationships hypothesized between Miocene apes, such as *Kenyapithecus* in Africa and *Graecopithecus/Ouranopithecus* in Europe, and *Australopithecus* cannot at the present time be demonstrated by fossil evidence. This is because there is a gap between 8.0 and 4.5 million years ago in the fossil record of hominids. In East Africa, only the fragmentary Lukeino (Figure 10–7), Lothagam, and Tabarin fossils have been recovered in this time range. At Sahabi, Libya, dating from 5 to 6 million years ago, a skull fragment and a leg bone (fibula) have been discovered. They are so fragmentary that even their identification as hominoid has not been generally acknowledged. These East and North African fossils are tantalizing but they constitute insufficient evidence to establish the evolutionary origins of the australopithecines. More paleoanthropological exploration and research are needed to address this problem.

Middle Awash, Ethiopia   The broad paleontological significance of the Afar region of Ethiopia was first brought to light by the French geologist Maurice Taieb in the 1960s. Further explorations in the 1970s by Taieb, Donald Johanson, Yves Coppens, and John Kalb focused on the Hadar locality in the central Afar, and, in 1981, a multidisciplinary team led by J. Desmond Clark of the University of California, Berkeley, undertook a comprehensive survey of the Middle Awash region south of Hadar. Joining the team in the same year, Tim White became project director of paleontological research working alongside Berhane Asfaw and other researchers from the National Museum in Addis Ababa.

In 1981 the paleontological research team found at the site of Maka on the eastern side of the Awash River the first Pliocene-age hominid fossil in the Middle Awash, that of an adolescent left proximal femur. This specimen, dated by associated faunal remains that are comparable to those found at Laetoli, Tanzania, is approximately 3.5 to 4.0 million years old. In the same year at the nearby site of Belohdelie, a second

Figure 10–7 • The Lukeino specimen, a lower second molar, part of the scarce evidence currently available documenting hominid evolution from 5 to 8 million years ago.

hominid was recovered; this one consisted of seven skull fragments, three of which were from an adult frontal bone. Again on the basis of associated fauna, the Belohdelie fossils are dated at older than 4.0 million years. Morphologically, the femur and skull fragments are similar to their counterparts recovered at Hadar and were attributed to *A. afarensis.*

Explorations of this area in the late 1980s moved to the paleontologically rich Aramis locality on the west bank of the Awash River. The sediments of this region are separated by several volcanic tuffs, and initial dating of the Gaala Vitric Tuff complex located below the Aramis hominid fossils provides a maximum age of 4.4 million years for the hominids. The fossil hominids, which total more than 90 specimens, represent most of the skeleton and include foot, leg, and pelvic remains. Initially named *Australopithecus ramidus* (*ramid* means "root" in the Afar language) by its discoverers (White et al., 1994) it was subsequently renamed as a distinct genus, **Ardipithecus ramidus** (*ardi* means "ground" or "floor" in the Afar language, thus, "ground ape") (White et al., 1995) on the basis that it is the most apelike hominid ancestor known. *Ardipithecus* is also set apart from other known hominid species by its characteristic upper and lower canines that are larger relative to the postcanine teeth, and more incisiform in configuration and less projecting than those of other Miocene hominoids (Figure 10–8). Its canines and molars also show thinner enamel than do other hominids. In addition, the fossil bones of the left arm of a single individual found there display a mosaic of characteristics that resemble those of both hominids and apes.

Kanapoi and Allia Bay, Kenya   A new series of fossils were found by a team led by Meave Leakey and Alan Walker at two sites located near Lake Turkana: Kanapoi to the southwest of the lake, where nine dental, cranial and postcranial pieces were found; and Allia Bay on the eastern rim of the lake, which yielded twelve additional specimens. These fossils fall between 3.9 and 4.2 million years based on their stratigraphic position within dated tuff sequences. The Leakey team (1995) has named these specimens *Australopithecus anamensis* (*anam* means "lake" in the Turkana language of the region). The teeth are similar to those of *A. afarensis* except that the canine of *anamensis* is larger in size and usually more asymmetrical, possessing a long and robust root. The teeth differ from *Ardipithecus* by possessing thicker tooth enamel. The tibia that was recovered at Kanapoi comes from the same (upper) level as did the earlier discovered distal humerus and shows bipedal characteristics. Leakey and Walker believe that *A. anamensis* represents one of a number of early emerging, variable hominid species that all were based on the novel bipedal adaptation. Peter Andrews of the British Natural History Museum (1995) observes that while all of these so-called species may have been phylogenetically hom-

Ardipithecus ramidus—the most primitive species of hominid presently known.

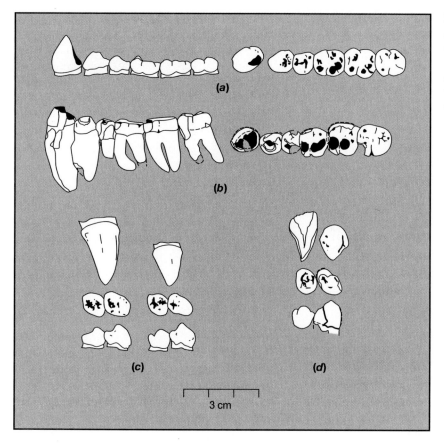

Figure 10–8 • (*a*) Side and occlusal views of *P. troglodytes* dentition compared to (*b*) *A. ramidus;* (*c*) side views of upper canines, and side and occlusal views of *P. troglodyte* compared to (*d*) *A. ramidus.*

(a)

(b)

(c)

(d)

3 cm

inids, they seem, ecologically anyway, to be more closely similar to apes.

Laetoli, Tanzania The first major finds of australopithecines in eastern Africa are at Laetoli, in northern Tanzania (Figure 10–9). "Laetoli" is a Maasai word referring to a small flowering shrub, abundant in the area. The site is some 50 kilometers (30 miles) to the south of Olduvai Gorge, and was the site of the previously mentioned discovery of an australopithecine canine by Louis Leakey in 1935. Following the discovery of some fragmentary hominid fossils, Mary Leakey reinstituted collection there in 1974. Garniss Curtis at the University of California, Berkeley, used the potassium-argon method to date a sample of volcanic ash to 3.7 million years ago.

The hominid fossils from Laetoli were originally ascribed to the genus *Homo* by Mary Leakey. As such they represented the earliest known occurrence of this genus in the fossil record, fully 1.5 million years earlier than well-dated *Homo* fossils from other sites, such as Omo. The detailed description of the fossils by White, however, re-

 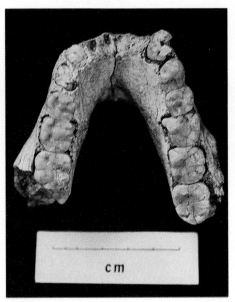 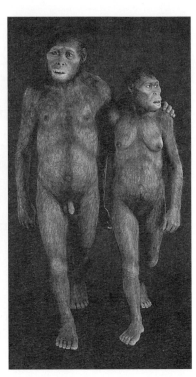

Figure 10–9 • Laetoli footprint trail (left), LH4 mandible of *A. afarensis* (center), and one possible behavioral reconstruction of the Laetoli hominids (right).

tuff–a geological deposit composed of volcanic ash.

vealed that they possessed a number of primitive traits, not expected in specimens belonging to the genus *Homo.* Although the specimens were similar to South African *Australopithecus africanus,* a new species, *Australopithecus afarensis,* was named based on the combined fossil hominid sample from Laetoli and the Afar site in northern Ethiopia (Johanson in Hinrichson, 1978; Johanson, White, and Coppens, 1978; see Boaz, 1988).

In 1976 the remarkable discovery was made that the volcanic ash layer (known as a "**tuff**") at Laetoli had preserved footprints of animals living when the ash was deposited 3.7 million years ago. Among these animal tracks were trails of two hominids, walking side-by-side (Figure 10–9). These footprints of walking hominids constitute the earliest evidence of bipedalism in the hominid fossil record. On the basis of the size of the feet the height of the hominids was estimated to have been between 119 and 139 centimeters (3.9 to 4.6 feet). Other scientists used the estimated size of the hominids and the length of their stride, and inferred a slow rate of speed at which they were walking, which however needed to be adjusted because of the relatively shorter lower limbs and stride length of *A. afarensis.* Mary Leakey suggested that by the difference in their size, the footprints were probably those of a male and a female.

Hadar   The most abundant fossil evidence for early australopithecines comes from Hadar, dated somewhat later in time than Laetoli. It is located some 1,600 kilometers to the north of Laetoli, in the Afar Depression of northern Ethiopia. The first hominid fossils to be discovered at Hadar were a distal thigh bone (femur) and the proximal shin bone (tibia), which fit together to form a knee joint (minus the knee cap). The angle at which the femur articulated with the tibia in the fossil from Hadar was like a hominid's and unlike an ape's. The femora in hominids slant downward to the knees that are quite close together, whereas the femora are aligned with the long axis of the tibia and the knees are widespread in apes. This was a clear indication from anatomy that the early australopithecines at Hadar were bipedal, a confirmation of the evidence from Laetoli.

Further discoveries at Hadar confirmed it as one of the most productive of hominid fossil sites. Among the sample, consisting of between 35 and 65 individuals, were the largely complete skeleton from Hadar (Afar) Locality AL288, nicknamed "Lucy" (Figure 10–6), and a concentration of remains of some 13 individuals from AL333, nicknamed the "First Family" (Figure 10–10). These remains constitute the most complete evidence that anthropologists have so far of this most distant time period of hominid evolution. Potassium-argon dates have bracketed the age of the Hadar hominids between 2.8 and 3.4 million years ago. Study of the fossils has revealed that early australopithecines possessed a high degree of sexual dimorphism (Figure 10–10). Australopithecine males, although larger than females, did not have proportionately larger canines, an important difference from sexually dimorphic non-human primates. This difference implies that canines had ceased to be used in intraspecific display and in male–male aggressive competition. The Hadar hominid finds also confirmed estimates from the footprint evidence at Laetoli that the early australopithecines had been small. "Lucy," for example, was estimated to have been less than 4 feet tall, although males would have been taller and larger.

The Sample of East and South African Early Australopithecines   Anthropologists have now carefully compared the East and South African samples of australopithecines. Dating at the South African cave sites has never been clear, because it has been based on relative ages, as ascertained by the evolutionary stages of the fossil vertebrates contained in the assemblages. Nevertheless, the ages of Sterkfontein and Makapansgat can be estimated to be between 2.5 and 3.0 million years old. Makapansgat appears to be somewhat earlier than Sterkfontein and Taung may be somewhat later (Figure 10–11).

Recent work has shown that both African groups of early australopithecines (*A. afarensis* and *A. africanus*) are similar. They both possess relatively large canines, a tendency for a nonbicuspid premolars (like apes), a high degree of sexual dimorphism and a face that is "dished" or depressed in the area around the nasal opening. Differ-

Figure 10–10 • Sexual dimorphism in *Australopithecus afarensis* shown in a comparison of AL 333w-60 (top) and AL 333w-12 (bottom) mandibles.

ences that have been pointed out between the eastern African sample from Laetoli and Hadar, on the one hand, and the South African hominids on the other, include a more primitive pattern of blood drainage in the brain, a compound temporo-nuchal bony crest at the back of the skull, and a smaller cranial capacity in the former. These differences led to the creation of the separate species name, *Australopithecus afarensis*. Other experts are of the opinion that the differences that are seen are to be expected in populations composed of individuals possessing their own somewhat variable characteristics. These latter anthropologists (e.g. Tobias, 1980) combine the eastern and southern African australopithecines into *Australopithecus africanus*. A third group (e.g. Falk, Olsen, and Senut) consider that there were already two australopithecine species present at Hadar.

Skull morphology is the most important criteria for recognizing early, or gracile, *Australopithecus* because most of the important anatomical and behavioral adaptations of the species are reflected in the skull. Three general adaptations account for cranial form: brain size, erect posture (bipedalism), and use of the teeth.

The relatively enlarged brain gives *A. afarensis* and *A. africanus* a somewhat globular head shape compared to modern apes' (Figure

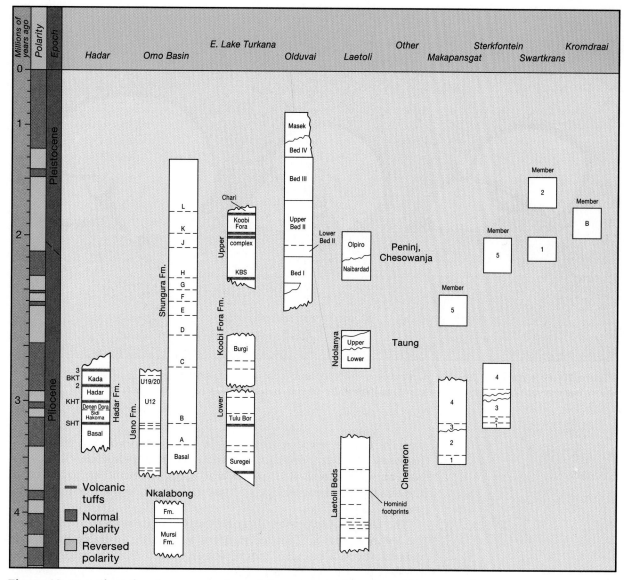

Figure 10–11 • Chart showing a comparison of the eastern and southern African australo-pithecine sites by age.

10–12). This shape is emphasized by the lack of the heavy ridges for muscular attachment seen in the ape, the exceptions being the presence of small temporo-nuchal and sagittal crests on some specimens of *A. afarensis.* One of the muscles of mastication, *temporalis,* which can be felt in the "temple" region, is less developed, particularly in its front part, in *A. africanus* than in *A. afarensis.* This muscle attaches to a slight ridge, the temporal line, halfway up the side of the cranial vault

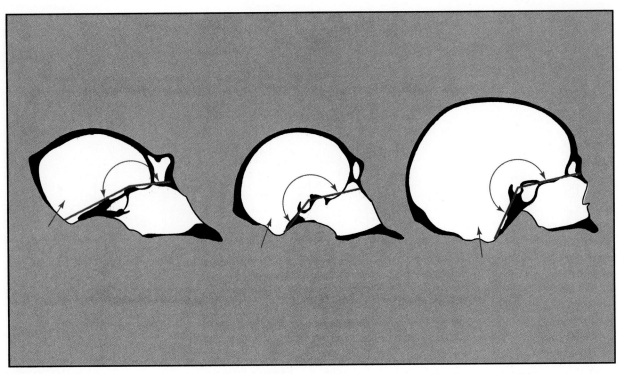

Figure 10–12 • Ape (gorilla, left), *A. africanus* (middle), and human (right) skulls, drawn in midline sections to show basicranial flexion and with arrows indicating the direction and position of the foramen magnum.

in *A. africanus,* most *A. afarensis,* and *Homo.* In gorillas, male chimpanzees, some *A. afarensis,* and robust australopithecines the *temporalis* muscles of both sides of the head meet in the midline at the top of the skull and a heavy ridge of bone is formed, known as the sagittal crest.

The face of *A. afarensis* protrudes less than in modern apes because the anterior teeth are smaller. *A. afarensis* and the australopithecines in general show a peculiar morphology in that the nose region is depressed relative to the rest of the face. The functional significance of this "dished face" morphology is related to a relative increase in bone thickness of both sides of the nose and back along the maxillae that hold the large hominid molars (Rak, 1983). Erect posture in the australopithecines may have also placed a premium on facial reduction for head balance.

Overall the gracile australopithecine face is orthognathous, pushed in under the braincase, in a form similar to that of later hominids. The facial skeleton has moved backward and downward and the back of the braincase has rotated forward, a process known as **basicranial flexion** (Figure 10–12). Thus the opening through which the spinal cord enters the brain, the *foramen magnum* (Latin, meaning "great

basicranial flexion–the hinging of the base of the skull and the hard palate together to form a more acute angle; seen in both australopithecine lineages.

window"), is located halfway between the front and the back of the skull so that the head is balanced on the vertebral column. In the knuckle-walking apes the *foramen* is positioned more posteriorly and its opening is slanted more towards the back of the skull than in hominids, characteristics related to the more horizontal posture of these animals. Heavy neck muscles hold up and move the head. In australopithecines a reduced face, basicranial flexion, a centrally placed foramen magnum, and a lack of heavy neck musculature are cranial features that reflect bipedality.

Pilbeam has applied the term **megadont,** meaning "large-toothed," to refer to the relatively large molar size of early hominids as compared to apes. Teeth are the most abundant remains of the gracile australopithecines. Their structure parallels that of later hominids of the genus *Homo*: generally large and wide incisors relative to canines, canines functionally similar to incisors, and lower third premolars which generally do not wear or hone against the back of the upper canines, as in apes. In certain aspects, however, australopithecines are more primitive. Their canines are generally larger than those in *Homo*, the lower third premolar is less "squared" in appearance and may even have a wear facet for the upper canine, the molars are generally longer relative to their width and they possess a complicated wrinkled ("crenulated") surface pattern. Australopithecines, like all hominids, possess thick enamel on the top surfaces of the molars, a characteristic also shared with some apes, such as the modern orangutan and *Sivapithecus*. Thick enamel increases the functional lifetime of the tooth, especially when the diet is abrasive. The larger and crenulated molars of australopithecines provided them with increased surface area for grinding food, which probably was more fibrous and tougher to chew than that of later *Homo*.

The form and shape of the mandible in gracile australopthecines has been of interest because in certain individual specimens it is markedly V-shaped. Interest has centered on whether or not this characteristic separates all *Australopithecus* from later (or perhaps contemporaneous) species of *Homo* that had a more "parabolic" shape to their mandibular outline. There seems, however, to be an intergradation in V- and parabolic shape in early hominid mandibles found in the same locality. There are even rare examples of V-shape in modern human mandibles. The shape of the mandible is a function of the width of the *symphysis* (the region in the front holding the incisors), the length of the *corpus* (the region along the sides holding the molars), and the distance between the condyles articulating with the skull base. A V-shaped mandible results when a small incisor region is combined with a long molar region and a relatively large brain (a wide cranial base accounts for widely spread mandibular condyles). Australopithecine populations had a higher percentage of individuals with V-shaped mandibles, due primarily to long molar rows, than individuals with parabolic-shaped mandibles.

megadont—"large-toothed," referring to the relatively large molars of hominids; Boaz (1983) has suggested that "megamylic" ("large-molared") is a more accurate term.

Australopithecine Phylogeny

Australopithecus africanus has been considered for some years to represent the hominid ancestral to the genus *Homo*. But in their study of the Laetoli and Hadar australopithecines, Johanson and White (1979) suggested that only *Australopithecus afarensis* was ancestral to *Homo* and that *A. africanus* was ancestral to the later robust australopithecines (Figure 10–13). The morphological similarity between the specimens ascribed to *A. afarensis* and *A. africanus,* respectively, seems to argue against this proposal, as does the consequent lack of an ancestor to the *Homo* lineage after 2.8 million years ago, the upper date at the Hadar site (Boaz, 1988). Most anthropologists now hypothesize *A. afarensis* as the ancestor of *A. africanus.* As will be discussed in Chapter 11, the earliest members of the genus *Homo* show a number of similarities to "gracile" australopithecines, specifically *A. africanus,* and this argues for an evolutionary sequence from *Australopithecus africanus* to *Homo*.

There are no certain occurrences of australopithecines outside Africa. G.H.R. von Koenigswald reported some fossils (single teeth) from mainland China that he bought in Hong Kong and which he considered to be australopithecines. These specimens, however, are undated and are insufficient evidence to confirm the presence of the genus *Australopithecus* in China. Three mandibles collected in Java were considered by J. T. Robinson, an expert on the South African australopithecines, to be robust australopithecines. But most other anthropologists consider these specimens to be large individuals of early *Homo*.

The temporal range of australopithecines, as determined by absolute and relative methods of dating, are circa 4.3 to 2.3 million years ago for early and gracile australopithecines (*Ardipithecus ramidus, Australopithecus afarensis* and *Australopithecus africanus*).

Figure 10–13 • Four possible evolutionary schemes for early hominids.

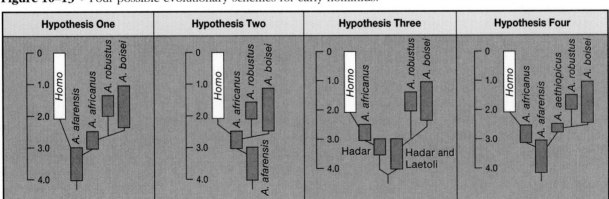

FRONTIERS

The Earliest Australopithecines and Human Origins

by Alan Walker

Present-day Lake Turkana in northern Kenya is over 150 miles long and has an area of about two and a half thousand square miles. Because the lake dominates the local landscape, it is difficult to imagine that the lake was not always present, yet geological evidence clearly shows that for most of the last 4.5 million years, there was no lake. Instead, through most of this period there was only a huge, flat floodplain associated with the proto-Omo river that drained southwards from the Ethiopian highlands. The earliest of the several relatively brief lacustrine periods (when a lake was formed), just over 4.0 million years ago, was associated with sediments that contain the earliest known species of *Australopithecus.*

The first specimen of this species, a single distal humerus, was collected from the site of Kanapoi, south of Lake Turkana, by a Harvard expedition in the 1960s. Unfortunately, Kanapoi was at the time poorly dated and determining the fossil's affinities was difficult. Recent expeditions led by Meave Leakey have established new facts about both of these issues. The Kanapoi sediments were laid down by a river that built its delta out into the ancient lake between 4.2 and 4.0 million years ago, according to age determinations using the new and quite accurate method of single crystal

laser fusion argon-argon analysis. Leakey's expeditions have collected additional fossil teeth, jaws, cranial parts, and limb bones from Kanapoi, as well as similar fossils from slightly younger sediments (dated to between 3.9 and 4.0 million years ago) at Allia Bay, across the modern Lake Turkana from Kanapoi. Leakey and her colleagues named a new species based on the combined Kanapoi/Allia Bay sample. They call it *Australopithecus anamensis,* using the word for "lake" (*anam*) from the Turkana language.

To define a new species, biologists must differentiate between the new material and that of older similar species of comparable age. Leakey and her colleagues compared *Australopithecus anamensis* to other known early hominids, namely the more recent *Australopithecus afarensis* from between 3.6 and 2.9 million years ago and the slightly older *Ardipithecus ramidus* from about 4.4 million years ago.

This study showed that the new species belongs in the genus *Australopithecus.* First, the enamel on the teeth of the new specimens is thick, as is the enamel on all other australopithecines. Second, *Australopithecus anamensis* shows marked sexual dimorphism in body size, with males being considerably larger than females—another feature found in all species of *Australopithecus.* Finally, *Australopithecus anamensis* is clearly bipedal as is *afarensis* and other later species. A tibia from Kanapoi shows clear anatomical adaptations that make the knee stable in a bipedal position—adaptations that are lacking in quadrupedal apes. It has an ankle joint that places the foot at a right an-

gle to the long axis of the shin, rather than being angled closer to the tibia, as in apes. However, bipedalism is not the only locomotor adaptation of *Australopithecus anamensis.* A radius of this species, together with the original humerus from Kanapoi, shows that these animals had powerful forelimbs. These facts make it likely that, despite being bipedal, they could still climb effectively and may have spent substantial time in the trees. However, the new material could not be included in *Australopithecus afarensis* because *anamensis* has retained primitive features that are lacking in *afarensis.* Such features are today known only in African apes.

The new material also differs from *Ardipithecus ramidus* in a number of cranial and dental features, such as the thin enamel on all of the *ramidus* teeth, which contrasts with the thick enamel of *anamensis.* There is at present no published evidence about the locomotor pattern of *ramidus,* but it is found with many forest-dwelling species that suggests a closed habitat. Like *ramidus, Australopithecus anamensis* is found with animals that lived in an extensive gallery forest along the ancient rivers or their deltas. For example, there are six species of monkey found at Allia Bay. It is most likely that *anamensis* was also forest-dwelling.

Paleoanthropologist and anatomist Alan Walker is Professor of Anthropology at Pennsylvania State University. He has worked many years at fossil sites dating from the Miocene to the Pleistocene in East Africa, especially in Kenya.

HOMINID MORPHOLOGY AND BEHAVIOR

Although interest has been concentrated on hominid brain evolution since the first discoveries of fossil hominids, studies of fossil **endocasts** (casts of the inside of the cranial cavity) have yielded disappointing results. The external form of the brain is variable, making its study based on crania difficult. Additionally, too little is known regarding the function of the modern human brain for anthropologists to be confident in assessing the functional capabilities of early hominid brains.

The cranial capacity of *Australopithecus afarensis* is known to lie between approximately 375 and 425 cubic centimeters, and between 400 and 600 cubic centimeters for *A. africanus,* roughly equivalent to the brain sizes of modern apes. There is one important difference, however. Body size in gracile *Australopithecus* is smaller than in the modern gorilla or even chimpanzee. *Australopithecus* had a brain-to-body size ratio that was larger than in modern African apes (Figure 10–14). A relatively larger brain implies that reorganization of neurons had taken place and that australopithecine behavior had become in some respects more complex and elaborate than that which we see in living apes.

Historically, brain size has figured prominently in the classification of fossil hominids. At one time it was proposed that a brain volume of 800 cubic centimeters was a hominid "**cerebral Rubicon**." Australopithecines, it was argued, fell below that value and thus should not be considered hominids. This argument not only failed to recognize the smaller body size of australopithecines (and thus relatively larger brain size) but was inflexible in disregarding the known principle that biological populations show variability in any trait. Modern humans, for example, show a range in brain capacity from under 1,000 to over 2,000 cubic centimeters, and it is certain that past hominid populations showed similar degrees of variability.

Initially, there had been high hopes of understanding australopithecine behavioral capabilities from brain morphology as determined from cranial endocasts. Such attributes as speech, tool use and sociality were expected to have observable neurological correlations. Unfortunately, although the brain is composed of specific convolutions that are known to be associated with certain functions in living people (see Figure 12–13 on page 426), the morphological and behavioral correlates can be difficult to interpret. A recent debate between Dean Falk and Ralph Holloway over the identification of the **lunate sulcus** in the Taung endocast is one example. Part of the problem lies in the variability of brain structures. Endocasts also do not preserve precise surface detail of the brain because they are actually impressions of the inside of the cranium, not the outside of the brain. The tissues which in life lie between the skull wall and the brain to cushion it (the meninges) obscure the smaller convolutions and surface features. The known gracile australopithecine endocasts, however, do suggest a greater degree of folding and a larger

endocast–a three-dimensional replica of the inside of the brain case, revealing what the exterior of the brain would have looked like.

cerebral Rubicon–The Rubicon is the Italian river crossed by Caesar during his return from Gaul to conquer Rome, and is used figuratively as a "decisive step;" cerebral refers to the brain; the term implies a typological and artificial threshold of absolute brain size in definitions of hominid taxa.

lunate sulcus–a groove in the cerebral cortex of humans associated with speech; "lunate" refers to "moon" or crescent shape of this wrinkle on the surface of the brain.

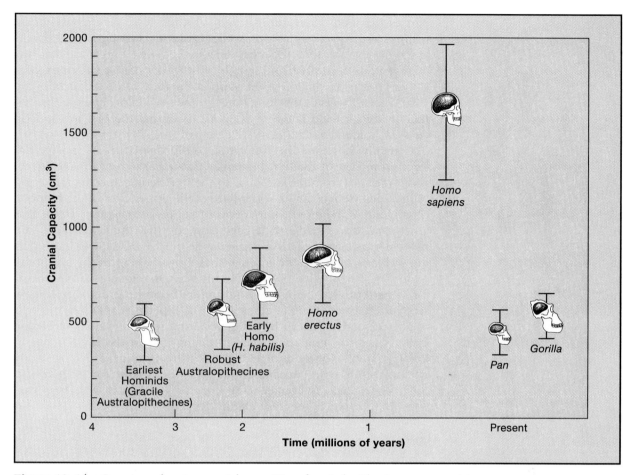

Figure 10–14 • Drawings showing cranial capacities of australopithecines compared to species of *Homo* and living African apes.

number of convolutions in comparison to the brain morphology of the living apes. These features indicate greater neurological complexity in australopithecines.

The pelvic, shoulder girdle and limb bone remains that have now come to light confirm that the gracile australopithecines were bipeds. There is a difference of opinion on the degree to which they used their upper limbs in locomotion, if at all, and whether *A. afarensis* may have had significant foot and lower limb adaptations for climbing (Susman and Stern, 1986). Expanding this debate, Ron Clarke and Phillip Tobias (1995) report on four articulating hominid foot bones originally discovered in 1980 from Member 2 at the site of Sterkfontein, South Africa. Labeled Stw 573 and nicknamed "little foot," these fossils are considerably older than the other Sterkfontein fossils, all of which are derived from the more recent Members 4 and 5. Consisting of a talus, navicular heal, medial cuneiform and first metatarsal, which together make up part of the medial longitudinal arch of a left foot, they show human features at the back of the foot, while displaying strikingly apelike traits at the front of the foot, the most remarkable being a great toe that was divergent, or opposible, and mobile. The Sterkfontein foot bones, possibly as old as 3.5 million years, support the idea, as do the teeth of the East African fossils of this time range, of an "evolutionary experimentation" within a wide range of adaptations during the first few million years of hominid evolutionary divergence.

Certainly, however, the adaptation to bipedalism seems to have differed from that of modern humans. *Australopithecus* had a relatively wider distance from the hip joint to the muscle attachments at the top of the thigh (femur) and a wider flare of the upper crest of the hipbone (ilium, one of the three components of the pelvis) (Figure 10–10). This arrangement provided a wide base of support for the lower limbs in a bipedal stance, as well as strong leverage in lifting the lower limbs during walking. In *Homo* the hip joint has moved closer to the top of the femur and lateral edge of the ilium, in order to expand the birth canal for larger-brained infants. The australopithecine morphology is now recognized as an efficient, albeit different, bipedal adaptation.

Overall body size can be estimated from the dimensions of certain fossil bones by comparing them to dimensions of the same bones in known samples of modern humans and living primates whose body weights are known. Recent estimates of body size for *A. afarensis* range approximately from 30 to 80 kilograms and for *A. africanus* from 30 to 70 kilograms (Jungers, 1988).

AUSTRALOPITHECINE PALEOECOLOGY AND BEHAVIOR

In Dart's original (1925) paper he pointed out the arid nature of the habitat in which *A. africanus* must have lived at Taung. This environment would not have been habitable for an ape, assuming extinct apes had similar ecological adaptations to those of the forest-living gorilla or chimpanzee of today. Further research has shown that *A. afarensis* and *A. africanus* lived in both arid and more well-watered environments in eastern and southern Africa (Figure 10–15). It is clear that even without the use of stone tools and fire, gracile australopithecines were able to adapt to a variety of environmental conditions, but apparently only in Africa.

Within the past decade interest in hominid paleoecology has increased, partly because of the realization that environment is an important variable in determining social behavior in primates and partly because of the debate on the **single species hypothesis** (Wolpoff, 1973). This hypothesis held that all early hominids (*Australopithecus* and early *Homo*) lived in a cultural ecological niche with widely overlapping adaptive capabilities. Only one species could exist at any one time in the same area. If two species had been present, the principle of

single species hypothesis–the hypothesis advanced by Milford Wolpoff and others in the 1970s and 1980s that only one hominid species could have lived at any one time in the past.

Figure 10–15 • Reconstructed environment at Laetoli, to show the more open spectrum of early australopithecine habitats. Environments at other early australopithecine sites may have been significantly more wooded or even forested.

Figure 10–16 • Leopard mandible showing correspondence of canine with holes in robust australopithecine skull from Swartkrans.

competitive exclusion would have come into play. By this principle one species would have driven the other to extinction by expropriation of environmental resources, the primary one of which is, of course, food. Discoveries since the hypothesis was proposed have now demonstrated that, although there was only one species of gracile australopithecine living during the African Plio-Pleistocene at any one time, two species of hominids (early *Homo* and robust *Australopithecus*) and, therefore, two types of "proto-cultural" hominid behavioral adaptations, coexisted later on. Thus, the assumptions of the hypothesis, particularly those concerning the cultural capabilities of early hominids at this time, were incorrect. Early hominid adaptations may have been quite similar to those of other coexisting species, but apparently were not identical to them and, therefore, did not totally overlap them.

The paleoecology of *Australopithecus* is reflected in the types of animals and plants and the geological conditions associated with these hominids in fossil deposits. It is important to undertake taphonomic studies in order to determine how these remains came to be buried together in order to understand how they might have been associated in life. Such studies, important in hominid paleoecology, have shown that hominids in the South African cave sites were probably the remains of carnivore kills (Figure 10–16), while East African open-air sites contain hominids that had died under a variety of conditions.

Figure 10–17 • Excavated pyramid of numbers of mammals from Locality 398 at Omo (2.3 million years ago), showing relative numbers of hominids, carnivores, and other large mammals.

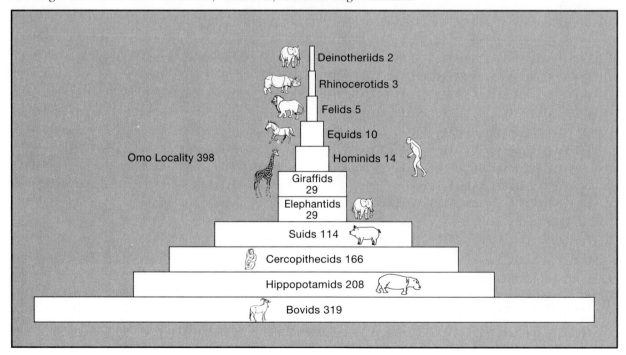

In the early South African cave sites, *A. africanus* has been found in association with a high percentage of bush-adapted, as opposed to grassland-adapted, antelopes, an association that indicates a more bush-covered habitat than the same area today. This paleoecological picture of South Africa is supported by similar vegetational reconstructions for two early australopithecine sites in Ethiopia (Omo and Hadar). The fauna from Laetoli, on the other hand, indicates markedly dry, grassland conditions. However, surface water such as streams and water holes were present. It is likely that early hominids were dependent on these because hominids, as many other mammals, need to drink water at least once a day.

Figure 10–18 • Dental development in modern humans and chimpanzees. Solid lines represent the age of formation of the tooth crown, dashed lines the period of root formation. Tooth eruption is indicated by E. Black dots on both charts represent the development of corresponding teeth in *A. africanus*, and suggest that *A. africanus* had an ape-like, rather than humanlike, pattern of dental development. (From Fleagle, 1988)

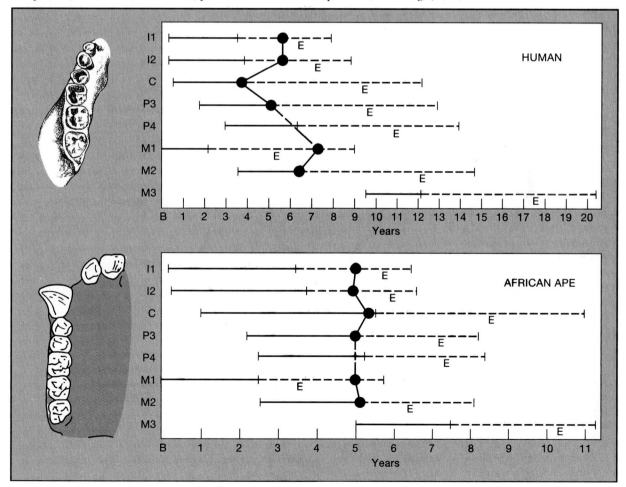

On the basis of dental morphology, the diet of the gracile australopithecines was probably omnivorous. However, excavations at Omo indicate that australopithecine individuals occur in similar numbers to large mammalian carnivores. If confirmed by further taphonomic analyses this would indicate that these early hominids and carnivores occupied similar positions in the food chain (Figure 10–17).

A number of sites are known where animal and gracile australopithecine bones intermingle, but no recognizable animal remains survive from australopithecine meals. At one time, Dart considered damaged baboon crania from South Africa to represent australopithecine prey. The damage to these skulls is now thought to have been caused by rock fragments pushing against the surface of the bone while the skulls were being buried in the consolidating cave breccia.

Gracile australopithecines seemed to have died quite young. It is possible to reconstruct age at death by the wear of the teeth. A study by Alan Mann (1975) on South African australopithecines showed the mean age at death to be a modern human equivalent age of 22 years. Considering the small size of these early hominids and their consequent faster maturation rates, they would have been biologically older at 22 years of age than modern humans. Mann suggested that australopithecines had a prolonged period of infant dependency, similar to modern humans. Recent work on the pattern of dental development and eruption (Figure 10–18; Bromage and Dean, 1985; Smith, 1986; Conroy and Vannier, 1987) has indicated that australopithecines may have had a more ape-like, short, and rapid period of growth as infants.

Comparative primate studies have shown that important aspects of social structure in savanna or savanna-woodland-dwelling primates vary in response to the environmental conditions in which they occur. Group size usually increases and multimale groups generally occur. This suggests relatively large one-male or shifting multimale social groups for the early australopithecines (Table 10–3).

Specific analogies have also been drawn between certain primates, particularly the baboon and chimpanzee, and *Australopithecus*. A major contribution in this area has been the demonstration by Jane Goodall that chimpanzees fashion and use tools in obtaining food (see Chapter 9). Stones are occasionally used by both chimpanzees and baboons in aggressive throwing or in breaking open hard objects, but they are never purposely chipped. *Australopithecus* can be expected to have shown at least an equivalent degree of tool use.

Chimpanzee groupings are also affected in a predictable way by a change from forest to savanna-woodland, in a manner that mirrors a major ecological and behavioral change in hominid evolution. Several primatologists have shown that meat-eating and predation, as well as bipedal walking, occur more frequently in chimpanzees that live in more open vegetation habitats, such as forest fringe environments.

Table 10-3   Group Sizes and Habitats of Nonhuman Primates, Indicating a Possibly Large, One-Male Grouping for Australopithecines

	Grade I	Grade II	Grade III	Grade IV	Grade V
Species	*Galago* sp. *Aotus trivirgatus*	*Lemur* sp. *Hylobates* sp.	*Alouatta palliata* *Gorilla gorilla*	*Macaca mulatta* *Pan troglodytes*	*Papio hamadryas* *Theropithecus gelada* *?Australopithecus*
Habitat	Forest (Nocturnal)	Forest	Forest/Forest Fringe	Forest Fringe/Tree	Grassland or Arid
Size of Group	Usually solitary	Very small groups	Small to occasionally large parties	Medium to large groups; *Pan* groups inconstant in size	Medium to large groups; variable size in *T. gelada* and probably *P. hamadryas*
Reproductive units	Pairs where known	Small family parties	Multimale groups	Multimale groups	One-male groups

Adapted from Crook and Gartland (1966).

Early proto-hominids likely possessed such behavioral flexibility, which allowed them to adapt from the typical primate habitat, the forest, to a savanna (grassland) environment in a manner similar to the modern chimpanzee's. Among other implications, these findings show that meat eating in hominids has a primate behavioral analogue and did not have to evolve *de novo*.

ROBUST AUSTRALOPITHECINES

The robust australopithecines were a group of hominids that are known to have lived in eastern and southern Africa from 2.5 million years ago to about 1 million years ago (see Grine, 1988). Their presence has not yet been confirmed outside Africa. They were specialized para-human creatures (Figure 10–19), apparently not in modern humans' direct ancestry, but coexistent with early members of the genus *Homo*. The causes of both the evolutionary origin and eventual extinction of the robust australopithecines remain obscure.

Much of the characteristic robust australopithecine cranial morphology is related to a specialization for heavy mastication. One student of these hominids has termed them "chewing machines." Characteristic morphology includes a sagittal crest along the midline of the skull and heavy cheek bones (zygomatic arches) to support large muscles of mastication. The face is characteristically "dished" as in australopithecines generally but is more heavily constructed than in the gracile species to withstand the forces generated in chewing. To lighten the weight of the

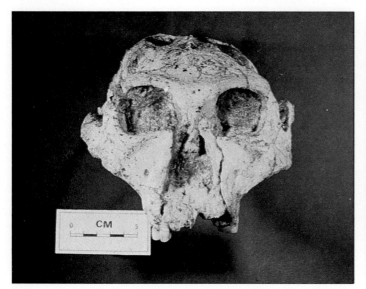

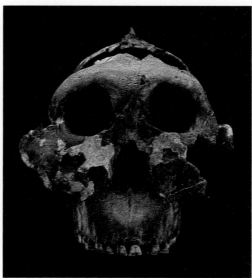

Figure 10–19 • The skulls of *Australopithecus robustus* (Swartkrans 48), left, and *Australopithecus boisei* (Olduvai Hominid 5), right.

head, large areas of the skull have developed internal air cells inside the bone. The East African species, *A. boisei,* and the South African *A. robustus,* sometimes referred to as *Paranthropus,* seem similar in all these respects except that the former appears to be larger and more robust.

From the known cranial endocasts, robust australopithecines apparently possessed brains of an absolute size close to the earlier gracile australopithecines'. However, since the robust forms probably were of somewhat larger body size, they would have had a relatively smaller brain.

The teeth of these hominids are specialized for high-bite-force grinding. The chewing surfaces of the molars are expanded; premolars have also become larger and molar-like in form; and the incisors and canines, for cutting and tearing food, are quite reduced in size. Robinson put forth the so-called **dietary hypothesis** to account for this dental pattern. He proposed that the robust australopithecine was a vegetarian who had to eat large quantities of food to sustain its bulk. The dentition of the smaller gracile australopithecine, on the other hand, with its relatively larger incisors and canines and smaller molar surface areas, was adapted to a more varied diet that may have included meat. Studies on dental wear using the scanning electron microscope (Grine and Kay, 1988) have demonstrated a difference in molar wear in the South African gracile and robust australopithecines, although it has not been exactly as predicted by the dietary hypothesis. Robust hominids had more pitting on their molars, indicating a diet significantly higher in tough food objects such as seeds, nuts, or bark. Gracile australopithecines had more longitudinal scratches indicating a diet, based on analogy with modern primates, including significantly more fruit and

dietary hypothesis–hypothesis advanced by John T. Robinson that differences in the dentitions of the gracile and robust australopithecines were to be accounted for by differences in dietary adaptations, the former eating a more omnivorous diet and the latter eating a more herbivorous one.

foliage. Charles Peters of the University of Georgia has also suggested that the high bite forces generated by the robust australopithecine dentition could also have served as a good adaptation for meat eating.

The postcrania of robust australopithecines is poorly known. On the basis of extremity bones and pelvic fragments the stature of these hominids had been estimated at between 145 and 165 centimeters with a weight range of 40 to 90 kilograms (Jungers, 1988), somewhat larger than the gracile australopithecine. The arm may also have been relatively longer. Although some foot bones in *A. robustus* suggest a divergent big toe, and, thus, an ape form of locomotion, indications from the pelvis and lower limb bones, as well as the central placement of the foramen magnum, strongly suggest well-developed bipedalism.

The robust australopithecines were originally thought to have been the gorillas of the hominid family, large, heavily built creatures living in forested habitats. Initial paleoecological results from the South African caves seemed to support this scenario. Robust australopithecine cave sites had a higher incidence of angular sand grains, presumably washed quickly into the cave and not scattered and rounded over time by wind action. This was interpreted to indicate relatively wet conditions, or greater rainfall at the time of deposition than at present.

Studies on the fauna in both South and East Africa have not resolved this issue. Some studies have indicated that dry-adapted antelopes predominate in the robust australopithecine sites, indicating drier, not wetter, conditions. Other studies indicate that robust australopithecines may have preferred wooded or bushier habitats.

A number of intriguing paleoanthropological problems still surround the robust australopithecines. According to the dietary hypothesis one might expect these hominids in relatively large numbers in fossil deposits, because herbivores are generally more abundant than are omnivores/carnivores in ecological food chains. In fact they occur in virtually the same percentages as the supposedly omnivorous gracile early hominids (Table 10–4). The present best estimate of robust australopithecine adaptation is that of a bipedal, hard-object feeding omnivorous dweller of either woodlands or grasslands within an overall savanna environment.

Another paleoanthropological dilemma associated with the robust australopithecine is ecological niche separation between this hominid and the contemporary *Homo habilis* (see Chapter 11). Hominids are generally considered culture-bearing primates, but how could two such species live in the same environment without one eventually ecologically excluding the other? Perhaps the skill of tool use was exclusive to *Homo*. Robust australopithecines are found in sites in which Oldowan stone tools are also found and, in some cases, where *Homo* is lacking. Despite the absence of *Homo* fossils from these sites, they may have left their stone tools there. General opinion seems to lean toward robust australopithecines lacking the ability to fashion stone tools, but the question is still open.

Table 10-4 • Relative Numbers of Robust Australopithecines and *Homo* Specimens at Some East African Sites[1]

Locality/Level	Robust	*Homo*	Ratio Robust/*Homo*
Omo			
E	10	3	3.3 : 1
F	19	7	2.7 : 1
G	18	10	1.8 : 1
K	1	1	1 : 1
Koobi Fora			
KBS	27	15	1.8 : 1
Okote	20	10	2 : 1
Burgi	2	17	0.1 : 1
Olduvai			
I	1	11	0.1 : 1
II	4	7	0.6 : 1
Totals	102	81	1.3 : 1

[1]Numbers of specimens from the sites sampled in this table are relatively equal, a phenomenon at variance with what one would expect from the dietary hypothesis of Robinson. Data from White (1988).

Phylogenetic origin of the robust australopithecines is postulated by some to be from *A. africanus* (Figure 10–13). Discovery of the "Black Skull" (KNM–WT15000) at West Lake Turkana, Kenya, dated to 2.5 million years ago, has weakened this interpretation because there is now near overlap in dates for *A. africanus* and *A. boisei,* suggesting that *A. boisei* had an earlier origin.

Robust australopithecine species seem to persist in Africa until shortly after the appearance of the relatively advanced *Homo erectus* (see Chapter 11). Washburn has suggested that this culturally endowed early human species was able to ecologically outcompete the robust australopithecine and thus drive the latter to extinction. Another possibility is that as *Homo erectus* increased in size through evolutionary time, groups required greater food resources and territory, and *H. erectus* were able to physically outcompete robust australopithecines. A third possibility is that ecological change to drier conditions did in the robust australopithecines.

 SUMMARY

Hominids are those hominoids that are adapted to bipedalism, or walking on two legs. Australopithecines are the earliest known hominids in the fossil record, appearing at the boundary of the Miocene and

Pliocene Epochs in Africa. A number of adaptations characterize australopithecines and set them apart from apes. In addition to adaptations related to bipedalism, these include larger brain-to-body size, larger molar teeth compared to body size, and relatively small canine teeth. Hominids are rare in the fossil record and this may be because they occupied large home ranges and were rarely concentrated in one area where they might easily be fossilized. There are two broad categories of australopithecines: "gracile" or early australopithecines, and "robust" australopithecines, that appear later in the fossil record. Robust australopithecines are characterized by very large molar and premolar teeth and relatively diminutive front teeth. Australopithecines seem to be broadly adapted to savanna or woodland habitats. One or the other of the early gracile australopithecines gave rise to the genus *Homo*. The robust australopithecines became extinct about 1 million years ago.

 ## CRITICAL-THINKING QUESTIONS

1. What are the characteristics that define the Family Hominidae?
2. Compare and contrast gracile and robust australopithecines.
3. Name two reasons that hominid fossils are relatively rare in the fossil record.
4. Why did Raymond Dart believe that the australopithecines possessed an osteodontokeratic tool culture?
5. Discuss australopithecine discoveries at Hadar and Laetoli.
6. Describe the probable australopithecine econiches.

 ## SUGGESTED READINGS

Brain, C.K. 1981. *The Hunters or the Hunted? An Introduction to African Cave Taphonomy*. Chicago: University of Chicago Press. An important book on how bones become buried and fossilized and how we can reconstruct past ecology from fossilized remains.

Clark, Wilfrid E. Le Gros. 1978. *The Fossil Evidence for Human Evolution: An Introduction to the Study of Paleoanthropology*. Chicago: University of Chicago Press. A classic by one of the architects of modern paleoanthropology, dealing with evolutionary anatomy and the importance of anatomy in reconstructing phylogenetic relationships.

Corruccini, R.S., and R.L. Ciochon (eds.). 1994. *Integrative Paths to the Past: Paleoanthropological Advances in Honor of F. Clark Howell*. Englewood Cliffs: Prentice Hall. Essays in honor of one of the great paleoanthropologists. A book for the student who wishes to pursue some of the major paleoanthropological questions of the day.

Dart, Raymond. 1959. *Adventures with the Missing Link*. New York: Harper. The story of the discovery of the Taung Child, its interpretation, and the follow-up research in South Africa by the discoverer of *Australopithecus africanus*.

Grine, F. E. (ed.). 1988. *Evolutionary History of the "Robust" Australopithecines*. New York: Aldine de Gruyter. The most comprehensive treatment of these fascinating "near-humans."

Johanson, Donald C. and Maitland Edey. 1981. *Lucy, the Beginnings of Humankind*. New York: Simon and Schuster. The story of the discovery and interpretation of *Australopithecus afarensis,* co-authored by the individual most responsible for bringing this new hominid species to light.

Reader, John. 1981. *Missing Links: The Hunt for Earliest Man*. Boston: Little Brown. A beautifully illustrated volume about the discovery of early hominids, their interpretations, and the history of the field.

Tattersall, Ian. 1995. *The Fossil Trail: How We Know What We Think We Know about Human Evolution*. New York: Oxford University Press. A new book by American Museum of Natural History paleoanthropologist Ian Tattersall, stressing the importance of cladistic methodology in hominid evolutionary studies.

Tobias, Phillip V. (ed.). 1985. *Hominid Evolution: Past, Present, and Future*. New York: Liss. The proceedings of the Taung Jubilee International Symposium in 1985. A book edited by eminent paleoanthropologist Phillip Tobias in honor of the fiftieth anniversary of the discovery of Taung, discussing many of the themes and research directions that have characterized paleoanthropology in the last fifty years.

The Genus Homo

The Brain, a Hallmark of Humanity

Teeth

Skull and Jaws

Body Size and Limbs

Homo habilis
Age of *Homo habilis*
Homo habilis and Other Species
  of Early *Homo*

The First Stone Tools
Paleoecology and Behavior

***Homo erectus* Comes onto the Scene**
Paleoecology and Behavior
  of *Homo erectus*
Homo and Robust
  Australopithecines

The Appearance of *Homo sapiens*
Evolutionary Origins
  of *Homo sapiens*
Archaic *Homo sapiens*
Homo sapiens sapiens
Homo sapiens neanderthalensis
Behavior of Early *Homo sapiens*
Evolutionary Relationships
  in *Homo sapiens*

Summary

Critical-Thinking Questions

Suggested Readings

Homo habilis—earliest generally recognized species of the genus *Homo.*

Homo erectus—primitive species of the genus *Homo,* generally considered to have evolved from *Homo habilis* and to be the ancestor of *Homo sapiens.*

Homo sapiens—species that includes modern humans as well as archaic *Homo sapiens.*

endocranial volume—synonymous with cranial capacity—the amount of space inside the skull, occupied in life by the brain and brain coverings.

When Linnaeus set forth his classification of animals in 1742 he proposed five species of *Homo,* based on geographic and largely hypothetical differences. Because Linnaeus did not specify a type specimen for *Homo* (he merely said, "*homo nosce te ipsum*", meaning "humanity know yourself"), the implied type specimen of *Homo sapiens* is that with which Linnaeus was most familiar, presumably himself! Thus, anthropologists have had to establish a working definition of the genus and species that can serve to distinguish modern humans from more primitive and earlier hominids.

There are now three species of *Homo* generally recognized by experts: **Homo habilis, Homo erectus,** and our own species, **Homo sapiens.** Some paleoanthropologists now recognize two additional species, *Homo ergaster* and *Homo rudolfensis,* within what most others consider *Homo habilis.* As a group they are distinguished from *Australopithecus* by a larger cranial capacity, indicating a larger brain, which is successively larger from *habilis* to *erectus* to *sapiens.* Members of the genus *Homo* also have shorter molars, smaller canine teeth, and more lightly constructed skulls generally lacking "dished faces" and cranial crests. Body size increased dramatically in the *Homo* lineage, especially with *Homo erectus.* Based on current evidence, members of the *Homo* lineage were stone tool-making and culture-bearing hominids, in probable contrast to australopithecines.

THE BRAIN, A HALLMARK OF HUMANITY

Perhaps the trait most widely believed characteristic of *Homo* is an enlarged brain in relation to body size. Brain size can be relatively accurately predicted from the **endocranial volume,** the space of the brain cavity inside the skull. But this determination is also somewhat larger than true brain size because of the thickness of the membranes that cover the brain (the *meninges*) and the *venous sinuses* that contain blood between the inside of the skull and the outside of the brain (see Appendix 1).

Body size and body weight of primates exist in a constant relationship to various dimensions of their skeletons. Using relationships with limb bones, anthropologists can compute the body weight and size of fossil hominids. With both brain size and body weight estimates, one

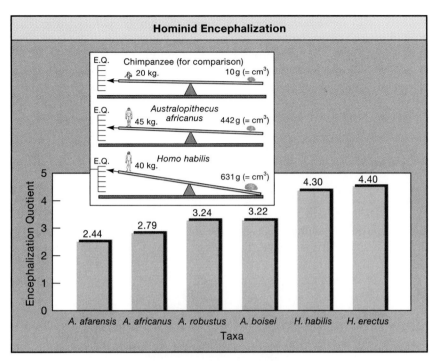

Figure 11–1 • Graph of hominid cranial capacity, body weight, and encephalization quotients.

can determine the degree of **encephalization**—the size of the brain in relation to body weight. *Homo* has an encephalization quotient higher than any australopithecine (Figure 11–1).

Expansion of the relative size of the brain indicates increased cerebral ability and intelligence, but only in a very general sense. There is great variation in cranial capacities between individuals in modern human populations, with no apparent correlation between size and function. Nevertheless, in considering the hominid fossil record we suspect that as cranial capacity increased in *Homo,* there were also significant organizational changes within the brain that did enhance function.

The human brain evolved to such a large size and to such complexity because of strong selective forces. There are many hypotheses that have been advanced to account for its phenomenal growth. Theories have generally emphasized one or another of the components in the total adaptation of early *Homo* that may be considered "prime movers" or first causes for encephalization. Tool use and increasing cultural socio-behavioral complexity in the evolving *Homo* lineage has been long in the forefront of hypothesized selective reasons for an increase in brain size (Washburn, 1960). This formulation also implicated cooperative hunting by males, but it is now realized that female social cooperation in food getting would have been of equivalent if not greater selective importance, because more of the daily caloric intake of modern hunter-gatherer groups derives from female-collected food sources (Tanner, 1986). Bipedalism has also been involved in some scenarios of

encephalization–the process of extreme brain enlargement in the *Homo* lineage.

human brain evolution because it "freed the hands" for tool use. This hypothesis has now had to be discarded in the main because it is clear that *Australopithecus* was bipedal by 3.7 million years ago, long before the large expansion of the brain seen in the genus *Homo*. Other ideas (see Falk, 1989; Foley, 1990) have implicated the selective importance of language, ecological parameters, diet, and, recently, the circulatory patterns in the head as a cooling mechanism for an enlarged brain.

TEETH

The teeth as a whole, but particularly the back teeth, underwent reduction in size in *Homo* compared to the dentition of the ancestral gracile australopithecines (Figure 11–2). The molar teeth are more squared in outline, viewed from above, than they are in australopithecines. The

Figure 11–2 • *Homo habilis* (OH 7) dentition, top, compared to that of *Australopithecus africanus* (Sts 52), bottom.

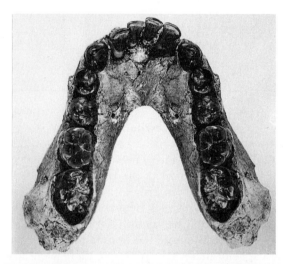

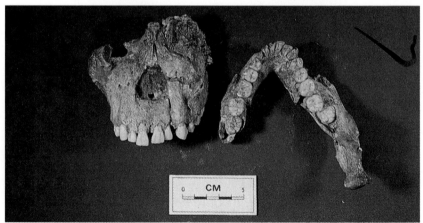

canines are relatively smaller. The third premolar, which in australopithecines tends to be as large as, or larger than, the fourth premolar, is generally relatively smaller in *Homo*.

The grinding teeth, the molars and the premolars, have generally lost their complex enamel wrinkling ("crenulation") in *Homo* (Figure 11–2). The function of the crenulation in australopithecines was probably to increase surface area, particularly in younger individuals where jaw strength was less. With advancing age the crenulations wore down to a flat surface area, although the genus retained thick enamel on the tops of the molars characteristic of hominids.

SKULL AND JAWS

The changes that we have seen in the size of the brain and in the teeth are reflected in the parts of the body skeleton which hold them. The increased size of the brain, around which the skull bones develop during embryonic growth, accounts for a higher skull vault in *Homo* than in *Australopithecus* (Figure 11–3). Anthropologists have developed sev-

Figure 11–3 • Crania and faces of *A. africanus* (Sts 5), *H. habilis* (KNM-ER 1470 and KNM-ER 1813), and *H. erectus* (KNM-ER 3733 and Choukoutien [Zhoukoudian]).

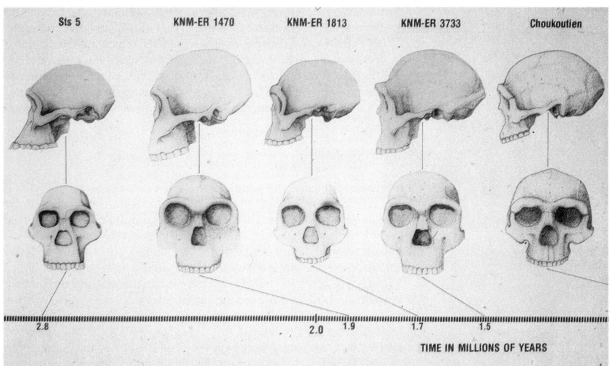

eral measurements that express this change, such as height of the skull above the ear opening and the curvature of the frontal bone (frontal angle).

In *Homo,* the part of the skull that holds the teeth, the maxilla, and the jaw or mandible, are decreased in size and bone thickness because the teeth are decreased in size. Because the dentition is not as large, the muscles of mastication that move the teeth are not as heavily developed. Thus, in *Homo* the bony face protrudes less (is less prognathous and more orthognathous), the zygomatic arch is smaller, the mandible is lighter in construction, and the temporal lines are reduced in size.

BODY SIZE AND LIMBS

Body size and weight have increased substantially during the evolution of the genus *Homo*. This increase over *Australopithecus africanus* is seen most dramatically in the near six-foot reconstructed adult height of the 1.5 million-year-old *Homo erectus* skeleton (KNM-WT 15000) from the site of Nariokotome in West Turkana, Kenya (Brown et al., 1987). There was a change in relative lengths of limbs. *Homo* is characterized by longer lower limbs (thigh length and leg length) compared to trunk length, and perhaps relatively shorter upper limbs (arm length and forearm length) (Figure 11–4). Increase in lower limb length meant an increased length in *Homo*'s walking stride, allowing the attainment of greater speeds over greater distances. This may have been an important pre-adaptation for hunting of larger animals, which are characteristically "run down" over long distances by modern hunter-gatherers. Larger body size was of advantage in interspecific interactions, such as displacement competition for food (in scavenging, hunting, or gathering) with other species, and in avoiding predation.

HOMO HABILIS

The earliest species of the genus *Homo* was first discovered at Olduvai Gorge in l960. Louis Leakey, Phillip Tobias, and John Napier named the new finds *Homo habilis* in l964. The species name had been suggested to Leakey by Raymond Dart, and it means "dexterous" or "handy," on the assumption that this and not the contemporary *Australopithecus boisei* fashioned the stone tools at Olduvai Bed I.

The naming of *Homo habilis,* thereby indicating a species distinctly different from both the preceding *Australopithecus africanus* and the later *Homo erectus,* sparked controversy. Some anthropologists, such as C. Loring Brace, considered the fossils ascribed to *Homo habilis* to be early *Homo erectus,* which will be discussed later in this chapter. Later discoveries have weakened this position by demonstrating that *H. habilis* and *H. erectus* show distinct differences in morphological

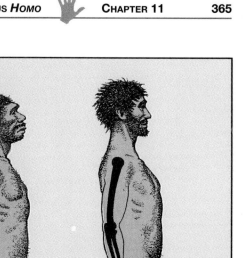

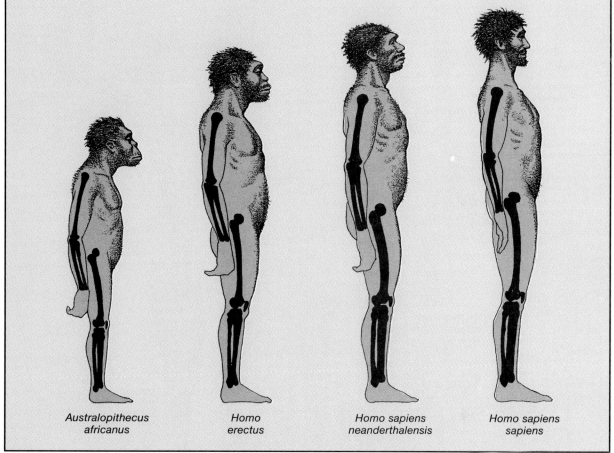

| Australopithecus africanus | Homo erectus | Homo sapiens neanderthalensis | Homo sapiens sapiens |

Figure 11–4 • Diagram showing intermembral indices (length of the forelimb divided by length of the hindlimb) of *Homo* and *Australopithecus.*

patterns, even if certain measurable traits of individual fossils overlap (Tobias, 1991). Other paleoanthropologists, such as John T. Robinson, initially considered the fossils on which *Homo habilis* was based to represent an East African variant of *Australopithecus africanus.* Further fossil discoveries which documented more of the *Homo habilis* bony face, skull, and teeth also weakened this position, although certain individuals such as Richard Leakey have continued to believe some small-brained *Homo habilis* fossils are actually *Australopithecus africanus.* Figure 11–5 presents two schemes that have been proposed for the evolution of early *Homo* over the last several years.

Since 1964 other specimens of *Homo habilis* have been discovered in eastern Africa—at East Lake Turkana (Leakey and Leakey, 1978) and Omo (Boaz and Howell, 1978). Renewed work at Olduvai yielded a fragmentary skeleton of *Homo habilis,* Olduvai Hominid 62 (Johanson et al., 1987). This sampling, along with the earlier Olduvai finds, shows

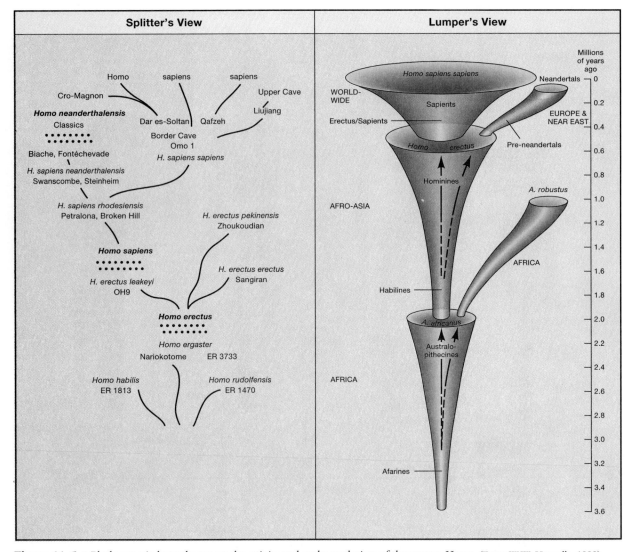

Figure 11–5 • Phylogenetic hypotheses on the origin and early evolution of the genus *Homo*. (From W.W. Howells, 1993)

that *Homo habilis* probably had a relatively larger body size than gracile australopithecines, but apparently had a more marked degree of sexual dimorphism than later *Homo*. The skeleton OH62, for example, was a quite small individual, probably a female weighing between 30 and 39 kilograms, compared to the large, probably male members of the species, weighing between about 50 kilograms and possibly up to over 90 kilograms (see McHenry, 1988, however, who contests that *habilis* was larger than gracile australopithecines). All *Homo habilis* dentitions show decreased molar tooth size, in comparison with australopithecines (both the gracile and robust varieties, but especially the latter). The facial skeleton of *Homo habilis* is also reduced in forward projection, a result of the generally smaller size of its teeth (Figure 11–3). The face shows the smoothly curved maxilla and parabolic-shaped mandible that differentiate it from the australopithecine dished face.

The recognition of an early species of *Homo* contemporaneous with robust australopithecines in eastern Africa led researchers to question whether the same or similar species might be found in the South African cave sites. At Swartkrans Robert Broom had discovered and named some skull and jaw fragments "*Telanthropus capensis*." On re-examination it became apparent that these fossils belonged to the genus *Homo,* but the jaw was much younger in geological age than the skull. This was determined by relating the type of cave sediment still adhering to the fossils with the stratigraphy of the cave. The skull was assigned to early *Homo* because it resembled *H. habilis* and the jaw was considered probably *H. sapiens.* The presence of *H. habilis* has been confirmed by this and more recent discoveries in South Africa.

It is still a mystery whether *H. habilis* extended outside sub-Saharan Africa. A skull of a juvenile hominid found by G. H. R. von Koenigswald at Modjokerto, Java (Indonesia) prior to World War II served as the type specimen for a species named by him *Homo modjokertensis.* It was initially considered to be as old as 1.9 million years, and recent redating by Carl Swisher and colleagues has confirmed this date, despite some opinion that the specimen is younger, of middle- to late Pleistocene age (see Pope, 1988b). Other hominid fossils in Java which have been considered of comparable age to the juvenile skull and which were thought to possibly represent the adult form of this species are equally suspect in terms of their age and provenance. All the Javan specimens are likely *Homo erectus,* despite some morphological similarities between them and *Homo habilis,* and until more complete fossils are discovered in Java and their geological contexts better defined, there is little fossil support for hypothesizing an extra-African species of *Homo* similar to *H. habilis.*

There is also evidence that has been brought forward to suggest that although fossils of early *Homo* have not been found in Eurasia, their stone tools have been. Stone tool occurrences have been reported by Dennell (1988) from Pakistan in sediments with dates in excess of 1.6 million years old, and by Bonifay (1989) from France in sediments in excess of 2 million years old. Both claims will need to be bolstered by more supporting data and geological analysis if scientists are to accept these dates, which are currently much earlier than agreed upon for most of the hominid fossils in Eurasia.

Age of *Homo habilis*

The dating of Olduvai Bed I was the first application of the new method of potassium-argon dating to an important paleoanthropological problem—the age of *Homo habilis* (and *Australopithecus boisei*). J. F. Evernden and Garniss Curtis of the University of California, Berke-

Figure 11–6 • KNM ER-1470 skull from Koobi Fora, Kenya.

ley, reported in 1965 a date of 1.73 million years for a tuff, a potassium-rich layer of volcanic ash, in Olduvai Bed I. The great antiquity thus indicated for early *Homo* was a surprise, because Olduvai Bed I had been estimated on biostratigraphic grounds at a maximum of about 1 million years old. In time, the dating was confirmed by more analyses at Olduvai, by comparisons of fauna and potassium-argon dates from other sites, particularly Omo, and by **paleomagnetic dating.** Olduvai in fact was the site of pioneering work on the paleomagnetic time scale and lent its name to the "Olduvai Event," a time of normal polarity (when a magnetic needle would have pointed to what we consider north today) during the Matuyama Reversed Epoch.

When the age of the earliest appearance of *Homo habilis* was questioned, it was not for being too old, but for being too young. Richard Leakey's team had discovered a skull of *Homo habilis,* now well-known by its museum accession number as KNM-ER 1470 (Figure 11–6) some meters below a tuff at Koobi Fora, East Lake Turkana, Kenya. The dating of the tuff, known as the "KBS Tuff," served as the major anthropological test case for a new variant of the potassium-argon method, argon 40–39 dating. The date obtained for the KBS Tuff was 2.6 million years old. Richard Leakey suggested on this basis that the *Homo* lineage was almost three million years old, adding some time to account for the laying down of the sediment between the 1470 skull and the KBS Tuff.

Because the **biostratigraphic age** of the fauna associated with 1470 did not match 3-million-year-old sections at the nearby Omo site, the age of the KBS Tuff was hotly debated. In the meantime, Clark Howell's team discovered a partial skull of *Homo habilis* at Omo dated at 2.0 million years ago, only somewhat older than Bed I at Olduvai. Finally the question was resolved by independent potassium-argon analyses at a number of laboratories. The KBS Tuff was deposited 2.0 million years ago, and the probable reason for the initial error was the "inherited argon" from older rocks that had become incorporated into the dated sample. General consensus now holds that *Homo habilis* had its beginnings as early as 2.4 million years ago, and disappeared by about 1.5 million years ago, when *Homo erectus* came onto the scene (Table 11–1 on page 383).

paleomagnetic dating–the matching of a sequence of strata with the dated pattern of changes in magnetic orientation through time, thereby dating the sediments.

biostratigraphic age–the relative placement of a fossil site by the comparison and matching of the animal species found there.

Homo habilis and Other Species of Early *Homo*

Some paleoanthropologists who have studied the fossils of early *Homo* from East and South Africa now think that several species of early *Homo* co-existed. One of the species names that has been suggested is *Homo ergaster* (Groves and Mazek, 1975). Another is *Homo rudolfensis* (Alexeev, 1986). This splitting of the early *Homo* fossils into a number of separate species has received some mainstream paleoanthropological support. Wood (1992), for example, accepts *Homo ergaster* as a large-bodied, fully bipedal species distinct from the smaller and partially arboreal *Homo habilis*. He suggests that *Homo rudolfensis* is the early African version of *Homo erectus,* as represented by later Asian specimens. However, most experts still accept the single taxon *Homo habilis* as accommodating the variation that is seen in the fossil of early *Homo* (Tobias, 1992).

THE FIRST STONE TOOLS

It is likely that early australopithecines such as *A. africanus* had developed tool making to a high degree, at least by nonhuman primate standards. However, paleoanthropologists have found only hints of australopithecine bone tools, utilized at such sites as Swartkrans, South Africa, notwithstanding the possible "osteodontokeratic" tools from South Africa (pp 333–334). **Stone artifacts**—pieces of rock that by their context or their pattern of breakage indicate hominid modification—have never been found in clear association with gracile australopithecines. They are absent at Laetoli, lower Omo, Hadar, lower Sterkfontein, Makapansgat, and other sites where only gracile australopithecines are known.

The advent of stone tool-making is a major event in hominid evolution. It requires a knowledge of rock types (only hard, crystalline rocks make adequate stone tools), locating source areas for these rocks, an understanding of the properties of rock fracturing (Figure 11–7), and the ability to produce functional tool designs. These abilities are far beyond the interest or aptitudes of apes, even though captive bonobos have been taught to chip stones, and chimpanzees have been observed in the wild to use unaltered stones to crack nuts. Chimpanzees also fashion simple tools for catching termites by stripping small branches off twigs (pp 296), and by crumpling leaves for use as sponges. Chimpanzees are thus able to conceptualize how the intrinsic properties of certain objects can be used to augment their food-getting capabilities, but in the wild they apparently do not make tools that cut.

Why and how did early *Homo* start using stone tools? The general answer is almost certainly in order to increase efficiency or predictability of food getting. Other animals that use stone—apes, sea otters, or certain birds—do so in order to eat nuts, mussels, eggs, or some other food items not otherwise accessible to them. Early *Homo* discovered that flaked stone tools can cut—a principle that still underlies many of our food preparation techniques (grating, slicing, paring, blending, chopping, etc.). With the increased cutting edge surface of a stone flake tool and the force with which it could be used, early *Homo* was able to match the biting and chewing efficiency of much larger and stronger animals with much more impressive dentitions.

stone artifacts—stones broken or flaked by hominids in order to be used as tools, or unmodified stones found in geological circumstances indicating that hominids carried them and placed them at a site.

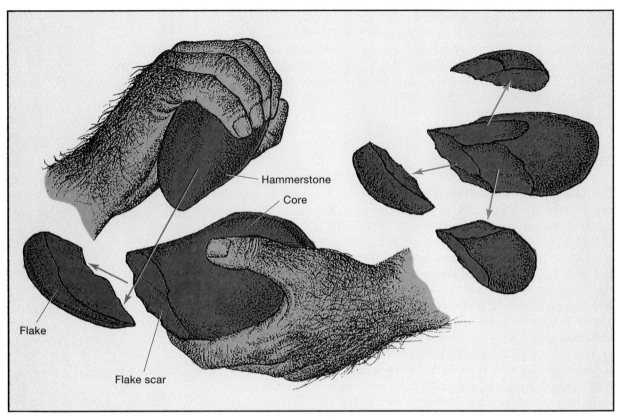

Figure 11–7 • Rock fracturing by early stone tool-making hominids; the making of a core and flakes of early (Oldowan) stone tools.

cut marks–incisions left on bone as a byproduct of skinning or cutting muscle off the bone with stone tools; uniquely characteristic of hominids but sometimes difficult to distinguish from carnivore bite marks or scratch marks made by sand grains.

Another argument for the development of stone tools is that they were used as weapons for protection against predators and for aggressive purposes against other hominids. Although chimpanzees and even baboons have been seen to throw stones at predators or intruders, these stones are naturally occurring and unaltered. This hypothesis does not explain the utility of flaking stone in order to obtain sharp edges, because none of the earliest stone artifacts can be seen as long-range spear or projectile points.

The earliest stone tools that are more than merely battered pieces of quartzite are termed Oldowan, after Olduvai Gorge. Mary Leakey has categorized them into those tool types shown in Figure 11–7. Basically, there are two jobs for which these tools were used—cutting and bashing. Cutting tools were used primarily to dismember carcasses for meat. Recent research at Olduvai, Koobi Fora, and Senga (Zaire) has revealed **cut marks** left on the animals' bones when the muscles were cut off. Bashing tools were used primarily to break open long bones for their fatty marrow. Fatty foods are a particularly valued commodity among

modern hunter-gatherers, and the thousands of smashed bone fragments at Olduvai attest to the antiquity of this predilection (Potts, 1988).

Paleoecology and Behavior

Homo habilis lived in areas of sub-Saharan Africa not remarkably different from the savannas and savanna woodlands that one can still see
today in places such as Serengeti, Maasai Mara, and Kruger National
Parks. The fauna were also similar, although several of the animals then
alive, such as chalicotheres, deinotheres, saber-toothed cats and si-
vatheres, no longer exist. Trees, for fruit and shade, were generally
scarcer than in *A. africanus* times. Early *Homo* groups were well-integrated into this environment, although they probably competed with
robust australopithecines, wild dogs, hyenas, and other carnivores for
meat, and with robust australopithecines, baboons, and perhaps some
pig species for fruits, vegetables, nuts, and roots.

Archaeologists have found evidence of *H. habilis* having butchered
and eaten hippopotamus and deinothere, as well as numerous small
antelopes and other animals. A major question is whether early *Homo*
hunted and killed these animals, or scavenged carcasses left by carnivores, drought, or disease. A definite answer to this question is not yet
possible, but it seems likely that *H. habilis* individuals did not have the
technical capabilities to kill animals much larger than themselves.

Because *H. habilis* had increased in body size and because trees
were relatively sparse, individuals were not as free to climb into trees
when danger threatened. Probably for these reasons *H. habilis* built
shelters on the ground that served as a refuge from predators, provided
shade in the day, and were warm at night. The earliest such structure
has been found at Olduvai (Figure 11–8). It is a circle of large stones
that probably served as the groundwork for a structure of sticks,
branches, or skins.

Randall Susman and J.T. Stern have suggested a modification of this
model of terrestrial-living *H. habilis*. They suggest that the strong hand-
flexing muscles, the attachment areas of which can be seen on the fossil hand bones of *H. habilis* from Olduvai, indicate hanging and climbing (and perhaps sleeping) in trees. However, these heavy hand flexors
would also have been needed for using heavy, crude, and quickly
dulled Oldowan tools, and this seems an equally plausible explanation
considering the environmentally open paleoecological setting for *H.
habilis*.

The population density, home range size, and group size are important ecological parameters of the behavior and adaptation of *H. habilis*.
Foley (1990) has suggested that as home range size increased, perhaps
to take advantage of greater foraging or hunting opportunities, so did
brain size in the *Homo* lineage. Excavations at Omo and ecological calculations based on body size have given us estimates of *H. habilis* pop-

Figure 11–8 • Environmental reconstruction of *Homo habilis* at Olduvai Bed I/II, with stone circle at site DK which may have served as a base for a hut-like structure or wind break.

ulation density, around 1.0 individuals per square kilometer (Boaz, 1979). We can estimate early *Homo* home range size at about 10.5 square kilometers, and the average number of individuals in a group at about 16, values not unlike those of modern foraging peoples. The population density, home range size, and group size calculated for *Homo habilis* are all somewhat larger than those of *A. africanus,* but smaller than those of *A. boisei.*

Other aspects of *H. habilis* behavior we must deduce from analogy to modern hunter-gathers. The females likely gathered plant foods, while males cooperated in hunting for small game and scavenging for meat, an important source of protein. Containers of some sort must have been used for carrying food and other necessities, and may even have been invented by *A. africanus.* A nuclear family of a male, one or more females, and offspring was probably the basic economic unit in early *Homo* groups. Kinship with others outside the family likely was recognized as a principle which organized sharing of meat and of other valued food resources, and which regulated alliances both within the group and with other groups. *H. habilis* groups were seminomadic and moved in relation to availability of food and water, but some researchers have suggested that they had a "home base," a camping place to which all individuals returned after foraging or hunting, and where food was shared (Isaac, 1979).

HOMO ERECTUS COMES ONTO THE SCENE

The evolutionary trends toward relatively greater cranial capacity, orthognathy, dental reduction, and greater body size which had begun in *H. habilis,* continued in its descendants. The skull also began to change to a very distinctive form—vault bones became very thick, the area over the eye sockets came to protrude markedly into brow (supraorbital) ridges, the back of the skull (occiput) developed a horizontal ridge known as the **occipital torus** , and the area along the sagittal suture became raised into a low "keel," called the **sagittal keel,** with flattened areas extending laterally from it. Hominids with this distinctive morphology began to appear in Africa at 1.5 to 1.6 million years ago. They are classified in the species *Homo erectus* (Rightmire, 1990).

The type specimens defining *Homo erectus* were discovered in the 1890s in Java by Eugene Dubois, a Dutch physician and physical anthropologist. The most diagnostic specimens were a skull cap, showing the thick cranial vault, the prominent brow ridges, and the sagittal keel characteristic of *H. erectus,* and a partial femur. The femur had a straight shaft unlike the femora of apes, and it indicated bipedality. Dubois therefore named the new species *Pithecanthropus* ("Greek, meaning ape-man") *erectus.* Because these were the oldest and most anatomically primitive human fossils found up to that time, Dubois had borrowed the term "*Pithecanthropus*" from the famous German evolu-

occipital torus–a horizontal raised ridge of bone at the back of the *Homo erectus* skull.

sagittal keel–a low rounded elevation of bone along the midline of the top of the *Homo erectus* skull.

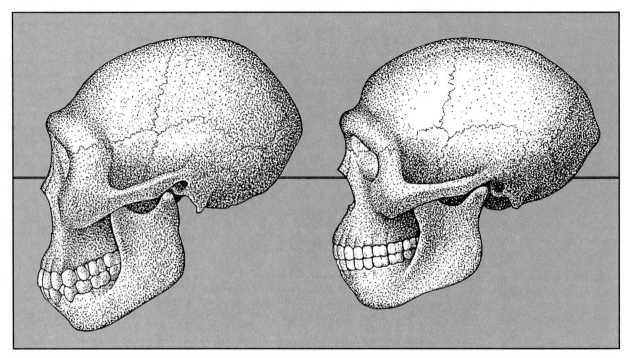

Figure 11–9 • Drawing of a reconstructed skull of an African *Homo erectus* (KNM WT 15000) from West Lake Turkana (left), compared with an Asian *Homo erectus* from Zhoukoudian (right). (After Alan Walker and Franz Weidenreich; art by Raymond Smith)

Zhoukoudian–Middle Pleistocene cave site of *Homo erectus* near Beijing, China.

tionist Ernst Haeckel. Haeckel had used the term many years earlier to refer to the hypothetical "missing link" between apes and humans. Since Dubois's pioneering studies, many additional *H. erectus* fossils have been discovered in Java, including a complete skull.

The biggest sample of *H. erectus* fossils, however, was discovered in China (Figure 11–9), at the cave site of **Zhoukoudian** near Beijing in the 1920s and 1930s. These fossils, of what was known popularly as "Peking Man," were described in a series of excellent monographs by Franz Weidenreich. After making casts of the specimens, Weidenreich arranged for the specimens to be sent to the United States for safekeeping at the outbreak of World War II. The Japanese invasion of China occurred after Weidenreich left China and, on the very day that the fossils were leaving with a detachment of U.S. marines, the marines were captured and the fossils were lost, never to be relocated. Weidenreich's detailed descriptions and the casts have served as our best source of knowledge of the anatomy of *H. erectus*.

Zhoukoudian is dated by both radiometric and paleomagnetic methods to between 230,000 and 500,000 years ago (Pope, 1988b). Despite recent critical review of the paleontological and archaeological data from the cave (Binford and Ho, 1985; Binford and Stone, 1986), the Zhoukoudian evidence seems secure in indicating the use of fire, the occupation of a single site for a long period of time, and the eating and probably hunting of large animals (Pope, 1988a, b).

Paleoecology and Behavior of *Homo Erectus*

Homo erectus was the first hominid species that we know extended its range outside Africa. As groups pressed into more northern latitudes, they experienced greater seasonal temperature and climatic fluctuations. The colder temperatures likely were important in one of the biggest cultural developments in human history—*fire.*

The date that hominids first harnessed fire has recently come into question. Evidence of fire—charred bones, pieces of charcoal, and fire-cracked rocks—were long ago found with *H. erectus* at Zhoukoudian. Recent excavations at the sites of Chesowanja and Koobi Fora in Kenya, dated at 1.4 million years ago—that is, about one million years earlier than Zhoukoudian—have revealed fire-hardened clay. The clay in the soil could have been the result of a naturally occurring bush fire set by lightning, but the investigating archaeologists claim that the close intermixing of human artifacts with the baked clay means that the fire was of human manufacture. If this early date for the discovery of fire by humans is upheld by further investigation, early and not latest *Homo erectus* would have been responsible. But what of the correlation of fire and colder climates? These Kenyan sites are almost on the equator. One possible answer is that by 1.4 million years ago glacial periods began to effect worldwide cooling trends. One way of measuring the history of worldwide temperature changes is by the deep sea oxygen isotope curve (Figure 11–10), whose oscillations to colder and colder temperature toward the Pleistocene may explain this early use of fire.

It has also been suggested that *Homo erectus* was the first hominid to adapt culturally to forest habitats (Pope, 1988a), making use of bamboo and other nonstone materials. This emphasis on nonstone tools may explain the archaeological record associated with *Homo erectus* in Asia—that of relatively unsophisticated "chopper/chopping tool" assemblages largely lacking the hand axes that are found during this period in Africa and Europe—that preserves what is perhaps a skewed view of the true cultural capabilities of Asian *Homo erectus.*

The stone tools that *H. erectus* made were more sophisticated than those of *H. habilis.* Beginning archaeology students with practice can generally make Oldowan choppers, but few attain the skill to make a hand ax (Figure 11–11), the bifacial stone tools with greatly increased cutting edges frequently found associated with *H. erectus.* The assemblages of stone artifacts that include hand axes are referred to by most archaeologists as **Acheulean,** after the site of Saint Acheul in France. The Acheulean first appears in Africa during Bed II times (1.5 to 1.2 million years ago) at Olduvai, and probably evolved from the "Developed Oldowan," an advanced type of chopper tradition. "Scrapers,"

Acheulean–Stone tool culture characterized by "hand axes" flaked on two sides, thus termed "bifaces."

Figure 11–10 • Deep sea oxygen isotope curve for paleoclimate with evolutionary events in hominid evolution. (From Boaz and Burckle, 1984)

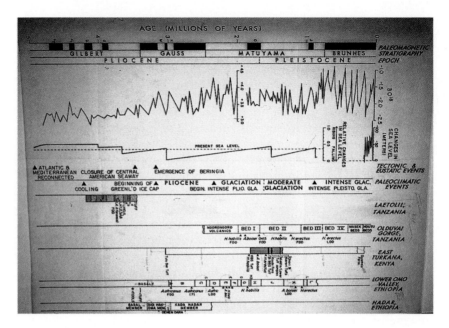

flat-edged flaked stone tools, became important during *H. erectus* times, possibly for preparing animal skins for use as clothing.

Hunting large animals was instituted by later groups of *H. erectus*. The best evidence is at the sites of Torralba and Ambrona in Spain, where hominids apparently killed and butchered several elephants 500,000 years ago. No human fossils have been found at these sites, but the age of the elephant fossils points to late *H. erectus* or earliest *Homo sapiens* as responsible for the hunt. Hunting large animals has important implications for human behavior. One animal could provide enough meat for a large group, and because it had to be eaten all at once (there was no way to store it), more complicated systems of sharing based on kinship and reciprocity must have developed. Since hunting large animals was also more dangerous and difficult than catching and killing smaller animals, more complex hunting strategies evolved.

One aspect of the behavior of *H. erectus* that has occasioned a number of hypotheses has been the discovery at Zhoukoudian that the brains of individuals found in the cave had been removed after death. Despite a recent dissenting opinion, most researchers hold that the foramen magnum had been broken to provide access to the brain. This sort of damage is not characteristic of hyena or other carnivore damage. *Cannibalism* is still a reasonable interpretation for the hominid skulls found at the site (Weidenreich, 1938).

Homo and Robust Australopithecines

Figure 11–11 • Acheulean hand ax.

As we have seen, *Australopithecus boisei* and *A. robustus* apparently lived side-by-side with *Homo habilis* and later with *H. erectus* in sub-

Saharan Africa. How two species of early hominids ecologically co-existed, and why the robust australopithecines died out around one million years ago, is unknown. Part of the problem is our ignorance of the cultural capabilities of the robust australopithecine. Humans have been said to occupy an ecological niche that is cultural, that is, they adapt relatively rapidly to changing conditions by cultural means, not by long-term physical changes effected by natural selection. How the cultural or proto-cultural adaptations of *Homo* and robust australopithecines allowed them to avoid competition and to co-exist remains a question. There have been intriguing suggestions: early *Homo* had a cooperative ecological arrangement with *A. robustus,* with the latter protecting the former from predators while scavenging from its leftover meat; the two species were both carnivores specializing in hunting prey of different sizes, thus avoiding competition; they lived in different habitats and, thus, did not actually come into contact or use the same resources; and one species, *Homo,* was an omnivore whereas the other was a herbivore. Major steps toward understanding early hominid diet are needed before anthropologists will be able to solve this question. Robust australopithecines probably did use tools of some sort (Susman, 1988), but one suggestion is that, like chimpanzees, they never conceptualized "cutting." As *H. erectus* increased in body size, there would have been a greater need for a larger home range area, and ecological competition with robust australopithecines, probably for food, would have become more and more intense. The competitive edge went to *H. erectus,* with its large brain, and the robust australopithecines became extinct. Other hypotheses attribute the extinction of robust australopithecines to environmental cooling in the Pleistocene or to competition with species other than *H. erectus,* such as pigs. Although environmental changes may have played a role, ecological competition usually occurs between closely related species and therefore similarly adapted organisms. By understanding more of the robust australopithecines and their extinction, we will learn more of both *H. habilis* and *H. erectus.*

THE APPEARANCE OF *HOMO SAPIENS*

In the several decades following Darwin's publication in 1859 of the theory of natural selection, scientific and popular interest in human origins burgeoned in Europe and America. There was extremely little fossil evidence, so most research concentrated on comparative studies of the living primates and human beings in terms of human origin. Emphasis has been placed on the importance for human evolutionary emergence of human locomotion (bipedalism), the opposable thumb of the grasping human hand, the very large human brain, and other attributes, depending on the author (Bowler, 1989). Mainstream conceptions as enunciated by Sir Arthur Keith and Sir Grafton Elliot Smith centered on

FRONTIERS

Multiregional Evolution in the Genus *Homo*

by Milford Wolpoff

Multiregional evolution is a model of population variation and evolutionary change in a widespread, geographically diverse species that is internally subdivided. Applied to ourselves it begins with the obvious—human beings today form a single polytypic species, with multiple, constantly evolving, interlinked, populations. Population dynamics can be partially explained through clinal theory (see Chapters 4 and 13), the histories of populations, their habitats, and the consequences of population placements relative to other populations. Multiregional evolution proposes that this has characterized human evolution at least since the world outside of Africa was first colonized, starting with early members of the genus *Homo*.

The web of population relations comes from the widespread admixture created by population movements and exogamy ("marrying out" of the group). We understand from mi-tochondrial DNA (mtDNA) studies in chimpanzees that genic exchanges are very widespread even without social rules. In humans, the relationships of populations, languages, and cultures are multiple and complex, and there are even more pathways for genic exchanges. Populations, languages, and cultures each descend from, or are rooted in, multiple antecedents. They divide and merge in a matrix of changing patterns called ethnogenesis, in which each can have several ancestors and several descendants. The ethnogenic pattern is likened to the channels of a river that can separate and recombine numerous times. The continued population interactions and the exchanges that it implies mean that there can be no link between language, culture, and biology, a hallmark of modern humanity. Such a pattern cannot possibly be topologically transformed into a branching one, and therefore no branching analysis or analysis that assumes branching evolution, such as the "Out-of-Africa" model, can validly address *Homo sapiens* evolution.

This interconnected pattern is the background for the processes of change and diversification, in which there is both long-lasting diversity and species-wide evolution. Far-flung differences are linked by gradations of continuously varying features that reflect gradients in selection and/or genic exchanges between adjacent populations. The opposing forces of genic exchange and selection, or drift, will invariably form clinal balances. One cannot overwhelm the other, which is how the apparent contradiction between geographic diversification and common evolutionary trends is resolved.

Long-lasting genetic differentiation created by clinal balances is commonly thought to be the main cause of human racial variation today. It is the central contention of multiregional evolution that shifting clinal balances extend far into the past, for the entire history of *Homo sapiens*. While the details of the balances varied with the ongoing process of evolution, local continuities for certain features lasted for long periods of time. These account for observations of regional continuity, and at the same time create the potential for a historical as well as an adaptive dimension to modern population variation.

Humans evolved as an interconnected polytypic species from a single origin in Africa about 2 million years ago. While African populations attained high numbers and came to encompass considerable variation,

---

Cro-Magnon—a cave site in southern France, used to refer to Late Pleistocene anatomically modern humans in Europe.

Neandertal—a cave site in Germany, used to refer to a Late Pleistocene human population in Europe and part of the Middle East; termed *Homo sapiens neanderthalensis*.

the primacy of the enlarged human brain in differentiating humans from their closest primate relatives in the slowly growing fossil record. A large cranial capacity came to be accepted as the hallmark for human status.

Discoveries in the European Late Pleistocene demonstrated the existence of anatomically modern, large-brained people ("**Cro-Magnon**" named after the cave site in which they were found). The discovery of **Neandertal** fossils, which showed different morphology, was interpreted by many to indicate the existence of a second, more primitive human lineage in the Pleistocene in addition to Cro-Magnon. This in-the small population effects during initial colonizations as humans first expanded out of Africa reduced local variation and helped establish regional differences in more peripheral areas, at the edges of the population. Some regional differences were subsequently maintained through isolation-by-distance and adaptive variation. A very few of the enduring features, but not the population themselves, persisted for long periods of time, helping trace lines of descent. This persistence of features is known as regional continuity.

Continuities in adaptive characteristics are an expected product of the evolutionary process and may well be the most common form of regional continuity. They are commonly expressed as exaptations—adaptive changes that are based on pre-existing morphology. The existing morphology has the potential for equivalence—the same requirements met in different ways. For instance, marginal ridges and crown curvature are manifestations of upper incisor "shoveling" that provided equivalent means of expanding incisor size in a limited space along the tooth row. We might think of an adaptive landscape in the Pleistocene with several different adaptive valleys. An Asian population gets stuck in one valley (with straight crowns and large marginal ridges) while a European population gets stuck in another (with curved crowns and only moderate marginal ridges). They can stay this way for a long time because selection keeps pushing them down in, even in the face of genic exchanges, assuming that it is important to have large incisors in small spaces. However, the predominant evolutionary pattern was created by advantageous changes that spread widely through the matrix of interconnected populations, linked by both genic exchanges and the common background of the evolving cultural system whose elements also could spread. Most modernizing features arose at different times and places and dispersed independently.

When the powerful homogenizing effects of the Holocene colonizations—the population expansions and replacements—are taken into account, there are three domains where evidence strongly supports the multiregional interpretation. First, regional continuity is evident in several different areas, for instance in Asia, Australasia, and Europe (minimally through the Upper Paleolithic). This is the evidence, albeit greatly expanded, that the model was first developed to explain. Second, the multiregional pattern emphasizes the independent ori-gin of different features and therefore is supported by the fact that modern humans cannot be uniquely defined in all regions. Today's modernity was created by the coalescence of different characteristics that appeared at various places and times. Third, some gene systems underwent bottlenecks; others could not have. Different genetic systems have different histories, ruling out the possibility of a single recent population bottleneck. Instead, the pattern of nucleotide diversity shows a long period of small population sizes, and the distribution of mitochondrial lines exposes evidence of long-term genic exchanges between the populations. The geographic pattern of variation reveals Africa to have had much larger past population sizes than other regions, as predicted.

Milford Wolpoff, Professor of Anthropology at the University of Michigan, is a paleoanthropologist who has worked on many parts of the hominid fossil record. He is known particularly for developing the "single species hypothesis" and the "multiregional hypothesis," which he discusses here.

terpretation came to be known as the **presapiens hypothesis** because it tended to accept fossils for the human lineage that possessed advanced features and to reject possible human ancestors that appeared too primitive, usually interpreted as being too "ape-like" or having too small a cranial capacity.

The greatest support for the presapiens hypothesis came from the **Piltdown** "discoveries," a series of hoaxed human fossils from Sussex, England, made between 1908 and 1912. The age of these specimens was supposed to have been the earliest, geologically speaking, of any found up to that point—Early Pleistocene or Pliocene. Yet the cranial vault of

presapiens hypothesis—a phylogeny that holds that there was a long-standing lineage of human ancestors characterized by "modern" morphology that lived side-by-side with a more primitive lineage of hominids not ancestral to modern humans; originally applied to Cro-Magnons and Neandertals.

Piltdown showed the enlarged brain characteristic of modern *Homo sapiens*. Its jaw, which was later shown to be that of an orangutan, was of course interpreted to be ape-like. Piltdown's spurious morphology was to confuse phylogenetic interpretation of hominid evolution for many years. Fortunately, however, the growing fossil record, especially that of the small-brained australopithecine, slowly changed the belief that a pre-eminently large human brain appeared early in hominid evolution.

The time of appearance of the earliest members of the species *Homo sapiens* is still an unsolved question. Several recent discoveries indicate that *Homo sapiens* was on the scene earlier than many paleoanthropologists previously thought (Figure 11–12). General opinion has held that 250,000 years ago was a reasonable estimate for the appearance of *Homo sapiens*. The discoveries of skulls from Petralona, Greece, dated at over 230,000 years old, and from Bodo, Ethiopia (Figure 11–13), that could be as old as 500,000 years, have demonstrated the presence of the earliest *Homo sapiens*. These specimens have retained so many primitive features in their morphology that some authorities have included them within the species *Homo erectus*. But a number of characteristics seem to indicate to most workers that these and other later specimens from Africa and Asia fit into a framework of worldwide appearance of *Homo sapiens* at about 500,000 years ago. The major specimens now attributed to earliest *Homo sapiens* are listed in Table 11–1.

The phylogenetic history of anatomically modern humans has been a topic of paleoanthropological concern for well over a hundred years. The earliest discovered fossils of extinct human populations were those of a subspecies of *Homo sapiens,* the well-known Neandertals. More has been written about Neandertals than about any other group of fossil hominids, although within the grand sweep of hominid evolution, they represent a geographically and restricted phenomenon. *Homo sapiens neanderthalensis,* as the subspecies is now known, occupies a much more important place in the history of anthropological method and theory than in the history of the human species.

Molecular studies have thrown some light on the timing and place of origin of anatomically modern *Homo sapiens,* although consensus on the significance of these findings has not yet been reached (Eckhardt, 1989). Studies of mitochondrial DNA (Cann et al., 1987; Vigilant et al., 1989), popularly known as the **"African Eve" Hypothesis,** have shown that the basic division in human populations is between sub-Saharan African populations and the rest of the world and that the greatest genetic distances in the human species occur in Africa, with the Khoisan (Bushman) being the most divergent population. Despite a dissenting opinion (Templeton, 1993), these results indicate that Africa is the most likely home of most of the mtDNA genetic diversity of the human species. By analyzing the data for mtDNA evolution among human populations it has been proposed that all living human popula-

Piltdown—a fraudulent series of specimens composed of a human skull and a modern ape jaw, made public between 1908 and 1912 at Sussex, England.

"African Eve" Hypothesis—the hypothesis, based on studies of mitochondrial DNA, that all modern humans descended from one closely related population, or even from one woman, living in Africa approximately 100,000 to 200,000 years ago.

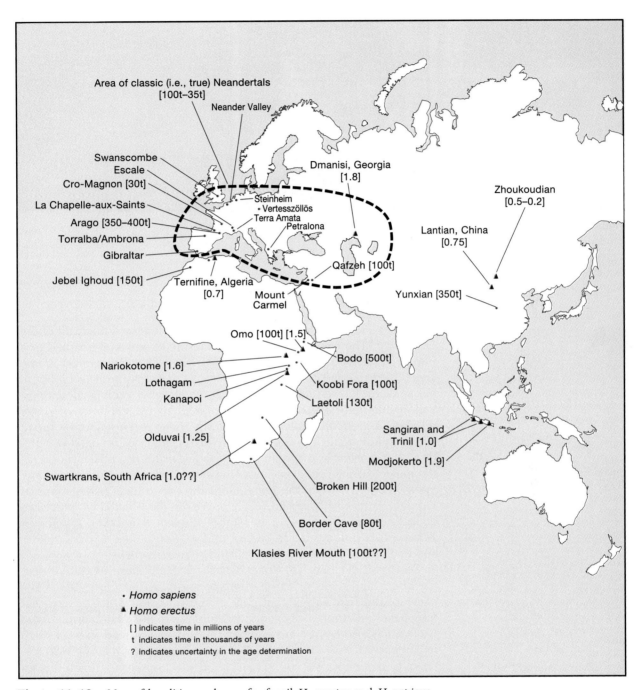

Figure 11–12 • Map of localities and ages for fossil *H. erectus* and *H. sapiens*.

tions derived from ancestors who came from Africa between about 140,000 and 290,000 years ago.

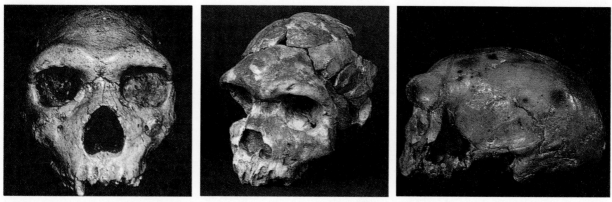

Figure 11–13 • Grade 1 archaic *Homo sapiens* skulls from (left to right) Petralona, Greece; Bodo, Ethiopia; and Dali, China.

Evolutionary Origins of *Homo sapiens*

As we have seen, *Homo erectus* managed to colonize virtually all of the Old World. The species was clearly widespread and well-adapted to a number of environments. Although we know that the earliest *Homo sapiens* superseded *Homo erectus,* because their fossils occur higher in the stratigraphic sequence, the timing, geography, ecological settings, and evolutionary contexts for this replacement are still areas of active research. Did *Homo sapiens* evolve from *Homo erectus* across a broad front worldwide, or did the former evolve from one localized population of *H. erectus* and spread out to populate the rest of the world, as the molecular interpretations now indicate? Could there have been any interbreeding between the immigrants and the resident populations or were the latter totally replaced? There is even the possibility, which we consider remote, advanced by some scholars that other species of *Homo* existed alongside *H. erectus* and *H. habilis* (see Groves, 1989), and that one of these may have given rise to *H. sapiens.*

The fossil evidence of *Homo sapiens* is much more extensive than the bones and teeth of early *Homo* or australopithecines. This is because of the relatively recent date of these fossils, which means that they have undergone less geological alteration and destruction. *Homo sapiens* has also been a more geographically widespread species, even in comparison to *Homo erectus.* The taxonomy of *H. sapiens* is also historically complex. We adopt here a "**grade**" system for evolutionary stages of *H. sapiens,* presented in Table 11–1 with the major specimens at each grade. The geological ages of specimens are important for piecing together the sequence of events in their evolutionary history, and it is important to recognize that fossil specimens in the same grade may be of substantially different ages in different parts of the world.

grade–a level of organization or morphological complexity in an evolving lineage of organisms.

Table 11-1 • Major Fossil Specimens of *Homo,* Including Grades of *Homo sapiens*

Taxon	Locality	Specimen Number	Body Part	Geological Age
Homo habilis	Olduvai Gorge, Tanzania	OH (Olduvai Hominid) 7 ("Olduvai Hand")	Partial hand skeleton	1.8 million years
		OH 8 ("Olduvai Foot")	Partial foot skeleton	1.8 million years
		OH 13 ("Cinderella")	Partial skull	1.6 million years
		OH 24 ("Olduvai George")	Partial skull	1.9 million years
		OH 62 ("Son of Lucy")	Fragmentary skeleton	1.8 million years
	Omo, Ethiopia	L894-1	Fragmentary skull with teeth	1.9 million years
[also classified by some as *Homo rudolfensis*]	East Turkana, Kenya	KNM ER (Kenya National Museum, East Rudolf) 1470	Skull lacking teeth	1.9 million years
[also classified by some as *Homo ergaster*]		KNM ER 1813	Complete skull with teeth	1.9 million years
Homo erectus	West Turkana, Kenya	KNM WT 15000 ("Turkana Boy")	Nearly complete skeleton, with skull and dentition	1.6 million years
	East Turkana, Kenya	KNM ER 3733	Complete skull with dentition	1.5 million years
	Swartkrans, South Africa	SK 847	Partial skull with partial dentition	circa 1.5 million years
	Trinil, Indonesia	Trinil 1	Skull cap	circa 1.0 million years
	Modjokerto, Indonesia	Modjokerto 1 "Modjokerto Infant"	Partial skull	?1.9 million years
	Sangiran, Indonesia	Sangiran Skull IX	Complete skull and dentition	circa 1.5 million years
	Dmanisi, Georgia	Dmanisi 1	Mandible with teeth	circa 1.4–1.6 million years
Homo sapiens "Grade 1"	Bodo, Ethiopia	Bodo 1	Skull	circa 500,000 years
	Petralona, Greece	Petralona 1	Skull	over 230,000 years
	Dali, China	Dali 1	Skull	230,000–180,000 years
	Heidelberg	Mauer 1	Mandible with teeth	circa 300,000 years
Homo sapiens "Grade 2"	Steinheim, Germany	Steinheim 1	Skull lacking teeth	circa 150,000 years
Homo sapiens "Grade 3A"	Neandertal, Germany	Neandertal 1	Skull cap and partial skeleton	circa 50,000 years
	La Chapelle-aux-Saints, France	La Chapelle 1	Skull and mandible with teeth	circa 50,000 years
Homo sapiens "Grade 3B"	Omo, Ethiopia	Omo 1 and 2	Skulls lacking faces	120,000 years
	Qafzeh, Israel	Qafzeh I–XI	Skulls and Postcronia of a number of individuals	100,000 years

Data from Wood (1992).

The most primitive representatives of *Homo sapiens* (Grade 1) appear between 400,000 and 500,000 years ago. They are characterized by a rounded skull vault, lacking the sagittal keel and pronounced occipital bun of *H. erectus* (Figure 11–13). The brow ridges are still prominent, but unlike *H. erectus,* the ridges are thickest over the medial part of the orbit and they blend smoothly into the frontal bone behind. The cranial capacity of Grade 1 *Homo sapiens* is expanded compared to *Homo erectus,* although both are substantially lower than modern human values. The changes in the teeth from *H. erectus* to *H. sapiens* are limited to slight reduction in overall size.

So far as the fossil and geochronological records indicate, earliest *H. sapiens* occurred throughout the Old World, except probably in the northernmost latitudes. Broken Hill or Kabwe (Zambia), Bodo (Ethiopia), and Salé (Algeria) have provided ample evidence of earliest *Homo sapiens* in Africa. Petralona (Greece), the mandible from Mauer near Heidelberg (Germany), and the skull fragments from Bilzingsleben (Germany) are among the earliest evidences for *Homo sapiens* in Europe. Numerous fossil remains from Ngangdong (Indonesia) and a skull from Dali (China) attest to earliest *Homo sapiens* in Asia. Some of these fossils, particularly Mauer, Bilzingsleben, and Ngangdong, have been referred to in the past as belonging to *H. erectus.* As the morphological dividing line between the two species may have been thin, this confusion might be expected given that populations of intermediate morphology existed during the transitional period between *H. erectus* and *H. sapiens.* Our greater knowledge of the ranges of morphological variability in both *H. erectus* and earliest *H. sapiens,* because of new discoveries, now seems to warrant the attribution of these fossils to *H. sapiens* (Howell, 1986). The morphology of these specimens makes a good case for the evolution of *Homo sapiens* from *Homo erectus.*

What do the anatomical changes seen in earliest *H. sapiens* connote in terms of changes in behavior or adaptation, and what selective forces caused them to evolve? There is no clear answer to these questions, however, because anthropologists have yet to explain the major anatomical peculiarities of *H. erectus.* We do not know why the sagittal keel or the occipital torus disappeared, because we do not know what forces accounted for their presence in the first place. Hypotheses include differences in size and shape of certain parts of the brain and changes in chewing forces, but none so far are fully satisfactory. One trend is clear, however, and that is increasing cranial capacity. Selection in earliest *Homo sapiens* strongly favored greater brain size and presumably greater cerebral ability.

Archaic *Homo sapiens*

Homo sapiens Grade 2 probably ranges in time from approximately 300,000 to somewhat less than 100,000 years ago, although the ages of the fossils in many cases are unclear. The skulls of this grade have lost the *erectus*-like characteristics and their vaults are higher.

The evidence for these hominids in Europe and Africa is good (Figure 11–12). The Saccopastore (Italy), Arago (France), and Ndutu (Tanzania) specimens are the best representatives. Two partial skulls from Swanscombe (England) and Steinheim (Germany) have been intensively studied, and they occupy important positions in hominid evolutionary studies. Both specimens were cited in support of the "presapiens" hypothesis, mentioned earlier. Asia so far has yielded few if any *H. sapiens* fossils of Grade 2. *H. sapiens* Grade 2 provides a good evolutionary source for both Grade 3A (Neandertal) and Grade 3B (anatomically modern *Homo sapiens*).

Homo sapiens sapiens

Anatomically modern humans (*Homo sapiens* Grade 3B or *Homo sapiens sapiens*) appear around 100,000 years ago in the Old World. Major specimens documenting this apparently gradual evolutionary step from *H. sapiens* Grade 2 are found at several localities in both Africa and Asia. In Europe and the Middle East the Neandertals were replaced between 34,000 years ago in Western Europe and about 40,000 years ago in the eastern Mediterranean. New dates from Israel indicate that the anatomically modern Qafzeh cranium is 100,000 years old, suggesting that both anatomically modern and Neandertal lineages may have existed side by side in the Middle East (Stringer, 1990). *H. sapiens sapiens* lacks the very heavy brow ridge development, the midfacial prognathism and the forward positioning of the teeth characteristic of Neandertals. The postcranial skeleton shows that *H. sapiens sapiens* individuals were in general taller than Neandertals.

The geographic range of these early humans extended to Australia some 40,000–50,000 years ago, and eventually to North and South America, by way of a land bridge across what is now the Bering Strait. The date of the human presence in the Western Hemisphere is disputed. From the fossil evidence, humans were undeniably present by 10,000 to 12,000 years ago, but stone tools found at various localities in North and South America indicate a human presence in the New World as early as 37,000 to 40,000 years ago, and perhaps earlier.

Homo sapiens neanderthalensis

By a strange linguistic turn of chance "Neandertal" means "valley of the new man," a very appropriate name for the site which provided the first generally recognized human fossil. It was named for Joachim Neumann, a Dusseldorf clergyman and hymn writer of the mid-seventeenth century who wrote under the name of "Neander," meaning "new man" in Greek. "Thal" (later "tal") is German for "valley."

Limestone quarrymen found remains of a skeleton, which they thought might be a bear, at a cave in the Neandertal in 1856. They shoveled the bones out of the cave, losing many pieces in the process, and informed the local schoolmaster, Johannes Fuhlrott, that they were there if he chose to collect them. Fuhlrott is described as "one of those pedagogues so numerous in Germany who wander industriously about their native environment, examining every form of life and every stone they come across, and thus perform valuable small scale services to science" (Wendt, 1956:217). In this case it was quite a large-scale service, for Fuhlrott and an anthropologist from Bonn, Herman Schaafhausen, recognized and described for the first time an extinct human (Figure 11–14), which, in 1864, the British anatomist W.B.R. King named *Homo neanderthalensis* (it is now recognized as a subspecies of *Homo sapiens* by most workers although Stringer [1990] is in favor of resurrecting it as a separate species name).

The Neandertal discovery sparked a scientific controversy unrivaled in length in a field known for controversy. One side maintained that the fossils documented an extinct species intermediate in morphology

Figure 11–14 • Drawing of characteristic Neandertal skull morphology, compared to *Homo sapiens sapiens*.

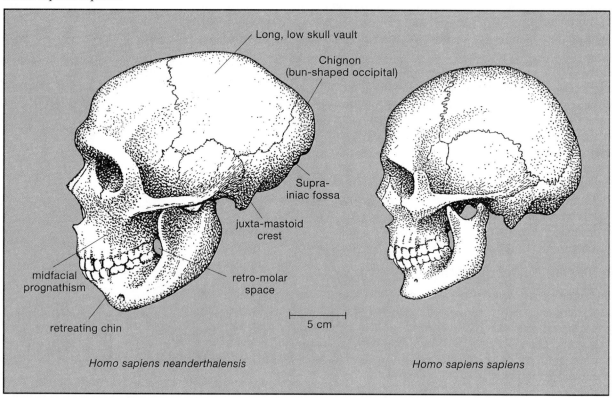

Homo sapiens neanderthalensis   Homo sapiens sapiens

between humans and the apes, and the other maintained that they represented an aberrant, perhaps pathological, modern human. With the discovery of additional Neandertal-like skulls from the cave of Spy (pronounced "spee") in Belgium in 1886 and the rediscovery of a Neandertal skull first found at Gibraltar in 1848, the former side prevailed. But, as with most long-standing scientific debates, both sides were partially right and partially wrong. We now know from increased fossil samples that the Neandertals are very similar to modern *H. sapiens* and do not in any meaningful way resemble apes. They are, nevertheless, morphologically distinct at a subspecific level and represent an extinct race of *H. sapiens*. Although some anthropologists have used the term "Neandertal" to refer to fossil hominids in various parts of the Old World, most agree that the term should be restricted to Late Pleistocene fossils of Europe and Southwest Asia sharing a specific morphological pattern. Neandertals date to the period of about 100,000 to 34,000 years ago.

The most well-known anatomical trait of Neandertals is their heavy brow ridge. As in early *Homo sapiens,* this is thickest medially, unlike that of *Homo erectus*. The middle portion of the face, around the nasal opening, protrudes greatly in Neandertals, and the teeth as a whole are moved forward relative to the skull vault. Because of this anatomical change, there is a gap, called the **retromolar space,** to be seen in lateral view behind the last molar (Figure 11–14). The forward projection of the face and teeth and the pointed occiput, retained from early *H. sapiens,* give to the Neandertal skull a low, flat appearance, even though its known range of cranial capacities is greater than the mean in modern humans. The facial skeleton and cheek bones are less strongly constructed and less massive than in early *H. sapiens*. Earlier authors considered a chin, the point in the midline of the front of the mandible, to be lacking in Neandertals. Actually it is variably present but it tends to be obscured by the far anterior placement of the front teeth and their supporting bone (Figure 11–14).

Why the teeth in Neandertals are positioned so far forward is still a question, but their **midfacial prognathism** and brow ridge formation are almost certainly related to it. The bone forming the brow ridges transfers the forces from the face generated by the anterior teeth. C. Loring Brace has argued that the unique rounded wear on the incisors of Neandertals suggests that they used their teeth to process skins or to hold objects. Although this hypothesis helps to explain the heavy brow ridges and tooth wear in Neandertals, it does not account for the anterior position of the teeth.

Most parts of the Neandertal skeleton are known. Overall body size had increased, certainly in comparison with average *H. erectus* and probably also relative to earlier *H. sapiens*. This body size increase may likely have been effected by an adaptation to cold climatic conditions. A general principle known as Bergmann's Principle states that animals in a related group tend to be larger in colder climates (Chapter 14).

retromolar space—a gap to be seen between the last upper molar and the ascending ramus of the mandible when articulated with the skull.

midfacial prognathism—forward projection of the bony nose region of the skull; characteristic of Neandertals.

The limb bones of Neandertals show them to have been powerfully built, "stocky" individuals. Otherwise, with two major exceptions, the anatomy of the limbs and axial skeleton of Neandertals were similar to ours. The Neandertal scapula shows a deep groove for attachment of the *teres minor* muscle. This muscle contracts to counteract the medial rotational force of very strong arm flexors, thus refining flexing movements used in throwing or pounding. Neandertals also show a thin and elongated pubic arch in the pelvis. This increases the diameter of the birth canal and may be related to a relatively large head size in Neandertal newborns.

Behavior of Early *Homo sapiens*

Material culture and artifactual remains left by *H. sapiens* are progressively more abundant the closer we approach the present. These remains and their contexts provide archaeologists with important bases for interpreting early human behavior.

Early *Homo sapiens* of Grades 1 and 2 used stone tools classified as within the Lower Paleolithic or Old Stone Age. Acheulean hand axes remained a distinguishing component of these cultures, except in Asia where modified chopping tools or nonlithic tools apparently served similar purposes.

Neandertals, whose primarily **Mousterian** flake tools are considered Middle Paleolithic, show the first indications of many cultural aspects that we recognize as "human." Burial of the dead (even with flowers, as indicated by pollen analysis at Shanidar Cave, Iraq), implies a belief in life after death. The discovery of fossils of old, physically handicapped or virtually toothless Neandertal individuals (Figure 11–15) means that groups to which they belonged cared for and helped to feed them. Special arrangements of bear skulls and deer bones suggest magical hunting rites. A few pieces of crude polished bones and ivory with scratches indicate the first beginnings of artistry. A single tooth with a hole drilled in it, possibly worn as a necklace, and intentional cranial deformation show early ideas of personal esthetics and perhaps group identity. There are clear indications that some Neandertals were wounded or killed with spears or by blows to the head (Figure 11–16). Although evidence for fossil *H. sapiens* groups in areas other than Europe and the Middle East is less complete, it is likely that their behavior was generally similar.

When modern *Homo sapiens* appears in Europe, so do stone tools made from "blades," elongated pieces of stone deftly struck off a core (Figure 11–17). These tools signal the beginning of the **Upper Paleolithic.** There is significant regional variation in these tool traditions, suggesting greater cultural differences between groups. The preferential pattern of site locations near river courses seen in southern France may be correlated with an increased use of fish and birds in the diet. We find

Mousterian–a Middle Paleolithic stone tool culture characterized by prepared flakes struck off a core.

Upper Paleolithic–a series of Late Pleistocene cultures typified by a diversification of traditions and stone tools made from blades struck from cores; associated with anatomically modern humans.

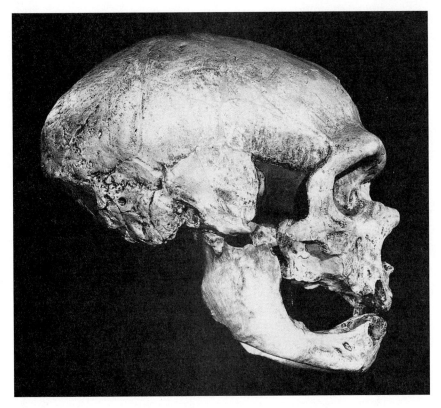

Figure 11–15 • *H. sapiens neanderthalensis*—Edentulous, old individual, from the cave site at La Chapelle-aux-Saints, France.

substantially more reindeer skeletal remains in European sites at this time, suggesting preferred utilization of these animals for food and for antler tools. Modern *Homo sapiens* controlled fire more adeptly, constructing stone-lined hearths that generated more heat and in which fires could be banked. Impressive cave art in the form of paintings (Figure 11–18) and figurines occur. Materials from distant sources, such as marine shells and flint, indicate long-distance trading contacts or individual movements. Population density was probably higher, or at least people congregated in relatively large groups (perhaps in response to local food abundance) for part of the year, as indicated by larger site sizes.

Evolutionary Relationships in *Homo sapiens*

As discussed earlier in this chapter, the accumulated fossil evidence seems to indicate to most scholars that *Homo sapiens* evolved from *Homoerectus*. This hypothesis has been seriously questioned only recently by authors who consider that *Homo erectus* was too "specialized" anatomically to serve as a possible ancestor for *Homo sapiens*. The discovery of *erectus*-like *Homo sapiens* (Grade 1) hominids makes this suggestion unlikely.

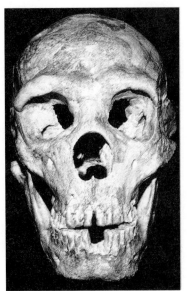

Figure 11–16 • Neanderthal specimen from Shanidar (Shanidar I, showing evidence of cranial fracture in the left eye orbit).

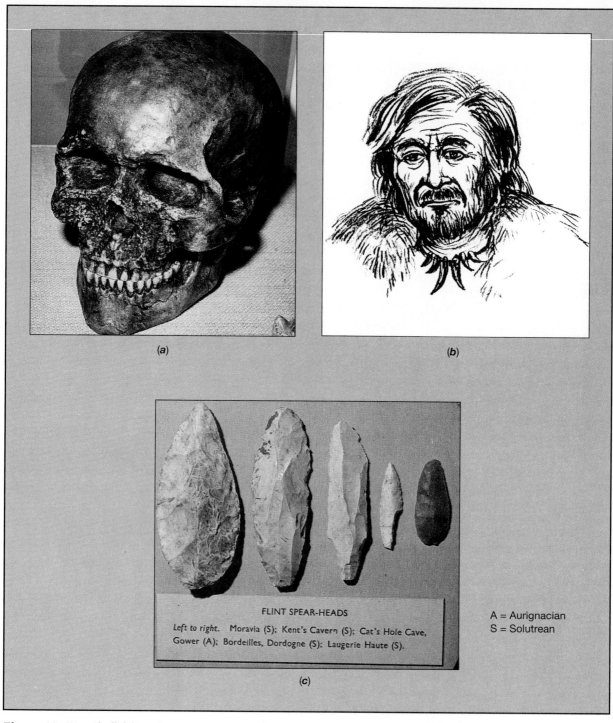

(a)

(b)

FLINT SPEAR-HEADS

Left to right. Moravia (S); Kent's Cavern (S); Cat's Hole Cave, Gower (A); Bordeilles, Dordogne (S); Laugerie Haute (S).

A = Aurignacian
S = Solutrean

(c)

Figure 11–17 • Skull (*a*) and artistic reconstruction (*b*) of Cro-Magnon; Upper Paleolithic stone tools commonly associated with anatomically modern *Homo sapiens* in Europe (*c*).

Figure 11–18 • Painting on wall of a prehistoric cave discovered in 1995 in the Vallon Pont d'Arc region of France dating to the Solutrean, circa 20,000 years ago.

It is generally agreed that *H. sapiens* Grades 1 and 2 are representative of populations ancestral to anatomically modern humans. However, the geological dating and the geographic placement of the sites yielding these fossils, as well as the constraints on evolutionary hypotheses placed by the emerging molecular data, have led to three major hypotheses on the origins of modern humans (Stringer, 1990).

The **Out-of-Africa Model** (Figure 11–19), which is consistent with the "African Eve" Hypothesis discussed earlier, has been advocated by paleoanthropologists Günter Bräuer and Christopher Stringer and geneticists Allan Wilson and Rebecca Cann. It holds that an African population of anatomically modern *Homo sapiens,* as exemplified by fossils such as those from the Klasies River site in South Africa, left Africa about 100,000 years ago. This population spread over the entire Old World and accounts for all the racial differences seen in the fossil record and in modern populations. This model considers *all* the pre-modern *Homo sapiens* fossils in Eurasia extinct side branches, unrelated to the lineal ancestors of modern human beings. This model fits

Out-of-Africa Model—evolutionary hypothesis that holds that modern humans evolved first in Africa and then spread out over the rest of the world, displacing or driving to extinction other populations.

Figure 11–19 • Two models of *Homo sapiens sapiens* phylogeny.

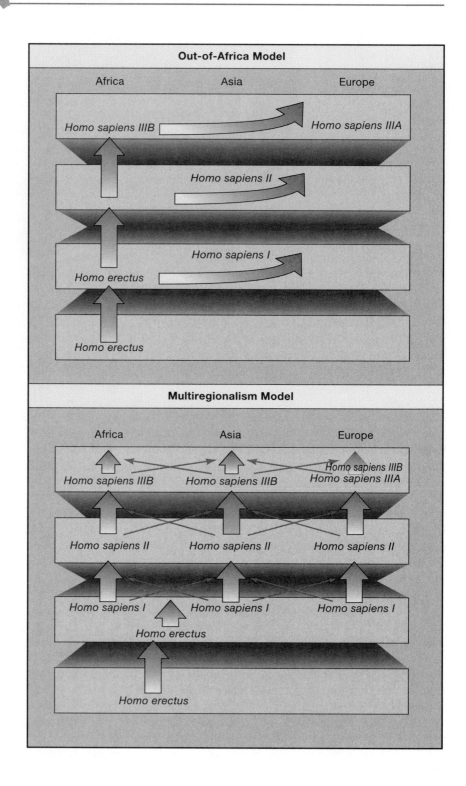

the genetic data the best but fails to account for some of the apparent morphological continuities that are seen from earlier fossil populations in the same areas. For example, Asian populations today have a high proportion of shovel-shaped incisors, as do Asian *Homo erectus* and archaic *Homo sapiens* in the same region, and modern Europeans have projecting midfacial regions and relatively heavy brows, just as do the archaic *Homo sapiens* in that area.

The **Hybridization Model,** advanced by Erik Trinkaus, Fred Smith, and others, accounts for these morphological continuities by suggesting that the human populations migrating out of Africa did replace the older populations in the same areas, but there was gene flow as the immigrants interbred with the resident populations. The resulting genetic intermixture could account for the mixture of anatomical traits seen in the anatomically modern populations. This model is less consistent with the molecular interpretation, which maintains that there is no evidence for genetic intermixture after the divergence from the ancestral *Homo sapiens* population in Africa.

The third model can be termed the **Multiregional Model** and can be traced back to Franz Weidenreich. Its current primary advocate is Milford Wolpoff. This model rejects the one-region (African Eden) origin and molecular interpretation of Cann and Wilson. It instead regards regional ancestral populations of *Homo sapiens* as the major genetic evolutionary pathways to anatomically modern humans. There must have been some genetic interbreeding between regional populations of *Homo sapiens* to have maintained the biological unity of the species and its ability to interbreed, but this model holds that this interbreeding was of lesser importance than maintained by the second model. The support for the third model comes primarily from one interpretation of the paleontological record, and its accommodation of the available molecular data is poor.

Where then do Neandertals fit in human evolution? The position of Neandertals in this evolutionary picture is still debated. One school, termed "pre sapiens," analogous in this case to the Out-of-Africa model, has considered populations of *H. sapiens* Grade 2, as indicated by Steinheim and Swanscombe, uniquely ancestral to *H. sapiens sapiens,* with Neandertals, therefore, an evolutionary dead end, supplanted or perhaps wiped out by Cro-Magnon populations. The school promoting the "Neandertal Phase" hypothesis, analogous here to the multiregional model, holds that Neandertals were directly ancestral to modern *Homo sapiens*. There are some cogent anatomical arguments supporting the latter interpretation, at least in Europe, but the rapidity of the transition from *H. sapiens neanderthalensis* to modern *Homo sapiens* and the localized nature of Neandertals argue against their being ancestral to modern *Homo sapiens* on a species-wide, global scale.

Neandertals were most likely a geographic variant, a race of *H. sapiens,* which differentiated in Europe and Western Asia because of at least partial geographic isolation. Expanded glaciers in northern and

Hybridization Model—evolutionary hypothesis that suggests interbreeding between emigrant African populations and resident human populations in other parts of the world.

Multiregional Model—evolutionary hypothesis that suggests primary continuity from earlier to later human populations in each area of the world, with some gene exchange between populations.

mountainous regions and extensive bodies of water formed by glacial melt waters reduced gene flow during the next to last (Riss) and last (Würm) Pleistocene glaciations (Figure 11–20). They disappeared when very arid conditions, which affected southern Asia and northern Africa, may have forced populations we now recognize as modern *Homo sapiens* into Europe, as the coldest period of the last glaciation approached. There may have been at least some interbreeding, explaining transitional morphology in a few specimens, and cultural exchange, explaining some continuities observed in the archaeological record. But because Neandertals occupied a relatively restricted area and their population densities were probably lower, they likely were genetically swamped and thus became extinct as a distinct population.

Figure 11–20 • Paleogeography of late Pleistocene Europe with *Homo sapiens* sites noted; glaciers are shown in grey, montane forests in brown, deserts in tan, and water in blue. (From Boaz et al., 1982)

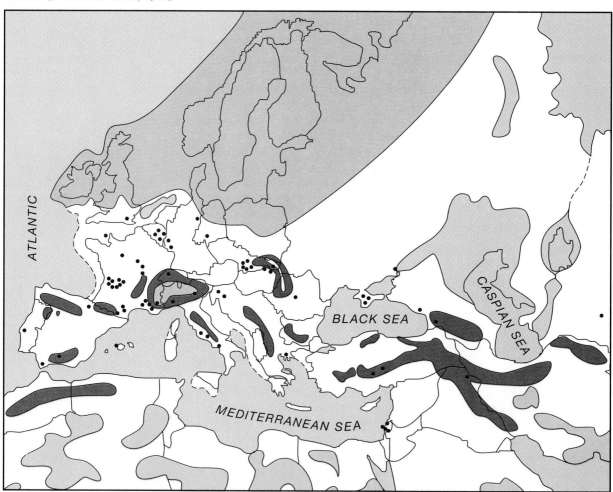

Nevertheless, certain Neandertal characteristics, such as heavy brow ridges and facial prognathism, persist in some modern populations.

Phylogenetic interpretation of the fossil record of *Homo sapiens* has now been significantly augmented by the data and perspectives that molecular studies have contributed to this question. Research into modern human origins can now draw from paleontological, genetic, and paleoecological data bases to formulate more sophisticated and more defensible hypotheses for this best known period of hominid evolution.

SUMMARY

The evolutionary history of the genus *Homo* is a story of expansion of a series of species out of Africa, not once but several times. The earliest members of *Homo* had brains even larger than did australopithecines, and this trend of increasing brain size has been sustained through to our own species, *Homo sapiens*. Other evolutionary trends are decreases in the size of the dentition, face, and jaws. The first species of *Homo* seen in the fossil record is *Homo habilis,* a species that appears at about 2.4 million years ago in sub-Saharan Africa. Its appearance is coincident with the first discovery of stone tools, and there is a strong presumption that *Homo habilis* was the maker of the stone tools, even though robust australopithecines were also present. *Homo erectus* succeeds *Homo habilis* and is the species that spreads out of Africa and into Eurasia. It is typified by a larger brain, thick cranial bones, heavy brow ridges, and other identifying cranial traits. By about 500,000 years archaic *Homo sapiens* fossils are known from Africa and Europe. These show a number of similarities to the earlier *Homo erectus* and are likely lineal descendents. Anatomically modern *Homo sapiens* appears by 100,000 years ago in Africa and by 30,000 years ago has spread to Australia and by 12,000 years ago has extended to the Americas. Neandertals were a subspecies of *Homo sapiens* that lived in Europe during the late Pleistocene and were extinct by 32,000 years ago. There is lively debate concerning the exact evolutionary relationships of species of the genus *Homo,* and a developing interaction of paleoanthropological and biomolecular research approaches.

CRITICAL-THINKING QUESTIONS

1. What criteria are used to distinguish the genus *Homo* from the genus *Australopithecus?*
2. Who found and named *Homo habilis?* Why was this find so important?
3. Draw a hominid phylogeny including a probable time frame for each member. Include the corresponding type specimen.
4. What factors contributed to the widespread acceptance of the Piltdown discovery?

5. Discuss Neandertals and their placement in the hominid lineage.
6. Who was "Mitochondrial Eve"?

 ## SUGGESTED READINGS

Aiken, M.J., C.B. Stringer, and P.A. Mellars (eds.). 1993. *The Origin of Modern Humans and the Impact of Chronometric Dating: A Discussion*. Princeton, N.J.: Princeton University Press. A volume discussing the important new methods of accurately dating fossil sites in the period of time covering the evolution of anatomically modern humans.

Bowler, Peter. 1986. *Theories of Human Evolution: A Century of Debate, 1844–1944*. Baltimore: Johns Hopkins University Press. A detailed and fascinating book on the history of the ideas and hypotheses of human origins.

Ciochon, Russell, and John G. Fleagle (eds.). 1993. *The Human Evolution Source Book*. Englewood Cliffs, N.J.: Prentice Hall. A collected book of readings of major recent papers in human evolution.

Falk, Dean. 1992. *Braindance*. New York: Henry Holt. A book on the evolution of the human brain as understood by a study of fossil brain endocasts.

Isaac, G. L. and Elizabeth McCown (eds.). 1976. *Human Origins: Louis Leakey and the East African Evidence*. Menlo Park, Calif.: W.A. Benjamin. A series of chapters covering both fossil and archaeological reviews of the Early Pleistocene record of African early *Homo*.

Jones, Steve, Robert Martin, and David Pilbeam (eds.). 1992. *The Cambridge Encyclopedia of Human Evolution*. Cambridge: Cambridge University Press. A useful compendium and reference volume.

Klein, Richard. 1989. *The Human Career: Human Biological and Cultural Origins*. Chicago: University of Chicago Press. A general treatment of the archaeological, ecological, and paleoanthropological changes that characterize human evolution.

Leakey, Richard, and Roger Lewin. 1992. *Origins Reconsidered: In Search of What Makes Us Human*. New York: Doubleday. A review of the theories of human behavioral and morphological evolution from the starting point of Richard Leakey's discoveries of early *Homo* in Kenya.

Rightmire, G. Philip. 1990. *The Evolution of Homo Erectus: Comparative Anatomical Studies of an Extinct Human Species*. Cambridge: Cambridge University Press. A review of the anatomy and evolutionary relationships of this fossil human species intermediate between early *Homo* and *Homo sapiens*.

Smith, Fred, and Frank Spencer (eds.). 1984. *The Origins of Modern Humans: A World Survey of the Fossil Evidence*. A good review of the major finds of anatomically modern *Homo sapiens* and a sampling of the hypotheses explaining their evolution.

Trinkaus, Erik (ed.). 1989. *The Emergence of Modern Humans: Biocultural Adaptations in the Later Pleistocene*. Cambridge: Cambridge University Press. An up-to-date account by some of the major workers in the field on new dating, new archaeological discoveries, and new morphological analyses relating to the evolutionary transition to anatomically modern humans.

The Evolution of Human Social Behavior

Human Behavioral Evolution
Primate Behavior
Baboon Models
Ape Models
Studies of Modern Carnivores

**Archaeology's Insights
into Cultural Development**
Paleobehavior

**Model Building and
Ethnographic Research**

**Reconstructing Early Human
Behavior**
Historical Overview
New Behavioral Models
Emerge: Bipedalism
Brain Size
Cerebral Laterality: Two Brains
in One
Speech Areas of the Cortex
Language
Art, Symbolism, and Speech
Anatomical Evidence
for Speech

Summary

Critical-Thinking Questions

Suggested Readings

HUMAN BEHAVIORAL EVOLUTION

Reconstructing the path of human behavioral evolution has proved to be difficult, perhaps even more so than tracing our physical evolution, because the data are less concrete and many times of fleeting duration. Because we cannot travel back in time, piecing together human behavioral evolution is hampered by the lack of firsthand observation. Our knowledge is constrained by the extent of the fossil record and the archaeological remains and by the accuracy of anatomical reconstructions. The models that these data have generated remain speculative because they are based on many unknowns. They require the reconstruction of the unique morphologies and behaviors of early humans, as well as the habitats in which they lived, reproduced, and adapted.

Sketches of early human lifeways passed down from nineteenth-century authors contain largely imaginary descriptions of large-brained, apelike ancestors whose primitive behaviors were gradually forged into the modern form. This view of human evolution initiated by expansion of the human brain was cut short with the realization that our earliest australopithecine ancestors had brains no larger than those of modern apes and had survived for millions of years without stone tools. Current behavioral reconstructions may be affected by subtleties that lie within our own subconscious. As Fedigan (1986) remarks, "[i]n many cases reconstructions of the past are in some respects also reflections of the present." Misia Landau (1984) pointed out that models of human evolution follow a standard Western cultural narrative tradition (stories). In this tradition the typical "hero" emerges: "man" who conquers "his" obstacles, and perseveres against all odds. This tradition favors public, not domestic, aspects of human culture and production rather than reproduction, limiting the role of women to bearing and raising of children. These roles, Landau notes, largely reflect Western cultural beliefs that, in her view, have been incorrectly generalized into accepted universals of natural human behavior (Figure 12–1).

There are two issues in reconstructing behavioral evolution. First, one must determine the limitations of the data sets used, that is, how much information can be usefully acquired from any one source; and, second, one should be able to construct flexible models that will arrange, as well as explain, the information that we have.

Figure 12–1 • Behavioral scenarios from Misia Landau (1984). Prominent researchers (listed in the left column) since Darwin have rearranged the sequence of events that led up to the evolution of modern humans. Each model consists of the same elements, although in varying order of appearance.

John Tooby and Irven DeVore of Harvard University, in addressing the problems of behavioral evolution described two kinds of models. These are examples of *deductive reasoning* in science (see Chapter 1). The first kind, **referential models,** are ones in which a closely allied living species is used as a model for an extinct one that is "less amenable to study." Alliance between the living species and its referent is based on some illuminating characteristic or cluster of characteristics that the living form probably shared with the extinct one. Hunting, gathering, scavenging, and other behaviors have been used as a focus to explain human behavior, and on that basis a baboon, chimpanzee (common and pygmy), or social carnivore have been chosen as a referent. The second kinds of models, ones that Tooby and DeVore prefer, are **conceptual models.** Rather than using one particular living species as a direct model, they use information from many sources to create a model that is, on the one hand, a theoretical composite of many data sets, and, on the other, unique in that it is not exactly like any one of them.

Before a conceptual model can be developed the following three determinations must be made: the set of principles that govern the model; the time framework (or phylogenetics) during which these principles apply; and, the extent to which the data sets are useful in constructing the model. In regard to the first point, behavior is selected to follow specific strategies that work to promote, at least on one level, inclusive fitness. All species unalterably follow the same evolutionary laws and face the same ecological forces. Specific conditions (such as environment) that determine the interaction of these principles for each specific case, however, do vary. In addition to following strategies that promote *inclusive fitness* (see Chapter 7), selected primate traits must be (1) *adaptive compromises,* that is, they will have both costs and benefits; (2) *behaviorally flexible,* allowing members of groups to act individualistically; and (3) important in regard to *each stage in the life cycle.* No single age or sex group is more important to the model than any other. Tooby and DeVore summarize:

> Any account of hominid evolution that concentrates only on males, or only on females, or suggests that any specific age-sex class is responsible for hominid evolution is defective. Both "Man the Hunter" and "Woman the Gatherer" analyses suffer from this problem.

There are two additional concerns that will affect the final outcome of a model of human evolution. The distinctive set of evolutionarily significant adaptations that humans have made at any given point in time is probably far more extensive than we realize, and by concentrating on only a few well-described adaptations, such as hunting or gathering, other equally important adaptations may be overlooked. It may also be true, that if the study of human evolution is approached as a process

referential models–hypotheses of behavioral evolution using a "reference" species as a model based on shared traits or characteristics of a living species and an extinct species under study.

conceptual models–hypotheses of behavioral evolution constructed using data from a number of sources, models of which may not correspond closely to the behavior of any living species.

consisting of a number of distinct stages, all of which could be affected by different selective forces, then the model will have to be designed to take into account many different reconstructions, rather than a single one. Models that minimize the contribution of a trait at one stage, for example, the importance of hunting as a subsistence strategy for *Australopithecus,* could then be reconsidered and the importance of hunting evaluated at the appropriate time in the sequence of behavioral adaptations.

Culture and cultural evolution are a shared paradigm between biological anthropology and the other subfields of anthropology. In constructing a model of human evolution four main sources of data offer insights. Guided by current evolutionary theory, scenarios for hominid divergence and the emergence of human culture should be consistent with (1) the available human *fossil evidence,* (2) the behavioral data from *studies of the nonhuman primates* in the wild, (3) the detectable remains of hominid behavior as revealed by *archaeological research,* and (4) the *ethnographic research* on modern hunters and gatherers. Because the human fossil record has already been discussed in Chapter 10 the remaining three sources of data will now be further explored.

Primate Behavior

Few aspects of past behavior leave behind a fossil record. Wear on teeth, bumps and ridges on bones, stone artifacts, a trail of footprints—these are all indications of past behavior. They either record one particular incident or indicate habitual behavior. But the richness of everyday interactions among individuals and the details of everyday life cannot be known from the fossil record alone. To fill in the blanks concerning the lives of early hominids many anthropologists have used the detailed knowledge of the behavior of our closest living primate relatives. The human evolutionary framework implies a continuity with ancestral forms and thus, commonality with other closely related living primates. Shared behavioral traits with humans are considered *homologous,* that is those derived from common inheritance. For this reason the study of the behavior of nonhuman primates has proved useful in interpreting human behavior and provides many insights into the human condition. For example, psychologist Harry Harlow and his research group at the Wisconsin Regional Primate Research Center studied the learning processes of the nonhuman primates. They demonstrated similarities between humans and the nonhuman primates in what is learned, how it is learned, and, within the developmental sequence, when it is learned.

The idea that culture is a unique human characteristic is misleading, because certain aspects of the behavior of monkeys and apes can be considered cultural. If culture is, in part, learning ways of doing things and passing them on from one generation to the next, then such be-

Figure 12–2 • Japanese macaque washing a potato.

haviors as potato washing among the Japanese macaques (considered "precultural") or termite feeding, as seen in chimpanzees, is "protocultural" behavior. In the instance of the Japanese macaque, monkeys were fed sweet potatoes in order to entice them out of the hills so that primatologists could study them on open beaches. Potatoes strewn in the sand presented a problem for the monkeys because the sand which adhered to the potatoes made them difficult to eat. One young female solved the problem by dropping the potato into a nearby pool of fresh water and washing the sand from the potato (Figure 12–2). By observation other animals followed suit and the potato washing tradition began. Subsequent generations of Japanese macaques continued the behavior established by the single female until almost all of the troop ate their potatoes in this manner.

The definition of culture, however, is elusive. Anthropologists themselves have not reached a consensus in defining this concept. Keesing (1974) reviewed the concept of culture and considered it within two broad viewpoints. Some anthropologists see culture as an *adaptive system based on **technology*** (Harris, 1979), whereas others see it as a *conceptual system dependent on **language*** (Goodenough, 1981). Parker and Russon (1995) sought to define culture on the basis of parallels between human and nonhuman **cognition** and traditions. They believed that because human culture is defined on the basis of language that a broadened definition of culture should include nonhuman abilities that could have set the stage for the emergence of human systems. They recommend that many core features of cultural anthropology, psychology, and biology should be incorporated in a comparative functional definition of culture and argue:

> Cultures are representations of knowledge socially transmitted within and between generations in groups and populations within a species which may aid them in adapting to local conditions (ecological, demographic, or social).

technology–tool-making and tool-use, including construction of structures, clothing, fire, weapons, and all other aspects of "material culture."

language–verbal communication, using speech, uniquely characteristic of humankind.

cognition–self-awareness and the acquisition of knowledge, including the processes of perceiving, recognizing, conceiving, judging, sensing, reasoning, and imagining.

cosmology–awareness and knowledge of the universe, its origins, and its workings.

The beginnings and development of human culture must have occurred as a process whereby younger members of the group, who, by observing the behavior of older individuals, adopted, improved, and later passed on better and more efficient ways of doing things. As humans came to depend on more intricate behavior and technology for their survival, a cultural tradition arose. Tool use and manufacture, and other forms of food and object manipulation must have been at the root of cultural development. As brain size increased and humans became concerned with **cosmological** aspects of their surroundings and the intricacies of nature, cultural rules expanded. As populations became larger and as individuals developed sedentary ways of life, such aspects as property rights, economics, and politics were dealt their own set of cultural rules, further complicating human behavior.

Baboon Models

One of the earliest attempts to use data from nonhuman primates in the wild to explain human behavior was DeVore and Washburn's study of baboons of the Amboseli Game Reserve in Kenya. To these anthropologists the baboons provided an excellent referent model to explain how hominids could have differentiated from earlier nonhuman primate forms. They reasoned that early hominids became distinct by exploiting the resources of the savanna and survived by a social system of defense provided by the protective behavior of large males. This rigidly organized male dominance hierarchy was based on the bonding and cooperation of adult males moving in a carefully structured defense formation that guarded the nucleus of defenseless and smaller females and their infants.

Subsequent studies of baboons have de-emphasized male dominance and aggression and stressed the importance of female matrilines as the organizing force of baboon social organization (Strum, 1987; Altmann and Altmann, 1970). Although the baboon model has not totally been abandoned, the key elements from which it was constructed have changed as knowledge of the intricacies of their social behavior has expanded. Some researchers suggest that early humans and baboons may not have coexisted in environments similar to the modern African savanna. Additionally, behavioral comparisons between humans and baboons rely more on analogous behaviors than homologous behaviors because modern humans and baboons are not as genetically close as are humans to the African apes.

Ape Models

The close genetic relationships that humans share with the great apes prompted the development of other models that focused on ape behavior (Wrangham, 1987). Behavioral and ecological observations of apes have been used to generate and test hypotheses about early human social organization and behavior (Kortlandt, 1962, 1972; Tanner, 1987), and ape behavioral traits have been compared with those of humans to determine which traits may be derived from a hominid-ape common ancestor (Table 12–1).

Chimpanzee social organization has been described as possessing the essential ingredients that might have been found in early hominid forager groups (McGrew, 1992; Wrangham et al., 1994). Chimpanzees live in large communities of individuals who recognize each other and who are not mutually antagonistic when they meet. They also form smaller parties of individuals who generally travel and forage together over longer periods of time. Group composition is relatively fluid, and membership, with the exception of mothers and their dependent offspring, also fluctuates. The importance of the mother–infant bond

Table 12–1 • Some Human and Ape Behavioral Traits Compared

Behavioral Traits	African Apes	Humans
Surveillance and Defense Against Predators	Yes	Yes
Defense and Maintenance of Resources Within Home Range or Territory	Yes	Yes
Generally Hostile Intergroup Relationships	Yes	Yes
Variable Territorial Defense	Yes	Yes
Inheritance of Resources Within Home Range or Territory	Yes	Yes
Protection Against Infanticidal Conspecifics	Yes	Yes
Social Network	Closed	Semi-Closed
Dominance Hierarchies	Yes	Yes
Mating System	Promiscuity	Polygynous
Length of Sexual Relationship	Short-Term	Long-Term
Male Food and Resource Provisioning to Females	Rare	Common
Shelter Construction	Single Nests	Communal Housing
Inheritance of Status, Wealth, and Possessions	Matrilineal Status Only	Yes

Data from Wrangham (1987) and Taub and Mehlman (1991).

stresses the **matrifocal unit** rather than a **nuclear family.** Chimpanzees have learned to make a variety of simple tools and weapons leading to the hypothesis that early hominids did the same. In fact, populations of chimpanzees that are well habituated to a human presence are observed to use tools on a daily basis.

Social ties between adult males and females are usually made on the basis of kinship instead of sex, as copulations are generally casual and opportunistic with females usually showing few preferences for one male over others. The development of long-term sexual bonds in the gibbon show that little evidence exists to connect that with the "loss of estrus," as seen in human females. For example, female pygmy chimpanzees copulate throughout their monthly cycle and are not pair-bonded, whereas monogamous, pair-bonded gibbons do not show loss of estrus. The idea of a loss of estrus and its coupling with monogamy, therefore, is not well supported by the data.

Goodall and other primatologists studying chimpanzees in the wild made startling discoveries about the eating habits of these apes. As a result, the dividing line between humans, supposedly omnivorous, and

matrifocal unit–a family unit based around the mother.

nuclear family–a family unit consisting of a father, mother, and offspring.

chimpanzees, supposedly **frugivorous** became blurred with the discovery that chimpanzees ate meat. Meat is a prized food item and tends to be eaten most commonly during the dry season or when there is a lack of fruit. However, chimps are not well-adapted to meat eating. Chimpanzees who eat meat frequently engage in **coprophagy,** re-ingesting their own feces because their gastrointestinal tract has not adequately digested the fibrous meat. Work by Peters and O'Brien (1981) shows that in Africa humans and chimps have substantial overlap in the plant species they eat. However, at some time in the evolution of the human diet a significant shift occurred towards a greater proportion of meat.

Tool use, especially stone tool use, has been thought to have evolved in early hominids for hunting or at least cutting open, dismembering, and dividing up animal carcasses. Observations on wild chimpanzees have argued against this hypothesis. Chimps are successful hunters, but generally hunt without tools. Although there is a reported case of a male chimp throwing a rock at a group of bush pigs after which some chimps pursued, captured, and ate a piglet from the group (McGrew, 1979) most of the tool use observed in wild chimps is undertaken by females. Most of the habitual tool use patterns involve subsistence activities for acquiring or processing food. These activities are what Parker and Gibson (1979) describe as **tool-aided extractive foraging,** such as termite fishing (Goodall, 1988). Likewise, chimpanzees in West Africa have been observed gathering nuts and cracking them with stones, female chimps engaging in this behavior more frequently than males (Boesch and Boesch, 1981). Several authors have speculated that gathering plant foods was the primary hominid adaptation and that tool use began, not for hunting by males and meat eating, but rather for plant-food gathering, primarily, on the part of females.

African apes have been used as models for the locomotor adaptations of the common ape-human ancestor. Washburn posited a *knuckle-walking phase* through which human ancestors passed. He pointed to a number of anatomical similarities, such as limited abduction of the human wrist (movement to the thumb side), and positional similarities, such as football lineman in a four-point stance, to underline this argument. Tuttle, however, in a detailed comparative anatomical study (1975), found no vestiges of a knuckle-walking adaptation in the modern human hand or forelimb. Neither have the earliest hominid fossils evinced any anatomical characteristics recalling a knuckle-walking ancestry. More fossil evidence will be required to answer the question of what sort of locomotion the common ape-human ancestor had. It appears unlikely, however, on present evidence that a modern chimp or gorilla provides a good model for this stage of hominid evolution.

Limited bipedalism has been observed in chimps and gorillas, usually for no more than a few meters. About 85% of the time that chimpanzees are bipedal they are engaged in eating activities or in gathering food. In these cases, chimpanzees might stand upright and reach

frugivorous–fruit-eating.

coprophagy–the ingestion of feces.

tool-aided extractive foraging–hypothesis that early hominid tool use was aimed at securing hard-to-obtain foraged foods, mainly by females, as opposed to hunting by males.

Figure 12–3 • Chimpanzee bipedalism during aggressive display.

out or hold themselves up by grasping on to an overhead limb. There are several other reasons for ape bipedality including: (1) carrying objects; (2) raising the line of sight over visual obstructions, usually tall grass; and (3) displaying aggression (Figure 12–3). The leading hypothesis for the adaptive advantage of early hominid bipedalism is that it allowed efficient long distance locomotion and foraging.

Studies of Modern Carnivores

Studies of large mammalian carnivores, such as lions, spotted hyenas and African hunting dogs, have also provided important clues to early hominid behavior, based on reasoning from behavioral analogy and adaptation to environments similar to those inhabited by early hominids. One study by Schaller and Lowther (1965) showed the relevance of carnivore ecology to early hominid evolution. These authors pointed out that early pre-stone-tool-using hominids, such as *A. afarensis* and *africanus,* probably made their living by both hunting small animals and scavenging, as do other carnivores. If early hominids hunted in groups then their social organization might have resembled that of social carnivores. To test this idea Schaller and Lowther simulated an opportunistic hunting/scavenging australopithecine lifestyle in the Serengeti Park in Tanzania and found that a successful hunt could sustain a small group if their diet was supplemented by gathered vegetable food. Although this study only demonstrated that hunting could be a possible alternative for early hominids within their overall subsistence strategy, it sustained the notion that carnivore hunting practices could be a useful way of looking at how hominids may have hunted.

Additional analogies have since been drawn between early hominids and carnivores. For example, early hominids may have had large territories to defend, and adults may have cooperated in food getting and sharing with young or infirm members of the group, as do some modern social carnivores. These comparisons underline the fact that, although australopithecines arose from a primate base, selection for a social opportunistic and omnivorous way of life significantly altered the trajectory of hominid evolution.

ARCHAEOLOGY'S INSIGHTS INTO CULTURAL DEVELOPMENT

Paleobehavior

"Behavior fossils" consist of the remains or traces of human activity in the fossil record. Such remains consist of **artifacts** (Latin, meaning "made by skill"), usually stone tools, as well as the actions that these tools had on other objects, such as the **cut marks** they may have made on bone (Figure 12–4). Cut marks may be important in establishing the fact that hominids rather than other scavengers, such as hyenas, utilized the bone for food. Other "behavior fossils," such as the footprint trails from the site of Laetoli (Chapter 10), preserve no bone but they do record the passage of hominids.

Some behavioral capabilities can be determined from fossil bones themselves. From the fossilized remains inferences can be made concerning *body size and shape, locomotor abilities,* and from the dental patterns, aspects of *diet.* The earliest hominids were small-brained and apparently highly sexually dimorphic (somewhere in range between a chimpanzee and a gorilla), with a distinctive dentition characterized by nonsectorial canines whose tips barely projected above the level of the other teeth (Chapter 10).

The relatively small size of the hominid canine teeth (Figure 12–5) is curious and has prompted a number of hypotheses about their supposed reduction. Assuming that the ancestral proto-hominid had large canines, these teeth could have been reduced as a consequence of *weapon use* in their place (a bioenergetic model); as a consequence of *selection by females* who saw their loss as less of an aggressive threat to them and their offspring (a sexual selection model); or perhaps as a consequence of *rotatory chewing* to process more fibrous food that produced flatter surfaces on the rest of the teeth (a feeding model). However, changes in anatomical structure are usually foreshadowed by changes in behavior, and unless the exact nature of selection and the selective agent can be identified it is frequently difficult to sort out causes and effects. An analysis, using the scanning electron micro-

artifacts–any object that humans (or apes) have modified or created to perform a task.

cut marks–marks left on bone from tools used to extract the meat.

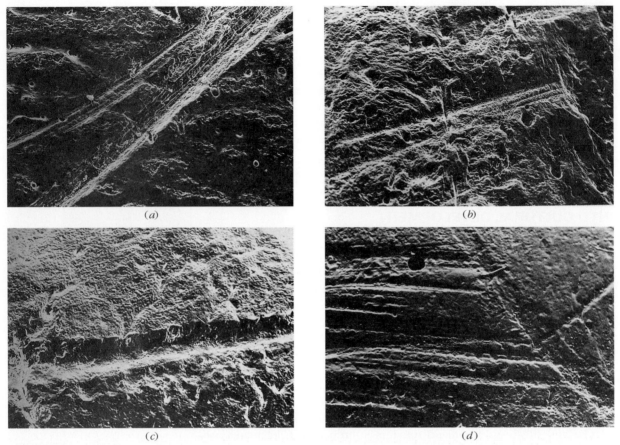

Figure 12–4 • Micrographs show (*a*) experimental cutmarks made with a stone tool on a modern bone to match (*b*) the same cutmarks found on a fossil from Kenya (FxJj site); (*c*) a toothmark produced by a modern hyena's chewing on a recent bone; and (*d*) a fossil bone from Olduvai Gorge (FLK Zinj site) showing cutmarks made by hominids using stone tools and later toothmarks made by a carnivore.

scope, of tooth shape and tooth wear patterns indicates an omnivorous diet for early humans. The dentition shows that our ancestors ate a variety of different foods with no clear specialization for meat shearing, seed grinding, or bone gnawing.

As reviewed more extensively in Chapter 10, the archaeological record is a source of information for understanding the origin of the human cultural adaptation. The earliest dated stone artifacts are found in East Africa and are approximately 2.5 million years old. The industries that are represented at these sites are called "Oldowan" or "Mode I" and represent a technology capable of producing such tools as hammer stones, simple cores, and retouched and unmodified flakes in combination with waste fragments. Isaac and Crader (1981) were among the first researchers to look at this empirical evidence and to consider what possible processes led to formation of Mode I sites.

Researchers Kathy Schick and Nicholas Toth of the Center for Research into the Anthropological Foundations of Technology (CRAFT) at

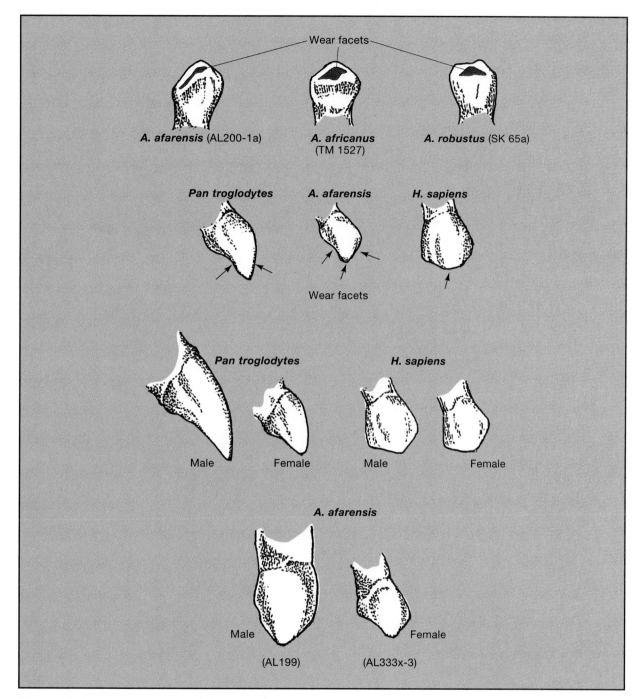

Figure 12–5 • Human canine teeth from *A. afarensis* to *H. sapiens.*

Figure 12–6 • Different hypotheses used to explain how bones and stones might be found in association at a specific site (top). Hypothesis X: whole carcasses are removed from a kill site to a safe place where stone tools are cached. Hypothesis Y: parts of a carcass are butchered and removed to a safe place for feeding in trees; butchering tools are brought in as needed. Hypothesis Z: hominids butcher a carcass and remove pieces to a home base.
Site dynamics (bottom): various influences that might affect the nature and composition of bones and artifacts at a site.
(From Isaac, 1980)

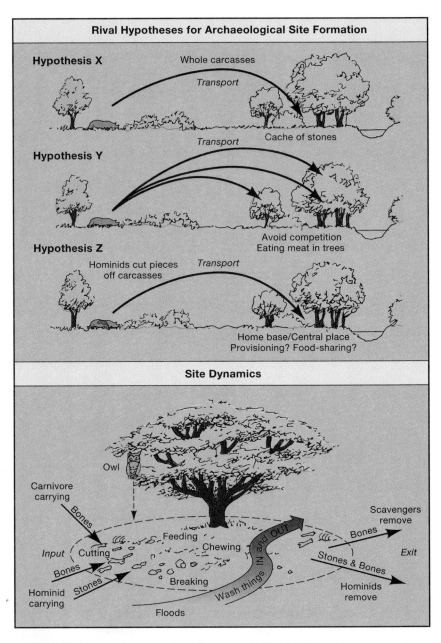

Early Stone Age–an archaeological term referring to the earliest period of stone artifact manufacture, extending from the appearance of the first stone tools at some 2.5 million years ago, to the Middle Stone Age, some 100,000 years ago.

Indiana University believe that these Early Paleolithic sites are a unique and valuable record of early hominid activities. Although these sites provide behavioral information not readily accessible from the fossils themselves, they also present a unique set of problems to researchers (Schick, 1991). Considering that they are the "*prima facie* evidence of hominid activity" **Early Stone Age** sites provide us with only a limited number of cultural features that contain information about behavior, unlike later archaeological sites that contain structures, hearths, or well-defined areas of activity. For example, understanding the usage of a tool simply from its form or shape is difficult. As Schick points out "'choppers' may not have been used to chop, nor 'scrapers' to scrape, while flakes typologically defined as 'waste' may have served as vitally useful cutting implements."

What about the nature of the site itself? Some concerns revolve around our ability to discriminate between those site patterns possibly produced by hominid activity and those produced by other (nonhominid) agencies, such as carnivores (Figure 12–6). Having drawn the conclusion that the primary nature of the site is the result of hominid presence, how could the archaeological patterns be affected by noncultural forces? For example, for sites associated with water-laid sediments, how much has the process of burial by water altered the original pattern left by the hominids? When water-transported materials are redeposited, the site will reflect this process by moving material around with or without any apparent loss. Additionally, the site may become enlarged and changed in shape beyond its original boundaries, the density of artifacts may be reduced, and changes may occur in spatial relationships between artifacts and bones. As a result, an attempt must be made to delineate patterns produced by specific hominid and non-hominid activities. In some cases archaeologists can reconstruct or conjoin flaked artifacts to their original shape from flake scatters. This **conjoined artifact** may provide evidence for on-site tool manufacture or off-site transport of raw materials (Figure 12–7).

Schick and Toth provide a case study from their excavation at Koobi Fora site FxJj 50. From the evidence excavated at this site, they conclude that by 1.5 million years hominids were no longer collecting stone material for immediate needs, presumably bringing stone onto sites, flaking or using it for that moment, and then discarding it before they moved on. At this site the pattern seems to be one of a "complex overlay of material flaked prior to incorporation to the site area, flaked further at the site, and much of it, subsequently, removed from the site."

Comparisons with chimpanzees in terms of tool transport are illuminating. Chimpanzees seem to use a "least distance" strategy in making their transport decisions, first locating a food source, in one case a nut grove, then finding a source of stones which they use to crack open the nuts. Transport of stone in these cases is never more than a few tens of meters (Boesch and Boesch, 1984). Koobi Fora and other sites in East Africa give evidence of stone transport of more than 10 kilometers from the original source to the site where it was excavated. This evidence suggests that hominids were carrying stone around on a regular basis, not for a specific objective within a short distance, but with forethought for the possible need of the material should food or other resources be encountered.

The question still remains, what do these accumulated stone artifacts and associated remains mean? Glynn Isaac (1984) developed the **home base sharing model** of early human behavior. In a number of sites

Figure 12–7 • Conjoining flake material to its original shape.

conjoined artifact—a stone tool whose various flakes and fragments have been refitted to approximate the original stone from which the tool was made.

home base sharing model—hypothesis that posits a central living place to which early hominid hunters and gatherers returned daily.

stone transport model—
hypothesis that early hominids stored stone tools for later use at certain spots on the landscape.

where tools are found in dense patches along with the bone remains of many species, Isaac suggested that humans consistently carried food and possessions back to home bases. To Isaac, these sites represented camps where different members of a social group consistently returned after foraging for necessities and where a variety of social and economic behaviors took place.

Looking at the same data, Potts (1984) noted that the animal bones were marked by both carnivore teeth and by stone tools, adding new interpretations to the ongoing debate over the significance of the associated faunal remains with regard to the way early hominids obtained food. Were these remains the result of hominid scavenging of the refuse left behind by carnivores, or were the remains the result of hominid hunting and modified later by the action of scavenging carnivores? Whatever the case, Potts put forward the argument that the high density of bone and tools represented an accumulation over a five to ten year period and argued against the home base interpretation. Some ethnographic data on modern hunters and gatherers do support this notion in that they rarely occupy a campsite for long periods of time. From the available evidence, Potts does not think we can assume any type of sharing or division of labor activities. He argues that these sites represent areas where hominids brought their food and processed it quickly with stored stone tools. He contends that home bases were not possible until hominids gained control of fire, which would have made them safe from predators.

Because the question remained as to why so many stone tools are found at some sites (more than could be reasonably explained as being simply left there in storage or "cached"), Schick (1987) proposed the **stone transport model.** She suggests that the buildup of early hominid sites was a by-product of a well-established stone transport system. She believes that stone transport was a regular behavior pattern of early humans who anticipated and planned for "unknown and unseen problems," therefore, sites should show the importation of some ready-made tools and the removal of others, which they do. Sites located near plentiful resources that the hominids used should have proportionally greater numbers of tools; and that also seems to be the case.

Isaac (1984) concluded that the data base of human evolution will always remain limited. Models, he feels, can never be fully substantiated "purely by recovering bones, stones, and pollen from layered prehistoric deposits." Besides archaeological data, potentially useful ethnographic information of modern peoples needs to be explored.

MODEL BUILDING AND ETHNOGRAPHIC RESEARCH

Before the advent of agriculture and the domestication of plants and animals about 12,000 years ago, people lived as nomadic foragers. Evidence of human occupation—tool use, cut marks on animal bones, home bases associated with the remains of collected plants, and the use of fire—all point to a hunting and gathering subsistence pattern through the Late Paleolithic. Anthropologists Richard Lee and Irven De-Vore believe that some modern hunters and gatherers can provide insight to further explain how prehistoric patterns might have worked. They found that modern groups are usually small and mobile with a fluctuating membership. Surpluses of anything were not prominent, as the mobility of the group constrains the accumulation of goods. Individuals within groups usually do not maintain exclusive rights to resources. In general, although a well-defined division of labor exists, the emphasis on the sharing of resources creates a basis for an equality of the sexes, or sexual egalitarianism. Lee and DeVore reasoned that prehistoric nomadic groups might have been organized on the same basis.

In reality, though, no social system of any modern peoples replicates past cultural stages. Although the cultural adaptations of modern hunters and gatherers may be closer to those of earlier humans than are those of technologically modern peoples, they, too, have evolved. Archaeologist Leslie Freeman believes that all social-cultural systems have specialized in response to their own unique geographical region and resources; thus, it is problematic to interpret the archaeological data solely in light of current hunter-gatherer behavior, because their specializations reflect their own recent environmental constraints. Gibson (1993: 266–267) questions the information processing capabilities of early hominids. She suggests that only after early hominids reached levels achieved by modern adolescents would sophisticated "hunting and gathering strategies involving divisions of labor and the linguistic communication of complex factual knowledge of ecology, animal behavior, and climatic fluctuations have become possible." She does not believe the early australopithecines had such capacities and that models suggesting that early hominid behaviors mimicked those of modern hunters or gatherers are probably incorrect.

RECONSTRUCTING EARLY HUMAN BEHAVIOR

Historical Overview

Three characteristics, historically, have been used to emphasize the differences between human and nonhuman primates: *bipedalism*; our *large brain*; and our ability to *communicate symbolically* with language. Using these three characteristics a number of models of early human behavior emerged to sort out what came first and why these adaptations developed.

In *Descent of Man and Selection in Relation to Sex,* Darwin (1871) believed that the human brain was the primary feature that initially separated humans from their closest relatives, the African apes. Darwin viewed increased brain size as important in terms of the technological behavior that developed from it. He believed our ancestors became skillful tool-makers, producing weapons that allowed the males to become efficient hunters. Darwin did not ignore bipedalism in his model of human evolution, but it was clear that it was of secondary importance. Darwin believed that bipedalism arose when the ancestral hominid came "to live somewhat less in the trees and more on the ground" as a response to "a change in its manner of procuring subsistence or to a change in the conditions of its native country" (Darwin, 1871:135). Darwin also helped to develop the idea of sexually dimorphic behavior. Men were courageous, inventive and sexually competitive. Females in his view, leaned more towards the nurturing, housemaking, and the reclusive aspects of behavior. Darwin saw selection as operating almost exclusively on the males, producing larger, more colorful and stronger individuals than the smaller, more drably ornamented females (as in birds). The evolution of women was viewed by the "coat-tails" approach: women evolved primarily because of men. Incest and close kin mating taboos as well as marriage practices were developed to alleviate sexual jealousy and regulate sexual behavior.

Social groups of early hominids were thought to have progressed from a "promiscuous horde," as seen to some extent among the nonhuman primates, to groups of small hunting bands made up of monogamous or polygamous units in which the only recognized kinship relations were **matrilineal.** Social evolution climaxed with the more complex patrilineally organized societies. Friedrich Engels, the socialist philosopher, saw the invention of agriculture as the primary stimulus for a patrilineal society. With domestication of plants and animals came the accumulation of property. As a consequence patrilineal descent systems evolved to control the disposition of property, including wives and children.

New Behavioral Models Emerge: Bipedalism

By the turn of the century as the number of fossil finds increased, anthropologists created new models of human evolution. These models differed from those of Darwin. The fossil discoveries showed that our earliest ancestors possessed brains similar in size to those of living apes, but differed from the apes primarily in their bipedal mode of locomotion. From the 1940s onward, discoveries of postcranial remains from many sites in South and East Africa confirmed that locomotor changes had preceded cranial changes. Bipedalism, it seemed, was an ancient form of locomotion and, perhaps, the most ancient of all of the hominid anatomical specializations. After the discovery of the Laetoli footprints, there could no longer be any doubt in the matter.

Why did bipedalism become the predominant form of hominid locomotion? The shift to bipedalism certainly was not made without costs, because it placed early humans at a disadvantage, should they find themselves in the midst of predators they could not outrun. Others argued that hominids could outdistance potential predators, if they had a

matrilineal–descent through the female line.

head start. In terms of energy consumption hominid bipedalism is as efficient as mammalian quadrupedalism, providing both are moving at normal speeds (Taylor and Roundtree, 1973).

Bipedalism provides a selective advantage in other behaviors (Figure 12–8) such as carrying objects (Hewes, 1964), displaying threat behavior (Wescott, 1967), or foraging for widely dispersed food sources (Sigmon, 1971). However, the most pervasive explanation revolves around the question of tool use, as stated by Washburn (1960) in his article entitled "Tools and Human Evolution":

> Substantial, adaptively important use of objects goes back millions of years before [tool-use] can be proved from the archaeological record. The nature

Figure 12–8 • Theories as to the origin of human bipedalism. (Adapted from Jeanne Sept)

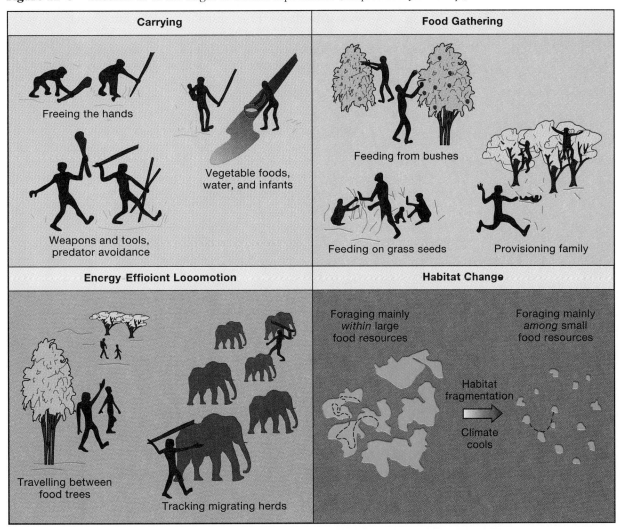

of the evidence leads to underestimating the importance of tools in the early part of human evolution and to over-estimating the intelligence of humans before *Homo sapiens*.

S. L. Washburn and Jane Lancaster's (1968) article entitled the "Evolution of Hunting," depicted men as the active and aggressive procurers of food, defending their families and supplying food through hunting. Women were viewed as dependent, staying close to a home camp, and trading sex for protection and provisions.

During the 1970s a shift in emphasis away from hunting as the major means of obtaining food was prompted by studies of many nonhuman primates, especially the chimpanzees, and by studies of modern-day hunters and gatherers. Lee, who studied the South African !Kung people, concluded that on the average, hunting produced only about 35% of the total food supply, while women's gathering activities contributed the rest. These data showed that in most modern hunter-gatherer societies women are not economically dependent on men for provisions and most often produce more than men do. Women were also not sedentary. Lee's studies showed that women were away from their base camps for at least as many hours and covered as many miles as the men. At the same time they often carried infants and other heavy objects (Figure 12–9).

The matrifocal, matrilineal nature of most non-human primate societies also altered ideas about the male role and male associations with females. From this information new models of early hominid behavior were developed to incorporate female gathering, carrying, and sharing foods with their young, emphasizing the mother–infant bond and kin relationships. In 1971 the first of these revisions appeared in an article entitled "Woman the Gatherer" by Sally Linton. Reciprocal sharing, she believed, occurred first among members of a kin group and was not

Figure 12–9 • !Kung San women foraging.

based on the establishment of sexual bonds or sexual exchange. She argued that, where hunting did occur, the first hunters shared food not with sexual partners, but with mother and siblings who had shared food with them. Additional insight was provided by Adrienne Zihlman of the University of California, Santa Cruz, who stressed that obtaining plant foods with tools was the important event that promoted the development of bipedalism, as well as the invention of ways to carry food and/or infants while walking long distances. These ideas were also supported by Lancaster (1978) and Isaac (1978, 1980). They hypothesized that males and females ranged separately in small groups and engaged in specialized activities in order to find different foods to share and then carried tools and food back to home bases (Galdikas and Teleki, 1981). Leibowitz (1983) countered by stating that food getting with tools was initially unspecialized and undifferentiated by age or sex. She believed that early hominid populations only barely replaced themselves, and that only with the invention of fire and projectile weapons, approximately during the time of *Homo erectus,* did humans finally accumulate surplus food and establish practices leading to the first appearance of a sexual division of labor.

Parker and Gibson (1979:373) developed the concept of *tool-aided extractive foraging* that focused on behaviors that were designed to benefit offspring, such as maternal food sharing, and maternal assistance in obtaining hard-to-get-at or hard-to-process foods, such as nuts, ants, termites, and honey. It was hypothesized that mothers, using tools, extracted and processed foods and then shared this food with young offspring who had not yet developed tool-using behaviors. Gibson (1993) continues by saying that "such food sharing may have selected for communication capacities similar to those of children just learning to talk." They emphasize that these practices favored the elaboration of sensorimotor and symbolic abilities similar to those of two-year-old children. This analysis based on the supposed information processing abilities of earliest hominids suggest that they had diverged from apes by increasing their tool-using, linguistic, and social capabilities. The growing dependence on tool-aided extracting foraging practices, Parker and Gibson believe, was the primary basis for the ape-human split.

Building on these ideas, King (1994) developed a **diachronic** model that viewed tool-aided extractive foraging as important not only in terms of obtaining difficult-to-get-at foods, but also in terms of the donation of information from the adults to the immatures. Her hypothesis is that the more primates are dependent on tool-aided extractive foraging the more donated information is required to accomplish difficult tasks. This situation selected for greater cognitive abilities that, in turn, resulted in the ape-human split.

Whether or not tool-aided extractive foraging was the important variable in the split of the hominids from the apes, as King (1994:101) remarks, it "is consistent with the suggestion that hominids donated

diachronic–historical; extending through time.

FRONTIERS

Were Our Ancestors Hunters or Scavengers?[1]

by John D. Speth

Modern humans frequently eat meat, and often in prodigious amounts. The fact that we eat animal flesh, doesn't seem like anything noteworthy or unusual, and might seem almost trivial were it not for the fact that our closest living relatives, the primates, for the most part do not. If we are descended from a primate ancestor, and primates are largely vegetarians, then hunting, especially of large and dangerous prey, must somehow have played a pivotal role in transforming a small-brained quadrupedal ape into a brainy, tool-making, bipedal human. Charles Darwin, in fact, believed that hunting was so fundamental that he used it as the basis for a theory of human origins that, somewhat modified, still remains very persuasive today.[2]

In its modern form, Darwin's "hunting hypothesis," holds that this transition began during the Miocene, when global climatic conditions steadily deteriorated, becoming cooler, drier, and more markedly seasonal. Many species of great ape, adapted to the forest, were unable to cope with these dramatic habitat changes and became extinct. However, some populations successfully adapted to the changing conditions by turning to the one obvious new resource that the expanding grasslands offered—huge herds of grazing antelopes and other herbivores. But to kill these animals, these puny "proto-hominids" needed effective, sharp-edged cutting and piercing tools. Gradually, a positive feedback relationship emerged, in which increasing reliance on tools by the hominids favored a bipedal or two-legged stance in order to free their hands, as well as greater intelligence (and hence larger brain size) as they came to rely more and more on tools

and other forms of learned or culturally mediated behavior.

However, despite its elegance and compelling simplicity, various lines of evidence are now beginning to raise serious doubts about the validity of this "hunting hypothesis." The new evidence and insights are coming from many different sources, including detailed ethnographic studies of the world's last remaining groups of hunters and gatherers, as well as from the fields of archaeology and taphonomy.

Hunters and gatherers (or foragers) are peoples who live entirely or largely without agriculture or animal husbandry. In such societies, there is a fairly strong positive correlation between latitude and proportion of meat (or fish) in the diet. Not unexpectedly, in the arctic and subarctic plant foods contribute only minimally to the diet.[3] As one continues toward the equator, the contribution of plant foods to the larder of many forager groups, particularly those living far from the sea, steadily increases, reaching as much as 60 to 80 percent by weight of the total food intake among many of the groups that live in the tropics.[4]

These observations have led to a change in perspective which, in turn, has led anthropologists to question whether, if plant foods constitute a major part of the diet among many tropical latitude foragers today, was this perhaps also true of early hominid diet in the distant past, since our earliest ancestors evolved in the African tropics. This suggests that the "hunting hypothesis" may be overly simplistic in downplaying or ignoring the role of plant foods (and of course nonsubsistence factors) in this process.

Since the pioneering work of the Leakeys in the 1950s and 1960s at Olduvai Gorge, Tanzania, our understanding of the archaeological record of early hominids has improved dramatically. The repeated association of tools and bones seemed incontrovertible proof that early hominids were avid and highly successful hunters.

While archaeology was uncovering "hard" evidence of past human activities, another field—taphonomy—was beginning

to explore other issues. Taphonomy is the study of the processes that can alter and distort an assemblage of bones from the time an animal dies until its bones become incorporated into the fossil record.[5] Taphonomic studies began to make it clear that the mere juxtaposition of stone tools and animal bones did not demonstrate that the bones were the food remains of early hominids. Flowing water could have brought the two together in a channel deposit, or hyenas and humans could each have taken advantage of the same shade tree but at slightly different times, producing a fortuitous association of bones and tools. However, some of the early sites where stone tools and animal bones occur together do in fact represent places where hominids butchered animal carcasses. The best evidence is provided by unambiguous cutmarks on many of the bones produced by sharp-edged flakes, and by use-wear studies of some of the stone tools themselves, which reveal distinct polishes on their edges shown by experimental work to be the product of meat-cutting.[6] Other, somewhat less direct and hence more controversial evidence includes the fact that bones of many different species occur together in a single place, a pattern clearly distinct from that found at hyena or lion kills.[7, 8]

But the taphonomic studies of these sites have raised a different issue, one that has far-reaching implications for the "hunting hypothesis." Many of the bones at these sites have gnaw marks, punctures, and other clear evidence of carnivore damage. Additionally, the less dense parts of limb elements, those with lots of porous, "spongy" tissue, are almost always conspicuously underrepresented. Detailed studies of the feeding behavior of many different carnivores suggest that these bones have most likely been destroyed or carried off by hyenas.

Did humans kill the animals and hyenas scavenge the remains that littered the campsite once its human occupants had left? This scenario of course would be entirely compatible with the traditional "man the hunter" view. Or did lions or hyenas kill the animals and humans merely scavenge the carcasses for edible scraps of meat and marrow after the carnivores had finished feeding or were driven off by the humans? Today, most scholars are now convinced that the latter is more likely.[9]

This discovery marks a radical turning point in our understanding of our distant past. Archaeologists have often been criticized for relying too heavily on analogies with living primates and hunter-gatherers in arriving at their reconstructions of the past. The fear is that we are simply "creating" a past that is nothing more than a mirror image of the present. But in the hunting/scavenging debate we have discovered a pattern in the past that has no modern analogue. No living primate or human group obtains its meat primarily by scavenging.

If we accept the view that early hominids were basically scavengers, not hunters, what role did scavenging play in hominid origins and evolution?

Observations suggest that early hominid scavengers would have been most likely to encounter the partial remains of medium-sized animals from which they could have gleaned scraps of meat and marrow. If they transported the edible parts back to a central place to process them in comparative safety (and perhaps to share with other members of the group), these marginal skeletal elements are the ones that we would expect to find in greatest abundance in early hominid archaeological sites such as at Olduvai. Initial study of the animal bones from several of the major Olduvai localities, in fact, found that these elements far outnumbered bones from more meaty parts of carcasses, seemingly clinching the scavenging argument.

But the debate didn't stop there. Were early hominids passive or active scavengers, that is, did they have to wait until hyenas and other predators had finished feeding on a carcass or were they instead capable of driving them away soon after the kill? Scavenging studies have revealed interesting facets of hyena behavior, which shed light on this question. During the dry season, when many of the herbivores stay much closer to permanent water sources, hyenas often leave lion kills untouched or only partly devoured. The reason for this seasonal difference in hyena feeding behavior appears to be related to their fear of lions, which are much more likely to ambush them in the dense thickets near these water holes. This suggests that the opportunities for hominid scavenging are likely to have been greater during the dry season than during the rainy season, and close to water sources, assuming of course that early hominids were less intimidated in vegetated areas by lions than modern hyenas seem to be.

The idea of hominids scavenging where hyenas feared to go may not be as far-fetched as it might at first seem. Hyenas and lions do much of their hunting at night. On the other hand, early hominids, like ourselves, may not have been very adept at foraging in the dark and may instead have been most active during the heat of the day, taking advantage of a time when the big carnivores are much less active.

Obviously at stake in this entire debate is much more than just the issue of whether early hominids were scavengers rather than hunters, but whether they actually possessed the necessary cognitive and organizational sophistication to plan, coordinate, and carry out successful hunts of large and dangerous prey. And in the process we are gradually piecing together a picture of where we came from, tracing the complex chain of events that gradually transformed a small-brained quadrupedal ape into the unique creature that we are today.

Notes

1. Portions of this chapter are reprinted by permission of the publisher from John D. Speth, "Carnivory," in R. Dulbecco, ed., *Encyclopedia of Human Biology*, vol. 2 (Copyright © 1991 by Academic Press, Inc.).

2. Charles Darwin, *The Descent of Man and Selection in Relation to Sex* (London: Murray, 1871).

3. Brian Hayden, "Subsistence and Ecological Adaptations of Modern Hunter/Gatherers," in Robert S. O. Harding and Geza Teleki, eds., *Omnivorous Primates: Gathering and Hunting in Human Evolution* (New York: Columbia University Press, 1981), pp. 344–421.

4. Richard B. Lee, "What Hunters Do for a Living, or, How to Make Out on Scarce Resources," in Richard B. Lee and Irven DeVore, eds., *Man the Hunter* (Chicago: Aldine, 1968), pp. 30–48.

5. Anna K. Behrensmeyer and Andrew P. Hill, *Fossils in the Making: Vertebrate Taphonomy and Paleoecology* (Chicago: University of Chicago Press, 1980); C. K. Brain, *The Hunters or the Hunted? An Introduction to African Cave Taphonomy* (Chicago: University of Chicago Press, 1981).

6. Lawrence H. Keeley and Nicholas Toth, "Microwear Polishes on Early Stone Tools from Koobi Fora, Kenya," *Nature* 293 (1981): 464–465.

7. Henry T. Bunn, "Patterns of Skeletal Representation and Hominid Subsistence Activities at Olduvai Gorge, Tanzania, and Koobi Fora, Kenya," *Journal of Human Evolution* 15 (1986): 673–690.

8. Shipman, "Scavenging or Hunting in Early Hominids: Theoretical Framework and Tests," *American Anthropologist* 88 (1986): 27–43.

9. Henry T. Bunn and Ellen M. Kroll, "Systematic Butchery by Plio/Pleistocene Hominids at Olduvai Gorge, Tanzania," *Current Anthropology* 27 (1986): 431–452.

John D. Speth is currently Professor and Curator of North American Archaeology at the Museum of Anthropology, University of Michigan, Ann Arbor.

more information than did other primates, and that information donation increased during human evolution." This observation is important
for the discussion in Chapter 14 on the evolution of childhood as a
stage in the human life cycle.

In 1981, Owen Lovejoy of Kent State University proposed a model of
human evolution in his publication "The Origin of Man." In this model,
tool use, hunting, gathering, or scavenging were not the primary selective agents for human bipedalism. Rather the success of the earliest
hominids was due primarily to their ability to increase their reproductive rate and to lower their rate of infant mortality. He suggested that
early hominids, in contrast to chimpanzees who produce an infant only
once in about four years and who have usually only five live offspring
in a lifetime, were able to increase their reproductive success by reducing the mobility of lactating mothers and by being provisioned by
bipedal males. In this model, gathering became an important male activity rather than a female one. Lovejoy proposes that a number of in-
novative primate behaviors evolved. For example, provisioning of de-
pendents on the whole is not a characteristic of primates, and even
minimal sharing of food by "tolerated scrounging" is rare (Isaac, 1978).
In addition, using the common chimpanzee as an example, the vast
majority of sharing (more than 80%) occurs within the matrifocal family. Further, in contrast to the Lovejoy model, chimpanzee females are
mobile, quite capable of carrying their young while moving across the
terrain and at the same time finding food for themselves. There seems to
be no relationship between females on the move and higher infant mortality, and there is no reason to suspect that early human females were
not as hairy as chimpanzees which would allow their infants to cling effectively to them while traveling bipedally. Other data suggest that
chimpanzee reproduction may not be as different from that of modern
human female hunter and gatherers as the Lovejoy model assumes.

Parker (1987) revised the Lovejoy model by claiming that females
were not exclusively provisioned but were otherwise "courted" by
males with gifts of especially nutritious and/or hard-to-get foods. Bipedal behavior would have had a selective advantage of allowing the
females to accurately assess the size of the male, the size of his gift, and
the size and tumescence of his genitals. According to Parker bipedal locomotion arose through sexual selection; it was a part of the male reproductive strategy of "nuptial," or courtship, feeding of estrous females. The model is consistent with some primate field data on pygmy
chimpanzees that show males and females sharing food during copulations (Kurodo, 1984).

The possibility that environmental change had something to do with
the emergence of bipedalism has been promoted by several authors
(Brain, 1980; Boaz and Burckle, 1985; Vrba, 1988). They believe that
there is good evidence to suggest that about 5.5 million years ago at
the close of the Miocene and, later, about 2.5 million years ago, a shift

to cooler world climates resulted in major forests giving way to grasslands. During the earlier shift, bipedalism may have arisen as an adaptive response to covering the distances required by larger home ranges in the relatively treeless grasslands (Vrba, 1988; Stanley, 1992) (Figure 12–10). This model states that a shift to open savanna environments stimulated greater reliance upon a bipedal form of locomotion that in turn may have had something to do with increased tool use, and the beginnings of the hominization process. However, recent evidence from studies of forest-living chimpanzees, to a certain extent, contradicts this notion. Boesch-Ackermann and Boesch (1994:10–11) compared the behavior of chimpanzees in the Tai Forest with chimpanzee populations living in more open environments and have shown that "the forest chimpanzees use more tools, make them in more different ways, hunt more frequently and more often in groups, and show more frequent cooperation and food sharing." These authors believe that the environment, no doubt, plays an important role in the evolution of behavior, but disagree that the open savanna had much to do with the behaviors that we have come to believe characterize the early hominids. In addition they cite new paleoecological studies that suggest our ancestors, in fact, lived in tropical rain forests (Bailey et al., 1989; Rayner et al., 1993).

Brain Size

The advance of paleoanthropological knowledge of human behavior depends not only on new discoveries of fossil crania and brain endocasts, but also on the advancement in knowledge about the workings of the modern human brain. The brain is the repository of culture and it moderates all conscious behavior from the most biologically expedient to the most sublime. The large size and complexity of the human brain form the most important components of the anatomical and phylogenetic definition of the genus *Homo*. Our knowledge of the evolution of the brain is derived from neurophysiological and anatomical studies of living species, and comparative studies of endocasts of fossil species.

From about two million years onward some selective advantage resulted in larger brain size leading to greater intellectual and symbolic abilities. The expansion of the brain was, no doubt, related to a number of factors that might have included a shift in the way humans procured food, for example, towards a greater reliance upon hunting or more effective scavenging of larger game, aided by an increasingly sophisticated technology that produced stone tools.

The evolution of large brains, however, was not without its drawbacks. First, larger brain size in the adult human meant larger brain size in the neonate, creating more complications in the birth process, exacerbated by a pelvis designed for bipedal locomotion (Figure 12–11).

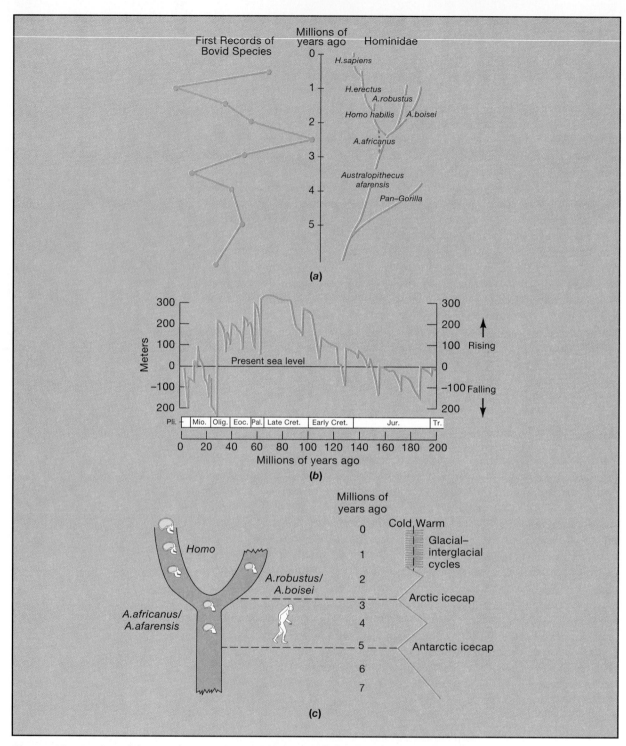

Figure 12–10 • Bipedalism and environmental change. Various indicators of environmental change: (*a*) the appearance of certain species of herbivores (bovids), (*b*) lowered sea levels, and (*c*) the expansion of Arctic and Antarctic ice caps suggest cooler world climates in which forest areas would be replaced by more treeless grasslands, possibly encouraging selection for bipedal locomotion in certain groups of Late Miocene hominoids.

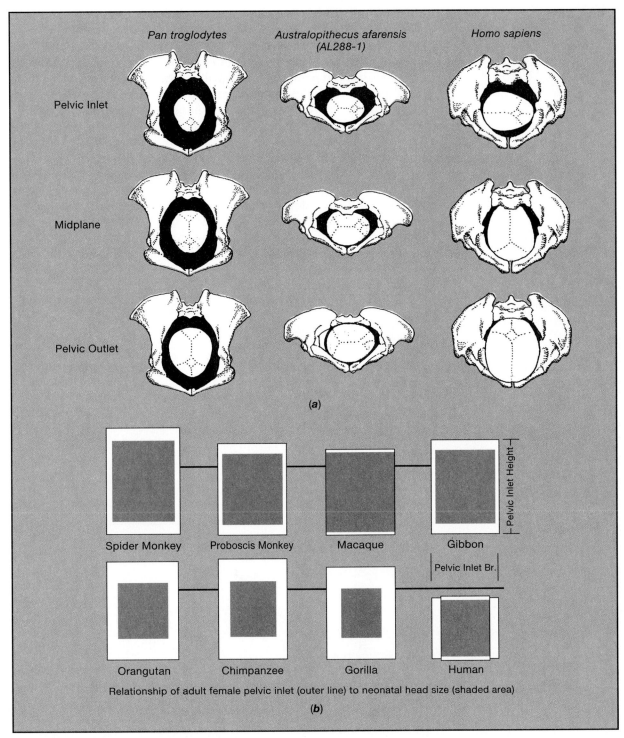

Figure 12–11 • Pelvic size and neonate delivery in various primates, showing the very large head size of the human neonate. ([*a*] From Tague and Lovejoy, 1986; [*b*] From Schultz, 1941)

The smaller-brained *Australopithecus* probably had no more problems with birth than chimpanzee mothers (Leutenegger, 1987), because neonate head size was most likely smaller than the opening of the birth canal. As the brain enlarged (Figure 12–12), however, several factors emerged that compensated for a smaller birth canal. First, infants were born at increasingly less mature states which minimized head size, and, second, the female pelvis changed in shape to maximize the area of the birth canal. Although these solutions alleviated some obstetrical problems, they caused others. At some point human infants lost their ability to successfully cling to the bodies of their mothers and possessed at birth such poorly developed locomotor skills that much greater effort and care was required from the mother. At this point a sexual division of labor may have developed, causing males and females to join together in more stable and longer term bonds. Modifications of the pelvis involving expansion of the birth canal may also have placed certain limitations on female locomotion, especially on running.

Figure 12–12 • Brain growth curve in human infant and chimpanzee from conception to adulthood. (From Vrba, 1994)

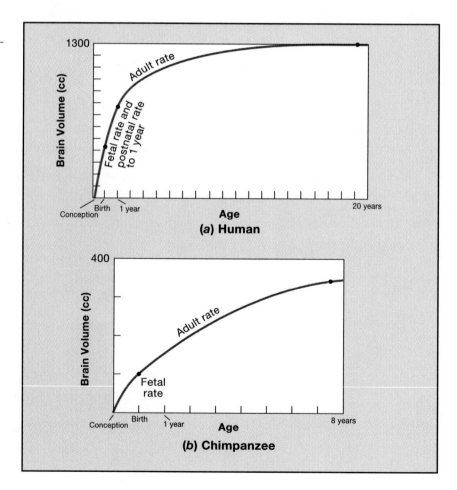

Cerebral Laterality: Two Brains in One

In Chapter 5, the basic structures of the mammalian brain were outlined. Continuing this discussion, the neocortex is divided into two cerebral hemispheres. Each, as early research proved, has somewhat different functions. But what functions do the two hemispheres divide up and to what degree? Some speculated that these differences were minor and that each hemisphere could take over the functions of the other. Others thought that there might be two entirely different brains, connected together only by a nerve tract passing from one side to the other. Actually, between the hemispheres lies a large tract of fibers, called the **corpus callosum** (Latin, meaning "hard body"), that connects the two halves.

Early investigations into the functions of the right and left hemispheres were conducted by Roger Sperry and his colleagues at the California Institute of Technology, who began a series of unique tests on individuals who had "split brains." These patients had histories of "grand mal" epilepsy, a neuroelectrical storm in the brain that disrupts all activity, and had undergone radical neurosurgical resections of the corpus callosum. Surgeons hoped that this procedure would prevent the epileptic seizure from spreading across to both hemispheres when it appeared. The operation was quite successful in not only reducing the severity of the attacks, but also in reducing the frequency of them in both hemispheres. Even more surprising, the patients seemed to have no mental impairment whatsoever. What was a major structure like the *corpus callosum* for if cutting it produced no obvious defects? (Figure 12–13). In order to find out Sperry carefully designed a series of experiments. He used the fact that the medial side of the retina of the eye sends fibers into the optic nerve that cross over to the opposite-side cerebral hemisphere. In contrast, the outside, or lateral side, of the retinal surface projects to the same-side cerebral hemisphere. If a split-brain patient looked straight ahead, then Sperry could flash visual information to the right visual field which would end up only in the left visual cortex and vice-versa. But it was necessary to flash the information for only an instant. Otherwise, the patient's eyes would wander over the screen, and the information would wind up in the other hemisphere.

Sperry could now test the capabilities of each isolated hemisphere. A word flashed to only the left hemisphere could be spoken and could be written by the right hand, but not the left. A different word flashed to the right hemisphere could not be spoken or written by the right hand, but could be written by the left hand! Sperry received the Nobel Prize in 1981 for his work in demonstrating that speech, writing, and calculation are centered in the left hemisphere. The right hemisphere has a number of capabilities that the left does not have. It can copy three-dimensional diagrams whereas the left cannot. The right hemi-

corpus callosum–the fiber tract connecting the two halves of the brain across the midline.

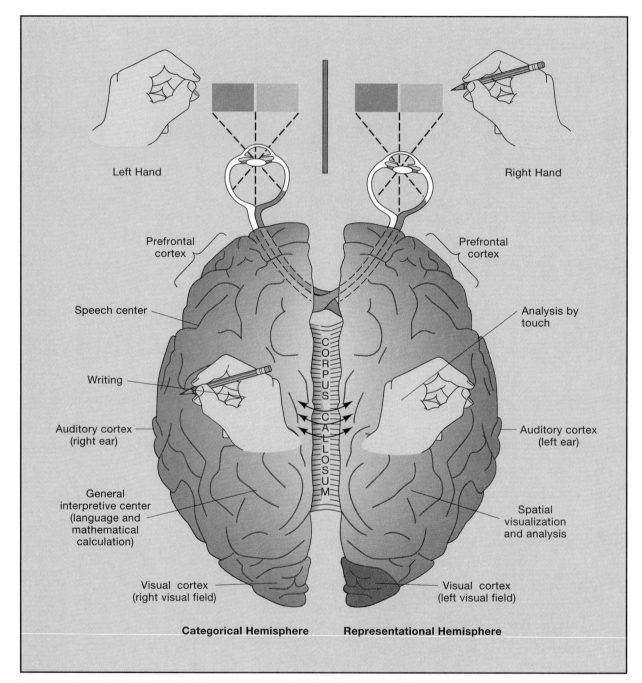

Figure 12–13 • The "split brain," showing the cerebral hemispheres and the corpus callosum.

sphere can understand speech, can think abstractly, and may be important in the appreciation of music.

Why did evolution produce this unusual specialization of the two
sides of the cerebrum? One suggestion is that only one hemisphere is
needed to control a midline structure, such as the tongue. Probably by
chance, the left hemisphere assumed this function. Similarly, handedness may have evolved because greater hand skill, whether the right or
the left, was needed in early hominid tool making. Another suggestion is that as the hominid brain expanded, the left assumed the computer-like capability of calculation and the right became memory storage. (However, current popular thinking that people are either
"right-brained" or "left-brained," and that "right-brained" people are
artistic–intuitive while "left-brained" people are practical–analytic, is
faulty and simplistic.)

Speech Areas of the Cortex

In 1863 the French physical anthropologist and physician Pierre-Paul
Broca announced a discovery based on autopsies of brains of individuals who had lost the ability to speak coherently prior to death. In all instances he found that the brain had sustained an injury to the "posterior
third of the third frontal convolution." He correctly inferred from this
observation that speech ability was localized in this particular part of
the brain, now known as **Broca's Area.** Individuals with brain damage
to this area can utter only short disjointed fragments of sentences, if he
or she can speak at all. The most surprising aspect of Broca's findings
was that the brain injuries were all only in the left hemisphere. With a
sample size of eight cases, Broca shied away from the conclusion that
the speech center was always on the left side of the brain. Yet years of
subsequent research have confirmed that this is the case in 95% of individuals. Broca was one of the first researchers to discover that the cerebral hemispheres have different functions.

In 1874 the German physiologist, Karl Wernicke, located an area of
the temporal lobe that is the center for understanding speech, now
known as **Wernicke's Area.** Damage to Wernicke's Area results in lack
of comprehension of both spoken and written language, although the
patient can still speak. This area of the brain lies just above the auditory cortex, the part of the temporal lobe that analyzes sound. Like
Broca's Area, Wernicke's Area shows differential development in the
two hemispheres: it is bigger on the left side. Interestingly, Wernicke's
Area is also larger on the left than on the right side in the chimpanzee,
which lacks verbal language (Figure 12–14). Speech loss can occur if
other parts of the brain are injured. For example, if motor areas of the
brain that control the muscles of the vocal apparatus are damaged and
paralysis occurs, speech is also affected.

Broca's Area–portion of the
cerebral cortex (posterior part of
the inferior frontal gyrus, usually
on the left side) that is essential
for the motor control of speech.

Wernicke's Area–portion of the
cerebral cortex (parts of the parietal and temporal lobes near the
lateral sulcus, usually on the left)
that is responsible for understanding and formulating coherent speech.

Figure 12–14 • Language centers of the brain.

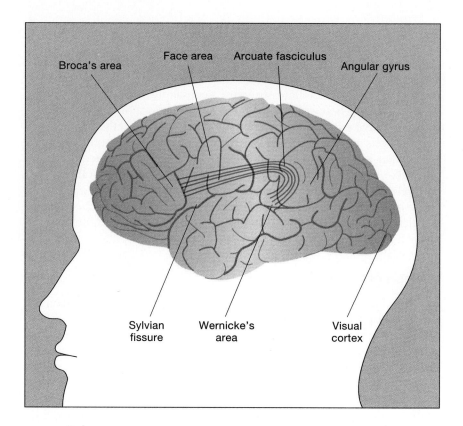

Language

The debate involving the first appearance of spoken language focuses on whether or not it played a role in the evolution of modern *Homo sapiens* (Conkey, 1980). Alternatively, language may have emerged earlier in human evolution, perhaps, as far back as the earliest members of the genus *Homo,* but at what point and to what extent is unclear. King (1994:131) believes that human communicative behavior, including social information transfer and language, should be studied as a continuum with that of other primates. Human language can best be understood when compared and contrasted with other forms of information transfer that do not rely on language.

In 1957, Noam Chomsky of MIT was one of the first researchers to challenge the idea that language is an exclusively cultural phenomena. He argued that the way in which language develops makes it more likely that linguistic ability is innate or instinctual. He surmised that the brain must have a built-in program that can put together an inexhaustible array of sentences from a limited number of words. Because sentences that individuals produce often consist of novel combinations of words it would be difficult to explain such creations solely on the basis of past experiences. He further observes that children before the age of two learn grammatical structure rapidly without any formal training. More recently Stephen Pinker (1994) also of MIT has reaffirmed the Chomskian position, but disagrees with Chomsky in that language abilities emerged as a result of an increase in brain size passing a cultural threshold with the emergence of modern *Homo sapiens.* Pinker believes that spoken language, in some primitive form, emerged as the result of natural selection early in prehistory. He asserts that the human brain enlarged as a result of the gradual elaboration of language structures and that language provided a survival advantage for early hominids as they developed a hunting and gathering mode of subsistence.

Provocative as these ideas are, how can they be tested? At the onset the task is formidable because scarcely any direct evidence exists, except rare endocasts of fossil brains that are seldom detailed enough to conclusively show the presence or absence of language centers. Other evidence is circumstantial and involves examinations of (1) the prehistoric material culture, (2) anatomical reconstructions of fossil vocal tracts, and (3) linguistic analysis of modern languages in order to reconstruct ancient forms. Each of these will be examined in turn.

Lynn Schepartz (1993) of the University of Michigan provides us with some useful definitions of language. First, she notes that language has both internal (cerebral) and external (vocal tract) components. The internal components involve conscious thought that includes "complex mapping and simulation of the world" around us. The external components are basically behavioral expressions that include gestures, vocalizations, and articulate speech. **Speech** is defined as "a coordination of activity of both the brain and the vocal apparatus." Spoken language is unique to humans. The nonhuman primates cannot be taught to speak in any human sense because their brains do not possess the anatomical structures for speech. With the evolution of intelligence human ability to communicate more effectively through language must also have developed.

In determining the origin of language some believe that it is important to know when humans first gained the ability to name objects. Washburn (1960) believed that the situation which originally led to naming was tool making of a kind more complicated than that performed by wild chimpanzees. Others believe that some early form of language may have arisen as a more sophisticated system for communicating the location and type of dispersed food, or of important individuals such as close kin. Such vocal communication may have also become more elaborate as a response to the requirements of coordinating individuals in cooperative hunting (Parker, 1985; Parker and Gibson, 1979).

Aiello and Dunbar's hypothesis, that the size of the brain is the key to understanding cognitive ability and language, is based on a close relationship between relative neocortex size, group size and the amount

Speech–the set of verbal sounds that is used by humans in language.

of time needed to devote to "social grooming." They believe that group size is limited by the number of relationships that an individual can successfully monitor and this, in turn, is limited by the relative size of the neocortex. They predict that larger hominid group size would have been too great to be sustained by methods of social grooming such as those used by nonhuman primates, and conclude that language evolved as a binding mechanism in order to use social time more efficiently. These authors suggest that language would be the logical adaptation that would allow early hominids to exchange information about individuals who might not be immediately present, thus maintaining group cohesion and also coordinating group members' behavior that would become increasingly more difficult to do through personal contact alone.

Certainly as time went on language would have played a more important role in encoding complex cultural rules involving ritual, the control and regulation of reproduction and resource distribution, and other rules that ritually transform people's reproductive status through important rites of passage (Hockett and Asher, 1964).

William Calvin (1994: 102) of the University of Washington School of Medicine believes:

> We need to understand how our ancestors remodeled the ape's symbolic repertoire and enhanced it by inventing syntax. Wild chimpanzees use about three dozen different vocalizations to convey about three dozen different meanings. They may repeat a sound to intensify its meaning, but they do not string together three sounds to add a new word to their vocabulary.

Humans use about the same number of sounds as do chimpanzees, however, in human language it is not the sounds that have meaning but the combination of sounds put together as words. About the evolution of language, Calvin ponders the question of how and at what point our ancestors replaced the ape system of "one sound, one meaning" with the human system that uses individually meaningless sounds in meaningful combinations.

Attempts to answer this question use interpretations based on the archaeological record. In terms of language, to what extent can technological ability be correlated with neurological complexity? Toth and Schick (1992) caution that technological change is Lamarckian in that it occurs according to need and to demand. Unlike anatomical change that often occurs quite slowly, technological development usually proceeds independently at a much faster rate. As Toth and Schick point out, "the challenge is to identify what patterns of material culture in the prehistoric record have implications for intelligence and language."

The earliest Oldowan or Mode I stone tools are technologically quite simple, consisting mainly of discarded cores used for flake production. Toth and Schick believe there is little evidence that early hominid tool makers might have had a "mental template" for constructing Oldowan tools. The final shape of the "tool" was probably more determined by a matter of size, shape, and raw material of the rock being flaked. Wynn (1988) agrees, and believes that the construction of Oldowan tools involved only rote learning of a sequence of specific actions that could be transmitted visually.

On the other hand there are at least four factors that suggest early hominids had greater forethought than is shown by modern apes: (1) Recent experiments in ape stone tool making shows that the judgment for the correct angle and force of impact required to match early stone tools may be beyond the intellectual capabilities of chimpanzees (Figure 12–15). (2) Toth (1985) has shown that these early tools were flaked usually by right-handed individuals. He points out that flakes were most often struck off the cores in a clockwise turning direction, consistent with right-hand working (Figure 12–16). We know that handedness is related to cerebral dominance, and whereas asymmetrical specializations of the hemispheres can be demonstrated in the non-human primates, in humans handedness is considered as a preadaptation for language (Falk, 1980). (3) Within Mode I technology, transport of raw materials and food occurred over considerably greater distances than that observed for chimpanzees. (4) The excavated accumulations also reveal a more intensive use of tools.

Figure 12–15 • Kanzi, a pygmy chimpanzee, making a stone tool.

Mode II, or the Acheulean, tool tradition presents a different picture. The skills required to make these artifacts are much more sophisticated. Acheulean tool makers had the ability to conceive of a predetermined shape and to construct it. They had the ability to flake and produce a straight cutting edge and, apparently, with cultural standardization, they could produce consistently shaped tools. If the Acheulean tool makers had limited or no language skills, their geographic dispersion would have made cultural uniformity difficult. This being the case it could have accounted for the lack of Acheulean tools in the Far East.

Paleoenvironmental evidence suggests that few differences existed between Middle and Upper Paleolithic mammalian faunas in Europe. Evidence also shows that in both periods game drives and selective ambush hunting indicate extensive cognitive capacities for earlier, as well as later, forms of *Homo sapiens* (Chase, 1989). As a consequence, archaic *sapiens* populations, including Neandertal, were probably capable of a wide variety of procurement strategies that show cognitive ability equal to that of modern *Homo sapiens*. The recent excavations at Kebara Cave, Israel, reveal specialized uses of the living area by Neandertals that suggest substantial cognitive ability. For example, hearths and a thick accumulation of bone characterized by cut-marks and relatively little carnivore gnawing were found in the central area of the cave. There was also evidence of the removal of bone and larger lithic refuse from the central area, perhaps an indication of cleanliness (Bar-Yosef and Vandermeersch, 1993).

Figure 12–16 • Handedness and tool use. Flakes 1–3 are removed from their core, one after the other, in a clockwise direction characteristic of an individual who is right-handed.

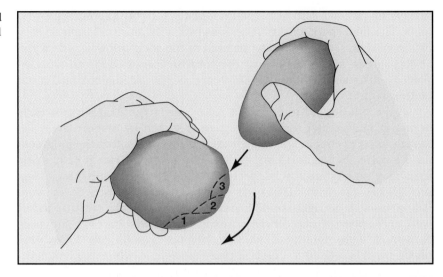

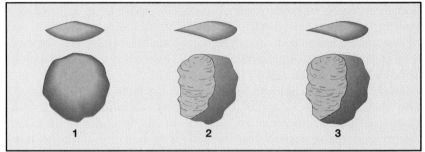

Art, Symbolism, and Speech

Most examples of artwork are unquestionably associated with modern *Homo sapiens,* and they are found relatively late in the record, well after 35,000 years ago. Although it is rare, the evidence for Lower and Middle Paleolithic art, not associated with modern humans, is, perhaps, more to the point of understanding the origin of language. Although earlier archaic *Homo sapiens* may have lacked the modern ability to verbalize, their conceptual ability witnessed in their artwork supports the notion that they possessed speech to some extent (Table 12–2). The oldest example of artwork of this age, thus far discovered, is a figurine of exaggerated female human form dated to about 230,000 years ago that was excavated from the Acheulean site of Berekhat Ram, Israel (Figure 12–17) (Goren-Inbar, 1986). A more recent find, dating about 100,000 years ago from the Middle Paleolithic site of Tata in Hungary, is a mammoth tooth carved into a plaque and subsequently covered with red ochre powder (Schwarcz, 1982). Later within this period from the La Ferrassie burials in France engraved pieces and notched bone were discovered (Simek, 1992). The earliest Mousterian burials themselves should also be considered as evidence for symbolic behavior, as

Table 12–2 • Behavioral Characteristics and Language of Modern Humans[1]
Prism-shaped stone-tool blades produced by indirect blows
A well-developed bone/antler/ivory technology
Very small tools (microliths) used as part of composite tools
Mechanical devices such as the spear thrower, and bow and arrow technology
Heat treatment of raw materials to enhance their flaking properties
Projectile points and knives produced by controlled pressure, versus percussion
Artifacts consisting of ground stones
Ceramic vessels
Needles for sewing
Wall (parietal) and movable (mobiliary) art representative of living subjects

[1]These characteristics are associated with anatomically modern humans, whether due to increased cerebral capacity or accumulated cultural evolution

Adapted from Toth and Schick (1993).

the human body becomes a symbol once it is provided a burial (Schepartz, 1993).

Contemporary with these art forms are examples of objects that were, presumably, used as body ornamentation. This evidence provides additional insight into the evolution of symbolic behavior and speech. Ornamentation is one form of communication (Wobst, 1977). Ornaments name individuals, either their owner or their maker, and the use of shared ornamentation can be used to identify a member of a group (Wiessner, 1990). Alexander Marshak (1989) has offered evidence for body ornamentation beginning with the Lower Paleolithic, believing that as early as 110,000 years ago pierced animal teeth and bone were used as beads or pendants. Although some of this evidence has been questioned (White, 1993), clearly the "explosion" of ornamentation and art in the European Upper Paleolithic represents:

> [A] continuation and intensification of a symbolic capacity that is evident for earlier populations of hominids. This shift in the frequency of symbolic evidence marks a change in the use of symbolism (rather than its evolution) unrelated to the origin of modern *Homo sapiens* (Schepartz, 1993).

Anatomical Evidence for Speech

Interest in the evolution of cognition, such as sequential thinking and planning, has been revived by Binford (1989). Although most recognize the possibility that hominid behavior in the past may not have been cognitively structured as it is now, paleoneurologists are in complete agreement that the brains of archaic *Homo sapiens,* especially the Neandertal's, are morphologically similar to modern human brains.

Figure 12–17 • Acheulean figure from Berekhat Ram.

In the early 1970s, Lieberman and Crelin (1971) began pioneering research on vocal tract reconstruction, comparing the shape and position of the tract in modern humans and infants, nonhuman primates and fossil hominids. They described the supra laryngeal vocal tract of the Neandertal male from La Chapelle and compared it to that of a modern human newborn. In both they found lacking the elongation and bending of the tract that develops later in young juveniles of modern *Homo sapiens*. These authors concluded that the La Chapelle male, like the modern newborn, was limited in his ability to produce some vowels and consonants and stated that, "Even if he were able to make optimum use of his speech-producing apparatus, the constraints of his supra laryngeal vocal tract would make it impossible for him to produce 'articulate' human speech, i.e., the full range of phonetic contrasts employed by modern man" (1971:217). They conceded, however, that the brain itself might have been "sufficiently well developed for him to have established a language based on the speech signals at his command."

Following this work were a number of critical studies of other specimens of archaic *Homo sapiens* indicating, contrary to Lieberman and Crelin, that many of them might be capable of human speech. Other criticisms were leveled on the basis that the La Chapelle fossil is too pathologically altered to justify any conclusions on speech capabilities (Frayer, 1992) and that errors may have been made in the original reconstruction (Houghton, 1993). Kathleen Gibson of the University of Texas (1994) showed that the range of variation in the shape of modern human vocal tracts is not as limited as previously thought. She has demonstrated that Neandertal-like configurations of the tract have been observed in certain modern individuals who were capable of modern speech. Certainly, more comparative anatomical work on vocal tracts and the exact relationship of speech to individual variations of shape and position is needed.

Additional insights into the language origins problem have come from an entirely different corner of research, that of linguistic analysis. Johanna Nichols of the Department of Slavic Languages at the University of California, Berkeley, recently proposed that the common ancestor of modern languages must be at least 100,000 years old. In a paper presented at the annual meeting of the American Association for the Advancement of Science (1994), she described her analysis of grammatical features, including transitive and intransitive verbs, subject—object relationships, and the gendering of nouns and singular/plural distinctions. She assigned an average age of 5,000 years for each language family and a branching rate of 1.6 languages per family. She concluded that, if there were a single common language, it would take about 100,000 years for it to differentiate into the number of different languages that presently exist.

The varied lines of evidence presented in this section show that a relationship exists between language and technology that preceded the late arrival of modern *Homo sapiens*. From the evidence at hand the exact links between them remain insufficiently clear to allow a completely satisfactory reconstruction of the evolution of language and cognition. Certainly more information is necessary from many fields such as neurology in order to shed further light on ape and human cognitive abilities. As Gibson (1991) wrote:

> We need to rethink the theoretical terms in which this information is organized. The very notions of language, intelligence, technology and society remain ill-defined and contentious as ever, and our evolutionary speculations continue to be bound by powerful root metaphors of Western thought.

 ## SUMMARY

The discovery that hominids were fully bipedal at least as early as two million years before the appearance of recognizable stone tools "decoupled Darwin's compelling trinity of bipedalism, tool-use and brain expansion" (Tooby and DeVore, 1987). Once this was recognized, bipedalism, as a unique form of locomotion and as a feeding adaptation, demanded an independent explanation from those that might explain the evolution of the human brain, technology, and language.

Conceptual models are the most appropriate ones to use in reconstructing early human behavior patterns. These models use different data sets in their construction, such as ape language and cognition studies, the fossil and archaeological record, and paleoneurology, but as selection acts on all categories of individuals and at each stage in the life cycle, models must take into account the fact that no one age or sex group is more important in any account of human evolution than any other. However, reconstructions have proved difficult because much of the evidence either is unavailable or sketchy at best.

Every line of evidence presents a slightly different perspective on human behavioral evolution. The fossil record with its reconstructions can show what early humans looked like; the archaeological material can show what our ancestors were capable of doing; and studies of the living primates can provide clues as to how early hominids behaved in a social setting. Each line, however, has its own pitfalls. The nonhuman primates have been evolving separately for millions of years. This muddies the waters as to exactly what we can learn from them. The fossil and archaeological records are fragmentary, and, in regard to stone tools, we have little idea exactly what the tools were used for. Finally, a major problem emerges with the realization that there are no modern representations of past cultural stages. Modern hunter/gatherers have also evolved, and their own cultural adaptations reflect recent environmental constraints.

Our knowledge of the communication systems of the nonhuman primates has increased considerably through the efforts of many researchers. Apes do not speak as we do, because they lack the neurological structures for human language. More complicated language may have arisen early in our evolutionary history, certainly before the emergence of modern *Homo sapiens,* but at what point in time and to what extent speech began still eludes us.

 ## CRITICAL-THINKING QUESTIONS

1. When constructing an evolutionary theory for hominid divergence, what four factors must be incorporated? Elaborate on each of these.
2. Briefly explain how studies done on baboons, apes, and carnivores contribute to the understanding of human evolution.
3. How have studies of tool kit technology aided in understanding early hominid feeding techniques? Describe the various theories.
4. List and describe the costs and advantages bipedalism had on the evolution of early human behavior.
5. Outline the experiments conducted by Roger Sperry and give their significance in understanding brain functioning.
6. In what ways did the use of the Neandertal La Chapelle specimen limit the understanding of speech production in archaic *Homo sapiens?*

 ## SUGGESTED READINGS

Calvin, W. H. 1991. *The Ascent of Mind: Ice Age Climate and the Evolution of Intelligence.* New York: Bantam Books. Discusses the question of why humanity increased its mental facilities fourfold during the Ice Ages that spanned 2.5 million years. Examines the possible link between climates and intelligence and postulates that cold climates forced humans to increase their mental activity.

Gibson, K. R., and T. Ingold (eds.). 1993. *Tools, Language and Cognition in Human Evolution.* New York: Cambridge University Press. Interdisciplinary study of the question of how humans evolved as creatures who can make and use more complex tools, communicate in more complex ways and engage in more complex forms of social life than any other species. Questions the idea that the evolution of tool making and language are interrelated phenomena.

Iaccino, J. F. 1993. *Left Brain–Right Brain Differences: Inquiries, Evidence, and New Approaches.* Hillsdale, N.J.: Lawrence Erlbaum Assoc. Publishers. Volume addresses the issue of cerebral asymmetries as it encompasses perceptual, physiological, comparative, and cognitive fields as these contribute to the question of human nature. Up-to-date research findings on brain lateralization with particular emphasis on gender and handedness.

Khalfa, J. (ed.). 1994. *What Is Intelligence?* New York: Cambridge University Press. A collection of essays that review the latest work on intelligence. One view of intelligence is that knowledge plays an active, rather than passive role. In other words, what makes someone intelligent is what they know. Contributors agree that intelligence is much more than cognitive. It is social, perceptual, and to a certain extent, illogical.

King, B. J. 1994. *The Information Continuum*. Santa Fe, N.M.: School of American Research Press. Interdisciplinary perspective that discusses the evolution of social information transfer in nonhuman and human primates. Describes the ability of primates to obtain, use and transfer information that is critical to their survival and reproduction.

Pinker, S. 1994. *The Language Instinct*. New York: William Morrow. Volume argues to the point that spoken language, in some primitive form, emerged early in human prehistory and is instinctual. Contrary to earlier beliefs Pinker asserts that the human brain enlarged as a result of the gradual elaboration of structures that underlie language, a result of natural selection.

Savage-Rumbaugh, E. S., J. Murphy, R. A. Sevcik, K. E. Brakke, S. L. Williams, and D. Rumbaugh. 1993. *Language Comprehension in Ape and Child*. Chicago: University of Chicago Press. Discusses research into the linguistic capacities of apes and their ability to produce words along with their ability to comprehend. Volume addresses this issue through experimental comparisons of language comprehension of a two-year-old child and an eight-year-old bonobo. Develops a model of evolution of language that suggests the potential for language comprehension preceded the appearance of speech, speech being linked to fully adapted bipedalism.

Springer, S. P., and G. Deutsch. 1985. *Left Brain, Right Brain*. (Revised Edition). New York: W. H. Freeman. Also discusses issues involved with cerebral asymmetries and of assigning functions to specific regions of the brain. Includes topics of right hemisphere language in split-brain patients, the nature of the visuospatial superiority of the right hemispherc, an immunological theory of left-handedness and new cerebral imaging techniques.

Tanner, N. M. 1983. *On Becoming Human*. New York: Cambridge University Press. Describes one model involving the transition from ape to human and the reconstruction of early human social life. It suggests that plant gathering with tools by females for obtaining sufficient food to share with their offspring was a very early innovation. Examines the role of women and children, as well as men, stressing the sequential development of important economic innovations.

Human Biology and Variation

The Nature of Human Genetic Variation

How Variation Is Measured

The Process of Geographical Isolation

Early Studies of Human Variation
What is "Race"?
Inadequacy of Traditional Racial Classifications

Genetic Markers Can Trace Population Relatedness

Natural Selection Causes Human Variation
Blood Group Polymorphisms
The HLA System
Lactose Intolerance
Skin Pigmentation

Genetic Influence on Behavioral Variation
Twin Studies
Race, IQ, and Social Class
Alcoholism
Schizophrenia

Summary

Critical-Thinking Questions

Suggested Readings

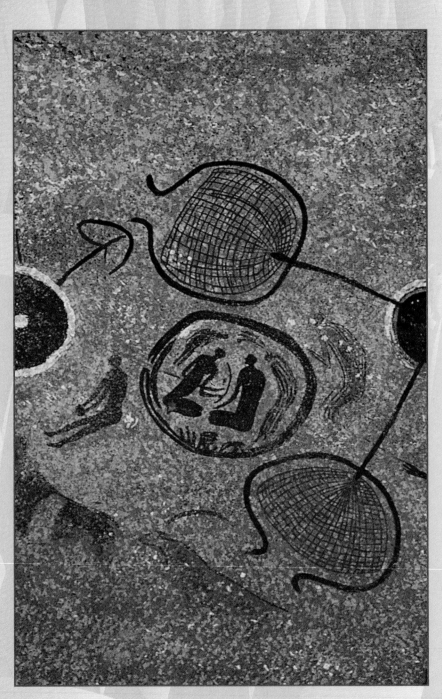

A cross-section of human individuals shows the extent to which we vary (Figure 13–1). Humans are one of the most morphologically variable species of living animals, and part of the reason this **variation** exists is because members of our species occupy many diverse habitats. Yet the exact genetic basis of this variation must be quite small. Biochemical evidence shows that humans and chimpanzees differ genetically by between 1–2% and that this amount of difference was accumulated over a period of approximately 7 million years. The human gene pool has apparently changed very little since the widespread appearance of anatomically modern humans about 35,000 years ago. Humans today remain genetically nearly identical to our upper Paleolithic pre-agricultural hunter-gatherer ancestors (Eaton, Konner, and Shostak, 1988).

Given these facts, why do modern humans appear to vary so much from one another and what are the factors responsible for this inherited variation? In the study of human evolution we have only a few examples providing explanations for the patterns of variability that exist within the species. In this chapter we will review what we know about human variation, attempt insofar as possible to explain this variability at the genetic level, and discuss the evolutionary framework in which these characteristics have come to exist. What we will *not* do in this chapter is summarize the vast amounts of data collected in the past on human variability unless they can offer specific insights into general principles or illustrate specific issues.

THE NATURE OF HUMAN GENETIC VARIATION

Inherited characteristics are variable at all levels of our biology, down to the genes. These characteristics include features of our external appearance—hair and skin color, facial features, and stature, among others—and of our internal characteristics—our blood types and our abilities to digest or metabolize certain substances. All these characteristics we have inherited from our parents and from our ancestors before them. We as individuals cannot, for the most part, change our genetic makeup, nor can it change in response to different environmental conditions. Inherited variation lies in the reshuffling of genes within populations from one generation to the next. As we saw in Chapters 3 and 4, inherited variation is a critical component in the action of evolution by

variation–in biological anthropology, the genetic and physical differences within and between human populations.

Figure 13–1 • College-aged individuals showing physical features that are found in some of the world's population. Based solely on the criteria of physical appearance, biological diversity in humans is substantial.

natural selection. We study inherited variation to understand how evolutionary forces have acted and continue to act to produce modern human populations.

There are important patterns to human biological variation. All individuals within a species do not vary equally from one another. Individuals within one family vary to some degree from one another in their characteristics, but they also share significant genetic, anatomical, and even behavioral similarities due to their close genetic bonds. There is also a geographical component to variation—individuals drawn from indigenous populations at the far north of Greenland and at the tip of southern Africa will show a great degree of difference, although they are still clearly within the same zoological species, *Homo sapiens* (Figure 13–2). As a rule, the amount of variation between individuals

Figure 13–2 • Degrees of genetic variation based on geographic distance. For small populations, variation increases rapidly with increasing distance. This increase in variability is less marked in larger populations.

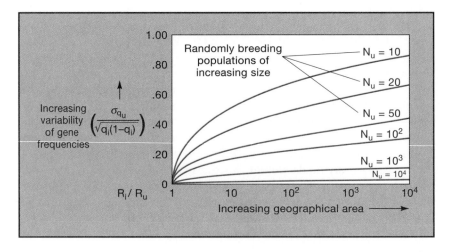

increases with distance: the farther away individuals' populations are, the more they tend to differ. Conversely, individuals who live close together within a populaton tend to resemble one another both genetically and morphologically. These patterns are the result of and are maintained by the forces of evolution: selection, migration, and genetic drift.

However, a population must pay a price for its variability; it is called **genetic load.** Where selection rather than neutrality is responsible for the creation of polymorphisms, a number of genotypes less favorable than the optimum are maintained in the gene pool. A definition provided by the geneticist J. F. Crow in 1958 describes the genetic load of a population as the proportional decrease in fitness relative to the fitness of an optimum genotype. These genotypes act then to lower the reproductive potential of those individuals who possess them by causing disease, and in some cases, death. Genetic loads may be calculated for all loci and may differ considerably one from the other depending upon the lethality of the genotypes. In the sickle-cell anemia example that we will describe later on in this chapter, the minimum genetic load must be calculated based on those deaths both caused by the lethal homozygous recessive genotype (about 4% of the population) and those deaths caused by malaria in individuals who possess either the normal homozygous or the heterozygous genotypes. As a rough rule of thumb a high genetic load usually follows a high degree of genetic variability.

HOW VARIATION IS MEASURED

Biological anthropologists study anatomical variation both qualitatively and quantitatively, that is, both in terms of traits that are either present or absent and in terms of traits that vary in degree. Thus, they collect observations on the presence, absence, or frequencies of **genetic markers,** or they collect observations on the variations of certain markers, such as finger print patterns, or dermatoglyphics. For example, certain populations have the qualitative anatomical trait of ridges of enamel on the back edges of their upper incisor teeth, a feature known as "shovel-shaped" incisors (Figure 13–3). Moderate to marked shovel incisors are almost universal in populations from the Far East, including Eskimos and American Indians (Carbonell, 1963). In other populations very few individuals show even slight development of this trait (Brues, 1977). On the other hand, quantitative traits such as body size (from tall to short), skin and hair pigmentation (from black to white), and hair form (from straight to curly) vary in all populations. Frequency differences of traits between populations are expressed in terms of differences in mean values of a normal or "Gaussian" curve. For example, the mean height in one population may be 3.5 centimeters greater than that of another population, yet the entire range of adult height may be found among individuals in each of the two populations.

genetic load—the deleterious or lethal effects that accompany genetic variation in a population, measured by the number of recessive lethal genes carried by individuals in a population; also called genetic burden.

genetic markers—traits whose genetic causation are known and which can be used in the study of populations.

Figure 13–3 • Top, a view of the upper dentition of a modern human (a European) from the inside of the mouth. The inside surface of the middle incisors is smooth, lacking the characteristic indentations seen in the two isolated middle incisors, pictured below, from the *Homo erectus* site of Zhoukoudian in north China. Termed shovel-shaped incisors because this indentation gives the tooth a shovel-like appearance, these teeth are found more frequently in modern Asian peoples and their close kin, such as Native Americans, than in other human populations. Shovel-shaped incisors are also found with a high frequency in Asian archaic *H. erectus* and *H. sapiens* specimens, suggesting a regional continuity in evolution from Asian *H. erectus* through archaic *sapiens* to modern Asians.

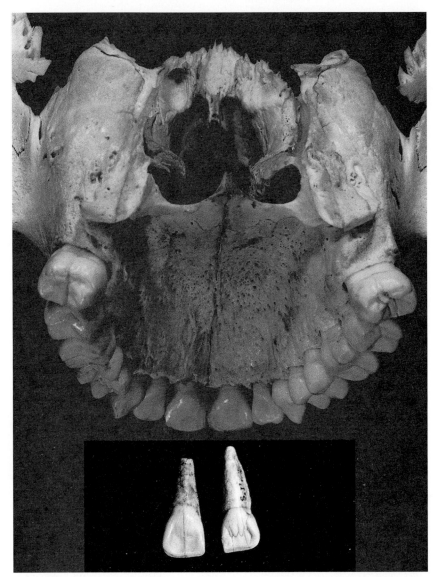

antibodies—immune or protective proteins evoked by specific substances (antigens) in the body.

Measuring genetic variation is important because it is by this means that the effects of natural selection on human populations can be studied. Let us take as an example of a quantitative genetic marker the human ABO blood groups. The various blood types of this system are found in individuals in all populations, but the types vary in frequency from one population to another. We can illustrate how genetic variation is measured in human populations.

Scientists who detect genetic markers have used the mammalian immune system as one of their primary research tools. An experimental mammal, frequently a rabbit, is used as a factory for generating very specific molecules, **antibodies,** that can recognize the genetic marker.

Table 13–1 • Worldwide Distribution of the ABO Blood Group[1]

Geographic Area	Sample Size	Blood Type				Allele Frequency		
		O	A	B	AB	A	B	O
Europe								
Belgium	40,960	.46	.43	.08	.03	.27	.06	.67
Finland	1,445	.35	.41	.16	.08	.29	.13	.58
France	30,810	.42	.45	.09	.04	.29	.07	.67
Greece	55,334	.43	.38	.13	.05	.25	.11	.64
Iceland	187	.65	.28	.06	.01	.14	.02	.84
Ireland	36,879	.54	.32	.11	.03	.19	.07	.74
Italy	11,679	.46	.36	.13	.05	.23	.09	.68
Eastern Europe								
Russia (Leningrad)	54,447	.35	.37	.20	.08	.26	.15	.59
"Lapps" (Russia)	123	.20	.59	.16	.05	.41	.11	.48
"Armenians" (Russia)	44,632	.29	.50	.13	.08	.35	.11	.54
Uzbekistan	2,400	.31	.32	.27	.11	.24	.21	.55
Czechoslovakia	80,518	.34	.42	.17	.08	.29	.13	.58
Asia								
Siberia	653	.28	.25	.34	.14	.21	.27	.52
Japan	12,253	.30	.37	.23	.10	.27	.19	.54
Nepal	5,000	.30	.37	.24	.10	.27	.18	.55
Vietnam	114,022	.42	.22	.31	.06	.15	.20	.65
Middle East								
Iran (Fars)	16,368	.41	.28	.24	.07	.19	.17	.64
Israel (Ashkenazi)	465	.38	.40	.16	.06	.27	.11	.62
Egypt	10,000	.36	.34	.24	.06	.23	.17	.60
Africa								
Nigeria	9,240	.52	.24	.21	.03	.14	.13	.73
Upper Volta	948	.44	.23	.29	.04	.15	.18	.67
Botswana Kung!	114	.70	.25	.03	.02	.15	.02	.83
Republic of South Africa	2,526	.46	.28	.21	.05	.18	.14	.68
Pacific Islands								
Hawaii (Natives)	4,670	.41	.53	.04	.02	.33	.03	.64
Easter Islands	1,056	.32	.66	.01	.01	.42	.10	.58
Americas (Natives)								
North America (Cherokee)	166	.95	.04	.02	.00	.02	.01	.97
(Pawnee)	80	.58	.40	.03	.00	.23	.01	.76
Greenland (Eskimos)	377	.36	.55	.05	.04	.35	.05	.60
Guatemala	331	.95	.03	.03	.00	.02	.01	.97
Brazil	594	.98	.01	.00	.00	.01	.01	.98

[1]Shows from worldwide population samples the frequencies of the ABO blood groups and the frequencies of the A, B, O alleles. Populations with high frequencies of blood type "O" tend to be peripheral in Europe and Asia, with the highest frequencies reaching nearly 100% among Native Americans. Frequencies of "A" are higher in Europe and in Native Americans of western North America. The "B" blood group is almost totally absent from Native American populations. It reaches its highest frequencies in Central Asia and North India.

From Mourant, et al. (1976).

polygenic–a trait controlled by interaction of genes at more than one locus.

subspecies–a geographically defined population within a species, the individuals of which tend to share certain physical and genetic traits but who are nevertheless interfertile with other members of the species; a race.

race–a biological term meaning subspecies, or a geographically defined population within a species; not synonymous with "ethnic group" or other socio-politically or culturally defined terms referring to group identity.

In the case of the ABO blood system, known Type O blood serum from a human, for example, is separated into its red cell and serum components, and then some of the latter is injected into a test rabbit. The rabbit's immune system then creates antibodies that "recognize" the foreign human Type O serum antibody. The same procedure is repeated to develop antibodies for Type A and Type B blood groups. The researcher then takes vials of this various anti-A, anti-B, and anti-O antigens for testing a human population. If centrifuged serum from a human subject causes a vial of the rabbit anti-O antigen to react and clump up into a cloudy mixture, then that subject has Type O blood. Blood serum from Type A or Type B individuals will not cause a reaction to anti-O antibodies. We then deduce that the subject has a genotype of OO.

Human populations vary in frequencies of the different ABO blood types, and they can be distinguished in part on the basis of these frequencies (Table 13–1). American Indian groups, for example, have a very low proportion of B blood types and a relatively high proportion of O blood types compared to most other human populations.

Certainly as markers, the frequencies of particular alleles among the various blood group systems can serve to detect genetic affinity between groups. Although too much reliance should never be placed on single-locus analysis, this approach may clarify questions involving the origins of certain peoples. For example, the suggestion that the Hungarian gypsies originated in India, one following from a linguistic comparison of these two populations, can be supported by the frequency distribution of the ABO blood group system.

Most genetic markers are not visible to a human observer. It is impossible, for example, to tell whether a person has A, B, or O Type blood by looking at any of his or her external features. However, external features also may serve to define human populations. In many cases though, the underlying genetic cause of these traits is not simple and cannot be tied to any one gene. Although the genetic control for some discrete anatomical traits is known (McKusick, 1989), for many traits, such as stature or skin color, the exact genetic causes are unclear. As a number of loci and their alleles must be responsible for such measurable features they are referred to as being under **polygenic** ("many gene") control.

THE PROCESS OF GEOGRAPHICAL ISOLATION

Changing gene frequencies in geographically defined populations is evolution in action. The formation of geographically delimited populations within a species is sometimes termed "raciation" (Harrison et al., 1990). **Subspecies** or **races** created by raciation represent these geographical subdivisions or populations which differ in gene frequencies.

The factors creating subspecies or races take into account (1) partial geographic and partial genetic isolation that may exist between populations at any point in time; (2) the amount of time in which gene flow has been reduced between two populations, and (3) mutations that may occur and spread in one population but not in another.

Today sophisticated techniques, such as protein electrophoresis (Chapter 3), have allowed us to look at many genetic systems in order to compare different individuals within a population, or to compare populations and subspecies. We can quantify these differences. At the DNA level, where the base pairs can be directly sequenced, the average individual is somewhat less than 1% different in sequence from any other randomly chosen individual. However, this 1% difference represents thousands of different genetic combinations when one considers there are 3 to 4 $\times$ 10^9 base pairs in the human haploid genome. The average human is also heterozygous at from 5 to 15% of his or her genes. If we compare individuals and populations it appears that up to 80% of all variation in humans is found within any one population, and only 20% of the variation is found in differences between populations (Figure 13–4).

There are no single features of modern populations that clearly set one group off from the next. What defines a race is a suite of morphological and genetic features that statistically can be related to the origin of a particular population group in a geographical location. In today's

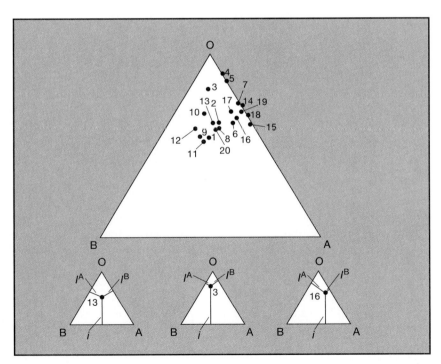

Figure 13–4 • Heterozygosity of individuals compared to that of populations. Three-axis diagram shows ABO blood group alleles from 20 different human populations from various regions of the world: 1–3, Africa; 4–7, American Indians; 8–13, Asia; 14–15, Australian Aborigines; 16–20, Europe. Human races are only marginally more heterozygous than individuals within one race. (From Lewontin, 1982).

populations the results of migration make the definition of races a complex question resolvable only by studies of quantitative traits. But this lack of precision in defining modern human races does not mean that population structure and the process of race formation were not important in human evolution. Our knowledge of both the human fossil record and the human genome indicate that an understanding of human population history is important in understanding our modern genetic diversity.

EARLY STUDIES OF HUMAN VARIATION

Darwin showed that inherited variation was a key element in natural selection. Scientists interested in human evolution thus began in the nineteenth century to study human variation and to interpret variation in evolutionary terms. The first attempts were clumsy.

The prevailing theoretical and philosophical debate concerning human origins before and around Darwin's time was between supporters of the unitary (**monogenic**) and of the separate (**polygenic**) origin of the human species. Debate centered on whether the differences seen in modern populations were of such a degree that different human groups should be considered separate species, or whether they were varieties of the same species. Those who emphasized the differences, such as the early American anthropologist Samuel G. Morton (1799–1851) of Philadelphia in his *Crania Americana* (1839), were strong proponents of polygenism. Polygenists supported the clear-cut separation of the major human races, usually into separate species. Monogenists emphasized the similarities among populations and pointed to the criterion of interfertility between individuals of the different groups. Monogenism had the support of Western religious doctrine because it upheld the single origin of humanity, in accordance with the Book of Genesis. Major proponents of monogenism were Johann Friedrich Blumenbach and Erasmus Darwin, the grandfather of Charles Darwin (1731–1802).

The interplay of monogenic and polygenic conceptions of human origins and human variability has had a great effect on human evolutionary theory. For example, there were polygenist propositions that vastly overestimated the evolutionary longevity of human races. One hypothesis held that modern western Europeans as a racial group descended directly from a common human-orangutan ancestor; another hypothesis advanced in Germany in the 1940s suggested that the German "Aryans" had descended uniquely from a Miocene ape, *Dryopithecus germanicus*. Prior to the modern population understanding of variability within species and how subspecies and races were reflections of this variability, there was a widespread belief in "pure" races. Variability is now accepted as a natural aspect of a population and not as a deviation from some ideal "type."

monogenic–in the history of anthropology, relating to a single or unitary origin of the human species, connoting that all human races were part of one species; an early point of agreement between the Church and Darwinism.

polygenism–in the history of anthropology, relating to a multiple origin of the human species, connoting that human races were different species; used by some to defend slavery and by others to justify colonial mistreatment of indigenous peoples.

What Is "Race"?

The initial ideas about human **races** were developed around a series of "types," defined by morphological or metric features of body, head, facial, or hair forms. If an individual possessed the one or two characteristics considered essential for inclusion in that type, then that was the type or race he or she was assigned to. There are problems with this "typological" approach. First, there is little provision for variability. And second, there is no provision for cases that are on the ends of the distributions of populations, for example, an individual who has as parents members of two different populations. However, physical traits that earlier anthropologists found to be characteristic of certain populations or "races" may still provide guides to understanding population variability today, even though we now have better ways to study and explain differences among human groups.

Anthropology has been involved since its inception in the study of human variation. Blumenbach, the founder of biological anthropology, studied the variations in cranial form in living human groups and categorized them into five major "races," which he termed "Caucasian," "Mongolian," "Malayan," "Ethiopian," and "American." Blumenbach, foreshadowing modern population biology, however, stressed that his division of the human species was arbitrary because in reality he said "One variety does so sensibly pass into the other that you cannot mark out the limits between them." As more and more research is undertaken on the molecular evolutionary aspects of human populations, conceptions of human races are changing radically. We will review both traditional and newly emerging views of human variation.

In these early studies chief among skeletal indicators of racial affinities was cranial form, and physical anthropologists spent a good deal of time over the years measuring differences, compiling vast quantities of data, and determining numerous indices. Cranial form is measured by the cranial (cephalic) index, the breadth of the skull divided by its length multiplied by 100 (Figure 13–5). Individuals with cephalic indices below 75 were "long-headed" or dolichocephalic, and individuals with indices greater than 80 were "short-headed" or brachycephalic. Those between the two extremes were called mesocephalic. Today most of the Mediterranean populations are brachycephalic and the western Europeans are dolichocephalic, but worldwide variation is such that this index has been of relatively little use by itself in determining population affinities. Because there is no evidence that significant differences in cranial capacity exist between geographical groups, different cranial shapes simply represent different ways evolution took in providing a housing for the brain. The German-American anthropologist Franz Boas (1858–1942) undertook an important study of European immigrants to America in the early part of this century that showed that cranial index could change between parents and their offspring. Thus, the environment, and not genetics alone, could be important in determining the cranial index.

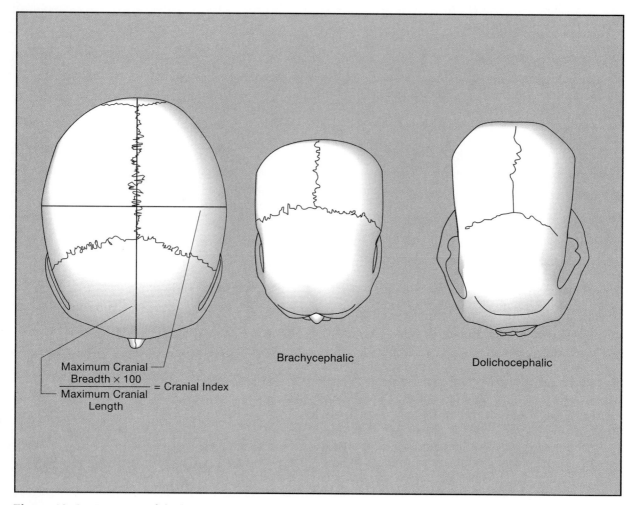

Brachycephalic

Dolichocephalic

$$\frac{\text{Maximum Cranial Breadth} \times 100}{\text{Maximum Cranial Length}} = \text{Cranial Index}$$

Figure 13–5 • Extremes of the human skull form as measured by the cranial index.

From Blumenbach's time other classifications, primarily based on external morphological characteristics, have put forward between three and seven major races with many micro races. Geographical distributions and genetic markers have been used to defend or to refute the boundaries of the major racial lines. For example, one classification (Coon, 1962) distinguished five human races with a number of smaller geographical variants or "micro races": (1) "Caucasoids" (a typological term deriving from the Caucasus Mountain region of western Russia) including peoples living in Europe, western Asia, North Africa, most of India, as well as the Ainu of Japan; (2) "Mongoloids" (the name deriving from the general region of Mongolia) including peoples living in East Asia, Indonesians, Polynesians, Micronesians, American Indians, and Eskimos; (3) "Australoids" (from Australia and surrounding islands) including Australian aborigines, Melanesians, and the "Negritos" of

South Asia, and Oceana; (4) "Congoids" (from the Congo River region of western Africa) including most of the peoples living in Africa south of the Sahara; and (5) "Capoids" (from the Cape of Good Hope region of southern Africa), also termed "Khoisan" or "Bushman" and Hottentots. The major racial divisions of this more recent classification are quite similar to those originally proposed by Blumenbach, who had included the Indians within his "Caucasian" category.

There has been a long-standing historical confusion in anthropology concerning the interrelationships of race, language and culture, a confusion which is manifested in common usage as well. Standard U.S. Government usage requests individuals applying for jobs to fill in the "ethnic group," which used to be termed "race." The categories used by the U.S. Government are *Hispanic,* largely a language-based term, referring to Spanish speakers (but these individuals can be "White," "Black," or also "Native American"); *African-American* and *Asian-American,* geographically based terms which can relate to real population affinities; *Native American,* which can refer to a wide array of geographic populations of broadly Asian affinities ranging from Florida to Alaska to the Pacific Islands; and *White,* a purely descriptive grouping based on skin color, or *Caucasian,* an old term referring to a European "type" from eastern Europe. Widely used terms such as "Jewish" and "Muslim" have a clearly religious connection. But do these connote separate "races" because they share certain genetic characteristics distinct from other human populations, separate linguistic groupings because they share a common original language (Hebrew and Arabic, respectively), or separate cultures because they are bound together by common religions, Judaism and Islam, respectively? Or are they all three? What about a population that has a very distinguishing physical characteristics, such as the small stature of the Central African Mbuti (pygmies), but that is not linguistically distinct, instead speaking the languages of their Bantu neighbors? What about the case when two populations, such as the Hopi and Navaho Indians, are physically and genetically very similar but have quite different languages, as well as cultural adaptations to the same environment? There are no straightforward answers to these questions although it is clear that the categories "race," "language," and "culture" should be decoupled from one another, as they can all vary independently.

The prevailing conceptions of the biological unity or disunity of the human species have had far-reaching and often negative effects on such disparate areas as social mores, religious doctrine, educational planning, public health policy and medical practice. That is why we must realize that "race" is not synonymous with "ethnic group," and such "racial" categories as governments have found expedient, be they for (a) discriminatory purposes, such as the apartheid system of South Africa ("blacks" were classified by the "pencil test," that is if one's hair was curled enough to hold a pencil, one was black regardless of other attributes or parentage); for (b) obtaining the privileges associated with

FRONTIERS

Dissecting the Human Genome

by Kenneth K. Kidd and Judith R. Kidd

What is the human genome? The human genome is the approximately 3 billion nucleotide base pairs organized into 23 pairs of chromosomes that each individual possesses. It is also the variation in these 3 billion base pairs as well as the organization of the variation among individuals both within and between human populations. The human genome, like the genome of any other complex species, is not homogeneous. It is composed of a variety of elements that vary from individual to individual. Just as a single representative "consensus" sequence of the genome (the objective of the Human Genome Project) will be a major aid to understanding the function and expression of all human genes, a detailed description of variation in sequence (the objective of the Human Genome Diversity Project) will be a crucial element in understanding our evolutionary history as a species.

The genome contains clues to aspects of our evolutionary history such as human and primate relationships and origins, where and when we arose as a species, and how different populations are related. There are also clues to the social structures of populations, for example, whether there has been a pattern of marrying outside the group ("exogamy") or marrying within the group ("endogamy"). [The genome also carries traces of migrations of individuals between populations and of whole populations.] Finally, there are important indications from human genome data as to how we have adapted, and are presently adapting, to our environments, especially as affected by such parameters as disease, diet, and altitude.

Two recent scientific developments are allowing us to examine these clues as never before and are revolutionizing the field of physical anthropology. First, extraordinarily large amounts of data and molecular resources are now being produced by the Human Genome Project. This project is a major international research effort to sequence the human genome with primary emphasis on functional genes and their genetic controlling elements. Understanding which DNA sequences control morphology and how they control it will allow physical anthropologists to understand better how we evolved from our hominoid ancestors and the genetic changes involved in adapting to new niches. Second, the vast and ever-increasing amount of DNA sequence variation being discovered is relegating the classical markers of variation, such as blood groups and serum protein polymorphisms, to a minute fraction of the known variation available to study. Such data are coming from the Human Genome Diversity Project (HGDP), which is being organized to coordinate the systematic and broadly representative study of genetic variation at the DNA level. It is the huge amount of hitherto unknown genetic variation now being characterized that makes feasible such a project to understand human diversity and variation and ensures the successful coordination of the work necessary for it.

The results of some of our own research on DNA variation indicate the types of understanding of the human species that we expect to come from the HGDP. The data at the DNA level are beginning to suggest scenarios

---

panmictic—"all mixing," referring to populations in which the breeding structure approximates the condition in which an individual male or female has the same probability of mating with another individual of the opposite sex anywhere in the population.

a certain group, such as claiming a tribal affiliation with an American Indian group (for example the Cherokee Indians require 1/8 genetic descent from a "full-blooded" Cherokee), or for (c) attempting to rectify societal inequities, as in the case of the U.S. government's Affirmative Action programs. All these are quite distinct from the scientific definition of "race." In this book, we are dealing with the biological study of human variation, as defined by biological attributes of populations, and not with the hybrid categories erected for social ends.

When population biological theory began to exert an important influence in human evolutionary studies in the 1940s, an opinion predominated that human populations had been for the most part **panmictic** (Latin, meaning "all mixing") in the past, that is they had for the geographical and temporal origin of humans. Preliminary work on both nuclear and mitochondrial DNA variation corroborate paleoanthropological evidence for an African origin for *Homo sapiens* (Stoneking, 1993; but see Templeton, 1993, and Bowcock et al., 1994). The continuous nature of the distribution of variation within the human species is another emerging conclusion. Although as yet fragmentary, data on the global distribution of DNA variation demonstrate the continuous distribution of genetic variation between populations. Variation is being seen as quantitative rather than qualitative, that of frequency and not type. For example, virtually all of the polymorphic alleles originally discovered and characterized in Europeans are seen in nearly all populations in all regions of the world. The HGDP is also helping us to understand the effect of the speciation events and different species histories separating humans from their nearest primate relatives. We are beginning to observe that *Homo sapiens,* compared to other living hominoids (*Pan troglodytes, Pan paniscus, Gorilla gorilla,* and *Pongo pygmaeus*) has far less DNA variation. If these observations prove to be more than anecdotal, they will shape both our view of the nature of the speciation events that separate us from our evolutionary cousins and our understanding of the effects of differing species-wide population structures on genetic variation.

We are better able than ever before to study who we are as a species, where we came from evolutionarily and geographically, and how we came to be what we are today—a single species, genetically quite homogeneous, yet with a rich and fascinating genetic and population diversity.

References

Bowcock, A.M., A. Ruiz-Linares, J. Tomfohrde, E. Minch, J.R. Kidd, and L.L. Cavalli-Sforza. 1994. High resolution of human evolutionary trees with polymorphic microsatellites. *Nature* 368:455–57.

Cavalli-Sforza, L.L., P. Menozzi, and A. Piazza. 1993. Demic expansions and human evolution. *Science* 259: 639–46.

Deinard, A.S. and K.K. Kidd. 1995. Levels of DNA polymorphism in extant and extinct hominoids. In S. Brenner and K. Hanihara, eds., *The Origin and Past of Modern Humans as Viewed from DNA.* New Jersey: World Scientific, pp. 149–70.

Kidd, K.K. and J.R. Kidd. 1996. A nuclear perspective on human evolution. In A.J. Boyce, ed., *Molecular Biology and Human Diversity.* Cambridge: Cambridge University Press, in press.

Kidd, J.R., K.K. Kidd, and K.M. Weiss. 1993. Human genome diversity initiative. *Human Biology* 65:1–6.

Stoneking, M. 1993. DNA and recent human evolution. *Evolutionary Anthropology* 60–73.

Templeton, A.R. 1993. The "Eve" hypothesis: a genetic critique and reanalysis. *American Anthropology* 95: 51–72.

Kenneth K. Kidd is Professor of Genetics at Yale University School of Medicine and has helped to develop the Human Genome Diversity Project.

Judith R. Kidd is Research Scientist in Genetics at Yale University School of Medicine and an active investigator into human genetic variation.

interbred freely over almost their entire range. The range for humans was over most of the Old World after the time of *Homo habilis* and over most of the entire world except Antarctica for *Homo sapiens.* This theoretical predisposition meant that there must have been relatively little racial differentiation because of the high degree of gene flow between geographic regions in the human past.

General opinion now holds that, although human species seem to have passed the thresholds from one ancestral species to its descendent across the species' worldwide range in a more or less synchronous fashion, there is also strong evidence in certain anatomical markers for regional continuity. For example, we do see a high incidence of shovel-shaped incisors in Asian *Homo erectus* and modern Asian (and

American Indian) human populations and in the midfacial prognathism of Late Pleistocene European populations and modern Europeans. This means that, although there has been enough gene flow between regions in the past to insure that all human populations are interfertile and thus in the same species, there has also been enough regional inbreeding to account for higher incidence of certain traits in geographically defined human populations.

Inadequacy of Traditional Racial Classifications

Genetic studies have now added substantially to our understanding of human population variability. The reconstruction of gene lineages in some ways parallels the use of discrete anatomical marker traits in deciphering the history of human variation in the past. New molecular studies have not supported the traditional human racial divisions based on morphology. Cavalli-Sforza and Edwards (1967) used the available genetic data to categorize fifteen distinct human populations. Mito-

Figure 13–6 • The mitochondrial DNA phylogeny of *Homo sapiens* and the geographical component of genetic variation. (From Cann, et al., 1987)

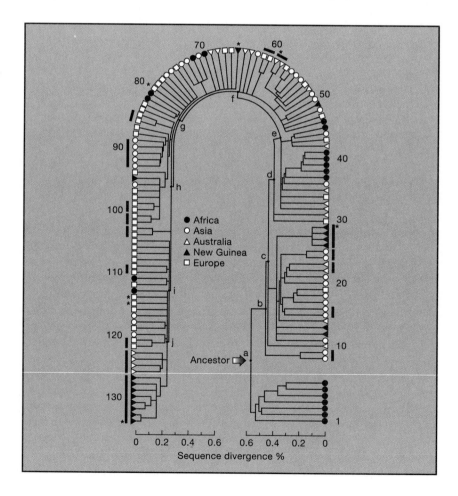

chondrial DNA (MtDNA) studies have been at the forefront of this research. Cann (1988) and colleagues have surveyed worldwide mtDNA diversity and analyzed the data in terms of cladistic patterns (Figure 13–6). They suggest that the major division in human races lies at a split between Euro-Asian and African populations. The degree of genetic polymorphism in Africa is five times that of the rest of the world's populations. Using these data and the criteria of genetic distance as indicative of race, the traditional racial category of "Africans" would have to be broken up into a number of separate races equal to those traditionally defined. For example, mtDNA data has shown that an individual from English ancestors is more similar genetically to an individual from Japanese ancestors than are two individuals drawn from any number of contiguous African populations. Future work in molecular anthropology will undoubtedly change our understanding of human races even further.

GENETIC MARKERS CAN TRACE POPULATION RELATEDNESS

Neutral mutations, discussed first in Chapter 3, are one source of variation that contributes to the formation of genetic polymorphisms in human populations. The spread of neutral mutations within populations is the result of genetic drift, as we have seen in Chapter 4. In Chapter 3, we showed how two selectively neutral alleles, where there is no apparent advantage of one allele over the other, may coexist over a considerable period of time. The frequency of the resulting polymorphic genotypes varies over time only by chance.

At that time we briefly discussed the fact that sections of the DNA molecule exist with no apparent function; that is, they do not code for polypeptide chains. These sections consist of short runs of nucleotides repeated in tandem perhaps thousands of times. We have known for a number of years about some of these noncoding tandem repeats called, **satellite DNA,** that are found at the chromosome centromere. Other nonfunctional tandem repeats have also been identified and labeled according to their size as either minisatellite or microsatellite DNA loci. Although these have been known since the late 1970s what we have not known until recently is that they, like many of their functional counterparts on DNA, are also polymorphic: there are different numbers of repeats in different individuals. These loci, which we have already called VNTRs (variable noncoding tandem repeats), are found by the hundreds and are distributed across all chromosomes.

There are a number of reasons why VNTRs are potentially useful for study by anthropologists. As they make up the noncoding regions of the DNA, being relatively unaffected by natural selection, their observed variability must be selectively neutral. As we have seen in our studies of primate phylogeny, neutral polymorphisms are more useful

satellite DNA—DNA that consists of short sequences repeated many times in the genome; so named because it forms a subsidiary "satellite" band when DNA is spun in a laboratory centrifuge.

than selectively maintained polymorphisms for analyzing the relatedness of species. Because VNTR polymorphisms also appear by chance and are fixed by genetic drift, their high rate of production makes them especially useful for studying how populations within species are related and for estimating the amount of genetic distance that separates them. The greater the number of polymorphisms and the higher the rate of heterozygosity, the more useful VNTRs can be in resolving issues of recent human migration history and, perhaps, even the issue of the origin of modern *Homo sapiens* (Harding, 1992).

Neutral mutations either within the noncoding sections of the DNA, like the VNTRs, or within the coding sections of DNA, expressed as variable amino acid sequences in polypeptide chains, such as the serum albumins, have proven useful in evolutionary studies. However, we may also consider the role of neutrality at higher levels in the phenotype. For example, several known variable phenotypes might fall into the category of neutrality because none has been demonstrated to affect individual fitness. The first example involves the excretion of a substance called **methanethiol.** Probably a single dominant allele controls the excretion of methanethiol once it has entered the body's system, usually after an individual has eaten asparagus. One estimate of the frequency of this allele in an English population is 0.23 (23 in 100). Carriers of this allele can be identified because of the strong odor of their urine. Individuals, on the other hand, who are homozygous for the recessive allele can eat as much as a pound of asparagus without any detectable odor. Studies have not confirmed any selective advantage for either the excretion or nonexcretion of methanethiol.

The enzyme **betamin** controls the breakdown of the red pigment in beets. This enzyme is manufactured by individuals who possess the dominate allele and it breaks down the pigment betacyanin, leaving the urine free of color. Homozygote recessives do not produce the enzyme, and as a consequence, when these individuals consume moderate amounts of beets their urine appears red as the pigment is excreted. Frequency of the recessive allele, again from an English sample, is about 0.31. No selective advantage is known to be served by the ability to excrete betacyanin.

A third example that is also under genetic control involves the ability to taste different substances. R. J. Williams, a biochemist, investigated taste sensitivity for a number of substances and found that individuals had different "taste profiles" or responses to the different substances used (Williams, 1951). For example, while 251 individuals said that sugar tasted sweet, 21 unrelated individuals reported a bitter taste. Identical twins usually agreed in their responses, indicating the genetic basis for differences in one's ability to taste.

Of all of the substances used to determine taste differences, the chemical phenylthiocarbamide (**PTC**) is the best known and the most commonly used. This substance to some people tastes exceedingly bit-

methanethiol–a chemical breakdown product of asparagus with a detectable odor, excreted by individuals heterozygous for the gene.

betamin–an enzyme, produced by a dominant allele, that breaks down betacyanin, the red color in beets.

PTC–phenylthiocarbamide, also known as phenylthiourea; its peculiar taste, for "tasters" with the dominant allele, derives from a nitrogen-carbon-sulfur group in the chemical structure of the molecule.

ter, whereas to others it has no taste at all. Nontasters are recessive homozygotes. In this case, however, although it is difficult to prove, selection may favor the dominant allele. Among individuals who have the thyroid condition known as nodular goiter, the proportion of nontasters is higher than can be expected by chance. Likewise, tasters are reported to have fewer dental caries than nontasters. Correlations such as these, however, are not necessarily conclusive proof of a causal relationship.

Neutrally selective genetic markers such as methanethiol excretion, betacyanin excretion, and PTC tasting ability are useful in studying population movements and gene flow, because their frequencies are probably not be affected by selection. The movement of genes through populations can be tracked by gene frequencies, revealing (as discussed in Chapter 4) a gradient of populations each successively less genetically related. These gradients in populations are termed **clines.**

cline–a gradient of genotypes or phenotypes over a geographic range; in the opinions of some researchers a better description of the geographic distribution of human variation than "races."

Figure 13–7 • Allele frequencies of dry cerumen in humans from Asia to Europe, an example of a cline.

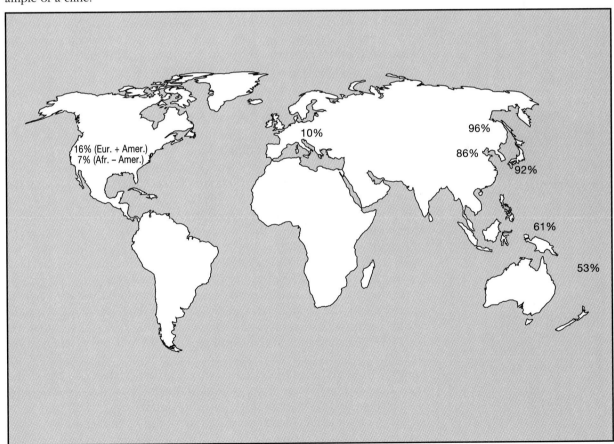

cerumen—ear wax; a waxy secretion of glands located in the external ear canal.

malaria—from Italian for "bad air," from the original, mistaken belief that the disease was air borne; occasionally fatal disease caused by a protozoan infecting the red blood cells and transmitted from one carrier to another by the bite of a female *Anopheles* mosquito; symptoms include chills, sweating, and convulsions.

Some researchers prefer to use this term to describe human variation rather than the term "race."

A particularly good example of a cline in human populations is the incidence of **cerumen** or ear wax types in Eurasia (Figure 13–7). In northern China dry cerumen, that is "nonsticky" ear wax, occurs in 96% of the population. These individuals are homozygous for the recessive allele that causes dry cerumen. In western Europe, on the other hand, over 90% of individuals have "wet" cerumen, a very different type of ear wax, one that has a high lipid content, indicating high frequencies of the dominant wet cerumen allele.

Over the geographical area intervening between northern China and western Europe there is a gradient of cerumen types, with dry frequencies increasing west to east and wet frequencies increasing east to west. Because no selective advantage has been determined for the two cerumen types—both types apparently serve to provide a protective barrier to small foreign particles entering the ear canal—their frequency variations have been interpreted on the basis of selective neutrality and are indicative of past gene flow. Historically, the major event that may account for this cline is the Mongol invasion, a mass movement of northern Asian peoples into western Asia and Europe in the fifth century AD. The degree of gene exchange has decreased from western Asian to western European populations as numbers of northern Asian migrants has decreased towards the west.

NATURAL SELECTION CAUSES HUMAN VARIATION

Although biological anthropologists and geneticists have documented much variation in human populations, under most circumstances they have been unable to ascertain either the selective advantages or the evolutionary forces that produce the variation. Where we know something about them, the reason is an unusually large fitness difference among individuals within the study population. Such a situation exists for sickle cell hemoglobin. In this example, individuals in West Africa who are heterozygous (Hb^{A}Hb^S) with the mutant allele for the beta chain of hemoglobin have protection against **malaria**.

Hospital data demonstrate that normal hemoglobin patients can be infected with the malarial parasite 20% more frequently than those individuals who were heterozygous. One particular study showed that out of 1,013 heterozygotes, 132 or only about 13% had heavy parasite infestation, whereas out of 2,858 AA homozygous individuals 955 or about 33% tested for the same degree of parasitic infection. The death rate due to malaria for homozygous individuals is also considerably higher than that for the heterozygous individuals.

Such a high genetic load, or death rate of the homozygous recessive, suggests that this genetic accommodation between humans and the malarial parasite is a relatively recent one. About 4% of the population is lost (due to the lethal homozygous mutant combination Hb^{s}Hb^s) so that about 32% of the population can be protected from the effects of malaria. However, a 4% death rate per generation is a severe genetic load.

In the best of situations natural selection over time should favor possible alternative solutions that reduce genetic load. An "ideal" solution would be a single locus protection against malarial infection that is not detrimental to individuals carrying the mutant gene. In theory, other solutions that would lower the genetic load might arise if additional loci and other alleles were to become involved, or if the homozygous mutant condition were to become less lethal. Both of these solutions have in fact evolved.

Adaptation through evolution can occur only when a population has sufficient variability. Mutations, the source of population variability, do not occur because they are needed. Rather, the process of mutation is continuous and random. As the environmental situation changes, some mutations will by chance turn out to be adaptive. Given the relative infrequency, however, of mutational events and the finite nature of populations (there are only so many individuals in any given species), we would not expect to find the same identical adaptation in two different populations. Throughout the Old World many human populations have been exposed to malaria (Figure 13–8), but genetic adaptations to malaria are varied. In Africa, for example, the adaptation of highest frequency is sickle-cell hemoglobin (Hb^s). In Southeast Asia a different mutant (Hb^e) works to protect individuals from malaria. Hb^e, however, is much less lethal than Hb^s when in the homozygous state.

Hb^s, Hb^e, and a West African allele, Hb^c are found in fairly large areas of the world at heterozygote frequencies of 10% to 30%, the highest in populations in tropical Africa and in a few locations around the Mediterranean and in India. In addition to these, at least three other variants exist whose local heterozygote frequencies may reach 50%.

In areas where Hb^s and Hb^c both occur, the frequency of Hb^s is lower than that of Hb^c. Predictably the Hb^c allele with its higher degree of fitness (lower genetic load in the homozygous recessive genotype) is spreading. Although heterozygotes for Hb^s/Hb^c are clearly at a disadvantage, this combination is not as lethal as the Hb^s homozygote, exemplifying how natural selection acts in reducing genetic load.

Time is again the important ingredient. If a situation requiring some genetic intervention persists for a long enough period and certain chance factors (mutations) occur enabling alternative solutions, a shift will take place from a single-locus to a two-locus (or more) mechanism. Substantiating this prediction, we again look at West African and Mediterranean populations in which other loci exist that contain specific alleles whose frequencies correlate with the presence of malaria. At one of these loci, alleles produce the enzyme **G6PD** (glucose-6-phosphate dehydrogenase), important in red blood cell metabolism. Where the frequency of Hb^s is high, the mutant forms of the G6PD

G6PD–glucose-6-phosphate dehydrogenase, an enzyme necessary for red blood cell metabolism; G6PD deficiency is caused by recessive genes and can result in the disease "favism."

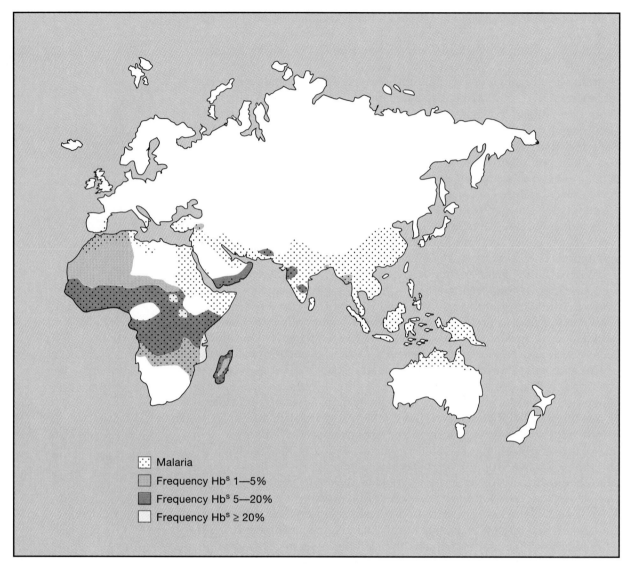

Figure 13–8 • Malarial areas of the Old World and frequencies of the Hb[s] allele. Higher frequencies of Hb[s] correspond with higher frequencies of sickle-cell anemia.

gene, leading to deficiency in the enzyme, are also found (Greene, 1993).

Under ordinary conditions carriers of one of the G6PD deficiency alleles exhibit no abnormal effects. Only if a carrier is administered an antimalarial drug will he or she develop anemia. Anemia will also occur if a carrier eats or comes into contact with the pollen of the fava bean, *Vicia faba*. The disease caused by G6PD deficiency and brought on by the fava bean is commonly known as "favism," and is characterized by fever, abdominal pain, anemia, and coma. It was originally found chiefly in Italy and was associated with long-term diets of the raw bean. G6PD deficiency is now known to be widespread in populations exposed in the past to malarial infection. In Israel, for example, among Kurdish Jews the frequency of the G6PD deficiency alleles may reach higher than 60%. The unexpected relationship between G6PD and malaria demonstrates how evolution in some human populations responded to malaria and developed a defense that affected red blood cell metabolism, which must have in some way protected individuals against the lethal effects of malaria.

The second locus which has been associated with malaria possesses alleles that are concerned with the synthesis of the various polypeptide chains that make up the hemoglobin molecule. Individuals who have one of the alleles for β **Thalassemia** have defective hemoglobin due to the partial suppression of the formation of the normal β chain. As a consequence, these individuals may be anemic. On mainland Italy the frequency of the heterozygotes for β Thalassemia reaches 20%, and in some Sardinian populations it approaches 40%. The high frequencies of these genotypes in many populations and the frequent severity of the anemia suggest that natural selection should be reducing these frequencies through differential fitness. That this has not occurred is again good evidence of natural selection at work, maintaining the high frequencies of the thalassemia alleles in a balanced polymorphism. We presume that the counteracting selection is for protection against malaria, and as with sickle-cell hemoglobin and G6PD deficiency, a lowered efficiency of red blood cell activity and metabolism apparently retards the propagation of the malarial parasite. When the frequencies of the anemia-producing alleles are examined, they, like the Hb^s allele, are high in areas where malaria is also prevalent.

A third condition known as α-Thalassemia involves the α chain of the hemoglobin molecule. Normally there are four α alleles. Deletions may occur so that individuals may have one, two, three, or four α alleles missing. The *AO* combination, with all four genes deleted, is most frequent in Southeast Asia. The *A+* combination, with at least one deletion, occurs thoughout Africa and Southeast Asia, and is especially common in New Guinea (up to 80% of the population). The α-Thalassemias may have also reached their high frequency in tropical regions because heterozygotes are protected against malaria (Haldane, 1949).

Malaria may also be involved in the genetics of the red blood cell antigen system, the "Duffy" blood group (denoted fy+). Most individuals in the world are Duffy+ and possess the antigen on their red blood cells. However, in West Africa, the Duffy negative allele (fy−) is quite common. Apparently one of the species of the malarial parasite (*Plasmodium knowlseii*) uses this antigen as a receptor to attach and enter the red blood cell. If the antigen is lacking the parasite cannot attach and invade the red blood cell and reproduce. The lack of this antigen, then, in a malarial environment is adaptive.

thalassemia—from Greek meaning "sea blood," in reference to the blood's "dilute" nature; genetic disorders affecting hemoglobin metabolism that can range from negligible clinical effects to fatal anemia.

A study on the relationships between malaria, β-Thalassemia, and G6PD deficiency alleles was undertaken in Sardinia. Here the frequency of the alleles was correlated with altitude, the interpretation being that malaria inversely affected individuals living in villages at higher altitudes (Figure 13–9). The prediction borne out by this study was that, as the effects of malaria on the human population diminished, the incidence of malaria-related alleles would also decrease in frequency.

The malarial example illustrates the interaction between disease, genetics, and natural selection. It also shows how changes in cultural patterns can have an effect on human biological evolution. With the introduction of agriculture in Africa between 0 and 500 A.D., populations moved into mostly uninhabited tropical areas to practice this new type of subsistence. Clearing the forests improved the environment for the mosquitoes that carried the malarial parasite and, in turn, increased the chances for malarial infection among the newly situated human populations. Although the majority of these new immigrants must have developed malarial infections to one degree or another, those individuals who by chance carried an allele for sickle-cell anemia or any of the other alleles already described now had a selective advantage over their "normal" neighbors.

Figure 13–9 • Incidence (average frequency) of G6PD deficiency and the thalassemia trait among villagers on the island of Sardinia. These traits are lower at higher altitudes, away from coastal malarial areas.

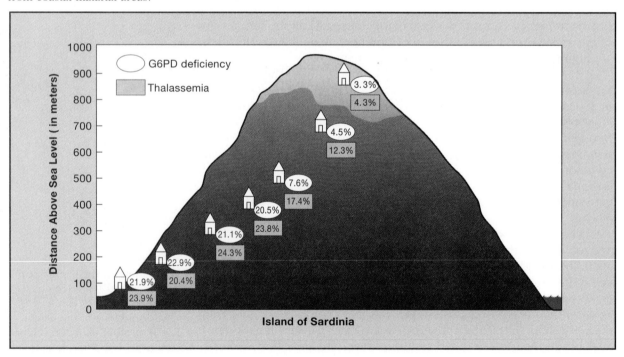

Thus, a heterogeneous group of genetic variants of various red cell components (including hemoglobin S,C,E, α- and β-Thalassemia, and G6PD deficiency) appear to impart in common an increased fitness in malarial environments, the end result of which is the production of a common phenotype, one in which the red cell environment is less favorable for the malarial parasite.

Blood Group Polymorphisms

The idea of transfusing the blood of one individual into that of another dates back several centuries; however, the initial results were far from encouraging. As early as the seventeenth century blood transfusions were attempted, but the patients often died, and although physicians at the time were not certain what caused death, transfusion as a practice was abandoned for a while. Why some patients survived transfusion was not correctly answered until the turn of this century by Karl Landsteiner (1868–1943). He discovered what ultimately became one of the most widely known genetic systems, the **ABO blood group.** The ABO system is the primary blood antigen system and it is in daily use to match blood types for transfusions. Individuals may have an A, B, AB, or O blood type. The genotypes for these types are AA or AO, BB or BO, AB, and OO, respectively.

The ABO system was the first of many blood groups to be discovered, and the reason that it was first is relatively simple. Individuals who do not have the A antigen possess a preexisting, "natural" antibody to A. Likewise, individuals who lack the B antigen possess anti-B. In this respect the ABO system is different from other blood group systems, such as the **Rh blood group,** in that in these latter systems antibodies are not initially found within an individual if certain system antigens are absent. Antibodies that do exist to specific antigens are manufactured at the time foreign antigens are introduced, as for example, by transfusion. Because of this difference, the reaction to foreign antigens of the ABO system is immediate, whereas in the other systems, reactions may be delayed. In short, the likelihood of discovering the ABO system increased because it is the first to respond to foreign substances.

When incompatible blood is mixed together, a reaction results between the antigens present on the surface of the red blood cell and the antibody to it, which is present in the blood of a recipient. The antibody acts to change the surface structure of the foreign red blood cells so that these cells clump together in clots. These clots are capable of blocking small blood vessels, often with the fatal results observed by seventeenth century and later physicians.

The vast quantity of data on different frequencies of blood groups in human populations around the world might be explicable on the basis of chance and genetic drift. Clearly, various polymorphic situations exist among the dozen or so blood group antigen systems. Frequencies of

ABO blood group—blood group system discovered by Landsteiner in 1900 defined by agglutination (clotting) reactions of red blood cells to natural anti-A and anti-B antibodies. Blood type A reacts to only anti-A, type B reacts only to anti-B, type AB reacts to both, and type O reacts to neither.

Rh blood group—a complex system of blood antigens originally discovered by Landsteiner and Wiener in 1940 using blood from the rhesus monkey, which lent the first two letters of its name to the system. Rh antigens are controlled by 8 major genes or gene complexes yielding some 18 different phenotypes.

the different blood groups have been shown to vary geographically, as Table 13–1 on page 443 demonstrates. How might natural selection have played a role in the origins of this variation in the first place?

When we look carefully at the data, we see that blood group polymorphisms cannot result from neutral mutation and genetic drift. Even under drift situations polymorphisms will tend to be eliminated by chance, given enough time (Chapter 4). One clue explaining blood group polymorphisms comes from their great antiquity. Antigens for the ABO system, for example, have been found to exist in all mammals and even in birds. The fact that polymorphisms still exist after such vast amounts of time demands the explanation that these polymorphisms must be balanced polymorphisms. Yet for a balanced polymorphic situation to exist some selective advantages must be found for the heterozygote. In a few examples that we have for heterozygotes the opposite has been found to be true. Heterozygotes are at a disadvantage in examples that involve **hemolytic incompatibility** between the mother and her fetus for both the ABO system and, especially, the Rh system (Figure 13–10).

Until quite recently, heterozygous fetuses were at direct risk for spontaneous abortion, a risk that increased as the mother conceived succeeding offspring. The blood group data, therefore, presents a considerable paradox. The existence of multiple alleles, on the one hand, can be explained only by a balanced polymorphic situation, yet this hypothesis is weakened in a number of significant examples that clearly show that the supposedly favored hetrozygote may be fatally at peril.

Blood group antigens stimulate the production of antibodies, which, in turn, function to eliminate foreign substances, including disease causing agents, from an individual's circulatory system. Most of the studies attempted so far, however, have looked at individual antigen systems, such as the ABO system, and studied the various gene frequencies as if they existed in isolation from the other antigen systems. As with malaria, one, two, and perhaps three independent systems, each having something to do with the blood environment, may interact to produce a combined heterozygote advantage. In the blood group systems a dozen different antigen groups have been identified. If each one of these evolved as a response to a particular situation, such as malaria, we should easily be able to identify a causal relationship. That we have not yet been able to do so strengthens our assumption that the multiplicity of the blood groups themselves are the results of natural selection over long periods of time. The interactions of these systems should be the focal point for evolutionary investigations. With this thought in mind let us turn to the second best known blood group: the Rh system.

Rh incompatibility occurs in a pregnancy in which the fetus is an Rh+ (Dd) heterozygote while the mother is Rh− (dd). Because of the nature of the placental membrane, D antigens on the red blood cell

hemolytic incompatibility– destruction of red blood cells caused by the action of antibodies, resulting in release of hemoglobin into the plasma.

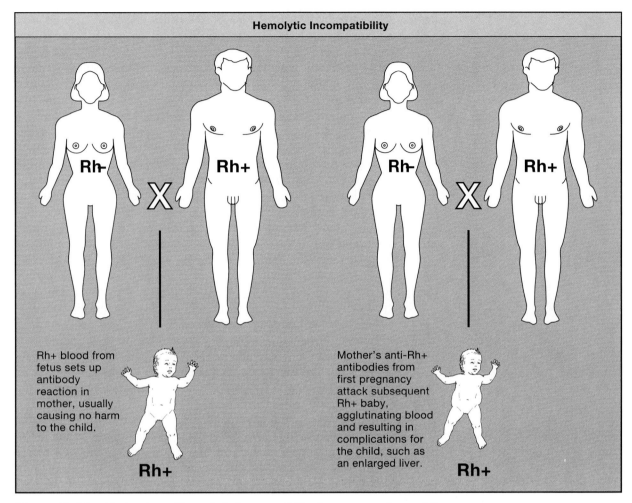

Hemolytic Incompatibility

Rh- X Rh+

Rh- X Rh+

Rh+ blood from fetus sets up antibody reaction in mother, usually causing no harm to the child.

Rh+

Mother's anti-Rh+ antibodies from first pregnancy attack subsequent Rh+ baby, agglutinating blood and resulting in complications for the child, such as an enlarged liver.

Rh+

Figure 13–10 • Mechanism of hemolytic incompatibility between mother and fetus.

from the offspring may cross over into the blood supply of the mother. As the mother has no D alleles, her immune system responds by manufacturing an antibody to them, anti-D, which functions, as all antibodies do, to agglutinate the foreign D antigens and remove them from the mother's system. However, as red blood cells can cross the placental barrier from fetus to mother, so can the maternal anti-D antibodies travel from mother to offspring. If enough maternal anti-D is transferred to the fetus, it can incur hemolytic disease.

A mother's first pregnancy is generally a safe one, at least in regard to hemolytic disease. Under normal conditions no blood passes directly between mother and fetus. But about the time of birth fetal red blood cells can transfer between the fetus and mother, at which time the mother's immune system begins to produce anti-D antibodies. In subsequent pregnancies residual anti-D antibodies can have a cumulative effect and do serious harm to the fetus.

If the fetus dies of hemolytic disease, its two alleles, D and d, are lost to the population gene pool. If a balanced polymorphism favoring the heterozygote genotype did not exist and each of the alleles D and d were of equal fitness, chance processes alone would lead to the loss over time of one or the other. In the Rh example hemolytic incompatibility clearly selects against the heterozygote, yet both D and d alleles remain in the gene pool. That this is true is a puzzle for human geneticists. The case of double incompatibility between the Rh and ABO blood groups may shed some light on the solution.

Like the Rh system, the ABO system also provides situations that may result in hemolytic incompatibility in the fetus. In fact, all ABO phenotypes are potentially incompatible if the fetus possesses an antigen that the mother does not. Cohen (1970a,b), supporting earlier work, showed how maternal–fetal pairs who were doubly incompatible for both ABO and Rh ran less risk of fetal death than if the fetus was incompatible only for one system or the other. We do not know why this is the case.

The protective effect of double incompatibility for the Rh system is better understood. Apparently, antibodies to A or B, which may normally circulate in the mother's system, attack those fetal red blood cells if they manage to get into the maternal circulation. The fact that the fetal red blood cells are destroyed thus prevents the mother's body from recognizing the presence of the D allele in the first place, preventing the production of the anti-D antibody.

Recognizing the possibility of many more instances where multiple incompatibility will have a selective advantage allows us to look at the blood group frequency data from a new perspective. Through future research multiple loci analysis will probably shed light on the remainder of the blood group polymorphisms.

The HLA System

If the blood groups provide us with puzzling paradoxes, the immune system and the **HLA** (Human Lymphocyte Antigen) system are even more complex. The antigens of the HLA system are found on the surface of almost all body cells, perhaps most importantly on the leukocytes (Greek, meaning "white cells"), the white blood cells, and they function to protect the body from foreign substances by first recognizing and then, eliminating them. These antigens are coded on chromosome 6 at seven closely linked loci, A, B, C, D, D_r, Dq, and Dp. Additional loci and the I_r genes, controlling the immune response by determining the level of antibody response, are also found near the HLA loci.

At least 23 alleles (or antigens) have been discovered at the A locus, 47 at B, 8 at C, 19 at D, 16 at D_r, 3 at Dq and 6 at Dp. In combinations of two, these allelic systems can produce an enormous number of genotypes, certainly more than all of the known red blood cell group

HLA—Human Lymphocyte Antigen system; a white blood cell antigen system important in the immune response.

systems put together. Some of the allelic combinations are found in all human populations; others are restricted to specific geographic groups. Some interesting correlations have been discovered, for example, linking HLA B8 and intolerance to gluten, protein contained in wheat and barley. Apparently, the frequency of this allele in European populations is related to the shortness of time peoples have engaged in agriculture, lowest in those groups that adopted agriculture early in their history, higher in those that adopted agriculture more recently.

Inherited differences in HLA antigens of tissue are medically important in situations where the tissue of one individual is grafted onto that of another. The rejection of the graft, tissue incompatibility, is less severe if the antigens of the host and those of the donor are identical or closely related. The complex of antigens found in the blood groups and **histocompatibility** of HLA systems may well be responses to various disease causing agents, a sophisticated and complex system that has been evolving for a long period of time. In theory, the complexity of these systems would be the practical and anticipated result of natural selection.

Lactose Intolerance

The kinds of foods eaten by individuals in most societies are largely recent history. Domestication of plants and animals occurred only some 10,000 years ago, and our current diet is derived mainly from the success of this agricultural "revolution." Although this "revolution" came about in many cultures of the world more or less simultaneously, specific cultures adapted to new foods in different ways. Intolerance to gluten is one example of how people from different geographic regions adapt differently to new diets. The United States government learned this lesson when agencies responsible for foreign-aid programs discovered that food shipments of powdered milk to needy countries were being destroyed by the people it was meant to feed (Figure 13–11). Milk contains the sugar lactose that in cow's milk amounts to 4 to 5% of the total volume, but in powdered or condensed milk may be as high as 15 to 38%. For milk sugar to be digestible, the enzyme **lactase** is needed to break lactose down to its component sugars, glucose and galactose. Although it is true that nearly all mammals, including humans, produce enough lactase at birth, enzyme production falls off sharply once adulthood is reached. Most adults in the world are lactose intolerant; therefore, their consuming milk products being shipped as aid produced diarrhea and cramps. To individuals already weakened by hunger these additional problems could be life threatening.

Lactose intolerance in humans may be an adaptation that prevents adults who can eat other foods from consuming milk on a regular basis, thereby preventing them from directly competing with their young for nourishment. The evolutionary significance of lactase deficiency may also be viewed in terms of the ways different populations utilize

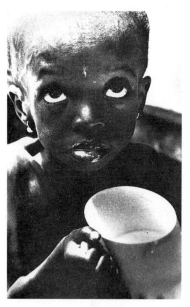

Figure 13–11 • Well-intentioned relief shipments of powdered milk only exacerbated the health problems of many already starving, lactose-intolerant Biafrans.

histocompatibility–immunologic similarity or identity of tissues; used in referring to tissues appropriate for grafting in medical procedures.

lactase–a sugar-splitting enzyme that helps to produce glucose ("blood sugar") and galactose ("brain sugar") from lactose ("milk sugar").

milk products. As a way of avoiding spoilage many peoples have fermented their raw milk, producing from it yogurt and cheese. In both these foods lactose is already broken down into its component sugars before ingestion. In some European groups, where adults continued to drink raw milk, selection pressure may have been for maintenance of an enzyme throughout adult life that allowed these populations to utilize an available food source.

Skin Pigmentation

The anatomy, physiology, and genetics of the skin and its coloration are complicated. The skin is composed of two layers, an outer epidermis and an inner dermis (Figure 13–12). The epidermis, which concerns us here, in turn has thin but significantly different levels: (1) the outermost *stratum corneum* (Latin, meaning "horny layer") composed of dead and dying skin cells, (2) the translucent *stratum lucidum*

Figure 13–12 • The structure of human skin, showing the melanin-containing *stratum granulosum.*

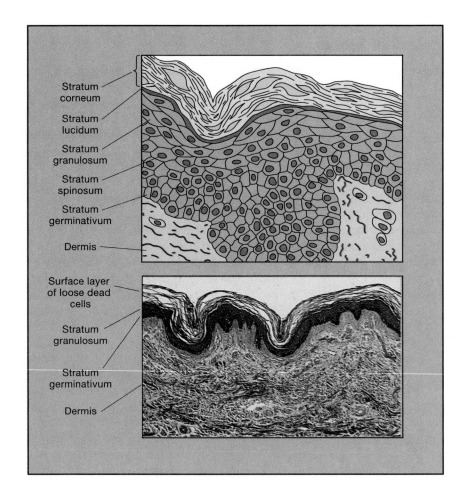

(Latin, meaning "light layer"), and (3) the pigment-containing levels *stratum granulosum, stratum spinosum,* and *stratum germanitivum,* from which new epidermal cells are made. Because the outer two layers of the epidermis are translucent the coloration of the lower levels of the epidermis are what determine skin color. Coloration, on a light to dark scale, depends upon the pigment, **melanin.** Melanocytes, cells found in the *stratum germinativum,* produce this brown pigment; actual skin color depends upon how active melanocytes are in producing melanin, since the number and density of these cells are the same in light- and dark-skinned individuals. In lighter skin one environmental factor affecting coloration is the sun's ultraviolet radiation. The red color of a "sunburn," the body's first response to excessive ultraviolet light, is the result of a concentration of hemoglobin near the skin's surface. Normal light or "white" skin is usually pinkish anyway, because of the red pigment in hemoglobin, that shows through the translucent upper skin layers. A "suntan," the body's usual second response to excessive UV light, can also darken lightly pigmented skin by stimulating the production of additional melanin.

The genetics of skin color is not completely understood. Some researchers believe that, rather than a single locus of a major gene, many loci and their multiple alleles work in combination to determine a person's pigmentation.

One of the most common misconceptions about race concerns skin pigmentation. The lay public, in particular, often confuses race with skin color, as in "white race," "people of color," and "black race." Skin color is, indeed, a very noticeable anatomical characteristic of inherited human variation. However, it is not in itself a reliable indicator of population affinities. For example, Africans, the Dravidians of southern India, and native Austral-Asians may all have darkly pigmented skin, but otherwise they share no particularly close genetic affinities. They are probably more closely related to lightly pigmented populations than to one another. This conclusion implies that skin color has been under rather strong selective forces and has changed relatively rapidly in recent human evolutionary history. To understand the variation in human skin color we must investigate its adaptive significance.

The colonial American physician John Mitchel (ca. 1700–1768) was the first to recognize the nature of human pigmented skin from his treatment of African-American slaves on plantations in Virginia. He realized that dark skin color was not due to a circulating fluid but was instead a static characteristic of the basal part of the epithelium. He hypothesized that dark skin color was an adaptation to a tropical climate and that the original complexion of humankind had been a "dark swarthy" (see Spencer, 1986:83–84).

Human skin serves in a general adaptive sense to regulate the penetration of UV light. In the lower latitudes near the equator which experience intense UV radiation, pigmented epidermal skin serves to block the harmful rays of the sun from reaching the dermis. This prevents

melanin–from Greek meaning "black," a dark brown or black pigment that occurs in the skin and hair.

sunburn and, eventually skin cancer from developing. For these reasons dark skin color has a great adaptive advantage for peoples of equatorial regions. That peoples living farther away from the Equator are subjected to lesser amounts of ultraviolet radiation does not explain why lighter skin color is characteristic of those regions. The question of why lightly pigmented skin evolved is not so clearly answered.

We do know that sunlight, in addition to producing harmful effects on the human body in excessive amounts, also has beneficial effects. Vitamin D is produced in the skin and subcutaneous tissue when light penetrates and is absorbed there. Although Vitamin D can also be eaten in the form of fish or fortified milk, experimental results indicate that most of the body's content of the vitamin derives from sunlight. Vitamin D, once it is in the body, is acted on by the kidneys and liver to produce derivatives that serve to facilitate: (1) calcium exchange in the formation of bone, and (2) calcium absorption in the intestinal wall. If Vitamin D is insufficient during growth, a condition known as **rickets** develops. In this disease the lower limbs become bowed outward and the pelvic bones are deformed because the bones are under-mineralized by a lack of calcium. Rickets can be treated successfully either by exposure to ultraviolet light or by administration of Vitamin D. Rickets has occurred frequently in many populations, such as African-Americans, whose darkly pigmented skin does not allow sufficient sunlight to penetrate to the dermis or with poor dietary intake of Vitamin D. Incidences of pelvic deformation among women of this group may reach as high as 15% (Molnar, 1992). The fossil record also shows that rickets occurred in the Neandertals in Ice Age northern Europe. With these facts in mind, many researchers believe that a more lightly pigmented skin in areas of reduced solar radiation would have been advantageous, because dark skin would have reduced the already limited sunlight needed for Vitamin D synthesis and lead to a Vitamin D deficiency.

Thus, a model explaining the distribution of skin pigmentation was developed on the basis of Vitamin D requirements for individuals living in different environmental conditions. The Vitamin D hypothesis, however, fails to explain conclusively why various shades of skin color persist at different latitudes. Whereas an excess of Vitamin D can cause vitamin poisoning, affect proper kidney functioning, and cause calcification of soft tissues and abnormal calcification on bone, research has shown that excessive exposures to UV light does not lead to such high levels of Vitamin D that toxicity occurs. While dark-skinned peoples are about six times slower than light-skinned peoples in producing the maximum amount of Vitamin D, this is still adequate, all other environmental conditions being equal. Robins (1991) has leveled other criticisms at the Vitamin D hypothesis, claiming rickets to be a disease of urbanization, not one particularly worrisome to our Paleolithic ancestors.

rickets–from Old English, meaning "twisted," a disease caused by deficiency of Vitamin D and characterized by the symptoms of poor calcification of bones, skeletal deformities, disturbance of growth, and generalized muscular weakness.

One other explanation for skin color distribution is based on wartime observations of different groups of soldiers and the effects cold climates had on them. Data confirmed in controlled studies showed that light-skinned soldiers were four times less likely to suffer frostbite than dark-skinned soldiers. Although the reason for this is not clearly understood, lighter-skinned people may have an advantage in cold climates, that is, they suffer less from injury by the cold, and this may have been a main factor that selected for lighter skin in early human populations migrating northward from Africa.

Clearly, skin color has adaptive value for people living under different environmental conditions. Nevertheless, the picture is clouded by many factors that may have contributed to the overall pattern of skin color distribution of modern peoples. We can be confident, however, that skin color is a product of natural selection and not a characteristic that can be or should be used as the primary criterion to delimit one specific population of people from another.

GENETIC INFLUENCE ON BEHAVIORAL VARIATION

Although human behavior has as its primary component the patterned learned behavior adopted by living and growing up in a society (*culture*) (Figure 13–13), many human behaviors also have a direct genetic basis. In contrast, among the social insects individual behavior is almost entirely genetically programmed and is limited to specific sets of tasks that each animal performs from birth to death. As the range and flexibility of insect behavior is limited, so also is the genetic variability upon which it is based. Among the mammals, primates show the highest amounts of behavioral variability. Humans, of course, have reached a level epitomizing an adaptation of behavioral flexibility and adaptability to diverse environments. How much of this variability is due to the responsiveness of culture and learning, and how much is due to genetic variation, has been examined by our looking at behavioral differences between groups where cultural and genetic influences can be minimized. For example, studies on the differences in males and females in the same culture, coupled with a functional interpretation of hormonal differences in behavior, attempt to relate behavior to biological sex differences. Studies of identical twins, who share the same genes, but may have different cultural experiences as they mature, have also provided important insights into the interplay of genetics and culture in behavior.

Part of the folklore of any human culture are stories describing behavioral differences. Of these, those stories that describe differences between men and women are probably the most common. For example, before the advent of empiricism Aristotle thought that men had more teeth than women. It would have been simple for Aristotle to

Figure 13–13 • The process of enculturation—learning a culture.

open up the mouths of a number of men and women and simply count teeth, but he never did. The idea that men are more "intelligent" than women has been shown in scientific studies to be insupportable, but for centuries this idea has remained in place. It was not until 1920, for example, that society held women to be competent to vote in the United States. In many countries of the world, women's suffrage has yet to come to pass.

Twin Studies

Identical (monozygotic) twins who have been reared apart provide one of the simplest and most powerful focuses for disentangling the influence of environmental and genetic factors on human characteristics and their variable expression (Figure 13–14). The published report of *The Minnesota Study of Twins Reared Apart* (Bouchard et al., 1990) offers a basis for understanding the contributions of genetics versus environmental influences.

Assuming first that genetic and environmental factors are uncorrelated and combine additively, the following expression can be developed to account for total observed variance of any particular characteristic.

$$V_{total} = V_g + V_e + V_m$$

where V_g is the variance due to genetic differences, V_e is the variance due to environmental or experiential factors, and V_m is variance due to measurement error. In the twin study, V_m has been estimated at about 10% of V_{total}. For traits such as IQ, V_g has a surprisingly high (approximately 70%) heritability as reported in these studies. This suggests that, although parents may be able to affect their children's rate of cognitive skill acquisition, they probably have little influence on the ultimate level attained. These findings do not imply that traits like IQ cannot be enhanced. In fact, a recent survey (Flynn, 1987) that covered 14 countries showed that the average IQ test score has significantly increased in recent years. The Bouchard study did not define or limit what might be conceivably achieved in an optimal environment, but it did indicate that in the broad middle class of an industrial society, two-thirds of the observed variances of IQ could be traced to genetic variation.

Race, IQ, and Social Class

Figure 13–14 • Identical twins studied in the Minnesota Study.

The heritability of intelligence has been difficult to predict, because the actual genetic basis of intelligence is not well understood. The Minnesota Twin Study may provide us with one estimation of heritability, but we must consider a number of other factors before we can apply the data from specific individuals to whole populations.

In a variety of ways, quantitative individual differences in intelligence can be recognized and these differences may roughly indicate the genetic component that relates to them. However, when we step away from measurements based on individual differences and attempt to extrapolate from and apply them to broader categories, such as populations, we must ask additional questions. One question concerns the range of intelligence for all populations. Is there any evidence to suggest that whole groups of people fall below (or rise above) some hypothetical worldwide average?

The consequences of the answers to these questions are not simply academic. For example, only 20 years ago the Commonwealth of Virginia had a law in effect that allowed the state to sterilize any individual without requiring his or her consent if the state found them to be mentally deficient. This law, which the Supreme Court upheld in 1927, permitted the state to perform over 7,500 sterilizations during the period 1924 to 1972. In theory, such a law had the potential to be extended to include whole groups of people considered to be "mentally" inferior.

What is "intelligence" in reality and how has it been measured? From a biological point of view we might consider intelligence as a manifestation of the innate intellectual capacity of the brain (Birdsell, 1981). However, innate intelligence cannot yet be defined in precise genetic terms. Psychologists have usually looked at intelligence on the basis of what can be measured by testing such skills as memory, problem solving, ability to synthesize information, and motivation (more difficult to measure). Some psychologists have listed up to 120 different components for intelligence (Bodmer and Cavalli-Sforza, 1976).

Intelligence is usually measured by administering a standardized test to an individual and then scoring that test. One common intelligence test is the well-known Stanford-Binet IQ test. **IQ** or "intelligence quotient" measures a person's "mental age" based on the test score and divides it by his or her chronological age. The test sets the average response at 100 with the range for average intelligence falling between 90 and 110. Because the test supposedly measures a number of abilities, often individuals score differently on the various test sections. Furthermore, over an individual's life span an IQ can change as much as 30 points due to a number of factors, not the least of which may be the individual's overall improvement in taking tests.

The IQ test, originally developed in France by psychologist Alfred Binet (1857–1911), was designed to identify children who might be learning disabled and, subsequently, require special education. Today, test scores between individuals of different groups have been used to set educational policy on the assumption that whole groups of people might be incapable of using certain educational opportunities.

In the United States the most questionable use of IQ testing has been in response to a fairly consistent and large body of data that sug-

IQ–Intelligence Quotient; a score on a standardized psychological test designed in western Europe and North America to measure "an individual's aggregate capacity to act purposefully, think rationally, and deal effectively with his environment."

gests the average IQ of African-Americans to be about 15 points below that of white Americans. In a number of cases (Jensen, 1969, 1980) educators and others have attributed these differences to genetics. This contention, however, is rejected by most anthropologists and evolutionary biologists. A number of tests have confirmed their stance. If white Americans on the average were more intelligent than African-Americans and the difference were due to genetics, African-Americans with a high degree of European admixture should do better on IQ tests than African-Americans who do not have a high degree of European admixture. They do not. Again, if this model were correct those African-Americans who did score the highest should have the highest degree of European admixture. They do not.

Japanese children from a socioeconomically disadvantaged group, the Buraku-min, scored on the average 16 points below other Japanese children, roughly a comparable difference between white Americans and African-Americans. Yet there is no genetic distinction of the Buraku-min as a group. In fact, they can be distinguished from other Japanese only by their place of birth or current residence. Such examples, indicate that "intelligence" as measured by standardized tests has a strong environmental component (Birdsell, 1981:386–387).

Other environmental factors affecting IQ scores—diet, disease, educational quality, and social class—all must figure into the formula. Also the design of IQ tests is socioeconomically based because of the cultural differences between those making up such tests and those taking them. No one yet has constructed a culture-free IQ test and probably never will. Therefore, in large measure, the IQ test applied across cultural or ethnic boundaries provides only a quantitative assessment of how great or little relevance the questions have to test takers.

Alcoholism

A widespread folk myth is that men can consume more alcohol with less effect than can women. However, this myth may contain some truth. In terms of size, men and women are often different. On average, women are smaller than men and thus women are more affected than men by the same amount of alcohol consumed. On the other hand, this observation fails to explain the fact that, when men and women of equal size drink identical quantities of alcohol, invariably the women tend to get intoxicated more rapidly. Women, it turns out, produce far less of a crucial enzyme in the lining of their gastro-intestinal tracts than do men (Figure 13–15). This enzyme, **alcohol dehydrogenase,** acts to break down alcohol, reducing the amount before it gets into the bloodstream. Because of the reduced amount of enzyme, women absorb about 30% more alcohol than men.

Men who are alcoholics have about half as much alcohol dehydrogenase as their healthy counterparts, but alcoholic women show almost

alcohol dehydrogenase—an enzyme that converts alcohol in the body to the chemical compounds known as aldehydes.

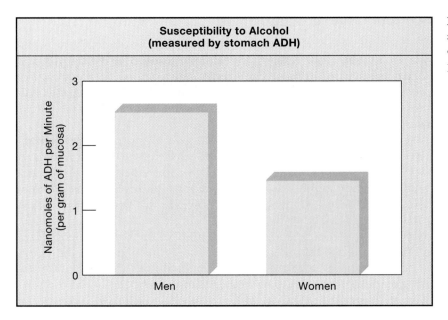

Figure 13–15 • Production of alcohol dehydrogenase after consumption of alcohol, compared in men and women.

no enzyme activity at all, which may explain why alcoholic women suffer more heavily from liver damage then do alcoholic men (Yoshida et al., 1991). Thus, alcohol consumption and the extent of intoxication could be related to a particular biochemical variability between the sexes. The question of why this variability exits, however, requires an explanation.

Undoubtedly one of the oldest intoxicants used by humans is alcohol. As with most other intoxicants and hallucinogens, ethnographic data suggest that its ingestion generally falls within the realm of male behavior and outside the realm of what is considered to be proper female behavior (Mandelbaum, 1965:282). Many reasons may exist for this, reasons that vary culturally. However, in hunting and gathering as well as traditional societies, any drug or alcohol use for women of childbearing years is usually culturally prohibited (Saunders, 1980:67), intoxication being known to have important reproductive consequences both pre- and postnatally. Evidence from a number of cultures shows that this prohibition may be suspended for postmenopausal women (women beyond the age of childbearing). If we could demonstrate that for a considerable time regular alcohol use was predominantly a male activity, we might conclude that selection was operating to provide some protection against what clearly is a poison to the system. The genetics of this protection would be what they seem to be—sexually dimorphic. Certainly, more work needs to be done before the evolutionary implications of these observations can be confirmed. It does show, however, that an evolutionary perspective can be useful in generating new models of understanding variability.

Schizophrenia

We know of numerous situations in which mutant dominant or recessive alleles may cause disease, for example, **muscular dystrophy** and **aortic aneurysm.** In these cases as in many others, the frequency of occurrence of the mutant alleles is an equilibrium situation that balances the rate of mutations created against the rate of mutations lost as a result of an individual's death.

Recently the unlikely case for a balanced polymorphism for **schizophrenia** (Greek, meaning "split mind") was investigated by Allen and Sarich (1988). Other, earlier studies have shown that there is about a tenfold variation in the rates of expression of schizophrenia in different human populations. On the average, however, schizophrenia occurs at a frequency of about 1% worldwide. Using this 1% figure as a guide, coupled with demonstrated reduced fertility of the overt schizophrenia genotypes, we see that the genotype is being maintained in the population at a frequency far greater than mutation rates would allow. Studies attempting to demonstrate higher than average fertility in the relatives of schizophrenics have so far proven inconclusive; however, an absolute selective advantage of only 5% would be enough to maintain the polymorphism. But it would be very difficult to detect.

For this situation to exist at all, the decreased fitness of overt schizophrenia must be balanced by a corresponding increase in fitness of individuals who carry the gene(s) but do not manifest the pathological condition. In this case, Allen and Sarich propose that heterozygote individuals possess an unusually high rate of social creativity that gives them their advantage.

To explain this phenomenon from an evolutionary perspective, Allen and Sarich suggest that an increasingly fit role may have existed for the individual who could, to a greater extent than most, reject the prevailing opinions of the day and, thus, in a "mundane" way promote changes in technology and behavior. According to Allen and Sarich, among those individuals who possess the schizophrenia gene(s), a balance will occur between those who can handle the condition productively and those who cannot. Once the marginal gain in fitness equals the loss of fitness experienced by those overt schizophrenics, a genetic equilibrium balance point for the polymorphism is reached.

Unlike the malarial example the loci and gene(s) for schizophrenia have so far been difficult to detect. Potential tests for schizophrenia are based on the knowledge that diagnosed schizophrenics, as well as their relatives, show increased sensitivity to the drug dopamine, possibly because these individuals have elevated dopamine receptor densities in various parts of their brains. In an evolutionary sense, schizophrenia might be viewed as a condition that increases in frequency with the rise of complex societies. In such societies social dysfunction may be better tolerated than in more traditional ones.

muscular dystrophy–an inborn abnormality of muscle tissue that leads to lack of function and deterioration.

aortic aneurysm–weakening of the wall of the aorta artery, a condition which can lead to rupture of the aorta and death.

schizophrenia–from Greek meaning "split mind," a group of mental disorders which may be characterized by delusions, hallucinations, and withdrawal of an individual's interest from other people and the outside world.

An evolutionary model can offer explanations for the apparent worldwide differences in schizophrenia. In Micronesia, for example, where some island populations exhibit no evidence of schizophrenia, the absence of this condition might be due to genetic drift. In Taiwan, where aboriginal Taiwanese groups are found to have much lower rates of schizophrenia than those found among ethnic Chinese who also live on the island, the frequency differences might be reflective of genetic differences in the two populations. Whatever the final outcome of our understanding of the variability in the incidence of schizophrenia, evolutionary models offer the chance of new predictive models and greater insight into worldwide differences.

Whatever the ancient origins and functions of genetic variability are, repercussions of variation in contemporary society are pervasive and important. A human species whose members did not vary genetically with respect to significant cognitive and motivational attributes and who were uniformly average by current standards would have created a very different society than the one we know. Modern society not only augments the influence of genotype on behavioral variability, but permits this variability to contribute reciprocally to the rapid pace of cultural change.

 ## SUMMARY

Humans are one of the most biologically variable of animal species, a fact that reflects the wide range of environments and habitats in which people live. Biological anthropologists measure this variability both quantitatively, as in stature and weight, and qualitatively, as in the presence or absence of the shovel-shaped incisor. Although the level of heterozygosity (between 10 to 15%) at loci among individuals within a population is only slightly lower than the differences seen between populations, population variation shows a geographical component that is a result of evolution. Local, geographically defined populations of humans are sometimes termed "races." "Race," however, is a term that has been frequently misused and is not synonymous with "ethnic group." Although we know that geographically isolated populations develop their own unique characteristics by mutation, genetic drift, and natural selection, it is difficult to categorize human "races" because of the continual ebb and flow of genetic exchange that occurs between individuals. It is also not scientifically useful to do so. Modern genetic studies show that some traditionally measured characteristics, such as skin color, are not good guides to actual population groupings.

The evolutionary forces of mutation, genetic drift, migration, and natural selection contribute to other aspects of human variability. Certain characteristics arise in individuals and spread by chance that have no discernible selective advantage. Such examples may be found in the variable excretion of methanethiol. Other variable conditions, such as sickle-cell anemia, provide heterozygotes in malarial areas an advantage in their ability to resist the disease. Much of the variability in human populations is not so clearly understood, yet a selective advantage must be present to account for the enormous numbers of combinations that exist among the blood groups and the HLA systems.

There may be considerable genetic influence on behavioral variation, as well as on morphophysiological variation, an area where twin studies have been useful, especially in the area of the inheritance of intelligence. No convincing evidence, however, exists for genetic differences in intelligence between human populations, IQ tests being too societally or subculturally based to provide any objective framework for measure.

In other areas, such as in the studies of alcoholism and schizophrenia, an understanding of variation coupled with an evolutionary perspective has generated new models of understanding these conditions in terms of their prevalence and distribution in different societies.

 ## CRITICAL-THINKING QUESTIONS

1. Name three factors that influence human biological variation.
2. Describe the process of geographical isolation and the role it plays in human biological variation.
3. Explain the heterozygote advantage selected for in malarial regions and how this relates to human genetic variability.
4. Is skin color a good indicator of a person's racial group? Elaborate.
5. Are IQ tests a valid indication of intelligence? Explain.
6. Discuss the theory of balanced polymorphism of schizophrenia.

 ## SUGGESTED READINGS

Brues, A. 1977. *People and Races.* New York: Macmillan Publishing Co. Discussions of genetics and human variation and the concept of race. This 8-chapter volume focuses on specific aspects of human variation such as blood groups and pigmentation. It concludes with a statement on new and future races of humankind.

Harrison, G. A., J. M. Tanner, D. R. Pilbeam, and P. T. Baker. 1988. *Human Biology. An Introduction to Human Evolution, Variation, Growth, and Adaptability,* 3rd. ed. Oxford: Oxford University Press. Detailed text that reviews the subjects of human evolution, human genetics, biological variation in modern human populations, human growth, and human ecology. The concluding section includes the subject material of nutritional ecology, climatic adaptation, disease, and population stability.

Johnston, F. 1973. *Microevolution of Human Populations*. Englewood Cliffs, N.J.: Prentice Hall. Population genetics and the Hardy-Weinberg equilibrium are discussed in relation to natural selection and microevolution in human populations. Major contribution of this text is its discussion of the search for natural selection.

Molnar, S. J. 1992. *Races, Types and Ethnic Groups: The Problem of Human Variation,* 3rd. ed. Englewood Cliffs, N.J.: Prentice Hall. Discussions include the biological basis for human variation, the perception of human differences, and the distribution of those differences in world populations. The text reviews what we know about the adaptive value of human variation. Race, behavior, and intelligence, along with some speculations on the future of the human species, are also discussed.

Woodward, U. 1992. *Human Heredity and Society,* St. Paul, Minn.: West Publishing Co. General review of genetics, evolution, populations, and species. Includes discussions of human behavior and intelligence, social Darwinism, sociobiology, and genetic engineering.

The Human Life Cycle: Human Biology, Growth, and Adaptability

Human Growth Studies
How Growth Is Defined
How Growth Is Measured
The Seven Stages of Human
  Growth
Genetic and Hormonal Control
  of Growth
Growth and Development:
  A Guide to Evolutionary
  History
Secular Trends in Growth
  and Maturation
Growth and Development
  in Different Human Groups
Responses to Modernization
  and the Urban Environment

**Human Adaptability
  to Environment**
Heat and Cold
Light and Solar Radiation
High Altitude

**Nutritional and Dietary
  Aspects of Adaptation**

**Modern Life and Human
  Evolution**

Summary

Critical-Thinking Questions

Suggested Readings

We have seen how populations adapt to changing environmental conditions over time. This is evolution, a long-term response involving changes in the genetic makeup of a population. As a result of evolution, the human organism is, as indeed all organisms are, a palimpsest[1] of physiological and morphological adaptations. Some of these basic adaptations are very old, extending back to early vertebrate and even prevertebrate ancestors (see Chapters 2 and 5). Others are much more recent evolutionary acquisitions.

We have already determined that individuals in a population vary genetically from one another (see Chapter 4). Variability in gene pools offers the possibility that some individuals will be successful under different environmental situations or if the environmental conditions in which a population adapted changes in some way. The **genetic plasticity** of a species is the degree to which individuals can survive under increasingly diverse environmental situations. The different ways that individuals respond to changing environmental circumstances are measures of a species' genetic plasticity. Throughout an individual's life cycle, a dynamic interaction exists between environment and physiology, and this interaction is the subject of this chapter.

The study of a species' ability to adapt to different environmental conditions and the relation of this ability to the evolution and biology of the population is the study of **adaptability.** This term refers also to an individual's reaction to changes in environmental conditions, and it includes any biochemical, physiological, or behavioral response that improves its ability to function. Within the genetic limits of any species, each individual can, in varying degrees, make short-term changes in his or her physiological response to specific environmental situations as they are encountered. In higher altitudes, for example, one of the body's responses to hypoxia, that is, the lowering of the level of oxygen in the blood, is to increase both breathing and heart rate. This response assists the body, to some degree, by increasing both blood flow and the partial pressure of oxygen in the lungs.

---

[1]A palimpsest (Greek, meaning "scraped over") was a parchment that had been reused several times through which earlier writings could be seen when the parchment was held up to the light. The term here is a metaphor, indicating the visibility of both recent and ancient aspects of human adaptation.

genetic plasticity–ability of a developing organism to alter its form and function in conformity with demands of the immediate environment.

adaptability–range of physiological and anatomical changes and adjustments allowed by a species' adaptation.

In this chapter on adaptability the subject of growth and development is also examined. The study of growth is important from at least two different perspectives. First, as J. M. Tanner (1988), the British growth specialist, put it: growth is a mirror of the condition of society. Growth rates and development respond to the environmental conditions that surround an individual during its life. Less than optimal environmental conditions can retard the realization of the genetic potential of an individual, as for example, in the case of stature, which will not be recouped even as that individual matures. Second, the study of growth provides important clues towards an understanding of evolution (Bogin, 1995).

HUMAN GROWTH STUDIES

The process by which human beings develop biologically from conception to death is termed *growth*. The details of the growth process are the keys to understanding the unique attributes of a species' adaptation. In a sense an individual "grows into" the adaptive niche characteristic of adult members of the species to which it belongs. The study of human growth is a broad field and one to which biological anthropologists and human biologists have made and continue to make significant contributions. Tanner suggests in his *A History of the Study of Human Growth* (1981) that there were three main "impulses," or themes, in the development of the field. Understanding the motivations of researchers on the subject of human growth and development is important to our assimilation of this material into human natural history.

First, there have been social motivations for growth studies. Investigations of physical and physiological development of children began, for example, in Britain in response to the child labor reform movement during the nineteenth century. At this time, eruption of the second molar began to be taken as a sign that puberty had been attained, and thus employable age had been reached. The second molar thereby became known as the "factory molar."

Second, there have been studies of growth motivated by medical concerns. Included in this category are studies undertaken to monitor the physical and developmental progress of children. The earliest modern studies in biological anthropology in the United States, and the first anthropology doctorate granted (to A.F. Chamberlain in 1892, at Clark University, Worcester, Massachusetts), were in human growth studies supervised by Franz Boas. Boas, sometimes referred to as "the father of American anthropology," undertook in the late 1890s large-scale anthropometric studies of American school children in order to establish for the U.S. Department of Education standards for weight and height at each chronological age. Also included in this category of growth studies are those relating to nutritional requirements for normal growth, the effects of environment on growth, and medical aspects of growth and its abnormalities.

Third, there are evolutionary studies of growth, prompted by a desire to understand the interaction of growth and the evolutionary biology of the human species. Although of the three kinds of study these have the longest history, extending back to Buffon and later Haeckel, there have been fewer of them. Haeckel's famous "ontogeny recapitulates phylogeny" theory (Figure 14–1) is the most well-known of these early studies. Louis Bolk's (1926) **homunculus theory** of human evolution was the most clearly enunciated version of the idea that early human fossils would be discovered looking very much like fetal and pre-adult stages in human development. Bolk's conviction that early human fossils would show the large brain characteristic of human newborns was disproved by fossil discoveries of relatively small-brained (by human standards) australopithecines and the unmasking of the Piltdown hoax (Chapter 11).

From an evolutionary perspective the study of growth and maturation over time can tell us something about the forces of selection for specific characteristics. For example, the human fossil record shows that the earliest members, the australopithecines, were relatively short in stature (about 130 cm.) and small in cranial capacity (about 400 cc.). The succeeding species, members of the genus *Homo,* on the other hand, were as tall as the average of modern *Homo sapiens* and possessed a brain size about twice that of the earlier group. Clearly, selection favored increases in these two areas of growth.

The study of growth is also important as an assessment of how successful a population is at any point in time in terms of its overall adaptation to the environment. How well the nutritional needs of individuals in a population are met is, perhaps, best reflected from studies of growth rate and maturation. But other variables, such as pollution, stress, and family structures, too, can affect patterns of growth. These will be discussed later in this chapter.

Comparing the rates of growth between closely related species can also provide important insight into the different biology of each (Figure 14–2). Brain growth rate in humans is different from that in the apes. The accelerated fetal brain growth rate in humans (see Chapter 5) continues postnatally to about one year of age. In the apes postnatal brain growth slows to the adult rate immediately after birth. This is in part due to the extension of childhood years in humans as well as a reflection of the birth process. In humans, birth is a difficult process, as large headed newborns exceed the normal dimensions of the mother's birth canal. Such a situation at birth demands the smallest head size (and, thus, brain size) that is, one only substantial enough to sustain life. The accelerated rate of postnatal brain growth is a way by which, at least in the sense of motor development, the less developed humans at birth "catch-up" with the comparably aged apes.

homunculus theory—held that human ancestors when discovered would look similar to early stages of modern human development.

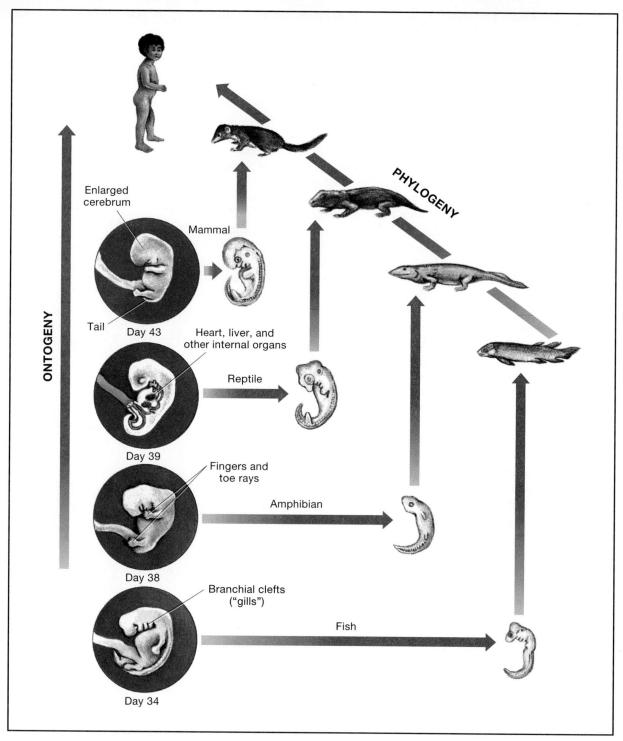

Figure 14–1 • Early stages of human embryological development recall stages of vertebrate evolution from fish to animals. Ernst Haeckel recognized the phenomenon and
coined the phrase "ontogeny recapitulates phylogeny," but it is now appreciated that the
recapitulation pertains only to the early phases of growth and development of ancestral
species, not to the adult forms of species themselves.

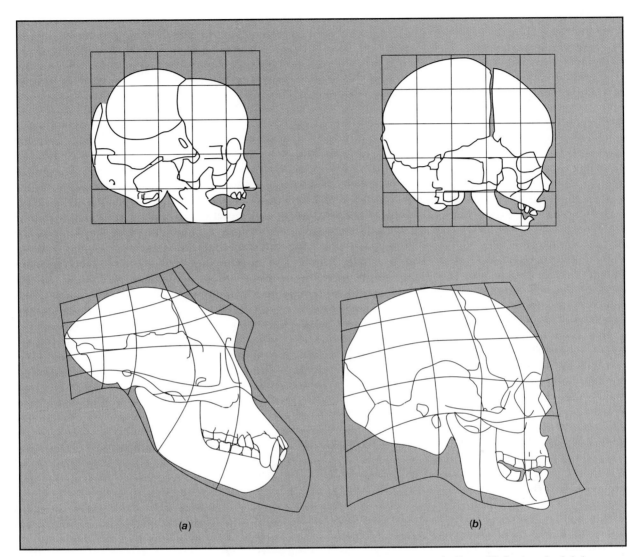

Figure 14–2 • Transformation grids comparing (*a*) fetal and adult chimpanzee skulls to (*b*) fetal and adult humans. The relative amount of distortion of the grid lines overlying the adult skull proportions indicates the amount of growth of different parts of the skull. (From Bogin, 1988)

How Growth Is Defined

Although growth is the increase in size of an organism and its parts during development, it is sometimes distinguished from **development,** that is, that part of growth that occurs prior to birth and consists of the differentiation of various tissues and body parts of the embryo and fetus. "Growth" has sometimes been defined as "increase in size," "development" as "increase in tissue diversity." Here, both growth and development are treated as pre- and postnatal growth and as components of the same continuous process.

development–embryological differentiation of organs and tissues; sometimes considered the earliest stage of growth.

interstitial growth–growth by new cell formation throughout the mass of a structure, tissue, or organ.

appositional growth–growth by adding of layers at a specfic point or plane.

allometry–proportional growth of one body structure to another or to overall body size.

isometric–a direct or linear relationship of the growth of one structure to another.

Growth takes place in several ways. The most common pattern for growth is an increase in the number of cells. In nonregenerating tissue this is usually followed by an increase in the size of cells or by an increase in the space between cells. Soft body structures, such as the brain or muscles, develop by **interstitial growth,** where cells proliferate from many centers within the structure. Muscle tissue represents a unique pattern of growth in that fibers are formed by the fusion of several cells, which means that each fiber has more than one nucleus. Hard or rigid structures, on the other hand, such as bones or teeth, develop by **appositional growth,** the laying down of new layers on top of those already formed. Counting these layers can tell us how old an individual is or was. Dean and Benyan (1989) have used the microscopic growth lines in tooth enamel to calculate the ages at death of australopithecines. Growth does not proceed at the same rate in all tissues (Figure 14–3). Indeed, differential growth, defined as the relative growth rates between two structures, is an important distinguishing characteristic between species.

An important component of differential growth is **allometry,** the relative change in size of structures compared to each other or compared to overall body size. The relationship between one part of the body and another may be direct, or **isometric,** expressed in mathematical form by $y=bx$ (where y is the size of the part, x is the size of another, and b is the times larger or smaller part x is of part y). Alterna-

Figure 14–3 • Relative growth rates of reproductive tissues and brain size, compared to overall body size.

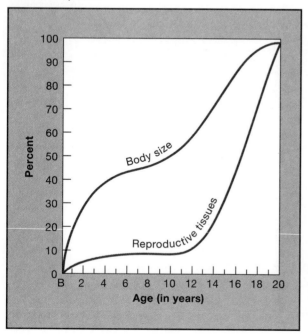

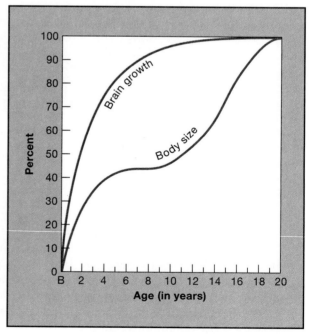

tively, the relationship between the sizes of body parts x and y may be allometric, that is, one of the parts changes in size proportionally to the other. This relationship is expressed by the relationship $y=bx^k$, where k is a certain power indicating that body part x increases or decreases with respect to changes in y. An example of allometry at work during human growth is the relationship between head height and overall body length or height. At birth the ratio of head height to body length is 1:4, and during growth it decreases to 1:7.5 in the adult.

How Growth Is Measured

Biological anthropologists who study growth are also called **auxologists.** They measure growth and other physical attributes of living humans, using instruments designed for the purpose. The subdiscipline that is dedicated to the measurement of the human body is known as **anthropometry.** As in the study of skeletal remains, a number of landmarks (Figure 14–4) have been defined for the living body. These serve to standardize measurements and comparisons between human groups and between individuals.

There is a good but not absolute correlation of chronological age with measures of skeletal maturation, dental eruption, and increase in overall body size. Variation may be due to (1) a different genetic profile for the population to which an individual belongs, determining the onset of growth of certain parts of the body; (2) variations in nutrition both pre- and postnatally that may retard or maximize growth potential; and (3) normal population variation in the onset of growth for individual characteristics. In assessing age by the use of biological criteria as many criteria as possible should be used to insure the most accurate estimate. Even so, precision within a range of error of between two and three years is usually the best that can be accomplished. A well-known case of skeletal age detective work involved the "Princes of the Tower" (Figure 14–5), who were put to death either by King Richard III or King Henry VII of England during the War of the Roses. If the ages of the two boys could be determined by their skeletons to plus-or-minus a year the crime could be pinned historically on either Richard III or Henry VII by the dates of their reigns. But taking into account the variability that can occur, the best that biological anthropologists could do was estimate a three- to four-year period of time that overlapped with both kings' reigns.

The Seven Stages of Human Growth

There are seven stages of growth (Bogin, 1995): **embryonic** which takes place before birth, during which there is rapid growth but little differentiation in function of various tissues; prematurity up to the adult condition that takes into account the stages of **infancy, childhood, juvenile,** and **adolescence,** during which a balance between growth

auxology–the study of growth.

anthropometry–the portion of physical anthropology concerned with measurement of the human body.

embryonic–that period of growth prior to birth, especially weeks 3 through 8; growth during the last six months of gestation is sometimes referred to as fetal growth.

infancy–earliest stage of post-partum growth, extending from birth to the time of weaning.

childhood–the period of growth from weaning to the attainment of adult brain size.

juvenile–the period of growth between attainment of adult brain size and the onset of puberty.

adolescence–the period of growth between puberty and the attainment of full adult stature and sexual maturity.

Figure 14–4 • Somatological landmarks used in measurements and assessments of growth. From Georges Olivier, *Practical Anthropology,* copyright © 1969. Courtesy of Charles C. Thomas, Publisher, Springfield, Illinois.

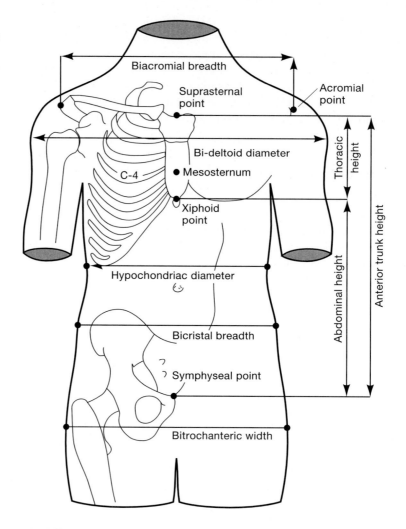

and differentiation of tissue functions exists; **maturity,** when functional activity is the primary activity and a steady replacement of cells takes place; and **old age,** when the rate of cell death is greater than the rate of replacement. Primates have a proportional relationship between the length of the seven stages that remains relatively constant throughout the order (Figure 14–6). As maximum life span increases, the embryonic, prematurity, maturity, and old age life periods proportionately lengthen. Humans have the longest life span of the primates and the longest period of prematurity growth.

Bogin has characterized each of the stages of prematurity with both biological and behavioral features. Infancy is defined as that period where the individual is nourished almost exclusively by its mother's milk. This stage ends upon weaning which in preindustrialized societies occurs at about three years of age. Childhood is a period of continued dependency, characterized by reliance upon others for feed-

maturity–life cycle stage typified by steady state replacement of cells and cessation of growth.

old age–life cycle stage typified by a greater rate of cell death than replacement.

Figure 14–5 • "Princes of the Tower" as a forensic case in age determination. Variability in skeletal maturation did not allow their murder to be pinned on Richard III or Henry VII.

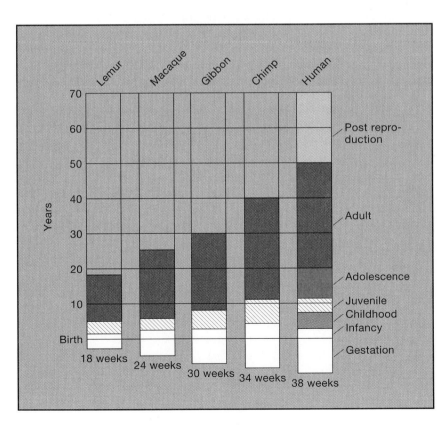

Figure 14–6 • Progressive prolongation of the life stages among the primates.

ing and protection, and ends when the growth of the brain (in weight) has reached the adult size, somewhere about seven years of age. The juvenile period is inserted between the end of childhood and puberty, the onset of which for girls is at about age ten and for boys at about two years later. Postpubescent growth and the development of secondary sexual characteristics marks the adolescent stage which ends when adult stature and full reproductive maturity is reached. On the average adolescence ends, and maturity or adulthood begins, by about 19 years of age for women and 21 to 25 years of age for men.

The human pattern of growth after birth is unique among the mammals. Several stages, such as childhood and adolescence, have no counterpart in the growth patterns of other animals. For the largest brained member of the primates the relatively slow physical growth of childhood holds advantages in that it extends the period of brain development and provides time for the development of technical as well as social skills. In addition, Bogin (1995:53) believes that childhood should also be viewed as a feeding adaptation where the child may be provisioned with food by kin, removing this exclusive burden from the mother.

Evolutionarily speaking, there is a reproductive advantage to humans in shortening the length of infancy by inserting childhood between the end of infancy and the juvenile period. The childhood stage frees the mother from nursing and the "inhibitions of ovulation related to continuous nursing." Thus, human females have a potentially shorter interval between births of offspring, an adaptation offering a reproductive advantage over the closely related apes (Table 14–1). The reduction of the birth spacing interval, a characteristic of "r-selection" (see

Table 14–1 • Comparative Fertility in Three Different Human Groups and in the Chimpanzee

	Chimpanzee	!Kung (Botswana)	Agta (Philippines)	Ache (Paraguay)
Menarche (Age in years)	8.8	16.6	17.1	14.3
Age at First Birth (Years)	14	19.9	20.1	18.5
Birth Spacing (Years)	5.6	4.1	3.05	3.2
Fertility Rate (Average Number of Children)	2.0	4.7	—	—
Average Reproductive Life-Span (Years)	25–30	36	—	—

Data from Smith (1992).

Chapter 4), enables humans to produce more offspring as compared to apes, who in this regard are more "K-selected."

Bogin also believes that "the allometry of the growth of the human child maintains an infantile, or neotenous, appearance which stimulates nurturing and care-giving behaviors in older individuals." Multiple caregiving can be quite common among human groups. For example, among the Aka pygmies of Africa, infants as young as four months of age have been observed being exchanged up to eight times per hour among caregivers (Hewlett, 1991). This, presumably, would lead to a substantial increase in early information sharing than if the infant, and later child, were confined as the sole responsibility of its mother.

The stage of human adolescence is also unique among the primates in that it is marked by a rapid acceleration in growth of the skeleton that accompanies the onset of sexual maturation. The sex-specific order of growth does not usually vary between individuals who may be early or late maturers, well or poorly nourished, dwell in rural or urban settings, or whose origins differ geographically. Growth seems to seek a *target,* rather than to proceed according to a strict schedule. If a spurt in growth that would normally have occurred at a certain age is delayed because of poor nutrition or illness, when conditions improve, then there is a rapid period of growth later on to "catch up." This aspect of growth is termed **canalization,** because there are certain channels or paths that it will follow. For normal and healthy individuals this growth spurt at its peak for stature velocity averages 9 to 10.3 cm/year in boys and 7.1 to 9.0 cm/year in girls (Tanner et al., 1976). This growth spurt is primarily responsible for the average 12.6 cm in height difference between males and females. The timing of adolescent growth is different for males and females (Figure 14–7). Females complete the growth spurt before becoming fertile. Males, on the other hand, begin the growth spurt after they have begun to produce sperm.

Although males and females take separate paths of growth through adolescence, during this period both sexes learn the necessary skills it takes to become functioning adults in their societies. Bogin believes that:

> The dramatic physical changes that girls experience during adolescence serve as efficient advertisements of their sexual and social maturation. So efficient in fact that they stimulate adults to include adolescent girls in their social circles, while encouraging the girls themselves to initiate adult social interactions (p. 57).

In girls, adolescence begins about the age of 12.5 years at menarche, usually followed by a period of one to three years of sterility. During this period menstrual cycling occurs but without ovulation. Females, also, do not attain adult pelvic inlet size until 17 to 18 years, as the pelvis has its own slower pattern of growth from that of the maturation

canalization–the directed trajectory of growth in certain directions even if normal growth spurts are delayed.

Figure 14–7 • Adolescent spurt in height growth for girls and boys.

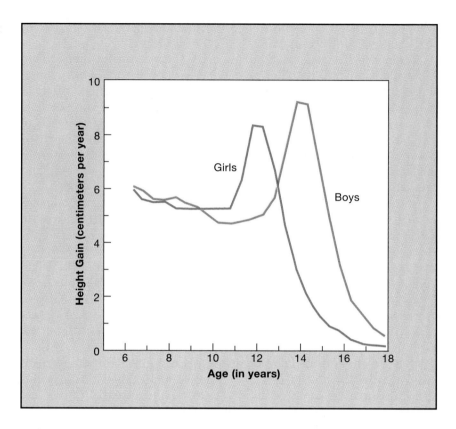

of the reproductive tract. Taking everything into account a female does not reach adult reproductive maturity until about the age of 20 to 24 years. Younger mothers face higher risks of spontaneous abortion and give birth to babies of lower than average birth weight at rates about twice as high as those of older females. Is there a reproductive advantage to this pattern of female adolescence? Bogin is convinced that the difference in infant survival rates is significant for first born humans whose mothers have greater experience in raising them because of adolescent learning. Studies of the nonhuman primates show that between 50 to 60% of the first born offspring die as compared to about 44% of infants of hunter-gatherer groups such as the !Kung. This is a significant advantage of nearly 16%.

The pattern of development for boys differs from that of girls in that boys become fertile at an early age and then attain adult size and the physical appearance of adult males. The median age for sperm production is about 13.4 years, yet cross-cultural evidence shows that few males are successful as fathers until they reach an age somewhere in their twenties. In the United States, for example, statistics report that only 4% of all births are fathered by men under 20 years old. The survival advantage of adolescence for boys is that, with increasing blood testosterone levels, they become more interested in adult activities and begin to behave more like adult males, while at the same time continuing to look like boys. As Bogin observes:

> Because their adolescent growth spurt occurs late in sexual development, young males can practice behaving like adults before they are actually perceived as adults. [Additionally] . . . competition between men for women favors the older more experienced man. Since such competition may be fatal, the child-like appearance of the young and cute, but hormonally-primed, adolescent male may be life-saving, as well as educational . . .

Bogin summarizes his argument for the adaptive value of adolescence with the following: though they are still infertile, adolescent girls are perceived by adults as adults, and this maximizes their ability to learn female adult social roles. Boys, on the other hand, are sexually mature while they learn male adult social roles, but they are not perceived as adults nor are they taken seriously in their attempts to model adult behavior. The advantage to the adolescent growth spurt is that this unique style of social and cultural learning can occur.

Genetic and Hormonal Control of Growth

The genetic message for growth is mediated through the production of secretions from glands (Latin, meaning "acorns" because of their usually small size) known as *endocrine glands* (Figure 14–8). These glands lack long tubes or ducts and are therefore sometimes called "ductless glands", and they connect internally to the body's blood system (thus accounting for their name; endocrine meaning "separating inside"). Several secretions of endocrine glands, known as *hormones,* are important for growth in human beings. The most important of these is **somatotropin** or growth hormone, which is secreted by the **pituitary gland** at the base of the brain. The secretion of the growth hormone does not occur on a continual basis; rather, it is secreted episodically, and may be affected by a number of factors, including stress and exercise. The actual secretion of the growth hormone is regulated by the **hypothalamus** which, depending on conditions, may itself secrete hormones that stimulate or inhibit growth hormone production in the pituitary gland.

Thyroid hormone, secreted by the thyroid gland in the neck, is also important in growth from birth through adolescence. The lack of either of these hormones in sufficient quantities will result in retardation of growth and smaller size. The artificial administering of growth hormones and their chemical substitutes (steroids) enhances muscle development in athletes, but it also leads to hypertrophy, or excessive development, and damage to certain internal organs, especially the liver. At adolescence gonadal hormones (from the ovaries in the female and

somatotropin–pituitary or growth hormone, important in initiating the adolescent growth spurt.

pituitary gland–an endocrine gland at the base of the cerebral cortex.

hypothalamus–part of the ancient forebrain; located "below the thalamus" at the base of the brain's third ventricle, and important in autonomic nervous system functions such as endocrine gland activity.

thyroid hormone–also known as thyroxine, an iodine-containing hormone secreted by the thyroid gland and important in regulating the rate of tissue metabolism.

Figure 14–8 • Endocrine glands of the human body.

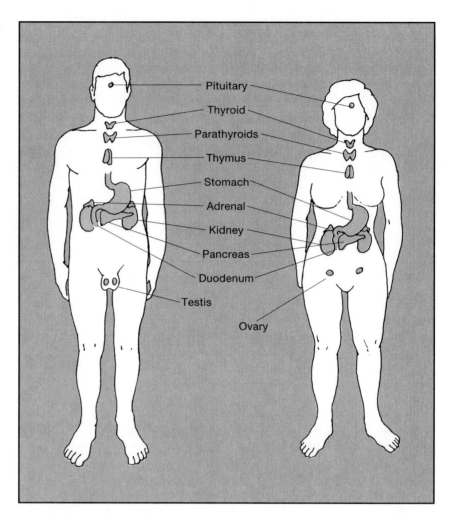

from the testes in the male), particularly *testosterone* in the male, and the hormone secreted by the adrenal gland (above the kidney), *androgen,* are added to the already present pituitary and thyroid hormones.

Growth and Development: A Guide to Evolutionary History

The study of growth is one important way biologists shed light on how evolution works. Earlier in this chapter it was noted that there is a general correspondence in the stages of a species' embryological growth and the major stages of its phylogenetic history. That this is so is not surprising. Evolution utilized the structural blueprint at hand to adapt to new conditions. Thus, the preceding evolutionary stages were incorporated into the new developmental plan, not supplanted by that plan. As evolution has proceeded, the end results of development and growth of species through time have changed dramatically, but the early stages of differentiation have been much more conservative. For this reason the embryos of sharks, chickens, dogs, and humans are all similar, but as growth proceeds the species-specific pattern becomes more clearly expressed. It is also important to recollect that Haeckel's hypothesis, "ontogeny recapitulates phylogeny," serves only as a general rule, because selection can act on embryological stages of development. The brain in human embryos, for example, shows relatively more growth than the brain in embryos of other species at the same level of development. Nevertheless, the sequence in which structures develop reflects to some degree the sequence in which they evolved. This principle can be of use when paleontologists attempt to determine the "primitive" or "derived" nature of anatomical traits. The embryological development of the horse, for example, clearly shows that its single-toed foot develops from a five-toed appendage, a conclusion well-documented in the fossil record.

One of the ways in which evolution produces species differences is by altering growth patterns, that is, by retarding, accelerating, or truncating the growth of certain parts of the body relative to others. Generally, species that are far removed phylogenetically from one another diverge in their patterns of growth early in their developmental histories. More closely related species diverge in growth patterns much later. The later stages of growth have been the foci of evolutionary changes that separate humans from our closest primate relatives. Human and chimpanzee embryos are virtually indistinguishable until just before birth. A chimpanzee embryo, for example, could grow into near-human form if its brain and lower limbs grew relatively faster or for a longer time, and its lower face, canine tooth, and arms grew more slowly or for a shorter time. The evolutionary changes in rates of growth are termed **heterochrony** (McKinney and McNamara, 1991).

There are two categories of heterochrony. The first alters growth patterns by retarding the growth of certain parts of the body while normal sexual development proceeds. This results in an adult of the new species looking like the juvenile form of the ancestral species. This juvenilization is known as **pedomorphosis** (Latin, meaning "child body;" *neoteny,* a closely related term, was introduced in Chapter 5).

Pedomorphosis is important in human evolution because it explains many specific human anatomical traits. Adult humans in many characteristics resemble juvenile nonhuman primates (see Figure 14-2). Like infants of other species adult humans have relatively large heads, the head is flexed toward the ventrum of the body, the body is largely hairless, and there is a relatively high retention of body fat. There are likely a number of selective reasons for these pedomorphic characteristics in humans. No doubt large brain size (accounting for a large head), bipedalism (accounting for balanced or "flexed" head position), regulation of temperature (relating to hairlessness allowing effective sweating), and long-term energy storage (accounting for fat retention) all play a role in the selection for pedomorphic characteristics.

heterochrony–Greek meaning "different time;" refers to the changes in rate of growth characteristic of species' evolutionary divergence from an ancestral species.

pedomorphosis–the retention of a juvenile stage in some part of a descendent species' morphology or behavior, in comparison to its ancestral species.

peromorphosis–the extension of growth or "adultification" of some part of the morphology or behavior of a descendant species, in comparison to its ancestral species.

secular trends–trends in growth or morphological characteristics that are attributable to transient environmental factors, such as nutrition and disease, and not to genetic adaptation.

The second category of heterochrony is **peromorphosis,** or adultification of body form. Evolution can produce species differences by continuing growth for a longer period of time, accelerating development in some of the life stages, or adding additional stages to the end of the life cycle of descendant species. An example of peromorphosis in human evolution is the growth of the relatively long lower limbs (Shea, 1993).

Secular Trends in Growth and Maturation

The reduction in the number of infectious diseases and overall improved nutrition has allowed certain populations to achieve more of their genetic potential for growth and has contributed significantly in three ways. In many countries we have, over time, observed increases in height and weight and a decrease in the age of menarche. Because these trends are not always confined to the upper economic segment of a population, we deduce that a better balance in diet with the regular consumption of essential minerals and vitamins must certainly be more important than some single factor increase, such as calories. We study **secular trends,** those that we observe from one generation to the next, to understand the effects, over time, of nutrition, socioeconomic factors and general health conditions on populations.

In Western Europe and North America studies have demonstrated several important trends. Tanner (1981) has shown that there was a decrease in the age of menarche of about a year: from average ages of between 15 to nearly 17 in the 1800s to the current 12.5 to 14.5 years in the 1940s (Figure 14–9). However, women in advantaged socioeco-

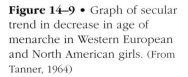

Figure 14–9 • Graph of secular trend in decrease in age of menarche in Western European and North American girls. (From Tanner, 1964)

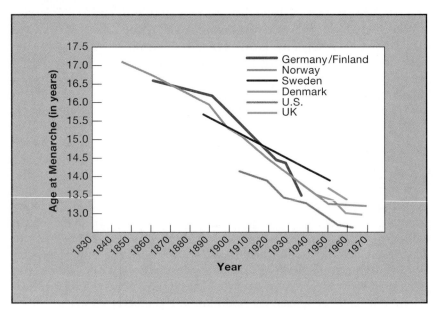

nomic conditions have an onset of menstruation earlier by between 12 and 18 months compared to poor women. This is primarily due to the generally better level of nutrition in the advantaged group. Studies have shown that when lean body mass (LBM) has reached a critical point, or in another measure, when the proportion of fat compared to muscle mass (one measure of overall nutrition) has reached a certain point, menarche will occur. The ratio of body fat to lean body mass prior to puberty is about 1 to 5. At menarche this ratio increases to about 1 to 3.

In one of the classic studies of human growth, the anthropologist Franz Boas measured the stature and head diameters of European immigrants to the United States, and then compared them to the same measurements of their children who were born and reared in the United States. He found that stature in the children was somewhat higher than in their European parents and that head diameters were larger as well. At the same time, secular trends were observed in European-American males who lived in North America. At all ages, males living in the 1960s were taller than their counterparts living in 1880 (Figure 14–10).

Growth and Development in Different Human Groups

The genetic messages for growth may differ from one human population to another. For example, Landa and Foglia (1977) found that Australian aborigines showed growth curves similar to Europeans' up to the age of five to six years of age. After that point the length of the lower limbs in aborigine children increased rapidly, at the relative expense of sitting height. Adult aborigines have on average longer legs than do Europeans. Similar patterns also show up when comparisons

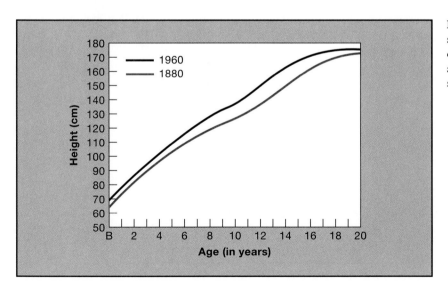

Figure 14–10 • Comparison of stature between American-born children of European descent and earlier populations of the same heritage. (From Malina, 1975)

between individuals of European and African descent are made (Figure 14–11).

Bogin, Wall, and MacVean (1992) studied two ethnic groups in Guatemala: Mayas and *ladinos*. Mayan children are on average shorter than *ladino* children of the same age. Is this difference due to genetic differences or to nutritional and environmental differences? Some researchers have argued that the small size and delayed maturation of malnourished populations, such as the Maya, is a genetic adaptation to their poor environmental conditions. This being the case, then no amount of social improvement will improve growth. The mean difference in height between Mayan and *ladino* boys is established during childhood and maintained without significant change during adolescence. Girls of the two groups, on the other hand, established differences in mean height during childhood that increased during adolescence, and Mayan girls, even though their adolescent period was shorter than *ladinas*, had a slower rate of growth at all ages. In contrast to the Mayan boys, Mayan girls do not show a delay in maturation. From many studies it seems that girls in general possess genetics that

Figure 14–11 • (*a*) Africans and Australian aborigines have longer legs compared to Europeans and Asians, relative to sitting height. (*b*) Olympic 400m runners. Comparison of physiques of two individuals, European (left) and African (right), both having the same sitting height. (From Tanner, 1964)

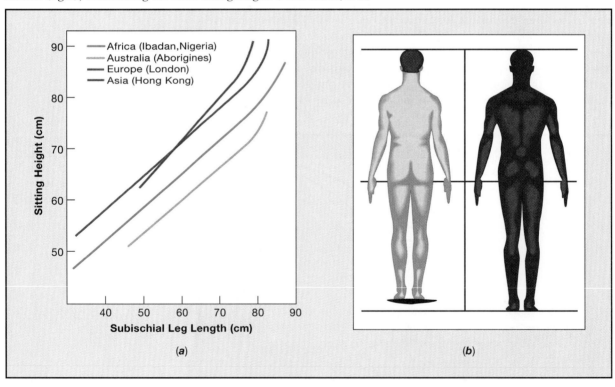

(a)   (b)

override or "buffer" some environmental effects on adolescent growth. As a consequence, Mayan girls appear to proceed through adolescence more in accordance with genetically determined timing for development than Mayan boys.

Although genetics may play a greater role in the timing of growth in girls than in boys, it is not necessarily a useful explanation for the differences between the two ethnic groups of children. Comparing the Mayan and *ladino* study to others in which poor nutrition and health are environmental factors, similar patterns of difference emerge. Data from rural India and Gambia reveal boys who, along with the Mayans, show slower growth velocities and longer periods of growth during childhood and adolescence and end up significantly shorter in stature than cohorts who are better nourished and healthier.

Secular studies of Mayan children living in Florida and Los Angeles, California, have shown that these immigrants are significantly taller and heavier than Mayan children living in Guatemala. Although they are still shorter, on the average, than children of African-Americans or Mexican-Americans living in the United States, they appear to be in the process of a trend leading to increased stature. The average increase of 5.5 centimeters in height for Mayan children reared in the United States is substantial. This illustrates clearly the fact that socioeconomic improvement is an important factor influencing growth, and that the greater the deprivation the more it affects growth potential.

Another example of the interaction of genetic and environmental causes in growth is a study of the Japanese (Tanner, 1989). Japan had a trend, beginning about 1950, of steadily rapid growth in children with a consequent increase in height as adults. This trend was caused, presumably, by increasingly high standards of nutrition and medical care following World War II. Although this trend has stopped in Japan today, and, on average, adult Japanese are still somewhat shorter than their Western contemporaries, trunk to leg proportions now are similar in both groups. These data show that the overall height increases can be entirely accounted for by increases in leg rather than trunk length, and that socioeconomic conditions can somehow affect overall growth patterns and the regulating genes of growth of the lower limb.

A case in which genetics overrides environment is among the Efe pygmies of eastern Zaire (Figure 14–12), studied by Bailey (1991). The Efe are among the smallest of modern humans, males averaging 142 cm (4 ft. 8 in.) and females 135 cm (4 ft. 5 in.). Efe babies at birth are smaller than babies born to a neighboring group, the Lese, even though nutritional and environmental factors are close to equal. Efe show slower growth throughout childhood and a slower peak velocity of growth at adolescence. Their small body size has evolved through natural selection, possibly for greater heat dissipation in their hot, humid environment, or possibly in response to negotiating dense forest undergrowth.

Figure 14–12 • The Efe of eastern Zaire.

Tanner makes an important distinction between the nutritional effects on rate of growth during development and those affecting the adult condition. He observes that nutrition appears to affect rate first: growth slowdowns occur in undernourished children (along with the young of animals in general). This regulation of growth is an important adaptation among animals to counter the uncertainties of the food supply; that is, as a conservation method, slowdowns are periods awaiting better times for growth optimization. Tanner (1989:130) concludes:

> Man did not evolve in the supermarket society of today, but in small tribal communities, most of the period nomadic, following a usually precarious food supply. (Hence we can cope with periodic malnutrition better, perhaps, than with overfeeding.)

Responses to Modernization and the Urban Environment

Living in modern urban environments has put other kinds of stress on human populations. Changes in diet, in the routine of physical activity, in stress levels and in lifestyle may all, in various ways, affect human biology. Any of these factors may have an immediate effect on increasing blood pressure, for example, that in itself can contribute to many health problems, such as heart disease and stroke (Figure 14–13). There also may be longer term consequences that affect growth.

In previous sections we have discussed the fact that, in our evolutionary history, urban life has been a relatively recent cultural situation. Up until 1950, much of the world's population still lived as peasant

Figure 14–13 • One example of the effects of modernization on male diastolic blood pressure is that blood pressure tends to increase with age. These are common findings in studies such as this one, performed in the Gilbert Islands, South Pacific. (From Eaton et al., 1988)

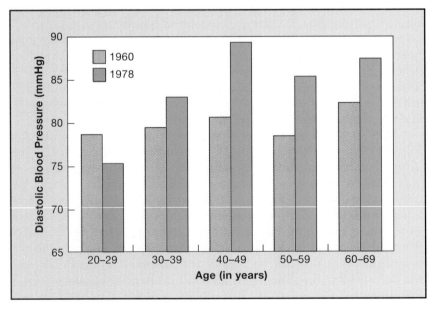

farmers in small social groups, much as humans have done since the agricultural revolution 12,000 years or so ago. Urban life has created both environmental and social situations that have considerably modified our earlier lifestyles. While improvements in health and nutrition have allowed individuals in many populations to reach more of their genetic potential for growth, urban environments have exacted a price.

To give one example, although the majority of the world's societies permit some use of tobacco and alcohol, consumption has been overwhelmingly reserved for males; however, urban environments allow the relaxation of these cultural rules and sometimes encourage women of childbearing years to drink and smoke. Both tobacco and alcohol use are clearly responsible for poor fetal health and slower postpartum growth: the average birth weight of children born to women who smoke is less than that of children born to women who do not smoke (Figure 14–14). Although there is medical controversy as to just how much alcohol pregnant women can safely consume, an excess can cause "fetal alcohol syndrome," which may result in newborns who have overall smaller body size, smaller heads with possible facial deformities, organ disorders, and a chance of reduced intelligence.

Psychological stress also has been proven to be a factor affecting growth. Infants and children who have been exposed to continual emotional stress from family breakups, among other factors, show reduced growth patterns. Psychological stress may contribute to a reduced appetite and difficulty in sleeping. We know, for example, that growth hormones are commonly secreted into the blood stream during the first few hours of sleep. If the normal level of growth hormone is

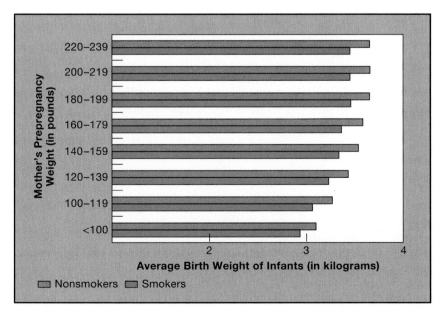

Figure 14–14 • Effects of mothers' smoking during pregnancy on birth weight. (From Eaton et al., 1988)

reduced as a consequence of disturbed sleep, overall growth may also be reduced.

Certainly urban societies, as opposed to traditional ones, are affected by greater levels of many different kinds of pollution. For example, some decreases in average height may be attributable to the presence of toxic waste and noise. In a study of Japanese children who lived close to Osaka International Airport, Schell and Ando (1991) concluded that their observations of shorter than average height in their sample could be attributed to noise pollution, and psychological stress generated by continual noise, which creates disturbed sleep patterns and reduced secretions of growth hormones. Urban families with a small number of siblings show faster growth patterns than families with a large number of children (Weiner, 1989). This suggests that the general stress and noise levels of large families living in restricted confines also slows the growth of offspring.

HUMAN ADAPTABILITY TO ENVIRONMENT

Individual humans respond physiologically to changes in many different environmental conditions. However, it seems that whereas humans adapt to a wide range of climates, climate apparently has little effect on growth rate. If the age at menarche is used as one criterion of growth rate, studies show that for well-nourished girls this event is not perceptibly affected by major climatic differences. For example, girls in Nigeria average 14.3 years of age at menarche, while Eskimo girls average 14.4 years of age. Compare this to the average 13.2 years of age for girls raised in Burma who grow up in hot climates where temperatures frequently reach 45°C. All three of these groups also closely approximate the age of menarche of European girls (Tanner, 1988:384).

Newman (1970) characterized humans as "linear in build, large, meaty, hairless, and sweaty." These attributes came about by adaptation to a certain set of environmental conditions (hot, dry, terrestrial) and a certain ecological niche (large terrestrial home range, omnivorous, and culture-bearing), yet they allow the human species to be extremely adaptable throughout a range of modern environments. By understanding the limits of human adaptability and how adaptation to the environment takes place we can understand much more of the essence of human biology.

Human adaptability to changing environmental conditions consists of genetically shaped responses within the range that is characteristic of the species' *adaptation,* as determined by natural selection (see Chapters 3 and 4). Adaptation by natural selection occurs between generations and is mediated by differential reproduction. Individuals during their lifetimes can do nothing to affect their adaptation. However, within their range of adaptive responses individuals react to changes in their environment in three different ways. (1) **Acclimatization** is accommo-

acclimatization—long-term physiological adaptation, which may have some morphological effect, but which occurs during the lifetime of one individual and which is not passed on genetically.

dation over a period of months or years to environmental conditions, acclimatizing to living in high mountains is an example. (2) **Acclimation** is short-term physiological response to changed environmental conditions. Acclimating over several days to a new time zone, as in "jet lag," or light-skinned individuals acclimating to increased exposure to sunlight by **tanning,** are examples. (3) **Habituation** is an even shorter-term accommodation to a temporary environmental stimulus. Tuning out the monotonous sound of an air-conditioner during a lecture is an example. Individuals within populations, as well as entire populations, may differ in their thresholds and responses to stimuli.

Heat and Cold

Biological anthropologists have studied the various shapes and dimensions of people around the world using the ecological rules known as *Bergmann's Rule* and *Allen's Rule,* introduced in Chapter 3. Bergmann (1847) observed that in a single warm-blooded species that ranged over a wide area, those populations in the colder regions were larger in body size than those in the hotter regions. This is so because of physical laws governing heat dissipation or conservation. A smaller animal has a relatively large surface area compared to its body mass. Its body therefore acts as a radiator transferring internal body heat to the surrounding air. As an animal's body size increases, its surface area relatively decreases, as does the amount of body heat it transfers to the air. In fact, if body shape stays the same, there is a standard mathematical relationship: if body size increases body surface area increases two dimensionally (by surface area squared), but body mass (weight) increases three dimensionally (by mass cubed). Thus by simply getting larger and exposing relatively less surface area, individuals within a species can conserve body heat in colder climates (Figure 14–15).

Shape of the body can also change in response to climatic temperature differences across the range of a species. Allen's Rule (Allen, 1877) holds that the appendages of populations inhabiting hotter climates will be larger and longer than in colder climates, for the same functional reasons of heat dissipation and conservation. Polar bears, for example, have shorter ears than grizzlies, which have shorter ears than black bears.

Whether Bergmann's and Allen's Rules work for the human species is at present debated. There are studies which show that adult populations inhabiting hot climates, such as the pygmies of Central Africa, southern African Khoisan, and the Semang of Borneo, have relatively large surface/body mass ratios, compared to populations that live in colder climates, such as Eskimos and Germans (Newman, 1975). However, it has also been pointed out that all human populations pass through in their growth from birth to adulthood that same range of surface-area-to-body-mass seen in adults of all modern human populations (Schreider, 1963). Thus, children of all populations are more

acclimation–short-term physiological adaptation, occurring over a period of several hours to several days.

tanning–a response of lightly pigmented skin after exposure to sunlight that increases the amount of melanin in the cells of the skin; an example of acclimation.

habituation–neurophysiological mechanism for "tuning out" unwanted stimuli, an accommodation that takes only a few minutes.

Figure 14–15 • Weight regressions in different human populations. Bergmann's Rule: Body size increases with decreasing temperature of the habitat. (After Roberts, 1953)

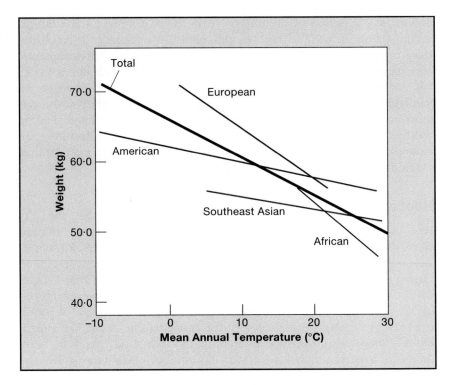

"heat-adapted" because they have relatively greater surface area and adults are more "cold-adapted" because they have relatively greater mass. If Allen's and Bergmann's Rules hold up as generalizations for the human species, their effects would therefore be expected to be seen in increased mortality in childhood in cold climates, and decreased fitness with fewer offspring in adulthood in hot climates. These relationships have yet to be sustained by controlled research results.

Allen's Rule predicts that cold-adapted human populations should have relatively short limbs and hot-adapted populations should have relatively long limbs. This generalization seems to hold up better than overall body size. The long limbs of Nilotic Africans and the short limbs of the Eskimos are the two extremes. However, in the human species cultural attributes, such as clothing, fire, and shelter, alter the direct ecological relationships that other mammals have with their environments. For this reason Bergmann's and Allen's Rules may not be as clearly expressed in the human species as in some other species.

Physiological responses to heat and cold constitute human **thermoregulation,** an important part of the human adaptation. Humans have a tropical origin, a fact demonstrated not only by the fossil record but by human biology. No other indication of this origin is stronger than the range of temperature at which human beings achieve thermal equilibrium, that is neither gaining or losing heat. This temperature for

thermoregulation—controlling the body's temperature by a number of physiological and behavioral means.

a naked adult at rest is approximately 25°C (77°F), depending on humidity. Once sweating starts, either because of exercise or increasing temperature, the temperature of the skin is maintained at between 35°C and 36°C (95°F and 102°F) (Newman, 1975). When internal body temperature or local skin temperature increases, **eccrine sweat glands** in the skin become active, producing a watery liquid that evaporates, cooling the skin. When internal body temperature decreases the body produces more heat by muscular contraction (shivering), by increasing the body's metabolic rate, and by **vasoconstriction,** the contracting of the small arterioles near the skin's surface to reduce the temperature of the skin. An even older physiological response to cold is "goose bumps." This is a reflex standing-up of hairs which served to increase the insulating effect of fur that disappeared from the hominid body probably several million years ago.

If the temperature continues to drop, a "warming response" can be seen in European and Asian populations, in which the hands or feet become vasodilated to increase circulation and raise the temperature of the extremity. Africans do not show this response, which seems to be a genetically controlled part of thermoregulatory physiology evolved by northern hemisphere, cold-adapted populations.

Light and Solar Radiation

Physiological responses to solar radiation and light occur in the skin, whether it is pigmented or relatively less pigmented. The most well-known response of lightly pigmented skin to exposure to solar radiation is *tanning*. Melanocytes in the epidermis of the skin produce melanin-containing skin cells which give a darker cast to the skin, thus protecting the dermis from potentially harmful ultraviolet radiation. Exposure to sunlight also increases the rate of skin cell division, resulting in a thicker and more protective external layer of the skin. If the length of exposure to solar radiation exceeds the adaptive ability of the skin to tan and thicken itself, sunburn or *erythema solare* will result. Repeated sun burning can lead to skin cancer in later years.

The **pineal body** at the base of the brain (where the French philosopher Descartes thought the soul was located) controls daily rhythms relating to light and dark (Cardinali and Wurtman, 1975). The primitive human adaptation to light was undoubtedly tropical, with day length virtually the same all year long. But, as hominids expanded into increasingly northern and southern latitudes, they had to adapt to changing day lengths. As yet, the details of this adaptation are poorly understood. But we have ample evidence that, when days shorten or lengthen with the seasons, humans can suffer emotional changes. Light therapy, in which an individual is subjected to bright, intense light, has been found to be an effective treatment for some conditions, such as symptoms of depression in night shift workers resulting from light dep-

eccrine sweat glands–glands that excrete a watery liquid over much of the surface area of the head, face, neck, and upper body during heat stress.

vasoconstriction–the contraction of small blood vessels next to the skin's surface; a response to cold.

pineal body–small, cone-shaped part of the brain (thought by French philosopher René Descartes to be the site of the soul) located below the *corpus callosum*; synthesizes the hormone melatonin, which is important in mediating estrus cycling in mammals, and reacts to ambient light in the environment.

rivation. Furthermore, modern people spend much of their lives, particularly in the winter months, indoors. Their relationship to light has changed in three major ways: the spectrum of artificial light has changed, the irradiance level is drastically different, and the number of hours per day that an individual is exposed has increased dramatically.

High Altitude

Today over 25 million people live in high plateau environments (over 2,500m) in places such as Ethiopia, South America, and Tibet, in spite of the apparent stresses these altitudes cause. Two important stresses, lowered air temperature and atmospheric pressure, are particularly important to sustained life. Air temperature at 5,000 meters, for example, in tropical latitudes averages about 0°C, and declines in latitudes farther from the equator. In all latitudes, atmospheric pressure at 5,000 meters is reduced by one-half that encountered at sea level.

Living at high altitude, that is, greater than about 3,000 meters (9,840 feet) above sea level causes a number of physiological changes. Biological anthropologists have studied these changes in order to learn how rapidly nonacclimatized individuals can adapt to the low oxygen levels (**hypoxia**) found at high altitudes. For visitors to these altitudes, as we have described in the first part of this chapter, the immediate response to hypoxia is the increase in breathing and heart rate. Although this response increases partial oxygen pressure in the lungs and, at the same time, blood flow, it also contributes to difficulty in sleeping and to bouts of hyper- and hypoventilation.

A longer term physiological response to lower oxygen pressure is the reduction, somewhere between 20 to 30%, in the amount of oxygen that the body can absorb. As a consequence, work capacity for high altitude visitors is diminished. One study did suggest, however, that individuals who grow up in high altitudes somehow acclimatize themselves and, in terms of oxygen consumption (and, thus, work) capacity, measure closely to those individuals born at sea level (Frisancho et al., 1973). Although hypoxia is the primary stress factor in high altitude environments, there are others, such as high solar radiation, cold, aridity, rough terrain, and a limited nutritional base (Mazess, 1975).

On the other hand, the widespread belief does not hold that an important physiological response to altitude is increased red blood cell count. Although the red blood cell count is somewhat higher than normal at sea level, rather than helping to increase the ability of the body to absorb oxygen, it is probably no more than simply one added indication of hypoxic stress (Harrison et al., 1988: 477). Likewise, whereas some studies do suggest that chest growth may be more rapid in high altitude children, resulting in a commonly observed barrel shape, it is not certain whether hypoxia, by itself, negatively affects other aspects of growth.

hypoxia–a condition of reduced oxygen supply to tissues despite adequate blood supply.

NUTRITIONAL AND DIETARY ASPECTS OF ADAPTATION

Humans are omnivores. They and their primate ancestors have eaten a very wide range of plant and animal foods with little or no preparation for many millions of years (Harding and Teleki, 1981; Table 14–2). This adaptation confers a large degree of dietary adaptability, but it has its limits.

Although the idea that early hominids in general consumed large quantities of meat is probably fallacious, at least one known fossil individual must have suffered a great deal before her death in consequence of overindulging in one type of scavenged or hunted meat. Alan Walker of Pennsylvania State University (Walker et al., 1982) described one of the most complete *Homo erectus* skeletons dated about 1.6 million years from the upper member of the Koobi Fora Formation at East Lake Turkana. This partial skeleton, KNM-ER 1808, showed pathological changes consistent with a condition known as **hypervitaminosis A,** possibly acquired as a result of consuming carnivore liver, which is inherently rich in concentration of vitamin A. Liver, perhaps more than any other organ meat, is easy to consume, requiring little preparation and, as fire may not have been used at this time, no cooking. For comparison, 100 grams of the liver from a herbivore may contain somewhere between 44,000 to 50,000 I.U. of vitamin A, whereas the same quantity of carnivore liver contains 1.3 to 1.8 million I.U. At the time of KNM-ER 1808 there may have been a major dietary shift coupled to a large increase in meat eating, if the evidence at Koobi Fora of the first stone tools associated with animal bones is any indication. Unlike carnivores who can

Table 14–2 • Daily Diet of Pre-Agricultural Humans[1]		
	Grams[2]	Percent Total Energy
Protein	250	33
Animal	190	
Vegetable	60	
Fat	70	21
Animal	30	
Vegetable	40	
Carbohydrate	340	46
Total Fiber	150	
	1130	100

[1]Based on an average modern human hunter-gatherer diet of 3000 kilocalories, composed of 35% meat and 65% plant foods.
[2]Represents weight less water content. Weight of actual ingested food is 2250g (5 lbs.). Equivalent food weight for same energy in modern American diet is 3 lbs.
From Eaton et al. (1988).

hypervitaminosis A–condition resulting from excessive ingestion of vitamin A, resulting in increased pigmentation of the skin, loss of hair, and eventually to bleeding in the bones; the latter symptom being the means of diagnosing the condition in the KNM-ER 1808 *Homo erectus* skeleton.

store large quantities of vitamin A obtained from their prey, humans had to learn which parts of a carcass were poisonous to them.

In more recent times early polar explorers reported symptoms consistent with hypervitaminosis A after eating the liver of polar bears, seals, and their own husky dogs. Acute hypervitaminosis A, causing such conditions as peeling off of skin, convulsions and vomiting, diarrhea, and headaches, is still a fatal disease, and fairly common in infants who either accidentally ingest or are unknowingly provided excesses of vitamin A by their parents.

In other situations in which we have seen changes as a result of adaptation, normal human liver levels of vitamin A remain, even today, within herbivore ranges. This indicates that there was little, if any, tendency toward a dietary modification that would have enabled hominids to consume what must have been a fairly common and otherwise nutritious food for them: carnivore liver.

With the advent of fire and cultural food preparation techniques, the potential range of edible foods expanded. Or did it? Newman (1975) suggested that the early hominid reliance on animal meat relaxed selection on the body's synthesis of several important amino acids. Although hominids lost the ability to synthesize these substances, they were not at a selective disadvantage because their diets supplied these essential nutrients. However, during the Neolithic Revolution, that period of time about 10,000 years ago in the Middle East when farming and village life became predominant and the food supply more stable, the overall human diet may have been less nutritious with a dependence on single plant food staples. A similar problem exists in many of the world's cultures today, such as those in which dependence on rice or manioc has led to malnutrition and even nutritional diseases.

Jared Diamond, physiologist at the University of California, Los Angeles, describes (1993) recent studies of a diabetic epidemic on the Pacific island of Nauru and points out other problems when changes in diet occur. Only a few generations ago the 5,000 or so Micronesians living on this island engaged in a lifestyle which depended upon fishing and subsistence farming. However, the discovery of phosphate deposits and the substantial income that mining this substance produced dramatically changed the Nauruan energetic way of life. Now virtually all food is imported, the caloric intake is more than double the norms set by the nearby Australians, and obesity is practically universal. **Non-insulin-dependent diabetes mellitus** (NIDDM) that, prior to 1950 was unknown in this population, now affects almost two-thirds of adults by the age of 55 to 64, contributing to most nonaccidental deaths and one of the world's shortest life spans.

Unfortunately, this example is not uncommon among developing peoples in other parts of the world. It is the extent of the problem on Nauru that is remarkable. Studies, however, show that the epidemic may have passed its peak, though not because of a decline in the envi-

non-insulin-dependent diabetes mellitus—metabolic disorder with a strong dietary component associated with its onset, characterized by abnormally high sugar content in the blood (hyperglycemia) and imperfect combustion of fats and carbohydrates; frequently associated with obesity, kidney disease, and hardening of the arteries (atherosclerosis).

ronmental risk factors. Rather it appears that natural selection has reduced the number of individuals who are genetically susceptible to NIDDM. Because it often occurs in women during their peak reproductive years, it results in increased stillbirths and less than half as many live births than in women who are not susceptible to the disease. As a consequence, over a few generations the number of islanders who possessed the lethal NIDDM genotype has been reduced.

This question remains to be answered: If NIDDM represents a major world health problem (50 million diabetics are estimated in China and India alone by the year 2000) then why is the genotype so common? One hypothesis was proposed by J. V. Neel (1962), which he labeled the "**thrifty genotype.**" Neel suggested that whenever the daily food supply becomes sparse and varies unpredictably in amount, the individuals with an advantage would be those who, during times when food is plentiful, could convert most of their ingested calories into fat through quick insulin release. Because these calories will be stored instead of immediately burned, they can be drawn on during times when food is scarce. Under such circumstances the NIDDM genotype would be advantageous, but it could lead to a diabetic condition in individuals recently introduced to modern diets of food high in calories and a regimen of little exercise that would burn these calories off. As Boyd Eaton, Marjorie Shostak, and Melvin Konner (1989) conclude:

> Our bodies today simply haven't "learned" that there is no longer an advantage to carrying extra weight. We are still essentially Late Paleolithic hunters and gatherers, and our appetite-control centers continue to operate as if the food surplus may come to a crashing halt at any time. We persist in storing up against that eventuality and, because the shortages fail to materialize, we become obese. Fat people . . . are stocking up for a famine that never comes.

MODERN LIFE AND HUMAN EVOLUTION

As we have said, adaptable as the human organism is, it is nevertheless true that well over 90% of the species' evolutionary history has been spent in tropical environments, in small groups of related individuals, eating for the most part low sugar, high fiber foods and leading physically demanding lives. Modern, technologically advanced humans, many of whom lead sedentary lives and eat highly processed foods that are high in sugar, salt, and polyunsaturated fats, suffer from "diseases of civilization" that are virtually unknown among technologically primitive hunter-gatherer peoples (Table 14–3). Among these are **hypertension** and the related problem of heart attack, cancer, gastric ulcers, and stress-related disorders. Studies also show among urban dwellers an increase in blood pressure and **serum cholesterol** levels (Table 14–4), and a

thrifty genotype—the adaptation of storing "excess calories" as fat, and then burning them during periods of famine or scarcity of food.

hypertension—persistently high blood pressure; above 140 mm Hg systolic (contraction) and 90 mm Hg diastolic (dilation) pressures of the heart.

serum cholesterol—cholesterol is a lipid (fat), deriving from the diet, that when in high concentrations in the blood serum causes lesions and plaque build-up in arteries.

Table 14–3 • Diseases of Civilization: The Leading Causes of Death in the United States

Cause of Death	Percent of Total Deaths
Heart Disease (chiefly coronary atherosclerosis)	37.0%
Cancer (Lung, colon, rectum, breast, and prostate cause 54% of cancer deaths)	22.1%
Stroke	7.3%
[Accidents	4.5%]
Chronic Obstructive Lung Disease	3.4%
Pneumonia	3.2%
Diabetes mellitus	1.8%
Atherosclerosis (not including heart or brain, but including aortic aneurysm)	1.8%
[Suicide	1.4%]
Cirrhosis	1.3%
Total	83.8%

From Eaton et al. (1987).

tendency for higher blood pressure to increase with age. In contrast, traditional populations show lower blood pressure and no tendency for blood pressure to increase with age (Little and Baker, 1988). In an attempt to counter some of the deleterious effects of civilized life Eaton and colleagues (1987) have suggested a "Paleolithic prescription," which calls for the return, within modern technological limits, to many of the practices of diet and exertion employed by our ancestors.

On the other hand, our Paleolithic ancestors never faced the problems of overpopulation (Figure 14–16). Quite the contrary. Rather than curbing the birth rate, societies, until recently, attempted to maximize child production and minimize infant mortality. Today, the world population problem poses a new challenge to human adaptability and may force significant changes only vaguely contemplated by modern peo-

Table 14–4 • Serum Cholesterol Values in Different Human Hunter-Gatherer Groups

Population	Average Serum Cholesterol Value
Hadza (Tanzania)	110
Eskimos (Canada)	141
San (Botswana)	120
Aborigines (Australia)	139
Pygmies (Zaire)	106
Caucasians (United States)	210

From Eaton et al. (1987).

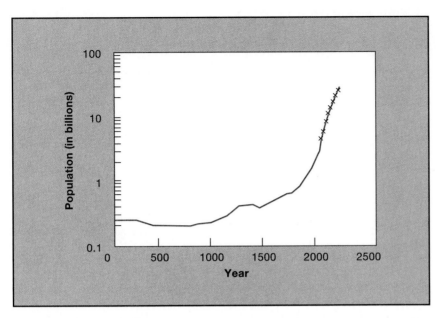

Figure 14–16 • World population growth and growth estimates. "X's" represent projected growth, given no change in the current world birth rate.

ples. The one-child policy, which China has set in motion, even though morally repugnant to some, may presage things to come in many of the world's societies.

There are other less dramatic possibilities for change. Our diet, as we have seen, is a mixture of plant and animal foods. Whether we hunted or scavenged, animal proteins have been a necessary component of our diet, because they are relatively complete in their contents of essential amino acids. Proteins found in the plants that humans consume are usually deficient in one or more essential amino acids. Even today in many parts of the world animal protein is almost the only way to secure a complete and balanced pattern of amino acids in a diet consisting predominantly of plant foods. However, conditions of overpopulation require a hard look at land use because they make us view the domesticated animal as a competitor to humans. Cropland produces 10 to 20 times the amount of human food that we can obtain from animals grazing on the same land. In fact, animal efficiencies in returning as human food the nutrients they consume is only between 15 to 25%, which means there is a 75 to 90% loss of calories consumed in the form of carbohydrates and fat (Almquist, 1966).

As all of our food originates in plants, the animal is only a converter. What has kept animals in use as converters? Originally, they earned their place by their value in locating and converting food items that humans could not, or would not, consume, such as seeds, roots, and wild grasses. They also provided the amino acids that could not be obtained from other sources. Today, however, under the conditions of the modern feed lot, where animals consume supplemental food that humans could use, animal food is an ever-increasing luxury. Furthermore with the advances in genetic engineering plant varieties have been devel-

FRONTIERS

The Growth of Pastoral Turkana Children

by Michael Little

In the early 1980s, researchers from the fields of ecology, anthropology, and human biology undertook a study of pastoral Turkana nomads with a view toward better understanding the health and patterns of adaptation of this unusual people. The part of northwest Kenya where the Turkana people live is a semi-arid savanna or tropical grassland that is a part of the rift valley system of East Africa. These savanna lands are hot throughout the year, with low rainfall that is concentrated in only a few months in a typical tropical monsoon pattern. Seasonal drought occurs each year, while more serious droughts may occur once or twice each decade. Turkana pastoralists adapt to this inhospitable environment by moving their herds of camels, cattle, sheep, goats, and donkeys in search of green vegetation and water for the animals. They subsist on the products of their livestock, which include milk, blood, and meat, by direct

consumption and by trading these products for other foods.

The research project included investigations into several facets of Turkana life, namely (1) diet and nutrition, (2) growth and development, (3) reproduction, (4) adult size and body composition, (5) physical activity, and (6) disease. The six categories are all highly interrelated. Accordingly, it is important to understand the disease, dietary, and physical activity statuses of children in order to understand and interpret their patterns of growth. We found, for example, that the Turkana diet, high in milk products, provides an abundance of protein (up to four times the daily requirement), yet energy in the form of calories is quite limited. Reproduction was discovered to be a complex issue. Although fertility is relatively high, so also is infant mortality, and births tend to be highly seasonal, reflecting some environmental limits placed on fertility. Among adults, height is tall and comparable to that of adults in the United States, although body weight is quite light. Hence, physiques of Turkana are tall and very linear, with relatively small muscle sizes and minimal body fat. The limited energy input from food is expended in the moderate and occa-

sionally vigorous activities of herding and tending livestock and managing the household settlement. As might be expected, levels of physical fitness are good. Disease has only been studied to a modest degree. It appears, however, that parasites are not a serious problem for the nomads, yet certain endemic diseases, such as malaria, produce considerable sickness and contribute to deaths at all ages.

During the course of a decade or more of research, we did anthropometric measurements of size and body composition of more than 1,500 Turkana men, women, and children. The earliest research concentrated on simple description of growth at different ages. Later research dealt with comparative studies of nomadic and settled Turkana (those who cultivate irrigated plots of land), especially with regard to problems of nutrition, maternal health and breastfeeding, and pregnancy rates. One of the problems currently being explored is the influence of seasonality in food availability and seasonal hunger on growth rates in children as well as seasonal influences on fertility in adults.

Heights and weights of nomadic Turkana from one year of age to adulthood were compared with those of the fiftieth (average) and the fifth (95% and

oped that are no longer deficient in particular amino acids. Cereal and oil seed protein are deficient, for example, in the amino acid, lysine. A mutant corn, however, was developed some years ago that was not deficient in lysine.

Our knowledge of nutrition can help to improve our efficiency in how we use plant food. Protein blending, adding soybean, which contains a surplus of lysine, to corn, and supplementing this mixture with a synthetic methionine (lacking in soybean) would produce an adequate diet. Technologically, as the world population situation becomes more critical, we can gradually shift from a diet based on animal food greater) percentiles of the U.S. population of similar ages. Several interesting things were noted about the Turkana growth curves. First, growth in height is below U.S. values throughout childhood, adolescence, and early adulthood up to about 23 or 24 years of age, at which time, Turkana catch up to U.S. young adults. This is an extraordinarily late maturation in size, but it reflects a prolonged but steady growth into the early twenties. Full adult height for U.S. girls is achieved at about 16 years of age and for U.S. boys is at about 18 years. We can not be absolutely sure, but this prolonged growth in Turkana youths is probably the result of limited calories or energy in the normal nomadic diet and a conservation of energy needed for growth. The tall stature may be "driven" by the high protein intake from milk. A second interesting observation is in the very low body weights of both boys and girls, the average of which hovers at or below the fifth percentile of U.S. youth. This extreme linearity or thinness of physique is characteristic of East African pastoralists, and is probably produced by a combination of limited food energy intake and a genetic tendency toward linearity. It may also be related to the hot climate since heat is better handled by individuals with relatively thin physiques. Finally, girls seem slightly better off than boys after age 16 years since body weights are slightly above the U.S. fifth percentile for girls but well below the U.S. fifth percentile for boys. This may mean that young women of marriageable age are better nourished than young men due to differences in food access (women are responsible for milking the animals).

Contributions made by this research on Turkana growth are twofold: First, it has yielded valuable information about Turkana children, their health, and their adaptability within the context of their population, culture and environment. This is the integrated aspect of growth. Second, it has added to our understanding of the general processes of growth under a variety of environmental conditions. Studies of non-Western societies, such as the Turkana, provide a breadth of experiences and environments, both physical and behavioral, that enable us to know more about general patterns of human growth in all its dimensions.

Suggested Readings

Dyson-Hudson, R. 1989. Ecological influences on systems of food production and social organization of South Turkana pastoralists. In V. Standen & R.A. Foley, eds., *Comparative Socioecology: The Behavioral Ecology of Humans and Other Mammals.* Oxford: Blackwell, pp. 165–93.

Galvin, K.A. 1992. Nutritional ecology of pastoralists in dry tropical Africa. *American Journal of Human Biology* 4:209–21.

Little, M.A. 1989. Human biology of African pastoralists. *Yearbook of Physical Anthropology* 32:215–47.

Little, M.A. 1995. Growth and development of Turkana pastoralists. In P.N. Peregrine, C.R. Ember, and M. Ember, eds., *Research Frontiers in Anthropology: Advances in Archaeology and Physical Anthropology.* Englewood Cliffs, NJ: Prentice Hall.

Michael Little is Professor of Anthropology at State University of New York, Binghamton. He is a specialist in human growth and development and a former president of the American Association of Physical Anthropologists.

to one predominantly derived from plants. Although such an adaptation will pose no physiological problem, such changes will inevitably be strongly culturally challenged by our traditional eating patterns and may become acceptable only after no alternative exists.

The crowded, noisy, and generally "artificial" conditions of modern urban life are very recent environments for humans to live in (Cavalli-Sforza, 1983). The consequences to human biology and psychology are profound though still not fully understood. Yet cities being cultural entities, they are environments that can be changed if necessary to better fit human adaptations evolved over millions of years (Briggs, 1983).

SUMMARY

This chapter reviews many of the issues surrounding human growth patterns and the adaptability of modern humans to a wide variety of habitats. Growth patterns in all species are, to a certain extent, reflections of their evolutionary history. The prolonged period of human adolescence, coupled with the delayed maturation of the brain, is adaptive to the needs of our species to learn. Furthermore, the rapid catchup period of growth for the first year after birth advances the newborn to the same stage of locomotor ability achieved at birth by the smaller brained, but less dependent, apes.

In addition to evolutionary concerns, the study of growth patterns provides a measure of how well a population is adapted to its environment. Poor nutrition, pollution, stress, and a number of sociological factors, such as family size, can retard growth, reducing the genetic potential for adult stature. Different populations around the world, however, respond differently to adverse conditions. Secular studies of Japanese children showed that growth retardation in that population occurs primarily in the lower limbs rather than affecting trunk height. Studies of growth show us how much genetics is involved in regulating rates and stages, and how much the environment can modify the genetic program. Studies of boys versus girls, for example, shows that nutritional factors affect girls' maturation much less than they do boys'.

Allometry is the study of differential growth, the relative change in the size of one structure compared to another. Neoteny describes the situation in which growth of certain parts of the body is retarded while normal sexual development proceeds. Neoteny, or pedomorphism, helps explain why humans have retained so many juvenile characteristics as adults, such as a relatively high retention of body fat.

Human individuals have adapted to a wide range of environments, even though for millions of years our ancestors were primarily a tropical species. In the course of this adaptation humans have responded to changes in temperature, light, and altitude among many factors that are now part of the broad human ecosystem. Humans have evolved unique ways of coping with diverse climates by thermoregulation: sweating to cool the body, and vasoconstriction of the extremities to maintain heat. Those living in high altitudes have adapted to low oxygen levels by increasing the breathing and heart rate. The fact that humans are especially adaptable has allowed us to explore and survive in Arctic as well as tropical climates.

Humans have a varied diet, but it is clear that there are limits to our adaptability to consume too much of any particular food. Many plant foods lack essential amino acids, and, if eaten without supplements, can cause deficiencies and, ultimately, disease. On the other hand, too much of certain kinds of meat, carnivore liver, for example, can result in a vitamin A overload that can also cause disease.

Perhaps the most telling limitations of our diet come from studies of "modern" diseases of the heart and arteries, those related to high blood pressure and diabetes. Modern lifestyles that incorporate high sugar, salt, and saturated fats, coupled with a lack of exercise, have proved to be a deadly combination. Modern medicine is investigating the consequences of our urban adaptation, and some practitioners have suggested a "Paleolithic" prescription that recommends a return to many of the practices of diet and exercise of our pre-agricultural ancestors.

 ## CRITICAL-THINKING QUESTIONS

1. Define growth in terms of biological development.
2. Describe the seven stages of human growth.
3. Explain allometry and how it can be used to better understand growth relationships.
4. How do different environments affect human variation?
5. How did the advent of fire affect nutritional diversity?
6. In what ways has human development responded to modernization and urban living?

 ## SUGGESTED READINGS

Bogin, B. 1988. *Patterns of Human Growth*. New York: Cambridge University Press. Text on human growth written from an evolutionary point of view. Attempts to place human growth into an ecological and phylogenetic context.

Eveleth, P. and J. M. Tanner. 1991. *Worldwide Variations in Human Growth*. 2nd ed. New York: Cambridge University Press. Text in the comparative studies of growth including 82 tables presenting the means and standard deviations of various anthropological measures and indices. Exhaustive list of references to other growth studies.

Tanner, J. M. 1989. *Foetus into Man: Physical Growth from Conception to Maturity,* 2nd ed. Cambridge: Harvard University Press. Text describes the process of growth in children, the maturation rate of different tissues, the chromosomal and endocrine control of sexual differentiation *in utero* and the further differentiation that takes place at puberty. Explores further the interaction of genes with the environment.

The Modern Human Condition in Evolutionary Perspective: Applied Biological Anthropology

**Premises and Goals
  of Applied Biological
  Anthropology**
Definition
Human Adaptation and the
  Modern Environment

**Biomedical Anthropology
  and Evolutionary Medicine**
Sudden Infant Death Syndrome
Neonatal Jaundice
Coping with the "Diseases
  of Civilization"
Human Populations, Infectious
  Diseases, and Parasites
Structural Problems
What is the Birth Environment
  for the Human?

Forensic Anthropology
Facial and Dental
  Reconstruction
Skeletal Reconstruction
Cause of Death
Human Rights Investigations

**Applied Aspects
  of Anthropometry**
Eugenics
Design Uses
Biometric Security Uses

**Evolutionary Perspectives
  on Brain and Behavior**
Treating Brain-Injured
  Children

**Anthropological Lessons
  for Education**

**Biological Anthropology,
  Human Ecology,
  and Quality of Life**

Summary

Critical-Thinking Questions

Suggested Readings

The subject of human evolution has excited both the public and scientific imaginations for many years. But the application of biological anthropological knowledge has lagged behind the intellectual popularity of the subject. Although many professional and lay people alike may have known about, and even been fascinated with, australopithecines and Neandertals, they would have doubted whether these dusty relics of our evolutionary past had any relevance to our current life and problems. There are signs that this attitude is now changing. We now know that our hominid ancestors can teach us a tremendous amount of useful information about how to conduct our daily lives.

As the perspective of evolutionary biology has pervaded both the natural and social sciences, so also has it affected such applied areas as medicine, psychotherapy, education, and conservation. We begin this chapter with a discussion of the basis for applying biological anthropology to the modern human condition.

PREMISES AND GOALS OF APPLIED BIOLOGICAL ANTHROPOLOGY

Although a distinct discipline of **applied biological anthropology** is still developing, biological anthropologists have been active in practical applications of their research for many years. One of the most prominent nineteenth century German biological anthropologists, Rudolf Virchow (Figure 15–1), founded the public health service in Berlin, for example. And the great French anthropologist, Paul Broca, made many contributions to medical treatment of brain disorders. In the twentieth century the list of applications of biological anthropological research is diverse and wide ranging, from designing the dimensions of fighter plane cockpits, to assistance in apprehending criminals, to urban planning. This chapter will discuss the major areas of applied biological anthropology, keeping in mind that the field is a dynamic one and new applications are being developed every year.

Definition

There are certain common attributes of applied biological anthropology that set it off from other disciplines that may be concerned with the same

applied biological anthropology—use of the method and theory of biological anthropology to solve problems or address questions of practical significance.

Figure 15–1 • Rudolf Virchow, one of the first applied physical anthropologists, who founded the public health service in Berlin in the late 1800s.

subject. In general, applied biological anthropology is "holistic, evolutionary, cross-cultural, comparative, and population-based" (Lasker, 1991:2). For example, an anthropological research project on the incidence of disease in a certain population will generally differ from a project in the public health field of **epidemiology** by investigating more biological parameters than the presence or absence of disease and whether patients survived or died. Anthropologists bring an approach that includes a broad comparative perspective on human biological response to the environment, and thus may look at, in addition to the manifestations of the disease in question, birth weights of babies, growth rates of children, and many other biological parameters termed **subclinical** that may escape medical attention. Anthropologists are also human evolutionary biologists; they consider the overall human adaptive response within the contexts of evolution, different cultures, and different environments. Biological anthropology becomes applied biological anthropology when it focuses on solving practical problems of human well-being.

Anthropology is a population-based biological science, and, unlike medicine, it does not specifically focus on the individual (Figure 15–2). Its conclusions are statistical and its statements are probabilistic. This aspect of anthropological research is very important for physicians or other health professionals to remember when using anthropological data. An example will suffice. A six-month-old child is brought in for his medical checkup and is found normal except that the examining nurse notes that he seems to have an enlarged head. A second appointment is made for the child with a growth specialist, who measures the child's head and compares his measurements with an anthropological study of head growth. The specialist finds that according to the study the child is in the 95th percentile of children his age, that is only 5 out of 100 children would have heads as large as his at his age. Despite the fact that there is no indication of abnormal brain function in the child and no indication of pressure inside the head creating an enlargement, the growth specialist recommends further tests, including a brain scan. The parents do not want this procedure performed on their child unless absolutely necessary. At this point a biological anthropologist enters the picture and is able to show by reference to the results of a second study that the child has head dimensions in the same proportion in the general population as his parents, who both have large heads. Anthropologists do not make individual diagnoses, nor should they, but they do show that the child's head dimensions are within the "normal" population limits of the original growth studies. The parents decide, after consultation with their child's physician, against a brain scan.

Human Adaptation and the Modern Environment

Human beings are remarkably adaptable, as we have seen in the last chapter. But there are limits to this adaptability. Obviously people cannot live in underwater or outer space environments without the aid of

epidemiology–the study of the geographic distribution, spread, and control of disease.

subclinical–referring to a disease condition that is below the threshold of medical diagnosis.

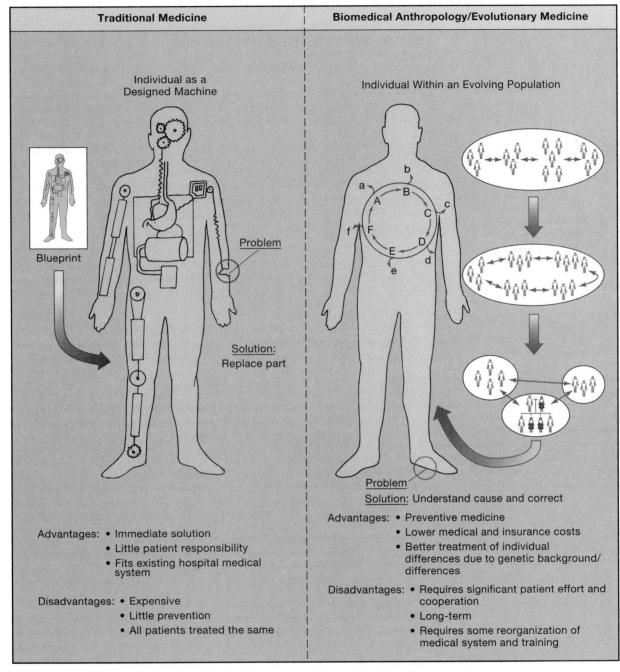

Figure 15–2 • Difference in approach of traditional medicine and biological anthropology as regards the individual. Traditional medicine is more typological and focuses on the individual, while anthropology places the individual within the context of a population.

sophisticated technology. Life in these environments is limited to short-term exploration and is clearly outside the range of habitats to which we can adapt, as defined by human evolutionary history. But are there less obvious examples of a lack of fit between human beings and their environment? The answer is a definite yes, and for those of us living in the technologically sophisticated Western world, many of the examples of this lack of fit are close to home.

Applying knowledge of human evolution to the problems of modern humankind is made necessary by the conflict between the conditions of the modern world and basic human adaptations, as we have studied throughout this book. This idea is known as the **Discordance Hypothesis,** a term applied by Eaton and Konner (1985) in biomedical anthropology but one which can be used equally well in a wider context. The evolutionary perspective that applied biological anthropology provides can help people bring their living environment into closer congruence with their biological adaptation as human beings.

Underlying the goal of "concordance" in applied biological anthropology is the realization that natural selection has produced through millions of years of evolution a good fit between human adaptive capabilities and the environment, as these have "**co-evolved**." Instead of viewing human beings as simply machines that need to be fixed when they break, malfunction, or wear out, an evolutionary perspective indicates that, more than this, human beings are the product of a long process of change that has perfected a certain way of solving problems and getting work done. A static machine metaphor for human adaptation has been replaced by the more sophisticated idea of a **feed-back system** that has been designed and perfected over immense spans of time and under many different circumstances. This approach fosters a new appreciation for the "wisdom of the human organism" and perhaps a little less human arrogance in regard to engineering human progress. Like the proverbial auto mechanic who ignores the directions and ends up with a few pieces left over of the engine he has just re-assembled, applied human scientists who ignore the overall evolutionary context of human biology and behavior may well find that their solutions to human problems are less than optimal. If human beings think that they can devise a better system than evolution, they must first at least know how that system operates.

The agenda of applied biological anthropology, then, is **adaptationist.** There is an assumption that, if a trait or characteristic is present in human beings, then there is or was some adaptive reason for it to be there. Not all evolutionary scientists agree. Stephen Jay Gould, for example, holds that specific traits may be the result of evolutionary processes more random than adaptation. The nipples on male humans (Figure 15–3), he points out, never had an adaptive reason to be there and do not have an adaptive reason today because men cannot and do not suckle infants. Despite the fact that men in some South Sea Pacific cultures are known to use their nipples as pacifiers for infants, Gould is

Discordance Hypothesis–the thesis that human biology and behavior, as shaped by evolution, are at odds with modern human environments.

co-evolution–the concept that organisms sharing the same environmental resources will evolve along with one another, as well as with environmental changes.

feed-back system–in information theory, the concept that change in one step of a loop will affect a subsequent step that will in turn affect the starting point.

adaptationist–the theoretical position that most if not all morphological and behavioral traits of a species have been crafted by natural selection to adapt that species to its adaptive niche; criticized by S.J. Gould as the "Panglossian paradigm," from Voltaire's *Candide,* in reference to Dr. Pangloss's explanation that "all things are for the best."

 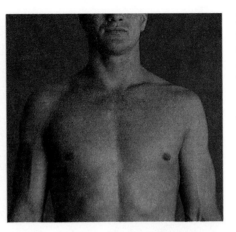

Figure 15–3 • Human pectoral nipples. The male nipple is cited as a possible example of a biological trait with no adaptive value, but the female nipple is an important reproductive adaptation for suckling infants. Viewed in a populational context, the male nipple is a reflection of an important species adaptation to infant care, shared with other mammals.

largely correct in this assessment if one focuses only on individuals. A focus on the species, however, reveals that breasts are a very important part of the biology of reproduction. Men have nipples because women have nipples with which to suckle infants, a trait that insures infant survival; it finds expression in males because of similarities in the early embryological development of males and females.

The goals, then, of applied biological anthropology are to construct an explanatory framework for the many physical and behavioral traits of the human species within evolutionary and environmental contexts and to seek ways to maximize their function. These are broad goals, and they will certainly be applied much more widely in the future of this still new discipline. This chapter will discuss the major areas of applied biological anthropology to date.

BIOMEDICAL ANTHROPOLOGY AND EVOLUTIONARY MEDICINE

One definition of medicine is applied biological anthropology. Physicians take the principles of normal human structure and function, the provinces of biological anthropology (and the related fields of anatomy, physiology, biochemistry, and genetics), and apply them to patients in whom normal structure and function have gone awry. Biomedical anthropology is the field that specifically relates knowledge of human biology and evolution to medical research and treatment of disease. Medicine has long recognized this close connection, and biological anthropologists who teach gross anatomy are frequently among the first instructors that entering medical students encounter (Figure 15–4). But until recently this connection between biological anthropology and medicine was viewed as largely static. Using the machine metaphor again, anthropologists and anatomists were needed to supply the parts, but the physicians, the master engineers, knew how to put them together. An old medical joke compared anthropologists and anatomists to the mapmakers of Paris—very

Figure 15–4 • Rembrandt's *The Anatomy Lesson* (painting). The role of biological anthropologist within medicine as gross anatomist is changing. Biomedical anthropology and evolutionary medicine are now more clinically relevant applied subfields of biological anthropology.

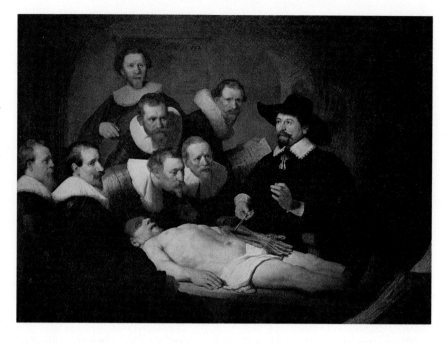

good at describing all the precise locations of buildings and houses but totally oblivious to what went on inside. Medicine became more concerned with the machine-like functioning of genes and cells, and less with the overall functioning of the organism.

New initiatives, however, in biomedical anthropology have begun to have an effect in medicine. Perhaps the most noticeable of these is **evolutionary medicine,** also sometimes termed Darwinian medicine (Williams and Nesse, 1991). Evolutionary medicine is the study and treatment of the causes, distributions, and cultural correlates of disease within a framework of evolution by natural selection. It is one of the most important new areas of applied biological anthropology and holds particular relevance to people's everyday lives.

The following case studies represent the range of issues dealt with by biomedical anthropologists and physicians who work in evolutionary medicine.

Sudden Infant Death Syndrome

evolutionary medicine–the application of evolutionary principles and deductions from biological anthropology and human biology to the practice of medicine; also termed "Darwinian medicine."

Sudden Infant Death Syndrome–"crib death" or "cot death;" sudden and unexpected death of apparently healthy infants, usually between 3 weeks and 5 months of age.

Anthropologist James McKenna of Pomona College was by training an expert in non-human primate mother-infant behavior, when he became interested in the problem of human **Sudden Infant Death Syndrome** (SIDS). SIDS, also known as "crib death," is the leading cause of death of very young infants in the United States. Standard medical research has failed to either find a cause or a cure for the syndrome. McKenna believed that the practice, very unusual from an evolutionary and nonhuman primate standpoint, of parents isolating young infants in a crib away from themselves had something to do with the problem. He undertook extensive studies of other cultures in which there are standard parent–infant "co-sleeping" arrangements and of other primates where infants and mothers sleep together (Figure 15–5), and he found that SIDS did not occur. In association with medical researchers he then began to investigate the neurological development of infants dying of SIDS. This research strongly implied that these infants were neurologically not yet fully capable of breathing on their own during sleep, and needed the pacemaker effect of nearby maternal breathing and heartbeat (McKenna et al. 1990). Further work showed that co-sleeping young infants responding to parents' movements slept less deeply and were less likely to stop breathing during deep, uninterrupted sleep. McKenna's research is continuing but his evolutionary approach has succeeded in directing research away from a search for elusive viruses or hidden trauma as a cause of the innumerable infant deaths resulting from SIDS deaths.

Neonatal Jaundice

Newborn babies may develop a yellowish cast to the skin (Figure 15–6), similar to that of jaundiced adults, between the second and fifth days after birth. Adult jaundice is a condition in which the pigment known as **bilirubin,** caused by a normal breakdown of red blood cells, builds up in the body, due to impaired liver function or to a lack of necessary enzymes to break hemoglobin down. Very high levels of bilirubin entering the brain can cause symptoms like those of tetanus. Neonatal jaundice is also due to an elevated amount of bilirubin and has been explained as a byproduct of a still immature and not fully functioning liver. Traditionally, it was treated primarily by phototherapy, the application of bright light, which oxidizes the excess bilirubin and makes the yellowish pigmentation disappear. One evolutionary explanation for this treatment was that early hominids normally lived outdoors and newborn babies would have normally been exposed to significantly greater amounts of light than modern indoor-living babies receive.

Two biomedical anthropologists, John Brett and Susan Niemeyer (1990), questioned this treatment and also the medical reasons for it. They contend that the presence of bilirubin enables a newborn's body to rid itself of **free radicals** which can damage developing tissues, particularly the brain. While the baby was in its mother's uterus her bloodstream and immune system removed these and other harmful substances. Excess bilirubin, contend Brett and Niemeyer, is an excellent way that evolution has produced of protecting a baby's first few days in its own oxygen-rich environment before its own immune system is fully functioning. They further argue that under normal conditions

Figure 15–5 • Co-sleeping human infant and mother; co-sleeping nonhuman primate infant and mother.

bilirubin–a bile pigment from the liver that results from the breakdown of hemoglobin in red blood cells; bilirubin normally circulates in the blood in a complex with albumin but can increase in certain pathological conditions such as hepatitis.

free radicals–highly reactive "active" molecules of oxygen (mainly O_2^-) formed from the breakdown of oxygen molecules in the body.

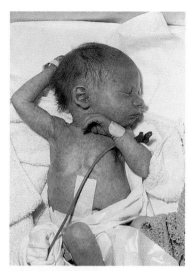

Figure 15–6 • Neonatal jaundice.

bilirubin is excluded from the brain and that, if it is present there, another disease is responsible, not neonatal jaundice. They suggest that pediatricians do not need to treat this "disease" and that they should not tamper with a process that has been designed by millions of years of evolution and that still works well. A news report on this research noted that "diseases have been abolished with drugs and vaccines before; to do away with one by force of argument might be a first" (*The Economist,* 1993).

Coping with the "Diseases of Civilization"

At the same time that Western medical researchers were making advances in understanding the genetic mechanisms of diseases and their more effective treatment, biological anthropologists studying the health and physiology of non-Western peoples made the startling discovery (Chapter 14) that the very diseases that Western medical practitioners considered an intrinsic, genetically coded part of human biology did not account for any major part of the mortality or **morbidity** of hunter-and-gathering peoples. Such maladies as cancer, stroke, heart attack, and diabetes, termed "diseases of civilization" (Table 14–3) by Eaton and colleagues et al. (1988), simply did not occur. Instead, trauma, parasites, and infectious diseases were identified as the major killers of non-Western peoples. Another important discovery was that many individuals in hunter-gatherer groups, and by extension early hominids, who survived the high mortality period of early childhood lived remarkably healthy lives and had excellent chances of living to advanced ages.

The genetic code of hunter-gatherers is largely the same as that of "civilized" populations because all human beings alive today are part of the same biological species. The conclusion from this research was, then, that there must be something about the environment or life styles of Westerners that caused disease which otherwise would not occur.

Obesity and the Human Ecology of Fat Deposition   Recent medical surveys indicate that some 20% to 30% of Americans are overweight, defined as 20% or more above the "normal" mean weight for their height. This is an astounding percentage when one considers that there are strong societal and medical forces that encourage individuals to moderate food intake, increase exercise, and lower body weight. But obesity continues to be a major health problem for Americans, as well as many other populations, and contributes directly or indirectly to heart disease, high blood pressure (hypertension), diabetes, and musculo-skeletal problems ranging from back pain to flat feet.

There are four types of fat in the human body defined on the basis of their location in the body and how they are metabolized (Björntorp and Brodoff, 1992). (1) *Brown fat* is found mainly in babies and young infants and functions to provide heat to keep them from hypothermia. It exists on the back between the shoulder blades. (2) *Subcutaneous*

morbidity–showing evidence of disease or infection.

fat occurs over almost all the body, but is found especially in the abdominal region and in the female breasts. It is directly related to "excess nutrition" built up during times of plenty. It serves as a long-term reservoir of energy and is metabolized during periods of famine or starvation. (3) *Hip/Thigh fat* is found predominantly in adult females and shows a different metabolic pattern than generally distributed subcutaneous fat. This fat serves solely as an energy reservoir for pregnancy and lactation; even in cases of near-starvation, females who are not pregnant or are not nursing do not metabolize this energy reservoir. (4) *Intra-abdominal fat* occurs inside the abdominal cavity especially in a structure that drapes over the stomach known as the greater omentum. Males have a predominance of this type of fat, which is metabolized the most rapidly of all the types of fat. It is a short-term energy reservoir that may have evolved to assist males in the short-term fasting that accompanies hunting. In modern humans it is this fat deposit that when excessive is associated with increased risk of heart disease.

Except for brown fat, human fat deposits are an adaptation for storing energy in a seasonal round of feast or famine, the "thrifty genotype" (see Chapter 14). Hunter-gatherer studies indicate that in the wet season of the year when food is plentiful individuals build up their fat reserves only to use them during the dry season when food is scarce. The percentage of fat compared to bone and muscle in the body fluctuates from about 10% to 15% in men and between about 20% to 30% in women (Eaton et al., 1988:63). In modern humans of the Western world, however, there is no season of scarcity and thus the fat reserves that build up in the body remain there unless exercise or moderation of food intake (dieting) take place.

Obesity contributes to high blood pressure by creating an internal physiological environment in which *cholesterol* builds up and plaque is deposited on the inside walls of arteries, constricting their diameters (Figure 15–7). The heart must pump harder to push the blood through these constricted arteries. When the arteries of the heart itself become constricted or occluded, the heart muscle can no longer get adequate oxygen for its work and a heart attack results.

Diverticulitis   Over millions of years, hominids have evolved their eating patterns, which are also related to the "feast or famine" seasonal round. Ancient diets had a high proportion of roughage—fibrous fruits and plant material low in energy but filling, and relatively small amounts of high-calorie animal fat and sugar. Nevertheless, natural selection ensured that the latter foods were craved, for the balance in diet and the excess energy that they conferred. Similar cravings occur with certain important minerals, particularly salt, a very necessary component in a thirsty, sweaty hominid (see Chapter 14). Potato chips and pizza, both loaded with fat and salt, are both excellent examples of what early hominids, not knowing any better, might have imagined as the ideal food. But not only does excess dietary fat in people con-

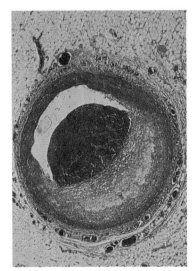

Figure 15–7 • Inside of artery showing buildup of plaque, which causes high blood pressure and, in turn, contributes to heart disease.

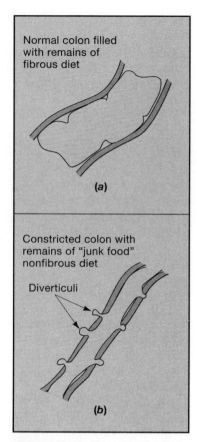

Figure 15–8 • Cross-sections of human colon with (*a*) normal fibrous diet, and (*b*) with junk-food diet and diverticuli.

diverticulitis–inflammation of an outpocketing of the wall of the large intestine.

gastric ulcer–an inflammation of the lining of the stomach.

sympathetic nervous system–part of the autonomic nervous system that is distributed in nerves leaving the thoracic and lumbar parts of the spinal cord; mediates activity of cardiac muscle, smooth muscle, and glands.

fever–elevation of body temperature above normal; in disease caused by infection by microorganisms.

tribute to heart disease, as noted above, and excess sodium (versus potassium) also raise blood pressure, but these sorts of "junk foods" also lack the fiber that early hominid foods had.

The lack of dietary fiber leads to chronically underfilled large intestines, that part of our digestive tracts that stores large volumes of the undigestible components of dietary intake (Painter and Burkitt, 1975). In consequence, the large intestines contract into smaller and smaller diameters, and the increased pressure inside creates small outpocketings of the intestinal walls known as "diverticuli" (Figure 15–8). When these become infected and burst, a serious disease known as diverticulitis results. **Diverticulitis** can be avoided by eating a diet high in fiber and plant roughage.

Breast Cancer   Eaton (1994) has recently related the late onset of first pregnancies in Western women and the high proportion of reproductive time they spend nonpregnant and without nursing infants as the primary contributing factors to breast cancer. In a comparative study of Asian and American women, Eaton noted that early onset of menarche, late menopause, fewer number of children born, and lower frequency of suckling infants all positively correlate with higher incidences of breast cancer. Mechanisms for this correlation are still under study.

Ulcers and Other Stress Indicators   **Gastric ulcers** are virtually unknown in hunter-gatherers. They constitute another "disease of civilization." The cause of ulcers is not generally agreed upon but stress is strongly implicated in their onset. A contributing cause is excessive irritation of the stomach lining, which can occur as a byproduct of constant production of stomach acid, a response of the **sympathetic nervous system** to anxiety, a poor diet composed of highly acidic content, such as excessive coffee, and hereditary predisposition. Recent medical research has indicated that treatment of ulcers with antibiotics is effective, suggesting that another factor may be bacteria (Marshall, 1993). Whatever the exact cause of ulcers, the life style factors of modern Western society have a causative role in the disease, and evolutionary medicine may yet play a major part in finding a better treatment.

Human Populations, Infectious Diseases, and Parasites

Evolutionary medicine has also contributed to a better understanding of the response of the human body to disease. Williams and Nesse (1991), for example, note that the increased body temperature (**fever**) that frequently accompanies infectious disease is actually adaptively beneficial, because it creates an internal environment in which enzymes can work faster and bacteria can be killed more effectively. The standard medical practice of reducing fever thus may actually work against the patient's best interests. Children with chicken pox whose low-grade fevers were lowered actually recovered from the disease more slowly than children whose fevers were untreated (Ewald, 1994).

Populations of some hunter-gatherers have exceedingly high levels of parasite loads in their bodies, as was probably the case over most of our evolutionary history. The Mbuti pygmies of Zaire, for example, have elevated white blood cell counts and widespread occurrence of malarial, **bilharzia,** and other parasites. Indications are that the relative parasite loads of our ancestors were high and we probably have a number of genetically defined defense mechanisms as holdovers of our adapting to these loads. Sometimes these mechanisms themselves, as in the case of sickle-cell hemoglobin which evolved as a defense against the malarial parasite (Chapter 13), result in disease.

Another recent discovery also demonstrates this co-evolutionary relationship between a genetic defense and disease. This is the case of **cholera,** a bacterial disease that can cause death by dehydration though diarrhea, and **cystic fibrosis,** an inherited disease caused by a recessive gene in homozygous condition that results in a number of pathological pancreas, lung, and other physiological functions (Figure 15–9). Cystic fibrosis is the "most common, fatal, homozygous recessive disorder of the Caucasian population" (Gabriel et al., 1994: 107). In populations of European ancestry 5% of individuals carry one gene, leading to 1 in 2,500 live births being homozygous and affected with the disease. Why the gene is so common has been a mystery. New research with genetically engineered strains of mice by Sherif Gabriel and colleagues at the University of North Carolina has shown that cystic fibrosis individuals are immune to cholera toxin. These individuals of course die of cystic fibrosis, but heterozygote individuals are protected from the cholera toxin at a 50% level. Because cholera must have taken a heavy toll in the evolutionary past of European populations, a bal-

bilharzia–infection by the parasitic blood fluke *Schistosoma,* which lays its eggs in the liver; leads to liver and occasionally kidney damage; also known as schistosomiasis.

cholera–infectious disease caused by the bacterium *Vibrio cholerae,* and spread usually by contaminated drinking water; the bacteria produces a number of toxins causing acute diarrhea, severe dehydration, electrolyte depletion, and circulatory collapse with a fatality rate near 50% in untreated cases.

cystic fibrosis–hereditary disease of children and young adults affecting the pancreas and exocrine glands and associated with chronic lung disease.

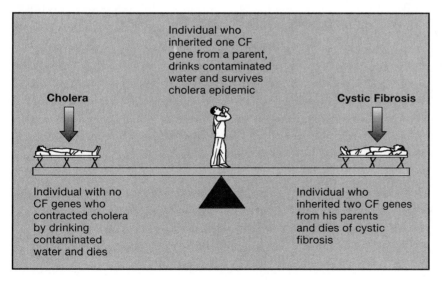

Figure 15–9 • Schematic view of the balanced polymorphism of cholera (left), cystic fibrosis (right), and heterozygote CF gene carrier, protected against cholera (middle).

anced polymorphism (see Chapter 13) exists, and we can explain through this evolutionary mechanism the high percentage of cystic fibrosis genes in the population.

Structural Problems

A number of medical problems that beset human beings are traceable to our bipedal stance and locomotion, a relatively recent adaptation in evolutionary terms. And as body size has increased in human evolution and obesity in modern Westerners becomes more common, some of these problems have become more severe.

Beginning with our feet, we note that they may have many problems that are related to our ancestors' being climbing hominoids. Morton in the 1930s first related foot structural problems to evolutionary history, and these observations have been updated by Olson and Seidel (1983). Basically, the ape foot is a grasping organ designed by evolution for holding on to large vertical branches and supporting the body with the foot inverted (sole facing inward). The human foot, on the other hand, is a rigid supporting organ that, although built on the basic ape plan, supports the body's weight with the sole of the foot flat on the ground. The human **longitudinal arch** in the foot is an important component of our ability to stride and "toe-off" in walking and is a feature lacking in the ape foot. The human great toe, brought into line with the other toes, plays an important role in stabilizing the longitudinal arch, but if, like that of apes, it diverges away and is mobile, flat feet result (Figure 15–10). When body weight in a standing human presses down, a rolled in or "pronated" foot results. This condition can cause foot pain from the excessive muscle effort needed to compensate for the lack of skeletal and joint support.

The knee joint is a rather fragile part of the human body, as runners and football players will readily admit. This fragility is also a residue of our nonbipedal heritage. Joints have a functional trade-off between strength and mobility. The knee joint is a quite mobile and very shallow joint formed between the distal end of the femur, which sits on the flat top of the tibia, and is rimmed with an up-lipped cartilage ring known as the **meniscus,** and the knee cap, or patella, in front (Figure 15–11). The evolutionary heritage of our knee joints is the ability to flex and extend through a wide range of movement while supporting the weight of the body, usually with a pronated foot, which grasps the vertical support, for example a tree trunk. Thus, the lateral (outside) ligaments that support the knee joint are the strongest, exactly the opposite to the force administered in football tackles to the lateral side of the knee. The knee is similarly not adapted to the vertical forces resulting from long distance running on hard pavement, exercise which can result in ligament and meniscus tears and pain. Fortunately, running with cushioning shoes can help alleviate this problem.

longitudinal arch–the upwardly arched structure composed of bones and connecting ligaments on the medial side of the human foot.

meniscus–from Latin meaning "lens;" the cartilage rimming the articular surface of the tibia at the knee joint and which forms a basin for the articular end of the femur.

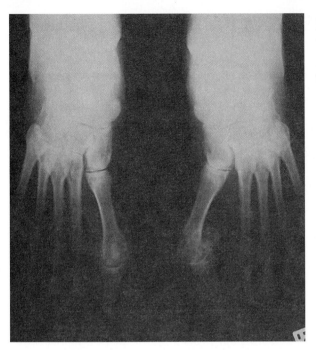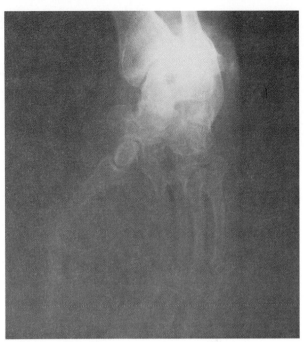

Figure 15–10 • X-rays showing hypermobility of the first metatarsal and hallux in the human foot (left), leading to *pes planum* or flat feet, compared to the normal condition in the gorilla foot (right). (From Meleisa McDonell)

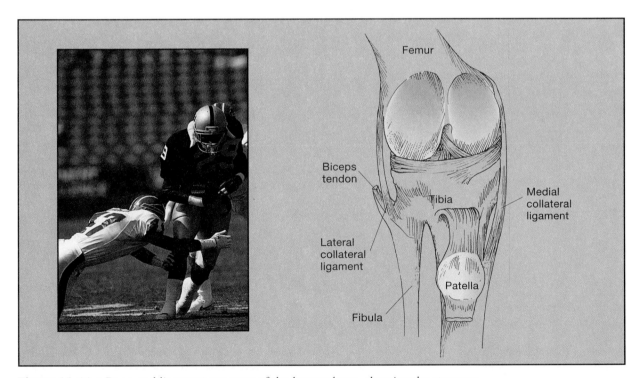

Figure 15–11 • Bone and ligament structure of the human knee, showing the stronger structures on the lateral side, with inset of side tackle in football, tearing medial collateral ligament.

What is the Proper Birth Environment for the Humans?

Modern Western medicine has tended to treat birth as a medical emergency, replete with surgical suites, white masks, and high technology intervention. Such an atmosphere, along with other, nonmedical, factors such as aberrations in malpractice insurance coverage, has led to the extremely high rate (more than 25% in some hospitals) of **Cesarean section** births, in which the fetus is surgically removed from the mother's uterus. Cesarean sections not only cost the patients and their insurance companies a lot of money because of the surgery and the extended period of hospital stay needed for recuperation, but they enforce mother–infant separation at birth because the mother is usually under general anaesthesia. Modern hospital practice also changed birth from an extended family event to a standardized medical procedure in which the mother is isolated from the family, even from the father.

Wenda Trevathan of New Mexico State University (1987) studied human birth practices from an evolutionary perspective and concluded that many of the standard hospital procedures used in Western births needed to be reconsidered in light of comparative and evolutionary anthropology. Her recommendations have found wide support and are now being applied in birth centers and hospitals throughout the United States. Natural childbirth, that is, without anaesthesia and surgical intervention unless required by medical emergency, results in babies born into a less hostile environment, one which offers less stress for mother and infant during birth; lets mothers breast feed immediately; develops better mother–infant and family bonds; and shortens the hospital stay and recuperative time for the mother.

FORENSIC ANTHROPOLOGY

Forensic anthropology is the applied side of that branch of biological anthropology known as skeletal biology, also termed **osteology.** It is the study of human skeletal remains for the purpose of solving crimes and personal identification (Ubelaker, 1995). Forensic anthropologists collaborate extensively with law enforcement officers, the military, international human rights organizations, and medical examiners' offices. Not surprisingly, forensic anthropology is the largest applied subdiscipline of biological anthropology.

Facial and Dental Reconstruction

Perhaps the oldest and most well-known, but also most problematical, aspect of forensic anthropology is facial reconstruction, widely popularized by the 1981 murder mystery and subsequent movie the life of *Gorky Park* (by Martin Cruz Smith). The Russian forensic anthropologist in this story, who recreates the face of one of the victims from the

Cesarean section–incision through the abdomen and uterus for delivery of a fetus; the name derives from Julius Caesar, whose mother arranged for this method of delivery to assure the proper astrological sign for her son.

osteology–study of bones.

skull, is based on the late Mikhail Gerasimov of the University of Moscow, perhaps the most well-known practitioner of facial reconstruction in the last several decades. In the West, facial reconstruction has been less widely practiced in forensic anthropology because of its arbitrariness. Years ago it was shown that one skull can lead to markedly different facial reconstructions, depending on the sculptor. Although the skull can provide a general outline to the face and average tissue thicknesses can provide some indications of soft part anatomy (Figure 15–12), many of the facial features that are critical to personal identification leave no marks on the skull. Nevertheless, facial reconstruction remains one weapon in the arsenal of the forensic anthropologist that may be used when all else fails. Ubelaker (1995) suggests that facial reproduction is "used only to inform the public through the media that the remains of a person of that general appearance has been recovered." This publicity may lead to further leads in solving the case.

Skeletal Reconstruction

Forensic anthropologists use many clues left on bones to determine the identification and history of a skeleton. Using standard osteological techniques (Chapter 5), an experienced specialist can determine sex, age, and population affinities ("race") if the remains are complete enough. Any remnants of clothes associated with the bones can give valuable clues as to weight and height. Teeth are particularly useful in identifying individuals, because of their idiosyncratic nature and because they can be matched to dental records. A telltale gap between the front teeth proved the most important single determining factor in forensic anthropologist Clyde Snow's positively identifying the Nazi SS officer Josef Mengele, the Auschwitz "Angel of Death," from a skull exhumed in Brazil (Joyce and Stover, 1991). Occasionally a photograph of a missing individual may be matched with a skull by a process of

Figure 15–12 • One skull, two stages of the forensic reconstruction made from it and a photograph of the victim in life. (Courtesy Gene O'Donell, FBI)

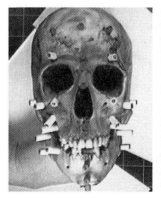
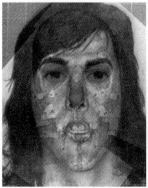

FRONTIERS

Evolutionary Medicine

by S. Boyd Eaton, M.D.

In prestigious universities around the world, theoretical physicists are attempting to find a modern day Holy Grail. They want to unravel basic relationships between the four fundamental natural forces—gravity, electromagnetism, and the strong and weak forces of atomic nuclei—with the ultimate aim of integrating these into a "unified field theory." A Nobel Prize awaits this achievement, which will rank with the discoveries of Newton and Einstein.

On a less exalted plane, evolutionary medical theory attempts to unify or integrate important disciplines related to health care: genetics, epidemiology, pathophysiology, and disease prevention. Genetics deals with the building blocks basic to all biomedical science. Epidemiology studies disease distribution: for example, why breast cancers are more common in Boston than in Tokyo. Pathophysiology seeks to explain disease mechanisms: just how does an elevated serum cholesterol level lead to atherosclerosis? And, of course, disease prevention is dedicated to finding lifeways that can delay or forestall indefinitely the development of serious illnesses. Evolutionary theory is central to all these endeavors and provides a conceptual framework that facilitates the interrelationship of each to the others.

Health status reflects the interaction of genetic makeup (for individuals) or the gene pool (for populations) with lifestyle factors:

Genes (+) Lifestyle = Health Status

When viewed as an equation, our gene pool represents the constant, over time, because humans living in the twentieth century are less than 0.005% different, genetically, from their preagricultural ancestors of 10,000 years ago. In contrast, lifestyle factors can change drastically in only a generation or two; therefore, they represent the equation's variable element.

Members of recently studied gatherer-hunter societies, present-day surrogates for our Late Paleolithic ancestors, have cholesterol levels averaging less than 150 mg/dL and their diets provide superample amounts of antioxidant vitamins. In contrast, the "new" (in evolutionary terms) life circumstances of affluent Americans show elevated average serum cholesterol concentrations to over 200 mg/dL and reduced antioxidant intake. Pathophysiologically, this phenomenon results in greater production of oxidized cholesterol (specifically, oxidized low density lipoprotein cholesterol, or LDL); it is this material which accumulates within developing

overlaying the images in a computer, controlling for orientation and exact measurements (Ubelaker and O'Donell, 1992).

Cause of Death

Forensic anthropologists categorize most trauma that they can detect in bony remains to (1) gunshot wounds, (2) blunt force trauma, or (3) sharp force trauma. These types of damage are readily identified in broad outline, but the details can be bedeviling. For example, if a skeleton shows both gunshot and blunt force trauma, which injury caused death? Or, if a victim was killed by blunt trauma to the head, and the accused murderer claims that the victim was kicked in the head by a horse rather than being hit with a hammer, can the forensic anthropologist distinguish between these two types of blunt trauma force? If a suicide victim's skeleton lying in a remote wooded area has been chewed by carnivores, can the forensic anthropologist distinguish these long bite marks on the bones from knife cuts? And can anthropologists atherosclerotic plaques and leads ultimately to hardening of the arteries, heart attacks and strokes.

Epidemiological studies increasingly link breast cancer incidence to reproductive events. Early menarche, delayed first birth, failure to breast-feed, lower parity (number of births), and late menopause are all significant risk factors. In each instance, the reproductive experience of women in Western nations heightens susceptibility: compared with foragers, we Americans experience menarche earlier, are older at first birth, breastfeed far less, have fewer babies, and our menopause occurs later. The experience of Japanese women is closer to that of foragers than is that of Americans, hence the epidemiological findings (higher incidence of breast cancer in Boston than in Tokyo) might have been anticipated.

In the light of evolutionary medical theory, health promotion recommendations reprise the life circumstances of our ancestors, either directly, as for diet and exercise, or indirectly, as for reproductive factors. Early first birth and increased parity would be socioeconomically disadvantageous for most women, but, fortunately the hormonal correlates of these factors can be recreated independently by endocrinological manipulation (in much the same way that oral contraceptives permit birth control) thereby substantially increasing the women's resistance to carcinogenesis.

Traditional medical practice historically has been oriented toward diagnosis and treatment of disease. Now, as economic considerations exert ever more influence on the health care system, we must place more emphasis on the importance of health promotion activities. However, the American public has become somewhat disenchanted with the conflicting results of epidemiological studies and with advice about diet and exercise that seems to fluctuate as capriciously as the stock market. The unifying influence of evolutionary medical theory can combat this jaundiced view by providing a consistent, rational framework for health promotion recommendations, a logic for ordering research priorities, and a compelling incentive for individual preventive activities.

The scientific impact of evolutionary medicine pales beside that expected from the unified field theory of physics, but its effect on health care costs, and, more importantly, on the well-being of individuals in affluent nations will nevertheless be profound.

S. Boyd Eaton, M.D., is Adjunct Professor of Anthropology at Emory University, and is a pioneer in the development of evolutionary medicine.

be confident enough of their conclusions to testify in court in cases where their expert testimony may be critical in determining the guilt or innocence of the defendant? These and similar questions make forensic anthropology a challenging subdiscipline of applied biological anthropology (Iscan and Kennedy, 1989).

Human Rights Investigations

As challenging as identifying individual criminal cases may be for forensic anthropologists, identifying the victims of state-sponsored human rights abuses can be even more so. Joyce and Stover (1991) describe the long-term work of Clyde Snow and the Argentine Forensic Anthropology Team (EAAF) in unearthing and identifying the remains of thousands of "the Disappeared," mainly young political dissenters who were detained, tortured, and executed without trial by the military junta that ruled Argentina in the late 1970s. Risking death threats and overcoming bureaucratic obstacles, Snow and his team succeeded in

Figure 15–13 • Excavation of anonymous graves, the Avellaneda Cemetery, Buenos Aires, by the Argentinian Team for Forensic Anthropology, 1988.

focusing attention on and investigating a number of the execution-style murders of over 9,000 missing individuals. Working with the courts, Snow's forensic team excavated a number of cemeteries and known burial places of individuals (Figure 15–13) and matched up medical and dental records of persons reported missing with exhumed skeletons. To gain an estimate of the magnitude of the problem they gathered cemetery records thoughout Argentina that showed that after the 1976 military coup numbers of anonymous burials rose drastically in those cemeteries located near prisons and detention centers. Absolute numbers of anonymous burials rose dramatically between 1976 and 1977, the height of the military's repression. There was a demographic shift as well. Before the coup most of the anonymous burials had been destitute men older than 35 years of age. The percentage of individuals between the ages of 21 and 35 buried in unmarked graves rose from 15% before 1976 to 56% after the coup. After the coup, anonymous burials of those who had died from gunshots rose from about 4% to more than 50% (Joyce and Stover, 1991:260–261). These figures and statistics provided irrefutable evidence of the thousands of the Argentinian "Disappeared" who would, in the main, never be identified further.

Snow, testifying at the trial of the Argentinian military junta, was able to provide identities of specific missing individuals known to have been arrested by the military and graphic proof of their execution-style murders. In one of their greatest legal triumphs Snow and his team succeeded in 1987 in forcing the extradition from the United States to Argentina of Carlos Suarez Mason, known as "el pajarito,"[1] who was in charge of most of the illegal detention centers during military rule and authorized most of the kidnappings around Buenos Aires. This forensic project was one of the largest and most politically sensitive human rights cases in which anthropologists have been involved.

Molecular forensic anthropology also played a part in the resolution of the human problems associated with the Argentinian "Disappeared." In 1984, Mary-Clair King, a geneticist at the University of California, Berkeley, developed a genetic screening test for determining the relatedness of grandparents to missing children. Using specific traits or "genetic markers," King and her Argentinian collaborator Ana Maria Di Lonardo used the HLA (Human Lymphocyte Antigen, Chapter 13) proteins for testing grandpaternity (Di Lonardo et al., 1984). This was necessary because, when the government death squads abducted and executed political opponents, they also abducted their victims' children, whom they adopted out to Argentinians who were in favor with the government. Grandparents of these unfortunate children wanted to determine if their grandchildren were still alive, in the hope of being reunited with them. In one case, King and Di Lonardo took small blood

---

[1]"little bird" in Spanish, "because of his prominent nose and his tendency to flee the country" (Joyce and Stover, 1991:286).

samples from an eight-year-old girl suspected of being the child of a Disappeared couple, along with samples from the girl's grandparents. Although a retired police chief and his wife claimed the child to be their biological daughter, the HLA tests conclusively proved the girl to be the granddaughter of the Disappeareds' parents. Consequently, the courts awarded custody to her maternal grandmother.

APPLIED ASPECTS OF ANTHROPOMETRY

Anthropometry, literally "measure of humankind," was defined by Aleš Hrdlička in 1939 (Stewart, 1952:5) as "the systematized art of measuring and taking observations on man, his skeleton, his brain, or other organs, by the most reliable means and methods, for scientific purposes." Unfortunately, one of the main applications of anthropometric data was **eugenics,** the control of human reproduction to meet standards deemed advisable by those setting the standards. Although the goal of the eugenics movement was the "improvement" of the human species, the movement was undone by its use during the Holocaust of World War II to destroy millions of humans deemed "genetically inferior" by the Nazis. The specter of white-coated anthropologists measuring people's heads and then sending the people off to death camps on the basis of their cephalic indices, presumably indicating Jewish, Gypsy, or Slavic affinities, is one that should rightfully haunt the discipline.

Eugenics

Most biological anthropologists would like to forget that the eugenics movement, most active from the late nineteenth century to the mid-twentieth century, ever happened. Its prepopulation-based, typological theoretical foundations, used to defend and institutionalize what we today consider blatant **racist** policies, however, did happen and had profound effects on society (Shipman, 1994). In addition to the well-known case of World War II Germany, where extermination of people not conforming to a social ideal of racial homogeneity was coupled with selective human breeding experiments, conducted at birth centers called **lebensborns**, eugenic ideas were widespread and widely practiced in other countries. In the United States well into the twentieth century enforced sterilization was required by law in many states to prevent mentally deficient individuals from producing offspring. If we mistakenly think that these attitudes are a thing of the past we need only look to the institutionalized **ethnic cleansing** in Bosnia, Serbia, and Croatia during the 1990s, policies every bit as chilling as those of the Holocaust.

Somatotyping, is a method of measuring and classifying the human body on the basis of its form and proportions and was devised and perfected by William H. Sheldon (1898–1977). Trained as a psychologist

eugenics–the promulgation of a system of controlled reproduction based on a desire to either enhance some individuals' reproductive success or inhibit others', based on attributes of those individuals.

cephalic index–see Chapter 13 pg 447.

racist–a policy or opinion that unfairly generalizes real or perceived characteristics of a specific ethnic group, population, or "race" to every member of that group, and which may be used to deny resources or fair and equal treament to an individual on the basis of their membership in that group.

lebensborns–during World War II, a system of government-sponsored "birth centers" in Germany dedicated to the eugenic ideal of propagation of a "pure" racial type.

ethnic cleansing–policy followed during the 1990s in the Balkan countries of the former Yugoslavia to justify the killing and forced removal of noncombatants, including children, belonging to ethnic minorities.

ectomorph–in somatotyping, an individual type characterized by linear and thin body build.

mesomorph–in somatotyping, an individual characterized by muscular body build.

endomorph–in somatotyping, an individual characterized by fleshy and heavy body build.

and physician, Sheldon believed that there was an intrinsic relationship between body build and behavior. He gathered thousands of somatotypes in the form of photographs in order to find correlations between such attributes as criminality and insanity and body form. His system was based on three body types: **ectomorphs,** who were thin and also termed "linear" or "asthenic;" **mesomorphs,** who were muscular in build and also termed "medium" or "sthenic;" and **endomorphs,** who were heavy in build and also termed "lateral" or "hypersthenic." His classification system was based on three numbers, which represented for each individual a ranking in each of the three body type categories. Sheldon's descriptive system has proved of use to later researchers on the varieties of human body form (Carter and Heath, 1990), but his correlations with behavior, as set forth in such books as *The Varieties of Human Physique* (1940), *The Varieties of Temperament* (1942), and *Varieties of Delinquent Youth* (1949), have now been universally rejected as insupportable by objective criteria. Nevertheless, Sheldon's work at the time was part of mainstream physical anthropology and was considered to be one of the most promising applications of the discipline. Sheldon's photographic program at 31 colleges and universities in the United States was aimed at gathering somatotype data from male and female undergraduates, a project based reputedly on eugenic motives. In 1995, the photographs became the focus of controversy when much of the collection was removed from the National Anthropological Archives and destroyed by the universities at which they had been taken, on the basis that they represented an invasion of privacy of the students photographed (Rosenbaum, 1995). Sheldon's work can perhaps best be viewed as representative of the prebiological and even prescientific ideas of **somatomancy** (Hunt, 1985), characteristic of part of the old physical anthropology. This folk method of interpreting an individual's behavioral characteristics from the form of the body or parts of the body was also seen in **phrenology,** a popular method in earlier centuries of reading the bumps on the head, and **palmistry,** interpreting the lines on the palm of the hand.

somatomancy–a nonscientific or prescientific way of divining an individual's personal attributes, particularly behavior, from the form of some aspect of their body.

phrenology–the now-discredited method of interpreting behavioral and mental aptitudes of an individual from the combination of bumps on the head, popular in previous centuries.

palmistry–a type of somatomancy using the palm of the hand to "read" an individual's past and future; like astrology, a prescientific practice that has held on to the present day.

Design Uses

Perhaps more than at any other time, individuals on long airplane flights are aware of the dimensions of their seats, particularly if they are too small. The fact that seats on some planes *are* too small for many Americans, who in general are larger and heavier than many other international passengers, attests to the need for accurate anthropometric data in the design of seating. When Yankee Stadium was built in 1922 a seat width of 19 inches was found to be adequate for the vast majority of patrons. When the stadium was renovated in 1978, however, the width had to be increased to 22 inches per seat to accommodate the larger posteriors of the American public, resulting in a net loss of 8,000 seats in the stadium.

Measuring the human body on an individual basis is a pretty standard procedure for most of us. A standard set of measurements is usually required in buying shoes, clothes, or sports equipment, particularly for growing children. If we question the accuracy of these measurements, we can try an article on for size, an effort that determines in the end whether we purchase it or not. For populations of individuals that are studied by anthropologists, however, accuracy and statistical validity are critically important. In projects where large numbers of individuals are involved and in which the methodology of trial-and-error is too expensive and time consuming, applied anthropologists must ensure the accuracy of the measurements, the representativeness of the sample population, and the effectiveness of the statistics in showing the key conclusions of the study.

The potential economic magnitude of anthropometric projects can be demonstrated by the example of automobile seating and "headroom." When Japanese and European cars first began to be imported into the United States they constituted an infinitesimal portion of the domestic market. Americans, having larger bulk and height, perceived them as "small" and "uncomfortable" and generally shunned them. But as car manufacturers discovered later, it is eminently possible to produce an automobile with a relatively small, fuel-efficient engine that at the same time has an interior of quite adequate and comfortable dimensions. When the oil crisis of the 1970s forced consumers to become more conscious of fuel efficiency, they discovered imported cars that now been engineered to American anthropometric standards. Japanese and European cars became increasingly popular, and in 1989 the Japanese-made Honda Accord became the best selling car in the United States.

There are many other uses and applications of anthropometric data. One of the largest generators and users of measurements of the human body is the military, which employs a number of physical anthropologists. These applied anthropologists assist in the design of uniforms, flight suits, helmets, seating for military vehicles, and many other articles needing accurate fits to be made to bodily form and size.

Figure 15–14 • Biometric security scanning device based on matching individual hand dimensions with computer files of the hands of security-cleared individuals.

Biometric Security Uses

A relatively recent application of anthropometric data has been in the field of biometric security, that is, protecting property and space by screening individuals on the basis of their unique bodily dimensions or characteristics. One device that has been developed measures very accurately an individual's hand (Figure 15–14). Accuracy is so precise that a large number of individuals' hand dimensions can be stored in a computer and recognized by a scanner to allow entry to individuals with security clearance.

EVOLUTIONARY PERSPECTIVES ON BRAIN AND BEHAVIOR

Treating Brain-Injured Children

In the 1940s a neurosurgeon in Philadelphia founded a clinical institute based on the long view of human evolution and development (Chapter 5). In 1955, child development specialist Glenn Doman founded from this beginning the Institutes for the Achievement of Human Potential. Reasoning that the human brain is the result of many millions of years of evolution, and that human growth and development mirror in many major ways these evolutionary stages (Chapter 13), he and his colleagues developed a controversial approach to the treatment of severely brain-injured children (Doman, 1974). Paleo-anthropologist Raymond Dart, the discoverer of *Australopithecus africanus,* became closely associated with the work of this institute. Despite having its methods questioned by mainstream clinicians, the Institutes for the Achievement of Human Potential has successfully treated many severely brain-injured children, those for whom no other treatment existed.

The basis of the treatment for brain-injured or mentally retarded children is a matrix of correlated behaviors (Figure 15–15). A child is evaluated and placed at a point on this developmental scale, which is then used to start treatment. Treatment consists primarily of an extensive regimen of self-initiated, patterned physical movements, beginning with same-side limb movements, progressing eventually to contralateral, alternating limb movements. These might be homologous to swimming movements of our early fish ancestors. The next stage is "crawling," which is forward movement flat on the belly with propulsion from the limbs, very similar to early amphibian locomotion. The child crawls for several kilometers each day. The child next progresses to the stage of "creeping," again for several kilometers each day, with the limbs drawn in under the body and the body raised up off the substrate. The child will frequently develop bipedal walking spontaneously from this point on, or he or she may be helped by an intermediate climbing or "brachiational" stage, one of the contributions of Raymond Dart to the treatment program. The Institute has a record of forty years of successful treatment of tens of thousands of children and has expanded its programs worldwide.

Because the Institute's program is an applied program of clinical treatment that is based on evolutionary theory, it is in this sense applied anthropology. But why it works is still more than a little problematical. Clearly part of the success of the program is based on the **equipotentiality** of the brain—the ability of one hemisphere to take over the functions of the other if disease or trauma has rendered a part of the other hemisphere nonfunctional. The Institute recognizes this ability by accepting for treatment patients with "vertical" rather than

equipotentiality–the ability of one cerebral hemisphere to assume the functions of the other if that side has been injured or damaged; the speech and language centers, normally in the left hemisphere, for example, can develop in the right hemisphere in the case of trauma or disease affecting the left hemisphere.

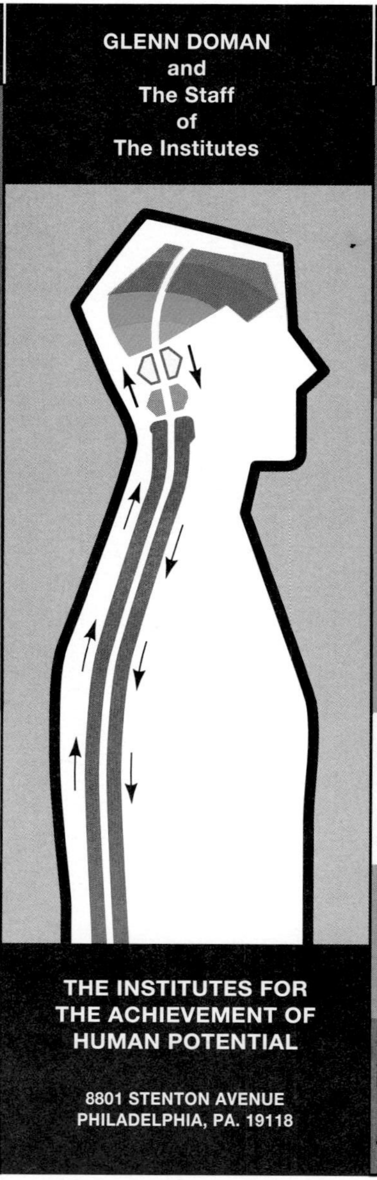

Figure 15–15 • Matrix of locomotor and cognitive development of children from the Institutes for the Achievement of Human Potential.

BRAIN STAGE	TIME FRAME	VISUAL COMPETENCE	AUDITORY COMPETENCE	TACTILE COMPETENCE	MOBILITY	LANGUAGE	MANUAL COMPETENCE
VII SOPHISTICATED CORTEX	Superior 36 Mon. / Average 72 Mon. / Slow 144 Mon.	Reading with total understanding / *Sophisticated human understanding*	Understanding of complete vocabulary and proper sentences / *Sophisticated human understanding*	Tactile identification of objects / *Sophisticated human understanding*	Using a leg in a skilled role which is consistent with the dominant hemisphere / *Sophisticated human expression*	Complete vocabulary and proper sentence structure / *Sophisticated human expression*	Using a hand to write which is consistent with the dominant hemisphere / *Sophisticated human expression*
VI PRIMITIVE CORTEX	Superior 18 Mon. / Average 36 Mon. / Slow 72 Mon.	Identification of visual symbols and letters within experience / *Primitive human understanding*	Understanding of 2000 words and simple sentences / *Primitive human understanding*	Ability to determine characteristics of objects by tactile means / *Primitive human understanding*	Walking and running in complete cross pattern / *Primitive human expression*	2000 words of language and short sentences / *Primitive human expression*	Bimanual function with one hand in a skilled role / *Primitive human expression*
V EARLY CORTEX	Superior 9 Mon. / Average 18 Mon. / Slow 36 Mon.	Differentiation of similar but unlike simple visual symbols / *Early human understanding*	Understanding of 10 to 25 words and two word couplets / *Early human understanding*	Tactile differentiation of similar but unlike objects / *Early human understanding*	Walking with arms freed from the primary balance role / *Early human expression*	10 to 25 words of language and two word couplets / *Early human expression*	Cortical opposition bilaterally and simultaneously / *Early human expression*
IV INITIAL CORTEX	Superior 6 Mon. / Average 12 Mon. / Slow 24 Mon.	Convergence of vision resulting in simple depth perception / *Initial human understanding*	Understanding of two words of speech / *Initial human understanding*	Tactile understanding of the third dimension in objects which appear to be flat / *Initial human understanding*	Walking with arms used in a primary balance role most frequently at or above shoulder height / *Initial human expression*	Two words of speech used spontaneously and meaningfully / *Initial human expression*	Cortical opposition in either hand / *Initial human expression*
III MIDBRAIN	Superior 3.5 Mon. / Average 7 Mon. / Slow 14 Mon.	Appreciation of detail within a configuration / *Meaningful appreciation*	Appreciation of meaningful sounds / *Meaningful appreciation*	Appreciation of gnostic sensation / *Meaningful appreciation*	Creeping on hands and knees, culminating in cross pattern creeping / *Meaningful response*	Creation of meaningful sounds / *Meaningful response*	Prehensile grasp / *Meaningful response*
II PONS	Superior 1 Mon. / Average 2.5 Mon. / Slow 5 Mon.	Outline perception / *Vital perception*	Vital response to threatening sounds / *Vital perception*	Perception of vital sensation / *Vital perception*	Crawling in the prone position culminating in cross pattern crawling / *Vital response*	Vital crying in response to threats to life / *Vital response*	Vital release / *Vital response*
I MEDULLA and CORD	Superior Birth to .5 / Average Birth to 1.0 / Slow Birth to 2.0	Light reflex / *Reflex reception*	Startle reflex / *Reflex reception*	Babinski reflex / *Reflex reception*	Movement of arms and legs without bodily movement / *Reflex response*	Birth cry and crying / *Reflex response*	Grasp reflex / *Reflex response*

GLENN DOMAN and The Staff of The Institutes

THE INSTITUTES FOR THE ACHIEVEMENT OF HUMAN POTENTIAL

8801 STENTON AVENUE PHILADELPHIA, PA. 19118

"horizontal" cerebral deficits. More surprising is that cerebral and language development stay in step with locomotor development (Figure 15–15), for still unclear neurological and developmental reasons. The work of the Institute is a good example not only of applied anthropology but also of how applications can lead back to questions of basic research, in this case how locomotor and cognitive development of the brain are interrelated.

ANTHROPOLOGICAL LESSONS FOR EDUCATION

Humans are set off from other animal species by the tremendous amount of information they transmit from one generation to the next. The sheer bulk of information requires a new concept: education. In the Western world education is formalized into schools, classes, and set patterns of social interaction between "teachers" and "students," but the concept of *learning* is pancultural. However, among hunter-gatherer groups, learning takes place in a much more relaxed atmosphere. Both a consideration of how learning takes place in non-Western human groups and in nonhuman primate societies may help educators adapt modern methods to the psychobiology of the human organism.

Most primate learning is also "play." This is nearly anathema to a traditional Western view of "school," which is frequently linked with

Figure 15–16 • Alloprimates (chimpanzees) learning by imitation and a modern Montessori school using imitative learning.

"work" to form "schoolwork," a description of what children should be doing as they learn. But as Sherwood Washburn and other anthropologists have pointed out, this view of human learning is short-sighted at best and totally ineffectual at worst. The best early learning and school programs now incorporate "fun" components into the curriculum, because if activities are fun, they are interesting. And if they are interesting they are learned and remembered.

Another lesson that anthropology has to teach educators is that human learning occurs in social environments. Primate learning is highly imitative (Figure 15–16). An individual sitting passively listening to a lecture, a student sitting alone reading a book, or a class watching a video on a television monitor—standard learning situations in modern society—are unusual situations, evolutionarily speaking. As educators have become more aware of the social aspects of learning, there has developed an increasing emphasis on interactive learning as we can see from elite private schools to public schools to science museum exhibits.

BIOLOGICAL ANTHROPOLOGY, HUMAN ECOLOGY, AND QUALITY OF LIFE

As biological anthropology succeeds in laying out the limits of human adaptation, opportunities to design better and more evolutionarily consistent living arrangements will increase. This area of applied biological anthropology is sometimes referred to as "human ecology."

Environmental pollution has become a major factor in lowering the standards of living for millions of people in the modern world. Increased noise pollution near busy airports leads to decreased birth weights in babies (Schell, 1991) and only recently, with modern medicine and nutrition, have secular trends in body size approached those of our Paleolithic hunter-gatherer ancestors (Chapter 13). Nevertheless, the dosage effects of the many substances foreign to our biological adaptations that are now common in our drinking water, in the foods we eat, and in the air we breathe create an environment that is hostile to human health and survival. Ridding our environment of these disease-causing substances while ensuring an adequate supply of food and energy to a growing world population is a major challenge for the entire human species. Applied anthropology will have much to contribute to the continuing search for a sustainable world ecosystem.

Anthropologist Lionel Tiger has argued in his 1992 book, *The Pursuit of Pleasure,* that all humans have some basic entitlements to certain aspects of the environment that are basically "normal" and therefore "pleasurable." If we accept this premise and its implication that society and governments should take it upon themselves to foster such environments, then much needs to be done. If, for example, Tiger is correct that expansive views of trees and bodies of water are "psycho-pleasures" born of human evolutionary adaptation over millions of years, then how do dwellers in urban glass towers surrounded on all sides by similar towers meet this need? If having an open fire with its warm glow, heat, and smoky smell are also evolutionary entitlements, how does the equally pressing need for clean air in our urban centers get met? These are not easy questions, but applied anthropology has contributed an important ingredient to the debate on human quality of life: an evolutionary perspective.

Another aspect of human ecology that perhaps is of even more importance than humans' relationship with the environment is intraspecific relationships. As more and more people are born and inhabit the earth, more and more crowding and interaction will become inevitable. The scale of the world's population of more than six billion people is simply incomprehensible to a hominid evolved out of a context in which groups of between 25 and 150 people were his or her entire lifelong social environment (Allman, 1994). The myriad of social and economic problems that besets the modern city-state—from racism to poverty to homelessness to unemployment to crime to bureaucratic inefficiency—are possibly symptoms of this discordance between human evolution and modern human living conditions. Perhaps if all is not well in the cityscapes of the modern world, then those environments need to be drastically changed. Modern urban environments need to mimic the small groups, the intimate settings, and the natural and unpolluted surroundings of our ancestors. Such a utopian solution is clearly very far off, but one thing remains certain. It will be easier to change our surroundings to fit our adaptation than to change our adaptation to fit surroundings that are outside the limits passed on to us from our ancestors.

 SUMMARY

Applied biological anthropology takes the lessons of anthropological research and relates them to solutions of real-world problems and concerns. It is "holistic, evolutionary, cross-cultural, and population-based." Much of applied biological anthropology is based on finding a resolution between the discordance of the human evolutionary past, to which we are still adapted, and modern living conditions. Biomedical anthropology and evolutionary medicine are concerned with the clinical aspects of this relationship. Anthropologists have studied such health problems as Sudden Infant Death Syndrome, various cancers and other "diseases of civilization," including obesity, cancer, and structural problems. Some presumed health problems or medical emergencies, such as jaundice in newborns, are not really problems at all. Forensic anthropology is the most well-known aspect of applied biological anthropology and helps to solve individual criminal cases as well as human rights cases. Applied anthropometry, although misused in the past, has a number of industrial applications that relate to fitting human populations to manufactured items, such as automobiles, and to devices for security. By using an evolutionary understanding of the brain, we can make significant new approaches to treating brain injuries and psychological disorders. How humanity copes with the increasing problems of global human ecology will have to take into consideration human evolutionary history and adaptation while maintaining a techno-logical infrastructure necessary for modern standards of living.

 CRITICAL-THINKING QUESTIONS

1. What is applied biological anthropology?
2. Discuss the "Discordance Hypothesis" of human adaptability.
3. Discuss three medical conditions and how knowledge of the evolu-tionary origins of these conditions has contributed to their treatment and prevention.
4. How can biological anthropology contribute to the investigation and solution of criminal cases?
5. Define "eugenics" and discuss how modern biological anthropology has contributed to society's altered view of this movement.
6. What contributions can applied biological anthropology make to im-proving the educational process?
7. What are some of the practical, applied reasons for our having a good knowledge of our early hominid forebears? Give examples.

 SUGGESTED READINGS

Allman, W.F. 1994. *The Stone Age Present*. New York: Simon and Schuster. An introduction to evolutionary psychology.

Doman, G. 1974. *What to Do About Your Brain-Injured Child, or Your Brain-Damaged, Mentally Retarded, Mentally Deficient, Cerebral Palsied, Emotion-ally Disturbed, Spastic, Flaccid, Rigid, Epileptic, Autistic, Athetoid, Hyperactive Child*. New York: Doubleday.

Eaton, S.B., M. Shostak, and M. Konner. 1988. *The Paleolithic Prescription, A Program of Diet and Exercise and a Design for Living*. New York: Harper and Row. One of the first books to establish the basis for evolutionary medicine, the application of anthropological principles to human disease, especially "dis-eases of civilization," in the modern world.

Ewald, P. 1994. *Evolution of Infectious Diseases*. London: Oxford Univ. Press. A view of the co-evolutionary relationships between human populations and contagious diseases.

Joyce, C. and E. Stover. 1991. *Witnesses from the Grave: The Stories Bones Tell*. New York: Ballantine. A popular book about the career of Dr. Clyde Snow, a forensic anthropologist.

Trevathan, W. 1987. *Human Birth: An Evolutionary Perspective*. New York: Al-dine de Gruyter. Looking at birth not as a medical emergency but as a normal life-cycle process of the human organism.

Williams, G.C. and R.M. Nesse. 1991. *The Dawn of Darwinian Medicine*. Quar-terly Review of Biology, 66:1–22. A succinct review of the evolutionary medi-cine movement.

The Language of Biological Anthropology: Human Anatomy

Finding one's way around the structures in the human body requires an understanding of some navigational terms. First, we must "pin down" the body. Anatomists have done this by defining **anatomical position,** a standard placement of the human body standing erect with head looking forward, arms at the side with palms facing forward, and feet flat on the ground facing forward. The front part of the body is termed **anterior** or **ventral** ("belly"). The back part of the body is termed **posterior** or **dorsal** ("back"). And upper and lower parts of the body are called **superior** and **inferior,** respectively. Anatomical structures are always defined in reference to anatomical position. For example, we would say that an acrobat's chin is inferior to his forehead even though he might be swinging upside down from a trapeze. When discussing limbs, **proximal** refers to a part near the center of the body, and **distal** refers to a part farther away from the body.

Anatomical position for nonhuman animals differs somewhat from that of humans. Because four-footed animals normally do not stand erect, their anatomical position is defined as facing forward with all four feet on the ground. Anterior, posterior, inferior, and superior, then, are defined in the context of this orientation. In comparative anatomy, unlike human anatomy, ventral is synonymous with inferior, and dorsal is synonymous with superior. This system of terminology is also used in describing the brain.

Planes in the body are also important to understand and visualize. A **median (or midsagittal) plane** cuts the body in half lengthwise, into right and left halves. **Sagittal** planes cut the body parallel to the left or right of the median plane. A **transverse plane** cuts the body in half crosswise, at a right angle to the long axis of the body. And a **coronal plane** cuts the body into ventral and dorsal halves.

Orientation and description of teeth also has its own terminology. We can think of a set of teeth as a triangle, with the apex at the front of the mouth. A direction along the tooth row towards this apex is termed **mesial,** and away from the apex is termed **distal.** The sides of teeth are termed **lingual** if they are on the side facing the tongue, and **labial** (for front teeth facing the lips) or **buccal** (for teeth facing the cheeks).

Basic Movements

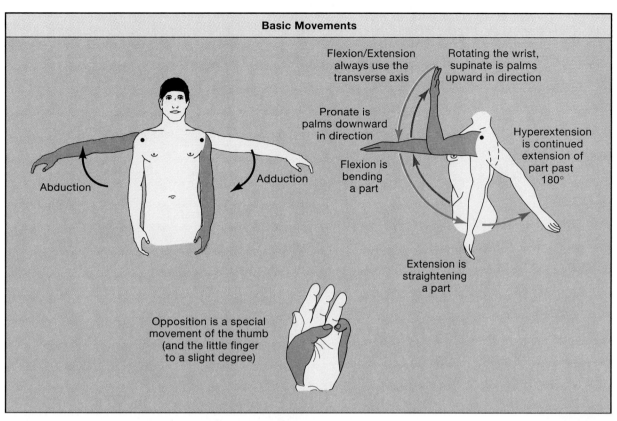

Flexion/Extension always use the transverse axis

Rotating the wrist, supinate is palms upward in direction

Pronate is palms downward in direction

Flexion is bending a part

Abduction

Adduction

Hyperextension is continued extension of part past 180°

Extension is straightening a part

Opposition is a special movement of the thumb (and the little finger to a slight degree)

Mammalian Tooth

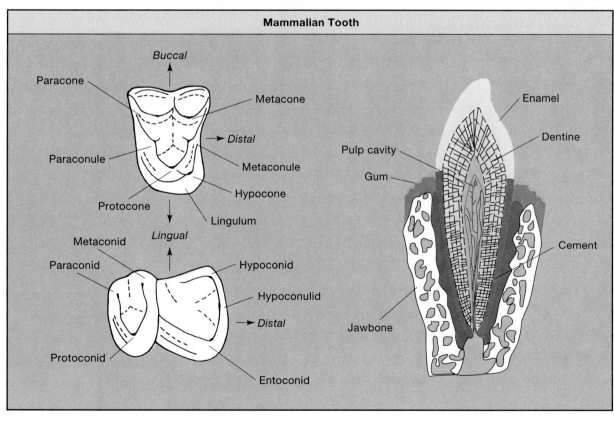

Buccal

Paracone

Metacone

Distal

Paraconule

Metaconule

Hypocone

Protocone

Lingulum

Lingual

Metaconid

Paraconid

Hypoconid

Hypoconulid

Distal

Protoconid

Entoconid

Enamel

Dentine

Pulp cavity

Gum

Cement

Jawbone

Planes and Orientations

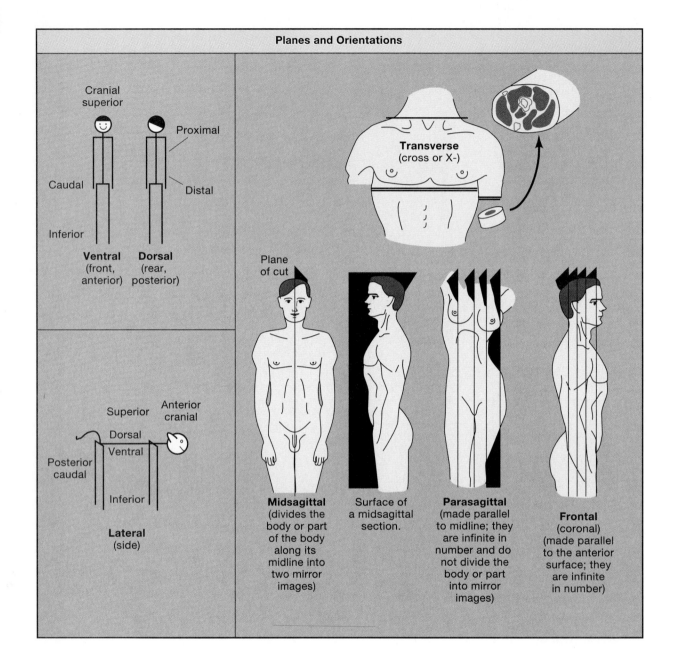

Cranial
superior

Proximal

Caudal

Distal

Inferior

Ventral
(front,
anterior)

Dorsal
(rear,
posterior)

Superior   Anterior
                cranial
Dorsal

Posterior   Ventral
caudal

Inferior

Lateral
(side)

Plane
of cut

Transverse
(cross or X-)

Midsagittal
(divides the
body or part
of the body
along its
midline into
two mirror
images)

Surface of
a midsagittal
section.

Parasagittal
(made parallel
to midline; they
are infinite in
number and do
not divide the
body or part
into mirror
images)

Frontal
(coronal)
(made parallel
to the anterior
surface; they
are infinite
in number)

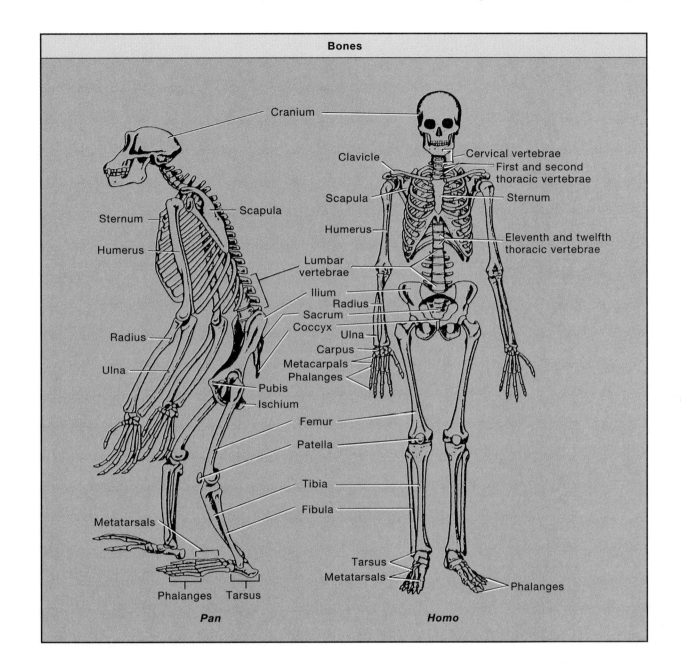

Bones

Cranium

Clavicle

Cervical vertebrae

First and second thoracic vertebrae

Scapula

Sternum

Humerus

Eleventh and twelfth thoracic vertebrae

Sternum

Scapula

Humerus

Lumbar vertebrae

Ilium

Radius

Sacrum

Coccyx

Ulna

Carpus

Metacarpals

Phalanges

Radius

Ulna

Pubis

Ischium

Femur

Patella

Tibia

Fibula

Metatarsals

Phalanges   Tarsus

Tarsus

Metatarsals

Phalanges

Pan

Homo

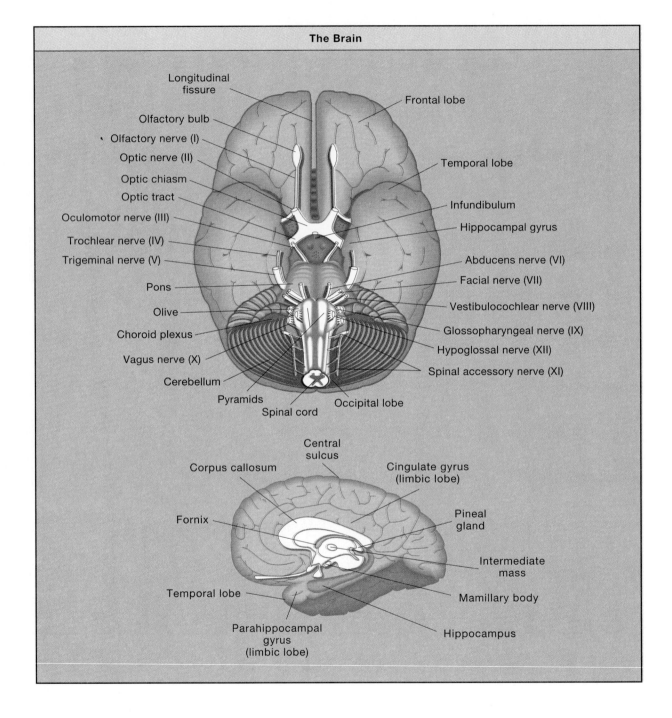

The Brain

Longitudinal fissure

Olfactory bulb

Olfactory nerve (I)

Optic nerve (II)

Optic chiasm

Optic tract

Oculomotor nerve (III)

Trochlear nerve (IV)

Trigeminal nerve (V)

Pons

Olive

Choroid plexus

Vagus nerve (X)

Cerebellum

Pyramids

Spinal cord

Frontal lobe

Temporal lobe

Infundibulum

Hippocampal gyrus

Abducens nerve (VI)

Facial nerve (VII)

Vestibulocochlear nerve (VIII)

Glossopharyngeal nerve (IX)

Hypoglossal nerve (XII)

Spinal accessory nerve (XI)

Occipital lobe

Central sulcus

Corpus callosum

Cingulate gyrus (limbic lobe)

Fornix

Pineal gland

Intermediate mass

Temporal lobe

Mamillary body

Parahippocampal gyrus (limbic lobe)

Hippocampus

The Language of Biological Anthropology: Geology

The geological time scale provides an important way to describe how old and in what time context ancient organisms lived. The largest categories of time in the geological time scale are termed **eras.** Eras are divided into **periods.** For the most recent two periods of geological time, there are also smaller divisions known as **epochs.** As methods of determining the absolute ages of fossil sites have improved, so have our ideas of the age limits of the various time boundaries been refined. These boundaries are shown in the table.

Geological Terminology

Time (millions of years ago)	Era	Period	Epoch	Etymology
0.01		Quaternary	Holocene (Recent)	"entirely recent"
			Pleistocene	"most recent"
1.6–1.8			Pliocene	"more recent"
5.5	*Cenozoic*		Miocene	"less recent"
22		Tertiary	Oligocene	"scanty recent"
40			Eocene	"dawn recent"
50			Paleocene	"ancient recent"
70		Cretaceous		"chalk-bearing"
140	*Mesozoic*	Jurassic		from Jura Mts., Switzerland
190		Triassic		"three-parts"
220		Permian		from region in Eastern Russia
280		Carboniferous		"carbon-bearing"
340		Devonian		from Devon, England
390	*Paleozoic*	Silurian		from Welsh tribe of Siluria
430		Ordovician		from Welsh tribe of Ordovices
500		Cambrian		from Cambria, Wales
570	*Precambrian*	Ediacaran		from Ediacara, Australia

The Language of Biological Anthropology: Biology and Taxonomy

The scientific discipline that studies naming is termed **taxonomy.** Although the naming of new species and the renaming of old species continually keeps classificatory schemes changing, scientists need to agree on the definition of the animal species and higher categories to which reference is being made. A formal taxonomic name at any level is known as a **taxon.**

All biological species are formally classified by a **binomial** system, under which they are assigned two, usually Latin, names. The first of these names, used alone, is the **genus.** Both names used together designate the **species** to which the animal is assigned.

Zoological classification is *hierarchical,* that is, organized in levels, one under another. In practice, the International Code of Zoological Nomenclature establishes the rules of taxonomy for animal species. There are many rules, but, basically, the Code says that names that were proposed first for a species always have *priority* over names proposed later. There must be a clearly designated type specimen with a description of the characteristics that distinguish its species from other closely related species. The classification can be somewhat arbitrary. For example, it does not matter if we call ourselves *Homo sapiens sapiens* or *Gorilla gorilla beringei* so long as everyone understands what group of animals is being referred to. Most classifications attempt to strike a balance between current taxonomic usage and recent findings in both paleontological and molecular realms. The full taxonomic classification of the human species, along with other living primates, is presented on the following page; common names of each classification are given in parentheses.

Kingdom Animalia (Animals)
  Phylum Chordata (Chordates)
    Subphylum Vertebrata (Vertebrates)
      Class Mammalia (Mammals)
        Subclass Eutheria (Placental Mammals)
          Order Primates (Primates)
            Suborder Prosimii (Prosimians)
              Infraorder Lemuroidea (Lemuroids)
                Family Cheirogalidae (Dwarf and Mouse Lemurs)
                Family Daubentoniidae (Aye-aye)
                Family Galagidae (Bushbaby)
                Family Indridae (Indri and Sifaka)
                Family Lemuridae (Lemur)
                Family Lepilemuridae (Sportive Lemur)
                Family Lorisidae (Potto and Loris)
              Infraorder Tarsioidea (Tarsioids)
                Family Tarsiidae (Tarsier)
            Suborder Anthropoidea (Anthropoids)
              Infraorder Platyrrhini (New World Monkeys)
                Family Cebidae (Cebid)
                Family Callimiconidae (Goeldi's Monkey)
                Family Callitrichidae (Marmoset and Tamarin)
              Infraorder Catarrhini ("Old World Primate")
              Superfamily Cercopithecoidea (Old World Monkey)
                Family Cercopithecidae (Cercopithecids)
                Family Colobidae (Langurs, Colobus)
              Superfamily Hominoidea (Apes, Humans, and Intermediates)
                Family Pongidae (Orangutan)
                Family Gorillidae (Gorilla)
                Family Panidae (Chimpanzee and Bonobo, or Pygmy Chimpanzee)
                Family Hominidae (Hominid)
                  Subfamily Homininae (Hominine)
                  Genus *Homo* (Human, "Man")
                    Species *Homo sapiens* (Human, "Man")
                      Subspecies *Homo sapiens sapiens* (Human, sometimes "anatomically modern human")

Glossary

ABO blood group—blood group system discovered by Landsteiner in 1900 defined by agglutination (clotting) reactions of red blood cells to natural anti-A and anti-B antibodies. Blood type A reacts only to anti-A, type B reacts only to anti-B, type AB reacts to both, and type O reacts to neither.

acclimation—short-term physiological adaptation, occurring over a period of several hours to several days

acclimatization—long-term physiological adaptation, which may have some morphological effect, but which occurs during the lifetime of one individual and which is not passed on genetically

Acheulean—stone tool culture characterized by "hand axes" flaked on two sides, thus termed "bifaces"

adapids—lemur-like prosimians, among the earliest strepsirhines

adaptability—range of physiological and anatomical changes and adjustments allowed by a species' adaptation

adaptation—biological change effected by evolution to accommodate populations to different environmental conditions

adaptationist—the theoretical position that most if not all morphological and behavioral traits of a species have been crafted by natural selection to adapt that species to its adaptive niche; criticized by S.J. Gould as the "Panglossian paradigm," from Voltaire's *Candide,* in reference to Dr. Pangloss's explanation that "all things are for the best"

adolescence—the period of growth between puberty and the attainment of full adult stature and sexual maturity

"African Eve" hypothesis—the hypothesis based on studies of modern human mitochondrial DNA, that all modern humans descended from one closely related population, or even one woman, living in Africa approximately 100,000 to 200,000 years ago

aggressive—tending toward or threatening physical injury

agnathans—primitive, "jawless" fish

agonistic—in ethology, referring to behavior that appears in aggressive encounters

alcohol dehydrogenase—an enzyme that converts alcohol in the body to the chemical compounds known as aldehydes

allele—alternate form of a gene

allometry—proportional growth of one body structure to another or to overall body size

amino acids—chemical building blocks of proteins

amniote egg—an egg characteristic of the reptiles that could be laid and developed out of water

Amphibia—class of vertebrates that includes frogs, salamanders, and extinct species living much of their lives on land but whose reproduction remains tied to water

analogous—similar because of adaptation for similar functions

androgen—any of a class of hormones that stimulates activity of the male sex organs or promotes development of male sex characteristics

anthropoids—"higher" primates, including the monkeys, apes, and humans

anthropology—the study of humankind

anthropometry—the portion of physical anthropology concerned with measurement of the human body

antibodies—immune or protective proteins evoked by specific substances (antigens) in the body

aortic aneurism—weakening of the wall of the aorta artery, a condition which can lead to rupture of the aorta and death

apomorphy—in cladistic terminology, a newly arisen or derived trait used in systematics

applied biological anthropology—use of the method and theory of biological anthropology to solve problems or address questions of practical significance

appositional growth—growth by adding of layers at a specific point or plane

archaeology—the anthropological study of past cultures, their social adaptations, and their lifeways by use of preserved artifacts and features

Ardipithecus ramidus—the most primitive species of hominid presently known, dating to 4 to 4.2 million years ago from northern Ethiopia.

artifacts—any object that humans (or apes) have modified or created to perform a task.

assort—the independent separation of pairs of genes on one chromosome from pairs of genes on other chromosomes; also known as Mendel's Second Law, or Law of Independent Assortment

auditory bulla—the bony covering of the middle and inner ear structures in primates

australopithecine—subfamily of the Hominidae containing the most primitive species within the family; characterized by relatively small crania, large cheek teeth, and according to some researchers enhanced climbing capabilities

Australopithecus afarensis—gracile species of *Australopithecus* found at sites in East Africa and dated from 4.0 to 2.5 million years ago; most famous representatives of this taxon are "Lucy" from Hadar, Ethiopia, and the Laetoli footprints in Tanzania.

Australopithecus africanus—the first species of *Australopithecus* to be named, based on the type of the Taung child; characterized by "harmonious dentition" and relatively "gracile" skull morphology, the species dates to between about 3 and 2.5 million years ago; represented at other sites in South Africa, and probably also in East Africa

Australopithecus anamensis—new species of *Australopithecus* discovered at two sites around Lake Turkana, described in 1995 by Meave Leakey and Alan Walker, and dated to 4.0 million years ago.

Australopithecus (=Paranthropus) aethiopicus—earlier form of robust australopithecines in East Africa dated from 2.6 to 2.3 million years ago; most famous representative is the Black Skull discovered in 1986 at a site on the western shores of Lake Turkana.

Australopithecus (=Paranthropus) boisei—robust australopithecines found at site in East Africa and dated from 2.4 to 1.3 million years ago; most famous representatives were found at Olduvai Gorge *(Zinjanthropus)* and East Lake Turkana.

Australopithecus (=Paranthropus) robustus—robust australopithecines found in cave deposits from South Africa and dated from 2.0 to 1.0 million years ago; most famous representatives were found at the site of Swartkrans, South Africa.

autosomes—referring to chromosomes other than the sex (X and Y) chromosomes

auxology—the study of growth

basal ganglia—structures in the forebrain of vertebrates that form part of the "R-Complex"

basicranial flexion—the hinging of the base of the skull and the hard palate together to form a more acute angle; seen in both australopithecine lineages.

behavior—patterns of animal activity over time

betamin—an enzyme, produced by a dominant allele, that breaks down betacyanin, the red color in beets

big bang theory—theory that the Universe had a clear beginning point typified by an explosion of stupendous proportions

bilharzia—infection by the parasitic blood fluke *Schistosoma*, which lays its eggs in the liver; leads to liver and occasionally kidney damage; also known as schistosomiasis

bilirubin—a bile pigment from the liver that results from the breakdown of hemoglobin in red blood cells; bilirubin normally circulates in the blood in a complex with albumin but can increase in certain pathological conditions such as hepatitis

biological anthropology—the study of human evolution, biology, variation, and adaptation

biostratigraphic age—the relative placement of a fossil site by the comparison and matching of the animal species found there

blending inheritance—the mixing in equal halves of the contributions of parents in their offspring

blue-green bacteria—simple, single-celled organisms, also called cyanobacteria, which are similar to the earliest life forms on earth

bonobo—*Pan paniscus,* a species of chimpanzee distinct from the common chimpanzee, *Pan troglodytes,* and living in a different, non-overlapping range—the Central Zaire forest basin; also termed the "pygmy chimpanzee" but its differences from the common chimp are more in terms of morphology and shape than size

brachycephalic—"short- or broad-headed"; referring to individuals with a cephalic index (breadth × 100/ length) above 80.

branchial arches—the tissue between the gill slits in the embryos of vertebrates.

breccia—from Italian, meaning "broken"; a geological term used to refer to the sediment found in cave deposits composed from rock fragments of widely varying sizes cemented together

Broca's Area—portion of the cerebral cortex (posterior part of the inferior frontal gyrus, usually on the left side) that is essential for the motor control of speech

bunodont—referring to low crowned cheek teeth

call—loud vocalization emitted for purposes of social communication

callithricids—marmosets and tamarins

canalization—the directed trajectory of growth in certain directions even if normal growth spurts are delayed

cartilage—a supporting tissue more elastic and flexible than bone (for example, the "gristle" in meat)

cartilage bone—bone formed by development from cartilage and growth at epiphyses, characteristic of vertebrate limb bones

catarrhines—Old World monkeys, apes, and humans

catastrophism—theory that earth history is explicable in terms of violent and sudden cataclysms that destroyed most living species, after which a new set of creations established new species

cebid—New World monkeys excluding marmosets and tamarins

cephalic index—in a living subject the head breadth × 100/head length

cercopithecines—Old World monkeys with generally omnivorous or graminivorous diets, frequently ground-living, and sometimes lacking tails

Cercopithecoidea—Old World monkeys

cerebral Rubicon—the Rubicon is the Italian river crossed by Caesar during his return from Gaul to conquer Rome, and is used figuratively as a "decisive step"; cerebral refers to the brain; the term implies a typological and artificial threshold of absolute brain size in definitions of hominid taxa

cerumen—ear wax; a waxy secretion of glands located in the external ear canal

cesarean section—incision through the abdomen and uterus for delivery of a fetus; the name derives from Julius Caesar, whose mother arranged for this method of delivery to assure the proper astrological sign for her son

childhood—the period of growth from weaning to the attainment of adult brain size

cholera—infectious disease caused by the bacterium *Vibrio cholerae*, and spread usually by contaminated drinking water; symptoms include severe diarrhea, dehydration, shock, and kidney failure

chordates—animals with a notochord and a dorsal nerve cord

chromosomes—structures composed of folded DNA found in the nuclei of the cells of eukaryotic organisms

cingulum—a "belt" (from Latin), connoting in the dentition a raised ridge of enamel encircling a tooth crown

cladistics—the common term for the study of the phylogenetic relationships among a group of related animals by reference to only derived traits shared in common

cladogram—branching diagram showing relative relationships among taxonomic groups of animals; not to be confused with a phylogenetic tree, which postulated ancestor-descendent relationships

cline—a gradient of genotypes or phenotypes over a geographic range

co-evolution—the concept that organisms sharing the same environmental resources will evolve along with one another, as well as with environmental changes

codons—the triplet of adjacent nucleotides that codes for a specific amino acid or that codes for a stop on termination of translation of that particular segment of DNA

cognition—self-awareness and the acquisition of knowledge, including the processes of perceiving, recognizing, conceiving, judging, sensing, reasoning, and imagining

collector bias—the selection that an individual makes in assembling a collection of specimens, which can vary from one individual to another

colobines—leaf-eating monkeys, mostly arboreal

communication—transmittal of information by sensory means

conceptual models—hypotheses of behavioral evolution constructed using data from a number of sources, models of which may not correspond closely to the behavior of any living species

conjoined artifact—a stone tool whose various flakes and fragments have been re-fitted to approximate the original stone from which the tool was made

consort relationships—pairing off of a female and male for the purposes of mating

continental drift—theory that continental plates move in relation to one another through and over the earth's crust, also known as "plate tectonics"

convergence—the evolution of similar traits in two distantly related animals, such as similar streamlined body form for swimming in dolphins and sharks

coprophagy—the ingestion of feces

corpus callosum—the fiber tract connecting the two halves of the brain across the midline

cortical homunculus—the localized map of the entire body as represented in the cerebral cortex

cosmology–awareness and knowledge of the universe, its origins, and its workings

cotylosaurs–"stem reptiles"; the earliest reptiles whose skulls like modern turtles had solid roofs; classified in subclass Anapsida.

Cro-Magnon–a cave site in southern France, used to refer to late Pleistocene anatomically modern humans in Europe

crossing over–the exchange of genes between paired chromosomes during cell duplication

cultural anthropology–the anthropological study of human societies, their belief systems, their cultural adaptations, and their social behavior

culture–learned aspects of behavior passed on from one generation to the next in human societies

cut marks–incisions left on bone as a byproduct of skinning or cutting muscle off the bone with stone tools; uniquely characteristic of hominids but sometimes difficult to distinguish from carnivore bite marks or scratch marks made by sand grains

cystic fibrosis–hereditary disease of children and young adults affecting the pancreas and exocrine glands and associated with chronic lung disease

deduction–inferring conclusions about particular instances from general or universal premises

deme–a population within which there is a high degree of gene exchange

demographic–relating to the age composition, proportions of the sexes, size, and other statistical parameters of a population

deterministic–referring to explanations or hypotheses that explain phenomena as caused by only one or two factors or variables

development–embryological differentiation of organs and tissues; sometimes considered the earliest stage of growth

diachronic–historical; extending through time

dietary hypothesis–hypothesis advanced by John T. Robinson that differences in the dentitions of the gracile and robust australopithecines were to be accounted for by differences in dietary adaptations, the former eating a more omnivorous diet and the latter eating a more herbivorous one.

diploid–having two sets of chromosomes, as normally found in the somatic cells of higher organisms

directional selection–selection that acts to move the mean of a population in one particular direction

Discordance Hypothesis–the thesis that human biology and behavior, as shaped by evolution, are at odds with modern human environments

diverticulitis–inflammation of an outpocketing of the wall of the large intestine

DNA–deoxyribonucleic acid, the chemical that carries the genetic code for all organisms

dolichocephalic–"long- or narrow-headed," referring to individuals with a cephalic index (breadth × 100/length) below 75

dominance rank–the relative hierarchical position of an individual in a social group

dryopithecid–family of apes known from the middle Miocene of Europe.

Early Divergence Hypothesis–hypothesis that there was an ancient evolutionary split (more than 15 million years ago) of African apes and humans from a common ancestor

Early Stone Age–an archaeological term referring to the earliest period of stone artifact manufacture, extending from the appearance of the first stone tools at some 2.5 million years ago, to the Middle Stone Age, some 100,000 years ago

eccrine sweat glands–glands that excrete a watery liquid over much of the surface area of the head, face, neck, and upper body during heat stress

ecological niche–the "ecological space" to which a species is adapted, including its habitat, diet, and behavior

ecology–the science that studies the biological relationships between species and their environment

ectomorph–in somatotyping, an individual characterized by linear and thin body build

ectotympanic–a separate bone covering the ear canal

electrophoresis–a technique of measuring the mobility of proteins in an electrified field, thereby testing the structural composition and genetic blueprint of the protein

embryo–the earliest stages of development, from fertilized egg to the differentiation of most of the major structures and organs. In humans the embryonic period is the first three months of development. At the beginning of the fourth month, the embryo is termed a fetus, and enters a phase primarily of growth.

embryonic–that period of growth prior to birth, especially weeks 3 through 8; growth during the last six months of gestation is sometimes referred to as fetal growth

encephalization–the process of extreme brain enlargement in the *Homo* lineage

endocast–a three-dimensional replica of the inside of the brain case, revealing what the exterior of the brain would have looked like

endocranial volume–synonymous with cranial capacity—the amount of space inside the skull, occupied in life by the brain and brain coverings

endomorph–in somatotyping, an individual characterized by fleshy and heavy body build

entotympanic–a separate bone of early primate ancestors that according to some workers accounts for the morphological origin of the auditory bulla

enzymes–a polypeptide that catalyzes or accelerates chemical reactions

epidemiology–the study of the geographic distribution, spread, and control of disease

epistasis–gene masking the effect of another gene

equipotentiality–the ability of one cerebral hemisphere to assume the functions of the other if that side has been injured or damaged; the speech and language centers, normally in the left hemisphere, for example, can develop in the right hemisphere in the case of trauma or disease affecting the left hemisphere

estrus–the period of maximum sexual receptivity

ethnic cleansing–policy followed during the 1990s in the Balkan countries of the former Yugoslavia to justify the killing and forced removal of non-combatants, including children, belonging to ethnic minorities

ethnocentrism–the pervasive belief present in all cultures that tends to lead individuals within a culture to view their own culture as superior to all others.

ethogram–the behavioral repertoire characteristic of a species

ethology–naturalistic study of animal behavior and its evolution

eugenics–the promulgation of a system of controlled reproduction based on a desire to either enhance some individuals' reproductive success or inhibit others', based on attributes of those individuals

eukaryotes–organisms that have a nucleus containing DNA in their cells

evolution by natural selection–Darwin's theory that inherited variability results in the differential survival of individuals and in their ability to contribute to offspring in succeeding generations

evolutionary medicine–the application of evolutionary principles and deductions from biological anthropology and human biology to the practice of medicine; also termed "Darwinian medicine"

exon–the expressed segment of a gene, separated from other exons by introns

exoskeleton–a hard and inflexible outer covering of the body of invertebrate animals, such as insects and crustaceans

family–a taxonomic grouping of similar genera

feed-back system–in information theory, the concept that change in one step of a loop will affect a subsequent step that will in turn affect the starting point

fever–elevation of body temperature above normal; in disease caused by infection by microorganisms

fibrinopeptide–blood protein related to blood clotting

field studies–in primatology, studies of species in their natural habitat, uninfluenced or influenced to a minor degree by interactions with humans

fist-walking–a terrestrial quadrupedal form of locomotion characteristic of orangutans involving the placement of the flexed first phalanges instead of the palms on the ground for support; similar in function but probably not homologous to knuckle-walking

fitness–the extent to which the genes of an individual survive in its descendants

fixed action patterns–inborn, genetically programmed behaviors that are always released by the same stimuli and always show the same sequence of actions

foraging strategies–behavior patterns which result in the discovery and procurement of food

fossils–remains of animals and plants preserved in the ground

founder effect–a type of genetic drift caused by sampling a small amount of genetic variation from the original population in a group of individuals colonizing a new area

free radicals–highly reactive "active" molecules of oxygen (mainly O^-) formed from the breakdown of oxygen molecules in the body

frugivorous–fruit-eating

fusion-fission social organization–social organization based on formation and dissolution of groups

G6PD–glucose-6-phosphate dehydrogenase, an enzyme necessary for red blood cell metabolism; G6PD deficiency is caused by recessive genes and can result in the disease "favism"

game theory–the analysis of win-loss combinations in any competitive relationship in order to determine strategy or to predict outcomes of the competition.

gastric ulcer–an inflammation of the lining of the stomach

gene pool–the shared genetic make-up of a population

genes–units of the material of inheritance, now known to be sequences of DNA.

genetic drift–gene frequency changes due to chance effects, not affected by selection; most common in small population sizes

genetic load–the deleterious or lethal effects that accompany genetic variation in a population, measured by the number of recessive lethal genes carried by individuals in a population; also called genetic burden

genetic markers–traits whose genetic causation are known and which can be used in the study of populations

genetic mutation–a heritable change in the genetic material, located in the sex cells, that brings about a change in phenotype

genetic plasticity–ability of a developing organism to alter its form and function in conformity with demands of the immediate environment

genetic polymorphism–the existence of two or more genetic variants within a population; can be a balanced polymorphism when selection favors the heterozygotes, as in sickle cell anemia

genetics–the study of heredity and variation

genotype–the genetic composition of an organism, as compared to phenotype, the manifestation of its genes

genus–a taxonomic grouping of similar species

globin–protein of hemoglobin which comprises red blood cells

glycolysis–the metabolic breakdown of sugar molecules to ATP in an oxygenless chemical environment

grade–a level of organization or morphological complexity in an evolving lineage of organisms

grooming behavior–slow systematic picking through the hair of another individual to remove foreign - matter; important in primate social interactions

habituation–neurophysiological mechanism for "tuning out" unwanted stimuli, an accommodation that takes only a few minutes

haploid–having a single set of chromosomes, as found in the sex cells or gametes of higher organisms

Hardy-Weinberg Equilibrium–a hypothetical condition in which there is no selection or other forces of evolution acting on a panmictic population and in which gene and genotype frequencies stay the same from one generation to the next

harem species–in primatology, social groupings characterized by one dominant male and a number of females and their young

hemolytic incompatibility–destruction of red blood cells caused by the action of antibodies, resulting in release of hemoglobin into the plasma

heterochrony–Greek meaning "different time"; refers to the changes in rate of growth characteristic of species' evolutionary divergence from an ancestral species

heterodonty–the condition of possessing teeth differentiated for different functions; contrasted with the homodont dentition of many reptiles, such as living crocodiles

heterozygous–bearing two different alleles at a genetic locus

histocompatibility–immunologic similarity or identity of tissues; used in referring to tissues appropriate for grafting in medical procedures

HLA–Human Lymphocyte Antigen system; a white blood cell antigen system important in the immune response

holotype–the single specimen on which a taxonomic name is based

home base sharing model–hypothesis that posits a central living place to which early hominid hunters and gatherers returned daily

home range–the area that a group or population inhabits and ranges over, the boundaries of which, unlike a territory, are not defended

homeothermy–the maintenance of constant body temperature; "warm-blooded"

Hominidae–the zoological family in which humans and their more recent fossil antecedents are classified; bipedal hominoids with increased brain-to-body-size ratio

hominine–referring to subfamily Homininae of the Family Hominidae containing the members sharing derived characteristics with modern humans; characterized by relatively large brains, small dentitions, and fully modern postcranial adaptations

hominoids—modern apes, modern humans, and their immediate ancestors

Homo erectus—primitive species of the genus *Homo,* generally considered to have evolved from *Homo habilis* and to be the ancestor of *Homo sapiens*

Homo ergaster—taxon assigned by some researchers to remains of *Homo* in East Africa but regarded by most as being an early representative of *Homo erectus*

Homo habilis—smaller species of early *Homo* that inhabited East Africa, dated from 2.0 to 1.6 million years ago; most famous representatives were first discovered at Olduvai Gorge (OH7) and later at East Lake Turkana (ER1813)

Homo rudolfensis—larger species of early *Homo* that inhabited East Africa, dated from 2.4 to 1.6 million years ago; most famous representative is skull #1470 from East Lake Turkana

Homo sapiens—species that includes modern humans as well as archaic *Homo sapiens*

homologous—similar because of common descent or common inheritance

homozygous—bearing two identical alleles at a genetic locus

Homunculus Theory—held that human ancestors when discovered would look similar to early stages of modern human development

hormones—a chemical substance produced by an organ or structure of the body which acts on or affects another distinct organ or structure

human biology—the branch of biology that studies human physiology and adaptation; closely related to biological anthropological study of the same topics

Hybridization Model—evolutionary hypothesis that suggests interbreeding between emigrant African populations and resident human populations in other parts of the world

hypertension—persistently high blood pressure; above 140 mm Hg systolic (contraction) and 90 mm Hg diastolic (dilation) pressures of the heart

hypervitaminosis A—condition resulting from excessive ingestion of Vitamin A, resulting in increased pigmentation of the skin, loss of hair, and eventually to bleeding in the bones; the latter symptom being the means of diagnosing the condition in the KNM-ER 1808 *Homo erectus* skeleton

hypothalamus—part of the ancient forebrain; located "below the thalamus" at the base of the brain's third ventricle, and important in autonomic nervous system functions such as endocrine gland activity

hypothesis—an explanation of a set of observations that can be disproved or falsified by additional observations or facts

hypoxia—a condition of reduced oxygen supply to tissues despite adequate blood supply

hypsodont—referring to high-crowned cheek teeth

imitative—relating to information gained through observing other individuals and not through one's own experience

imprinting—the fixation in an individual of a specific stimulus or set of stimuli during a particular period of sensitivity to learning that stimulus

inbreeding—the increased incidence of mating within a deme or population that results in an increase in homozygosity within the population

inclusive fitness—the relative reproductive potential of an individual within a group of related individuals in a population

induction—inferring a generalized conclusion from particular instances

infancy—earliest stage of post-partum growth, extending from birth to the time of weaning

infanticide—killing of infants

innate releasing mechanism—sensory cue that triggers a certain behavior or set of behaviors in an animal.

Insectivora—order of insect-eating mammals that includes shrews and tree shrews; similar to early Mesozoic mammals

inter-birth interval—the period of time between births

interstitial growth—growth by new cell formation throughout the mass of a structure, tissue, or organ

intron—noncoding sequence of DNA that is not transcribed by the mRNA

IQ (Intelligence Quotient)—a score on a standardized psychological test designed in western Europe and North America to measure "an individual's aggregate capacity to act purposefully, think rationally, and deal effectively with his environment"

isometric—a direct or linear relationship of the growth of one structure to another

juvenile—the period of growth between attainment of adult brain size and the onset of puberty

karyotype—identified and numbered arrangement of chromosomes

Kenyapithecus—a genus of fossil ape from the Middle Miocene of Kenya named by Louis Leakey in 1968

knuckle-walking—a terrestrial quadrupedal form of locomotion characteristic of chimpanzees and gorillas involving the placement of the flexed second phalanges instead of the palms on the ground for support

laboratory studies—in primatology, controlled studies of captive primates

labyrinthodonts—extinct, predaceous amphibians of the Carboniferous Period some of whom were ancestral to the first reptiles

lactase—a sugar-splitting enzyme that helps to produce glucose ("blood sugar") and galactose ("brain sugar") from lactose ("milk sugar")

lactation—in mammals the period of production of milk following birth of offspring, during which offspring are suckled by the mother

Laetoli—a site in northern Tanzania, south of Olduvai Gorge, where hominids were first found in the 1930's and again in the 1970's; dated to between 3.6 and 3.8 million years ago

Lake Turkana—hominid sites on both the east and west sides of Lake Turkana (formerly Lake Rudolf), closely associated with Omo and dating to between 4.0 and 1.4 million years ago

language—verbal communication, using speech, uniquely characteristic of humankind

laryngeal sacs—outpocketings at the sides of the voice box (larynx) used as resonating chambers in certain primates; remnants of the laryngeal sacs can be seen in human individuals who, like trumpet players and glass blowers, create high air pressure in their throats.

Late Divergence Hypothesis—hypothesis that there was a recent evolutionary split (5 to less than 15 million years ago) of the African apes and humans from a common ancestor

learn—remember information or experience and retain for use in future behavior

lebensborns—during World War II, a system of government-sponsored "birth centers" in Germany dedicated to the eugenic ideal of propagation of a "pure" racial type

limbic system—a mammalian adaptation of the primarily olfactory part of the forebrain, important in sexual and maternal behavior

linguistics—the anthropological study of languages, their diversity and connections, and the interaction of language and culture in society

linkage—the tendency of genes to be inherited together because of their location and proximity to one another on one chromosome

locomotion—the means of moving about

locus—a "place" on a chromosome or segment of DNA where a gene is located

longitudinal arch—the upwardly arched structure composed of bones and connecting ligaments on the medial side of the human foot

lunate sulcus—a groove in the cerebral cortex of humans associated with speech; "lunate" refers to "moon" or crescent shape of this wrinkle on the surface of the brain

macroevolution—large-scale change in gene frequencies or other biological traits in a species or higher level taxonomic grouping, generally over a relatively long period of time

malaria—from Italian for "bad air," from the original, mistaken belief that the disease was air-borne; occasionally fatal disease caused by a protozoan infecting the red blood cells and transmitted from one carrier to another by the bite of a female *Anopheles* mosquito; symptoms include chills, sweating, and convulsions

mammal-like reptiles—reptiles with a skull opening behind the eye (subclass Synapsida) and with differentiated teeth.

mandible—the lower jaw

marsupials—pouched mammals

matrifocal unit—a family unit based around the mother

matrilineal—descent through the female line

maturity—life cycle stage typified by steady state replacement of cells and cessation of growth

mean—the statistical average of a measurement of a population

megadont—"large-toothed," referring to the relatively large molars of hominids; Boaz (1983) has suggested that "megamylic" ("large-molared") is a more accurate term

meiosis—the process whereby eukaryote sex cells halve their DNA for combination with the sex cells of another individual

melanin—from Greek meaning "black;" a dark brown or black pigment that occurs in the skin and hair

membrane bone—bone formed by development from a connective tissue membrane, characteristic of vertebrate skull bones

meniscus—from Latin meaning "lens;" the cartilage rimming the articular surface of the tibia at the knee joint and which forms a basin for the articular end of the femur

menstruation—monthly, cyclic shedding of the lining of the uterus by nonpregnant female primates, particularly noticeable in humans

mesomorph—in somatotyping, an individual characterized by muscular body build

metabolic rate—the rate at which energy is expended in all the chemical reactions in an animal's cells and tissues

metabolism—converting energy sources in the environment to the uses of cell growth and activity

methanethiol—a chemical breakdown product of asparagus with a detectable odor, excreted by individuals heterozygous for the gene

microevolution—small-scale change in gene frequencies or other biological traits in a population or species over a relatively brief period of time

microfauna—the smallest members of a fauna, usually used in paleoanthropological research to refer to small mammals, such as rodents, insectivores, and prosimian primates

midfacial prognathism—forward projection of the bony nose region of the skull; characteristic of Neandertals

migration—the movement of a reproductively active individual into a population from a distant population, thus bringing new genes into that population

mitochondria—organelles within the cell with their own DNA that carry on energy metabolism for the cell

mitochondrial DNA—the DNA within the mitochondria, abbreviated as mtDNA; mtDNA evolves approximately 10 times faster than the DNA in the cell nucleus

mitosis—the duplication of the DNA during splitting of a cell and migration of each duplicated portion to a new cell

monogamous—referring to one male-one female pair bonding

monogenism—in the history of anthropology, relating to a single or unitary origin of the human species, connoting that all human races were part of one species; an early point of agreement between the Church and Darwinism

morbidity—showing evidence of disease or infection

morphology—the study of the form and anatomy of physical structures in the bodies of living or once living organisms

motor cortex—the part of the cerebral cortex located in the pre-central gyrus that controls voluntary movements of the body

Mousterian—a Middle Paleolithic stone tool culture characterized by prepared flakes struck off a core

multi-male groups—in reference to primate social organization, groups of primates where several dominant males live together in the same group

Multiregional Model—evolutionary hypothesis that suggests primary continuity from earlier to later human populations in each area of the world, with some gene exchange between populations

muscles of mastication—four paired muscles which connect the skull to the mandible and move the jaw upward and to the sides in chewing

muscular dystrophy—an inborn abnormality of muscle tissue that leads to lack of function and deterioration

mutation—any novel genetic change that may affect both genes and chromosomes. Such changes are spontaneous and random in occurrence. Mutations are the source of all variability in populations, and, if they occur in the sex cells usually during the formation of gametes, they hold the possibility of altering the Phenotypes in succeeding generations

natal residents—residents of a group born there

natural selection—the process of differential reproduction whereby individuals well-adapted to their environment will be "favored," that is, they will pass on more of their heritable attributes to the next generation than other, less well-adapted individuals

Neandertal—a cave site in Germany, used to refer to a late Pleistocene human population in Europe and part of the Middle East; termed *Homo sapiens neanderthalensis*

Neo-Darwinism—the combined theory of evolution by natural selection and modern genetics

neocortex—the evolutionary "new" part of the cerebral cortex

neurocranium—that part of the skull holding the brain

neutral mutations—mutations that are not acted upon by selection; neutral mutations accumulate at a more or less constant rate over time

non-insulin-dependent diabetes mellitus—metabolic disorder with a strong dietary component associated with its onset, characterized by abnormally high sugar content in the blood (hyperglycemia) and imperfect combustion of fats and carbohydrates; frequently associated with obesity, kidney disease, and hardening of the arteries (atherosclerosis)

nuclear family—a family unit consisting of a father, mother, and offspring

nucleic acid hybridization—method of assessing genetic relationships by splitting and then "re-annealing" strands of DNA from different species

observational learning—learning by seeing and hearing

occipital torus—a horizontal raised ridge of bone at the back of the *Homo erectus* skull

old age—life cycle stage typified by a greater rate of cell death than replacement

omnivorous—having broad choice in dietary requirements

omomyids—tarsier-like prosimians, among the earliest haplorhines

optimal foraging theory—a predictive theory based on food-getting behavior selected to balance a group's needs to find food against the costs of getting it

Oreopithecus—unusual middle-late Miocene European ape with suspensory adaptations in its postcrania but teeth unlike other fossil or living apes.

orthogenesis—mistaken view of evolutionary change always proceeding in a "straight-line," directed course

osteology—study of bones

Out-of-Africa Model—evolutionary hypothesis that holds that modern humans evolved first in Africa and then spread out over the rest of the world, displacing or driving to extinction other populations

ovulate—release of a mature egg cell from the female's ovary after which time it can be fertilized by a male sperm cell

paleoanthropology—the study of the physical characteristics, evolution, and behavior of fossil humans and their relatives, incorporating parts of biological anthropology and archaeology

paleomagnetic dating—the matching of a sequence of strata with the dated pattern of changes in magnetic orientation through time, thereby dating the sediments

palmistry—a type of somatomancy using the palm of the hand to "read" an individual's past and future; like astrology, a prescientific practice that has held on to the present day

Pangaea—the ancient supercontinent encompassing all of the earth's then-emergent land masses

pangenesis—Darwin's mistaken theory of inheritance based on hypothetical particles called "gemmules" that accounted for the inheritance of acquired characteristics

panmictic—"all mixing," referring to populations in which the breeding structure approximates the condition in which an individual male or female has the same probability of mating with another individual of the opposite sex anywhere in the population

paradigm—a framework for understanding and interpreting observations

parallelism—the evolution of similar traits in two closely related species, such as elongated hind legs for jumping in two small rodent species

paratypes—a group of specimens on which a taxonomic name is based

paromomyoids—plesiadapiform primates that had gliding adaptations

pedogenesis—evolution of "child-like" form in adult animals

pedomorphosis—the retention of a juvenile stage in some part of a descendent species' morphology or behavior, in comparison to its ancestral species

perineal—relating to the area between the anus and the external genitalia, the perineum

peromorphosis—the extension of growth or "adultification" of some part of the morphology or behavior of a descendent species, in comparison to its ancestral species

petrosal—a part of the temporal bone in the modern human skull; a separate bone in early primates

pheromones—hormones that produce their effect by the sense of smell

photosynthesis—synthesis of energy-containing glucose from carbon dioxide using sunlight; the major metabolic method of plants

phrenology—the now-discredited method of interpreting behavioral and mental aptitudes of an individual from the combination of bumps on the head, popular in previous centuries

phyletic gradualism—term coined by Stephen J. Gould to characterize Darwin's idea of evolutionary rate; slow, gradual change over long periods of time

phylogeny—the study of evolutionary relationships of organisms

Piltdown—a fraudulent series of specimens composed of a human skull and a modern ape jaw, made public between 1908 and 1912 at Sussex, southern England

pineal body—small, cone-shaped part of the brain (thought by French philosopher René Descartes to be the site of the soul) located below the *corpus* *callosum;* synthesizes the hormone melatonin, which is important in mediating estrus cycling in mammals, and reacts to ambient light in the environment

pituitary gland—an endocrine gland at the base of the cerebral cortex

placentals—evolved mammals with a very efficient reproductive system, which includes a placenta, a structure that provides the developing embryo with well-oxygenated blood

placoderms—early fish with biting jaws

plates—the portions of crust that move as a unit during continental drift

platyrrhines—New World monkeys

play—behavior that is not directed toward any clearly defined end result, such as food-getting, and which is frequently characteristic of young mammals

plesiadapiforms—archaic primates of the Paleocene and early Eocene Epochs

plesiadapoids—plesiadapiform primates that were generalized archaic primates and may have been ancestral to later primates

pliopithecid—medium-sized, folivorous apes known from the Middle-Late Miocene of Eurasia.

polygenic—a trait controlled by interaction of genes at more tha one locus

polygenic—referring to genes at two or more loci affecting a single trait

polygenism—in the history of anthropology, relating to a multiple origin of the human species, connoting that human races were different species; used by some to defend slavery and by others to justify colonial mistreatment of indigenous peoples in South America

polymer—a long chained molecule

polypeptide chain—a molecule consisting of a long chain of amino acids joined together by peptide bonds

population—a group of individual organisms within the same species living in one area and sharing genetic material

presapiens hypothesis—a phylogeny that holds that there was a long-standing lineage of human ancestors characterized by "modern" morphology that lived side-by-side with a more primitive lineage of hominids not ancestral to modern humans; originally applied to Cro-Magnons and Neandertals

predation rate—frequency of killing and eating of individuals of a prey species by one or several predator species

Primates—the zoological order of mammals that includes living and extinct monkeys, apes, and humans, as well as more primitive taxa

primatology—science that studies primates, usually primate behavior and ecology

proconsulids—Early to Middle Miocene catarrhines or primitive apes from Africa ranging in size from a small monkey to gorilla-sized.

prognathism—forward-protruding jaws (maxilla plus mandible) or lower face

prokaryotes—organisms like bacteria that lack a differentiated cell nucleus

promiscuity—sexual relations with a number of partners

propliopithecoids—anthropoid (catarrhine) primates from the Oligocene of Egypt, sometimes considered the earliest hominoids

prosimians—primates typified by small body size and frequently nocturnal adaptations in the living forms

PTC (phenylthiocarbamide)—also known as phenylthiourea; its peculiar taste, for "tasters" with the dominant allele, derives from a nitrogen-carbon=sulfur group in the chemical structure of the molecule

punctuated equilibrium—term coined by Stephen J. Gould and Niles Eldredge to characterize evolution typified by long periods of little or no change (stasis), interrupted by bursts of rapid change (punctuational events)

quantum evolution—stepwise evolutionary change

quantum theory of heredity—passing of traits as clear-cut quantifiable units not subject to subdivision; characteristic of Mendelian genetics

race—a biological term meaning subspecies, or a geographically defined population within a species; not synonymous with "ethnic group" or other socio-politically or culturally defined terms referring to group identity

racism—a policy or opinion that unfairly generalizes real or perceived characteristics of a specific ethnic group, population, or "race" to every member of that group, and which may be used to deny resources or fair and equal treament to an individual on the basis of their membership in that group

R-Complex—the most primitive, "reptilian" part of the "triune" brain model of Paul MacLean; the site of certain ritualisitic, stereotypical, and social communication behaviors

reductionistic—referring to explanations or hypotheses that explain phenomena in terms of only one or two correlated factors or variables

referential models–hypotheses of behavioral evolution using a "reference" species as a model based on shared traits or characteristics of a living species and an extinct species under study

replication–a duplication process requiring copying from a template, in this case the DNA molecule

reproduction–the creation of a new individual from a parental organism with the ability to survive and reproduce

reproductive isolating mechanisms–genetic separation of populations by geography, ecology, behavior, physiology, or anatomy

retromolar space–a gap to be seen between the last upper molar and the ascending ramus of the mandible when articulated with the skull

Rh blood group–a complex system of blood antigens originally discovered by Landsteiner and Wiener in 1940 using blood from the rhesus monkey, which lent the first two letters of its name to the system. Rh antigens are controlled by 8 major genes or gene complexes yielding some 18 different phenotypes.

rickets–from Old English, meaning "twisted," a disease caused by deficiency of Vitamin D and characterized by the symptoms of poor calcification of bones, skeletal deformities, disturbance of growth, and generalized muscular weakness

rifts–splits in the earth's crust where portions of crust begin to move apart

RNA–ribonucleic acid, a molecule similar to DNA except that uracil (*U*) replaces thymine (*T*) as one of its four bases; the hereditary material in some viruses, but in most organisms a molecule that helps translate the structure of DNA into the structure of protein molecules

sagittal crest–a bony crest running along the length of the top of the skull, formed by the attachment areas of the temporalis muscles from opposite sides

sagittal keel–a low rounded elevation of bone along the midline of the top of the *Homo erectus* skull

sampling error–the degree that a sample of a population misrepresents or is not reflective of the composition in some trait of a larger population because of chance

sarcopterygians–lobe-finned fish capable of some support of the body on land

satellite DNA–DNA that consists of short sequences repeated many times in the genome; so named because it forms a subsidiary "satellite" band when DNA is spun in a laboratory centrifuge

schizophrenia–from Greek meaning "split mind," a group of mental disorders which may be characterized by delusions, hallucinations, and withdrawal of an individual's interest from other people and the outside world

secular trends–trends in growth or morphological characteristics that are attributable to transient environmental factors, such as nutrition and disease, and not to genetic adaptation

segregation–the separation of recessive and dominant alleles during reproduction, allowing maintenance of their separate identities and later full expression of their traits; sometimes referred to as Mendel's First Law, or Law of Segregation

semi-free-ranging studies–in primatology, the study of primate groups that are in some way affected by or are dependent on humans, yet live more-or-less "normal" social lives

sensory cortexg–the part of the cerebral cortex located in the post-central gyrus that senses touch, temperature, and pain on all parts of the body

serum cholesterol–cholesterol is a lipid (fat), deriving from the diet, that when in high concentrations in the blood serum causes lesions and plaque build-up in arteries

sexual dimorphism–presence of two distinctly different forms of male and female individuals in a species

sexual reproduction–reproduction resulting from the exchange of genetic material between two parent organisms

sexual selection–selection within a species based on mate choice or competition within the species, usually between males

single species hypothesis–the hypothesis advanced by Milford Wolpoff and others in the 1970s and 1980s that only one hominid species could have lived at any one time in the past

social behavior–actions and interactions of animals within groups

social bond–linkage or tendency to associate between one or more individuals in a group

sociobiology–evolutionary study of social behavior emphasizing relative reproductive rates of success of individuals within a population

socioecology–evolutionary study of social behavior emphasizing the adaptation of species to their environment and ecological conditions

somatic mutations–a nonheritable change in the genetic material of the cells of the body

somatomancy—a nonscientific or prescientific way of divining an individual's personal attributes, particularly behavior, from the form of some aspect of the individual's body

somatotrophin—pituitary or growth hormone, important in initiating the adolescent growth spurt

special creation—the nonevolutionary theory associated with catastrophism that held that totally new species, unrelated to prior species, were created after extinctions

species—an actually or potentially interbreeding group of organisms in nature

speech—the set of verbal sounds used by humans in language

splanchnocranium—that part of the skull holding the mouth and jaws

standard deviation—in statistics, a measure of variance about the mean within any population; defined as the square root of the average of the squares of the deviations from the mean

stereoscopic vision—the ability to perceive depth by virtue of the fact that the fields of vision of each eye partially overlap, thus giving the brain information sufficient to reconstruct an accurate impression of depth or distance

stereotypic—referring to repetitive behavior reproduced without significant variation

sternal glands—glands located near the sternum or breast bone

steroids—family of chemical substances that includes many hormones, constituents of the body, and Vitamin D

stone artifacts—stones broken or flaked by hominids in order to be used as tools, or unmodified stones found in geological circumstances indicating that hominids carried them and placed them at a site

stone transport model—hypothesis that early hominids stored stone tools for later use at certain spots on the landscape

subclinical—referring to a disease condition that is below the threshold of medical diagnosis

subduction zone—an area where one plate is moving under another plate, creating earthquakes and volcanic activity

subspecies—a geographically defined population within a species, the individuals of which tend to share certain physical and genetic traits but who are nevertheless interfertile with other members of the species; a race

Sudden Infant Death Syndrome—"crib death" or "cot death"; sudden and unexpected death of apparently healthy infants, usually between 3 weeks and 5 months of age

symbiosis—the theory that formerly free-living primitive organisms came together to form a single organism, capable of metabolism and reproduction as a unit

sympathetic nervous system—part of the autonomic nervous system that is distributed in nerves leaving the thoracic and lumbar parts of the spinal cord; mediates activity of cardiac muscle, smooth muscle, and glands

synapsids—mammal-like reptiles characterized by a single temporal arch in their skulls, homologous to the cheek bone or zygomatic arch of mammals

systematics—the science of classifying and organizing organisms

tanning—a response of lightly pigmented skin after exposure to sunlight that increases the amount of melanin in the cells of the skin; an example of acclimation

taphonomy—the paleontological study of burial processes leading to the formation and preservation of fossils

taxonomy—the science of naming different organisms

technology—tool-making and tool-use, including construction of structures, clothing, fire, weapons, and all other aspects of "material culture"

testosterone—the most potent naturally occurring androgen, produced in the testes

thalassemia—from Greek meaning "sea blood," in reference to the blood's "dilute" nature; genetic disorders affecting hemoglobin metabolism that can range from negligible clinical effects to fatal anemia

theory—usually a set of hypotheses that withstands attempts at disproof and continues to successfully explain observations as they are made, thus gaining scientific support over time

thermoregulation—controlling the body's temperature by a number of physiological and behavioral means

thrifty genotype—the adaptation of storing "excess calories" as fat, and then burning them during periods of famine or scarcity of food

tissue—literally meaning "woven"; in anatomy referring to an aggregate of cells of the same type, which form a structural unit of the body.

thyroid hormone—also known as thyroxine, an iodine-containing hormone secreted by the thyroid gland and important in regulating the rate of tissue metabolism

tool-aided extractive foraging—hypothesis that early hominid tool use was aimed at securing hard-to-obtain foraged foods, mainly by females, as opposed to hunting by males

transcription—transfer of genetic information encoded in a DNA sequence to an RNA message

transformation—incorporation of another cell's DNA into a cell's own DNA structure

translation—synthesis of a polypeptide chain from an RNA genetic message

triune brain—the division of the human brain by Paul MacLean into three broad divisions based on phylogenetic and functional patterns

tuff—a geological deposit composed of volcanic ash

typology—"idealist" definition of an entire group by reference to a "type" which tends to ignore variation from that ideal

uniformitarianism—principle that processes observable today can account for past events in geological history

Upper Paleolithic—a series of late Pleistocene cultures typified by a diversification of traditions and stone tools made from blades struck from cores; associated with anatomically modern humans

variation—the range of differences in physical or genetic make-up across, within, and between populations of individuals of the same species

vasoconstriction—the contraction of small blood vessels next to the skin's surface; a response to cold

ventro-ventral position—two individuals facing each other with bodies in contact

vertebrates—animals with backbones and segmented body plans

vertical clinging and leaping—the method of locomotion characteristic of many living prosimians, and inferred to have been a method of locomotion in some early primates

Wernicke's Area—portion of the cerebral cortex (parts of the parietal and temporal lobes near the lateral sulcus, usually on the left) that is responsible for understanding and formulating coherent speech

Y-5 pattern—a pattern in the lower molars of five distinct cusps, separated by a backward (distally) facing Y-shaped groove; characteristic of hominoids

References

Aiello, L. C., and Dean, C. (1990). *Introduction to Human Evolutionary Anatomy*. Academic Press, San Diego, CA.

Aiello, L. C., and Dunbar, R. I. M. (1993). Neocortex size, group size, and the evolution of language. *Curr. Anthropol.* **34:** 184–193.

Alexander, R. D. (1974). The evolution of social behavior. *Annu. Rev. Ecol. Syst.* **5:**324–384.

Allen, J. S., and Sarich, V. M. (1988). Schizophrenia in an evolutionary perspective. *Perspect. Biol. Med.* **32** (1):132–153.

Allman, W. F. (1994). *The Stone Age Present*. Simon & Schuster, New York.

Almquist, H. J. (1969). The future of animals as food producers. *Proc. West. Poul. Dis. Conf., 18th,* University of California, Davis, 1969.

Altmann, S., and Altmann, J. (1970). *Baboon Ecology*. Univ. of Chicago Press, Chicago.

Andrews, P. (1987). Aspects of hominoid phylogeny. In *Molecules and Morphology in Evolution: Conflict and Compromise*. (C. Patterson, ed.), pp. 23–53 Cambridge Univ. Press, Cambridge, UK.

Andrews, P. (1992). Evolution and environment in the Hominoidea. *Nature (London)* **360:**641–646.

Andrews, P. (1995). Ecological apes and ancestors. *Nature (London)* **376:**555–556.

Andrews, P., and Cronin, J. E. (1982). The relationships of *Sivapithecus* and *Ramapithecus* and the evolution of the Orangutan. *Nature (London)* **297:**541–546.

Anon. (1993). Evolving Answers. *The Economist* 326 (7799):79–80.

Ashton, E., and Oxnard, C. (1964). Locomotor patterns in primates. *Proc. Zool. Soc. London* **142:**1–28.

Ayala, F. J. (ed.). (1976). *Molecular Evolution*. Sinauer, Sunderland, MA.

Badrian, A., and Badrian, N. (1984). Group composition and social structure of *Pan paniscus* in the Lomako Forest, Zaire. In *The Pygmy Chimpanzee: Evolutionary Biology and Behavior* (R. Susman, ed.), pp. 325–346. Plenum, New York.

Bailey, R., Head, G., Jenike, M., Owen, B., Rechtmann, R., and Zechenter, E. (1989). Hunting and gathering in tropical rain forest: Is it possible? *Am. Anthropol.* **91:**59–82.

Barash, D. P. (1983). *Sociobiology and Behavior*. Elsevier, New York.

Barrett, J. M., Abramoff, P., Kumaran, A. K., and Millington, W. F. (1986). *Biology*. Prentice Hall, Englewood Cliffs, NJ.

Bartholomew, G. A., and Birdsell, J. B. (1953). Ecology and the protohominids. *Am. Anthropol.* **55:**481–498.

Bauer, H. R. (1977). Chimpanzee bipedal locomotion in the Gombe National Park, East Africa. *Primates* **18:**913–921.

Beard, K. C. (1990). Gliding behavior and paleoecology of the alleged primate family Paromomyidae (Mammalia, Dermoptera). *Nature (London)* **345:**340–341.

Begun, D., Moya-Sola, S., and Kohler, M. (1990). New Miocene hominoid specimens from Can Llobateres (Valles Penedes, Spain) and their geological and paleontological context. *J. Hum. Evol.* **3:** 255–268.

Benefit, B., and McCrossin, M. (1993). New *Kenyapithecus* postcrania and other primate fossils from Moboko Island, Kenya. *Am. J. Phys. Anthropol.* **16** (Suppl.):55–56.

Bergmann, C. (1847). Über die Verhältnisse der Wärmeökonomie des Thiere zu ihrer Grösse. *Göttlinger Studien* **3:**595–708.

Beynon, A. D., and Dean, M. C. (1988). Distinct dental development patterns in early fossil hominids. *Nature (London)* **335:**509– 514.

Bianchi, N. O., Bianchi, M. S., Cleaver, J. E., and Wolff, S. (1985). The pattern of restriction enzyme-induced bonding in the chromosomes of chimpanzee, gorilla, and the orangutan and its evolutionary significance. *J. Mol. Evol.* **22:**323–333.

Biegert, J. (1963). The evolution of characteristics of the skull, hands, and feet for primate taxonomy. In *Classification and Human Evolution* (S. L. Washburn, ed.), pp. 116–145. Aldine, Chicago.

Binford, L. H., and Ho, C. K. (1985). Taphonomy at a distance: Zhoukoudian, "the cave home of Beijing Man?" *Curr. Anthropol.* **26:**413–442.

Binford, L. H., and Stone, N. M. (1986). Zhoukoudian: A closer look. *Curr. Anthropol.* **27:**453–468.

Birdsell, J. B. (1981). *Human Evolution: An Introduction of the New Physical Anthropology*. Houghton-Mifflin, Boston.

Bjorntorp, P., and Brodoff, B. N. (1992). *Obesity*. Lippincott, New York.

Blurton-Jones, N. (1987). Bushmen birth spacing: Direct tests of some simple predictions. *Ethol. Sociobiol.* **8:**183–203.

Boaz, N. T. (1977). Paleoecology of early Hominidae in Africa. *Kroeber Anthropol. Soc. Pap.* **50:**37–62.

Boaz, N. T. (1979a). Early hominid population densities: New estimates. *Science* **206:**592–595.

Boaz, N. T. (1979b). Hominid evolution in eastern Africa during the Pliocene and early Pleistocene. *Annu. Rev. Anthropol.* **8:**71–85.

Boaz, N. T. (1983). Morphological trends and phylogenetic relationships from middle Miocene hominoids to late Pliocene hominids. In *New Interpretations of Ape and Human Ancestry* (R. L. Ciochon and R.S. Corruccini, eds.), pp. 705–720. Plenum, New York.

Boaz, N. T. (1985). Early hominid paleoecology in the Omo basin, Ethiopia. In *L'Environnement des Hominidés au Plio-Pléistocène,* Fondation Singer-Polignac, pp. 283–312. Masson, Paris.

Boaz, N. T. (1988). Status of *Australopithecus afarensis*. *Yearb. Phys. Anthropol.* **31:**85–113.

Boaz, N. T. (1993). *Quarry. Closing in on the Missing Link*. Free Press, New York.

Boaz, N. T. (1996). *Eco Homo*. Basic Books, New York (in press).

Boaz, N. T., and Burckle, L. H. (1984). Paleoclimatic framework for African hominid evolution. In: Vogel, J.C., ed. *Late Cainozoic Palaeoclimates of the Southern Hemisphere*. Balkema, Rotterdam.

Boaz, N. T., and Howell, F. C. (1977). A gracile hominid cranium from upper Member G of the Shungura Formation, Ethiopia. *Am. J. Phys. Anthropol.* **46:**93–108.

Boaz, N. T., and Wolfe, L., (eds.). (1995). *Biological Anthropology: The State of the Science*. International Institute for Human Evolutionary Research, Bend, OR.

Bodmer, W. F., and Cavalli-Sforza, L. L. (1976). *Genetics, Evolution and Man*. Freeman, San Francisco.

Boesch, C. (1991). The effects of leopard predation on grouping patterns of forest chimpanzees. *Behaviour* **117:**220–242.

Boesch, C., and Boesch, H. (1984). Mental maps in wild chimpanzees: an analysis of hammer transports for nut cracking. *Primates* **25:** 160–170.

Boesch-Ackermann, H., and Boesch, C. (1994). Hominization in the rainforest: The chimpanzee's piece of the puzzle. *Evol. Anthropol.* **3:**9–16.

Bogin, B. (1995). Growth and development: Recent evolutionary and biocultural research. In *Biological Anthropology: The State of the Science* (N. T. Boaz and L. D. Wolfe, eds.), pp. 49–70. International Institute for Human Evolutionary Research, Bend, OR.

Bogin, B. (1988). *Patterns of Human Growth*. Cambridge University Press, Cambridge, England.

Bogin, B., Wall, M., and MacVean, R. (1992). Longitudinal analysis of adolescent growth of Ladino and Mayan school children in Guatemala: Effects of environment and sex. *Am. J. Phys. Anthropol.* **89:**447–457.

Bonifay, E. (1989). Un site du très ancien Paléolithique de plus de 2 m.a. dans le massif central français: Saint-Eble-le-Coopeto (Haute-Loire). *C. R. Acad. Sci., Ser. 2* **308:**1567–1570.

Borgerhoff Mulder, M. (1991). Human behavioral ecology. In *Behavioral Ecology: An Evolutionary Approach* (J. R. Krebs and N. B. Davies, eds.), 3rd ed. pp. 69–98. Blackwell, Oxford.

Bouchard, T. J., Lykken, D. T., McGue, M., Segal, N. L., and Tellegen, A. (1990). Sources of human psychological differences: The Minnesota study of twins reared apart. *Science* **250:**223–228.

Bowler, P. (1989). *Evolution: The History of an Idea,* rev. ed. Univ. of California Press, Berkeley.

Bown, T. M., Kraus, M. J., Wing, S. L., Fleagle, J. G., Tiffany, B. H., Simons, E. L., and Vondra, C. F. (1982). The Fayum primate forest revisited. *J. Hum. Evol.* **11:**603–632.

Boyer, S. H., Noyes, A. N., Timmons, C. F., and Young, R. A. (1971). Primate haemoglobins: Some sequences and some proposals concerning the character of evolution and mutation. *Biochem. Genet.* **5:**405–448.

Brain, C. K. (1972). An attempt to reconstruct the behavior of Australopithecus: The evidence for interpersonal violence. *S. Afr. Mus. Assoc. Bull.* **9:**127–139.

Brain, C. K. (1995). In *Paleoclimate and Evolution,* E. Vrba and N. Denton, (eds.). Yale Univ. Press, Princeton, NJ.

Brauer, G., and Smith, F. (eds.). (1992). *Continuity or Replacement? Controversies in Homo sapiens Evolution.* A. A. Balkema Press, Rotterdam, The Netherlands.

Brett, J., and Niemeyer, S. (1990). Neonatal jaundice: A disorder of transition or adaptive process. *Med. Anthropol. Q.* **4:**149–161.

Bromage, T. G., and Dean, M. C. (1985). Re-evaluation of the age of death of immature fossil hominids. *Nature* (*London*) **317:**525–527.

Brown, M. H. (1990). *The Search for Eve.* Harper & Row, New York.

Brues, A. (1977). *People and Races.* Macmillan, New York.

Bullough, V. L. (1981). Age at menarche: A misunderstanding. *Science* **213:**365–366.

Butzer, K. W., and Isaac, G. L. (eds.), (1975). *After the Australopithecines.* Mouton, The Hague/Aldine, Chicago.

Bygott, D. (1974). Agonistic behaviour and dominance in wild chimpanzees. Ph.D. Dissertation, Cambridge University, England.

Caccone, A., and Powell, J. R. (1989). DNA divergence among hominoids. *Evolution* (*Lawrence, Kans.*) **43:**925–942.

Calder, N. (1973). *The Life Game. Evolution and the New Biology.* Dell, New York.

Calvin, W. H. (1994). The emergence of intelligence. *Sci. Am.* October: 101–107.

Cann, R. L. (1988). DNA and human origins. *Annu. Rev. Anthropol.* **17:**127–143.

Cann, R. L., Stoneking, M., and Wilson, A. C. (1987). Mitochondrial DNA and human evolution. *Nature* (*London*) **325:**31–36.

Carbonell, V. M. (1963). Variations in the frequency of shovel-shaped incisors in different populations. In *Dental Anthropology* (D. R. Brothwell, ed.), pp. 211–234. Pergamon, Elmsford, NY.

Cardinali, D. P., and Wurtman, R. J. (1975). Methods for assessing the biological activity of the mammalian pineal organ. *Methods Enzymol.* **39:**376–397.

Carpenter, C. R. (1934). A field study of the behavior and social relations of the howling monkey (*Alouatta palliata*). *Comp. Psychol. Monogr.* **10:**1–168.

Carpenter, C. R. (1940). A field study in Siam of the behavior and social relations of the gibbon (*Hylobates lar*). *Comp. Psychol. Monogr.* **16:**1–212.

Carpenter, C. R. (1942). Sexual behavior of free-ranging rhesus monkeys, *Macaca mulatta. Comp. Psychol. Monogr.* **33:**113–142.

Cartmill, M., Hylander, W., and Shafland, J. (1987). *Human Structure.* Harvard Univ. Press, Cambridge, MA.

Cavalli-Sforza, L., and Edwards. (1967). Phylogenetic analysis: models and estimation procedures, *Amer. J. Human Genetics,* **19:**233–257.

Chapman, C. A., Fedigan, L. M., Fedigan, L., and Chapman, L. J. (1989). Post-weaning resource competition and sex ratios in spider monkeys. *Oikos* **54:**315–319.

Charles-Dominique, C. (1977). *Ecology and Behavior of Nocturnal Primates.* Columbia Univ. Press, New York.

Charteris, J., Wall, J. C., and Nottrodt, J. (1981). Functional reconstruction of gait from the Pliocene hominid footprints at Laetoli, northern Tanzania. *Nature* (*London*) **290:**496–498.

Chivers, D. J. (1974). The siamang in Malaya: A field study of a primate in a tropical rain forest. *Contrib. Primatol.* **4.**

Chivers, D. J. (1980). *Malayan Forest Primates: Ten Years Study in Tropical Rain Forest.* Plenum, New York.

Chomsky, N. (1957). *Syntactic Structures,* Ser. Janna Linguaram No. 11. 's-Gravenhage, Mouton.

Clark, J. D., Asfaw, B., Assefa, G., Harris, J. W. K., Kurashina, H., Walter, R. C., White, T. D., and Williams, M. A. J. (1984). Palaeontological discoveries in the Middle Awash Valley, Ethiopia. *Nature* (*London*) **307:**423–428.

Clarke, R. J., and Tobias, P. V. (1995). Sterkfontein member 2 foot bones of the oldest South African hominid. *Science* **269:**521–524.

Clutton-Brock, T. H., and Harvey, P. H. (1977). Primate ecology and social organization. *J. Zool.* **183:**1–39.

Cohen, B. H. (1970a). ABO and Rh incompatibility. I. Fetal and neonatal mortality with ABO and Rh incompatibility: Some new interpretations. *Am. J. Hum. Genet.* **22:**412–440.

Cohen, B. H. (1970b). ABO and Rh incompatibility. II. Is there a dual interaction in combined ABO and Rh incompatibility? *Am. J. Hum. Genet.* **22:**441–452.

Cohen, J. (1995). Population growth and earth's human carrying capacity. *Science* **269.**

Conkey, M. (1980). The identification of prehistoric hunter-gatherer aggregation sites: The case of Altamira. *Curr. Anthropol.* **21:** 609–629.

Conroy, G. C. (1990). *Primate Evolution.* Norton, New York.

Conroy, G. C., and Vannier, M. W. (1987). Dental development of the Taung skull from computerized tomography. *Nature* (*London*) **329:**625–627.

Coon, C. (1962). *Origin of Races.* Knopf. New York.

Corbet, G. B. (1970). Patterns of subspecific variation. *Symp. Zool. Soc. London* **26:**105–116.

Corruccini, R., and Ciochon, R. (eds.). (1994). *Integrative Paths to the Past.* Prentice Hall, Englewood Cliffs, NJ.

Cronin, J. E. (1983). Apes, humans and molecular clocks: a reappraisal. In *New Interpretations of Ape and Human Ancestry* (R. Ciochon and R. Corruccini, eds.), pp. 115–150. Plenum, New York.

Cronk, L. (1989). Low socioeconomic status and female-biased parental investment. The Mukogodo example. *Am. Anthropol.* **91:** 414–429.

Cronk, L. (1991). Human behavioral ecology. *Annu. Rev. Anthropol.* **20:**25–53.

Dart, R. A. (1925). *Australopithecus africanus:* The man-ape of South Africa. *Nature* (*London*) **115:**195–199.

Dart, R. A. (1949). The predatory implemental technique of *Australopithecus. Am. J. Phys. Anthropol.* **7:**1–38.

Darwin, C. R. (1859). *The Origin of Species by Natural Selection.* Murray, London.

Darwin, C. R. (1871). *The Descent of Man and Selection with Respect to Sex.* Murray, London.

Dawkins, R. (1979). *The Extended Phenotype.* Oxford Univ. Press, Oxford.

Dawkins, R. (1989) *The Selfish Gene,* 2nd ed. Oxford Univ. Press, Oxford.

Day, M. H. (1987). *Guide to Fossil Man.* Univ. of Chicago Press, Chicago.

De Jong, W. W. W. (1971a). Chimpanzee foetal haemoglobin: Structure and heterogeneity of the gamma chain. *Biochim. Biophys. Acta* **251:**217.

De Jong, W. W. W. (1971b). Structure of chain of chimpanzee haemoglobin A2. *Nature* (*London*) **234:**176.

Delson, E. (1977). Catarrhine phylogeny and classification: Principles, methods and comments. *J. Hum. Evol.* **6:**433–459.

Delson, E. (ed.) (1987). *Ancestors: The Hard Evidence.* Alan R. Liss, New York.

Delson, E. (1988). Chronology of South African australopith site units.

In *Evolutionary History of the "Robust" Australopithecines*. (F. E. Grine, ed.), pp. 317–324. de Gruyter, New York.

Delson, E. (1989) Oldest Eurasian stone tools. *Nature (London)* **340:**96.

Dennell, R. (1989). Reply to Hemingway, "Early artefacts from Pakistan?—Some questions for the excavators." *Curr. Anthropol.* **30:** 318–322.

DeVore, I. (ed.). (1965). *Primate Behavior*. Holt, Rinehart & Winston, New York.

de Waal, F. B. M. (1989). *Chimpanzee Politics: Power and Sex Among Apes.* Johns Hopkins Univ. Press, Baltimore, MD.

Dickemann, M. (1985). Human sociobiology: The first decade. *New Sci.* **108:**38–42.

Dickerson, R. E. (1978). Chemical evolution and the origin of life. *Sci. Am.* **239:**70–86.

Di Lonardo, A. M., Darlu, P., Baur, M., et al. (1984). Human genetics and human rights: Identifying the families of kidnapped children. *Am. J. Forensic Med. Pathol.* **5:**339–347.

Dixon, A. F. (1981). *The Natural History of the Gorilla*. Columbia Univ. Press, New York.

Dobzhansky, T. (1937). *Genetics and Origin of Species*. Columbia Univ. Press, New York.

Dohlinow, P. C., and Taff, M. A. (1993). Rivalry, resolution and the individual. Cooperation among male langur monkeys. In *Milestones in Human Evolution* (A. J. Almquist and J. A. Manyak, eds.), pp. 75–92. Waveland Press, Prospect Heights, IL.

Doman, G. (1974). *What to Do About Your Brain-Injured Child, or Your Brain-Damaged, Mentally Retarded, Mentally Deficient, Cerebral Palsied, Emotionally Disturbed, Spastic, Flaccid, Rigid, Epileptic, Autistic, Athetoid, Hyperactive Child*. Doubleday, New York.

DuMond, F. V., and Hutchinson, T. C. (1967). Squirrel monkey reproduction: The "fatted" male phenomenon and season spermatogenesis. *Science* **158:**1067-1070.

Dunbar, R. I. M. (1986). The social ecology of gelada baboons. In *Ecological Aspects of Social Evolution: Birds and Mammals* (D. I. Rubenstein and R. W. Wrangham, eds.). Princeton Univ. Press, Princeton, NJ.

Dunbar, R. I. M. (1989). Reproductive strategies of female gelada baboons. In *Sociobiology of Reproductive Strategies* (A. E. Rasa, C. Vogel, and E. Voland, eds.), pp. 74–282. Chapman & Hall, New York.

Dyson-Hudson, R., and Smith, E. A. (1978). Human territoriality: An ecological reassessment. *Am. Anthropol.* **80:**21–41.

Eaton, S. B., and Konner, M. J. (1985). Paleolithic nutrition: A consideration of its nature and current implications. *N. Engl. J. Med.* **312:** 283–289.

Eaton, S. B., Konner, M., and Shostack, M. (1988). *The Paleolithic Prescription: A Program of Diet and Exercise and a Design for Living*. Harper & Row, New York.

Eaton, S. B., Pike, M. C., Short, R. V., Lee, N. C., Trussell, J., Hatcher, R. A., Wood, J. W., Worthman, C. M., Blurton Jones, N. G., Konner, M. J., Hill, K. R., Bailey, R., Hurtado, A. M. (1994). Women's reproductive concerns in evolutionary context. *Quart. Rev. Biol.* 69: 353–367.

Eckhardt, R. B. (1989). Matching molecular and morphological evolution. *Hum. Evol.* **4:**317–319.

Edey, M. A. (1972). *The Missing Link*. Time-Life, New York.

Eibl-Eibesfeldt, I. (1975). *Ethology: The Biology of Behavior*. Holt, Rinehart & Winston, New York.

Ekman, P. (ed.). (1973). *Darwin and Facial Expression*. Academic Press, New York.

Eldredge, N., and Cracraft, J. (1980). *Phylogenetic Patterns and the Evolutionary Process*. Columbia Univ. Press, New York.

Epple, G. (1978). Reproductive and social behavior of marmosets with special reference to captive breeding. *Primates Med.* **10:** 50–62.

Eveleth, P. B., and Tanner, J. M. (1976). *Worldwide Variation in Human Growth*, IBP Synth. Ser. No. 8. Cambridge Univ. Press, Cambridge, UK.

Ewald, P. (1994). *Evolution of Infectious Diseases*. Oxford Univ. Press, London.

Fagan, B. (1992). *People of the Earth*. Harper Collins, New York.

Fairbanks, L. A. (1988). Vervet monkey grandmothers: Interactions with infant offspring. *Int. J. Primatol.* **9:**425–441.

Falk, D. (1980). Hominid brain evolution: The approach from paleoneurology. *Yearb. Phys. Anthropol.* **23:**93–107.

Falk, D. (1983). Cerebral cortices of East African early hominids. *Science* **221:**1072–1074.

Falk, D. (1986a). Hominid evolution. *Science* **234:**11.

Falk, D. (1986b). Reply to Holloway and Kimbel: Endocast morphology of Hadar hominid AL 162-28. *Nature (London)* **321:**536–537.

Falk, D. (1987). Hominid paleoneurology. *Annu. Rev. Anthropol.* **16:**13–30.

Falk, D. (1990). Brain evolution in Homo: The "radiator" theory. *Behav. Brain Sci.* **13:**333–381.

Falkner, F., and Tanner, J. M. (eds.). (1989). *Human Growth*. Plenum, New York.

Fedigan, L. (1986). The changing roles of women in models of human evolution. *Annu. Rev. Anthropol.* **15:**25–66.

Fitch, W. (1976). In *Molecular Evolution* (F. Ayala, ed.). Sinauer Press, Sunderland, MA.

Fleagle, J. G. (1988). *Primate Adaptation and Evolution*. Academic Press, San Diego, CA.

Fleagle, J. G., and Kay, R. F. (1987). The phyletic position of the Parapithecidae. *J. Hum. Evol.* **16:**483–531.

Flynn, J. R. (1987). Massive IQ gains in 14 nations: What IQ tests really measure. *Psychol. Bull.* **101:**171–191.

Foley, R. (1990). The causes of brain enlargement in human evolution. *Behav. Brain Sci.* **13:**354–356.

Ford, S. (1986). Systematics of the New World monkeys. In *Comparative Primate Biology* (D. Swindler and J. Erwin, eds.), Vol. 1, pp. 73–135. Alan R. Liss, New York.

Fossey, D. (1983). *Gorillas in the Mist*. Houghton-Mifflin, Boston.

Fouts, R. S., and Fouts, D. H. (1993). Chimpanzees' use of sign language. In *The Great Ape Project: Equality Beyond Humanity,* pp. 28–41. St. Martin's Press, New York.

Freeman, L. (1968). A Theoretical framework for interpreting archaeological materials. In *Man the Hunter* (R. Lee and I. DeVore, eds.), pp. 262–267. Aldine, New York.

Gabriel, S. E., Brigman, K. N., Koller, B. H., Boucher, R. C., and Smuts, M. J. (1994). Cystic fibrosis heterozyote resistance to cholera toxin in the cystic fibrosis mouse model. *Science* **266:**107–109.

Galdikas, B., and Teleki, G. (1981). Variations in subsistence activities of female and male pongids: New perspective on the origins of hominid labor division. *Curr. Anthropol.* **22:**240–256.

Gardner, B. T., and Gardner, R. A. (1971). Two-way communication with an infant chimpanzee. In *Behavior of Non-Human Primates* (A. Schrier and F. Stollnitz eds.), Vol. 4, pp. 117–184. Academic Press, New York.

Gardner, R. A., Gardner, B. T., and van Cautforts, T. E. (eds.). (1989). *Teaching Sign Language to Chimpanzees*. SUNY Press, New York.

Garn, S. M., and Shamir, Z. (1958). *Methods for Research in Human Growth*. Thomas, Springfield, IL.

Gebo, D.L. (1989a). Locomotor and phylogenetic considerations in anthropoid evolution. *J. Hum. Evol.* **18:**201–233.

Gebo, D.L. (1989b). Postcranial adaptation and evolution in Lorisidae. *Primates* **30:**347–367.

Ghiglieri, M. (1984). *The Chimpanzees of the Kibale Forest: A Field Study of Ecology and Social Structure*. Columbia Univ. Press, New York.

Gibson, K. (1991). Tools, language and intelligence: Evolutionary implications. *Man [N.S.]* **26:**255–264.

Gingerich, P. (1990). African dawn for primates. *Nature (London)* **346:** 411.

Goodall, J. (1977). Infant killing and cannibalism in free-living chimpanzees. *Folia Primatol.* **28:**259–282.

Goodall, J. (1986). *The Chimpanzees of Gombe*. Harvard University (Belknap Press), Cambridge, MA.

Goodenough, W. (1981). *Language, Culture and Society,* 2nd ed. Benjamin/Cummings, Menlo Park, CA.

Goodman, M. (1961). The role of immunochemical differences in the phyletic development of human behavior. *Hum. Biol.* **33:**131–162.

Goodman, M. (1962). Evolution of the immunologic species specificity of human serum proteins. *Hum. Biol.* **34:**105–150.

Goodman, M. (1973). The chronicle of primate phylogeny continued in proteins. *Symp. Zool. Soc. London* **33:**339–375.

Goodman, M., Barnabas, J., Matsuda, G., and Moore, G. W. (1971). Molecular evolution in the descent of man. *Nature (London)* **233:**604–613.

Gordon, T. P., Rose, R. W., Grady, C. L., and Bernstein, I. S. (1979). Effects of increased testosterone secretion on the behavior of adult male rhesus living in a social group. *Folia Primatol.* **32:**149–160.

Goren-Inbar, N. (1986). A figurine from the Acheulean site of Berekhat Rom. *Mitakufat Haeven* **19:**7–12.

Gould, S. J. (1981). *The Mismeasure of Man.* Norton, New York.

Greene, L. S. (1993). G6PD deficiency as protection against *falciparum* Malaria: An epidemiologic critique of population and experimental studies. *Yearb. Phys. Anthropol.* **36:**153–178.

Greenfield, L. O. (1980). Late divergence hypothesis. *Am. J. Phys. Anthropol.* **52:**351–365.

Gregory, W. K. (1927). Dawn man or ape? *Sci. Am.* **83:**230–232.

Gregory, W. K., and Hellman, M. (1926). The dentition of *Dryopithecus* and the origin of man. *Am. Mus. Anthropol. Pap.* **28:**1–123.

Greulich, W. W. (1976). Some secular changes in the growth of American-born and native Japanese children. *Am. J. Phys. Anthropol.* **15:**489–515.

Gribbin, J., and Gribbin, M. (1990). *Children of the Ice. Climate and Human Origins.* Blackwell, Oxford.

Grine, F. E. (1986). Dental evidence for dietary differences in *Australopithecus* and *Paranthropus:* A quantitative analysis of permanent molar microwear. *J. Hum. Evol.* **15:**783–822.

Grine, F. E. (ed.). (1988). *Evolutionary History of the "Robust" Australopithecines.* de Gruyter, New York.

Groves, C. (1989). *A Theory of Human and Primate Evolution.* Oxford Univ. Press, Oxford.

Guthrie, R. D. (1970). Evolution of human threat display organs. *Evol. Biol.* **4:**257–302.

Hafleigh, A. S., and Williams, C. A., Jr. (1966). Antigenic correspondence of serum albumins among the primates. *Science* **151:**1530–1535.

Hamburg, D. A. (1968). Evolution of emotional responses: Evidence from recent research on non-human primates. In *Science and Psychoanalysis* (J. Masserman, ed.), Vol. 12. Grune & Stratton, New York.

Hamburg, D. A., and McCown, E. (eds.). (1979). *The Great Apes. Perspectives on Human Evolution.* Benjamin/Cummings Press, San Francisco.

Hamilton, W. D. (1963). The evolution of altruistic behavior. *Am. Nat.* **97:**357–366.

Hamilton, W. D. (1975). Innate social attitudes of man: An approach from an evolutionary point of view. In *Biosocial Anthropology* (R. Fox, ed.). Malaby Press, London.

Hamilton, W. D. (1971). Selection of selfish or altruistic behaviors in some extreme models. In *Man and Beast: Comparative Social Behavior* (J. Eisenberg and W. Dillon, eds.). Smithsonian Institution Press, Washington, DC.

Harding, R. M. (1992). VNTR's in review. *Evol. Anthropol.* **1**(2):62–71.

Harding, R. M., and Teleki, G. (eds.). (1981). *Omnivorous Primates. Gathering and Hunting in Human Evolution.* Columbia Univ. Press, New York.

Harris, J. M., Brown, F. H., Leakey, M. G., Walker, A. C., and Leakey, R. E. F. (1988). Pliocene and Pleistocene hominid-bearing sites from west of Lake Turkana, Kenya. *Science* **239:**27–33.

Harris, M. (1979). *Cultural Materialism.* Random House, New York.

Harrison, G. A., Tanner, J. M., Pilbeam, D. R., and Baker, P. T. (1988). *Human Biology. An Introduction to Human Evolution, Variation, Growth, and Adaptability,* 3rd ed. Oxford Univ. Press, Oxford.

Harrison, T. (1986). A reassessment of the phylogenetic relationships of *Oreopithecus bambolii* Gervais. *J. Hum. Evol.* **15:**541–583.

Hausfater, G. (1976). Predatory behavior of yellow baboons. *Behaviour* **56:**44–68.

Hawkes, K. (1990). Why do men hunt? Some benefits for risky strategies. In *Risk and Uncertainty* (E. Cashdan, ed.). Westview Press, Boulder, CO.

Hawkes, K. (1991). Showing off: Tests of an hypothesis about men's foraging goals. *Ethol. Sociobiol.* **12:**29–54.

Hawkes, K., O'Connell, J., and Blurton-Jones, N. (1989). Hardworking Hadza grandmothers. In *Comparative Socioecology* (Standen and R. Foley, eds.), pp. 341–566. Blackwell, Oxford.

Hay, R., and Leakey, M. (1982). The fossil footprints at Laetoli. *Sci. Am.* **246**(2): 50–57.

Hayes, K. J., and Nissen, C. H. (1971). Higher mental functions of a home-raised chimpanzee. In *Behavior of Non-Human Primates* (A. Schrier and F. Stollnitz, eds.), pp. 60–115. Academic Press, New York.

Hewes, G. W. (1964). Hominid bipedalism: Independent evidence for food carrying theory. *Science* **146:**416–418.

Hildebrand, M. (1974). *Analysis of Vertebrate Structure.* Wiley, New York.

Hill, A., and Ward, S. (1988). Origin of the Hominidae: The record of African large hominoid evolution between 14 my and 4 my. *Yearb. Phys. Anthropol.* **31:**49–83.

Hill, K., Kaplan, H., Hawkes, K., and Hurtado, A. M. (1987). Foraging decisions among Ache hunter-gatherers: New data and implications for optimal foraging models. *Ethol. Sociobiol.* **8:**1–36.

Hinegardner, R. (1976). Evolution of genome size. In *Molecular Evolution* (F. J. Ayala, ed.), pp. 179–199. Sinauer, Sunderland, MA.

Hockett, C., and Ascher, R. (1964). The human revolution. *Curr. Anthropol.* **5:**135–168.

Holloway, R. L. (1981). The Indonesian *Homo erectus* brain endocasts revisited. *Am. J. Phys. Anthropol.* **55:**503–521.

Holloway, R. L. (1984). The Taung endocast and the lunate sulcus: A rejection of the hypothesis of its anterior position. *Am. J. Phys. Anthropol.* **64:**285–287.

Holloway, R. L., and Kimbel, W. H. (1986). Endocast morphology of Hadar hominid AL 162-28. *Nature (London)* **321:**536.

Holmquist, R., Miyamoto, M. M., and Goodman, M. (1988). Higher primate phylogeny. Why can't we decide? *Mol. Biol. Evol.* **5:**201–216.

Howell, F. C. (1965). *Early Man.* Time-Life, New York.

Howell, F. C. (1986). Variability in *Homo erectus,* and the question of the presence of this species in Europe. *Anthropologie* **90:**447–481.

Howells, W. W. (1993). *Getting Here.* Penguin Press, New York.

Hoyer, B. H., Van de Vilde, N. W., Goodman, M., and Roberts, R. B. (1972). Examination of hominoid evolution by DNA sequence homology. *J. Hum. Evol.* **1:**645–649.

Hrdy, S. B. (1977). *The Langurs of Abu.* Harvard Univ. Press, Cambridge, MA.

Hrdy, S. B., and Bennett, W. (1970). Lucy's husband: What did he stand for? *Harv. Mag.* **83**(6):7–46.

Irons, W. (1979). Cultural and biological success. In *Evolutionary Biology and Human Social Behavior* (N. Chagnon and W. Irons, eds.), pp. 257–272. Duxbury Press, Boston.

Isaac, G. L. (1978). The food sharing behavior of protohuman hominids. *Sci. Am.* **238:**90–109.

Isaac, G. L. (1980). Casting the net wide: A review of archaeological evidence for early hominid land use and ecological relations. In *Current Argument on Early Man* (L. Konigsson, ed.), pp. 226–251. Pergamon, Oxford.

Isaac, G. L. (1984). The archaeology of human origins: Studies of the lower Pleistocene in East Africa, 1971–1981. In *Advances in World Archaeology* (F. Wendorf and A. Close, eds.), pp. 1–87. Academic Press, New York.

Isaac, G. L., and Crader, D. C. (1981). To what extent were early hominids carnivorous? An archaeological perspective. In *Omnivorous Primates: Gathering and Hunting in Human Evolution* (R. Harding and G. Teleki, eds.), pp. 37–103. Columbia Univ. Press, New York.

Isbell, L. A. (1991). Contest and scramble competition: Patterns of female aggression and ranging behavior among primates. *Behav. Ecol.* **2:**143–155.

Iscan, M. Y., and Kennedy, K. A. R. (1989). *Reconstruction of Life from the Skeleton*. Alan R. Liss, New York.

Itani, J. (1954). *Japanese Monkeys in Takasakiyama*. Kobunsha, Tokyo.

Izard, C. (1971). *The Face of Emotion*. Appleton Century Crofts, New York.

Jensen, A. (1969). How much can we boost IQ and scholastic achievement? *Harv. Educ. Rev.* **39:**1–123.

Jensen, A. (1980). *Bias in Mental Testing*. Free Press, New York.

Jerison, H. (1973). *Evolution of the Brain and Intelligence*. Academic Press, New York.

Johanson, D. C. (1976). Ethiopia yields the first "family" of man. *Natl. Geogr.* **150**(6):790–811.

Johanson, D. C., and Edey, M. (1989). *Lucy's Child*. New York.

Johanson, D. C., and White, T. D. (1979). A systematic assessment of early African hominids. *Science* **203:**321–330.

Johanson, D. C., White, T. D., and Coppens, Y. (1978). A new species of the genus *Australopithecus* (Primates: Hominidae) from the Pliocene of eastern Africa. *Kirtlandia* **28:**1–14.

Johanson, D. C., Masao, F. T., Eck, G. G., White, T. D., Walter, R. C., Kimbel, W. H., Asfaw, B., Manega, P., Ndessokia, P., and Suwa, G. (1987). New partial skeleton of *Homo habilis* from Olduvai Gorge, Tanzania. *Nature* (*London*) **327:**205–209.

Johnston, F. E. (1964). The relationship of certain growth variables to chronological and skeletal age. *Hum. Biol.* **36:**16–27.

Jolly, A. (1966). *Lemur Behavior: Madagascar Field Study*. Univ. of Chicago Press, Chicago.

Jolly, A. (1985). *The Evolution of Primate Behavior,* 2nd ed. Macmillan, New York.

Jolly, C. (1970). The seed eaters: A new model of hominid differentiation based on a baboon analogy. *Man* **5:**5–27.

Joyce, C., and Stover, E. (1991). *Witnesses from the Grave: The Stories Bones Tell*. Ballantine Books, New York.

Jukes, T. H. (1966). *Molecules and Evolution*. Columbia Univ. Press, New York.

Jungers, W. L. (1988). New estimates of body size in australopithecines. In *Evolutionary History of the "Robust" Australopithecines* (F. E. Grine, ed.), pp. 115–125. de Gruyter, New York.

Jungers, W. L., and Stern, J. T. (1980). Telemetered electromyography of forelimb muscle chains in gibbons (*Hylobates lar*). *Science* **208:**617–619.

Kahn, F. (1943). *Man in Structure and Function,* 2 vols. Knopf, New York.

Kaplan, H., and Hill, K. (1985). Hunting ability and reproductive success among male Ache foragers: Preliminary results. *Curr. Anthropol.* **26:**131–133.

Kay, R. (1977). Diets of early Miocene African hominoids. *Nature* (*London*) **268:**628–630.

Kay, R., Thorington, R. W., and Houde, P. (1990). Eocene plesiadapiform shows affinities with flying lemurs not primates. *Nature* (*London*) **345:**342–344.

Keesing, R. (1974). Theories of culture. *Annu. Rev. Anthropol.* 73–97.

Keith, A. (1896). An introduction to the study of the anthropoid apes. *Nat. Sci.* **9:**316–326, 372–379.

Keith, A. (1899). On the chimpanzees and their relationship to the gorilla. *Proc. Zool. Soc. London,* pp. 296–312.

Keith, A. (1915). *The Antiquity of Man*. Williams & Norgate, London.

Kelley, J. (1987). Species recognition and sexual dimorphism in *Proconsul* and *Rangwapithecus*. *J. Hum. Evol.* **15:**461–495.

Kellogg, W. N., and Kellogg, L. A. (1933). *The Ape and the Child*. McGraw-Hill, New York.

King, M.-C. (1974). Evolution at two levels: Molecular similarities and biological differences between humans and chimpanzees. *Am. J. Hum. Genet.* **26:**49A.

King, M.-C., and Wilson, A. C. (1975). Evolution at two levels in humans and chimpanzees. *Science* **188:**107–116.

Klein, R. (1989). *The Human Career*. Univ. of Chicago Press, Chicago.

Klug, W. S., and Cummings, M. R. (1994). *Concepts of Genetics,* 4th ed. MacMillan College Publishing, New York.

Kohne, D. E. (1970). Evolution of higher organism DNA. *Q. Rev. Biophys.* **3:**327–375.

Kohne, D. E., Chiscon, J. A., and Hoyer, B. H. (1972). Evolution of primate DNA sequences. *J. Hum. Evol.* **1:**627–644.

Krogman, W. M. (1950). The physical growth of the child: Syllabus. *Yearb. Phys. Anthropol.* **5:**280–299.

Kuhn, T. S. (1970). *The Structure of Scientific Revolutions*. Univ. of Chicago Press, Chicago.

Kuroda, S. (1980). Social behavior of the pygmy chimpanzee. *Primates* **21:**181–197.

Kuroda, S. (1984). Interaction over food among pygmy chimpanzees. In *The Pygmy Chimpanzee: Evolutionary Biology and Behavior* (R. Susman, ed.). Plenum, New York.

Kurten, B. (1972). *Not From the Apes*. Pantheon Books, New York.

Laidler, K. (1980). *The Talking Ape*. Stein & Day, New York.

Lancaster, J. (1978). Carrying and sharing in human evolution. *Hum. Nat.* **1:**32–89.

Lancaster, J. (1984). Evolutionary perspectives on sex differences in the higher primates. In *Gender and the Life Course* (A. Rossi, ed.). Aldine, New York.

Landau, M. (1984). Human evolution as narrative. *Am. Sci.* **72:** 262–268.

Landau, M. (1991). *Narratives of Human Evolution*. Yale Univ. Press, New Haven, CT.

Langebartel, D. A., and Ullrich, R. H. (1977). *The Anatomical Primer*. University Park Press, Baltimore, MD.

Lartet, E. (1856). Note sur un grand singe fossile qui se rattache au groupe des singes supérieurs. *C. R. Hebd. Seances Acad. Sci.* **43:**219–223.

Lasker, G. W. (1991). Introduction. In *Applications of Biological Anthropology to Human Affairs* (C. G. N. Mascie-Taylor and G. W. Lasker, eds.), pp. 1–13. Cambridge Univ. Press, London.

Leakey, L. S. B. (1959). A new fossil skull from Olduvai. *Nature* (*London*) **184:**491–493.

Leakey, M. D., and Hay, R. L. (1979). Pliocene footprints in the Laetolil Beds at Laetoli, northern Tanzania. *Nature* (*London*) **278:**317–323.

Leakey, M. G. (1995). The dawn of humans: The farthest horizon. *Natl. Geogr. Mag.* September: 38–51.

Leakey, M. G., and Leakey, R. E. (1978). *The Fossil Hominids and an Introduction to Their Context, 1968–1974*. Koobi Fora Res. Proj., Vol. 1. Oxford Univ. Press (Clarendon), Oxford.

Leakey, M. G., Feibel, C. S., McDougall, I., and Walker, A. (1995). New four-million-year-old hominid species from Kanapoi and Allia Bay, Kenya. *Nature* (*London*) **376:**565–571.

Leakey, R. E. F., and Leakey, M. G. (1986). A new Miocene hominoid from Kenya. *Nature* (*London*) **324:**143–146.

Leakey, R. E. F., and Leakey, M. G. (1988). A new Miocene small-bodied ape from Kenya. *J. Hum. Evol.* **16:**369–387.

Leakey, R. E. F., Leakey, M. G., and Walker, A. (1988). Morphology of *Afropithecus turkanensis* from Kenya. *Am. J. Phys. Anthropol.* **73:**289–307.

Lee, R. B. (1980). Lactation, ovulation, infanticide, and women's work: A study of hunter-gatherer population regulation. In *Biosocial Mechanisms of Population Regulation* (M. Cohen, R. Malpass, and H. Klein, eds.), pp. 321–348. Yale Univ. Press, New Haven, CT.

Lee, R. B., and DeVore, I. (eds.). (1968). *Man the Hunter*. Aldine, Chicago.

LeGros Clark, W. E. (1960). *The Antecedents of Man*. Quadrangle Books, Chicago.

LeGros Clark, W. E. (1964). *The Fossil Evidence for Human Evolution*. Univ. of Chicago Press, Chicago.

LeGros Clark, W. E. (1967). *Man-Apes or Ape-Men. The Story of Discoveries in Africa*. Holt, Rinehart & Winston, New York.

Leibowitz, L. (1983). Origins of the sexual division of labor. In *Women's Nature: Rationalization of Inequality* (M. Lowe and R. Hubbard, eds.), pp. 123–147. Pergamon, New York.

LeMay, M. (1977). Asymmetries of the skull and handedness. *J. Neurolog. Sci.* **32:**213–225.

Leutenegger, W. (1987). Neonatal brain size and and neurocranial dimensions in Pliocene hominids: Implications for obstetrics. *J. Hum. Evol.* **16:**291–296.

Lewin, R. (1993). *Human Evolution: An Illustrated Introduction,* 3rd ed. Blackwell, Oxford.

Lewontin, R. C. (1972). The apportionment of human diversity. In *Evolutionary Biology* (T. Dobzhansky, ed.), Vol. 6, pp. 381–398. Plenum, New York.

Lieberman, P., and Crelin, E. S. (1971). On the speech of Neanderthal man. *Linguistic Inquiry* **11:**203–222.

Linden, E. (1992). Chimpanzees with a difference: Bonobos. *Natl. Geogr.* **181:**46–53.

Linton, S. (1971). Woman the gatherer: Male bias in anthropology. In *Women in Perspective: A Guide for Cross-Cultural Studies* (S. Jacobs, ed.), pp. 9–21. Univ. of Illinois Press, Urbana.

Livingstone. F. B. (1962). Reconstructing man's Pliocene pongid ancestor. *Am. Anthropol.* **64:**301–395.

Loomis, W. F. (1967). Skin pigment regulation of Vitamin D biosynthesis in man. *Science* **157:**501–506.

Lorenz, K. (1965). *On Aggression.* Harcourt, Brace, New York.

Lovejoy, C. O. (1981). The origins of man. *Science* **211:**341–350.

Lovejoy, C. O., Meindl, R. S., Pryzbeck, T. R., Barton, T. S., Heiple, K. G., and Kotting, D. (1977). Paleodemography of the Libben site, Ottawa County, Ohio. *Science* **198:**291–293.

Loy, J. (1987). The sexual behavior of African monkeys and the question of estrus. In *Comparative Behavior of African Monkeys* (E. Zucker, ed.), pp. 175–195. Alan R. Liss, New York.

Loy, J. (1992). Behavioral dynamics among primates: An overview. *Perspect. Primate Biol.* **4:**79–94.

MacLean, P. D. (1967). The brain in relation to empathy and medical education. *J. Nerv. Ment. Dis.* **144:**374–382.

MacLean, P. D. (1958). Contrasting functions of limbic and neocortical systems of the brain and their relevance to psychopharmacological aspects of medicine. *Am. J. Med.* **25:**611–626.

MacLean, P. D. (1990). *The Triune Brain in Human Evolution.* Plenum, New York.

Malina, R. M. (1975). *Growth and Development.* Burgess, Minneapolis, MN.

Malina, R. M. (1979). The effects of exercise on specific tissues, dimensions and functions during growth. *Stud. Phys. Anthropol.* **5:**21–52.

Margulis, L., and Sagan, D. (1986a). *Microcosmos: Four Billion Years of Evolution from Our Microbial Ancestors.* Summit Press, New York.

Margulis, L., and Sagan, D. (1986b). *Origins of Sex: Three Billion Years of Genetic Recombination.* Yale Univ. Press, New Haven, CT.

Marks, J., Schmid, C. W., and Sarich, V. M. (1988). DNA hybridization as a guide to phylogeny: Relations of the Hominoidea. *J. Hum. Evol.* **17:**769–786.

Marler, P. (1973). A comparison of vocalizations of red-tailed monkeys and blue monkeys, *Cercopithecus ascanius* and *C. mitis,* in Uganda. *Z. Tierpsychol.* **33:**223–247.

Marshack, A. (1989). Evolution of the human capacity: Symbolic evidence. *Yearb. Phys. Anthropol.* **32:**1–34.

Marshall, B. J. (1993). *Helicobacter pylori:* A primer for 1994. *Gastroenterologist* **1:**241–247.

Martini, F. and Timmons, M. (1995). *Human Anatomy.* Prentice Hall, Upper Saddle River, NJ.

Maynard Smith, J. (1964). Group selection and new selection. *Nature (London)* **201:**1145–1147.

Maynard Smith, J. (1966). Sympatric speciation. *Am. Nat.* **100:**637–650.

Maynard Smith, J. (1976). Group selection. *Q. Rev. Biol.* **51:**277–283.

Maynard Smith, J. (1978). *The Evolution of Sex.* Cambridge Univ. Press, Cambridge, UK.

Mayr, E. (1963). *Animal Species and Evolution.* Harvard Univ. Press, Cambridge, MA.

McFadden, (1985). An overview of paleomagnetic chronology with special reference to the South African hominid sites. *Palaeontol. Afr.* **23:**35–40.

McGrew, W. C. (1979). Evolutionary implications of sex differences in chimpanzee predation and tool-use. In *The Great Apes* (D. A. Hamburg and E. R. McCown, eds.), pp. 440–463. Benjamin/Cummings, Menlo Park, CA.

McGrew, W. C. (1981). The female chimpanzee as a human evolutionary prototype. In *Woman the Gatherer* (F. Dahlberg, ed.), pp. 35–73. Yale Univ. Press, New Haven, CT.

McGrew, W. C. (1988). Parental division of infant care-taking varies with family composition in cotton-topped tamarins. *Anim. Behav.* **36:**285–286.

McGrew, W. (1992). *Chimpanzee Material Culture.* Cambridge Univ. Press, New York.

McHenry, H. M. (1982). The pattern of human evolution: Studies on bipedalism, mastication, and encephalization. *Annu. Rev. Anthropol.* **11:**151–173.

McHenry, H. M. (1988). New estimates of body weight in early hominids and their significance to encephalization and megadontia in "robust" australopithecines. In *Evolutionary History of the "Robust" Australopithecines* (F. E. Grine, ed.), pp. 133–148. de Gruyter, New York.

McKenna, J., Mosko, S., Dungy, C., and McAninch, J. (1990). Sleep and arousal patterns of co-sleeping human mother-infant pairs: A preliminary physiological study with implications for the study of sudden infant death syndrome. *Am. J. Phys. Anthropol.* **83:**331–347.

McKusick, V. A. (1989). *Mendelian Inheritance in Man.* Johns Hopkins Univ. Press, Baltimore, MD.

Mellars, P. (1989). Major issues in the emergence of modern humans. *Curr. Anthropol.* **30:**349–385.

Meredith, H. V. (1971). Growth in body size: A compendium of findings on contemporary children living in different parts of the world. *Adv. Child Dev. Behav.* **6:**154–238.

Miles, H. L. (1990). The cognitive foundations for reference in a signing orangutan. In *"Language" and Intelligence in Monkeys and Apes: Comparative Development Perspectives* (S. Parker and K. Gibson, eds.), pp. 511–539. Cambridge Univ. Press, Cambridge, UK.

Molnar, S. (1992). *Human Variation: Races, Types, and Ethnic Groups,* 3rd ed. Prentice Hall, Englewood Cliffs, NJ.

Morant, G. M. (1950). Secular changes in the heights of British people. *Proc. R. Soc. London, Ser. B* **137:**443–452.

Morbeck, M. E. (1979). Forelimb use and positional adaptation in *Colobus guereza:* Integration of behavioral and anatomical data. In *Environment, Behavior and Morphology: Dynamic Interactions in Primates* (M. Morbeck, H. Preuschoft, and N. Gomberg, eds.), pp. 95–118. Fischer, New York.

Morrison, R. T., and Boyd, R. N. (1959). *Organic Chemistry.* Allyn & Bacon, Boston.

Mourant, A. E., Kopec, A. C., and Domaniewska-Sobczak, K. (1976). *The Distribution of the Human Blood Groups and Other Polymorphisms.* Oxford Univ. Press, London.

Napier, J. R., and Napier, P. (1967). *Handbook of Living Primates.* Academic Press, New York.

Napier, J. R., and Napier, P. (1994). *Natural History of the Primates.* MIT Press, Boston.

Napier, J. R., and Walker, A. (1967). Vertical clinging and leaping: A newly recognized category of locomotor behavior in primates. *Folia Primatol.* **6:**204–219.

Neel, J. V. (1962). Diabetes mellitus: A "Thrifty" Genotype rendered detrimental by "progress." *Am. J. Hum. Genet.* **14:**353–362.

Newman, R. W. (1970). Why man is such a sweaty and thirsty naked animal: A speculative review. *Hum. Biol.* **42:**12–27.

Nieuwenhuijsen, K., de Neef, K. J., and Slob, A. K. (1986). Sexual behaviour during ovarian cycles, pregnancy and lactation in group-living stump-tailed macaques (*Macaca arctoides*). *Hum. Reprod.* **1:**159–169.

Nishida, T. (1979). The social structure of chimpanzees of the Mahale Mountains. In *The Great Apes* (D. Hamburg and E. McCown, eds.), pp. 73–121. Benjamin/Cummings, San Francisco.

Olivier, G. (1969). *Practical Anthropology.* Thomas, Springfield, IL.

Olson, T. R., and Seidel, M. R. (1983). The evolutionary basis of some clinical disorders of the human foot: A comparative study of the living primates. *Foot & Ankle* **3:**32–341.

Oxnard, C. E. (1984). *The Order of Man: A Biomathematical Anatomy of the Primates.* Yale Univ. Press, New Haven, CT.

Oxnard, C. E. (1986). Comparative anatomy of the primates: Old and new. *Comp. Primate Biol.* **1:**719–763.

Pagels, H. R. (1982). *The Cosmic Code: Quantum Physics as the Language of Nature*. Simon & Schuster, New York.

Painter, N. S., and Burkitt, D. P. (1975). Diverticular disease of the colon. In *Refined Carbohydrate Foods and Disease* (D. P. Burkitt and H. C. Trowell, eds.). Academic Press, London.

Parker, S. T. (1985). A social-technological model for the evolution of language. *Curr. Anthropol.* **27:**671–639.

Parker, S. T. (1987). A sexual selection model for hominid evolution. *Hum. Evol.* **2:**235–253.

Parker, S. T., and Gibson, K. (1982). The importance of theory for reconstructing the evolution of language and intelligence in hominids. In *Advanced Views of Primate Biology* (A. B. Chiarelli and R. S. Corruccini, eds.), pp. 42–64. Springer-Verlag, Berlin.

Parker, S. T., and Russon, A. E. (1995). On the wild side of culture and cognition in the great apes. In *Reaching Into Thought* (A. Russon, K. Bard, and S. Parker, eds.), pp. 1–54. Cambridge Univ. Press, Cambridge, UK.

Partridge, T. (1986). Paleoecology of the Pliocene and lower Pleistocene hominids of southern Africa: How good is the chronological and paleoenvironmental evidence? *S. Afr. J. Sci.* **82:**80–83.

Patterson, J. D., and Linden, E. (1981). *The Education of Koko*. Holt, Rinehart & Winston, New York.

Pennington, R., and Harpending, H. (1988). Fitness and fertility among Kalahari !Kung. *Am. J. Phys. Anthropol.* **77:**303–319.

Peters, C. R., and O'Brien, E. (1981). The early hominid plant-food niche: Insights from an analysis of plant exploitation by *Homo, Pan,* and *Papio* in eastern and southern Africa. *Curr. Anthropol.* **22:**127–140.

Petter, J. J. (1965). The Lemurs of Madagascar. In *Primate Behavior* (I. DeVore, ed.), pp. 292–319. Holt, Rinehart & Winston, New York.

Pettigrew, J. D., Jamieson, B. G. M., Robson, S. K., Hall, L. S., Mcanally, K. I., and Cooper, H. M. (1989). Phylogenetic relations between microbats, megabats and primates (Mammalia: Chiroptera and Primates). *Philos. Trans. R. Soc. London, Ser. B* **325:**489–559.

Pfeiffer, J. E. (1983). *The Emergence of Man*. Harper & Row, New York.

Pickford, M., Senut, B., Ssemmanda, I., Elepu, D., and Obwona, P. (1988). Premiers résultats de la mission de l'Uganda. Palaeontology expedition à Nkondo (Pliocene du Bassin du Lac Albert, Ouganda). *C. R. Acad. Sci. Ser. 2* **306:**315–320.

Pilbeam, D. R. (1972). *The Ascent of Man*. Macmillan, New York.

Pilbeam, D. R. (1978). Rearranging our family tree. *Hum. Nat.* **1** (6):38–45.

Pilbeam, D. R. (1980). Major trends in human evolution. In *Current Argument on Early Man* (L. Konigsson, ed.), pp. 261–285. Pergamon, Oxford.

Pilbeam, D. R. (1986). The origin of *Homo sapiens*: The fossil evidence. In *Major Topics in Primate and Human Evolution* (B. Wood, L. Martin, and P. Andrews, eds.), pp. 331–338. Cambridge Univ. Press, Cambridge, UK.

Pilbeam, D. R., Rose, M. D., Badgley, C., et al. (1980). *Miocene Hominoids from Pakistan*. Postilla No. 181. Yale Peabody Museum, New Haven, CT.

Pilgrim, G. E. (1915). New Siwalik primates and their bearing on the questions of evolution of man and the Anthropoidea. *Rec. Geol. Surv. India* **45:**1–74.

Ploog, D. W. (1964). Verhaltensforschung und Psychiatrie. In *Psychiatrie der Gegenwart* (H. Gruhle, R. Jung, W. Mayer-Gross, and M. Muller, eds.), pp. 291–443. Springer-Verlag, Berlin.

Pope, G. G. (1988a). Current issues in Far Eastern paleoanthropology. In *The Palaeoenvironments of East Asia from the Mid-Tertiary* (E. K. Y. Chen, ed.), Vol. 2, pp. 1097–1123.

Pope, G. G. (1988b). Recent advances in Far Eastern paleoanthropology. *Annu. Rev. Anthropol.* **17:**43–77.

Pope, G. G., and Cronin, J. E. (1984). The Asian Hominidae. *J. Hum. Evol.* **13:**377–398.

Potts, R. (1984). Home bases and early hominids. *Am. Sci.* **72:**338–347.

Potts, R. (1988). *Early Hominid Activities at Olduvai*. de Gruyter, New York.

Premack, D. (1971a). Language in chimpanzee? *Science* **172:**808–822.

Premack, D. (1971b). On the assessment of language competence in the chimpanzee. In *Behavior of Non-Human Primates* (A. Schrier and F. Stollnitz, eds.), pp. 186–228. Academic Press, New York.

Premack, D. (1986). *Gavagai: On the Future History of the Animal Language Controversy*. MIT Press, Cambridge, MA.

Pusey, A. E., and Parker, C. (1987). Dispersal and philopatry. In *Primate Societies* (B. Smuts, D. Cheney, R. Seyfarth, T. Struhsaker, and R. Wrangham, eds.). Univ. of Chicago Press, Chicago.

Rak, Y. (1983). *The Australopithecine Face*. Academic Press, Orlando, FL.

Rayner, R. J., Moon, B. P., and Masters, J. C. (1993). The Makapansgat australopithecine environment. *J. Hum. Evol.* **24:**219–231.

Reader, J. (1981). *Missing Links. The Hunt for Earliest Man*. Little, Brown, Boston.

Reynolds, V. (1966). Open groups in hominid evolution. *Man* **1** (4):441–452.

Richard, A. F. (1985a). *Primates in Nature*. Freeman, New York.

Richard, A. F. (1985b). Social boundaries in a Malagasy prosimian, the sifaka (*Propithecus verreauxi*). *Intl. J. Primatol.* **6:**553–568.

Richard, A. F., and Schulman, S. R. (1982). Sociobiology: Primate field studies. *Annu. Rev. Anthropol.* **11:**231–255.

Rightmire, G. P. (1990). *The Evolution of Homo erectus*. Cambridge Univ. Press, Cambridge, UK.

Robins, A. H. (1991). *Biological Perspectives on Human Pigmentation*. Cambridge Univ. Press, Cambridge, UK.

Robinson, J. G. (1986). Seasonal variation in the use of time and space by the wedge-capped capuchin monkey, *Cebus olivaceus*: Implications for foraging theory. *Smithsonian Contrib. Zool.* **431:** 1–60.

Robinson, J. T. (1963). Adaptive radiation in the australopithecines and the origin of man. In *African Ecology and Human Evolution* (F. C. Howell and F. Bourliere, eds.), pp. 385–416. Aldine, Chicago.

Rodman, P. S. (1988). Resources and group size of primates. In *The Ecology of Social Behavior* (C. N. Slobodchikoff, ed.), pp. 83–108. Academic Press, San Diego, CA.

Rodman, P. S., and McHenry, H. M. (1980). Bioenergetics and the origin of hominid bipedalism. *Am. J. Phys. Anthropol.* **52:**103–106.

Romer, A. S. (1970). *The Vertebrate Body*. Saunders, Philadelphia.

Romer, A. S. (1971). *Vertebrate Paleontology*. Univ. of Chicago Press, Chicago.

Romero-Herrera, A. E., Lehmann, H., Joysey, K. A., and Friday, A. E. (1973). Molecular evolution of myoglobin and the fossil record: A phylogenetic synthesis. *Nature* (*London*) **246:**389–395.

Rose, K. D., and Fleagle, J. G. (1981). The fossil history of non-human primates in the Americas. In *Ecology and Behavior of Neotropical Primates* (A. F. Coimbra-Filho and R. A. Mittermeier, eds.), Vol. 1, pp. 111–167. Academia Brasiliera de Ciencias, Rio de Janeiro, Brazil.

Rose, M. D. (1976). Bipedal behavior of olive baboons (*Papio anubis*) and its relevance to an understanding of the evolution of human bipedalism. *Am. J. Phys. Anthropol.* **44:**247–262.

Rumbaugh, D. M. et al. (1977). The LANA project: Origin and tactics. In *Language Learning by a Chimpanzee* (D. M. Rumbaugh, ed.), pp. 87–90. Academic Press, New York.

Russell, D.A., and Séguin, R. (1982). Reconstruction of the small Cretaceous theropod *Stenonychosaurus inequalis* and a hypothetical dinosauroid. *Syllogeus* **37:**1–43.

Sade, D. S. (1991). Kinship. In *Understanding Behavior* (J. D. Loy and C. B. Peters, eds.), pp. 229–241. Oxford Univ. Press, New York.

Sadler, T. W. (1990). *Langman's Medical Embryology*. Williams & Wilkins, Baltimore, MD.

Sarich, V. M., and Wilson, A. C. (1967). Immunological time scale for hominid evolution. *Science* **158:**1200–1203.

Schaller, G. B. (1963). *The Mountain Gorilla: Ecology and Behavior*. Univ. of Chicago Press, Chicago.

Schaller, G. B., and Lowther, G. R. (1969). The relevance of carnivore behavior to the study of early hominids. *Southwest. J. Anthropol.* **25:**307–341.

Schell, L. M. (1991). Pollution and human growth: lead, noise, polychlorobiphenyl compounds, and toxic wastes. In *Applications of Biological Anthropology to Human Affairs* (C. G. N. Mascie-Taylor and G. W. Lasker, eds.), pp. 83–116. Cambridge Univ. Press, Cambridge, UK.

Schell, L. M., and Ando, Y. (1991). Postnatal growth of children in relation to noise from Osaka International airport. *J. Sound Vibr.* **151:** 371–382.

Schepartz, L. A. (1993). Language and modern human origins. *Yearb. Phys. Anthropol.* **36:**91–126.

Schick, K. D. (1987). Modeling the formation of Stone Age artifact concentrations. *J. Hum. Evol.* **16**(7/8): 789–807.

Schick, K. D. (1991). On making behavioral inferences from early archeological sites. In *Cultural Beginnings: Approaches to Understanding Early Hominid Life-ways in the African Savanna* (J. D. Clark, ed.), pp. 79–107. Dr. Rudolf Habelt GMBH, Bonn.

Schoch, R. M. (1986). *Phylogeny Reconstruction in Paleontology.* Van Nostrand Reinhold Co., New York.

Schopf, J. W. (1978). The evolution of the earliest cells. *Sci. Am.* **239:**110–138.

Schultz, A. H. (1924). Growth studies on primates bearing upon man's evolution. *Am. J. Phys. Anthropol.* **7:**149–164.

Schultz, A. H. (1933). Die Körper proportionen der erwachsenen catarrhinen Primaten, mit spezieller Berücksichtigung der Menschenaffen. *Anthropol Anz.* 10:154–185.

Schultz, A. H. (1936). Characters common to higher primates and characters specific to man. *Q. Rev. Biol.* **11:**259–283, 425–455.

Schultz, A. H. (1949). Sex differences in the pelves of primates. *Am. J. Phys. Anthropol.* **7:**401–423.

Schultz, A. H. (1960). Age changes in primates and their modification in man. In *Human Growth* (J. M. Tanner, ed.), pp. 1–20. Pergamon, Oxford.

Schultz, A. H. (1969). *The Life of Primates.* Weidenfels & Nicolson, London.

Schwarcz, H. P. (1982). New dates for the Tata, Hungary, archaeological site. *Nature* (*London*) **295:**590–591.

Schwartz, E. (1934). On the local races of the chimpanzee. *Ann. Mag. Nat. Hist.* [10] **13:**576–583.

Schwartz, J. (1987). *The Red Ape: Orangutans and Human Origins.* Houghton-Mifflin, Boston.

Seyfarth, R. M., Cheney, D. L., and Marler, P. (1980). Monkey responses to three different alarm calls: Evidence of predator classification and semantic communication. *Science* **210:**801–803.

Shapiro, H. (1979). *Peking Man.* Simon & Schuster, New York.

Sibley, C. G., and Ahlquist, J. E. (1987). DNA hybridization evidence of hominoid phylogeny: Results from an expanded data set. *J. Mol. Evol.* **26:**99–121.

Sibley, C. G., Comstock, J. A., and Ahlquist, J. E. (1990). DNA hybridization evidence of hominoid phylogeny: A reanalysis of the data. *J. Mol. Evol.* **30:**202–236.

Sige, B., Jaeger, J. J., Sudre, J., and Vianey-Liaud, M. (1990). *Altiatlasius koulchii* n. gen. et sp., Primate Omomyidae du Paleocene superieur du Maroc, et les origenes des euprimates. *Palaeontographica Abt. A* **214:**31–56.

Sigmon, B. A., and Cybulski, J. S. (eds.). (1981). *Homo erectus.* Univ. of Toronto Press, Toronto.

Simek, J. F. (1992). Neanderthal cognition and the Middle to Upper Paleolithic transition. In *Continuity or Replacement. Controversies in Homo sapiens Evolution* (G. Brauer and F. H. Smith, eds.), pp. 231–245. A. A. Balkema, Rotterdam.

Simons, E. L. (1965). New fossil apes from Egypt and the initial differentiation of the Hominoidea. *Nature* (*London*) **205:**135–139.

Simons, E. L. (1972). *Primate Evolution.* Macmillan, New York.

Simons, E. L. (1989). Human origins. *Science* **245:**1345.

Simons, E. L. (1990). Discovery of the oldest known anthropoidean skull from the Paleogene of Egypt. *Science* **247:**1567–1569.

Sinclair, D. (1989). *Human Growth After Birth.* Oxford Univ. Press, Oxford.

Small, M. F. (1989). MS monkey. *Nat. Hist.,* January:10–12.

Small, M. F. (1991). Sperm Wars. *Discover* **12**(7):48–53.

Smith, B. H. (1986). Dental developments in *Australopithecus* and early *Homo. Nature* (*London*) **323:**327–330.

Smith, E. A. (1992a). Human behavioral ecology. I. *Evol. Anthropol.* **1:**20–25.

Smith, E. A. (1992b). Human behavioral ecology. II. *Evol. Anthropol.* **1:**50–55.

Smith, H. M. (1960). *Evolution of Chordate Structure.* Holt, Rinehart & Winston, New York.

Smith, F. H., and Spencer, F. (eds.). (1984). *The Origins of Modern Humans.* Alan R. Liss, New York.

Smith, F. H., Falsetti, A. B., and Donnelly, S. M. (1989). Modern human origins. *Yearb. Phys. Anthropol.* **32:**35–68.

Smouse, P. E. and Li, W. H. (1987). Likelihood analysis of mitochondrial restriction-cleavage patterns for the human-chimpanzee-gorilla trichotomy. *Evolution* (*Lawrence, Kans.*) **41:**1162–1176.

Smuts, B. (1987). What are friends for? *Nat. Hist.* **92:**36–45.

Southwick, C. H., and Smith, R. B. (1986). The growth of primate field studies. *Comp. Primate Biol.* **2A:**173–191.

Spencer, F. (1986). *Ecce homo: An Annotated Bibliographic History of Physical Anthropology,* pp. 83–84. Greenwood Press, New York.

Spuhler, J. N. (1989). Raymond Pearl memorial lecture, 1988: Evolution of mitochondrial DNA in human and other organisms. *Am. J. Hum. Biol.* **1:**509–528.

Stanley, S. M. (1989). *Earth and Life Through Time* (2nd. ed.) W. H. Freeman, New York.

Stebbins, G. L. (1982). *Darwin to DNA, Molecules to Humanity.* Freeman, San Francisco.

Steklis, H. D. (1985). Primate communication, comparative neurology, and the origin of language re-examined. *J. Hum. Evol.* **14:**157–173.

Steklis, H. D. (1993). Primate socioecology from the bottom up. In *Milestones in Human Evolution* (A. J. Almquist and J. A. Manyak, eds.), pp. 39–74. Waveland Press, Prospect Heights, IL.

Stewart, T. D. (ed.) (1952). *Hrdlicka's Practical Anthropometry.* Wistar Institute of Anatomy and Biology, Philadelphia.

Stoneking, M. (1993). DNA and recent human evolution. *Evol. Anthropol.*: 60–73.

Stringer, C. B. (1990). The emergence of modern humans. *Sci. Am.* **263:**98–104.

Strum, S. C. (1987). *Almost Human. A Journey into the World of Baboons.* Random House, New York.

Stucky, R. K. (1990). Evolution of land mammal diversity in North America during the Cenozoic. In *Current Mammalogy* (H. H. Genoways, ed.), pp. 375–432. Vol. 2, Plenum, New York.

Sugardjito, J., te Boekhorst, I., and van Hooff, J. (1987). Ecological constraints on the grouping of wild orang-utans (*Pongo pygmaeus*) in the Gumung Lenser National Park, Sumatra, Indonesia. *Int. J. Primatol.* **8:**17–41.

Susman, R. W., and Garber, P. A. (1987). A new interpretation of the social organization and mating system of the Callitrichidae. *Int. J. Primatol.* **8:**73–92.

Sussman, R. L. (1988). Hand of *Paranthropus robustus* from Member I, Swartkrans: Fossil evidence for tool behavior. *Science* **240:** 781–784.

Suzuki, A. (1975). The origin of hominid hunting: A primatological perspective. In *The Socioecology and Psychology of Primates* (R. Tuttle, ed.), Mouton, The Hague.

Swisher, C. C., III, Curtis, G. H., Jacob, T., Getty, A. G., Suprijo, A., and Widiasmoro. (1994). Age of the earliest known hominids in Java, Indonesia. *Science* **263:**1118–1121.

Szalay, F. S. (1970). Late Eocene *Amphipithecus* and the origins of catarrhine primates. *Nature* (*London*) **227:**355–357.

Szalay, F. S., and Delson, E. (1979). *Evolutionary History of the Primates.* Academic Press, New York.

Tague, R., and Lovejoy, O. C. (1986). The obstetric pelvis of A.L. 288-1 (Lucy). *J. Hum. Evol.* **15:**237–255.

Tanner, J. M. (1981). *A History of the Study of Human Growth.* Cambridge Univ. Press, Cambridge, UK.

Tanner, J. M. (1990). *Foetus into Man,* revised and enlarged edition. Harvard Univ. Press, Cambridge, MA.

Tanner, N. M. (1981). *On Becoming Human.* Cambridge Univ. Press, Cambridge, UK.

Tattersall, I. (eds.). (1988). *Encyclopedia of Human Evolution and Pre-history*. Garland, New York.

Tattersall, I. (1993). *Human Odyssey: Four Million Years of Human Evolution*. Prentice Hall, Englewood Cliffs, NJ.

Taub, D., and Mehlman, P. (1991). Primate paternalistic investment: A cross-species view. In *Understanding Behavior* (J. Loy and C. Peters, eds.), pp. 51–89. Oxford Univ. Press, Oxford.

Taylor, C. R., and Rowntree, V. J. (1973). Running on two or four legs: Which consumes more energy? *Science* **179**:186–187.

Teleki, G. (1973). *The Predatory Behavior of Wild Chimpanzees*. Bucknell Univ. Press, Lewisburg, PA.

Templeton, A. R. (1985). The phylogeny of the hominoid primates: A statistical analysis of the DNA-DNA hybridization data. *Mol. Biol. Evol.* 2: 420–433.

Templeton, A. R. (1986). Further comments on statistical analysis of DNA-DNA hybridization data. *Mol. Biol. Evol.* **3**:290–295.

Templeton, A. R. (1992). Human origins and the analysis of mitochondrial DNA sequences. *Science* **255**:737.

Templeton, A. R. (1993). The "Eve" hypothesis: A genetic critique and reanalysis. *Am. Anthropol.* **95**:51–72.

Terbough, J. T. (1985). The ecology of Amazonian primates. In *Key Environments: Amazonia* (G. Prance and T. Lovejoy, eds.), pp. 284–304. Pergamon, New York.

Terbough, J. T., and Jansen, C. H. (1986). The socioecology of primate groups. *Annu. Rev. Ecol. Syste.* **17**:111–136.

Terrace, H. (1979). How Nim Chimpsky changed my mind. *Psychol. Today,* November: 65–76.

Tobias, P.V. (1980). "*Australopithecus afarensis*" and *A. africanus*: Critique and an alternative hypothesis. *Palaeontol. Afri.* **23**: 1–17.

Tobias, P. V. (1987). The brain of *Homo habilis*. A new level of organization in cerebral evolution. *J.Hum. Evol.* **16**:741–762.

Tobias, P. V. (1991). *The Skulls, Endocasts, and Teeth of Homo habilis. Olduvai Gorge,* Vol. 4. Cambridge Univ. Press, Cambridge, UK.

Tooby, J., and DeVore, I. (1987). The reconstruction of hominid behavioral evolution through strategic modeling. In *The Evolution of Human Behavior: Primate Models* (W. Kinzey, ed.), pp. 183–237. SUNY Press, Albany, NY.

Toth, N. (1985). Archaeological evidence for preferential right-handedness in the lower and middle Pleistocene, and its possible implications. *J. Hum. Evol.* **14**:607–614.

Toth, N. (1987). The first technology. *Sci. Am.* **256**:112–121.

Toth, N., and Schick, K. D. (1993). Early stone industries and inferences regarding language and cognition. In: *Tools, Language and Cognition in Human Evolution* (K. Gibson and T. Ingold, eds.), pp. 346–362. Cambridge Univ. Press, Cambridge, UK.

Toth, N., Schick, K. D., Savage-Rumbaugh, E. S., Sevcik, R. A., and Rumbaugh, D. M. (1993). *Pan* the tool-maker: Investigations into the stone tool-making and tool-using capabilities of a bonobo (*Pan paniscus*). *J. Archeol. Sci.* **20**:81–91.

Trevathan, W. (1987). *Human Birth: An Evolutionary Perspective*. de Gruyter, New York.

Trinkaus, E. (ed.) (1989). *The Emergence of Modern Humans: Biocultural Adaptations in the Later Pleistocene*. Cambridge Univ. Press, Cambridge, UK.

Trivers, R. L. (1971). The evolution of reciprocal altruism. *Q. Rev. Biol.* **46**:35–57.

Trivers, R. L. (1972). Parental investment and sexual selection. In *Sexual Selection and the Descent of Man* (B. Campbell, ed.). Aldine, Chicago.

Trivers, R. L., and Willard, D. E. (1973). Natural selection of parental ability to vary the sex ratio of offspring. *Science* **179**:90–92.

Tutin, C., and McGinnis, P. (1981). Sexuality of the chimpanzee in the wild. In *Reproductive Biology of the Great Apes: Comparative and Biomedical Perspectives*. (C. Graham, ed.), pp. 239–264. Academic Press, New York.

Tuttle, R. (1975). Parallelism, brachiation, and hominid phylogeny. In *The Phylogeny of the Primates* (W. Luckett and F. S. Szalay, eds.), pp. 447–480. Plenum, New York.

Tyson, E. (1699). *Orang-Outang, sive Homo sylvestris: Or; The Anatomy of a Pygmie Compared With That of Monkey, an Ape, and a Man*. Bennet, London.

Ubelaker, D. H. (1995). Latest developments in skeletal biology and forensic anthropology. In *Biological Anthropology: The State of the Science* (N. T. Boaz and L. D. Wolfe, eds.), pp. 91–106. International Institute for Human Evolutionary Research, Bend, OR.

Ubelaker, D. H., and O'Donnell, G. (1992). Computer-assisted facial reconstruction. *J. Forensic Sci.* **37**:155–162.

Valentine, J. W. (1978). The evolution of multicellular plants and animals. *Sci. Am.* **239**(3):140–158.

Van Shaik, C. P. (1983). Why are diurnal primates living in groups? *Behaviour* **87**:120–143.

Van Valen, L., and Sloan, R. E. (1965). The earliest primates. *Science* **150**:743–754.

Vigilant, L., Pennington, R., Harpending, H., Kocher, T. D., and Wilson, A. C. (1989). Mitochondrial DNA sequences in single hairs from a southern African population. *Proc. Natl. Acad. Sci. U.S.A.* **86**:9350–9354.

Vogel, J. C. (1985). Further attempts at dating the Taung tufas. In *Hominid Evolution: Past, Present, and Future* (P. V. Tobias, ed.), pp. 189–194. Alan R. Liss, New York.

Vrba, E.S. (1985). Environment and evolution: alternative causes of the temporal distribution of evolutionary events. *S. Afr. J. Sci.* **85**:229–236.

Vrba, E. S. (1975). Some evidence of chronology and palaeoecology of Sterkfontein, Swartkrans and Kromdraai from the fossil Bovidae. *Nature* (*London*) **254**:301–304.

Vrba, E. S. (1988). Late Pliocene climatic events and hominid and hominid evolution. In *Evolutionary History of the "Robust" Australopithecines* (F. Grine, ed.), pp. 405–426. de Gruyter, New York.

Wade, M. J. (1978). A critical review of the models of group selection. *Q. Rev. Biol.* **53**:101–114.

Walker, A. (1967). Locomotor adapations in living and fossil Madagascar lemurs. Ph.D. Dissertation, University of London.

Walker, A. (1993). The origin of the genus *Homo*. In *The Origin and Evolution of Humans and Humanness* (D. T. Rasmussen, ed.), pp. 29–47. Jones & Bartlett, Boston.

Walker, A., Zimmerman, M., and Leakey, R. (1981). A possible case of hypervitaminosis A in *Homo erectus*. *Nature* (*London*) **296**: 248–250.

Ward, P., and Zahavi, A. (1973). The importance of certain assemblages of birds as "information-centres" for food-finding. *Ibis* **115**(4):517–534.

Washburn, S. L. (1960). Tools and human evolution. *Sci. Am.* **203**: 63–75.

Washburn, S. L. (1963). Behavior and human evolution. In *Classification and Human Evolution* (S. L. Washburn, ed.), pp. 190–203. Aldine, Chicago.

Washburn, S. L. (1967). Behavior and the origin of man. The Huxley Memorial Lecture. *Proc. R. Soc. G. B. Irel.,* pp. 21–27.

Washburn, S. L. (1978). Human behavior and the behavior of other animals. *Am. Psychol.* **33**:405–418.

Washburn, S. L. (1985). Human evolution after Raymond Dart. 23rd Raymond Dart Lecture. In *Hominid Evolution: Past, Present, and Future* (P. V. Tobias, ed.), pp. 3–18. Alan R. Liss, New York.

Washburn, S. L. (1993). Evolution and education. In *Milestones in Human Evolution* (A. J. Almquist and J. A. Manyak, eds.), pp. 223–240. Waveland Press, Prospect Heights, IL.

Washburn, S. L., and Moore, R. (1980). *Ape into Human*, 2nd ed. Little, Brown, Boston.

Watson, J. D. (1976). *Molecular Biology of the Gene,* 3rd ed. Benjamin, Menlo Park, CA.

Weinert, H. (1932). *Ursprung der Menschheit. Uber den engeren Anschluss des Menschengeschlechts an die Menschenaffen*. Enke, Stuttgart.

Wendt, H. (1956). *In Search of Adam. The Story of Man's Quest for the Truth About His Earliest Ancestors*. Houghton-Mifflin, Boston.

Weiskrantz, L., Sanders, M. D., Marshall, J. (1974). Visual capacity in the hemianopic field following a restricted occipital ablation. *Brain* **97**: 709–728.

Wescott, R. W. (1967). The exhibitionistic origin of human bipedalism. *Man* **2**:630.

West-Eberhard, M. J. (1975). The evolution of social behavior by kin selection. *Q. Rev. Biol.* **46**:35–57.

Wheeler, P. E. (1984). The evolution of bipedality and loss of functional body hair in hominids. *J. Hum. Evol.* **13**:91–98.

White, F. (1986). Behavioral ecology of the pygmy chimpanzee. Ph.D. Dissertation, State University of New York, Stony Brook.

White, M. J. D. (1978). *Modes of Speciation*. Freeman, San Francisco.

White, T. D. (1988). The comparative biology of "Robust" australopithecines: Clues from context. In *Evolutionary History of the "Robust" Australopithecines* (F. Grine, ed.). de Gruyter, New York.

White, T. D., Suwa, G., and Asfaw, B. (1994). *Australopithecus ramidus,* a new species of early hominid from Aramis, Ethiopia. *Nature* (*London*) **371**:306–312.

White, T. D., Suwa, G., and Asfaw, B. (1995). *Australopithecus ramidus,* a new species of early hominid from Aramis, Ethiopia. *Nature* (*London*) **375**:88.

Whitten, T. (1982). *The gibbons of Siberut.* J. M. Dent, London, England.

Wiessner, P. (1990). Is there a unity to style? In *Uses of Style in Archeology* (M. Conkey and C. Hasdorf, eds.), pp. 105–112. Cambridge Univ. Press, Cambridge, UK.

Williams, G. C. (1966). *Adaptation and Natural Selection.* Princeton Univ. Press, Princeton, NJ.

Williams, G. C., and Nesse, R. M. (1991). The dawn of Darwinian medicine. *Q. Rev. Biol.* **66**:1–22.

Williams, R. J. (1951). Biochemical Institute Studies. IV. Individual metabolic patterns and human disease: An exploratory study utilizing predominantly paper chromatographic methods. *Univ. Tex. Publ.* **5109**:7–21.

Williams, S. A., and Goodman, M. (1989). A statistical test that supports a human/chimpanzee clade based on noncoding DNA sequence data. *Mol. Biol. Evol.* **6**:325–330.

Wilson, E. O. (1975). *Sociobiology: The New Synthesis.* Harvard Univ. Press, Cambridge, MA.

Wilson, R. S. (1976). Concordance in physical growth for monozygotic and dizygotic twins. *Ann. Hum. Biol.* **1**:175–188.

Winchester, A.M. (1972). *Genetics: A Survey of the Principles of Heredity.* 4th ed. Houghton-Mifflin, Boston.

Wobst, H. M. (1977). Stylistic behavior and information exchange. In *For the Director: Research Essays in Honor of James B. Griffin* (C. E. Cleland, ed.), Anthropol. Pap. No. 61, pp. 317–342. Ann Arbor Museum of Anthropology, Ann Arbor, MI.

Wolpoff, M. H. (1980). *Paleoanthropology.* Knopf, New York.

Wolpoff, M. H. (1989). Multiregional evolution: The fossil alternative to Eden. In *The Human Revolution: Behavioural and Biological Perspectives* (P. Mellars and C. B. Stringer, eds.), pp. 62–108. Princeton Univ. Press, Princeton, NJ.

Wood, B. A. (1992). Taxonomy and evolutionary relationships of *Homo erectus. Cour. Forschungsint,* Senckenberg, Frankfurt, Germany.

Wrangham, R. W. (1980). An ecological model of female-bonded primate groups. *Behaviour* **75**:262–300.

Wrangham, R. W. (1983). Ultimate factors determining social structure. In *Primate Social Relationships: An Integrated Approach* (R. Hinde, ed.), pp. 255–262. Blackwell, Oxford.

Wrangham, R. W. (1987a). Evolution of social structure. In *Primate Societies* (B. B. Smuts, D. L. Cheny, R. M. Seyfarth, R. W. Wrangham, and T. T. Struhsaker, eds.), pp. 282–296. Univ. of Chicago Press, Chicago.

Wrangham, R. W. (1987b). The significance of African apes for reconstructing human social evolution. In *The Evolution of Human Behavior: Primate Models* (W. Kinzey, ed.), pp. 51–71. SUNY Press, Albany, NY.

Wrangham, R. W., McGrew, W., deWaal, F., and Heltne, P. (eds.). (1994). *Chimpanzee Cultures.* Harvard Univ. Press, Cambridge, MA.

Wright, K. (1990). Cradle of mutation. *Discover,* September: 22–23.

Wynn, I. (1988). Tools and the evolution of human intelligence. In *Machiavellian Intelligence* (R. Byrne and A. Whiten, eds), pp. 271–284. Oxford Univ. Press (Clarendon), Oxford.

Wynne Edwards, V. C. (1962). *Animal Dispersal in Relation to Social Behavior.* Hafner, New York.

Yamagiwa, J. (1987). Intra- and inter-group interactions of an all-male group of Virunga Mountain gorillas. *Primates* **28**:1–30.

Yerkes, R. M., and Yerkes, A. W. (1929). *The Great Apes.* Yale Univ. Press, New Haven, CT.

Ziegler, T. E., Epple, G., Snowdon, C. T., Porter, T. A., Belcher, A. M., and Küderling, I. (1993). Detection of the chemical signals of ovulation in the cotton-top tamarin, *Saguinus oedipus. Anim. Behav.* **45**:313–322.

Zihlman, A. L. (1981). Women as shapers of human adaptation. In *Woman the Gatherer* (F. Dahlberg, ed.), pp. 75–120. Yale Univ. Press, New Haven, CT.

Zuckerman, S. (1932). *The Social Life of Monkeys and Apes.* Routledge & Kegan Paul, London.

Illustration Credits

CHAPTER 1 **1-1** Noel T. Boaz; **1-2** Blumenbach, Johann Friedrich. *De Generic Humani Varietate Nativa*, Editio tertia, Gottingae: Vandenhoek et Ruprecht, 1795. Reprinted in *The Anthropological Treatises of Johann Friedrich Blumenbach*, translated and edited by Thomas Bendyshe/The Burndy Library, Bibner Institute for the History of Science and Technology/The Granger Collection; **1-4** Bettman; **1-5** Gerry Ellis Nature Photography; **1-6** Dr. Gerhard Storch/Forschungsinstitut Senckenberg; **1-7** J. S. Kingdon/The Zoological Society of London, from J. R. and P. H. Napier, *The Natural History of the Primates* (The MIT Press), p. 141; **1-8** From *Phylogeny Reconstruction in Paleontology* by Robert M. Schock, pp. 173, 188, copyright © 1986 Van Nostrand Reinhold; **1-10** Thomas Huxley/Burndy Library, from Thomas Henry Huxley, *Evidence as to Man's Place in Nature*, London: Williams and Norgate, 1893; **1-11** Illustration by Whitney Powell from page 88 of *Promethean Fire* by C. J. Lumsden and E. O. Wilson, copyright © 1983 by the President and Fellows of Harvard College, reprinted by permission of Harvard University Press; **1-13** Noel T. Boaz/California Academy of Sciences.

CHAPTER 2 **2-1** From *Earth and Life Through Time* by Stanley. Copyright © 1986 by Freeman and Company, used with permission; **2-3** J. William Schopf. 1993. Microfossils of the Early Archean Apex Chert: New Evidence of the Antiquity of Life. *Science* 260: 640–646; **2-4, 2-5, 2-6** From *Chemical Evolution and The Origin of Life* by Richard E. Dickerson, illustration by Allen Beechel, copyright © 1978 by Scientific American, Inc., all rights reserved; **2-7** (photo) Phototake NYC; (line art) From Barrett/Abramoff/Kumaran/Millington, *Biology,* © 1986, reprinted by permission of Prentice Hall, Upper Saddle River, New Jersey; **2-8** From *Molecular Biology of the Gene*, Vol. I, Fourth Edition, by Watson et al., copyright © 1987 by James D. Watson, published by the Benjamin/Cummings Publishing Company; **2-9, 2-10** From Hinegardner, 1976, *Molecular Evolution*, F. J. Ayala ed., pp. 179–99, reprinted by permission of the authors; **2-11** epithelial cell, muscle cell: Runk Schoeberger from Grant Heilman/Grant Heilman Photography, Inc.; red blood cell: CNRI/Science Photo Library/Photo Researchers, Inc.; **2-12** Knoll, Andrew H.; **2-14, 2-17a, 2-18** Barrett/Abramoff/ Kumaran/Millington, *Biology,* © 1986, p. 134, reprinted by permission of Prentice Hall, Upper Saddle River, New Jersey; **2-15** From Kathleen Talaro and Arthur Talaro, *Foundations in Microbiology*, copyright © 1993 Times Mirror Higher Education Group, Inc., Dubuque, Iowa; **2-17b** Klug/Cummings, *Concepts of Genetics* 4/e, © 1994, p. 361, reprinted by permission of Prentice Hall, Upper Saddle River, New Jersey; **2-20** Knoll, Andrew H.

CHAPTER 3 **3-1, 3-4** Culver Pictures, Inc.; **3-3** North Wind Picture Archives; **3-6** (left) FPG International, (right) Photo Researchers, Inc.; **3-7** (top) Leonard Lee Rue III/Animals Animals/Earth Scenes, (bottom) American Museum of Natural History; **3-8** (left) The Stock Market, (right) Animals Animals/Earth Scenes; **3-10** Richard Pasley/Stock Boston; **3-11** Bettman; **3-12** Archive Photos; **3-13** Barrett/Abramoff/ Kumaran/Millington, *Biology,* © 1986, pp. 602, 603, reprinted by permission of Prentice Hall, Upper Saddle River, New Jersey; **3-15** Photo Researchers, Inc.; **3-17** Peter Menzel; **3-20** From *The Processing of DNA* by James E. Darnell, Jr., illustration by Jerome Kuhl, copyright © 1983 by Scientific American, Inc., all rights reserved; **3-21a** Barrett/ Abramoff/Kumaran/Millington, *Biology,* © 1986, pp. 622, reprinted by permission of Prentice Hall, Upper Saddle River, New Jersey; **3-21b** Klug/Cummings, *Concepts of Genetics* 4/e, © 1994, p. 361, reprinted by permission of Prentice Hall, Upper Saddle River, New Jersey.

CHAPTER 4 **4-5** Custom Medical Stock Photo; **4-6** VU/Stanley Flegler/Visuals Unlimited; **4-7, 4-10** From Wright, S., 1931, "Statistical Theory of Evolution," *Journal of American Statistical Association*, March 1931: 201–208; **4-8** Reprinted from *Genetics* by William Stans-

field, copyright © 1969 McGraw-Hill Co., reproduced with permission of the McGraw-Hill Companies; **4-9** Jerry Knab, Photo 29 Inc., from *Achondroplasia, Its Nature and Its Causes* by Jansen, Murk 1917; **4-11** David Barritt/Gamma Liaison, Inc.; **4-12** Illustration adapted from a drawing by Ian Worpole © 1990 *Discover* Magazine; **4-13** M. W. Tweedie/Photo Researchers, Inc.; **4-15** From Mettler/Gregg, *Population Genetics and Evolution, 2/E,* © 1988, p. 294, reprinted by permission of Prentice Hall, Upper Saddle River, New Jersey; **4-16** Adapted from *South African Journal of Science*, 61, 76 (1980), reprinted with permission; **4-17** (left) Tom McHugh/ Photo Researchers, Inc., (right) The Stock Market; **4-18** J. M. Macedonia; **4-19** Archive Photos; **4-20** (left) Frans Lanting/Minden Pictures; (center) J. M. Macedonia; (right) Stan Osolinski/Tony Stone Images.

CHAPTER 5 **5-1** From Barrett/Abramoff/Kumaran/Millington, *Biology,* © 1986, reprinted by permission of Prentice Hall, Upper Saddle River, New Jersey; **5-2** (left) Robert & Linda Mitchell Photography; (right) VU/Larry S. Roberts/Visuals Unlimited; **5-3** From Cartmill et al., *Human Structure,* Harvard University Press, 1987; **5-4** From *The Anatomical Primer* by D. A. Langebartel and R. H. Ullrich, 1977, University Park Press; **5-5** (top) From *Man In Structure and Function* by Fritz Kahn, copyright 1943 by Fritz Kahn and renewed 1971 by Alfred A. Knopf, Inc., reprinted by permission; **5-5** (bottom), **5-6** Martini/ Timmons, *Human Anatomy,* © 1995, reprinted by permission of Prentice Hall, Upper Saddle River, New Jersey; **5-11** (bird embryo) Visuals Unlimited; (human embryo) Photo Researchers, Inc.; **5-17** After Romer; **5-18** From *The Vertebrate Story* by Romer, Fig. 74, p. 116, copyright © 1970 Saunders, reprinted by permission of Academic Press, Inc., a subsidiary of Harcourt Brace & Co.; **5-19** From *The Triune Brain* by P. D MacLean, copyright © 1990 Plenum Publishing Corporation, reprinted by permission; **5-20** (left) DRK Photo; **5-23** Rod Williams/Bruce Coleman, Inc.; box photo p. 164 Glenn Conroy.

CHAPTER 6 **6-1, 6-2, 6-4, 6-6, 6-9** From *Primate Adaptation and Evolution* by J. G. Fleagle, copyright © 1988 Academic Press, reprinted by permission of Academic Press, Inc., a subsidiary of Harcourt Brace & Co.; **6-11** From *The Human Odyssey: Four Million Years of Evolution* by Ian Tattersall, p. 44, copyright © 1993, I. Tattersall, reprinted with permission; **6-13** Jean-Philippe Varin/JACANA/Photo Researchers, Inc.; **6-14** Redrawn from Napier and Walker, 1967, *Folia Primatologica* 6: 204–219, reprinted by permission of S. Karger A. G., Basel, Switzerland; **6-15** Dr. Elwyn L. Simons; **6-17** From "Egyptian Oligocene Primates: A Review," *Yearbook of Physical Anthropology* 38:199–238, 1995, E. L. Simons, reprinted by permission; **6-19** (left) S. F. Kimbrough/from Steven Stanley, *Earth and Life Through Time;* p. 541, W. H. Freeman and Company; **6-20** *Journal of Vertebrate Paleontology;* 4(4):570–74, copyright © by The Society of Vertebrate Paleontology; **6-21, 6-22, 6-24** From *Primate Adaptation and Evolution* by J. G. Fleagle, copyright © 1988, reprinted by permission from Academic Press; **6-23** Art Wolfe; **6-25** Art Wolfe/Tony Stone Images.

CHAPTER 7 **7-2, 7-4** N. DeVore/Anthro-Photo; **7-3, 7-5** From *Primate Adaptation and Evolution* by J. G. Fleagle, copyright © 1988, reprinted by permission from Academic Press; **7-7, 7-15** From *Primates in Nature* by Richard, copyright © 1985 by Freeman and Company, used with permission; **7-8** Anthro-Photo; **7-9** Reprinted with permission from "Squirrel Monkey Reproduction the 'Failed' Male Phenomenon and Seasonal Spermatogenic," F. V. Dumond (1967), *Science* 158:1067–1070, copyright © 1967 American Association for the Advancement of Science; **7-10** Dan McCoy/Rainbow; **7-11** Barbara Smuts/Anthro-Photo; **7-12** Bruce Coleman, Inc.; **7-13** Jim Moore/ Anthro-Photo; **7-14** R Wrangham/Anthro-Photo; **7-16** From *Primate Behavior: Field Studies of Monkeys and Apes* by Irven DeVore, 1965,

Harcourt Brace & Co., fig. 3–10, p. 70; **7-17** (left) Rod Williams/Bruce Coleman, Inc., (right) James H. Carmichael/Bruce Coleman, Inc.; **7-18** DRK Photo; **7-19** K. & K. Ammann/Bruce Coleman, Inc.; **7-20** Martin Rogers/Stock Boston; **7-21** Paul Symonds.

CHAPTER 8 8-1 Dieter and Mary Plage/Bruce Colman, Inc.; **8-5** original illustration by A. H. Schultz, reprinted with permission from the trustees of the Adolph H. Schultz Foundation, Zurich; **8-6** from John Buettner-Janusch, *Origins of Man: Physical Anthropology,* p. 298, John Wiley & Sons, Inc.; **8-7, 8-8** (top) Martini/Timmons, Human Anatomy © 1995, reprinted by permission of Prentice Hall, Upper Saddle River, New Jersey; (bottom) From Beard, K. C. and Godinot, M., 1988 *Journal of Human Evolution* 17:71–92; **8-9, 8-13, 8-21** From *Primate Adaptation and Evolution* by J. G. Fleagle, copyright © 1988, reprinted by permission from Academic Press; **8-10** Courtesy of G. Fischer, Jena, Germany, From R. Martin, 1914, Lehrbach der Anthropologie; **8-11** Animals Animals/Earth Scenes; **8-12** Robert E. Hynes/ National Geographic Image Collection; **8-14, 8-15** Art Wolfe; **8-16** VU/Joe McDonald/Visuals Unlimited; **8-18** From *New Interpretations of Ape and Human Ancestry* by Walker and M. Pickford, copyright © 1983, Plenum Publishing Corp., p. 325–52, reprinted by permission; **8-19** Pilbeam; **8-22, 8-24** From *Yearbook of Physical Anthropology* by D. R. Begun, copyright © 1994 John Wiley & Sons, Inc., reprinted by permission.

CHAPTER 9 9-1 From "Bonobo Sex and Society," by Franz B. M. de Waal, illustration by Laurie Grace, *Scientific American,* March 1995, copyright © by Scientific American, Inc.; all rights reserved; **9-2** From *Primate Adaptation and Evolution* by J. G. Fleagle, copyright © 1988, reprinted by permission from Academic Press; **9-3** From *Primates in Nature* by Richard, copyright © 1985 by Freeman and Company, used with permission; **9-4** The Zoological Society of San Diego; **9-5** Bruce Coleman, Inc.; **9-6** Robert Flaherty/Archive Photos; **9-7** From *The Mountain Gorilla* by George B. Schaller, Fig. 6.6, p. 285, copyright © 1963, reprinted by permission of George B. Schaller; **9-8** Edward Tyson, Orang-Outang, sive *Homo Syvestris: or The Anatomy of a Pygmie,* London: Thomas Bennet, 1699/The Burndy Library; **9-9** Gerry Ellis Nature Photography; **9-10** Illustration 3.1 from *The Chimpanzees of Gombe* by J. Goodall, copyright © 1986 by the President and Fellows of Harvard College, reprinted by permission of Harvard University Press; **9-11** (left) Wrangham/Anthro-Photo; (right) Nancy Nicolson/Anthro-Photo; **9-12** Peter Davey/Bruce Colman, Inc.; **9-13** Illustration 6.1 by David Minard (after D. Bygott) from *The Chimpanzees of Gombe* by J. Goodall, copyright © 1986 by the President and Fellows of Harvard College, reprinted by permission of Harvard University Press; **9-14** Anthro-Photo; **9-15** R. Van Nostrand/Photo Researchers, Inc.; **9-16** Elizabeth; Pugh; **9-17** (left) Petit Format/J. Da Cunha/Photo Researchers, Inc.; (right) Suzanne Szasz/Photo Researchers, Inc.; **9-18, 9-19** Irenaeus Eibl-Eibesfeldt/Aldine de Gruyter; **9-20** Malcolm Beaton/Caledonian Newspapers, Ltd.; **9-21** Gamma-Liaison, Inc.

CHAPTER 10 10-1, 10-7 Noel T. Boaz; **10-2** Brill Atlanta; **10-3** Figure of Swartkrans cave site by C. K. Brain, from *Paleoclimate and Evolution* by Vrba & Denton, eds., copyright © 1995 Yale University Press, reprinted by permission; **10-4** Adapted from *Encyclopedia of Human Evolution and Prehistory,* Tattersall, I., et al., Garland Publishing Co.; **10-5** Nanci Kahn/Institute of Human Origins; **10-6** Institute of Human Origins; "Australopithecine Skulls, Dentition," by E. L. Simons, from *Science,* 245:1345, Fig. 1, copyright © 1989 American Association for the Advancement of Science; **10-8** Reprinted with permission from *Nature* 371: 306–312, T. D. White et al., 1994, *Australopithecus ramidus,* a new species of early hominid from Aramis, Ethiopia, copyright © 1994 Macmillan Magazines Limited; **10-9** (left) John Reader/ Science Photo Library/Photo Researchers, Inc.; (right) D. Finnin/C. Chesek/American Museum of Natural History; **10-10** (left) W. H. Kimbel/Institute of Human Origins; (top,right) Dr. J. Francis Thackeray; (bottom, right) Phillip V. Tobias; **10-11** Adapted from Cooke, 1983 "Human Evolution: The Geological Framework," *Can. J. of Anthropology* 3: 143–161; **10-16** Brill Atlanta; **10-13** From *Human*

Evolution, 3rd ed, by R. Lewin, 1993, p. 118, reprinted by permission of Blackwell Science, Inc.; **10-18** From *Primate Adaptation and Evolution* by John Fleagle, copyright © 1988 Academic Press, reprinted by permission; **10-19** (left) Brill Atlanta; (right) Anthro-Photo.

CHAPTER 11 11-1 From H. M. McHenry, 1988, New Estimates of Body Weight in "Early Hominids and Their Significance to Encephalization and Megadontia in Robust Australopithecines" in *Evolutionary History of the Robust Australopithecines,* F. E. Grine (ed.), pp 133–40 (New York: Aldine de Gruyter), copyright © 1988 by Aldine de Gruyter; **11-3, 11-6, 11-10** Noel T. Boaz; **11-4** Neandertal and Modern Physique from J. J. Hublin in Pour La Science, No. 64, February, 1983, p. 63; **11-5** "The Lumper's View" from a schematic by Michael Day in Day, *Guide to Fossil Man,* London, Cassell, 1965, p. 173; "Splitter's Delight" from schematic by William Howells in Howells, *Getting Here,* Washington, Compass Press, copyright © 1993, p. 215; **11-12** (left) Paris Pavlakis, Ph.D.; (right) courtesy of and copyright by Eric Delson (City University of New York/American Museum of Natural History); **11-13** From *Human Evolution,* 3rd ed., by R. Lewin, p. 152, © 1993, reprinted by permission of Blackwell Science, Inc.; **11-15** Rota/American Museum of Natural History; **11-17** C. M. Dixon; **11-18** Gamma Liaison, Inc.; **11-20** From Vandermeersch, B. 1985, "Neanderthal Man and the Origins of Modern Man" in *Homo,* ed. Peretto, C., Venice: Cataloghi Marsilio, reprinted by permission of Marsilio Editori, Venice, Italy.

CHAPTER 12 12-1 Adapted from *Narratives of Human Evolution* by Landau, copyright © 1991 Yale University Press, reprinted by permission; **12-2** Irven De Vore/Anthro-Photo; **12-3** Anthro-Photo; **12-4** Pat Shipman; **12-5** From *The Human Career* by R. Klein, copyright © 1989 The University of Chicago Press, reprinted by permission; **12-6** From Glynn Isaac in F. Grine, 1986, *Journal of Human Evolution,* vol. 15, p. 813, Fig. 12, reprinted by permission of Academic Press Ltd., London, England; **12-7** Brill Atlanta; **12-9** M. Shostak/Anthro-Photo; **12-10, 12-11** From *Ancestors: The Hard Evidence* by E. Delson (ed.), copyright © 1985 Alan R. Liss, reprinted by permission of John Wiley & Sons, Inc.; **12-12** Elisabeth S. Vrba, "An Hypothesis of Heterochrony in Response to Climatic Cooling . . ." in *Integrative Paths to the Past,* Corrucini/Ciochon, eds., © 1994 p. 355, reprinted by permission of Prentice Hall, Upper Saddle River, New Jersey; **12-13** From Martini/ Timmons *Human Anatomy,* © 1995 p. 421, reprinted by permission of Prentice Hall, Upper Saddle River, New Jersey; **12-14** From "Language and the Brain" by Norman Geschwind, copyright © 1972 by Scientific American, Inc., all rights reserved; **12-15** Rose A. Sevcik/ Elizabeth Pugh; **12-17** Alexander Marshack.

CHAPTER 13 13-1 FPG International; **13-2** Adapted from Wright, S. (1943), "Isolation by Distance," *Genetics* 28: 114–138; **13-3** Alan Mann/University of Pennsylvania Museum; **13-4** From *Human Diversity* by Lewontin, copyright © 1982 by Scientific American Books, used with permission of W. H. Freeman and Company; **13-5** Molnar, Stephen, *Human Variation: Races, Types, and Groups,* 3/e, © 1992, p. 14, reprinted by permission of Prentice Hall, Upper Saddle River, New Jersey; From R. Martin, 1914, *Lehrbach der Anthropologie,* p. 523, Gustav Fischer Verlag Publishing Company, reprinted by permission; **13-6** Reprinted with permission from *Nature,* "Mitochondrial DNA and Human Evolution," R. L. Cann, M. Stoneking, A. C. Wilson, 325: 31-36, copyright © 1987 Macmillan Magazines Limited; **13-11** UPI/ Bettman; **13-12** (photo) Runk/Schoenberger/Grant Heilman Photography, Inc.; (line art) Martini/Timmons, Human Anatomy, © 1995, p. 91, reprinted by permission of Prentice Hall, Upper Saddle River, New Jersey; **13-13** Photo Researchers, Inc.; **13-14** D. Gorton/Time, Inc.

CHAPTER 14 14-2 From *Patterns of Human Growth* by Barry Bogin, copyright © 1988 Cambridge University Press, Cambridge, England; **14-3, 14-9, 14-10** Adapted from *Growth and Development* by R. Malina, copyright © 1975 by Burgess Publishing Co., an imprint of Burgess International Group, Inc., Edina, Minn.; **14-4** From Georges Olivier, *Practical Anthropology,* copyright © 1969, courtesy of Charles

C. Thomas, Publisher, Springfield, Illinois; **14-5** Paul Delaroche, "The Children of King Edward Imprisoned in the Tower," 1812, Louvre, Paris/Giraudon/Art Resource; **14-6** "Prolongation of Life Phases and Gestation in Primates" by C. O. Lovejoy, copyright © 1977, American Association for the Advancement of Science; **14-7** From Tanner 1962 in Harrison, et al.: *Human Biology*, 2nd ed., p. 320, fig. 20.1, copyright © 1977 Oxford University Press, reprinted by permission of Oxford University Press; **14-8** Barrett/Abramoff/Kumaran/Millington, *Biology*, © 1986, p. 382, reprinted by permission of Prentice Hall, Upper Saddle River, New Jersey; **14-11a** From Eveleth and Tanner, 1976; **14-11b** From Tanner "The Physique of the Olympic Athlete," G. Allen and Unwin, London, 1964; **14-12** Peacock/Anthro-Photo; **14-13, 14-14** From *The Paleolithic Prescription* by S. Boyd Eaton, Marjorie Shostack and Melvin Konner, copyright © 1988 by S. Boyd Eaton, M. D., Marjorie Shostack, and Melvin Konner, M. D., Ph. D., reprinted by permission of HarperCollins Publishers, Inc.; **14-15** After Roberts, *American Journal of Physical Anthropology*, 11: 533–58, copyright © 1953 John Wiley & Sons, Inc., reprinted by permission of John Wiley & Sons, Inc.; **14-16** "Recent World Population History A. D. 1 to 1990 and 1992 Population Projection of the U.N. from 1990 to 2150," from *Science*, Vol. 269, July 1995, J. Cohen, copyright © 1995 American Association for the Advancement of Science.

CHAPTER 15 15-1 Frank Spencer; **15-3** Photo Researchers, Inc.; **15-4** Rembrandt van Rijn, "The Anatomy Lesson," Mauritshuis, Den Haag/Art Resource; **15-5** (left) Black Star; (right) Photo Researchers, Inc.; **15-6** James Stevenson/Science Photo Library/Photo Researchers, Inc.; **15-7** Photo Researchers, Inc.; **15-10** Dr. Meleisa McDonnell/ United States National Zoo; **15-11** (photo) Long Photo Inc.; **15-12** Gene O'Donnell/FBI; **15-14** Recognition Systems, Inc.; **15-16** (left) Black Star; (right) Moore/Anthro-Photo; **15-20** From "What to Do About Your Brain-Injured Child" by Glenn Doman, © 1990, Glenn J. Doman, reprinted by permission of the author.

Tables

4-2 From *Genetics*, 4TH Ed. by A. M. Winchester, 1972, p. 423; **6-1** From *An Introduction to Human Evolutionary Anatomy* by L. Aiello & C. Dean. Copyright © 1990 Academic Press. Reprinted with permission.**7-1** From *Pimate Behavior: Field Studies of Monkeys and Apes* by Irven DeVore, Copyright © 1965 by Holt, Rinehart & Winston, Inc., and renewed 1993 by Irven DeVore, reproduced by permission of the publisher; **7-2** From Robinson, J. G. 1986, "Seasonal Variation in the Use of Time and Space by The Wedgecapped Capanchin Monkey, *Cebus Olivaceus:*," Smithsonian Contr. Zool. 431: 1–60. Reprinted by permission of Smithsonian Institute Press; **8-1** "Evolution at Two levels in Humans and Chimpanzee" by King and Wilson, *Science*, 188:107–116. Copyright © 1975 American Association for the Advancement of Science; **8-2** From Sibley C. G. and Ahlquist, J. E., 1987, *J. Molec. Evol.* 26:99–121, DNA hybridization evidence of hominoid phylogeny: results from an expanded data set. Reprinted by permission of Springer-Verlag, Inc.; **14-2, 14-3, 14-4** From *The Paleolithic Prescription* by S. Boyd Eaton. Marjorie Shostack and Melvin Konner, Copyright © 1988. Reprinted by permission of HarperCollins Publishers, Inc.

Index

A

Aardvarks, 168
ABO blood group, 442–45, 461–62, 464
Aborigines, 495, 496
Acclimation, 501
Acclimatization, 500–501
Acheulean tool culture, 375, 376, 388, 431
Achondroplasia, 111
ACTH (adenocorticotrophic hormone), 162
Active movement, 62
Adapis, 185
Adapis parisiensis, 253
Adapoids, 187, 188, 196, 200
Adaptability (*See also* Human adaptability)
   defined, 11
Adaptation, defined, 11
Adaptationist position, 518
Adaptive radiations, 139–40, 149–50, 155
   mammals and, 166–69
Adenine, 44, 47, 91, 92
Adolescence, 485–86, 488–91, 496–97
Aegyptopithecus, 198, 199, 260
African-Americans, 115, 468, 472
"African Eve" Hypothesis, 380, 390
Afropithecus, 259, 260, 264, 265
Aggressive behavior:
   hominoid, 285, 294–95
   human, 314–16
   primate, 191, 215, 218, 225–27, 236–38, 316
Agnathans, 140, 143
Agonistic encounters, 225, 226
Air bladder, 144–45
Aka pygmies, 489
Alanine, 48
Alarm call signaling, 233, 235, 236, 243
Albinism, 110
Albumin, 58–59, 89
Alcohol, 472–73, 499
Alcohol dehydrogenase, 472, 473
Allantois, 149, 150, 156
Alleles, 82, 84, 454

Allen's Rule, 501, 502
Allia Bay, Kenya, 336, 345
Allma, John, 192
Allometry, 484
Altiatlasius, 187
Altitude, adaptability to, 504
Amaurotic idiocy, 110
Ambrona, Spain, 375
American Indians, 444, 449–50
American race, 447
Amino acids, 40, 46–48, 52, 89, 91, 92, 96, 107, 272, 509,
   510
Ammonia, 40
Amnion, 149, 150
Amniote egg, 149, 150
Amphibians, 145–48
Amygdala, 161, 162
Anaerobic fermentation, 43
Analogous structures, 134
Anapsids, 153
Anatomy, 4, 5, 16, 542–46
Andes Mountains, 6–7, 38
Andrews, Peter, 336
Androgen, 224, 492
Androstenol, 307
Angwantibo, 189
Anirida, 110
Antarctica, 38–39
Anthropocentric view of evolution, 135
Anthropoids, 173–75, 177, 181, 194–200, 206
Anthropology, defined, 3
Anthropometry, 485, 533–35
Antibiotics, 96
Antibodies, 442, 444, 461–64
Aortic aneurysm, 474
Apes, 13, 261, 270 (*See also* Hominoid evolution; Hominoid
   social behavior; Primates)
   characteristics, 250–57
   differences from monkeys, 254
   geographic distribution of, 281, 282, 292
   models of behavior, 403–6
   molecular phylogeny of, 256

Apidium, 198
Apomorphy, 21
Applied biological anthropology, 514–41
    anthropometry, 533–35
    biomedical anthropology, 519–28
    defined, 515–16
    education and, 538–39
    forensic anthropology, 528–32
    human ecology, 539–40
    premises and goals of, 515–19
Appositional growth, 484
Arago, France, 385
Arambourg, Camille, 332
Arboreal mammals, 168
Archaeology, defined, 3
Archean Era, 136
Archontans, 182, 183
Ardipithecus ramidus, 323, 336, 337, 344, 345
Arginine, 48
Aristotle, 469–70
Armadillo, 72, 73
Arthropods, 62, 63
Artiodactyls, 168
Artwork, 432–33
Asfaw, Berhane, 335
Ashkenazi Jews, 117
Asparagine, 48
Aspartic acid, 48
Assort, 84
Atelines, 204
ATP (adenosine triphosphate), 42–43
Auditory bulla, 185, 186
Australoids, 448
Australopithecines, 258, 308, 323, 327–45, 344, 369
Australopithecus aethiopicus, 323
Australopithecus afarensis, 323, 333, 336, 338–42, 344–48
Australopithecus africanus, 323, 327–29, 333, 334, 338–42, 344, 348, 351, 356, 362–65, 373
Australopithecus anamensis, 336, 345
Australopithecus boisei, 323, 333, 334, 354, 356, 367, 373
Australopithecus prometheus, 335
Australopithecus ramidus (*See Ardipithecus ramidus*)
Australopithecus robustus, 323, 333, 350, 353–56, 376–77
Autosomes, 86
Auxologists, 485

B

Baboons, 204, 207, 212, 215, 216, 221, 222, 226, 227, 230, 231, 236, 352, 403
Bacon, Sir Francis, 26
Bacteria, 39–40, 47–49, 48, 53, 56, 96
Banding techniques, 86

Basal ganglia, 160, 161
Basicranial flexion, 342
Bateson, William, 81
Bats, 168, 173, 183, 187
Begun, David R., 260–61
Behavior, 13–15 (*See also* Social behavior)
Behavioral ecology, human, 312–13
Behavioral evolution, 123–28, 413–14 (*See also* Social behavior)
Belohdelie site, Ethiopia, 335–36
Berekhat Ram, Israel, 432, 433
Bergmann's Rule, 387, 501, 502
Betacyanin, 454, 455
Betamin, 454
Biblical Criticism, 26
Big bang theory, 34–36
Bilateral symmetry, 137, 138
Bilharzia, 525
Bilingsleben, Germany, 384
Bilirubin, 521–22
Binet, Alfred, 471
Bingham, Harold, 288
Binomial nomenclature, 17, 548
Biochemistry, 4
Biological anthropology:
    applied (*See* Applied biological anthropology)
    defined, 2, 3
    human biology and, 4
    language of, 15–19, 542–49
    paleoanthropology and, 4
    paradigms of, 7–10
    subjects of study, 10–15
Biomedical anthropology, 519–28
Biometric security, 535
Biostratigraphic age, 368
Bipedalism, 17, 168, 179, 180, 258, 305, 321, 324, 339, 347, 405–6, 413–17, 420–22
Birth environment, 528
Birth intervals, 283, 286, 313, 488–89
"Black Skull," 356
Blending inheritance, 77, 80, 82, 85
Blindsight, 159
Blood group polymorphisms, 461–64
Blood pressure, 507–8
Blue-green bacteria, 38, 39, 44
Blumenbach, Johann Friedrich, 7–9, 446, 447, 449
Boas, Franz, 447, 480, 495
Bodo, Ethiopia, 380, 382–84
Bogin, B., 485, 486, 488, 489, 491
Bolk, Louis, 481
Bones, 545
Bonobo, 254, 275, 280, 281, 299, 301–2, 317, 325, 404
Bony skeleton, evolution of, 142
Brace, C. Loring, 364, 387

Brachiation, 247, 252, 256
Brachycephalic, 447, 448
Brain:
    australopithecine, 340–43, 346–47, 398
    evolution of, 158–63, 166
    hominoid, 263, 264
    Homo, 360–62, 384
    human, 398, 413, 418, 421, 424–28, 546
    injuries, 535–37
    language and, 428–30
    primate, 177, 178, 240
Branchial arches, 136, 137, 144
Branisella, 200, 201
Brauer, Gunter, 391
Breast cancer, 524, 530, 531
Breccia, 329, 330
Brett, James, 521–22
Broca, Pierre-Paul, 427
Broca's Area, 427
Broken Hill (Kabwe), Zambia, 384
Broom, Robert, 329, 367
Brown, Frank, 332
Buffon, Georges-Louis, 202, 481
Bunodont, 168
Burckle, Lloyd H., 78–79
Burgess Shale, 62, 63
Burial of dead, 388

C

Callitrichids, 202
Calvin, William, 430
Cambrian Period, 62
Canalization, 489
Cann, Rebecca, 391, 393
Cannibalism, 311, 376
Capoids, 449
Capuchin monkeys, 229–30, 243, 273
Carbon, 34, 36, 40
Carbon dioxide, 40, 44, 78, 79
Carbonic anhydrase, 90
Carboniferous Period, 147–51
Carpenter, Clarence Ray, 211, 279, 281, 283, 302
Cartilage, 136
Cartilage bone, 142
Cartmill, Matt, 192–93
Catarrhines, 200, 201, 205
Catastrophism, 69
Catopithecus browni, 194–96, 198
Caucasian race, 447
Caucasoids, 448
Cayo Santiago Island, Puerto Rico, 225
Cebid, 200

Cells (*See also* DNA):
    earliest organisms, 51–55
    evolution of, 42–44, 51–55
    tissues, 134
Cell specialization, 55
Cenozoic Period, 151, 155, 166–68, 183, 188, 200
Central sulcus, 163
Cephalic indices, 447–48, 533
Cephalization, 137
Cercopithecines, 204, 207, 208, 224, 234, 263, 270
Cercopithecoidea, 204
Cerebral cortex, 158
Cerebral hemispheres, 425–27, 431
Cerebral Rubicon, 346
Cerebrum, 158
Cerumen, 455, 456
Cesarean section births, 528
Chagnon, Napoleon, 311
Chance sampling, 115–18
Charles-Dominique, P., 190
Chernobyl nuclear disaster, 104
Chesowanja, Kenya, 375
Child abuse, 311, 312
Childhood, 485, 486, 488
Chimpanzees, 13, 15, 20, 216, 228–29, 235, 247, 251, 253,
    254, 261, 264, 270–75, 280, 281, 290–99, 308–9, 325,
    352, 378, 403–5, 420, 430
Cholera, 525
Cholinesterase, 161
Chomsky, Noam, 428–29
Chondrodystrophic dwarfism, 110
Chordates, 62, 63, 135–39, 143
Chorion, 149, 150
Chromosomal theory of heredity, 86–87
Chromosomes, 61, 84, 87–89
Cingulate gyrus, 162
Cingulum, 180, 259, 543
Circulatory system, evolution of, 158
Cladistics, 21, 272, 273
Cladogram, 21, 22
Clark, J. Desmond, 335
Clark, Sir Wilfred Le Gros, 173, 192, 321, 333
Clarke, Ron, 347
Climate, 38, 78–79
Climbing heritage, anatomy of, 257–59
Clines, 18, 455–56
Cloning, 56, 97–98
Coacervate, 42
Codons, 47, 90, 96
Coelacanth, 145
Coelenterates, 138
Co-evolution, 518
Cognition, 402
Collagen, 90

Collector bias, 327

Colobines, 204, 205, 208, 226, 233, 234, 253, 308

Coloration, 124, 125

Color blindness, 110

Color vision, in primates, 177

Colugo, 168, 183, 186

Communication (*See also* Language):
  hominoid, 296, 298–302
  in nonhuman primates, 232–33, 235, 236

Competitive exclusion, principle of, 350

Computed tomography (CT), 164

Conceptual models, 400

Conditions, Uniformity of, 70

Condyle, 159

Congoids, 449

Conjoined artifact, 411

Conroy, Glenn, 164–65, 194

Consort relationships, 294

Continental drift, 37–39, 78, 187

Convergence, 21

Coppens, Yves, 332, 335

Coprophagy, 405

Core of earth, 35–37

Corpus callosum, 162, 425, 426

Corpus striatum, 160

Cortical homunculus, 163

Cosmology, 402

Cotylosaurs, 149

Creationism, 25–29

Cretaceous Period, 151, 156, 183

Crib death, 520–21

Crick, Francis, 89

Criminal investigations, 529–30

Crocodiles, 153

Cro-Magnon, 378, 379, 390, 393

Cronin, Helena, 124–25

Crossing over, 88

Crow, J. F., 441

Crust of earth, 35, 36, 38

Cultural anthropology, defined, 3

Culture:
  defined, 3, 402
  human social behavior and, 302, 305, 307, 313–16, 401–2
  as paradigm in biological anthropology, 8–9

Cursorial mammals, 168

Curtis, Garniss, 337

Cut marks, 370, 407, 408, 419

Cuvier, Georges, 69

Cyanobacteria, 39

Cynocephalus volans, 168, 183, 186

Cysteine, 48

Cystic fibrosis, 525–26

Cytochrome C, 52

Cytosine, 44, 47, 91, 92

D

Dali, China, 382–84

Dart, Raymond, 328, 333, 335, 348, 352, 364, 536

Darwin, Charles, 2, 6, 9, 68, 93–94, 221, 325, 377, 399, 418, 446
  behavioral evolution and, 123–25, 413–14
  development of natural selection theory, 71–77
  influences on, 67–70
  inherited variation and, 76–77, 80
  theory of inheritance, 80, 81

Darwin, Erasmus, 446

Deduction, 68, 400

Deep sea oxygen isotope curve, 375, 376

Delayed maturation, 164–65

Demes, 102

Dendropithecus macinnesi, 260, 262–64

Deoxyribonucleic acid (*See* DNA)

Dermopterans, 168, 183, 186, 187

Descartes, Rene, 503

Descent of Man and Selection with Respect to Sex, The (Darwin), 124, 413

Deterministic explanations of behavior, 219

Development, distinguished from growth, 483 (*See also* Human growth)

Devonian period, 143–46

DeVore, Irven, 212, 213, 400, 403, 413

De Vries, Sir Hugo, 81, 94

Diabetes, 506–7

Diamond, Jared, 506

Dietary hypothesis, 354, 355

Differential reproduction, 74–75

Dinosaurs, 149, 153, 154

Dionysopithecus, 268, 271

Diploid, 86

Directional selection, 118–19

Discordance Hypothesis, 518

Diseases of civilization, 508, 522

Displacement, 299

Diverticulitis, 523–24

Dmanisi, Georgia, 383

DNA (deoxyribonucleic acid), 13, 23, 24, 86, 325
  chemical structure of, 44, 45
  evolution, 47–50
  Human Genome Project, 450–51
  hydridization, 273–74
  introns, 93
  mitosis and meiosis, 60–61
  mutations of, 94, 96
  protein synthesis and, 46–47, 89–93
  repair systems, 55–57
  replication, 44, 46, 90–92, 94
  satellite, 453
  transcription and, 90–92
  translation and, 90–93

Dobzhansky, Theodosius, 29

Dolhinow, Phyllis Jay, 212
Dolichocephalic, 447
Doman, Glenn, 535–37
Dominance rank, 214, 226–28, 237–38, 284, 285, 316
Dominant gene, 82, 85, 86
Donisthorpe, Jill, 288
Dorsal nerve cord, 136–38
Dorso-ventral position, 289, 301
Double helix, of DNA, 90
Drimolen, South Africa, 323
Drosophila, 88
Dryopithecids, 268, 269
Dryopithecus, 260, 261, 268, 269
Dryopithecus germanicus, 446
Dubois, Eugene, 373
Duffy blood group, 459
Dunkers, 114
Dwarfism, 110, 111

E

Early Divergence Hypothesis, 264–66
Early Stone Age, 410
Earth, structure of, 35, 36
Eastern lowland gorilla, 287
Eaton, S. Boyd, 530–31
Eccrine sweat glands, 503
Ecological niche, 25
Ecology, defined, 25
Ectoderm, 137
Ectomorphs, 533
Ectotympanic bone, 196
Efe pygmies, 497
Eldredge, Niles, 122
Electrons, 36
Electrophoresis, 104, 107, 108, 445
Ellefson, John, 282, 283
Embryo, human, 150, 157
Embryology, 135, 142
Embryonic stage, 485, 492–93
Emlen, John, 289
Encephalization, 361
Enculturation, 469
Endocast, 346, 354, 429
Endocranial volume, 360
Endocrine glands, 491, 492
Endoderm, 137
Endogamy, 450
Endomorphs, 533
Endorphins, 161
Endoskeleton, 137
Engels, Friedrich, 414
English peppered moth (*Biston betularia*), 118–19, 122
Enlightenment, 3

Entotympanic bone, 186
Environmental sciences, 4
Enzymes, 44, 46, 56, 90, 96
Eocene Epoch, 183, 185–89, 193, 194, 196, 200, 201
Epidemiology, 516
Epilepsy, 163
Epiloia, 110
Epiphyses, 142
Epistasis, 86
Equipotentiality of brain, 536
Essay on the Principles of Population (Malthus), 68, 74
Estrus, 220–22, 234–35, 294, 404
Ethiopian race, 447
Ethnic cleansing, 533
Ethnocentrism, 314
Ethnogenesis, 378
Ethnology, 4
Ethogram, 127
Ethology, 126–27
Eugenics, 533–34
Eukaryotes, 51–55, 61
Evening primrose (*Denothera lamarckiana*), 94
Evolution (*See also* Human adaptability; Human behavioral evolution; Human growth):
    "African Eve" Hypothesis, 380, 390
    behavioral, 123–28, 413–14 (*See also* Social behavior)
    cells, 42–44
    versus creationism, 25–29
    hominid (*See* Hominid evolution)
    hominoid, 270–75
    Hybridization Model, 393
    interaction of climate and, 78–79
    Lamarckian, 71–72
    macroevolution, 122, 123
    microevolution, 121–22
    Multiregional Model, 378–79, 392, 393
    by natural selection, 2, 9–10, 68, 218, 240, 242, 377
    orthogenesis and, 135
    Out-of-Africa Model, 378, 391–93
    primate (*See* Primate evolution)
    vertebrate (*See* Vertebrate evolution)
Evolutionary medicine, 517, 520–28, 530–31
Exogamy, 450
Exons, 93
Exoskeleton, 136
Experiment, concept of, 6
Expression of the Emotions in Man and Animals, The (Darwin), 123
Extinction of species, 78, 121

F

Facial expressions, 232, 233, 297
Facial reconstruction, 528–29

Fairbanks, Lynn, 239
Falk, Dean, 346
Families, 17, 20
Family structure, 481
Fat deposition, 522–23
Favism, 458
Fayum Depression, Egypt, 194, 196–99, 201
Fear response, 314
Feed-back system, 518
Fejej, Ethiopia, 332
Ferns, 48
Fetal alcohol syndrome, 499
Fever, 524–25
Fibrinopeptide, 272
Field studies, 15, 211–13, 234–35
Fire, 374, 375, 389
"First Family," 339
Fish, DNA of, 49, 50
Fist-walking, 247, 258
Fitness, 118, 120–21
Fixed action patterns, 127–28, 303–6
Flying lemur or colugo (*Cynocephalus volans*), 168, 183, 186
Foraging strategies:
    hominoid, 295–96
    human, 312–13
    primate, 227, 228–30
Foramen magnum, 342–43
Forelimbs, 147
Forensic anthropology, 528–32
Fossey, Dian, 289, 293
Fossils, 3, 4, 6, 13, 17–18, 27–28
    defined, 25
Founder effect, 115–16
Freeman, Leslie, 413
Free radicals, 521
Frogs, 145, 159
Frugivorous, 405
Fuhlrott, Johannes, 386
Fundamentalists, 28
Fungi, 48, 49, 54
Fusion-fission social organization, 293

G

G6PD (glucose-6-phosphate dehydrogenase) deficiency, 457–60
Galagos, 181, 189, 191
Galápagos Islands, 6, 71–73, 76
Galton, Sir Francis, 80
Game theory, 312
Gangs, 315
Gastric ulcers, 524
Geese, 128
Gelada baboon (*Theropithecus gelada*), 18
Gemmules, 80, 81

Gene lineages, 23–25
Gene linkage, 87–88
Gene pool, 101
Genes:
    defined, 82
    structure of, 93
Genesis, 26, 28
Genetic death, 96
Genetic drift, 115, 117, 441, 453, 475
Genetic inheritance, 67 (*See also* Heredity)
Genetic load, 441
Genetic markers, 441, 442, 444, 453–56
Genetic mutations, 94
Genetic plasticity, 479
Genetic polymorphism, 119–20
Genetics, 4, 16, 34 (*See also* Heredity; Human biological variation)
    bases for, 81
    first use of term, 81
Genetic variation, 439–41
Genotype, 82, 84, 97, 107, 108, 112–13, 441, 464
Genus, 17, 20, 548
Geographical isolation, 72, 444–46
Geography, 4, 38–39
Geology, 4, 16, 69, 70, 547
Gibbons, 206, 216, 247, 248, 251–53, 255, 258, 260, 270, 273, 279–83, 404
Gibson, Kathleen, 434, 435
Gigantopithecus, 260, 265
Glaciations, 78
Global cooling, 78, 79
Globin, 272
Globus pallidus, 160
Glucose, 43–44
Glutamic acid, 48, 107
Glutamine, 48
Glycine, 48
Glycolysis, 43
Glyptodont, 72, 73
Golden monkeys, 233
Goldschmidt, Richard, 122
Gonadal hormones, 491–92
Gondwanaland, 36, 37
Gonococcus, 96
Goodall, Jane, 15, 279, 293, 296, 352, 404
Goodman, Morris, 58
Gorillas, 13, 19, 20, 227, 236, 247, 251, 253, 254, 264, 270–72, 275, 280, 281, 287–90, 325
Gorillidae, 254
Gould, Stephen Jay, 122, 518
Grade system, 382
Graecopithecus, 268, 335
Great apes (*See* Bonobo; Chimpanzees; Gorillas; Orangutans)
Green monkeys, 273
Gregory, William King, 183, 333, 399
Grooming behavior, 237, 294

Group living, advantages of, 213–15
Growth (*See* Human growth)
Guanine, 44, 47, 91
Guatemala, 496–97
Gulf Stream, 38

H

Habituation, 501
Hadar, Ethiopia, 323, 332–33, 336, 339–41, 344, 351, 369
Hadza people, 313
Haeckel, Ernst, 13, 14, 25, 135, 283, 373, 481, 482
Hall, K. R. L., 212
Hallux, 166
Hamburg, David, 240
Hamilton, William, 217
Handedness, 425, 427, 431, 432
Haploid, 86
Hapsburg Lip, 80
Hard palate, 159
Hardy, Godfrey, 104
Hardy-Weinberg equilibrium, 104–18
Harem species, 226, 227
Harlow, Harry, 239, 401
Hearing, evolution of, 147–48, 159
Heart, evolution of, 158
Heat and cold, adaptability to, 501–3
Heidelberg, Germany, 383, 384
Heliopithecus, 260
Hemoglobin, 89, 107, 456, 459, 467
Hemolytic incompatibility, 462–64
Hemophilia, 110
Hennig, Willi, 21
Heredity (*See also* Human biological variation):
    chromosomal theory of, 86–87
    Darwin's theory of, 80, 81
    laws of, 81–82
    principle of independent assortment, 84–86, 87
    principle of segregation, 82–84
Herschel, Sir John, 67
Heterochrony, 493–94
Heterodonty, 154–56
Heterozygosity, 82, 121, 445, 456, 462, 464
Hexosaminidase A, 117
Himalaya Mountains, 38
Hippocampus, 161, 162
Histidine, 48
Histocompatibility, 465
HLA (Human Lymphocyte Antigen) system, 464–65
H.M.S. Beagle, 70, 71
Holloway, Ralph, 346
Holmes, Gordon, 159
Holotype, 18
Home base sharing model, 411–12
Homeothermy, 157–58

Home range, 230, 281, 285, 289
Hominidae, 20
    defined, 17, 321
Hominid evolution, 11–13, 164–65 (*See also Homo;* Human behavioral evolution)
    australopithecines, 258, 308, 323, 327–45, 344
    bipedalism, 17, 324, 339, 347, 362
    characteristics of, 322
    definition of Hominidae, 321
    earliest hominids, 322–26
    morphology, 346–48
    paleoecology, 326, 327, 348–53
    taphonomy, 326–27
Hominines, 327
Hominoid evolution, 246–77
    apes, 250–57
    Eurasian, 268–70
    evolutionary relationships of, 270–75
    Late and Early Hypothesis, 264–66
    locomotion, 247, 251–53, 257–59, 261, 270, 285, 299
    Miocene fossil sites, 249
    phylogeny and timeline of, 249
    proconsulids, 259, 262–64
    teeth, 255, 259–61, 264, 267–68
Hominoid social behavior, 279–302, 403–5 (*See also* Human social behavior):
    aggressive, 285, 294–95
    birth intervals, 283, 286
    communication, 296, 298–302
    dominance rank, 284, 285
    foraging strategies, 295–96
    home range, 281, 285, 289
    hunting behavior, 308–9
    play, 285, 289
    reproductive strategies, 286, 289–90, 294, 299, 301
    tool use, 296, 317
    vocalizations, 281–83
Homo, 337, 338, 343
    brain, 360–62, 384
    fire use, 374, 375, 389
    robust australopithecines and, 353–56, 376–77
    skull and jaws, 363–64, 373, 382, 384–86
    social behavior, 371–72, 375–76
    teeth, 362–63, 366, 384, 385, 387, 409
    tool use, 367, 369–72, 375, 385, 388, 390
Homo erectus, 332, 356, 360, 364, 365, 367, 368, 373–76, 380–84, 381, 387, 389, 393, 442, 451, 505
Homo ergaster, 360, 368–69, 383
Homo habilis, 355, 360, 362–69, 383, 451
Homologous structures, 132, 134, 135
Homo modjokertensis, 367
Homo rudolfensis, 360, 368–69, 383
Homo sapiens, 13, 321, 360, 377–85, 442
    archaic, 384–85
    evolutionary origins of, 382–84
    evolutionary relationships in, 389–95

Homo sapiens, (con.)
  grade system, 382
  hand skeleton of, 253
  presapiens hypothesis, 378–79
  social behavior of, 388–89
  time of appearance of, 380
Homo sapiens neanderthalensis, 365, 378, 380, 385–89,
    393–95, 431, 433, 434
Homo sapiens sapiens, 365, 385, 386, 389, 391, 392
Homozygosity, 82, 112–14, 120–21, 456–57
Homunculus theory, 481
Hormones, 90, 220–22, 491–92
Horr, David, 284
Horses, 132, 169
Howell, F. Clark, 332, 368
Howler monkeys, 204, 211, 226
Hrdy, Sarah, 226, 227
Hughlings Jackson, John, 163
Human adaptability, 479, 500–511
  heat and cold, 501–3
  high altitude, 504
  light and solar radiation, 503–4
  modern life and, 507–11, 513, 516, 518
  nutritional and dietary aspects of, 505–7
Human anatomy, 542–46
Human behavioral evolution, 398–437
  ape models, 403–6
  archaeological sites and, 407–8, 410–12
  baboon models, 403
  bipedalism, 413–17, 420–22
  brain size, 398, 413, 418, 421, 424–28
  carnivore ecology and, 406–7
  culture and, 302, 305, 307, 313–16, 401–2
  ethnographic research, 412–13
  home base sharing model, 411–12
  language, 413, 428–35
  referential and conceptual models of, 400–401
  reproductive strategies, 420
Human biological variation, 10–11, 438–77
  alcoholism, 472–73
  blood group polymorphisms, 461–64
  early studies of, 446–49
  genetic influence on, 469–75
  genetic markers, 441, 442, 444, 453–56
  geographical isolation and, 444–46
  HLA (Human Lymphocyte Antigen) system, 464–65
  inadequacy of traditional racial classification, 452–53
  intelligence, 470–72
  lactose intolerance, 465–66
  measurement of, 441–44
  natural selection and, 456–69
  nature of genetic, 439–41
  schizophrenia, 474–75
  skin color, 466–69
  twin studies, 470
Human biology, defined, 4

Human ecology, 539–40
Human Genome Diversity Project, 450–51
Human Genome Project, 89
Human growth, 480–500
  defined, 483–85
  in different groups, 495–98
  genetic and hormonal control of, 491–92
  heterochrony, 493–94
  measurement of, 485
  responses to modernization, 498–500
  secular trends in, 494–95
  seven stages of, 485–91
Human rights investigations, 531–32
Human social behavior, 302–7, 310–17
  aggressive, 314–16
  behavioral ecology, 312–13
  culture and, 302, 305, 307, 313–16
  fixed action patterns, 303–6
  foraging strategies, 312–13
  imprinting, 305–6
  innate releasing mechanisms, 306–7, 310
  reproductive strategies, 313
  sexual behavior, 307, 310
  sociobiology and, 307, 310–12
Human species, taxonomic classification of, 16
Hunting strategies, 373, 375–76, 406–7, 416–20
Huntington's chorea (St. Vitus's Dance), 116–17
Hutton, James, 69
Huxley, Julian, 125
Huxley, Thomas Henry, 21, 22, 283, 325, 328
Hybridization Model, 393
Hydrogen, 34, 40, 90
Hylobates, 252, 282
Hylobatidae, 253
Hypertension, 507
Hypertrophy, 491
Hypervitaminosis A, 505–6
Hypothalamus, 161, 491
Hypotheses:
  biological anthropology and, 5–6
  defined, 5
Hypoxia, 504
Hypsodont, 168

I

Ichthyosaurs, 149, 153
Ignacius, 186
Imitative learning, 241
Immune system, 463–65
Imprinting, 305–6
Inbreeding, 112–14, 117
Inclusive fitness, 217
Independent assortment, principle of, 84–86, 87
Indri, 194

Inductive scientific method, 67
Industrial Revolution, 68
Infancy, 485, 486
Infanticide, 215, 226, 227, 295, 311
Infectious diseases, 524–25
Infraorders Adapiformes, 181
Inheritance (*See* Heredity)
Inherited variation, 74, 76–77
Innate releasing mechanisms, 306–7, 310
Insectivora, 166, 183
Institutes for the Achievement of Human Potential, 536–37
Intelligence, 470–72
Inter-birth interval, 226, 227
Interbreeding, 101–2
Intermembral indexes, of anthropoids, 206
International Rules of Zoological Nomenclature, 333, 548
Interphase, 87
Interstitial growth, 484
Intracellular Pangenesis, 81
Introns, 93
IQ (Intelligence Quotient) testing, 471–72
Iron, 34
Isaac, Glynn, 332, 411–12, 417
Isoleucine, 48
Isometric, 484

J

Japanese, 472, 497, 500
Jaundice, neonatal, 521–22
Jaws, evolution of, 143–44, 153, 159
Jenkin, Fleeming, 77
Johannsen, Wilhelm, 82
Johanson, Donald, 333, 335
Jolly, Alison, 190
Jones, Wood, 399
Journal of Researches (Darwin), 72
Jurassic period, 151, 155
Juvenile period, 485, 488

K

Kalb, John, 335
Kalodirr, Kenya, 263
Kanapoi, Kenya, 335, 336, 345
Karyotype, 86, 87
Kebara Cave, Israel, 431
Keith, Sir Arthur, 328, 329, 377, 399
Kelley, Steven, 98
Kellog, Winthrop, 293
Kenyapithecus, 260, 267, 268, 335
Kettelwell, H., 119
Kidd, Judith R., 450–51
Kidd, Kenneth K., 450–51

Kidney, vertebrate, 143
Kingdom, 62
Kinship systems, human, 311
Klasies River, South Africa, 391
Knuckle-walking, 247, 251, 259, 261, 288, 299, 326, 405
Koenigswald, G. H. R. von, 344, 367
Kohler, Wolfgang, 293
Komodo dragon, 160, 161
Koobi Fora, Kenya, 332, 368, 370, 375, 411, 505
Kromdaai site, 341
K-selection strategy, 177
Kummer, Hans, 212
!Kung people, 313, 416, 490
Kurt, Fred, 212
Kurtén, Bjorn, 11, 12

L

Laboratory studies, 211
Labyrinthodonts, 146, 147
La Chapelle, France, 383, 434
Lactation, 222
Lactose intolerance, 465–66
Laetoli, Tanzania, 323, 331, 333, 337–41, 349, 351, 369, 414
La Ferrassie, France, 432
Lake Turkana, Kenya, 323, 332, 341, 345, 365, 383
Lamarck, Jean Baptiste de, 71, 72, 77, 80
Lancaster, Jane, 416, 417
Lancelet, 137, 143
Landau, Misia, 398, 399
Landsteiner, Karl, 461
Language (*See also* Communication; Speech):
  defined, 402
  in human evolution, 413, 428–35
Langurs, 208, 212, 216, 226, 227
Laryngeal sacs, 284
Lascaux, France, 391
Late Divergence Hypothesis, 265–66
Laurasia, 36, 37
Law, Uniformity of, 70
Law of the succession of types, 73–74
Leakey, Louis, 267, 288, 289, 293, 296, 329–31, 337, 364, 419
Leakey, Meave, 336, 345
Leakey, Mary, 330, 337, 338, 370, 419
Leakey, Richard, 332, 365, 368
Learning, 538–39
  primate, 240–43
Lebensborns, 533
Lee, Richard, 413, 416
Lemurs, 125, 181, 187, 189–92
Lesser apes (*See* Gibbons; Siamangs)
Leucine, 48
Leukocytes, 464
Life cycle, human (*See* Human adaptability; Human growth)
Life on Earth, first evidence of, 39–41

Light and solar radiation, adaptability to, 503–4
Limbic system, 160–62
Limbs, evolution of, 144, 150, 154, 166, 167
Limnopithecus, 263, 264
Linguistics, defined, 3
Linkage of genes, 87–88
Linnaeus, 173, 360
Linton, Sally, 416–17
Little, Michael, 510–11
Lizards, 149, 161
Lobe-finned fish, 144–45, 147
Locomotion, 17, 154, 168, 177, 179, 180, 189, 204–6, 208,
   247, 251–53, 257–59, 261, 270, 285, 299, 305, 321, 324,
   339, 347, 405–6, 413–17, 420–22
Locus, 85
Longitudinal arch, 526
Lorenz, Konrad, 126–27, 216–17, 306, 314
Lorises, 181, 187, 189, 191
Lothagam mandible, 324, 325, 335
Lovejoy, Owen, 420
"Lucy," 339
Lukeino specimen, 335
Lunate sulcus, 346
Lungs, evolution of, 144
Lyell, Sir Charles, 69–70
Lysine, 48, 107

M

Macaques, 204, 207, 216, 222, 224, 231, 235, 402
McKenna, James, 520–21
MacLean, Paul, 160–62
McLean, William, 28–29
Macroevolution, 122, 123
Madagascar, 189–91
Makapansgat site, 333, 335, 339, 341, 369
Malaria, 107, 119, 120, 456–61, 525
Malayan race, 447
Malthus, Thomas, 68, 74
Mammal-like reptiles, 150, 152–54
Mammals:
   adaptive radiation and, 166–69
   evolution of, 155–59
Mandible, 159
Mandibular prognathism, 80
Mangabeys, 231, 233
Mann, Alan, 352
Mantle of earth, 35–37
Margulis, Lynn, 97
Marmosets, 194, 202, 204, 225, 226
Marshak, Alexander, 433
Marsupials, 156, 157
Mating strategies (*See* Reproductive strategies)
Matrifocal unit, 404
Matrilineal descent, 414

Maturity, 486, 488
Matuyama Reversed Epoch, 368
Mayr, Ernst, 17, 125
Mbuti pygmies, 525
Mean, concept of the, 102
Megadont, 343
Meiosis, 60–61, 88
Melanin, 467
Melanocytes, 467, 503
Membrane bone, 142
Memory, 158, 162
Menarche, 489, 494–95, 500, 531
Mendel, Gregor, 67, 81–84, 93, 94
Mendel's First Law, 82
Mendel's Second Law, 84, 87
Meniscus, 526
Menstruation, 222, 305
Mesocephalic, 447
Mesoderm, 137
Mesomorphs, 533
Mesozoic Period, 149, 151, 155, 156, 167, 183
Messenger RNA (m-RNA), 90, 92, 93
Messinian Event, 274, 275
Metabolic rate, 158
Metabolism, 39, 41, 42, 44, 46, 47
Metacarpals, 258
Metaphyta, 62
Metazoans, 62
Methane, 40
Methanethiol, 454, 455
Methionine, 48
Michod, Richard, 56
Microevolution, 121–22
Microfauna, 327
Micropithecus, 259, 264
Microtubules, 53–55
Middle Awash, Ethiopia, 323, 325, 335–36
Middle ear, 148, 159
Midfacial prognathism, 387
Migration, 114–15
Milankovich cycles, 78
Miller, Stanley, 40, 41
Miocene Epoch, 204, 247–49, 258–61, 263–65, 267–71, 274,
   324, 418
Mitchel, John, 467
Mitochondria, 52–55
Mitochondrial DNA, 53, 378, 452, 453
Mitosis, 60–61
Modjokerto, Java, 367, 383
Molecular biology, 4, 13, 16, 23–25, 34
Molecular clock, 58–59
Molecular genetics, 89–94
Molecules, 40–43 (*See also* DNA)
Moles, 168
Mongolian race, 447
Mongoloids, 448

Monkeys, 13, 247
   differences from apes, 254
   evolutionary origins of, 200–208
Monogamy, 225, 227
Monogenism, 446
Morbidity, 522
Morgan, T. H., 88–89
Morphology, 18
Morton, Samuel G., 446
Mother-infant relationship:
   human, 304
   primate, 238–40, 403
Motor cortex, 163
Mountain gorilla, 19, 160, 161, 287
Mount Bamboli, Italy, 269–70
Mount St. Helens, Washington, 38
Mousterian burials, 432
Mousterian stone tool culture, 388
Multi-male groups, primate, 225, 231
Multiregional Model, 378–79, 392, 393
Muscles of mastication, 250, 252
Muscular dystrophy, 474
Mutation, 77, 94–97, 105, 457
   achondroplasia, 111
   caused by single gene mutations, 110
   defined, 94
   Huntington's chorea (St. Vitus's Dance), 116–17
   neutral, 96, 112, 113, 453–54
   phenylketonuria (PKU), 117–18
   selection and, 97, 112, 113
   Tay-Sachs disease, 117, 118

N

Napier, John, 364
Nariokotome, Kenya, 364
Natal residents, 227
Natural selection, 2, 9–10, 68, 218, 240, 242, 377
   co-discovery of, 74, 75–76
   defined, 74
   development of theory, 71–77
   directional, 118–19
   genetic polymorphism, 119–20
   human biological variation and, 456–69
   mutation and, 97, 112, 113
Nauru people, 506
Ndutu, Tanzania, 385
Neandertals, 26, 114, 378–80, 383, 385–89, 393–95, 431, 433, 434, 468
Neocortex, 163, 240, 296, 425, 429, 430
Neo-Darwinism, 81
Neolithic Revolution, 506
Neonatal behavior, 303–4
Neonatal jaundice, 521–22
Neumann, Joachim, 385

Neurocranium, 142, 159
Neurotubules, 55
Neutral mutations, 96, 112, 113, 453–54
Neutrons, 36
New World monkeys, 181, 200–204, 206, 225–26
Ngangdong, Indonesia, 384
Ngorora specimen, 322–23
Nichols, Johanna, 434
Niemeyer, Susan, 521–22
Nilsson-Ehle, Herman, 84, 85
Nissen, Henry, 293
Nitrogen, 36
Nodular goiter, 455
Non-insulin-dependent diabetes mellitus, 506–7
Notharctus, 189
Notochord, 136–38
Nuclear family, 404
Nucleic acid hybridization, 273
Nucleus pulposus, 137, 138
Nuttall, G.H.F., 58
Nyanzapithecus, 264, 270

O

Obesity, 522–23
Observational learning, 213
Occipital torus, 373, 384
Old age, 486
Oldowan stone tools, 355, 370, 375, 408, 430–31
Olduvai Gorge, Tanzania, 30, 323, 330, 341, 364–68, 370–72, 383, 419
Old World monkeys, 181, 200, 203–8, 226, 247, 254
Olfaction, 232, 305, 307
Olfactostriatum, 160
Oligocene Epoch, 189, 194, 196, 198, 200, 201
Oligopithecus savagei, 198
Omnivorous species, 168
Omo, Ethiopia, 323, 327, 332, 337, 341, 349–52, 365, 368, 369, 371, 383
Omomyoids, 187, 196, 200
Oncogenes, 96
Ontogeny, 218
Optic convergence, 192
Optimal foraging theory, 229, 312
Orangutans, 20, 216, 247, 251, 254–55, 258–59, 261, 270, 271, 280, 281, 283–87
Orbital frontality, 174
Ordovician period, 143
Oreopithecus, 269–70
Organismal lineages, 23–25
Origin of Species by Means of Natural Selection (Darwin), 70, 74–76, 81
Ornamentation, 433
Orthogenesis, 135
Osborn, Rosalie, 288, 399

Osteodontokeratic, 334–4, 369
Osteology, 528
Ostracoderms, 142–43
Otters, 168
Ouranopithecus, 261, 335
Out-of-Africa model, 378, 391–93
Ovulation, 220–21, 222, 286, 305
Owen, Richard, 69
Owl monkeys, 225
Oxygen, 36, 41, 43, 44, 51
Ozone, 55

P

Paleoanthropology, 326
    defined, 4
Paleocene Epoch, 168, 183, 185, 187, 200
Paleoecology, 326, 327, 348–53, 371–72
Paleomagnetic dating, 368
Paleontology, 23–25
Paleospecies, 18
Paleozoic Era, 139, 148–49, 151
Palmistry, 534
Pangaea, 36
Pangenesis, 80, 81
Panidae, 253, 254
Panmictic populations, 450
Pan paniscus, 254, 275, 299, 301, 325
Pan troglodytes, 275, 290, 291, 299, 337
Paradigms of biological anthropology, 7–10
Parallelism, 21
Paranthropus, 354
Parapithecids, 198, 201
Parapithecus, 198
Parasites, 525
Paratypes, 18
Parental investment, 217
Paromomyoids, 186
Pasteur, Louis, 39
Patas monkey, 168, 237, 240
Patrilineal descent, 414
Pedogenesis, 136, 137
Pedomorphosis, 493
Peking Man, 374
Pelger anomaly, 110
Pelvic size, 421, 423–24, 489
Pelycosaurs, 153
Penicillin, 96
Perineal swelling, 221, 235, 294
Perissodactyls, 168
Permian Period, 149, 151, 152
Peromorphosis, 494
Peters, Charles, 355
Petralona, Greece, 380, 382–84
Petrosal bone, 185

Petter, Jean-Jacques, 190
Phalanges, 258
Phenotype, 84, 89, 97
Phenylalanine, 48
Phenylalanine hydroxylase, 117
Phenylketonuria (PKU), 117–18
Pheromones, 221
Photosynthesis, 43–44
Phrenology, 534
Phyletic gradualism, 122, 123
Phylogeny, 14, 20–27, 218
    animal kingdom, 133
    ape, 256
    australopithecine, 344
    defined, 13
    hominoid, 249
    Homo sapiens sapiens, 392
    primate, 181
    reptile, 151
Phylum Chordata, 62, 63, 135–39
Phylum Urochordata, 137
Physical anthropology (*See* Biological anthropology)
Pigs, 168
Piltdown forgery, 329, 379–80, 481
Pineal body, 503
Pinker, Stephen, 429
Pisum sativum, 81–84
Pithecanthropus erectus, 373 (*See also Homo erectus*)
Pituitary gland, 161, 162, 491
Placenta, 157
Placentals, 156, 157
Placoderms, 143–44
Planes of body, 542, 544
Plates, 38
Plate tectonics, 37
Platypus, 155
Platyrrhines, 181, 200, 201, 205
Play, 241–43, 285, 289
Pleistocene Epoch, 189, 284, 329, 374, 375, 377, 378, 379,
    394, 418
Plesiadapiforms, 181, 183–87
Plesiadapoids, 186, 188, 192
Plesiosaurs, 149, 153
Pliocene Epoch, 329, 335
Pliopithecids, 269
Pollex, 166
Pollution, 481, 500, 539
Polygenic inheritance, 85–86
Polygenism, 444, 446
Polymers, 41, 42
Polymorphisms, 119–20, 453–54
    blood group, 461–64
Polypeptide chain, 89–93
Pongidae, 253, 254, 271
Pongo, 271
Population (*See also* Mutations):

chance sampling, 115–18
  defined, 17
  directional selection, 118–19
  fitness, 118, 120–21
  Hardy-Weinberg equilibrium, 104–18
  inbreeding, 112–14, 117
  Malthusian theory of, 68
  migration, 114–15
  variation within, 102–4
Porpoises, 168
Post-central gyrus, 163, 166
Potto, 189, 191
Precambrian Period, 62
Pre-central gyrus, 163, 166
Predation:
  primate defenses against, 230–32
  rate, 224
Presapiens hypothesis, 378–79
Presbytis, 233
Primate evolution:
  anthropoids, 173–75, 177, 181, 194–200, 206
  characteristics, 173–81
  insectivore ancestry, 183
  locomotion, 177, 179, 189, 204–6, 208
  monkeys, 200–208
  plesiadapiforms, 181, 183–87
  prosimians, 13, 173–75, 177, 181, 187–91, 194
  suborders, 181–82
  teeth, 180, 193–95, 198, 201, 202, 207
  vision, 173–74, 176, 192
Primates, defined, 13, 173
Primate social behavior, 210–45
  advantages of group living, 213–15
  aggression, 191, 215, 218, 225–27, 236–38, 316
  birth and mother-infant bond, 238–40
  birth seasons, 223, 227
  communication, 232–33, 235, 236
  development of behavioral modeling, 215–19
  dominance rank, 214, 226–28, 237–38
  field studies, 211–13, 234–35
  foraging and feeding, 227, 228–30
  learning, 240–43
  predation defenses, 230–32
  reproductive strategies, 219–28
  types of social groups, 216
Primatology, defined, 15
Primordial soup, 41
Principles of Geology, The (Lyell), 69–70
Process (Actualism), Uniformity of, 70
Proconsul, 248, 260, 323
Proconsul africanus, 262, 264, 265
Proconsulids, 259, 262–64
Proconsul major, 262, 264, 265
Prognathism, 250
Prohylobates tandyi, 204
Prokaryotes, 51–53, 62

Proline, 48, 107
Promiscuity, 227, 286
Propliopithecoids, 198, 259
Propliopithecus, 198
Prosimians, 13, 173–75, 177, 181, 187–91, 194, 221
Proteins, 40
Protein synthesis, 46–47, 89–93
Protons, 36
Proto-sex, 56
Psychology, 4
PTC (phenylthiocarbamide), 454–55
Punctuated equilibrium, 122, 123
Purgatorius, 183, 185
Purines, 44
Pygmy chimpanzee (bonobo), 254, 275, 280, 281, 299, 301–2, 317, 325, 404
Pyrimidines, 44

Q

Quadrupedalism, 204, 205, 259
Quantum evolution, 122
Quantum theory of heredity, 82

R

Race, defined, 447
Races, Blumenthal's classification of, 7–9
Raciation, 444
Ramapithecus, 261, 264, 265
Rangwapithecus, 260, 270
Rape, 311–12
Rasmussen, Tab, 193
Rate (Gradualism), Uniformity of, 70
Ray-finned fish, 145
R-Complex, 160–62
Recessive gene, 82, 85, 86
Rectus abdominis, 138, 140
Redfield, Rosemary, 56, 57
Reductionistic explanations of behavior, 219
Referential models, 400
Regulators, 93
Religion, 26–27
Reproductive isolating mechanisms, 101
Reproductive strategies, 39, 41, 42
  hominoid, 286, 289–90, 294, 299, 301, 404
  human, 313
  mammals, 155–56
  primate, 177, 190–91, 219–28
Reptiles, evolution of, 148–54
Retinoblastoma, 110
Retromolar space, 387
Reversion, 80, 84
RH blood group, 461–64

Rhesus monkeys, 225, 227, 235, 461
Rhodesian man, 328
Ribosomal RNA (r-RNA), 92
Rickets, 468
Rifts, 37
Ring-tailed lemurs, 189, 191
RNA (ribonucleic acid), 47, 92
Robinson, John T., 344, 354, 365
Romer, Alfred, 150
Rumbaugh, Duane, 298–99

S

Saccopastore, Italy, 385
Sagan, Dorian, 97
Sagittal crest, 251
Sagittal keel, 373, 384
Sahabi, Libya, 325, 335
Sahulland, 76
Salamanders, 48, 49, 145
Salé, Algeria, 384
Salla, Brazil, 200
Samburu Hills hominoid, 323
Sampling error, 105
San Andreas Fault, California, 38
Sangiran, Indonesia, 383
Sarcopterygians, 144–45
Sarich, Vincent, 11, 12, 58–59
Satellite DNA, 453
Savage-Rumbaugh, Sue, 298
Scandentia, 183
Schaafhausen, Herman, 386
Schaller, George, 289
Schepartz, Lynn, 429
Schick, Kathy, 408, 411, 412, 430
Schizophrenia, 474–75
Scientific creationism, 28–29
Scientific method, 5–7
Scopes, John T., 28
Sea cows, 168
Sea floor spreading, 38
Seals, 168
Sea squirt, 136, 137
Secular trends in growth and maturation, 494–95
Segmentation of the body, 137
Segregation, principle of, 82–84
Semi-free-ranging studies, 211
Senga, Zaire, 370
Sensory cortex, 166
Septum, 162
Serine, 48
Serotonin, 161, 315–16
Serum cholesterol, 507, 508
Serum protein, 58–59
Sessile organisms, 62

Sex cells, 61, 64
Sex chromosomes, 86
Sex-ratio manipulation, 217
Sexual dimorphism, 124, 200, 207, 250, 251, 263, 283, 291, 339, 340, 473
Sexual reproduction, 56–57, 61, 62, 97–98
Sexual selection, 124–25
Shanidar Cave, Iraq, 388
Sharks, 144
Sheldon, William H., 533–34
Shell, 149, 150
Shovel-shaped incisors, 441, 442, 451
Siamangs, 252, 253, 258, 279, 283
Sickle-cell anemia, 106–7, 115, 119, 120, 441, 460
Sifakas, 191, 206
Silurian Period, 142
Silver leaf monkeys, 226
Simiolus, 260, 263
Simpson, George Gaylord, 122
Single species hypothesis, 348, 350
Sivapithecus, 260, 261, 264, 265, 268, 271
Sivapithecus parvada, 265
Skin color, 466–69
Skull, evolution of, 150, 153, 159
Sloths, 173
Smith, Fred, 393
Smith, John Maynard, 97, 217
Smith, Sir Grafton Elliot, 377, 399
Smoking, 499
Snakes, 149
Social behavior:
    hominoid (*See* Hominoid social behavior)
    Homo, 371–72, 375–76
    Homo erectus, 375–76
    Homo habilis, 371–73
    human (*See* Human social behavior)
    primate (*See* Primate social behavior)
    prosimian, 190–91, 194
Social bond, 219
Sociobiology, 215
    human, 307, 310–12
Socioecology, 217, 218, 234
Somatic mutations, 94
Somatomancy, 534
Somatotrophin, 491
Somatotyping, 533–34
Special creation theory, 69
Speciation, 122
Species, 17–18, 548 (*See also* Population)
Speech:
    anatomical evidence of, 433–35
    defined, 429
    loss, 427
Spencer, Herbert, 75
Sperry, Roger, 425
Speth, John D., 418–19

Spider monkeys, 204, 206, 227, 263
Spiny anteater, 155
Spirochetes, 53–56
Splanchnocranium, 144
Sports, 314
Spy, Belgium, 387
Squirrel monkeys, 243
Standard deviation, 102, 103
Stanford, Craig B., 308–9
Starfish, 138
Stars, 35, 36
Steinheim, Germany, 383, 385, 393
Stereoscopic vision, 174, 176, 192
Stereotypic aspects of behavior, 217
Sterkfontein, South Africa, 323, 333, 339, 341, 347–48, 369
Stern, J. T., 371
Sternal glands, 284
Steroids, 221, 491
Stone tools, 355, 367, 369–72, 375, 388, 408, 430–31
Stone transport model, 412
Stress, 481, 498–500, 524
Stringer, Christopher, 391
Structural problems, 526–27
Subclinical disease condition, 516
Subduction zone, 38
Subspecies, 18–19, 445
Sudden Infant Death Syndrome (SIDS), 520–21
Sundaland, 76
Supreme Court of the United States, 28, 29
Survival of the fittest (*See also* Natural selection)
    term coined, 75
Susman, Randall, 371
Sussman, Robert, 192–93
Swanscombe, England, 385, 393
Swartkrans, South Africa, 323, 330, 333, 341, 350, 367, 383
Symbiosis, 53
Sympathetic nervous system, 524
Synapsids, 153
Syndactylus, 279
Syndactyly, 116
Systematics, 16
Szalay, Frederick S., 192

T

Tabarin hominid, 324, 325
Taieb, Maurice, 332, 335
Tamarins, 202, 204, 221, 225, 226
Tanner, J. M., 480, 494, 497, 498
Tanning, 501, 503
Taphonomy, 326–27, 419
Tarsiers, 181, 189, 192, 206
Taste, 454–55
Tata, Hungary, 432

Taung, South Africa, 164–65, 323, 327–29, 333, 339, 346, 348
Taxonomy, 16–17, 548
Tay-Sachs disease, 117, 118
Technology, 402
Tectonism, 78, 79
Teeth:
    australopithecine, 327, 331, 336–40, 342–44, 351–53
    evolution of, 143, 150, 153–56, 164–65, 168, 169
    hominid, 322–24, 407–9
    hominoid, 255, 259–61, 264, 267–68
    Homo, 362–63, 366, 384, 385, 387, 409
    human, 441, 442, 451, 542, 543
    primate, 180, 193–95, 198, 201, 202, 207
Telanthropus capensis, 367
Terrace, Herbert, 298
Territoriality, human, 314–15
Tertiary Period, 78, 151
Testosterone, 224, 492
Thalamus, 162
Thalassemia, 459, 460
Theology, 26–27
Theory, defined, 5
Therapsids, 153, 154
Thermoregulation, 491, 502–3
Threonine, 48, 107
Thrifty genotype, 507
Thymine, 44, 47, 91, 92
Thymine dimers, 55
Thyroid hormone, 491
Tiger, Lionel, 539
Tissues, 134
Titis, 225
Tobias, Phillip, 347, 364
Tooby, John, 400
Tool use, 415–16
    Acheulean, 375, 376, 388, 431
    australopithecine, 333, 335, 352, 355, 369, 377
    handedness and, 431, 432
    hominid, 404, 405, 410–11, 418–19
    hominoid, 296, 317
    Homo, 367, 369–72, 375, 385, 388, 390
    Mousterian, 388
    stone tools, 355, 367, 369–72, 375, 388, 408, 430–31
Torralba, Spain, 375
Tortoises, 71–73
Toth, Nicholas, 408, 411, 430
Transcription, 90–92
Transferin, 90
Transfer RNA (t-RNA), 92–93
Transformation, 56
Translation, 90–93
Tree shrews, 168, 183
Triassic Period, 148, 150, 151, 154
Trinil, Indonesia, 383
Trinkaus, Erik, 393

Triune brain, 160–63, 166
Tryptophan, 48
Tuff, 368
Tulp, Nicolaas, 290
Turkana people, 510–11
Turkanapithecus, 260, 264
Twin studies, 470
Typology, 7–8
Tyrosine, 48
Tyson, Edward, 290

U

Ulcers, 524
Ultraviolet light, 467, 468, 503
Umbilical cord, 157
Undulipodia, 53–55
Uniformitarianism, 70
Universe, origins of, 3, 6, 34, 36
Upper Paleolithic, 388
Uracil, 47, 91, 92
Urban environment, 498–500, 511
Urochordates, 137
Ussher, James, 69

V

Valine, 48
Variation:
    human (*See* Human biological variation)
    inherited, 74, 76–77
Vasoconstriction, 503
Ventro-ventral position, 239, 289, 301
Vertebrate evolution, 131–71
    amphibians, 145–48
    chordates, 62, 63, 135–39, 143
    fish heritage, 139–40, 142–45
    homologous structures, 132, 134, 135
    mammals, 155–59
    reptiles, 148–54
Vertebrates:
    defined, 140
    diagram of traits, 141
Vertical clinging and leaping, 177, 189
Vervet monkeys, 232, 235, 236, 243, 316
Victoriapithecus maccinnesi, 204
Virchow, Rudolf, 81, 515, 516

Vision, primate, 173–74, 176, 192
Vitamin D, 468
VNTRs (variable noncoding tandem repeats), 453–54
Vocalizations:
    hominoid, 281–83, 430
    primate, 232, 233, 235

W

Walker, Alan, 168, 332, 336, 345
Wallace, Alfred Russel, 74, 75–76
Wallace Line, 75–76
Warm-bloodedness, 157–58
Washburn, Sherwood, 5, 30, 127, 212, 213, 242, 356, 403,
    415–16, 429, 538
Water vapor, 40
Watson, James, 89
Wegener, Alfred, 37
Weidenreich, Franz, 374, 393
Weinberg, Wilhelm, 104
Weismann, August, 81
Wernicke, Karl, 427
Wernicke's Area, 427
Western lowland gorilla, 287
Whales, 168
Whewell, William, 69–70
White, Tim, 335, 337
Wickramasinghe, Chandra, 29
Williams, George, 217
Williams, R. J., 454
Wilson, Allan, 12, 58, 391, 393
Wolfe, Linda D., 234
Wolpoff, Milford, 378–79, 393
Woolly monkeys, 204

Y

Y-5 pattern, 259
Yanomamö people, 311
Yemenite Jews, 117
Yerkes, Robert, 211, 293

Z

Zhoukoudian, China, 374–76, 442
Zihlman, Adrienne, 417

About the Authors

Noel T. Boaz is Director of the International Institute for Human Evolutionary Research at Central Oregon University Center in Bend, Oregon. A paleoanthropologist with many years of field experience in Africa, he was trained at the University of Virginia and the University of California, Berkeley, where he received his Ph.D. in Anthropology in 1977. Dr. Boaz's current research interests are in the earliest origins of the hominid lineage, ecological change and human evolution, and biomedical anthropology. Recent publications include *Quarry: Closing in on the Missing Link* (1993) and *Eco Homo*, an ecological history of the human species (forthcoming).

Alan J. Almquist is Professor of Anthropology at California State University, Hayward, where he is Chairman of the Anthropology Department. Dr. Almquist received his Ph.D. in Anthropology in 1972 at the University of California, Berkeley. A dedicated teacher, he has also headed the Clarence Smith Museum of Anthropology at Hayward and has undertaken fieldwork at early hominid sites in the Middle Awash, Ethiopia. Current research interests include the evolution of human sexual behavior and paleoanthropology. Recent publications include *Milestones in Human Evolution* (1993) edited with Ann Manyak, and a reader, *Human Sexuality* (1995) with Andrei Simic and Patricia Omidian.